Literacy

THIRD EDITION

Reading, Writing and Children's Literature

Gordon Winch
Rosemary Ross Johnston
Paul March
Lesley Ljungdahl
Marcelle Holliday

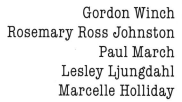

OXFORD

OXFORD

UNIVERSITY PRESS

253 Normanby Road, South Melbourne, Victoria 3205, Australia
Oxford University Press is a department of the University of Oxford.
It furthers the University's objective of excellence in research, scholarship,
and education by publishing worldwide in

Oxford New York

Auckland Cape Town Dar es Salaam Hong Kong Karachi
Kuala Lumpur Madrid Melbourne Mexico City Nairobi
New Delhi Shanghai Taipei Toronto

With offices in

Argentina Austria Brazil Chile Czech Republic France Greece
Guatemala Hungary Italy Japan Poland Portugal Singapore
South Korea Switzerland Thailand Turkey Ukraine Vietnam

OXFORD is a trade mark of Oxford University Press in the UK
and in certain other countries

National Library of Australia

Cataloguing-in-Publication data:

Literacy : reading, writing and children's literature.
3rd ed.
Bibliography.
Includes index.
For tertiary students.
ISBN 978 0 19555 126 6.

ISBN 0 19 555126 5.

1. Literacy - Australia. 2. Language arts (Primary) -
Australia. I. Winch, Gordon, 1930- .

372.60994

Edited by Venetia Somerset
Text and cover design by Patrick Cannon
Typeset by Linda Hamley, Melbourne
Proofread by Craig MacKenzie
Indexed by Neale Towart
Printed in Hong Kong by Sheck Wah Tong Printing Press Ltd

Brief Contents

Contents

| **PART I** | Reading | 1 |

GORDON WINCH AND MARCELLE HOLLIDAY

PART II   Writing

LESLEY LJUNGDAHL AND PAUL MARCH

PART III   Children's Literature   369

ROSEMARY ROSS JOHNSTON

List of Figures

List of Tables

Authors

Marcelle Holliday taught for eighteen years in primary and demonstration schools in New South Wales and South Australia before beginning work on the assessment of reading as part of the Australian Cooperative Assessment Project in 1980. She has since worked extensively on a range of projects in literacy including curriculum development, teacher professional development, and the development of effective literacy assessment materials. From 1997 to 1999 she played a major role in the design and implementation of the NSW Department of Education and Training Literacy Strategy, having responsibility for the reading component of the strategy. As part of this process, a widely acclaimed 'balanced approach to reading' was developed and the structure of a daily Literacy Session was refined and made available to all primary teachers in New South Wales. In 1998 Marcelle Holliday pioneered *Log on to Literacy*, a professional development program in the teaching of literacy that is delivered to teachers in isolated communities via the Internet. She has served as a council member of the Primary English Teaching Association, for which she has written and edited publications. She has presented papers and worked with teachers and trainee teachers at conferences and in seminars in Australia, the United Kingdom, the USA, and Sweden. She currently works as an education consultant and writer of online learning materials, and as a lecturer at the Australian Catholic University, New South Wales.

Rosemary Ross Johnston is an Associate Professor at the University of Technology Sydney, where she is Director of Teacher Education and Director of the Centre for Research and Education in the Arts. She has taught at primary, secondary, and tertiary levels. In 2000 she was H. W. Donner Guest Research Professor with the ChiLPA (Children's Literature: Pure and Applied) Project, an international project at Åbo Akademi University, Finland funded by the Finnish Ministry of Education. She remains as Expert Advisor with the project. She is Vice President of the *Fédération Internationale des Langues et Littératures Modernes* (FILLM, affiliated to UNESCO), was secretary of the International Research Society for Children's Literature (IRSCL, 1997–2001), was a Foundation Board member of the Australasian Children's Literature Association for Research (ACLAR), is a member of the International Board of the Montgomery Institute in Canada, was on the international committee of the Children's Literature Association (USA), and is a member of the Board of Governors of Dromkeen Australian Children's Literature Collection, as well as those of several schools. Dr Johnston's research covers both literary and pedagogical areas, and she has been key speaker at a number of international conferences. She is the invited author of a number of book chapters published both in Australia and overseas, and has been published in many national and international journals, including *Diogenes*, *Children's Literature in Education*, *Canadian Children's Literature*, *Bookbird*, *Diadromes*, *The Australian Journal of Language and Literacy*, and *Papers*. Her work has been translated into several languages including French, Greek and Arabic. She is the editor of *CREArTA*, an international, interdisciplinary journal in the arts.

Lesley Durrell Ljungdahl is a Senior Lecturer in the Faculty of Education at the University of Technology, Sydney, where she has taught in subjects on approaches to the teaching of reading, writing, and children's literature. She began teaching in London after obtaining a BA(Hons) in Language and Literature at the University of New South Wales in Sydney and later worked in Canberra and Sydney schools before being appointed to the William Balmain College (the Kuring-gai College of Advanced Education). Lesley is also a qualified librarian, holds a Master of Library Studies (McGill), and has worked as a secondary-school librarian in Montreal in the 1980s. Dr Ljungdahl is a past president of ATESOL (NSW) and has given conference presentations on literacy-related issues at national and international conferences. She has presented numerous papers on literacy at TESOL conferences (Teaching English to Speakers of Other Languages) in Baltimore, Long Beach, New York, and Vancouver. Recent publications in the *International Journal of Learning* have followed from presentations in Beijing, London, Havana, and Granada (2004). Her major book publication, *A Week in the Future*, highlights the work of Catherine Helen Spence (1825–1910), one of the first female authors in Australia. Dr Ljungdahl works with pre-service and postgraduate students in the teaching of language and literature, with a particular focus on the needs of students from a language background other than English. She has been a Visiting Scholar at Macquarie University and Sydney University (2005). She has regularly participated in teaching practicums in Kunming, the People's Republic of China, and in Apia, Western Samoa. Areas of research interest are literacies, TESOL education, international education and overseas practicums.

Paul March began his career in primary schools. He is currently Senior Lecturer and Associate Director of the Centre for Research and Education in the Arts, Faculty of Education, University of Technology, Sydney. He lectures in primary English curriculum studies as well as child drama. Among his publications are several co-edited academic texts: *Writing and Learning in Australia* (Oxford/Dellasta), *Teaching Writing K–12* (Dellasta), *The Teacher Is the Answer* (Centre For Reading, UTS) and chapters in academic research publications. He has presented papers at international conferences in the United Kingdom, the USA and Canada and has worked as an Adjunct Professor in Boston. He is involved in post-doctoral research in the semiotics of writing for children. He is active as an adjudicator and examiner for speech and drama and has had extensive experience in devising syllabuses for the Australian Speech Communication. He has also been active on committees for the International Reading Association and the Primary English Teaching Association.

Gordon Winch was previously Head of the Department of English at Kuring-gai College of Advanced Education, now the Lindfield campus of the University of Technology, Sydney and is currently a full-time author. He has taught in primary and secondary schools in Australia and overseas and holds a PhD in English and Education from the University of Wisconsin. His academic texts include *Teaching Reading: A Language Experience*, written and edited with Valerie Hoogstad, and *Give Them Wings: The Experience of Children's Literature*, written and edited with Maurice Saxby. He has written for children: *Barrington's Board Shorts*, *Popcorn and Porcupines*, *Samantha Seagull's Sandals* and *Enoch the Emu*, and more recently *Rodney Thinks of Food* (2002) and *Koala Sees the World* (2003). A collection of his comic verse, *Rhinos, Toucans and Woolly Dogs* came out in the same year. His new short chapter books include *The Amazing Matilda Mudpuddle*, *The Mighty Matilda Mudpuddle*, *The Invisible Matilda Mudpuddle* and *Matilda Mudpuddle and the X-ray eyes*. Gordon Winch's educational books on literacy for children, which include the Reading Rigby program, the Go Books Reading series, the Read Well, Write Well and Spell Well series, with Greg Blaxell and more recently Growing Up With Grammar, Conquering Comprehension and The Primary Grammar Dictionary. Many of these titles are sold around the world. He is currently a member of the Strategy Group of the Dymocks Literacy Foundation and acts on the selection panel of the Premier's Literacy Challenge, New South Wales. While working overseas in the 1970s, Dr Winch saw the need for a professional organisation for primary school teaching of English and was one of the founders and the first president of the Primary English Teaching Association (PETA), a position he held for six years.

Foreword

There have been many books published on literacy and almost as many published on children's literature. However, there are far fewer that attempt to cover both literacy and literature, and even fewer that remember to include writing as part of literacy. But one might still ask, 'why another book on literacy?' The short answer is that there is still much to learn about literacy and the way it is used and developed as part of life. I want to congratulate the authors of this significant book for the scope, quality, and freshness of their work.

I have known the work of the writers for many years. Indeed, I have been part of the same community of literacy scholars as the authors for almost thirty years. I worked with Marcelle Holliday on literacy curriculum reform in the late 1970s. I first encountered Gordon Winch's work at the same time and have been an active participant with all the authors in a range of professional and scholarly organisations throughout this period.

I feel quite privileged to have shared this period of growth in our understanding of literacy and the development of the Children's Literature field in Australia. This has been a significant time. In the 1960s the word 'literacy' was hardly mentioned in curriculum documents, textbooks, and professional organisations. We spoke of reading, spelling, writing, handwriting, speaking, listening, and literature as if they were separate entities. Literacy was defined much more narrowly than it is today, and was seen as the combined skills of reading and writing. These 'subskills' in turn were seen as sets of cognitive skills to be mastered. This was a very narrow view of all that we now recognise as literacy.

Reading was dominated by a concern for the development of word recognition skills, comprehension, and study and reference skills, as if each were separate sets of abilities to be mastered. Writing was often seen simply as 'composition' and received little attention beyond the teaching of surface features and grammar within the framework of narrative discourse. In fact, it was not until the mid-1970s that writing became a serious research pursuit and gained the interest from educators that it deserved. The explosion of 'process writing' under the bold and zealous leadership of scholars like Bob Walshe in Australia and Donald Graves in the USA was one of a number of key events that changed the way we viewed the primary and secondary English curriculum in Australia.

When one considers the last forty years it is possible to identify broad phases or themes in the teaching and research literature as well as in curriculum. In the 1960s the emphasis was on reading and writing as skills. The 1970s saw the emergence of process and meaning as twin concerns within the fields of writing and reading respectively, and an emergence in the latter stages of the decade of a concern for literacy as an integrated practice. In the 1980s we saw a strong concern among teachers and researchers to reconsider literacy as a linguistic phenomenon, a desire to make language form and structure more explicit to students, and the emergence of profiles and global assessment of literacy. The 1990s saw a concern for the sociocultural nature of literacy, and a desire to consider literacy not as a unitary skill but as multiple literacies, and finally, national action on literacy assessment and curriculum development became a reality.

Throughout these four decades children's literature continued to develop and grow in its own way with an explosion of new literary genres, new authors, excursions into reader response theory, the first multimedia texts, and so on. Non-fiction emerged as an even more exciting genre, with the boundaries between literature and factual genres being blurred. Indeed, the division between the traditional school reader and literature also began to break down, with literature finding its way increasingly into instructional programs. These were exciting times! Today, the buzz word is 'multiliteracies' as we consider how reading and writing relate to other sign systems. While the interest has been primarily with digital multimedia, it is interesting to contemplate that the picturebook was exploiting multimodality long before computers were invented.

This book is a product of its times. The opening pages provide a definition of literacy that recognises that literacy is seen differently from what it was forty years ago: an integrated set of practices that require literacy users to draw on multiple sign systems to make meaning. The pages that follow provide a detailed overview of many of the key developments that have shaped literacy research and practice to the present day and a wealth of practical ideas for teachers.

The challenge for all of us as teachers and students of literacy is to expand our literacy horizons. As a literacy researcher I have found that the more I have learned about literacy, the more questions this has posed for me. As a practising cognitive psychologist in the 1970s, I tried desperately to understand how the mind constructed meaning. As I developed greater precision in 'getting at' the cognitive processes that represented reading, I discovered linguistic complexity that made my quest more elusive. As I increasingly explored sociolinguistic aspects of literacy I began to see a social and cultural complexity to literacy that I hadn't recognised before. In the last ten years as I have explored the sociocultural dimensions of literacy I have continued to be amazed by new facets of literacy practices that previously had not been visible to me. I have come to see that while it is important to understand the cognitive processes that allow us to engage in literacy, this cannot be done in isolation from literacy's role as a set of social practices that have the potential to empower or exclude, and indeed to shape the very human relationships that are the essence of our being. I have also come to appreciate that literacy offers the power to inform or deceive, to express love or hate—to have an impact on the human condition.

But being positive, literacy has the potential to open up 'other worlds' (Cairney 1991). In the last six years I have also been struck by the enormous impact that cyber text and multimedia texts are having on the way we experience and use literacy in our world. The next decade will be one in which literacy will increasingly be characterised by the use of multiple sign systems to make meaning. The boundaries between written, visual, and real-world texts will blur as we seek to make sense of our worlds, using all that we have available to us. And yet, as I conclude my comments, I'm reminded that there is something inherently basic about literacy that will not change—the power of story. This is something that Harold Rosen constantly brought to our attention. Much of human experience and existence is lived out through narrative. There is immense power in 'story' to teach, to share, and to express all human emotions. This is indeed timeless.

In his wonderful story *The Stone Book*, Allan Garner (1976) tells the story of his English ancestors. In this brilliant tale, Mary expresses to her father the desire to have a book, a prayer book, to carry to chapel. This was a significant request to make of her stonemason father—not a man of letters, but of stone. Her wish was indeed granted, her father presenting her with the book she wanted. Garner tells it this way:

'There,' said Father. 'That'll do.'

He gave Mary a prayer book bound in blue-black calf skin, tooled, stitched and decorated. It was only by the weight that she could tell it was stone and not leather.

'It's better than a book you can open,' said Father. 'A book has only one story. And tomorrow I'll cut you a brass cross and let it in the front with some dabs of lead, and then I'll guarantee you'd think it was Lord Stanley's, if it's held right.'

Garner continues: 'And Mary sat by the fire and read the stone book that had in it all the stories of the world and the flowers of the flood'.

In a profound way, the old stonemason had learned something that it has taken literacy scholars and teachers many years to learn. Books have the power to be used to tell but a single story, and yet all the stories of the world are at our fingertips in the multiple signs that fill our world.

I want to thank the authors for asking me to write the foreword to this book. I trust that it will enrich readers' understanding of what literacy is and how it is nurtured and used as we relate one to another.

PROFESSOR TREVOR CAIRNEY
MASTER OF NEW COLLEGE
UNIVERSITY OF NEW SOUTH WALES

Preface

This book has been written to provide a suitable text for students in primary education and a resource for teachers. It places emphasis on both the theoretical and practical aspects of literacy and relates directly to everyday practice in the classroom.

Literacy: Reading, Writing, and Children's Literature is divided into three parts. Each part is written by different authors who explore the various aspects of literacy while giving attention to the obvious relationships among them. In doing so, the authors have provided day-to-day examples of classroom practice allocated specifically to the teaching of literacy in the school.

A text in three parts

In part I, *Gordon Winch and Marcelle Holliday* take what they call a 'balanced view of reading', which is widely held throughout the world today. They see reading, and literacy generally, operating in a sociocultural context where readers take on a number of roles depending on the situation, the text-type, and the nature of the reader. They explore the research relating to a range of aspects of reading and argue that both reading and writing depend on the simultaneous interaction of phonological–graphological, grammatical, and semantic information operating in varying contexts. They also explore the growing impact of literacy in the digital age and the influence of multiliteracies on communication.

Part 1 presents a balanced view of reading

Practical outcomes of reading are viewed chronologically. For example, chapters dealing with the child before school, the emergent reader, the developing reader, and the independent reader are considered. Shared, Guided, and Independent Reading are explored and assessment in reading is discussed in a range of possible types. This part provides the necessary amalgam of theory and practice that supports the underlying aim of the book.

An amalgam of theory and practice

In part II, *Lesley Ljungdahl and Paul March* consider writing in a sociocultural context also and see it developing in the classroom with other literacy skills. They believe that teachers should have a clear understanding of the nature of writing in society as well as a knowledge of ways it can be developed in the primary school years. Thus approaches and strategies for teaching writing are discussed, together with the skills of spelling, grammar, and punctuation and how they can be integrated to develop a polished text.

Part II places focus on writing development in sociocultural context

The authors see writing as a process—a process over which students gain greater control as they progress through the grades. It is therefore important for the young teacher to have a grasp of the different stages of the writing continuum and to be able to assess students' writing progress in order to devise suitable teaching practices and assessment. Although the focus of this part is on the practical skills of writing and the ways they can be achieved, the authors emphasise that writing itself is a creative act and a source of wonder and joy.

Writing is both a practical skill and a creative act

Rosemary Ross Johnston believes that children's literature is part of a literature continuum and that serious study of its theory can inform and enrich classroom practice. In part III, she

Part III stresses the importance of children's literature in the achievement of literacy

introduces the concept of Sustainable Creative Pedagogy in relation to language, literacy, and children's literature. She stresses the contribution that the study of children's literature can make to the multiple aspects of literacy, particularly critical literacy, and notes that children's books inscribe cultural attitudes and reflect in diverse ways the society that shapes them. She also stresses the importance, in a print-rich technological environment, of teachers modelling principles of lifelong learning and exposing children to books beyond their immediate needs and capacities. This must always be done with care and consideration for young students.

Children's literature offers diverse sites for practising and developing traditional literacy skills (not only reading and writing but also speaking and listening), for philosophical enquiry and the exploration of social issues, and for learning about multiliteracies including visual and cultural literacy. Children's literature is also a valuable resource in the multicultural, multilingual classroom.

Children's literature provides diverse sites for literacy skills in a social context

This part of the book has also been designed with classroom activities, often suitable for both primary and secondary contexts, that provide examples of how theoretical ideas can be applied in teaching. There is a strong emphasis on picturebooks, which, in their modern form, can be sophisticated and complex and are short and admirably suited to teaching practice.

New to this edition

The third edition seeks to enrich the content of the earlier book by addressing the increasingly significant influence of multiliteracies and the impact of the digital age. To do this, new chapters have been included where relevant, and special boxes are added to every chapter to address the effect of multiliteracy and digital age technology on the teaching of literacy skills. All chapters have been updated to reflect recent developments.

As well as the above, new 'In the Classroom' boxes have been added throughout the book to enhance the practical application of theory to classroom practice. Major revisions have been made to the chapters dealing with Handwriting and Spelling, and Punctuation and Grammar.

A new section is included in chapter 2 that reflects the important role of oracy in the classroom. 'Talking and listening' activities are integrated with reading and writing to improve overall literacy.

A new chapter on visual literacy provides a theorised and practical approach which will be of benefit to both primary and secondary teachers. Most chapters in Part 3 have been substantially rewritten.

Also, an overview of part and chapter titles has been included prior to the Contents to enable easy identification of the main contents of the book.

Key features of the book

Covers the spectrum of theory and practice in Australian schools

Literacy: Reading, Writing, and Children's Literature covers the spectrum of the theory and practice of teaching literacy in modern Australian primary schools. Its structure allows students to focus on the various aspects of literacy teaching and their practical outcomes. Students will be able to use the book over an extended period during their university courses and retain it as a suitable reference when teaching.

The text is designed to be used in all states and territories of Australia, and reference is made to each curriculum and literacy practice. Each part of the book—Reading, Writing, and Children's Literature—may be accessed separately or used with general courses on literacy. Critical thinking and discussion questions and activities are provided throughout and Further Reading and Web Links sections are provided, when relevant, at the end of chapters.

Designed for flexible use

A glossary of terms and a full index with cross-referencing are located at the back of the book, together with an appendix that lists contact details of organisations relating to literacy teaching in Australia. Words that are listed in the glossary are printed in the text in bold.

Provides for user-friendly access

An introductory Chapter Highlights box pinpoints the features of each chapter for easy access, while a Summary of the content is provided at the end of each chapter. This is followed by Critical thinking and study exercises, which will prove invaluable for students and teachers alike.

In this book the problem of the gender-neutral pronoun has been dealt with by using the masculine and feminine pronouns more or less alternately, unless a generic 'he or she' is needed.

The three parts of the book stress the developmental nature of literacy and provide examples of literacy teaching strategies across the primary school. Some of the material, particularly in the children's literature section, will also be helpful to secondary school teachers.

Contains scholarly comment and teaching strategies

Scholarly comment on various aspects of literacy is included in separate sections within the text to add depth to the discussion or to elucidate significant points. Literacy in Australia is considered in a world perspective and international research, theory, and practice are consulted throughout the text.

Guided Tour

Your navigation tools

Ease of navigation throughout the book is assisted by a complete Table of Contents, complemented by a brief Table of Contents and overview at the start of each Part.

Brief Contents

Contents

Reading
GORDON WINCH AND MARCELLE HOLLIDAY

PART 1

Overview

Chapter Highlights pinpoint the main topics of each chapter to assist navigation and identification of key issues.

2 SOME FACTORS RELATING TO READING

Chapter Highlights

- The writing system of English p. 18
- The sound system of English p. 23
- The importance of oral language p. 24
- In the classroom pp. 25 and 31
- Phonemic awareness and phonological awareness p. 26
- How readers operate p. 28
- Text and the locus of meaning p. 30
- Reading and technology p. 34
- Multiliteracies p. 35
- Literacy in the digital age p. 36
- The matter of dyslexia p. 37

Overview

There are many significant factors relating to the teaching of reading that every teacher should understand. These include the writing and sound systems of English, the importance of oral language, phonemic/phonological awareness and the locus of meaning. Modern technology is changing the face of reading and the question of dyslexia must be understood and kept in perspective. The above factors must be seen in the context of the socio-economic contexts in which students live and learn.

The writing system of English

English orthography can be described as an alphabetic writing system. The written symbols, the alphabet, represent the sounds, or phonemes (individual speech sounds), that allow a reader to distinguish between words. For example, in the words cat and fat, the two phonemes /k/ represented by 'c' and /f/ represented by 'f' allow the reader to distinguish the difference between the two words. There are forty-four or forty-five phonemes in English and because there are only twenty-six letters to represent them, the writing system presents special problems for the reader. To begin, some letters have to double up to represent the forty-five sounds.

To complicate things even more, English has borrowed from many different languages over its history and has kept many of the original spellings. As a result, we have different spellings of

> **English has an alphabetic writing system**

Margin notes highlight key concepts important to a student's understanding of literacy.

The importance of oral language

Oral language, or 'oracy', refers to the joint processes of listening and talking. 'Listening' can be described as the process of attending to and constructing meaning from spoken texts. It involves distinguishing the sounds of words, and being sensitive to the tone, pitch, stress, and pace of speech. 'Talking' can be described as the process of presenting meaning through the construction of spoken texts. It involves enunciating sounds appropriately, using tone, pitch, stress, and pace effectively, and using such nonverbal devices as gesture.

> **Oral language, or 'oracy', is made up of the joint processes of listening and talking**

We use oral language when we engage in social situations of which spoken interaction is a part, and the forms of oral language we use are governed by culturally accepted ways of using language. Listening, talking, reading, and writing have much in common since they all deal with the language user's attempts to construct and interpret meaning within social situations using elements of language.

Within the context of their families, children learn to use the basic structures of their home language before they go to school, and they gain control over almost all the sounds and many of the rules and principles related to the grammar of the language (although they are generally not able to talk about the grammatical features they are using). By school age almost all children have become competent users of the language spoken in their own community. This oral language competence forms a foundation for the learning of reading and writing.

> **By school age most children are competent users of spoken language. This ability provides the necessary foundation for learning to read and write, although it should be noted that deaf children, who may never learn to hear and speak, can learn to read.**

When children begin school they are ready to expand their spoken language competencies in response to new situations and demands, and to begin using oral language as a vehicle for learning in all areas of the curriculum. As children develop as oral language users, they will:

- understand that different social contexts require different oral texts
- use talk effectively to meet personal and social needs

Aids to learning

Summary of main points: a concise summary is provided at the end of each chapter to help students to identify the important issues covered in the chapter.

▶ **Summary**

1 Telling stories through images has a long and inspiring heritage in cultures across the world.
2 Visual literacy is related to signs, symbols and the theory of semiotics.
3 Traditional notions of literacy have a very strong visual element and this relates to what we can call the *visuality of literacy*.
4 As all literacy does, visual literacy pertains to transmission of ideas, exchange of meaning, and communication.
5 The interest in visual literacy highlights the emergence of new ideas about *visual language*.
8 Picturebooks play specifically to the visuality of literacy.
9 Signs, images, and paralinguistics—unspoken but visually expressed gestures, attitudes, and expressions—are all significantly culturally coded, and care must be taken in reading what they 'mean'.
10 The concept of the *visuality of literacy*, which refers to the significance of *seeing* in literacy—seeing the letters of the alphabet and reproducing them in multiple modes for others to see in multiple contexts—reminds us that

Critical Thinking and **Study Exercises** throughout the book are invaluable for students and teachers alike.

Critical thinking and study exercises

1 Discuss some of the principles of classroom assessment in relation to students' writing skills. A sample of a student's writing, accompanied by a student profile, may help you to direct the discussion.
   a What is considered 'correct' English?
   b Why should assessment be integral to classroom activities?
   c Why should assessment strategies be varied and cover a wide range of features?

a Suggest activities that are appropriate for self-assessment, group assessment and teacher assessment?
b Design a self-assessment sheet for a particular grade level and for a particular text-type. For example, list five items for a Year 2 class writing a narrative text.
3 Devise some 'authentic' writing assessment tasks for junior and/or senior grades in different areas of the curriculum, e.g. Mathematics,

Further Reading and **Web Links** are provided, when relevant, at the end of chapters.

Further reading

Angelillo, J. & L. M. Calkins 2002, *A Fresh Approach to Teaching Punctuation: Helping young writers use conventions with precision and purpose*, Scholastic Professional Books, New York.
Derewianka, B. 1998, *A Grammar Companion for Primary Teachers*, PETA, Sydney.
Partridge, E. 1953, *You Have a Point There*, Hamish Hamilton, London.
Snooks & Co. 2002, *Style Manual For Authors, Editors and Printers*, rev. 6th edn, Snooks & Co., John Wiley & Sons, Canberra.
Truss, L. 2003, *Eats, Shoots & Leaves: The zero tolerance approach to punctuation*, Profile Books, London.
Winch, G. & G. Blaxell 1999, *The Primary Grammar Handbook: Traditional and functional grammar, punctuation and usage*, rev. edn, Horwitz Martin, Sydney.

Web links

Book raps: http://rite.ed.qut.edu.au/old_oz-teachernet/projects/book-rap/about.html
Kim's Korner: www.kimskorner4teachertalk.com
Exploring English: Punctuation: shared-visions.com/explore/english/punct.html
OWL Online Writing Labs, Purdue University
Overview of punctuation. Includes some interactive exercises with answers. http://owl.english.purdue.edu/handouts/grammar/#punctuation
University of Ottawa: Punctuation
Includes section on identifying punctuation errors with exercises and explanations for correct use. www.uottawa.ca/academic/arts/writcent/hypergrammar/node227.html

Key topics and practical applications

In the Classroom boxes throughout the book illustrate the practical application of theory to classroom practice.

Literacy in the Digital Age boxes demonstrates the impact of technology on literacy. They provide ideas for using technology in the classroom.

Multiliteracies boxes throughout the book to highlight the importance and diversity of multiliteracy to all aspects of literacy.

Current and emerging issues are highlighted in relevant sections throughout the book.

 Iɴ ᴛʜᴇ ᴄʟᴀssʀᴏᴏᴍ

Systematic phonics in Early Stage 1 (Kindergarten/Prep)
The systematic teaching of phonics begins in Kindergarten (Prep). Approaches vary considerably. Some schools use one of the many published phonic programs; others devise their own method. Beginning teachers will be obliged to follow the approach used at a school and develop and modify it as they become more experienced. Below is an example of the approach used by one very experienced and successful teacher of children in their first year of school.

At the beginning of the year, I introduce the basic sounds, vowels and consonants, and use all kinds of examples of the sounds in words and in the stories the children meet.
There is a sound chart always at the front of the room and each morning I go over all of the sounds, almost as a drill. They love it!
When the children are writing their own stories, I hand out sound strips, 'magic wands' which they can

▶ Lɪᴛᴇʀᴀᴄʏ ɪɴ ᴛʜᴇ ᴅɪɢɪᴛᴀʟ ᴀɢᴇ

The idea of story worlds as a kind of virtual reality connects strongly to some of the e-literature experiences now available, particularly electronic literary theme parks ('real' virtual reality!). There are two main types of these:
1 *MUDs* (acronym for multi-user dungeons or domains, related to the idea of Dungeons and Dragons): synchronous chat rooms where participants log in and take on roles, using text.
2 *Story Palaces:* similar themed sites, often like cartoons, or may be elaborately decorated. Palaces may be story worlds or communal meeting places, and are built in cyberspace by a community of fans and enthusiasts, who can also construct and take on characters (avatars, realistic-looking or cartoon figures, available in all sorts of poses, often designed with costumes and props) and play out (in collaborative role-

Aʙᴏʀɪɢɪɴᴀʟ sᴛᴜᴅɪᴇs ᴡᴇʙ ǫᴜᴇsᴛ

'There has been much discussion lately on the news and in the newspapers about whether the Australian Government should make a formal apology to the indigenous people of Australia for the Government policies of the past which have affected them.'

'The Prime Minister has requested a group be appointed to help advise himself and other central community representatives on how Australian people view saying "Sorry" to the Aboriginal People.'

'You have been appointed to that Advisors' group, which consists of an historian, a reporter, a health worker, an anthropologist and a librarian. Together with your other team members, you are required to investigate the issue and then report back your findings.

Question: Should the Prime Minister and the Government say 'sorry' to the Aboriginal People? Why/why not? (bestwebquests.com)

Mᴜʟᴛɪʟɪᴛᴇʀᴀᴄɪᴇs

Literacy Session on 'monsters'
1 Use different communication media such as cartoons (*The Incredible Hulk*), film (*Shrek*), audio (*Beauty and the Beast* recorded story), paintings (Uccello's *St George and the Dragon*) to show how 'monsters' are portrayed.
2 Find illustrations and information on monsters from books and the Internet, e.g. dragons, Dracula, Frankenstein, Loch Ness Monster.
3 Incorporate these ideas into students' writing tasks, using the strategies of Shared, Guided and Independent Writing.

Shared Writing
The teacher and students suggest relevant words, phrases, and sentences that might describe monsters:

frightening, horrible
the shocking appearance; a dreadful lurch
The enormous ogre turned away.

Acknowledgments

The authors would like to thank Venetia Somerset, who edited the manuscript of the first and third edition with unrivalled skill and patience; Anne Mulvaney, who edited the second edition with equal professionalism; Debra James, Anna Martin, and Chris Wyness and his team at Oxford University Press who developed the second edition in its final form; and Lucy McLoughlin, Tim Campbell and Fleur Wilkins, who developed the third edition in its final form.

We would also like to extend thanks to the following people: Rhondda Brill and Gregory Blaxell for their work in the planning of the project; John Stannard, National Director of the National Literacy Strategy in the United Kingdom, for providing invaluable information; Professor Trevor Cairney, Professor of Education and Master of New College, University of New South Wales, Sydney, for his scholarly research and for the Foreword to this book; Ed Truscott, Past President of the Australian Literacy Educators' Association, for informed advice; Associate Professor Barbara Poston-Anderson for her contribution to the early literacy section; Phillipa Morris and the staff of the library at the Kuring-gai campus of the University of Technology, Sydney for their professional assistance; Rodney March, who contributed original art; Diana Parry, who took the photographs; members of the ChiLPA (Children's Literature Pure and Applied) Project in Finland; Annabel Robinson and Helen Cousens for research assistance; Malcolm Johnston, for photographs and research; Alan Robinson for the sketches in Chapter 29; Stephen Harris, Principal of Northern Beaches Christian School, for providing information on new technology in classrooms; David Costello, Principal, and the staff (especially Denise Petersen) and students of North Rocks Primary School for their help in the Writing part; and our colleagues, and the whole community of scholars in universities and professional associations, who have contributed directly and indirectly in ways too numerous to mention.

Special thanks are reserved for the principals, teachers, and children of the many schools who contributed examples of good literacy teaching. Particular mention must be made of Carmel McDonald, Principal of St Gerard's Primary School, Carlingford and Susan Hartigan with her class 1H; Robert Phipps, Principal, Judy O'Connell, and Stevon Orlando, The Hills Grammar School, Kenthurst; Mrs Gillian Moore, Principal, Lindall Watson and Linda Yeates, Pymble Ladies' College; Lorelle Shelley of Arden Anglican School; Brian Pennington, Principal of Sydney Grammar Preparatory School, St Ives and Rowena Lee, Head of the Junior School; David Costello, Principal of North Rocks Primary School; John Barbour and Stephen Baker of the Department of Education, Science and Training, and finally, special thanks to the undergraduate and postgraduate students at Kuring-gai campus of the University of Technology, Sydney and the international research students of the ChiLPA Project at Åbo Akademi University, Finland, who provided invaluable insights and refreshing reactions to our work.

The authors and publishers wish to thank copyright-holders for granting permission to reproduce illustrative material and textual extracts. Sources are as follows:

ABC Books for extracts from *A is for Aunty* by E. Russell; Blake Education Pty Ltd for extracts from *Sal and Sam at the Farm* and *Danny Dolphin's Nose* by G. Winch and G. Blaxell;

Cambridge University Press for the extract from *English as a Global Village* by David Crystal, 1997, Cambridge University Press; Childerset Pty Ltd for extracts from *Samantha Seagull's Sandals* written by Gordon Winch, illustrated by Tony Oliver; Christopher Little Literary Agency for the extract from *Harry Potter and the Philosopher's Stone* by J. K. Rowling, copyright © text Joanne Rowling 1997; Department of Education, Training and Youth Affairs, Canberra for extracts from *Mapping Literacy Achievement: Results of the 1996 National School English Literacy Survey* (1997) and *Australian Language and Literacy Policy 1991, Companion volume to the Policy Paper*; Education Department of Western Australia for the extract from *First Steps: Writing Developmental Continuum*, reproduced by courtesy of the Education Department of Western Australia; HarperCollins Publishers Australia for the extract from *The Bamboo Flute* by Gary Disher; Heinemann, Portsmouth, USA for the extract from *Bridges to Literacy* edited by De Ford, Lyons and Pinnell; Lothian Books for the extract from *Memorial* by Gary Crew, illustrated by Shaun Tan; Magabala Books Aboriginal Corporation for the extract from *Do Not Go Around the Edges* by Daisy Utemorrah and Pat Torres; Margaret Hamilton Books for extracts from *V for Vanishing* by P. Mullins and *Rain Dance* by C. Applegate and D. Huxley; NSW Department of Education and Training for the extract from *Teaching Reading: A K–6 Framework*, 1997 and the extract from Basic Skills Test (BST) 1997; Office of the Board of Studies, NSW for the extract from 'Reading Outcomes and Indicators', from English K–6 Syllabus © Board of Studies NSW, 1998; Omnibus Books for the extract from *Time for Bed* by Mem Fox and Jane Dyer, 1993; Pearson Education Australia for the extracts from *My Place* by N. Wheatley and D. Rawlins, 1987; Penguin Books Australia Ltd for extracts from *The Wolf* by Margaret Barbalet, illustrated by Jane Tanner, *The Fisherman and the Theefyspray* by Paul Jennings, illustrated by Jane Tanner, *Henry's Bed* by Margaret Perversi, illustrated by Ron Brooks, *John Brown, Rose and the Midnight Cat* by Jenny Wagner and Ron Brooks, *Hating Alison Ashley* by Robin Klein and *You and Me, Murrawee* by Kerrie Hashmi; Penguin UK for 'Ears for my Family' by Christine, from *The Language of Primary School Children* by Connie and Harold Rosen (Penguin Books, 1973) copyright © Schools Council Publications, 1973 and for the cover illustration of *Each Peach Pear Plum* by Janet and Allan Ahlberg (Viking, 1978) copyright © Janet and Allan Ahlberg, 1978; Random House Group Ltd for the extract from *Tidy Titch* by Pat Hutchins, *Zoo* by Anthony Browne, *Way Home* by L. Hathorn and G. Rogers and *The Werewolf Knight* by J. Wagner and R. Roennfeldt; Rondor Music (Australia) Pty Ltd for 'Telegraph Road' by Mark Knopfler; Scholastic, Inc. for extracts from *Let's Eat* by Ana Zamorano, illustrated by Julie Vivas; Gordon Winch for 'Sort of Brown', University of Queensland Press for the extract from *Lisdalia* by Brian Caswell; Walker Books Limited for extracts from *Mousewing* text © 1987 William Mayne, illustrations © 1987 Martin Baynton, *Owl Babies* text © 1992 Martin Waddell, illustrations © 1992 Patrick Benson, *Out and About* © 1988, 1998 Shirley Hughes, 'Who dat Girl?' © 1994 Valerie Bloom, from *A Caribbean Dozen* edited by John Agard and Grace Nicholls, illustrated by Cathie Felstead, *Chameleons are Cool* text © 1997 Martin Jenkins, illustrated by Sue Shields, *Beware, Beware* text © 1993 Sue Hill, illustrated by Angela Barrett and *Ginger* © 1997 Charlotte Voake; R. D. Walshe for the extract from *Writing and Learning in Australia*.

Every effort has been made to trace the original source of copyright material contained in this book. The publisher would be pleased to hear from copyright-holders to rectify any errors or omissions.

Introduction:
Literacy in the Modern World

What is literacy?

What can we take as a suitable definition of literacy for the modern world?

The Australian Language and Literacy Policy (1991) states:

What is a suitable definition of literacy? Literacy is the ability to read and use written information and to write appropriately in a range of contexts. It is used to develop knowledge and understanding, to achieve personal growth and to function effectively in our society. Literacy also includes the recognition of numbers and basic mathematical signs and symbols within text.

Literacy involves the integration of speaking, listening and critical thinking with reading and writing. Effective literacy is intrinsically purposeful, flexible and dynamic and continues to develop throughout an individual's lifetime.

All Australians need to have effective literacy in English, not only for their personal benefit and welfare but also for Australia to reach its social and economic goals.

A literacy definition for the modern world While this definition might have been adequate for the era of print-only literacy, it seems, now, to lack reference to the multitude of literacies that form part of the modern world. In these we might include technological literacies, the complex web of literate practices that have grown in conjunction with computer technology and other audiovisual modes of communication.

As Snyder has pointed out in *Silicon Literacies* (2002: 3),

We need an expanded definition which recognises that reading and writing, considered as print-based and logocentric, are only part of what people have to learn to be literate. Now, for the first time in history, the written, oral and audiovisual modalities of communication are integrated into multimodal hypertext systems made accessible via the Internet and the World Wide Web.

Whatever definition we choose, it must include those facets of literacy as we know it today: not only the basic view of literacy as the ability to read and write but also what are termed social literacy, critical literacy, mathematical literacy, and technological literacy. Essential to all aspects of literacy in Australia, nevertheless, is the ability to read and write in English.

Literacy is the ability to make and share meaning by constructing and interpreting texts. Texts may be oral or written, contain graphic elements, such as images, maps or tables, be paper-based or electronic. Many texts in modern society combine two or more of these elements.

Literacy also includes an understanding of the relationship between text and context and involves the integration of speaking, listening, and critical thinking with reading and writing.

The importance of literacy

Literacy is integral to success in modern society. It pervades almost every area of social interaction including education, work, leisure, communications, and business and is a key component of the information revolution. Its importance is underlined in the report of the National Inquiry into the Teaching of Literacy:

Literacy is integral to success in modern society

> The contents of this report and the processes leading to its production are grounded in two guiding propositions. First, skilled and knowledgeable young people are Australia's most valuable resource for the future. Second, teachers are the most valuable resource available to schools. Equipping young people to engage productively in the knowledge economy and in society more broadly is fundamental to both individual and national prosperity, and depends primarily on: the ability to speak, read and write effectively; and the provision of quality teaching. (Dept Education, Science and Training 2005: Preface)

Competence in literacy is essential if an individual is to participate fully in society—able to take part in the workforce, engage in democratic processes, and contribute to society. Literacy is also an essential component of social justice. It enables individuals to gain access to social resources and helps them to participate in social institutions. It can be a source of enjoyment and can contribute to individuals' widening knowledge and understanding of themselves and the world.

Literacy is an essential component of social justice

Literacy is crucial to young people's success at school. Students with effective literacy skills excel not only in English but also in other areas of the curriculum. Students' overall school performance and their successful transition from one stage of schooling to the next depends on a well-developed foundation of literacy skills and on the positive attitudes to learning that accompany these skills. Students need to have the necessary knowledge, skills, attitudes, and understandings to engage with the literacy demands of the curriculum and to participate effectively in society.

Denise Lievesley and Albert Motivans state: 'Literacy plays an essential role in improving the lives of individuals by enabling economic security and good health, and enriches societies by building human capital, fostering cultural identity and tolerance, and promoting civic participation' (2002: 8).

Most governments throughout the world give a high priority to the development of literacy skills in their populations. As part of basic education, literacy is seen as a key factor in a country's social and economic development. The UN Educational, Scientific and Cultural Organisation (UNESCO), as part of its education strategy, sees literacy as 'a fundamental human right'. The Director-General of UNESCO, as part of his message on International Literacy Day 2001, said:

Literacy is a fundamental human right

> We must never forget that literacy is indeed a cause for celebration: for individuals and their families and for society at large. Humankind has achieved spectacular progress in regard to literacy: there are now close to four billion literate people in the world. Moreover, many of today's rapid technological advances are focused on information and communication, which are central to the practice of literacy.

www.unesco.org/uis

Literacy as social practice

Literacy is embedded in our everyday lives

We can think of literacy not merely as a single skill, or even a set of skills, but as a way of operating with a variety of texts within particular sets of social situations. Whenever we use literacy we do so in the context of a social practice. We don't 'do' literacy. Rather, we engage in social situations of which literacy is an integral part. Literacy is embedded in the practices of our everyday lives. When we buy a car, do the shopping, visit the doctor, or pay a bill, we engage in social practices in which literacy is embedded.

There are culturally accepted ways of engaging in social practices and these can vary across cultures and over time. Greeting people, talking on the phone, sending greeting cards, sending text messages, even shopping, are social practices that vary across cultures and have changed over time. When these practices involve literacy, the forms of literacy also vary from culture to culture and from situation to situation. Out of a need to achieve these social purposes we reach for the skills of literacy.

Teaching children to be literate, therefore, should not be seen merely as providing them with a set of skills to transfer from situation to situation. Rather, it should involve teaching them about how to participate in, understand and gain control of the social practices of their society and the literacy practices that are embedded in them.

As James Gee says in his foreword to Lewis' *Literacy Practices as Social Acts*:

> Literacy-related social practices almost always involve a good many other things besides written language. They almost always include and integrate, along with written language, specific and characteristic ways of talking, acting, interacting, thinking, feeling, valuing, and using various sorts of symbols and tools. Becoming a participant in a specific social practice requires access offered by those already adept at the practice or those who 'own' and control it. (Lewis 2001)

Allan Luke and Peter Freebody take this concept further:

> History teaches us that 'literacy' refers to a malleable set of cultural practices that are shaped and re-shaped by different, often competing, social and cultural interests. As a result we do not view how to teach literacy as a 'scientific' decision, but rather as a moral, political and cultural decision about the kind of literate practices that are needed to enhance people's agency over their life trajectories and to enhance communities' intellectual, cultural and semiotic resources in print/multi-mediated economies. Literacy education is ultimately about the kinds of citizens/subjects that could and should be constructed. Teaching and learning isn't just a matter of skill acquisition and knowledge transmission or natural growth. It's about building identities and cultures, communities and institutions. And 'failure' at literacy isn't about individual skill deficits—it's about access and apprenticeship into institutions and resources, discourses and texts. (1995: 5)

Literacy and text

A multimodal concept of text

At the centre of an understanding of literacy is the concept of 'text'. A text is, essentially, any spoken, written, audio, or visual communication involving language. Many texts in modern society use varying combinations of all these modes. Whenever we use language to communicate we either construct a text or interpret a text constructed by someone else. In some instances, such as conversation, we construct and interpret a text simultaneously. We construct or interpret texts as part of engaging in social practices of which the text plays a part. For example, when we go shopping we interact with a range of texts as an integral part of that action; texts such as our shopping list, product labels, price tags, advertising signs or the growing total of our purchases on the checkout computer. And we interpret these texts in relation to our purpose, for example: 'How much sugar is in that brand of breakfast cereal?', 'Can I afford that coffee?'

When we speak or write we construct texts by making choices from the resources of the language system to achieve our particular social purposes. We decide how to present our texts using oral, written, audio, or visual means or a combination of these, depending on our purpose and audience. When we listen or read we create meaning from texts constructed by others by interpreting them within our particular social and cultural context.

The aim of any literacy program, therefore, should be to teach students to construct a wide range of texts, and to interpret a wide range of texts constructed by others within and beyond the social and cultural contexts in which they live.

Students should interpret and construct a wide range of texts

To do this, students need to understand that:

- different types of texts exist
- texts serve different social purposes
- texts are typically structured in particular ways
- we make choices from the resources of the language system to construct texts to achieve particular social purposes
- we choose how to present our texts depending on our purpose and audience
- we interpret texts constructed by others by understanding how and why particular texts have been constructed
- we use our knowledge of oral, written, and audiovisual text structures when we interpret texts constructed by others.

Literacy and technology: Literacy in the digital age

Literacy has always been closely bound up with technology. From earliest times, peoples have used technologies such as the clay tablet and papyrus to record ideas and stories, to save information, and to communicate across time and space. Over time, technological inventions such as the printing press, fountain and ballpoint pens, and the telephone prompted huge changes in the ways literacy, as part of social interaction, was practised.

The digital age extends our literate practices

Electronic technologies are part of the long list of technological advances called into the service of literate societies to improve their ability to communicate. But these new electronic technologies have opened the door to a whole new world of communication possibilities. It is important to point out, however, that the literacy practices that have developed alongside the technological inventions have done so because they meet the needs of socially grounded communication.

When we make use of the new technologies to engage in information-gathering and communication activities we are using literacy in new ways. When we use a mobile phone and send text messages, surf the Net, send emails or bank and shop online, use the fax or leave messages on answering machines, or listen to a song on our iPod or MP3, we are using the new technologies to meet our communication needs. New possibilities open up to us new ways of meeting socially grounded communication needs and these require, inevitably, new knowledge and skills. We need to learn how these new text forms are structured and what conventions apply to their use. We need to learn how these text forms operate in culturally significant ways to empower individuals and groups in society.

As Snyder says:

Central to all these changes is the altering of the landscape of representation and communication. We are in the midst of a shift from an era of mass communication to an era of individuated communication; from unidirectional communication from the centre to the mass, to multidirectional communication from many locations; from the 'passive' audience to the 'interactive' audience. (2002; 179)

And further:

In an electronically mediated world, being literate is to do with understanding how the different modalities are combined in complex ways to create meaning. People have to learn to make sense of the iconic systems evident in computer displays—with all the combination of signs, symbols, pictures, words and sounds. Language is no longer just grammar, lexicon and semantics: language now comprises a wider range of semiotic systems that cut across reading, writing, viewing and speaking. What looks like the same text or multimedia genre on paper or on screen is not functionally the same. It follows different meaning conventions and requires different skills for its successful use. Further, it operates in different social networks for different purposes as part of different human activities. Understanding these multimodal texts requires an interdisciplinary range of methods of analysis: linguistic, semiotic, social, cultural, historical and critical. (2002: 3)

We are living in a multiliterate world

We are facing a new world of literacy, a world in which the literacy skills of the paper-based text are no longer enough. Along with traditional literacy skills, we must now include facility with the many multimodal literacy practices that are made possible by the new technologies.

What, then, are the implications of these communication and information technologies for the classroom? What role should teachers play in helping their students to understand and use these new technologies? As Snyder states:

Literacy educators cannot be satisfied with merely identifying, describing and making familiar to students the new multimodal text types: this represents an increasingly inadequate response to the changes to literacy practices associated with the use of new technologies. We need to develop pedagogical and curriculum frameworks that seek to endow students with their place in the new global system, but also with the capacity to view that system critically. At the very least we can help our students to engage in local forms of cultural critique. (2002: 181)

Online learning

One of the fastest-growing areas of education is online learning. One significant project in this area is that of the Learning Federation, a consortium of the governments of Australia, the Australian States and Territories, and New Zealand. This project employs emerging technologies to produce world-class online curriculum content, which is freely available for students in a range of curriculum areas.

The products of the Learning Federation are known as Learning Objects. Learning Objects are 'chunks' of digital material (e.g. graphics, text, audio, animation, interactive tools), designed to provide students with multimodal learning opportunities that are engaging and interactive.

In the field of Literacy, learning materials are available in three areas: Text reception (reading and listening), Text production (writing and talking) and Critical literacy. All three areas use a wide range of multimodal elements to engage students and support them in authentic literacy tasks in a well-constructed virtual environment. The tasks are based on literacy outcomes and are closely linked to the syllabuses of the participating systems. Students are provided with appropriate feedback on their learning in a variety of supportive and engaging ways.

Comprehensive details about all learning objects are published on the Learning Federation website at www.thelearningfederation.edu.au.

Literacy standards

The authors of this book take the view that there is no sudden literacy crisis in Australian schools but that there are certain problems, particularly in specific areas where students are not achieving to their potential. This matter must be addressed.

The Programme for International Student Assessment (PISA) 2000 sheds light on world literacy standards

In 2000 the Organization for Economic Cooperation and Development (OECD) carried out the Programme for International Student Assessment (PISA) Survey of 15-year-olds in thirty-two OECD and other developed countries.

In its report of the survey results, *Knowledge and Skills for Life*, the OECD asks: 'Are students well prepared to meet the challenges of the future? Are they able to analyse, reason and communicate their ideas effectively? Do they have the capacity to continue learning throughout life? These are questions that parents, students, the public and those who run education systems continually ask' (OECD 2001).

The report provides some answers. It assesses how far students near the end of compulsory education have acquired some of the knowledge and skills that are essential for full participation in society. It presents evidence on student performance in reading, mathematics, and scientific literacy, reveals factors that influence the development of these skills at home and at school, and examines the implications for policy development.

Students taking part in PISA were asked questions based on a variety of written texts, ranging from a short story to a letter on the Internet and information presented in a diagram. They were assessed on their capacity to *retrieve* specified information, on whether they could *interpret* what they read, and on how well they could *reflect* on and *evaluate* it, drawing on their existing knowledge. For each of these three aspects of reading literacy, students were given a score based on the difficulty of the tasks they could perform. A combined score showed their overall reading performance. On the basis of this score each student was assigned to one of five reading levels.

PISA's results showed considerable variation in the levels of knowledge and skills among students, schools, and countries. The results showed differences in performances between males and females. They also showed that, in some countries, significant differences exist between student performance in the more 'routine' reading tasks of identifying information and reporting it, and tasks requiring reflection and evaluation.

Literacy standards are improving

The results showed also that students with more advantaged backgrounds tended to perform better, though the extent to which the socioeconomic background of students and schools affected student performance varied. Some countries have managed to mitigate the influence of social background and some have done that while achieving high overall mean performances.

However, there is still a long way to go before literacy is achieved throughout the world. The UNESCO Institute for Statistics (2002) provides the following figures. Almost 80 per cent of the world's population aged fifteen years and over is now literate, including more women than ever before. The new estimates and projections show a steady fall in the number of illiterate adults from 22.4 per cent of the world's population in 1995 to 20.3 per cent in 2000. On current trends the institute estimates that this should drop to 16.5 per cent by 2010.

Literacy standards in Australia

The results of the PISA survey were most encouraging for Australia. Almost 6200 15-year-olds from 231 Australian schools participated. In all three areas of reading, mathematical literacy, and scientific literacy Australia was above the OECD average. Only one country, Finland, outperformed Australia in literacy overall. Only Japan achieved better results than Australia in mathematical literacy and only Korea and Japan achieved better results in scientific literacy. Australia had one of the highest proportions of students of any country at the highest proficiency level (18 per cent compared with the OECD average of 10 per cent) and one of the lowest proportions of students at the lowest level (12 per cent compared to 18 per cent). In almost all Australian states and territories, the top 10 per cent of students achieved better results in reading than the top 10 per cent of students in even the highest performing country, which was Finland.

Australia has high ranking literacy standards

There are areas for concern in Australian literacy standards

There were some areas of concern for Australia in the PISA survey (see Lokan et al. 2001):

- Girls outperformed boys in all aspects of reading (as in all other countries in the survey).
- Australian students, as a group, performed relatively less well on reading tasks associated with continuous prose texts.
- Indigenous students were underrepresented at the highest proficiency level and overrepresented at the lowest proficiency level.
- Students' socio-economic background was significantly related to achievement in reading. Students from low socioeconomic backgrounds were twice as likely as students from high socioeconomic backgrounds to be in the lowest quarter of reading scores.
- Boys from low socioeconomic backgrounds, therefore, were much more likely to have low reading scores.

These results must nevertheless be seen in perspective. If they are examined carefully it is found that 12 per cent of the Australian students are in the sample whose literacy scores were at Level 1 (the lowest level), including 3 per cent below it. Although this percentage is considerably less than the OECD average for Level 1 and under of 18 per cent, translated into figures it means that 744 students in the Australian sample performed at Level 1 or below. If these findings were extrapolated across the whole school community the numbers would be very considerable indeed.

The way forward

What literacy skills will be needed for participation in society in the first decade of the 21st century? How will these skills be measured? How will we ensure that all children have access to the most advanced literacy learning?

Literacy skills for the 21st century

Snyder asserts:

> Indeed, it is likely that writing will remain an important medium of communication, probably culturally the most valued form, for some time yet. However, it is also likely that writing will become increasingly the medium used by and for the power elites of society. Issues of equal access to power and its use make it essential to ensure that all students have the opportunity to achieve the highest level of competence in this mode: print and writing must not be sidelined. But students require the opportunity to achieve the highest competence in *all* the varied modes of communication now available. It is not an either or: the challenge is to create pedagogical and curriculum frameworks in literacy education that are suitable for present conditions but that are also attuned to the multiple communication possibilities that an uncertain future might yield. (2002: 174)

The way forward in Australia

In 1996, the Australian state, territory and Commonwealth governments agreed on a national goal that 'every child leaving primary school should be numerate, and be able to read, write and spell at an appropriate level' (Australian Education Council 1989). In 2000, benchmarks, or minimum acceptable standards of performance in literacy and numeracy, were published by the Curriculum Corporation. The benchmarks are brief and simply expressed, and are intended for the general community as well as educators. They do not attempt to describe the whole of literacy learning but rather to represent the important and essential elements of literacy at a minimum acceptable level.

The National Literacy and Numeracy Plan provides a framework for the improvement of literacy and numeracy standards throughout Australia. and in a sense foreshadowed many of the recommendations of the National Inquiry into the Teaching of Literacy discussed below. Using the framework, each state and territory has developed a comprehensive plan to include assessment of all students to identify those at risk, those needing early intervention, and the professional development of teachers. The plan aims to provide all students in Australia, regardless of location, gender, ethnicity, or other factors, access to the enabling skills of literacy and numeracy that underpin learning at school.

The National Inquiry into the Teaching of Literacy, *Teaching Reading* (2005)

The National Inquiry into the Teaching of Literacy in its report, *Teaching Reading* (2005), has made specific recommendations for improving literacy standards in Australia. These are extensive and far-reaching. It emphasises, among many other initiatives, that effective literacy teaching must be 'grounded in rigorous evidence-based research', that current assessment of student literacy standards must be supported and extended, and that an 'integrated approach' to reading, which supports the development of oral language, vocabulary, grammar, reading fluency, comprehension, and the literacies of new technologies must be rigorously applied in teaching. It recognises that the teaching of literacy skills, particularly reading, is a highly developed professional skill, and that teachers must be properly equipped to teach reading in their training. It also recommends that specialist postgraduate studies in literacy be provided, as well as the identification in every school of a highly trained specialist literacy teacher with specialist skills in teaching reading. (See the full list of recommendations in the report Executive Summary, available on the Inquiry website: www.dest.gov.au/schools/literacyinquiry.)

Whatever the complexity of being literate in modern society—and particularly Australian society—may mean, it is nonetheless the achievement of a satisfactory level of reading and writing in English that underpins all literacy learning. We are mindful also of the rich diversity of languages in our country that does so much to enrich our cultural life.

In *English as a Global Village*, David Crystal points out that language diversity and the value of a common language are two sides of one coin.

- I believe in the fundamental value of multilingualism, as an amazing resource which presents us with different perspectives and insights, and thus enables us to reach a more profound understanding of the nature of the human mind and spirit.
- I believe in the fundamental value of a common language, as an amazing world resource that presents us with unprecedented possibilities for mutual understanding and thus enables us to find fresh opportunities for international cooperation. (1997: viii)

In Australia we are in an extremely fortunate position as we have both sides of the coin: a rich diversity of language background in our people and our common English language.

As Beard (1998) points out, nations around the world are not witnessing a large and visible downturn in literacy standards. In modern society there is now a demand for greater literacy skills and increased complexity in the ways literacy is used. This places schools and teachers in a pivotal position to assist students to attain the levels and varieties of literacy they will need in the future. They must decide what kinds of literacy practices they will value and promote. This is not a small matter but one of great importance for their students and for society in general. They will also need to concentrate more effectively on the areas of concern within the school community that have been specified by documents such as the PISA survey, internal assessment results carried out by states and territories within Australia, and the findings of such studies as the National Inquiry into the Teaching of Literacy discussed above.

Web links

UNESCO: www.unesco.org
Organization for Economic Cooperation and Development (OECD): www.pisa.oecd.org
Curriculum Corporation: www.curriculum.edu.au
Commonwealth Department of Education, Science, and Training: www.dest.gov.au

Reading

GORDON WINCH AND MARCELLE HOLLIDAY

PART 1

Overview

Reading is an integral part of literacy. Linked with listening, speaking, writing, and critical thinking it establishes the essential basis for literacy learning and literacy practice as they operate in the digital age.

Chapters 1 to 9 of this text are specifically devoted to reading and learning to read. In chapter 1, the authors have taken what they term a balanced view of reading, arguing that there is no one way of teaching a child to read. The best teaching practice emerges from a confluence of a number of theoretical positions and their practical outcomes operating in sociocultural context.

Fundamental factors in reading and learning to read are considered in chapter 2, including a discussion of the writing system of English, the sound system of English, the importance of oral language, the nature of phonemic awareness and its importance to reading, the way the eyes operate during reading, the locus and importance of meaning, the developing significance of technology in literacy learning, the necessary contribution to literacy learning from business and the community, and the matter of dyslexia.

In chapter 3 a model of the reading process is established, which forms a basis for sound practice in the classroom. The context and purpose of reading are discussed, together with the reading cue systems and the basic strategies of reading.

Chapters 4, 5, 6 and 7 deal with the development of reading in chronological fashion beginning with the child before school and ending with the student in the upper primary classroom. Examples of Shared, Guided, and Independent Reading are demonstrated to give a clear view of this practice in the primary school and specific attention is given to phonic instruction. The section opens with an overview of reading development.

Chapter 8 explores the issue of assessment in reading, illustrating the many forms and approaches which will result in the most effective programming, teaching, and monitoring in the teaching–learning cycle.

Chapter 9 ties the practical strands of literacy learning together in the Literacy Session or Literacy Block. It considers actual classroom practice during a Literacy Session with particular emphasis on the teaching of reading.

All chapters contain activities for students using this textbook, to be carried out both inside and outside the classroom. These are contained in critical and study questions at the ends of chapters and within 'In the classroom' boxes within the body of the text. This amalgam of theory and practice will provide a solid groundwork for students learning to acquire the necessary literacy skills to function in the modern world. Teachers who are engaging in the task of teaching reading to new generations of students in the primary school will appreciate the vital interconnection of listening, speaking, reading, writing, and children's literature in this text.

A feature of the third edition is the focus on reading in the digital age and the importance of multiliteracies. Each chapter contains specific boxes dealing with these two highly relevant aspects of reading instruction in modern schools, both in theory and practice.

A BALANCED VIEW OF READING

1

Overview

Reading is the process of constructing meaning from text, whether written or graphic, paper-based or digital. It is a purposeful, thinking act and meaning is always at the core. There has been disagreement in the past over the correct way to teach reading, but a balanced approach is now generally accepted. Phonics and other decoding skills need to be taught explicitly and systematically, but phonics is not enough; it is necessary but not sufficient. Reading in the modern world also requires the ability to understand and use texts for a wide range of purposes. Literature plays a significant role in the development of reading skills and writing has a reciprocal link with reading. The oral language of children is also very important. In the modern, digital age, multiliteracies are playing a significant role in literacy development. This book links theory with practice and 'In the Classroom' activities are interspersed throughout the text.

What is reading?

Reading is the process of constructing meaning from text, whether written or graphic, paper-based or digital. The text may be wholly print as in most novels, or contain visual elements such as illustrations, diagrams, maps, and graphs as in most children's books and many information books, magazines, and newspapers. Increasingly, the texts we read are presented electronically, and often interactively, and contain a mixture of screen print, graphic or visual elements, and even sound.

Reading is the process of constructing meaning from text

At the core of reading is meaning. Meaning is what we search for as we read (our goal) and it is also part of what we use to reach that goal (our guide). In constructing meaning from text, readers combine what they know about the world, the topic of the text, the grammatical structure of the language in which the text is written, and the way spoken language relates to the letters, words, visual elements, and symbols on the page.

Because reading is essentially a purposeful act, a reader seeks to fulfil some individual purpose by reading a text. Perhaps it is to enjoy a novel, or to find some information about plants for the garden. It may be to purchase a new car or to plan a holiday. Whatever the purpose, readers will bring to the reading task the skills and knowledge they have to fulfil that purpose. In the process they will learn more about what it means to be a reader.

Because reading is primarily a thinking task, readers relate what they draw from the text to what they already know about the topic, about texts of this type, and about the context. For example, when reading an information book about the wildlife of Kakadu, a reader might hope

Reading is a purposeful thinking act that can be described as bringing meaning to and taking meaning from text

to add to his knowledge about how climatic conditions and ecosystems relate to animal species and would expect to see illustrations and perhaps photographs of animals and birds. The reader may look at the credentials of the author and/or photographer and consider what their purpose was in producing the book; perhaps the book has been produced by a mining company. And she would take the book's publication date into account when considering if the information was up to date. Reading, then, can be described as a process of literate thinking and can be further defined as *bringing meaning to and taking meaning from text in a social and cultural context*. This definition provides a balance between the reader and the text. It also defines reading in terms of the context in which reading occurs and places meaning at the core of the process.

But what really happens? What does research tell us about reading and the best methods of reading instruction? What are the essential features of a balanced view?

Research and the teaching of reading

Research has not provided a perfect alignment with practice in the teaching of reading (Beard 1998), and the ways children learn and should be taught to read remain contentious issues (Scholes 1998).

Historically, there has been a sharp division among researchers and theorists about the teaching of reading. On one side stand those who stress decoding, phonics, and specific phonemic

There has been disagreement in the past about the way reading should be taught

awareness training for beginning readers with heavy emphasis on word recognition in its various forms, on the alphabetic writing system, and on the subskills that are claimed to make up the reading task. This approach has been described in various ways, such as a **'bottom-up' view of reading**, a code-based approach, a subskill approach, and a phonic approach. It has been heavily criticised for its limited vision of what reading is, for its lack of emphasis on comprehension of the text, and its playing down of the input that the reader makes to reading.

The 'bottom-up' or skill-based approach can be found in the writings of many theorists, from the past to the present: S. Jay Samuels and Philip B. Gough, for instance, and more recently Keith Stanovich and Charles Perfetti. It is misleading and inexact, nevertheless, to place these writers in a neatly defined category as their work crosses a wide range of theory and research.

On the other side stand those who are often termed '**top-down**' or whole-language theorists. They stress meaning as paramount in any approach to reading and devalue code as a substitute for context in word recognition. These theorists have been termed 'top-down' because of their emphasis on what the reader brings to print and on the primary importance of meaning generally. They are opposed to the subskill approach and view reading from a holistic point of view. They have been criticised for their lack of attention to the alphabetic system of English writing, for their overreliance on context in word recognition, and for their refusal to look squarely at research that shows high correlation between phonemic awareness and learning to read.

The 'top-down' or whole-language approach is found in the writings of Frank Smith, Kenneth and Yetta Goodman, Brian Cambourne, and others, but again caution must be exercised in describing these researchers because their works reflect a much richer vein of educational thought than a simple category can indicate.

As recently as 1998, Scholes, who supports the 'top-down' view, has stressed his strong opposition to the subsyllabic (phonemic) segments of speech as factors in literacy acquisition, arguing that developing an understanding of subsyllabic elements is a limited consequence of acquiring literacy in an alphabetic script and that positive correlations between phonemic awareness and reading skill are based on a misguided definition of reading. He also argues that phonemic awareness is a *consequence* of acquiring alphabetic literacy and not an engine for success.

R. S. Johnston (1998) attacks Scholes on the grounds that children have to recognise the 'building blocks of literacy' even though the ultimate purpose of reading is comprehension. She argues for a reciprocal relationship between reading skill and phonological awareness and states that using a learned knowledge of the alphabetic system of English spelling eases the burden on learning to read. She argues further that what skilled readers may need is orthographic knowledge (knowledge of the writing system), underpinned by an adequate but not particularly precise awareness of **phonemes** (sound units) in spoken words so that they can recognise printed words with ease.

Stuart (1998) also disagrees with Scholes, setting out a multidimensional view of reading that allows for two intersecting dimensions: word recognition and comprehension. She looks for agreement between the two antagonistic positions, arguing that perhaps all can agree that word recognition is a necessary part but not the whole of reading.

Fortunately there has been in recent years an emerging view of reading and acquiring reading, both from research and from ensuing practice, which can be termed a 'balanced view'. Before considering the current position we shall look at some important steps along the way.

Current theory and practice now support a balanced view

From the past to the present

In 1967 Jeanne Chall published a milestone text, *Learning to Read: The Great Debate*. The work was funded by the Carnegie Corporation in the USA and was written to draw some conclusions about current and past research on reading and learning to read. Chall put forward the view that learning the alphabetic code (variously termed by her as phonics, word analysis, decoding, and sound–symbol relations) was essential to beginning to read, although it was not all that was necessary. Other important factors were language, good teaching, and instructional materials at the appropriate level of difficulty.

Chall's seminal study pointed to the importance of teaching students to crack the alphabetic code

At about the same time as Chall was completing her studies, another project, commonly known as the First Grade Studies, was carried out and published by Bond & Dykstra (1967). This work was sponsored by the US Department of Health, Education and Welfare and experimentally compared various research methods. The First Grade Studies confirmed Chall's conclusions.

Chall (1999) drew attention to these facts and to following studies that had supported her views, in particular, Anderson et al. (1985), Adams (1990), and Snow et al. (1998), which essentially came to the same major conclusion as *Learning to Read*. Chall also referred in her paper to the Follow Through Studies—a large-scale investigation of compensatory education that extended into Year 3. Again, higher achievement occurred among those children learning from a direct instruction model with code (phonics) emphasis.

It should be noted, however, that Chall was eager to point out that many of her recommendations in *Learning to Read* and others of her writings included many of the practices

Phonics alone is not sufficient to teach a child to read effectively

that are commonly associated with whole language. She stressed that teaching only phonics—and in isolation—was not what she would support, that library books have an important place, and that children's writings should be incorporated into the teaching of reading. Likewise she warned against the over-teaching of phonics, 'leaving little time for the reading of stories and other connected texts' (1967: 531).

Stanovich (1994), while making the point that Chall saw the teaching of reading much more broadly than has been commonly accepted, argued that some children in whole-language

Explicit and systematic instruction is vitally important

classrooms do not pick up the alphabetic principle through simple immersion in print and writing activities but need explicit instruction in correspondences between spelling and sound. He argued that this fact was borne out by voluminous research evidence.

Modern cognitive research as reported by Perfetti (1995) and Stanovich (1994; Stanovich & Paula 1995) has made a number of contributions to views on the nature of reading and its application to the way reading should be taught. The position taken is that skilled readers read more words than they skip, use phonology when reading, and rely very little on the use of context for word recognition. Children benefit from learning how their writing system works. It is also argued that comprehension and the use of context are not sacrificed by following the above tenets of reading teaching.

Stanovich (1994) makes the point that essentially the 'reading wars' that have wasted so much energy can be reduced to having both sides say simultaneously, 'Some teachers overdo phonics' and 'Some children need explicit instruction in alphabetic coding'. The matter may not be as simple as this, but a defusing of the issue and a rapprochement between the two sides is beginning to appear in the literature, as explained below. It is important to remember that many good teachers continued to use a balance of both approaches in their classrooms while the reading debate was raging in academic circles.

The emerging situation

At the risk of trivialising the issue or ignoring the enormous amount of research and carefully woven theory that is available, it is necessary in a book of this nature to move to the current situation in the light of national and international movements in the field, with special emphasis on their practical outcomes. It is valuable to look at some recent reports and publications that point to a middle way between the extreme positions taken in the past. While various researchers have argued strenuously for a reading program based exclusively on one or other specific approach, the evidence is now overwhelming that no one element holds the key to the successful teaching of reading. Each element is necessary but none is sufficient on its own.

A consensus of opinion is appearing. Reading is neither 'top down' nor 'bottom up'

Beard (1998) draws attention to the fact that recent research-based models of early reading and fluent reading suggest that reading is neither 'top-down' nor 'bottom-up' in nature. Instead, as Adams Bruck (1993) in the USA point out, sources of contextual, comprehension, visual, and phonological–graphological information are used simultaneously and interactively by the reader. This is a similar bringing together, Beard argues, to that which operates in the composition of writing.

Substantial changes in how fluent reading is understood are incorporated in Beard's document, which refers to the British National Literacy Project. In particular, it draws attention first to the relationships between word recognition and context, and second to the role of phonological processing in reading. It is argued that fluent readers rely less on context for word recognition than was thought. They are experts at word recognition and are able to use their skills in rapid, effective reading, relying for comprehension on context and the knowledge they bring to print.

The hallmarks of skilled reading are fast word identification and rich context-dependent understanding of the text (Perfetti 1995). If we look at fluent, effective reading from a commonsense point of view, backed up as this is by a battery of research (Beard 1998), we realise that a balanced view is a logical and valuable one for the teacher of literacy. It opens the way to teaching children to read and write, bringing into play phonological–graphological, grammatical, and semantic information from a range of sources, and it allows teaching to be both balanced and focused on the needs of a child.

Skilled reading requires fast word identification and understanding of text

When it comes to working with fluent readers in a context that requires improvement in reading flexibility across a range of text-types, improvement in speed, skim reading, or reading in depth for specific and detailed information, the model holds up well: fluent readers are experts in word recognition, so much so that the process becomes automatic and higher reading skills can be taught through context and the use of improved strategies.

The role of phonological processing has been reconsidered, producing much more interest in the nature of the alphabetic writing system in English. Learning to read is not only learning to construct meaning from print but also learning how the writing system works and how it encodes the reader's language. Knowledge about the grammatical system of the language works in conjunction with phonological–graphological processing in fluent reading.

The British National Literacy Project has included these balanced findings in recommendations for practice in its Literacy Hour. Focus is placed on three broad dimensions of literacy: word-level work, sentence-level work, and text-level work, and each is incorporated in a structured hour of teaching.

A Literacy Session must be carefully structured and executed

An evaluation of the National Literacy Project was carried out by Sainsbury (1998) for the National Foundation for Educational Research. The test results showed that there was a statistically significant improvement in children's scores in the 250 schools that took part in the study, from autumn 1996 to summer 1998. This amounted to reading progress of between eight and twelve months above what was expected, with an equivalent rise in percentile rank.

It is important to note that effective teaching within the Literacy Hour was characterised by consistency, clear structure, high-quality interaction, and good pace, underpinned by thorough planning. Other aspects of the Literacy Hour and the balanced approach to literacy and the teaching of reading carried out in the project included a 30-minute designated period of whole-class teaching, 20 minutes of group and independent work, and 10 minutes of whole-class review, reflection, and consolidation. It was recommended that extra time might be needed for reading to a class, pupils' own Independent Reading, and extended writing. The introduction of a special period for the teaching of literacy has become the desired strategy for improving literacy skills in many Australian schools, where it is often termed the Literacy Session or Literacy Block. The structure and presentation of such a session is described in chapter 9.

The National Literacy Project recognised the need to provide well-designed, balanced models for teaching literacy and saw as a strategic task that schools would not be expected to 'reinvent the wheel' but would be informed about the best practice and be provided with the teaching skills to act on it.

Other factors seen as vital to the development of literacy skills included the need to exploit the reciprocal links between reading and writing. These links were recognised by Marie Clay (1972, 1991, 1998) and have been widely accepted. (See also 'Links between reading and writing' in chapter 19.) The value of the inclusion of nonfiction texts was now recognised and increasingly stressed. In addition, Shared, Guided, and Independent Reading approaches (see chapter 5) were incorporated into literacy teaching strategies. An increased emphasis was placed on the importance of grammatical knowledge and standard spelling, while children's literature was seen as being fundamental in developing the literacy skills of children.

Reading and writing have reciprocal links

It is interesting to notice how the National Literacy Project was influenced by research, theory, and practice from overseas: the work of Marie Clay in New Zealand; Halliday, Cairney, and Cambourne in Australia; Adams, Tierney, and numerous others in the USA; and Stanovich in Canada. Special reference was made to curriculum work in Australia that led the field in many aspects of literacy development. In particular, it emphasised the importance of the various text-types, including nonfiction, that students should read and write; this variety in genres related to the social purpose of the text concerned. Beard's well-documented Review of Research, however, can only touch on the sources and influences that came into play during the development of the National Literacy Project, although it shows clearly that the teaching of literacy has a significantly international flavour, particularly in this age of rapid and available communication.

The Report of the Literacy Taskforce in New Zealand (1999) also illustrates the emergence of an acceptance of commonly recognised principles and practice of teaching literacy. The document highlights the acceptance of a balanced model of teaching literacy and the general need for the highest quality teaching, the development of a culture of high expectations, close participation between home and school, and recognition of the need to cater for rising demands for literacy, especially with minority groups.

A balanced model of teaching reading is used in New Zealand

While New Zealand measures up well on international literacy standards, the report recognises that special intervention is needed. Its authors are also concerned about the polarisation of approach in the debate on phonics as against whole language. Some schools have moved to placing too great an emphasis on teaching skills in isolation in reading programs, while others have moved towards an exclusively whole-language approach with no systematic teaching of phonological awareness. Nevertheless, decisions on how to teach literacy are traditionally made at school level in New Zealand, with official guidance being made only at national level.

New Zealand's Literacy Taskforce (1999) recommends that a statement of best practice be drawn up and promulgated to schools. It is aware of the need to inform teachers of sound research that indicates that children should not rely on context as the primary or only strategy for working out unknown words, but should develop word-level skills and strategies as well.

Movement towards a balanced view of acquiring literacy is being seen in the USA, although professional teacher associations and governments are not always in agreement about the teaching of reading.

In the USA also, there has been a movement towards a balanced view of acquiring literacy, although states differ considerably. A good example is the position statement of the International Reading Association (IRA) Board (1998) on the teaching of reading. The board makes the point that although phonemic awareness is the best single predictor of successful reading acquisition—few scholars would dispute this—there is considerable disagreement about what this relation implies for reading instruction. Most researchers advocate attention to the development of phonemic awareness as part of a broad instructional program in reading and writing, keeping in mind that different children require different amounts of this instruction.

Some movement towards a balanced view of acquiring literacy is being seen in the USA

The Board notes that the relation between phonemic awareness and learning to read is reciprocal: interaction with print combined with explicit attention to sound structure in spoken words is the best vehicle of growth. The Board emphasises that instruction in phonemic awareness must not overpower other important aspects of literacy instruction.

The five points for good literacy instruction that conclude the statement show how the balanced view we have seen emerge in other countries is occurring also in the USA.

Five points of good literacy instruction within a balanced approach

- Offer students a print-rich environment within which to interact.
- Engage students with surrounding print as both readers and writers.
- Engage in language activities that focus on both the form and the content of spoken and written language.
- Provide explicit explanation of students' learning of the alphabetic principles.
- Provide opportunities for students to practise reading and writing for real reasons in a variety of contexts to promote fluency and independence.

In the USA the National Research Council's Committee on the Prevention of Reading Difficulties in Young Children (Snow et al. 1998) looked first at mostly convergent, but sometimes discrepant, research findings to provide an integrated picture of how reading develops and how its development can be promoted. Two very interesting points were made: effective teachers seemed able to craft a special mix of instructional ingredients for every child they worked with, and children with reading difficulties did not need radically different sorts of support but more intensive support. Excellent instruction was seen as the best intervention for children with reading problems.

The report points out that effective instruction in reading is built on a foundation that recognises that reading ability is determined by multiple factors; no prerequisite for success is sufficient by itself. The five requirements for initial reading instruction have perceived similarities with approaches discussed above:

- Use reading to obtain meaning from print.
- Have frequent and intensive opportunities to read.
- Be exposed to frequent, regular instances of the spelling–sound relationship.
- Learn about the nature of the alphabetic writing system.
- Understand the structure of spoken words.

The crucial importance of excellent reading instruction was at the centre of the Committee's recommendations: schools should be organised so that curriculum materials and support services function effectively.

Recommendations on detailed instructions are explicit in the report. They stress the careful teaching of words and their parts, the recognition of sight words as well as sound–symbol correspondences, comprehension by actively building linguistic knowledge, and the important link with writing. The report encourages independent reading outside school and the use of libraries. It also lists what are desirable accomplishments or outcomes at various grades, from kindergarten to Year 3.

Such specific outcomes are being extensively used in Australia and provide a sound basis for assessment across a spectrum of achievement.

The National Reading Panel of the USA

In April 2000 the National Reading Panel of the USA produced its major report on 'scientific research-based reading instruction'. The panel reported that for children to be good readers, they must be taught

- phonemic awareness skills—the ability to manipulate the sounds that make up spoken language
- phonics skills—the understanding that there is a relationship between letters and sounds
- the ability to read fluently with accuracy, fluency, and expression
- the application of reading comprehension strategies to enhance understanding and enjoyment of what they read.

The findings of the panel were translated into the 'No Child Left Behind' legislation, which identified the types of reading programs that were to receive US Federal Government funding and those that were not. In essence, only those programs that advocated a strong phonic approach were to receive such funding.

Unfortunately, many of the programs funded under this legislation have proved unsuccessful. In California, where vast resources were expended in putting the National Reading Panel recommendations into practice, the evidence is that reading test scores have dropped alarmingly and that California is one of the lowest states in terms of reading scores in the USA.

The reasons for this are complex. In hindsight, it is clear that the panel failed to consider many of the factors that could influence reading achievement, including socioeconomic status, cultural background, and the vast changes that digital literacies have made to the way we learn and use literacy in the modern world.

In addition, it may be that the definition of reading used by the committee was limited to the ability to decode and pronounce words automatically, so only research that looked at this aspect of reading was considered. Future research into the matter will provide a clearer answer to the problem. Thus a significant opportunity to influence the reading of an entire population has been lost because the panel members could not see beyond their own narrow definition of what it meant to be a competent reader in today's world.

Literacy Report in Australia

In Australia, in 2005, the then federal Minister for Education, Dr Brendan Nelson, also commissioned a nationwide review of literacy learning. Its report, *Teaching Reading: Report and Recommendations, National Inquiry into the Teaching of Literacy*, was released in 2006.

The review committee, which contained a wide range of experience and expertise, claimed to have dealt with the available authentic research in making this report. Some critics have argued that the findings are too limited and refer to reading only and that it is therefore not a true literacy report. Others have claimed that there is too little consideration given to socioeconomic factors and cultural diversity and the fact that literacy instruction goes far beyond decoding text. Teaching literacy skills in the digital age, it is argued, provides a much more complex scenario for the vast majority of students in today's Australian schools.

The report has not yet made its way into legislation and it will be both interesting and highly significant to observe the effect it will have on the preparation of teachers and the teaching and assessment of literacy in schools and universities.

IN THE CLASSROOM

Throughout the text there are constant applications of theory to classroom practice and examples of the ways literacy should be taught. These examples appear in the text itself, the Critical thinking and study questions at the end of each chapter, and in dedicated boxes within the chapters, titled In the Classroom.

Reading outcomes and indicators in Australia

Literacy outcomes, which present clear statements of the expected results of teaching, are becoming the norm in Australian syllabuses. They are supported by indicators of behaviour, which contribute to the achievement of such results. Reading outcomes, like other aspects of literacy, key into the National Literacy Benchmarks, which are used to report on student achievement.

Literacy outcomes and indicators key into National Literacy Benchmarks

Students should consult their particular state or territory syllabus for specific statements of such outcomes and indicators across the years of schooling.

New South Wales

The English K–6 Syllabus in New South Wales refers in detail to desired outcomes and indicators for learning to read and learning about reading. A breakdown of the desired outcomes, and a wide variety of possible indicators, are given for grades K (kindergarten) to 6 and are described in stages in the syllabus.

Outcomes and indicators are detailed and specific in the New South Wales English K–6 Syllabus

Indicators for the outcome 'Demonstrates developing reading skills and strategies for reading books, dealing with print and comprehending texts, Learning to Read—Skills and Strategies, Early Stage 1'(kindergarten), are thirty in number and cover a range of information relating to contextual, semantic, grammatical, graphological, phonological, textual, and computer aspects of reading. A sample of the types of indicators is:

- demonstrates awareness that print is an expression of meaning
- uses knowledge of grammatical structure of language to assist reading
- learns and articulates sound segments in words
- recognises sight words in printed texts
- hears and articulates sound segments in words
- recognises that words are made up of letters
- uses the illustration on the cover of the book to make predictions about what the story is going to be about when reading
- knows basic book conventions, i.e. can open book and hold book in correct way to look at pictures, can turn pages in correct order
- navigates through sections of computer software.

Victoria

There are close similarities in approaches among the states and territories

The Curriculum and Standards Framework (CSF II) in Victoria, now being replaced by the new Basics/Dimensions project, although not a detailed syllabus, makes it clear what students should know and be able to do. It, too, presents outcomes and indicators of achievement for the various levels of schooling.

For instance, at Level 1 (end of Preparatory Year) in Reading, outcomes and indicators are provided for the reading of texts and aspects of language comprising contextual understanding, and linguistic structures and strategies. Although the actual wording and the terminology may differ slightly from that used in the New South Wales syllabus, there is—as one would expect—close similarity between the two sets of expectations.

For example, indicators at this level demonstrate that, among other things, the child does the following:

- uses title, cover illustrations, and knowledge of a text topic to predict meaning in texts
- reads aloud simple texts, which include some high-frequency words and oral language structures
- identifies frequently used words in context, such as look, I, and me
- uses context and graphophonic information to make meaning
- names the letters of the alphabet and identifies some sound–letter relationships
- uses illustrations to extend meaning
- reads from left to right with return sweep and top to bottom
- uses terms associated with books and print, such as page, author, title, cover, illustrator
- reads and recalls simple messages, such as an electronic message.

A balanced approach to reading

In fact, across the Australian state and territory education systems there has been an adoption of a balanced view of reading and the way it should be taught. This statement is borne out in recent documents. The First Steps program in Western Australia states:

> A successful language program is one in which reading, writing, speaking and listening are integrated in a supportive and stimulating environment in which independent and reflective critical thinking is fostered.
>
> Children learn how language works when they are able to use it for purposes that are clear to them. They need to know that the purpose for reading is to make meaning. Some children believe that 'getting the words right' is the sole purpose of reading. These children are unlikely to be effective readers. (1994)

A balanced view of teaching reading is common to all states and territories

In Victoria the Early Years program in reading (Teaching Reading in the Early Years 1997) gives teachers clear guidelines for implementing a balanced approach to reading in the classroom.

> The program is based on the worldwide recognition of the significance of the early years of schooling to the acquisition of literacy. It was written as a result of extensive research into good literacy practice in Victoria and overseas and was informed by a wide range of literature relating to early literacy teaching and learning: 'A positive reading environment is significant in encouraging students to value reading and in supporting their reading development. Readers learn to read best in a community of readers. Involvement in appropriate literacy tasks, access to a wide variety of texts, and regular demonstration and modelling of literate behaviours encourage students to develop their reading.'

In New South Wales books in the Teaching Reading series (1997) provide teachers with theoretical underpinnings and practical classroom applications of a balanced approach to the teaching of reading.

> Students need a balanced reading program to develop contextual knowledge; knowledge about the sources of information; and skills in reading as code-breaker, text-participant, text-user, and text-analyst (see chapter 3): 'Teachers should ensure that every component of the reading program is covered explicitly and systematically. A balanced reading program enables students to develop as effective readers.'

A balanced approach in this book

A balanced approach to reading is the position taken in this book. It is in keeping with emerging views about literacy teaching throughout the world and offers the best access to successful practice. It provides the best opportunity for all students to acquire the skills of effective reading. The following are some essential features of such a position. A balanced approach to reading

1   places meaning at the core of all reading
2   recognises the interaction between reading and writing
3   recognises the importance of context in reading

Some essentials of a balanced approach to teaching reading

4 places equal emphasis on the development of semantic, grammatical, and phonological–graphological and visual/pictorial knowledge through explicit and systematic teaching
5 recognises the importance of students developing effective strategies for processing both paper-based and digital text
6 provides for instruction across a range of fictional and factual text-types including public and electronic texts
7 promotes a balance of Shared, Guided, and Independent Reading opportunities
8 bases instruction on effective assessment of students' needs and abilities.

Literacy: Government, business, and the community

The task of improving literacy is a combined responsibility

The task of improving literacy in Australia is increasingly being seen as a combined responsibility of the instruments of government, business, and the community, as well as schools. This type of involvement provides a special type of balance of its own. Developing literacy is not and should not be the task of the school alone. Specific initiatives in improving literacy standards at federal, state, and local government levels, as well as parental, community and business involvement, are becoming more and more evident.

The Federal Government has a wide-ranging brief

At federal level, the recent report of the National Inquiry into the Teaching of Literacy (Teaching Reading: Report and Recommendations, National Inquiry into the Teaching of Literacy, Department of Education, Science and Training [DEST], 2005) is a case in point. This far-reaching document is set to have significant effects on the teaching of literacy throughout Australia in the future.

During the years 2004–05, DEST, among other initiatives, furthered its priorities for improving literacy and other aspects of schooling through benchmarking literacy standards, making results in literacy available to parents, and implementing innovative programs such as the Tutorial Voucher scheme. This program offers parents $700 towards individual tutorial assistance for a child not meeting the 2003 literacy benchmark and it is estimated that the cost will be in the vicinity of $20.3 million. The significance of this initiative is great if the PISA results are considered. Although Australia ranks high in world literacy standards, the bottom quartile of achievers is well below desirable functional literacy. (See the DEST Annual Report, 2004–05 on the DEST website for further descriptions of Federal Government initiatives.)

The NSW Premier's Reading Challenge is a literacy initiative at state level

State governments are responsible for allocating funds to education generally and for the management and administration of public schools. The role of the Department for Education and Training, under its Minister, is of course much wider and more complex than this. Special initiatives, set up by the Minister, or in some cases by the Premier, can extend this role significantly, particularly in the area of literacy.

An example is the NSW Premier's Reading Challenge, which is designed to develop a love of books and improve standards of literacy in New South Wales schools. The Challenge, set up in 2001–02, is in its fifth year and is presented by the NSW Department of Education and Training, with principal support from the Dymocks Literacy Foundation and the Sun Herald, and associate support from OPSM and Syba Signs. At its inception, the Challenge involved 36 000 students; in 2005 there were 226 000 participating. The Challenge is constantly being modified. It was first set up to engage middle year students in years 5–8 and now involves students K–8. Books are constantly being added or removed from the lists, chosen by a panel of experts. Fiction, nonfiction, and poetry are included in the lists and a percentage of books accepted are the students' own choice.

The NSW Premier's Reading Challenge is widely accepted as a highly successful initiative in the area of reading and literacy. Similar Challenges, such as the Premier's Reading Challenge in Victoria, have been set up or are being set up in other states and territories.

A recent example in New South Wales is Kogarah Council's publication, *Games for Book Lovers*, based on character stories and themes found in classics and new literature. The book will be distributed to schools and public library services throughout New South Wales. Another example is the Newcastle City Council's ground-breaking new library, to be opened at Wallsend, which will offer extensive materials for loan, greater access to electronic resources, study space, and reading rooms.

Some examples at local government level

Involvement from business initiatives is now beginning to appear. One of particular note is the Dymocks Literacy Foundation, mentioned above. The Foundation went through its planning phase in 2002 and began operation in 2003. Its current form and planned development provide an interesting example of business involvement in literacy development.

A literacy initiative from business: the Dymocks Literacy Foundation

The Dymocks Group of booksellers operates in more than seventy-four communities throughout Australia and views literacy as fundamentally important in Australian life. The Foundation is well planned and carefully structured, operating under a Fundraising Manager, a Board of Directors, and a Strategy Group, which contains several high-profile members of the public to assist in the strategic direction of the Foundation.

The basic aim of the Foundation, a non-profit organisation, is to raise monies from multiple sources and distribute this funding to worthwhile literacy projects within the community. The Foundation aims not only to further the literacy development of young Australians, but to make the initiative one of the top foundations in Australia after three years of operation, providing millions of dollars and setting a model for corporate philanthropy in the business sector.

Plans drawn up by the organisation include involvement with the Premier's Reading Challenge Program for all New South Wales school students. This has been expanded from Years 5–8 to include all students from Years K–8, an increase of 528 per cent of students attempting the Challenge from its inception in 2001; supporting the Friday Night School in Victoria, which provides tutoring for refugee children to help them keep up at school, especially when they are speaking English as a second language; association with childcare centres to create awareness of the importance of literacy by involving their carers and parents; and also providing funds and books to the Royal Prince Alfred Hospital's baby follow-up program which targets premature babies who may suffer from later literacy deficiencies.

These types of literacy projects will target those in the Australian student population who have been singled out for special consideration by the PISA survey (discussed in the Introduction) as well as trying to intervene earlier and address the issue of literacy before it is too late.

Multiliteracies

The term 'multiliteracies' refers to the variation in communication in different cultural and social contexts and the spread of English throughout the global village. It refers also to the multimodal nature of making meaning through the interface of written-linguistic modes with visual, audio, gestural, and spatial forms to create new forms of literacy.

▶ LITERACY IN THE DIGITAL AGE

The digital age has brought a new dimension to reading and writing. Contemporary literacy includes the use of multimodal texts in a new communications environment, much more varied and more complex than just reading print or applying it to paper. The increasing prominence of visual, audio, gestural and spatial modes have produced a fast-changing literate world for the primary student to encounter and use. (See chapters XX and XX)

The new technologies and the metalanguage of the digital age have become the vehicle for communication through the Internet, the CD-ROM, the DVD, the mobile phone, the digital camera, and desktop publishing. Young people are now being deeply influenced by the World Wide Web (www) and other aspects of Information and Communication Technology (ICT). There is now 'a dynamic plurality of texts' producing new designs of literacy practice and meaning (Kalantzis et al. 2002). A new semiotic (sign-making) system now confronts the modern student of the digital age to decipher and use. Literacy theory, the literacy model, and its practical outcomes must accommodate the new technologies and the changing face of literacy itself. Modern syllabuses are constantly moving along this path.

Aspects of Multiliteracies and Literacy in the Digital Age are described in ensuing chapters throughout this book. These are shown in boxes in each of the chapters as well as in the relevant parts of the body of the text.

▶ Summary

1 Reading is bringing meaning to and taking meaning from text. It is a complex task.

2 Research has been inconclusive about the ways children learn to read and should be taught. Sharp divisions have occurred but common ground is now being found throughout the world and is being documented in international studies and reports.

3 Literacy outcomes and indicators are becoming the norm in Australian syllabuses and are aligned to National Literacy Benchmarks.

4 This book takes a balanced view of reading in line with emerging theory and practice.

5 The task of improving literacy must be seen as a total commitment from the whole community. It is not the task of schools alone. Parent and community involvement is significant but business involvement must be increased. The Dymocks Literacy Foundation is one such recent initiative.

6. Multiliteracy and the Digital Age are making rapid and dramatic changes to literacy

▷ *Critical thinking and study questions*

1   The beginning of this chapter puts forward a definition of literacy. Consider what you think is a suitable definition.

2. Discuss the two sides in the 'reading wars'. Attempt to isolate the main points of difference between a 'top-down' and a 'bottom-up' approach.

3   Consider how a balanced view of reading incorporates the best theory with the best practice in the light of the eight essential features listed above. Are there others? If so what are they?

4   Read one or two of the articles listed in the Bibliography that support a particular side of the argument for a 'top-down' or 'bottom-up' approach. Write a critique of the article(s).

5   Write a brief statement supporting what is termed 'a balanced view of reading' in this book. Use some of the evidence presented in this chapter.

6   What changes in your own literacy practice have occurred as a result of the 'Digital Age'?

7   What changes do you think might occur in literacy learning in classrooms within the next decade? (Try some lateral thinking.)

Further reading

Further reading for this chapter and others in parts I and II should include key journals on literacy such as the *Australian Journal of Language and Literacy* (ALEA), *Practically Primary* (PETA), *Reading Research Quarterly* (IRA), *The Reading Teacher* (IRA), and *Journal of Research in Reading* (UK Reading Association). These associations also publish specialist monographs on important literacy topics.

Anstey, M. & G. Bull (eds) 2003, *The Literacy Labyrinth*, 2nd edn, Pearson Prentice Hall, Sydney.

Cambourne, B. 1988, *The Whole Story*, Ashton Scholastic, Sydney.

Cope, B. & M. Kalantzis (eds) 2000, *Multiliteracies: Literacy learning and the design of social futures*, Routledge, London.

Gough, P. B. 1985, 'One Second of Reading'. In H. Singer & R. B. Ruddell (eds) *Theoretical Models and Processes of Reading*, 3rd edn, IRA, Newark, Del.

Holdaway, D. 1979, *The Foundations of Literacy*, Scholastic Australia, Gosford, NSW.

Samuels, S. J. 1985, 'Word recognition'. In H. Singer & R. Ruddell (eds), *Theoretical Models and Processes of Reading*, 3rd edn, IRA, Newark, Del.

Smith, F. 1971, *Understanding Reading*, Holt, Rinehart & Winston, New York.

Smith, F. 1973, *Psycholinguistics and Reading*, Holt, Rinehart & Winston, New York.

Unsworth, L. 2006, *E-Literature for Children: Enhancing digital literacy learning*, Routledge, London.

Unsworth, L. A. Thomas, A. Simpson & J. Asha 2005, *Children's Literature and Computer-based Learning*, Open University Press, Maidenhead, UK.

Web links

International Reading Association: www.reading.org
Australian Literacy Educators' Association: www.alea.edu.au
Primary English Teaching Association: www.peta.edu.au

2 SOME FACTORS RELATING TO READING

Overview

There are many significant factors relating to the teaching of reading that every teacher should understand. These include the writing and sound systems of English, the importance of oral language, phonemic/phonological awareness and the locus of meaning. Modern technology is changing the face of reading and the question of dyslexia must be understood and kept in perspective. The above factors must be seen in the context of the socio-economic contexts in which students live and learn.

The writing system of English

English orthography can be described as an alphabetic writing system. The written symbols, the alphabet, represent the sounds, or phonemes (individual speech sounds), that allow a reader to distinguish between words. For example, in the words *cat* and *fat*, the two phonemes /k/ represented by 'c' and /f/ represented by 'f' allow the reader to distinguish the difference between the two words. There are forty-four or forty-five phonemes in English and because there are only twenty-six letters to represent them, the writing system presents special problems for the reader. To begin, some letters have to double up to represent the forty-five sounds.

English has an alphabetic writing system

To complicate things even more, English has borrowed from many different languages over its history and has kept many of the original spellings. As a result, we have different spellings of the one sound, such as in *photo* and *foot*. Added to this, some sounds in our language, particularly the long vowels, changed quite dramatically at some time in the 15th century, so that the written symbols in English writing came to represent different sounds in the spoken language. This change is known as the Great Vowel Shift. For example, the word *five*, which was pronounced /fi: f/ (something like *feef*) in Chaucer's time, had become /fai:v/ (five) by Shakespeare's.

PHONEMES AND ALLOPHONES

Strictly speaking, 'phonemes' are abstract concepts and represent a range of actual sounds or phonetic realities called 'allophones'. There are great variations in dialects that contain a range of sounds representing the one phoneme. Take for example the different pronunciation of the /a/ phoneme in the word *bath* in British and American English. Consider also the difference in the sounds representing the /k/ phoneme in *key*, *cup*, and *cop*, which are slightly modified by the following vowel. These are allophones of the phoneme /k/.

If we consider also that many speech sounds in some dialects of English are different from those in other dialects, we have another mismatch between sound and symbol. Language is forever changing and this mismatch will continue and develop. Consider some vowel pronunciation differences found in American and Australian English. A real-life example makes the point. A mother of an Australian small child was visiting the Mid West American school that her daughter was attending. The teacher commented that the child was doing well with her spelling but insisted on beginning the word *octopus* with a u. Why? Why not? *Uktopus* is what the child heard her teacher say.

John Dewey (1971) calculated that for every 100 000 running words, English orthography averaged 9.1 spellings per consonant and 20.7 per vowel. There is certainly no perfect match between symbol and sound in English spelling. Although graphophonic (symbol–sound correspondence) information is an important facet of reading, if it were the only source available reading would be both difficult and slow. Fortunately it is not the only source. Kolers et al. (1970) say that if we did decode to sound for every written letter we would read no faster than thirty to forty words per minute. Smith (1973) argues further, stating that our short-term memory cannot hold more than four or five random letters at once, so that by the time we reached the end of a long word we could easily have forgotten the beginning.

In English there is no perfect match between sound and symbol

Regular features of English orthography

In spite of the limitations of orthography, there are features that are regular. They act as a valuable part of the available information we have when reading. For instance, although there is a poor match of symbol to sound in many spellings found in English, much of the written language is regular and predictable. Up to 80 per cent of symbol–sound relationships could be considered regular if we include the frequency of use of some of the letters that are used in English writing. The twenty-six letters of the alphabet, used as graphemes in writing, show considerable variations in consistency, but overall the correspondences between sounds (phonemes) and

Much of English orthography is regular and predictable. The vowels show most inconsistency

letters (graphemes) are very regular. A survey (Carney 1994) underlines this point: the phoneme /b/ is represented by the letter b 98 per cent of the time, the small exceptions being bb in words like rabbit (or bh in a few words imported from Hindi). The vowels show most irregularity: /i/ as in kid is represented by the letter i only 61 per cent of the time, with varied spellings in other cases: y in hymn, o in women, ui in build, and u in busy. Many common words contain these irregular spellings and cause problems in early reading—think of *are*, *were*, *come*, and *there*, for example. Teachers refer to them as 'sight' words and avoid decoding them phonically.

Phonic instruction must be carefully undertaken to reveal the consistencies and inconsistencies of the language

The important point is that in the early teaching of reading, teachers must show children how the speech sounds of English are mapped onto the written language. Phonic instruction must be carefully undertaken to show both the consistencies and inconsistencies and allow the child to gradually develop an understanding of how the writing system works. Children learn, first about the regularities of the English writing system and then later about its irregular functions such as the way the letter 'u' follows q or the 'silent' letter 'l' in a word like 'walking'. This extra information allows the child to reduce uncertainty and predict how the letter operates and what the word is. (See chapter 5 for more information on the teaching of phonics.)

English spelling is complicated in some of its instances, but it is not haphazard. Readers develop an expectation about the ways letters represent sounds and the order in which letters appear in English writing. George Bernard Shaw was not correct in saying that the letters in the nonsense word *ghoti* could spell 'fish' (*gh* as in *rough*, *o* as in *women*, and *ti* as in *nation*) because the consonant cluster *gh* is not found in English initially as the phoneme /f/, and the *gh* spelling of /f/ and the *ti* spelling of /sh/ are fairly rare, with the latter never found at the end of a word.

The linguists Chomsky & Halle (1968) pointed out that there is another underlying regularity in English spelling that readers understand and use when reading. This is the deep-structure similarity of pairs of words such as *line/linear*, *compose/composition*, and *anxious/anxiety*, irrespective of the fact that there is a marked difference in the pronunciation of the vowels within each pair of words. Readers ignore the surface–sound mismatch between the words because they recognise the similarity of paired words in meaning. Venezky (1967) drew attention to the bigger meaning-chunks of words that readers use when dealing with English spelling. The word *shepherd* is read as two meaningful chunks or 'morphemes', *shep* and *herd*, a *herder of sheep*.

WORLD WRITING SYSTEMS

Writing systems throughout the world are products of human invention and vary in how they operate. A child, learning to read in English, French or Italian, for instance, learns an alphabetic system that came from the Phoenicians and Greeks; in Japan, children learning to read Kana are dealing with a syllabic system; and Chinese children are confronted with a logographic script in which the writing units correspond to meanings or morphemes rather than to syllables or phonemes.

English is an effective writing system and is used worldwide

Native speakers of the language carry the rules relating to the above facts in their heads and use them automatically, as well as with surprising rapidity, when reading. English orthography overall is remarkably effective as a writing system and is used extensively throughout the world. The important thing is that when a child is learning to read in English, or any other writing system for that matter, he or she must learn the writing system concerned, specifically how it encodes the language, and apply this knowledge to the reading task. The question of the relationship of the text to meaning is as fascinating as it is controversial.

Olsen (1977), in an important paper, drew attention to the differences between speech, which he calls *utterance*, and written language, which he calls *text*. He argued that theories of reading and learning to read can be seen as expressions of rival assumptions about the locus of meaning: whether meaning is in the mind of the reader or in the text. He argued further that the Greek alphabet, from which our alphabet developed, gave writing an explicit quality and an autonomy that allowed it to place the meaning squarely in the text. The student's problem, it is argued by some, is to find out how to decode that meaning through the gradual mastery of subskills such as sound–symbol relationships, the recognition of words, and later comprehension of the text (Chall 1967; Gibson & Levin 1975). The opposing view (Goodman 1967; Smith 1973; Scholes 1998) is that readers bring meaning to the text, which allows them to predict words in context. Recent thinking has placed emphasis on the nature of the alphabetic system in reading and writing and on the importance of context, including social context. In other words, in a balanced view of reading the locus of meaning is to be found at once in the situation, the reader, and the text.

Recent thinking has placed emphasis on the importance of decoding and contextual information

The differences in oral language (Olsen's 'utterance') and written text in relation to reading have been well documented (Olsen 1977; Halliday 1979, 1985b; Winch 1988), but it is important also to note their interconnection. Children's oral language is a large part of what they bring to print, together with an understanding of the topic in question. Children use their oral language as a resource as they deal with written text and they do not confuse one with the other.

Scholes (1998) makes the point that seeing the English writing system as written speech is essentially wrong. (There are no truly phonetic writing systems, nor should there be.) It stems from the incorrect view (Bloomfield 1927) that to understand writing you must first convert it to speech. No, says Scholes. Children are smarter than that—in a relatively short time most of them realise that writing is not like speech.

As children increase their reading skills they become less willing to use phonological data alone to process writing. It must be noted, nevertheless, that this view does not contradict the view taken in this book—and increasingly throughout the world—that good readers are extremely good at word recognition as well as very good at bringing vital comprehension data to text. The point is, and it is Scholes' point also, that our writing system does not require pronunciation before comprehension, unless it is in the form of a linguistic joke, as in this Valentine's Day greeting: BEAM EYE VALE AND TINE BE COURSE ISLE OF EWE. This joke is, as Australian readers would readily recognise, the basis of Strine.

Good readers are effective at word recognition and comprehending text in context

OW DUZZY REDIT, MITE?
OIM STUFF TIFF EYE NO!

Figure 2.1   The Phonemes of English, showing points of articulation in the mouth: the vowels, the consonants, and the diphthongs

The Vowels in the Vowel Quadrilateral Showing the Speech Organs

i	as in	*seat*	sit
ɪ	"	*sit*	sɪt
ɛ	"	*set*	sɛt
æ	"	*sat*	sæt
ɑ	"	*cart*	kɑt
ɜ	"	*bird*	bɜd
ə	"	*alone*	əloʊn
ʌ	"	*hut*	hʌt
u	"	*boot*	but
ʊ	"	*put*	pʊt
ɔ	"	*sort*	sɔt
ɒ	"	*hot*	hɒt

Note that the IPA symbol /ɑ/ may also be written as /a/ as in c*a*rt.

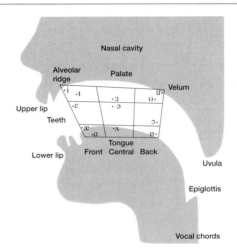

The Dipthongs

eɪ	as in	*day*	deɪ
oʊ	"	*so*	soʊ
aɪ	"	*try*	traɪ
aʊ	"	*down*	daʊn
ɔɪ	"	*boy*	bɔɪ
ɪə	"	*clear*	klɪə
ɛə	"	*dare*	dɛə
ɔə	"	*sore*	sɔə
ʊə	"	*tour*	tʊə

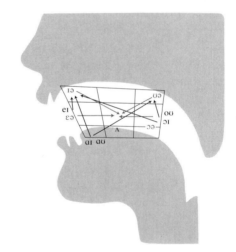

The Consonants

p	as in	*pet*	pɛt
t	"	*top*	tɒp
k	"	*kite*	kaɪt
b	"	*bed*	bɛd
d	"	*dog*	dɒg
g	"	*girl*	gɜl
f	"	*fan*	fæn
v	"	*van*	væn
θ	"	*thin*	θɪn
ð	"	*that*	ðæt
s	"	*sat*	sæt
z	"	*zoo*	zu
r	"	*rat*	ræt
ʃ	"	*ship*	ʃɪp
ʒ	"	*treasure*	trɛʒə
h	"	*hat*	hæt
tʃ	"	*chin*	tʃɪn
dʒ	"	*joke*	dʒoʊk
l	"	*log*	lɒg
m	"	*man*	mæn
n	"	*nail*	neɪl
ŋ	"	*long*	lɒŋ
j	"	*you*	ju
w	"	*will*	wɪl

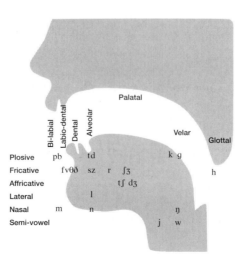

The sound system of English

In linguistics, the study of speech sounds, their production, description, and classification is called **phonetics**. **Articulatory phonetics** deals with the production of speech sounds by the human voice (for instance, where the sounds are made in the mouth and what physical features are involved). **Acoustic phonetics** deals with the nature of the sound waves involved in forming speech sounds.

It is important that a teacher understands the phonemic system of English

From the point of view of the teacher of reading, however, it is the nature of the phonemes of English that is important. Teachers deal with phonemes and the related phonic information such as letter–sound correspondence, the nature of vowel and consonant digraphs, blends, and onset and rime. Phonemes are the smallest meaningful sounds in a language that keep words apart. The sounds /p/ and /k/ in the words *pat* and *cat* are the phonemes that make the difference between the two words.

There are 45 phonemes in English. (Some linguists argue that there are 44, 46 or 47, depending on certain minor inclusions and exclusions). These phonemes can be represented by the International Phonetic Alphabet (IPA) as shown in Figure 2.1.

The representation of speech, using the IPA, a one symbol–one sound writing system, is used by speech therapists and linguists (in a much more sophisticated form) but not by teachers when teaching children to read. The nature of the IPA, however, provides us with a clear example and a better understanding of the sound system of English, which we use in teaching children to read.

hi ɪz maɪ brʌðə

He is my brother.

ðə trɛʒə ɪz ɪn ðə ʃɪp

The treasure is in the ship.

ɪtz əz hɛvi əz lɛd

It's as heavy as lead.

Phonetics, phonemics, and phonics

It is important for teachers to have an understanding of terms such as *phonetics*, *phonemics*, and *phonics*. The former two are linguistics terms, while phonics is essentially a method of teaching students to read and write using the relationship between sound and symbol.

Phonetics and phonemics are different from phonics

Linguists have been critical of teachers of phonics for their loose use of terms and in some cases, sheer inaccuracy. In a way, the linguists are correct. The description of the sounds made by *a, e, i, o,* and *u*, for instance, as long vowels in the words, *cake, eat, five, home* and *cute* is strictly incorrect in four of the five examples: the sound made by the letter *a* in the word *cake* is a diphthong (glided vowel), /eɪ/ the sound made by the letter *e* is correctly described, the sound made by the letter *i* is also a diphthong, /aɪ/, as in the letter *o* /oʊ/ and the letter *u* in this context makes two distinct sounds, /j/ and /u/.

Phonics provides a workable method of teaching children to decode and encode language

Nevertheless, phonics is necessarily simplified to provide a workable method for young children to decode (read) and encode (write) language. It is practical and workable in the hands of a skilled teacher, and provides vital access to phonological and graphological sources of information. It is a mandatory part of every reading and writing program and must be taught systematically and explicitly.

Phonics teaching will differ from school to school and no one approach is to be considered the perfect way to teach phonic skills. Further reference to phonics in practice is made in following chapters, particularly chapters 5 and 8, and a further discussion of the nature of phonics is carried out below in the section 'Phonemic awareness and phonological awareness'.

The importance of oral language

Oral language, or 'oracy', refers to the joint processes of listening and talking. 'Listening' can be described as the process of attending to and constructing meaning from spoken texts. It

Oral language, or 'oracy', is made up of the joint processes of listening and talking

involves distinguishing the sounds of words, and being sensitive to the tone, pitch, stress, and pace of speech. 'Talking' can be described as the process of presenting meaning through the construction of spoken texts. It involves enunciating sounds appropriately, using tone, pitch, stress, and pace effectively, and using such nonverbal devices as gesture.

We use oral language when we engage in social situations of which spoken interaction is a part, and the forms of oral language we use are governed by culturally accepted ways of using language. Listening, talking, reading, and writing have much in common since they all deal with the language user's attempts to construct and interpret meaning within social situations using elements of language.

By school age most children are competent users of spoken language. This ability provides the necessary foundation for learning to read and write, although it should be noted that deaf children, who may never learn to hear and speak, can learn to read.

Within the context of their families, children learn to use the basic structures of their home language before they go to school, and they gain control over almost all the sounds and many of the rules and principles related to the grammar of the language (although they are generally not able to talk about the grammatical features they are using). By school age almost all children have become competent users of the language spoken in their own community. This oral language competence forms a foundation for the learning of reading and writing.

When children begin school they are ready to expand their spoken language competencies in response to new situations and demands, and to begin using oral language as a vehicle for learning in all areas of the curriculum. As children develop as oral language users, they will:

•   understand that different social contexts require different oral texts
•   use talk effectively to meet personal and social needs

- listen for information and ideas in a growing number of contexts
- listen for enjoyment to stories, poetry, and factual texts
- use talk for a variety of purposes including to entertain and to share information, ideas, opinions, and feelings
- use talk to generate and clarify ideas in all curriculum areas
- use talk to take part in dialogue, discussion, drama, and games
- use talk to take part in group and individual presentations
- use talk in group processes and cooperative learning
- begin to talk about the grammatical features of language.

Oral language and reading

When children learn to read they use their knowledge of oral language as an important starting point. In learning to read, children discover that although spoken language can be written down, most written language is different from speech. They also learn what written language looks like. They learn that each written word on the page corresponds to one spoken word. We often see young children 'read' by running their finger along the line of text only to run out of spoken words before they reach the end of the line.

Children use their knowledge of oral language to make the link between speech and the written symbols on the page

The significant differences between spoken and written texts are realised by experience and careful teaching, and children begin to understand what different types of written texts are like. The reading of texts aloud to children is an important bridge between spoken language and reading because it helps them to understand what written texts, especially literary texts such as fairytales, sound like.

Differences between spoken and written texts are realised by experiencing many different texts and text-types

Early readers use their knowledge about word meanings and language structures, gained through experience with spoken language, in order to construct meaning from written texts. It is their knowledge of spoken grammar that tells them what to expect next in a written text, and it is their knowledge of vocabulary that helps them construct mental images from the texts they are reading. Children with a well-developed vocabulary will know not only words like 'big', but also others like 'huge', 'enormous', and 'gigantic'. In the early stages of learning to read, children develop their understandings of the correspondence between the sounds of language and the written symbols that represent these sounds.

IN THE CLASSROOM

Oral reading by the teacher: five helpful hints

The teacher's model of oral reading should be an inviting one.

- Rehearse your reading if you can and include a prop if one is available and appropriate. (Try a toy fox or hen for a reading of Pat Hutchins' *Rosie's Walk*).
- Indulge in some 'ham' acting to bring a story to life. (Dance like the bear in Pamela Allen's *Bertie and the Bear*)

- Use variations in pause, pace, volume, and pitch for dramatic effect ('OH NO YOU DON'T,' screamed the troll.)
- Always have your class ready to hear you read; it should be a treat, awaited with eagerness
- Serialise your reading with older students. (We'll stop now and find out what happens tomorrow).

Phonemic awareness and phonological awareness

Phonemic awareness refers to the ability of a speaker to hear, segment (divide up) and manipulate the sounds of speech

Phonemic awareness and phonological awareness are important concepts in reading and learning to read. Understanding what they refer to is significant for both theory and practice.

Phonemic awareness refers to an understanding of the smallest meaningful units of sound that make up oral language, remembering that there is a range of precise phonetic differences in each phoneme depending on such matters as dialect and where a phoneme exists in a word. (See the boxed discussion of allophones earlier.) Phonemic awareness is characterised by a speaker's ability to hear, segment, and manipulate sounds in speech, e.g. saying the first sound in the word *cat*, recognising the other sounds and blending them.

Phonological awareness is a more general term and can refer to larger segments than phonemes such as onset and rime, as in *b-ike*, and syllables, such as *un-der*. Sometimes the two terms are used interchangeably, but more often phonemic awareness is made the generic term in research and other literature.

Phonics, as described above, refers to the relationship between written letters and spoken sounds. When children are asked what letter makes the first sound in the written word *bat*, they are asked to call on phonic knowledge. It is a matter of making the relationship between sound and symbol. In order to do this they must be phonemically aware. Phonic analysis is a method of teaching word recognition by matching elements in writing with their corresponding sounds. This involves analysing consonants, vowels, blends, digraphs, diphthongs, and bigger segments such as syllables (*o-ver-take*), morphemes (*rein-deer*; *slow-ly*) or onset and rime (*b-ark*; *str-ing*). Phonic synthesis on the other hand is building up words from the sounds within them. There are many approaches to teaching phonics and a great deal of instructional material is available.

Phonics is an approach to teaching reading, pronunciation and spelling through the relationship between written letters (graphemes) and spoken sounds (phonemes)

It should be noted that some whole-language theorists have been opposed to the breaking up of words 'into bite-size but abstract little pieces' (Goodman 1986), which amounts to a disavowal of the value of teaching phonics out of the context of whole text. Others support phonics strongly (Stanovich & Paula 1995). Today there is widespread support for the inclusion of effective text-based phonics teaching in early reading programs. The National Literacy Project in Great Britain is a case in point and the National Inquiry into the Teaching of Literacy in Australia has made clear that 'direct systemic instruction in phonics during the early years of schooling is an essential foundation for teaching children to read' (2005: 11). Nevertheless, phonics or any graphophonic teaching should not overpower the teaching of reading. It must sit beside other approaches to reading in a balanced program that combines such systematic code instruction with the reading and writing of meaningful texts, both literary and factual.

Phonic instruction must be part of any balanced early reading program

PHONEMIC AWARENESS AND PHONETIC AWARENESS

Scholes (1998) correctly makes the distinction between syllabic awareness and subsyllabic awareness, arguing that manipulating subsyllabic particles (segmental phonemes), often called phonemic awareness, is really phonetic awareness (because the actual sounds differ so much). He uses the term Phonetic Segment Awareness (PSA) for the ability to manipulate individual segmental sounds as in the three sounds that make up the word *ball*, although the term 'phonemic awareness' is used widely and is accepted in the literature.

The importance of phonemic awareness

It is an established fact that phonemic awareness is a successful predictor of reading success (Stanovich 1994). It is a better predictor than many other candidates, including a child's IQ, although socio-economic factors do have a significant influence. The question of whether there is a causal link between phonemic awareness and learning to read is often debated without clear conclusions being reached. The important point is that there appears to be a strong reciprocal relationship between phonological segmentation and alphabetic coding skill and that these skills are mutually facilitative (Stanovich 1994). Lack of phonological sensitivity appears to inhibit the learning of the alphabetic coding system that underlies fluent word recognition. Although reading is essentially about bringing meaning to and taking meaning from print, it is also true that a child must learn the writing system and how it encodes his language.

Phonemic awareness is a successful predictor of reading success

The importance of phonemic awareness and phonemic processing is widely accepted (Beard 1998). Making the link with print through analytic and synthetic phonics (segmentation and blending) is the next step forward. For instance, 'Tell me the sounds in *cat*' (analytic); 'What do these sounds make when I put them together, *c-a-t*? (synthetic). The best way to develop phonemic awareness is by making it part of a broad instructional program in reading and writing so that young children are involved in language activities that help them recognise such things as initial sounds, **rhymes**, and the distinct speech energy rhythms that produce syllables (as in *cat. er.pil.lar*).

Children's phonological development appears to follow a clear pattern, from awareness of syllables to being aware of patterning in initial sounds (onsets) and rimes within syllables (*c-at*), to being aware of phonemes (Treiman & Zukowski 1996). Children will develop these skills at different rates and according to the focus of the teaching program. Rhymes, poems, songs, and shared books help to facilitate both phonemic awareness and reading through repetition, rhyme, and the pleasurable matching of sounds.

Children's phonological development follows a clear pattern

Although the precise relationship between phonemic awareness and learning to read may not be clear, its importance is recognised. The best teaching practice leading to reading acquisition combines interaction with print and explicit attention to the sound structure of words.

Perfetti, in his discussion of cognitive research and its importance to reading education, states: 'The fact that literacy and phonemic awareness can develop in tandem has implications for reading instruction. Rather than stressing phonological training in isolation, phonological training and word reading can be effectively linked together' (1995: 112).

Recent increased professional interest in the nature of phonemic awareness and its role in reading and writing has occasioned focus on the subject at conferences in Australia such as the 1999 Australian Literacy Educators' Association (ALEA) conference and the publications of discussion papers such as that of Freeman's *Phonemic/Phonological Awareness* (1998).

How readers operate

Visual and nonvisual information

It is obvious that the eyes are important in reading—you cannot read in the dark or with your eyes shut (unless you are reading Braille)—but there is a severe limitation on the *visual* information supplied by the eyes. They represent, in fact, only the camera that takes the picture and sends the information to the brain. It is the brain that converts this visual information into meaning and allows us to read. It supplies the *nonvisual* information that makes reading for meaning possible.

Readers use visual and nonvisual information

It can be argued that there is a trade-off between the two types of information: the more nonvisual information you have when you read, the less visual information you need. The opposite also applies. It must be noted, however, that this point of view is contentious. Perfetti (1995) argues that skilled readers fixate on most words on the page when they are reading for most purposes, from over 50 per cent to 80 per cent, with *content* words (nouns, verbs, adjectives, adverbs) featuring more than *function* words (articles, prepositions, etc.). He also argues that along with this dense sampling of the text the skilled reader relies on phonology to recognise the words in question and does not rely heavily on context for word recognition. This view is supported by Stanovich (1994), who found that context in word recognition was used less by skilled readers than by less skilled readers.

There is no doubt that skilled readers are experts at word recognition, and their ability is both rapid and automatic. Word recognition, however, is not reading in itself. Comprehension of the text is an essential component, as we have stated above. The balanced view taken in this book is that recent research has added to our knowledge of the way skilled readers operate in terms of word recognition but does not alter the fact that reading is a very complex matter relying on cues from a variety of sources—graphophonic, grammatical, and semantic—and that the reader's understanding of the written text is primary in any act of reading.

Word recognition is not reading in itself

Seeing and understanding

The more a reader understands the meaning of a text, the bigger the chunks she can read

Smith (1978) has used an interesting example to show how much reading can be achieved in a single glance. He refers to one of the oldest findings in experimental psychology, that four or five letters constitute the upper limit of how much can be seen at a single glance in a line of randomly selected letters such as those below.

x j p r q n o y r t v p s l m w k j l h z s p j m

He adds the interesting information that when the same number of letters is arranged in words, the brain can recognise twice as many letters in a single glance, although the amount of visual information is the same.

happy give when improve climb

If words are arranged in a sentence, the number of recognised letters in a simple glance is doubled again, so that the whole sentence is recognised. The visual information is made to go four times as far as with the random letters.

small seeds grow to tall trees

There are many factors associated with this finding. One is that the brain responds to the information arranged in a sentence more effectively than randomly arranged letters; another is that the redundancy in the language allows the reader to ignore much of the visual display and thus reduce uncertainty about the meaning; another again is the meaningful arrangement of the syntactic patterns of the words in example 3. It is also important to notice that the more the reader understands the meaning of the texts, the bigger the chunks of language he can recognise in a single glance.

Perfetti (1995) points out correctly that reading for gist or general understanding of a text allows readers to rely on fewer eye fixations when reading than if they were reading in depth, for detailed information (Just & Carpenter 1987). Winch, working with adults from 1990 to 1998 to improve reading flexibility and speed, confirms this (Australian Catholic University). When reading for gist, skilled readers can be taught to read at more than 1000 words per minute with limited sampling of the text and effective use of strategies such as reading for main idea and finding the key to paragraphs in first and last sentences. Readers in this process skip large sections of text and certainly many words, but still read effectively for that particular purpose.

Good reading strategies make for fast and effective reading

A large number of adult readers, many of them senior professional people in executive positions, read far too slowly, mainly because they tend to read everything at the same, often laborious, pace, failing to use metalinguistic knowledge relating to textual information that lies beyond the **lexical** level. In doing so they ignore the purposes for which they read.

How the eyes move during reading

Most people, when asked how the eyes move when reading, will answer that they move evenly from left to right. This is not the case. The eyes do not glide evenly along a line of print but proceed in a series of jumps (called 'saccades'). They jump and stop, jump and stop, during the reading process. The stops are called 'fixations' and are somewhat like the jumps and stops the eyes make when one looks around a room or watches a tennis match.

While reading, the eyes move in a series of jumps and stops; the stops are when the eye takes in information

Fluent readers make about four stops every second, and the time taken in moving the eye from fixation to fixation is very brief (about 1/1000 to 1/10 second) depending on the angle through which the eyes have to travel. It follows that for most of the time the eyes are stopped. This is just as well because while they are travelling the print is a blur that the brain ignores.

From this information we can see that reading occurs during fixations and that these occur about four times in a second. It is important to know that beginning readers and fluent readers change fixations at about the same rate. The difference is in what the brain processes during this time.

The eyes are the camera of the brain

Fluent readers make more effective use of the cue systems: they use graphophonic information; they handle the grammatical system skilfully; and they bring much more to print in terms of the world knowledge they possess, the breadth of their vocabulary, and their overall skill at *prediction*. This information about the fluent reader gives us important guidelines on how we should teach children to read. The important thing to notice is that good readers are good thinkers; they process larger chunks of print and use a variety of cue systems to do so. They do not see more, they *understand* more.

Figure 2.2

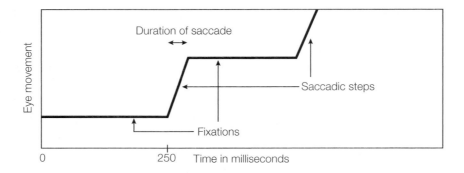

In speaking of the dense sampling of text described above, Perfetti (1995) agrees that the amount perceived in a single fixation is limited to the extent discussed. He concludes from this that readers, limited as they are by the eyes' inability to see much in a fixation, must sample a lot of words to read effectively. He does not address the matter of varying reading speeds by the adoption of strategies that allow the skilled reader to process large chunks of text as discussed above. Not every reading act requires the fixating and processing of most words on the page.

Other eye movements during reading also occur. Readers' eyes 'rove' around the page before and during reading, depending on the reading purpose and the level of concentration. Readers look back over text read at various stages of reading. These regressions are important to confirm or correct what has been read. It is also common for good readers to browse print by skimming through the text or scanning to find specific points. The latter techniques or strategies are valuable assets to a reader and can be successfully taught.

Readers' eyes 'rove' during effective reading

Text and the locus of meaning

Meaning lies somewhere between the writer and the reader

It must be noted that although meaning is seen to be at the core of all reading it is necessary to discuss where it resides, whether in the text, in some code within the text, in the reader's head, or in a combination of these. It is important to consider to what extent meaning is influenced by the social and cultural context of the writer and the reader. It could be argued that the text carries one meaning and that the reader's task is to find it. Another view might be that every reader comes to the text with a different set of skills and understandings and that there are therefore as many meanings as there are readers. Yet another view would be that there are aspects of a text that are common to all readers—the 'plain' or literal meaning of a text—while different levels of meaning would produce varying amounts of difference depending on the input of the reader and the social and cultural context.

Bloom (1956) produced a **taxonomy** of educational objectives that defined comprehension as exhibiting three types of behaviour in ascending order of reader input. Smith (1969) developed a further taxonomy that, although similar in many ways, extended the reader's input. She specified a series of skills that has been used widely by teachers. **Four levels of** Four levels of comprehension were included: the *literal* level in which a reader, **comprehension** among other things, identified, remembered, or recalled details and ideas; the *interpretive* or *inferential* level in which a reader concentrated on main ideas and further details, made contrasts, drew conclusions, generalised, and predicted; the *critical* level in which a reader judged, detected propaganda, analysed, and checked validity; and a final *creative* level in which a reader applied information to a new situation and responded emotionally. While these approaches appeared hierarchical, heavily cognitive, and skill-based, they provided teachers with a framework for discussion and questioning and were widely used. They did not, however, give enough attention to the social context in which situations occurred or the cultural background of the reader and what he brought to print. One method that gives attention to social context, while providing a framework for practice, is the Freebody & Luke (1990) concept of the four roles of the reader (see chapter 3).

IN THE CLASSROOM

An application of the four levels of comprehension is shown in questions that could be asked about the following short poem with, say, a fourth grade class.

Sort of Brown

Most things aren't any real colour
In my town;
They're sort of brown,
Like dust and dead leaves
And sleeves
That have been on people
For a day or two.
Most things aren't red or green
Or yellow or blue;
They're sort of brown,
I think.
Don't you?

Gordon Winch

For example:

Literal

1   What does the poet think 'sort of brown' things are like?

2   How does the poet describe 'sort of brown' sleeves?

3   What colours are not common in the poet's town?

Inferential

4   What other things in the poet's town might have been 'sort of brown' too?

5   What would the weather probably have been like if things were 'sort of brown' ?

Critical

6   The poet might have been in some kind of mood when he wrote this poem. How would you describe it?
     (Was he happy, sad, or just plain thoughtful?)

Creative

7   Some people have a favourite season of the year. What is your favourite season and why do you like it?

In the classroom of an experienced teacher, much of the comprehension work on 'Sort of Brown' would be carried out orally and would vary according to the ability, interests, and past experience of the class in reading poetry. For instance, at the literal level, the class might discuss what 'sort of brown' might really mean in the poem (brownlike, brownish, more brown than any other colour …). The discussion could move to the use of simile for comparison (like dust and dead leaves …). Which of the three is the most striking and original comparison? Why? Also how the poet uses rhyme, alliteration, and simple, shaved language for the desired effect.

Similar discussion could take place at the inferential, critical, and creative levels, extending and enriching the reading experience of the students.

Later, in chapter 5 and following, you will find more detail about the four roles of the reader. When you do, you will be able to compare and contrast the above questions with Luke and Freebody's approach.

Sociocultural views argue that comprehension and literacy can generally be seen only in their social and cultural setting: 'Texts are parts of lived, talked, enacted, value-and-belief laden

Reading occurs in a social context

practices carried out in specific places and at specific times' (Gee et al. 1996: 1, 3). Reading is thus a plural notion, '*readings* rather than *reading*', and must operate as a social practice. This idea views literacy and thus meaning or meanings more as ways of behaving and using literacy. It places emphasis on the language and literacy practices that a student brings to school from home and community, so that a teacher bases her practice on how the individual is behaving and on what she already knows.

These practices are not neutral and may not 'fit' with those of the school. School literacy practices may advantage some and disadvantage others, or, to use the terminology employed by this approach, may 'empower' or 'disempower' particular sociocultural groups. Literacy practice can thus become a political enterprise. It 'not only constructs the way an individual can operate in the world but also the way different cultural groups and agencies are structured and operationalised' (Anstey & Bull 1996: 153).

The above view is not universally accepted. Oakhill & Beard (1999) argue that while cultural factors are important, they play a secondary role. Close attention should be given to the necessary skills of literacy, which will allow children to learn to read, write, and understand. They question the concept of literacies as plural and argue that by equating literacies with various cultures and cultural practices there could be as many 'literacies' as there are cultures. Their perspective is that 'teaching literacy is primarily about teaching the skills of reading and writing, which once learned can be applied and extended in many ways that cover the broad definitions of literacy' (1999: x). These skills are the essentials that enable people to decipher the writing system or systems that they need to use. Oakhill & Beard's view, and that of the other contributors to their volume, is deeply influenced by cognitive psychology and empirical research relating to reading and writing.

Close attention must be paid to the essential skills of literacy

Literary theory and the locus of meaning

Literary theory also throws light on the locus of meaning in text. It places different interpretations on the place where meaning should reside and therefore how a reader comprehends. It also makes clearer how different approaches to reading have come to be.

Literary theory throws light on the locus of meaning in text

Put simply, the varying viewpoints of linguistic communication can be seen from the following diagram, which has been modified from that of the linguist Roman Jacobson.

WRITER   *CONTEXT*   *READER*
WRITING
CODE

The writer or *addresser* sends a message in writing to a reader or *addressee*. The message has a context and is sent through a medium, in this case writing.

Some literary theories focus on the writer's life or mind; others focus on the reader's experience; others focus on the nature of writing and the code; and others are more interested in the social context of the writing rather than the writing itself. There is a difference of opinion among critics as to where meaning really lies.

It is not difficult to equate some of the approaches to meaning (cognitive-psychological as opposed to sociocultural) with the positions discussed just above and to see how extreme positions can emerge. However, no matter how 'pure' a particular view of literary criticism may be, whether it is reader-dominated, code-dominated, or dominated by social context, no approach excludes the other entirely in explaining approaches to literary understanding and concomitantly to reading and the construction of meaning.

In the balanced approach to reading adopted in this book, the importance of the reader, the writer, the code, and the sociocultural context of the text are all considered as important in finding meaning and teaching children to read.

The reader, the writer, the code, and the context are all important in a balanced view

Applied to learning to read at school, this approach takes into account the varied experiences of language, world experience, and literary experience that a child brings to school. These understandings are included in the school's literacy program so that students can more readily bring meaning to and take meaning from text.

Some broad approaches to literature

It is too easy to oversimplify the complex world of literary theory and the above discussion touches only the surface. In part III Rosemary Ross Johnston explores it more deeply in terms of children's literature. However, certain approaches can be kept in mind while following the discussion in this section.

Early critics, when talking of literature and meaning, focused on the writer's personal experience, the social and historical background of the work, the human interest, and the imaginative thrust of the literature. They saw meaning as very much to do with the writer of the text.

Structuralist criticism, which places emphasis on the underlying structures or codes within the text, argues that the source of true meaning is found not in the writer or reader but in the system that governs the language. The **formalists**, too, concentrated on the text as a special use of language.

Reader-oriented theories offer yet another approach. They argue that unlike Jacobson's formalistic model, which places meaning in the text, no text has any meaning until it is read. The addressee, the reader, is the active agent in the making of meaning. There are 'blanks' in the text for the reader to fill and the reader's experience is at the heart of meaning.

Marxist criticism and to some extent feminist criticism place the focus on the social and cultural context of the writing with a view to changing the existing political and social order.

Reading and technology

In 1985 Jonathan Anderson wrote:

> Microcomputers are beginning to be a regular part of most schools … and imaginative teachers are finding a multitude of ways in which these new resources can promote learning. For reading and language teachers especially, microcomputers can be powerful allies. For a start they are highly motivating. More importantly, almost any interaction with microcomputers involves reading and writing of some kind. (1985: 203)

A prophetic statement

It is interesting to observe how prophetic Anderson's statements were, although he probably did not envisage the dramatic explosion of computer use in education that followed. He considered various aspects of computers in home and school: interactive software, including games; the computer and reading, writing, listening, speaking, thinking; simulation and database applications; the computer as a tool to develop reading skills; word-processing in its many aspects; and the potential of the computer for future literacy development.

Since that time and the advent of cheaper computers, the increased sophistication of the technology and its breathtaking rate of change, the World Wide Web and its many manifestations such as email, the availability of the CD-ROM, the DVD, the iPod, the MP3, the digital projector and the explosion in the software available for use, the computer is with us in full force. Many schools have their own considerable array of computers, not only in the classroom and the special computer area, but also in the library, where the monitor has replaced the card index and computer skills (particularly reading skills) are at a premium. Major references are on CD-ROM and that doyen of all resources, the Encyclopaedia Britannica, now comes to us on compact disc. Many schools have their own websites, many students carry around their personal laptops, and

There has been an explosion in computer technology and its use

homework is done on the home computer with multimedia presentations and all the extra embellishment that desktop publishing can bring.

Current syllabuses contain specific and detailed requirements in computer use. Computer technology sits beside handwriting, and basic desktop computer publishing skills are written into syllabus outcomes. As a consequence, textbooks are beginning to address computer skills and subskills as part and parcel of their content. The sophisticated level of computer knowledge and skills required in current syllabuses is illustrated by the following list of specific outcomes and indicators in the current NSW English K–6 Syllabus (NSW Board of Studies 1998a: 43) at Stage 3, senior primary. To achieve at this level it is necessary that the student produces texts in a fluent and legible style and uses computer technology to present these effectively in a variety of ways and that he

Modern literacy syllabuses reflect the changes in the digital age

- uses computer software programs and associated technology to format a variety of texts
- locates and uses a **thesaurus**
- uses font and layout to suit particular audience and purpose
- chooses appropriate graphics to accompany text
- designs and organises information for a web page
- locates and uses columns or borders when appropriate
- adds graphics, changes spacing and style when publishing
- uses word-processing programs to design school or class newspaper, importing graphics and written texts from a range of sources
- uses multimedia authoring software to create published works incorporating text, graphics, sound, animation
- creates texts that incorporate graphics or tables when appropriate.

The above may once have seemed highly sophisticated but in the intervening years there has been so much development in many aspects of technology that, today, these would be regarded as minimum competencies. Technology has added a new dimension to students, learning of literacy skills.

The use of the computer illustrates how closely reading and writing are intertwined. Most syllabus statements related to use of the computer tend to focus on its writing or word-processing use, but it must be remembered that every writing act is also a reading act. A student who is unable to read cannot effectively use a computer except in the most limited sense.

Technology has enabled reading and writing to become increasingly intertwined

Reading the written text is only one facet. Instructions and the applications of the various techniques of word-processing alone require considerable reading skills. The reading of computer icons adds an extra dimension and extends the concept of reading itself. Other skills, such as using computer software to find information and using **hypertext** and graphic materials effectively, are also examples of reading using the computer. The teaching of reading will more and more include the teaching of the 'grammar' of the computer and students will become increasingly able to navigate the complexities of electronic text.

As computers become more readily available, students will become familiar with electronic mail and its reading and writing processes. Email itself is providing a different type of discourse to be read and the script of the text message is in itself a new writing system or a radically changed one. A new genre

Text on screen is becoming increasingly non-linear and multimodal

of written material is becoming available and new reading approaches are needed to deal with it. New, interactive study programs are beginning to appear on the market. These combine online Internet access with dedicated CD-ROMs to enable the creation of multimedia presentations, including sound and visual effects. They claim to be complete packages, even including built-in self-assessment in order to allow students, parents, and teachers to monitor progress. The rapid development of software available to help young children learn to read is another example of the use of the computer in reading. Software programs that assist in developing phonemic awareness, and interactive stories and games with a literacy base, are becoming increasingly common and of improved quality.

MULTILITERACIES

As stated in Chapter 1, modes of meaning other than linguistic are becoming increasingly important in modern literacy learning and practice. Visual meanings (e.g. page layouts in a picturebook and screen formats); audio meanings (music sound effects); gestural meanings (body language, advertising on TV); spatial meanings (environmental and architectural spaces) and multimodal meanings all interrelate in two or more dynamic ways, such as when one visits a shopping mall. Two key concepts, hybridity and intertextuality, help us describe multimodal meanings.

In hybridity, people create, innovate and articulate in new ways and structure new forms of meaning. One example is where the musical forms of Africa meet audio electronics and the commercial music industry and new meanings are created. Intertextuality, in one sense, refers to the ways new meanings are made in linguistic texts by the relationships to other texts. Janet and Allan Ahlberg's *The Jolly Postman and Other People's Letters* and their *Each Peach Pear Plum* are classical examples of this. Movies are full of these cross-references. These form intertextual chains and provide a richer meaning for the viewer. (See also Rosemary Ross Johnston's discussion of intertextuality in chapter 24.)

Electronic professional programs are becoming a reality at tertiary institutions, and education online now exists in most universities. For instance, at the University of New England three-quarters of the 13 000 external students are doing some of their course online (Ho 2000) and other examples are appearing every year.

Crossman (2000) takes the view that the new technology and the talking computer will make literacy as we know it obsolete during this century. He argues that human society is moving away from a print culture to an oral culture. His reasoning is both interesting and persuasive, although it fails to recognise two fundamental factors, among others: that spoken language is comparatively very slow—a reader can read infinitely faster than a listener can comprehend speech—and that written language is different from spoken language in many aspects. These differences have been discussed earlier. The power of written language, its distinctive quality, its richness, and its remarkable flexibility make it a vital part of being educated and, indeed, human.

The computer sits beside the book in literacy development and requires the reader to acquire new literacy skills

The computer will sit beside the book in the future. Just as film and television sit beside the book now, and often support reading by building up semantic knowledge, so will the computer act as both supplement and complement to the book. Likewise, voice-interactive computers will convey oral language with increasing effectiveness and sit beside telephone technology. The survival of print material in its many forms is not at risk although new devices for communication, such as the mobile phone and the iPod, will add a new dimension. Rosemary Ross Johnston discusses the survival of the book with reference to children's literature in part III (see chapter 20). In no way does the new electronic age herald the death of the book.

▶ LITERACY IN THE DIGITAL AGE

The book in the digital age

The massive search engine, Google, is in the process of scanning some 32 million books, just about every book written in the English language. It is doing this for two reasons: one to provide a giant 'card index', that will allow a reader to find books by searching the words in them, and two to provide the reader with a book in a different form. Google books will allow the reader to sample the text and then read the lot if desired (one would presume at a suitable price).

The digital book presents problems to authors and publishers in terms of copyright and consequent loss of income. (There are currently two lawsuits in the USA filed against Google, one by the United States Authors Guild and the other by the Association of American Publishers.) There may be nothing to fear. An outcome could be that people will buy more traditional books in paper form if they can find out about them more easily and can sample the digital text on screen. Similar fears were sounded when photocopiers were installed in libraries in the 1960s and 1970s. The result was the opposite of the expected, as pointed out by Peter Martin (2005): More books were sold, particularly among journals that were copied the most.

SMS in the digital age

Consider the growing use of text messaging (SMS) in the digital age. It is in effect a new form of speed writing or shorthand (Rest in peace Isaac Pitman.) which uses the resources of multimodal presentation to produce a text that is shorter and faster to read than ordinary handwriting or print. (That is, of course, after you have mastered it.). The young of the digital age have. Have you?

But it is not only the young and trendy who are texting. The classics are about to be given a drastic slimming by the British student mobile service, *dot mobile*, for easy student access and revision. (Reported by Martin Wainwright in *The Guardian* and reprinted in *The Sydney Morning Herald, 18.11.05.*). Take the opening of Hamlet's famous soliloquy:

> 2b?Ntb?=?

or the summary of the climactic ending of *Jane Eyre* :

> MadwyfSetsFyr2Haus.

This crafty shorthand can pick up dialect, too, as in F. Scott Fitzgerald's opening admonition in *The Great Gatsby* :

> MembaDatAldaPplnDaWrld-HvntHdDaVantgsUvAd.

which translated means 'Whenever you feel like criticising anyone, just remember that all the people in the world haven't had the advantages you've had.'

The texting of the classics has the support of eminent scholars and is seen as an underused and promising resource. Are we seeing a dramatic change in the nature of our writing system? Will it affect reading as well as writing or IZitjstaflshnDapan?

The matter of dyslexia

Dyslexia, (*dys* difficulty, *lexia* words) is a type of specific learning difficulty (SLD) that affects a person's ability to read and spell. It is characterised by difficulties in the decoding and encoding of single words, and reflects poor phonological processing. These problems spill over into writing and reading comprehension and generally poor progress in literacy development at school.

Symptoms in preschoolers include delayed speech, poor pronunciation, difficulty with recognising and learning rhymes, and difficulty with writing one's own name or retelling stories. Primary school children experience problems with reading single words, exhibit poor spelling, confuse certain letters when writing, find it difficult to understand grammar, and have a dislike of reading books.

It is important to remember that only about 5 per cent of the population are genuinely dyslexic and many of the symptoms are typical of poor achievers in language development, associated with a range of factors. These may include poor application, physical problems such as poor hearing, bad attendance at school, poor teaching programs, a non-English-speaking background, inadequate or broken schooling, and low intellectual ability. Most children who are poor achievers are not dyslexic in the true sense of the word.

Dyslexia is difficult to diagnose, and although it is recognised that the causes are neurobiological and genetic (it can run in families) the exact aetiology (cause) remains unknown. Dyslexia is not a symptom of low intelligence as such or a barrier to success. Some famous dyslexics include Leonardo Da Vinci, Hans Christian Anderson, George Washington, and Albert Einstein.

If a child is thought to suffer from dyslexia, professional help is required through a specialist educational psychologist or speech therapist, who can make an effective diagnosis and recommend treatment. Referrals can be made through a school, a doctor or the State Department of Education.

Finally, although true dyslexia cannot be cured, most dyslexics can be taught to read and go about their lives in an effective way. Also, improvement in language skills for dyslexics can be effected through one-to-one tutoring, using a multisensory approach, careful development of phonemic awareness and phonological coding, and the application of a range of methods to teach the fundamentals of reading. Skilled teachers know that some children respond to certain approaches better than others, but that all the basics must be covered. This is the balanced approach to teaching reading and literacy skills generally. It applies to a dyslexic child as to any other.

▶ Summary

1   English is an alphabetic writing system. It is important to understand the writing system when learning to read. Meaning is found in the text, the writer, and the reader. Writing is not just speech written down. Oracy is important in learning to read, and oral language skills provide the starting point for reading.

2   Phonemic and phonological awareness

are important concepts in learning to read. Phonemic awareness is different from phonics. There is an important relationship between phonemic awareness and learning to read. Readers use phonological–graphological, grammatical, and semantic information when reading.

3   Readers use visual and nonvisual information when reading. It is important to be aware of what readers see and understand when reading. Readers need to read flexibly, using different strategies for different purposes. When reading, the eyes move in jumps and stops; reading is carried out during the stops.

4   Literary theory throws light on the locus of meaning in text. Various critics argue that the meaning lies in the author, the author's intention, and the historical setting; others argue that it resides in the text; and others again that it is in the reader. A balanced view of reading places importance on each of the three.

5   Computers are becoming an integral part of literacy learning, both reading and writing as well as listening, speaking, and thinking. Current syllabuses contain specific computer teaching. The computer will sit beside the book. The book is not 'dead'.

6   Dyslexia applies to approximately 5 per cent of the population and its accurate diagnosis is important. Often the symptoms are typical of any poor reader and the teaching is fundamentally the same.

▷ Critical thinking and study exercises

1   English can be described as an alphabetic writing system. What implications does this have for learning to read?

2   Discuss the concept of 'phoneme' in linguistics and the way a 'phoneme' differs from an 'allophone' and a 'grapheme'.

3   Consider some of the strengths and weaknesses of our English writing system and discuss some reasons for its widespread use around the world.

4   Discuss in what ways the commonly held view that eyes move evenly from left to right when reading is wrong.

5   Discuss ways a teacher might develop phonemic awareness in a classroom during the first year of school.

6   If you take the view that reading is a plural notion (readings rather than reading), what would you say about reading a legal document such as a will or reading a train timetable?

7   Consider in what ways an indigenous child from the Torres Strait Islands might find it extremely difficult to read and respond to nursery rhymes that are common to English-speaking children.

Take as an example:

A Week of Birthdays

Monday's child is fair of face,
Tuesday's child is full of grace,
Wednesday's child is full of woe,
Thursday's child has far to go,
Friday's child is loving and giving,
Saturday's child works hard for its living,
But the child that's born on the Sabbath day
Is bonny and blithe and good and gay.

8   Read the following excerpt from a recent book on literacy. Discuss the position that might be taken by these writers on the nature of literacy.

To illustrate the operation of power, we would like to share three examples from the research on language and social power. These particular three have been chosen not because they illustrate empowerment, but because they show individuals being disempowered in the interplay of power in literacy events in classrooms. We share them not as a comment on the classrooms or the teachers, but as a comment on how power operates. (Anstey & Bull 1996: 171)

9 The English literary scholar I. A. Richards wrote:

> In most poetry, the sense is as important as anything else; it is quite as subtle, and as dependent on the syntax as is prose; it is the poet's chief instrument … and in the immense majority of instances we miss nearly everything of value if we misread his sense. (1929: 191)

Richards is talking about the 'plain meaning' of poetry. Where do you think he would place the locus of meaning of a poem: in the writer, the poem, or the reader? Give your reason and say where you think the meaning of a poem (or a piece of prose) resides.

10 Consider the ways the computer is used in your daily life. What uses could be described as part of literacy?

11 Use a 'crystal ball' to look into the future. Write a brief essay (about one page) on the way you think computers will be used to teach literacy in the school. Think about the library and the classroom in particular.

12 Test yourself on the examples in the 'Seeing and understanding' section in chapter 2 by glancing at each one separately. See how much of each you can read with one glance per example.

13 Redundancy refers to the fact that much of the information in our written language is a matter of overkill—there is much more than we need. To give an example, read these two sentences. As you can see, not all the information supplied in the fully printed form is necessary for you to read the sentences.

> *I r n in t e r ce last y r.*
> *I have two eyes and ears.*

Make up some examples of your own.

14 Test your knowledge of basic phonics by answering this short phonics quiz. (Answers on page 560.) How well did you do?

i Which of the following words ends with a consonant sound?
  a. elbow   b. happy   c. play   d. hill
  e. ago

ii A combination of 2 or 3 consonants pronounced so that each consonant keeps its own identity is called a
  a. silent consonant   b. consonant digraph
  c. diphthong   d. schwa or indeterminate vowel   e. consonant blend

iii Which of these words begins with a consonant digraph?
  a. stop   b. black   c. hand   d. strain
  e. none of them

iv The word that begins with a consonant blend is:
  a. chain   b. think   c. which   d. street
  e. show

v Which word begins with a voiced consonant digraph?
  a. shape   b. thin   c. sheep   d. the
  e. phone

vi Which word begins with an unvoiced consonant digraph?
  a. them   b. thirst   c. that   d. breath
  e. these

vii Which of the following words contains a short vowel sound?
  a. fat   b. fate   c. them   d. rip
  e. fine   f. boat   g. pot   h. cuts
  i. cute   j. cuddle

viii In phonics, which of these words contains what is termed a long vowel sound?
  a. rake   b. bet   c. wine   d. been
  e. coat   f. huge   g. father

ix Which words contain a vowel digraph?
  a. see   b. bread   c. look   d. short
  e. soup

x Which words contain a diphthong (two vowel sounds glided together). Note that some long vowels in phonics (/eɪ/ as in fate) are strictly diphthongs in linguistics, although they are called long vowels by teachers.

a. oil   b. out   c. ear   d. down   e. boy
f. catch   g. sail

xi How many phonemes are in each of the following words?

a. chase   b. parked   c. might
d. bough   e. broke

xii How many syllables are in each of the following words?

a. plough   b. particle   c. permeated
d. painted   e. recovered   f. undertaken

15 Have a discussion or write an exposition on '*the future of the book*'.

Further reading

Clay, M. M. 1991, *Becoming Literate: The construction of inner control*, Heinemann, Auckland.

Clay, M. M. 1998, *By Different Paths to Common Outcomes*, Heinemann, Auckland.

Kervin, L. 2005, 'Students talking about home-school communication: Can technology support this process?' *Australian Journal of Language and Literacy* 28(2): 150–63.

Meek, M. 1982, *Learning to Read*, Bodley Head, London.

Meek, M. 1988, *How Texts Teach What Readers Learn*, Thimble Press, Stroud, UK in association with PETA, Sydney.

Meek, M. 1991, *On Being Literate*, Bodley Head, London.

Unsworth, L. 2002, 'Changing dimensions of school literacies', *Australian Journal of Language and Literacy* 25(1): 62–77.

Winch, G. & V. Hoogstad (eds) 1985, *Teaching Reading: A language experience*, 2nd edn, Macmillan, Melbourne.

Web links

International Reading Association: www.reading.org
Australian Literacy Educators' Association: www.alea.edu.au
Primary English Teaching Association: www.peta.edu.au

3 TOWARDS A MODEL OF READING

Overview

Effective teaching of reading comes through an understanding of the components that form part of the reading process and of how these are used by skilful readers. Expert teachers provide their students with a range of experiences to build knowledge and skill in all of the elements that make up the reading process. This chapter explains what these elements are and how they relate to each other. Subsequent chapters show how this model can be translated into classroom practice. The model provided here is an attempt to describe the complex process of reading but, being a static model, it cannot fully portray the dynamic and interactive nature of the reading process.

The context and purpose of reading

A reader reads the notices and prices in a supermarket for a specific social purpose: to make the most of the visit by obtaining the required goods at the best possible price. Another reader who reads the editorial of a newspaper has a different social purpose: to obtain news and to find out what the editorial writer thinks about a particular subject. As well, each reader reads differently in terms of his cultural background, personal interests, reading ability, and intellectual skills. Different cultural groups and individuals bring different purposes and understandings to print and therefore react in different ways to it.

We read with a sociocultural purpose

Likewise, the text itself is subject to similar influences. The writer's social purpose and cultural background will affect the genre in which text is written: a church newsletter has a totally different social purpose from that of an instruction on how to build a model car. The cultural background of the writer would also be reflected in the text. *Bury My Heart at Wounded Knee: An Indian History of the American West*, would likely be very different from a history written by a white American rancher.

The writer's purpose is reflected in the text

These differences are often discussed in terms of **register**, which means the way a particular situation affects the language and meaning of a text. (See also part III p. XX.) It is reflected in the choice of vocabulary, grammar, and other features. Register is described as consisting of field, tenor, and mode. Field refers to the subject matter involved (the subject or topic may change the language used in the text); tenor refers to the people involved and their relationship (one would speak differently to different people and in terms of what one thinks of them); and mode refers to the type of language use, whether written in the case of reading or spoken in the case of oral language. Formal written language, for instance, is very different from colloquial speech). Each of these features helps to describe the rich context of literate practice, the register of the text.

Register describes the context of literate practice

Social and cultural context must be built into any model of reading, because meaning is influenced by a number of factors relating to writer, reader, and text (see chapter 2). That is, the reader, the writer, and the text are involved in the act of reading, operating in social and cultural context.

Different social and cultural contexts will affect the **genre** in which a text is written and each genre will have a different internal structure in terms of its grammar and its sequential makeup. An *information report* is significantly different from an *instruction*; an *exposition* is significantly different from a *narrative*. Also, readers must access the necessary aspects of graphophonic information in a text; they must have grammatical information and semantic information, which includes word meanings and knowledge of the real world.

Sociocultural context affects the genre of the text

GENRE OR TEXT-TYPE

Genre or text-type refers to the way a text is structured to achieve a particular purpose. There are various categories of text-type and their names (and definitions) sometimes vary according to the person who describes them. A useful description for our purposes is that texts can be termed literary or factual with various subcategories.

Literary text-types include narrative, poetry, and drama although, obviously, many of these overlap. Factual text-types and some of their particular characteristics have been helpfully classified by Derewianka (1991):

- **Recount:** an account of something that happened in the past.
- **Information Report:** facts and information about a topic.
- **Explanation:** an explanation of how or why things work.

- **Instruction (Procedure):** a description of how to do or make something.
- **Exposition:** arguing a case for or against something.
- **Discussion:** presenting two or more points of view on an issue.

Again, although it is understood that text-types overlap and we often find 'mixed' texts, these distinctions help teachers to focus on the different ways texts are structured and their characteristic language features.

As we saw in chapter 2, we use reading practices to serve our social purposes and to get things done. In every case the social interaction we are involved in to get what we want means being able to know and use the forms of reading that are part of that action. And the way we do these

We read to serve our social purposes and to get things done

things in our society differs from the way they do them elsewhere. So reading is embedded in the social and cultural contexts in which we live, work, learn, play, communicate, create, buy and sell goods and services, and are entertained. And what we read and how we read it depends very much on our purpose, what we

want to achieve. That's why 'reading' changes, depending on the context in which it is being used and what we are trying to do with it.

Selecting texts

Once we know what we want to achieve we set about looking for a text that will help us do this. Choosing the right text is crucial to being an effective reader. If you want to order a pizza you

Effective readers select the right text

don't use a TV guide, you use a menu from the local pizza place. If you want to find out about dinosaurs you don't use a cookbook, you look in an information book about dinosaurs, or go to the Internet. Many of the texts we use are already

embedded in the social context in which they operate: you go to a restaurant and the menu is on the table; you go to the railway station and the timetable is displayed on an information board. Other texts need to be sought out; we buy a TV guide to find out what's on next week; we buy a newspaper to find out what's happened in the world. And, of course, the Internet is rapidly becoming the text of choice for many of the functions we want to perform in society, from booking airline tickets to finding out about entertainment in a city we are visiting. As effective readers we become adept at selecting the right text to fulfil the need we have.

We know that texts are different depending on what purpose we want them to fulfil. A train timetable looks different from a recipe, and a novel is different from an encyclopaedia. These text

Texts are different depending on what purpose they fulfil in society

differences have evolved because they help the text to achieve its purpose. So a recipe lists the ingredients first because that makes it easier to get ingredients ready to cook the dish. An information report on whales has information in paragraphs because that makes it easier to understand the different aspects of

whales—where they live, what they eat, what they look like and so on. The text-types we know and use today evolved to meet the social purposes we wanted these texts to perform. In future there will be new and different types of text to meet new and different purposes of society. An Internet website is an example of a new type of text that has evolved to fulfil particular purposes.

So, in building a model of reading, we can begin by showing that *what* we read grows out of what we want to achieve within our particular social and situational context.

Figure 3.1   Choosing what to read

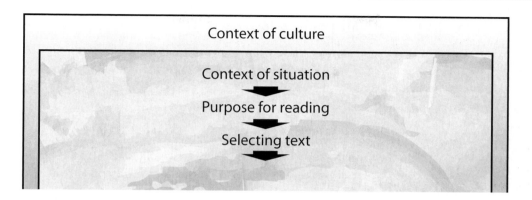

Multiliteracies

As pointed out previously, the term 'multiliteracies' helps to explain modern literacy practices. There are two important aspects to consider. The first refers to the differences created by cultural, social, and linguistic influences. These are becoming more significant as English is moving more to being a global or world language, a *lingua mundi*, as well as the common language of commerce, a *lingua franca*. This means that English, in its varied forms, is increasing in use around the world and is introducing a wider range of practices. Second, the new communication technologies are producing increasingly multimodal types of text. Written-linguistic forms of communication combine with visual, audio, gestural, and spatial modes, as stated above, to create new patterns of literacy, much broader than language alone. See Cope & Kalantzis 2002: 2–8. Some of the classroom applications of these changed practices are addressed in the following chapters.

Literacy practices

When we've chosen the text we want to meet our purpose, we need to know what to do with it. In other words, we need to know how to read and use this sort of text. Allan Luke and Peter Freebody (1990, 1999) have described a set of reading practices (previously known as reader roles) that effective readers use when they are interacting with texts to achieve particular purposes. These practices describe the kinds of things that effective readers do when they use texts to achieve their purposes in the world. Although the reading practices were originally intended to refer mainly to print texts, it is now widely accepted that these practices are a very effective framework for reading texts of all types including multimodal and digital texts. In most cases readers will use all of these practices interactively as they access, use, reflect on, and respond to the text they have chosen. These practices are described as effective literary practices.

We use different reading practices for different purposes

1. Code-breaking practices

Here the reader is concerned with the basic decoding of the print information of the text, working out what the words and sentences in the text are. The reader gives attention to letter-sound correspondences, whole words, sentences, paragraphs, semantic information, grammatical information (see cue systems below), punctuation, and word meanings. Readers also need to understand how to decode the images from print and digital texts. Code-breaking practices include understanding book and screen conventions and concepts about print such as left-to-right directionality and menu bars.

2. Text-participant practices

These practices refer to the ways the reader participates in constructing meaning from the text. Here the reader is concerned with what the text is saying in the context of the reader's own knowledge about the topic, and readers are usually better able to understand a text if they are familiar with the topic. The reader's concern is to access the literal and inferential meanings of the text. The 'literal meaning' is the plain sense of the text, what the text actually says. The 'inferential meaning' is the associated meaning, what the reader believes the writer is hinting at or implying. The reader needs to know how to construct meaning from the range of elements presented in the text. For example, an information book on the solar system requires the reader to use diagrams, pictures, labelled drawings, and tables as well as the printed part of the text. An Internet site requires the reader to understand how the different print, visual, and sound elements of the text work together.

3. Text-user practices

Text-user practices refer to the ways we use texts to achieve our particular social purposes. Here the reader is concerned with knowing about the structure of different texts and the ways they are used in different social situations (for example, a train timetable, a recipe, a movie, or a newspaper). The reader uses the text as part of acting in a particular social situation (whether at school or in the community). The reader may interact with others around the text, such as discussing characters' actions and motives, and participate in events in which the text plays a part, such as acting in a scripted play or making a purchase after seeing an advertisement for a product. Classroom discussions about texts such as narratives or poetry call on text-user practices.

4. Text-analyst practices

If we believe that texts are not neutral but have built into them the writers' points of view, assumptions and biases, we, as readers, are in a position to accept or challenge the views and assumptions provided in texts. Text-analyst practices refer to the ways readers critique the underlying and unstated assumptions in a text and the way a text attempts to position them as readers. The reader reads critically by considering the purpose of the text and the author's opinion, and considers the way the text portrays, for example, different social groups or scientific positions. The reader detects propaganda and bias and weighs the arguments presented.

The table below shows how readers can use these practices to access texts in different ways and for different purposes.

Table 3.1 Effective literacy practices

Code-breaking practices	*Text-participant practices*	*Text-user practices*	*Text-analyst practices*
In using code-breaking practices readers ask themselves questions such as 'What type of text is this?' 'How do I crack the code of this text?' 'What are the patterns and conventions of this text?' 'What can I see that I already know?' (words, letters, punctuation, images, screen layout) 'How will I work out those parts I don't already know?'	**In using text-participant practices readers ask themselves questions such as** 'What do I already know about this topic?' 'What is this text trying to say?' 'What are the possible meanings of this text?' 'How do the different elements in this text work together to present meaning?' 'Are the situations/characters/events in this text like any that I know?' 'What facts/information can I find in this text?' 'What do I know already?' 'What is new information?'	**In using text-user practices readers ask themselves questions such as** 'What is the purpose of this text?' 'How is this text constructed to achieve its purpose?' 'How would this text be used in the community?' 'How effective is this text in achieving its purpose?' 'In what ways can I use this text?' 'What activities can I (and others) do around this text?'	**In using text-analyst practices readers ask themselves questions such as** 'Whose interests are being served by this text?' 'What is this text trying to get me to think or feel?' 'Whose voices or opinions are missing from this text?' 'Does this text present a balanced point of view?' 'What action is the text trying to get me to take? Do I want to take this action?' 'What textual structures and features have been employed to present the text's position?'
Skills and strategies for being a code-breaker	*Skills and strategies for being a text-participant*	*Skills and strategies for being a text-user*	*Skills and strategies for being a text-analyst*
In using code-breaking practices readers need to ■ use and integrate semantic, grammatical and phonological/graphological cues ■ predict likely text and sentence structures ■ monitor their own reading and notice when an error (or miscue) occurs ■ cross-check information from one cue system against another (e.g. 'This word *looks* like 'house' but does that make *sense* in this sentence?') ■ self-correct by searching for more information and trying different options and by using strategies such as re-reading, reading ahead and checking illustrations ■ use and integrate knowledge about images ■ use and integrate knowledge about digital texts	**In using text-participant practices readers need to** ■ use their knowledge of word meanings and common English expressions to construct meaning with the text ■ use their knowledge about still and moving images, sound and interactivity to construct meaning with the text ■ understand how the grammatical structures in the text and the punctuation contribute to its meanings ■ understand how conventions of image-making contribute to the text's meaning ■ relate the text to their personal and cultural experiences and knowledge, including their experiences with other texts ■ participate in unpacking the literal and inferential meanings of the text ■ be able to understand how illustrations, diagrams, graphs and other pictorial features present meaning in the text ■ understand how layers of meaning are constructed in a text	**In using text-user practices readers need to** ■ know about the different social and cultural functions that texts perform (at school and in the community) ■ understand that these functions influence the way texts are structured ■ use texts for a range of purposes (e.g. for enjoyment, for finding information) ■ use texts as part of social action (e.g. use a recipe to make a cake, use an Internet site to gather information) ■ interact with others around a text (e.g. discuss how a text's structure contributes to its meaning)	**In using text-analyst practices readers need to** ■ talk about an author's purpose in constructing a text ■ talk about opinion, point of view and bias in texts ■ present an alternative position to the one taken in a text ■ compare texts on the same topic from different viewpoints ■ compare texts on the same topic in different media ■ talk about their agreement or disagreement with the ideas presented in a text ■ explain why people might interpret texts differently ■ talk about what the writer of the text believes ■ understand how a text's structure and features contribute to the way the text portrays ideas or issues ■ understand how a text's structure and features contribute to the way the text portrays different social and cultural groups and individuals

IN THE CLASSROOM

Prompting the reader

Teachers use knowledge of the sources of information or reading cue systems to assist students to work out unknown words when they read. Prompts can be specifically targeted to encourage the student to focus on one or other of the sources of information, e.g.

- What would make sense here? (semantic)
- What word would fit in this sentence? (grammatical)
- What letter does this word start with? What sound does it make in this word? (graphophonic)
- What does the picture tell you? (visual/pictorial)

The reading cue systems or sources of information

As we read, we use information from four different sources to construct meaning from the text we are reading. These sources of information are sometimes called cue systems because they provide us with the cues we need to access the text. In the past these cue systems referred only to print text, but in this model we have added visual or pictorial information because this is an important facet of nearly all texts produced and read in the modern world. When we read we draw on and combine information from these four sources continuously in order to read fluently. These sources of information or cue systems can be described as semantic information, grammatical information, phonological–graphological information, and visual/pictorial information.

Cue systems supply the reader with information to construct meaning

Semantic information

This system refers to the meanings in the text and in the mind of the reader. They include word meanings, subject-specific vocabulary, figurative language and meanings presented visually. Readers use semantic cues when they consider ideas, information, and feelings in a text. The more they call on their own knowledge that they bring to reading, the better they read. The topic of the text, the meanings of the words in the text, and the reader's knowledge of common or colloquial expressions, vocabulary, and figurative language all affect the operation of the semantic cue system.

Meaning is in the text and in the mind of the reader

It is this cue system that provides the main guide or monitor to readers as they read. It is by using their semantic knowledge that readers provide the answer to the question, 'Does this make sense?' It is usually when meaning is disrupted that readers go back in the text and use the grammatical and phonological–graphological knowledge to correct their earlier error.

Semantic information helps the reader to monitor meaning

It is the semantic cue system that enables the reader to link a new text to everything he already knows about the topic of the text or the setting of a narrative. This gives him tremendous power to unlock the meaning of the new text since he already has a mental frame of reference for what is being described. In scientific or technical texts, where this is linked with subject-specific vocabulary, the reader with a good bank of semantic knowledge has an enormous advantage over the reader without such knowledge.

It is important to note that the act of reading itself is one of the best ways of increasing semantic knowledge. As students read they add new words to those they already know and develop new concepts and understandings that strengthen and deepen their current knowledge. Many well-written factual texts make a point of clearly describing the meanings of key terms, often with the use of diagrams and illustrations. In this way readers are prompted to combine semantic and visual/pictorial information in order to understand the new or difficult words in the text.

Consider the difficulty you encounter when trying to read a text when you know little or nothing about the topic. In particular, imagine you know nothing about computers and try to read the following:

> *To move or delete buttons when the customize dialog box isn't open, hold down ALT and drag the button to a new location or off the toolbar.*

Or the following:

> *In your Word toolbox, you can customize existing menus by adding or removing commands, or you can create your own menus.*

Grammatical information

Grammatical information relies on the reader's knowledge of language and the way it works. Grammatical knowledge includes knowing how texts are constructed to achieve their purpose, how different types of sentences are structured, and how different types of words work to achieve meaning in a text. Two examples illustrate this system:

Grammatical information allows a reader to predict

> *She ____ the length of the pool using a backstroke style.*

> *He had one pet and she had two pet __.*

In the first case, a reader can predict that the word is *swam*, the past tense of the verb *to swim*; in the second, a reader can predict that the required **inflection** is *s*, so the word becomes *pets*. In each case the reader could easily supply the word or inflection without reference to the visual presentation of either. The fact that we can supply this information by calling on our linguistic knowledge of vocabulary and syntax (sentence structure) is also an example of redundancy in English: there is more information than we really need. Knowledge of the sentence structure of the language and word inflections such as -*s* and -*ed* is a vital component of reading. Grammatical knowledge gives important cues to what sentences say and mean. Grammatical cues are particularly important in reading English because its structural system relies more heavily on word order than is the case in other languages. Therefore the reader knows what type of word to expect next in a sentence.

Consider this example:

> *When I _____ coffee I always add _____.*

In the first instance we know that the missing word should be a verb, something I *do*. In the second instance we know it should be a noun, a *thing*. It is our grammatical knowledge that tells us this. This knowledge helps readers enormously in predicting what *kind* of word will come next. We often then need to check only one or two letters to predict what that word is. In checking we might find the following:

> *When I dr_____ coffee I always add su_____.*

This is often enough to confirm what the words are. Only if meaning is lost or the grammar of the sentence disrupted will the reader need to check more closely. A reader might misread the sentence as follows:

> *When I drink coffee I always add sung.*

It is grammatical knowledge that will tell the reader that this cannot be right and that she needs to re-read and to check more of the letters in the word.

Cohesive ties carry meaning across sentences

Linguists have pointed out that grammatical cues are carried across sentences and not confined within them. Words are connected throughout the text by special links called **cohesive ties**.

Chapman (1983), using insights derived from the linguists Halliday & Hasan (1976), has stressed the importance of these ties in reading. A simple example of one form of cohesive tie is shown in figure 3.2.

These cohesive ties are called **reference ties** and this particular example is called *anaphora* because the ties relate back to the original reference. There are many different types of cohesive ties in English. Others include *substitution* (using a different word): 'My *fishing rod* is a good *one*'; *ellipsis* (leaving out words): 'Jim is tall and (*he is*) strong'; *conjunctions* (linking words that join phrases, clauses, and sentences): 'The boy *and* his dog'; 'He turned quickly, *then* he ran'; and *related words*: 'The man was a *liar* and a *thief*'.

Grammatical knowledge also refers to knowledge about the ways texts are typically structured in our society to achieve their purpose. Grammatical knowledge at the text level tells readers what to expect next as they read a particular type of text. For example, a narrative will probably have a resolution after the complication, and a procedure will have a series of steps after the list of 'things you will need to achieve the task'.

Grammatical knowledge helps the reader know what to expect next in a text

Grammatical knowledge also tells the reader that paragraphs are 'bundles of information' which perform the function of organising the text, and that many paragraphs in factual texts have a topic sentence that signals what will be in the paragraph to follow. Cohesion in texts is also considered to be part of text-level grammar because it refers to ways different items are linked to enable us to 'track' meaning through the text.

Figure 3.2   Cohesive ties

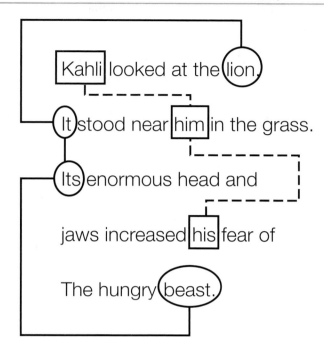

Phonological–graphological information

This information involves two types of language information, phonological and graphological information, and can be described as the phonological–graphological cue system. Although this cue system and its relation to phonemic awareness has been discussed above, it needs elaboration here as it is particularly important in word recognition.

Phonological information includes hearing the sounds, syllables, and morphemes in words and manipulating these sounds by exchanging and blending.

Graphological information includes knowledge of letters, letter clusters such as blends (*cl, bl*), digraphs (*ch, th, oa*), syllables (*syl.la.bles*), prefixes (*non-, anti-*), and suffixes (*-ness, -ation*). As well as these more common examples, graphological information includes concepts about print, such as spaces between words, directionality, punctuation, and book conventions such as page layout and sight words. There is some overlap here with the grammatical cue system because inflections such as past-tense markers like *-ed* and other affixes have a grammatical role to play.

'Graphophonic' is a term often used to describe the relationship between the graphic units of the language (graphological information) and the sounds they represent (phonological information) (Goodman 1973: 25). Readers make generalisations about the letter–sound and letter pattern–sound correspondences when reading. They extend this knowledge through the use of analogy and build up their skills at decoding written text when reading and encoding words when writing. Smith (1973) made the interesting point that these relationships are not strictly grapheme–phoneme correspondences but what he termed 'morphophonemic' (morpho- relates to meaning-bearing chunks of words called morphemes, as see-ing in 'seeing'), operating quite often at levels above the individual sound, which varies among dialects. Readers do in fact decode by using meaning-bearing letter groups that relate to sounds when they are reading. They also relate to blends (*bl-*) and the segments found in onset and rime (*bl-ack*). Simply sounding out the letters in a word (grapheme to sound) could often be confusing: 'In English as in many other languages the spelling system is fixed and standardised but the pronunciation is not. This means that correspondences will vary from dialect to dialect and that over time, changing phonology will loosen the fit of even the tightest alphabetical system' (Goodman 1973: 25)—so that simply decoding from symbol to sound is at best difficult and at worst, impossible!

Graphophonic information describes the links between sounds and letters

Figure 3.3   Cathy Wilcox illustrates some differences in pronunciation with impish wit and the licence permitted to the cartoonist. (SMH 25.7.05)

Table 3.2   Knowledge about the sources of information

Semantic	*Grammatical*	*Phonological*	*Graphological*
Students need experiences which will enable them to develop: • real-world knowledge about topics of interest and relevance to students including knowledge about everyday situations in the home and community • knowledge about topics being studied in all learning areas • conceptual knowledge about the world, e.g. concepts of size, shape, position, height, direction, orientation and time • vocabulary knowledge: – world meanings – common expressions – subject-specific vocabulary – figurative language	Students need experiences which will enable them to investigate: • grammar at the text level: – connecting words and phrases – content word chains throughout a text – how events are linked in a text by connectives such as *because*, *so*, *and* • grammar at the sentence level: – types of words in sentences, e.g. nouns, verbs, adjectives – sentence structure – clause structure in sentences – subject-verb agreement – correct tense – plurals – word order in phrases and noun and verb groups – word order in sentences – pronoun reference within sentences – connectives within sentences	Students need experiences which will enable them to develop: • phonological/ phonemic awareness: – hearing the sounds in words (rhyming, alliteration) – separating the sounds in words (isolation, onset/rime, segmentation) – manipulating the sounds in words (exchanging blending)	Students need experiences which will enable them to develop: • knowledge of book conventions: – page and book layout – front and back cover • concepts about print: – spaces between words – directionality (left to right and top to bottom) • sight vocabulary: – high frequency words – irregular words • letter knowledge: – individual letters – upper and lower case letters – letter clusters (syllables, prefixes/ suffixes) • punctuation: – capital letters – full stops – question marks – exclamation marks – commas – inverted commas – apostrophes – colons; semi-colons

The phonological–graphological cue system as a source of information can be represented in various ways. A useful table, 'Knowledge about the sources of information' is contained in the NSW Department of Education and Training document *Teaching Reading: A K–6 Framework* (1997) (table 3.2.) It also contains examples of semantic and grammatical sources of information discussed above.

Readers need to use the graphophonic cue system in conjunction with semantic and grammatical cues to ensure that they are reading the text accurately.

Thinking about meaning is always useful when trying to decode written text. Consider the following example.

> **Graphophonic knowledge helps the reader recognise whole words and work out how to pronounce new words. It works with semantic and graphophonic systems to construct meaning**

We need to raed olny the frsit and lsat lteetrs of a wrod to wrok it out wehn we use our smenaitc and grmmtaacial knolgedwe ecftfeevily.

TRADITIONAL APPROACHES TO WORD RECOGNITION

Traditional approaches to word recognition considered three categories of subskills: phonics, structural analysis, and sight words. Phonics was restricted to letter–sound correspondences; structural analysis included the rules of syllabification (the methods of dividing words into parts, roughly corresponding to the syllables of speech, having at least one vowel sound in every syllable) and the use of roots and affixes (prefixes and suffixes) in words (*un*-able; harm-*less*). A basic sight vocabulary was usually built up from words that were difficult to decode using phonic methods such as *there*, *their* and *through*). These subskills, although important, were often taught in isolation and were insufficiently linked with meaningful context.

Some common rules used for syllabification:

1   All syllables contain a vowel sound: book shelf.
2   When a second vowel appears in a word, the final e does not add another sound: gale
3   When two consonants exist between two vowels, the break comes between the consonants: wor king, but ter.
4   When a consonant exists between two vowels, the break occurs between the first vowel and the consonant: o pen.
5   When a word ends in le and is preceded by a consonant, the consonant and le make up a new syllable: bu gle and han dle.

Visual/pictorial information

Most texts in the 21st century use at least some visual elements, in addition to print, to help construct their meaning. This applies to print-based as well as electronic texts.

Visual elements in a text can

- *repeat the information that is in the print* in a different way by using some type of visual portrayal of what the print says, e.g. a graph showing the rainfall over several years in a particular place
- *add to what the print says* by giving more information or providing detail that is not in the print, e.g. a drawing of the main character in a novel
- *provide essentially different information* by depicting something not said in the print, e.g. an illustration of the relative sizes of planets in the solar system.

Note how the illustrations in Pat Hutchins' *Rosie's Walk* are integral to the meaning of the book. Without them the book has no real meaning. The illustrations change the register of the text. (See part III, p. xx.)

Visual elements in a text can include

Visual information becomes increasingly important as a component of modern text

- **pictures,** e.g. photos, drawings, comic strips, and moving images such as film and animation
- **diagrams,** e.g. tables, graphs, cut-aways, flowcharts, maps and plans
- **icons,** e.g. tabs, buttons, menu bars, drop-down menus, and cursors
- **design features**, e.g. page and screen layout, font, bolding and italics, spacing and movement

Each of these types of visual information needs to be understood by the reader if they are to effectively read the text as a whole. And, as well, the reader needs to know how to combine the visual information with the print information in a text in order to construct meaning.

The multimodal texts of Informational Communication Technology, such as those on the Internet, rely heavily on visual images that go well beyond written-linguistic forms of communication and extend the meanings of the messages they contain.

In reading a book about the solar system a reader might see, on one page

- several sections of print text in different sizes and fonts
- a satellite image (photo) of Earth
- drawings of the planets Mercury, Venus and Earth (not to scale)
- a diagram showing the sections of Earth's atmosphere
- a diagram showing the sections of Earth's core.

Readers use knowledge of the visual elements to increase their understanding of the text as a whole. The multimodal text of the Internet relies heavily on visual images

Not only does each of these images need to be understood, but the information they contain needs to be related to the print text.

The satellite image of Earth comes with this caption:

A satellite image of Earth, which has been coloured using a computer. In blue, you can see the water, which supports life on earth. Areas of forest are shown in red. Areas of forest which have been cut down are shown in green.

So a reader needs to look at the image, then read the caption, then look at the image again in order to understand what is being shown. The reading process is one of accessing and combining all the elements on the page or screen and thinking about what they mean and how they relate to each other in order to construct one's own understanding of what is being presented. It's no wonder, then, that readers often construct different meanings from the same text.

Figure 3.4 shows how reading cue systems and reading practices interact in the construction of meaning.

Figure 3.4   A Model of the Reading Cue System

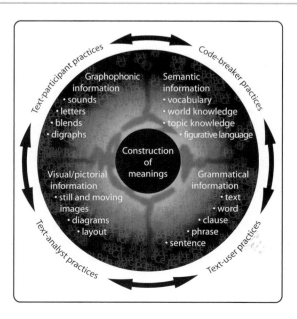

► LITERACY IN THE DIGITAL AGE

This chapter draws out and explains the elements that contribute to reading, and constructs a model to show how these elements interact with each other. Some reading models are based on the assumption, either explicit or implicit, that readers use only paper-based reading materials, but we know that readers today use both print and digital texts as part of participating in the modern world. It is important to consider how these reading experiences differ.

For example, there are significant differences between reading print on the page and reading print in a digital context. Paper-based print is static; it usually, but not always, goes from left to right across the page, and it cannot be changed in any way by the reader. Digital print, on the other hand, can move and change across the screen and can be altered in many ways by the reader at the touch of a key. Another important difference is how readers find information in paper-based and digital texts. Paper-based texts require the reader to use a table of contents or index to find the topic they want, and then scan the page of print to try to locate the required information or topic. Digital texts, however, can employ a search function which instantly locates the information on any topic through the use of key words and phrases. So, in a very real way, reading digital texts enables readers to be more in control of the reading process; that is, to be part of the construction of meaning from a text in a very dynamic way.

The basic strategies of reading

Good readers have good strategies that allow them to read effectively. A major difference between good and poor readers—and, in some ways, beginning readers—is that good readers have efficient strategies and poor readers do not. Many of these strategies are subsumed within the roles of the reader discussed above. Good readers use effective strategies as they take on the various roles.

Strategies provide an overall plan to gain meaning from text. Often termed metacognition, these strategies include skimming and scanning the text, sampling, predicting, confirming, understanding, and correcting errors in meaning as they occur. They also include re-reading parts of a text, changing reading speed, and questioning oneself during reading.

Strategies develop with age and experience, are important for effective reading, and must be

Good readers have good strategies

taught. Mastering these metacognitive strategies makes one an 'executive reader'. A useful diagram that illustrates the basic operation of this metacognitive technique in reading is shown in figure 3.5.

The first strategy is to sample the text. To do this the reader skims and scans the written text to obtain a quick overview of what it might contain, such as page layout, headings, paragraph lengths, or main ideas. Then significant aspects of the writing are selected that will lead the reader to obtain meaning.

Next, the reader uses the various sources of information, cue systems, to predict what the meaning will be, making use of semantic, grammatical, graphophonic, and visual information.

Finally, the reader confirms the meaning that has been gained and proceeds. If meaning has been lost the reader corrects, by searching the text for more information. This is done by going back along the line or up the page to find where the error occurred, or by looking at visual components that might provide further information. In correcting, the reader searches for more information and often compares one source of information with another. These strategies are just as important when reading printed and visual/pictorial parts of a text.

These global strategies illustrate that reading is very much a thinking process. Adept readers are good and flexible thinkers and they use an array of available information to arrive at meaning. Further strategies are outlined in chapter 8.

Figure 3.5   The basic strategies of reading

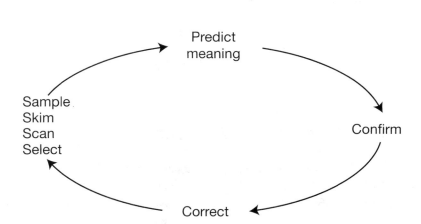

Viewing the reading model

Reading, then, is essentially an interactive cognitive task, a kind of literate thinking, in which the reader constructs meaning within a social and situational context. In essence, good readers have the correct bases to read well. These include perceptual ability (the ability to perceive accurately what is written in the text); language ability (the ability to communicate in the language of the text), and cognitive ability (the ability to think effectively).

We can develop a reading model

Good readers must make effective use of the cue systems, which rely on semantic, grammatical, graphological, and phonological and visual information. And they must use reading strategies effectively. These include the ability to sample, skim, scan, select, predict, confirm, and correct. In this way they read for meaning, as shown in figure 3.6.

In practice, all the facets represented in the model operate simultaneously and in a coordinated way.

Figure 3.6   Model of reading

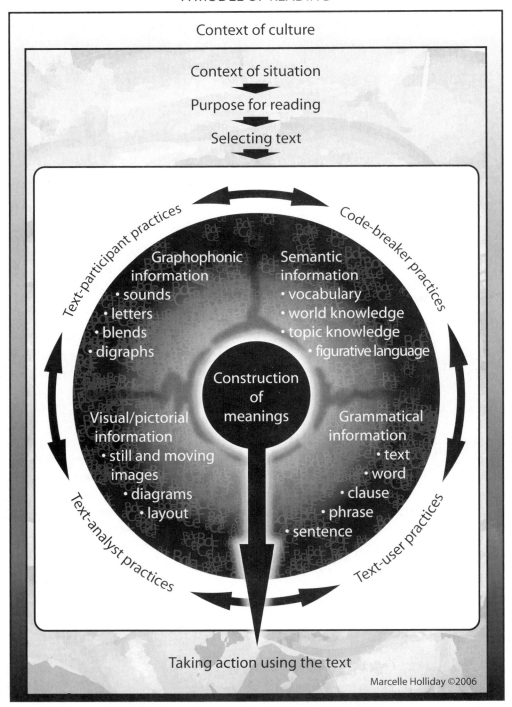

A MODEL OF READING

Context of culture

Context of situation

Purpose for reading

Selecting text

Text-participant practices

Code-breaker practices

Graphophonic information
• sounds
• letters
• blends
• digraphs

Semantic information
• vocabulary
• world knowledge
• topic knowledge
• figurative language

Construction of meanings

Visual/pictorial information
• still and moving images
• diagrams
• layout

Grammatical information
• text
• word
• clause
• phrase
• sentence

Text-analyst practices

Text-user practices

Taking action using the text

Marcelle Holliday ©2006

> ▶ **Summary**

1 The context of reading differs depending on the social purpose or cultural background of the writer and the reader.

2 Reading requires the use of cue systems: semantic, grammatical, phonological–graphological, and visual/pictorial.

3 Readers develop effective reading practices (code-breaker, text-participant, text-user and text-analyst) in order to access, understand, use and evaluate texts.

4 Good metacognitive strategies promote effective reading and produce 'executive readers'.

5 Reading in the digital age presents a new dimension to literacy.

6 A model can be developed to describe the reading process.

Critical thinking and study questions

1 Figure 3.6 attempts to show how reading operates in terms of necessary bases, the cue systems, and strategies available, and the various roles readers take in certain situations. Consider:

a how a reader might use semantic, grammatical, phonological–graphological, and visual cues in the code-breaker role while reading the following:

> *HOT*
> *It is hot.*
> *Sam is hot.*
> *Dad is hot.*
> *Mum is hot.*
> *The cat is hot.*
> *Sal is not.*

b how a reader who was an environmentalist would use semantic cues in the text-analyst role if he were reading a piece about logging native forests.

2 Read aloud the passage below.

> *The boys' arrows were nearly gone so they sat down on the grass and stopped hunting. Over at the edge of the wood they saw Henry making a bow to a small girl who was coming down the road. She had tears in her dress and tears in her eyes. She gave Henry a note which he brought over to the group of young hunters. Read to the boys, it caused great excitement. After a minute but rapid examination of their weapons they ran down to the valley. Does were standing at the edge of the lake making an excellent target.*

a Did you make any errors? Why do you think this was?

b Which source of information did you use to check that your reading made sense?

c Which source/s of information did you use to work out the following words: *bow, tears, read, minute, does*?

d Which source/s of information did you use to correct any errors you made?

e What does reading this passage tell you about how effective readers decode text?

3 What grammatical knowledge would you need to apply in order to work out the words that complete the following passage? (This is a cloze passage—see chapter 8.)

> *Thunderclouds*
>
> *Thunderclouds _____ made up _____ three things: air, water, and ice crystals.*
>
> *Inside a _____ there _____ violent movements of air currents.*

4   Select a children's book. Write down examples of questions you might ask a student to help her take on each of the four roles of the reader.

5   Discuss how any aspects of the model of reading described in this chapter could help you if you were teaching a child to read.

6   More than half of the visual information has been removed from this sentence. See if you can read it. In what way is this an example of redundancy in English orthography?

Reading is important to every child

7   Practise increasing your own reading speed by thinking more effectively. Try reading the opening sentence only of each paragraph of a page of print. This will make you take bigger *jumps* as you read. It is a good skimming technique. See if you can get the gist of the passage by reading this way.

8   The 31 173 verses of the Bible have been translated into SMS. Ecclesiastes 9, 10 now reads like this: *Wrk hard at wateva u do. U will soon go 2 da wrld of da dead, where no 1 wrks or thinks or reasons or knws NEting.* Consider how this type of text would affect a reader in his or her use of the main cue systems.Then consider what effect a widespread use of SMS might have on writing and standard spelling.

Further reading

Anstey, M. & G. Bull (eds) 2003, *The Literacy Labyrinth*, 2nd edn, Pearson Prentice Hall, Sydney.

Singer, H. & R. Ruddell (eds) 1985, *Theoretical Models and Processes of Reading*, 3rd edn, IRA, Newark, Del.

Unsworth, L. (ed.) 1993, *Literacy Learning and Teaching: Language as social practice in the primary school*, Macmillan, Melbourne.

Web links

Department of Education and Training (NSW): www.nsw.det.gov.au

Department of Education and Training (Vic.): www.det.vic.gov.au

Department of Education, Training and Employment (SA): www.dete.sa.gov.au

Commonwealth Department of Education, Science and Training: www.myread.org

THE CHILD BEFORE SCHOOL: THE BEGINNING OF LITERACY

4

Overview

Although children develop at different rates and in different ways, a broad description of the development of reading skills is helpful in providing quality teaching. The first stage can be described as the beginnings of literacy and extends from the time the child is born to his or her arrival at school. Speech development is rapid at this time and is important to later reading and writing achievement. Books, read to and shared with young children, provide the richest literacy experience and are vital to future success, while the plurality of texts children encounter in the modern world produce a new and expanded semiotic (meaning) system. The role of the parent in speaking and listening to children, in storytelling and in providing access to books, cannot be overestimated.

Reading development

Teachers strive to provide students with learning experiences that will result in their continued development as effective readers. But what does that development look like? What are its features? What can we expect to see as children develop the skills, knowledge and strategies of effective reading?

Chapters 4, 5, 6 and 7 look at reading development as it may occur from the years before school through to the end of primary school. An overview of typical reading development is provided here, followed by detailed chapters on the learning and teaching of reading at four points in the development continuum: before school, the early school years, and the middle and the later primary school years.

An overview of reading development and detailed teaching procedures can be described in three stages

Children's reading development shows a distinct pattern

Children develop as readers in different ways and at different rates and not all children will know or be able to do the same things at the same age. Nevertheless, it is possible to construct a broad description of the kinds of knowledge and skills children acquire as they develop towards proficiency in reading. Acquiring such knowledge and skills is, of course, dependent on the provision of quality learning experiences, both at home and at school, to build on what the child already knows and can do.

As children develop as readers they learn knowledge about texts and how they function in society, about meanings, about language, and about how the sounds of language relate to the letters and words on the page. They also learn skills in operating with texts in a range of reader roles that allow them to construct and interpret meaning from texts.

Tables 4.1 and 4.2 illustrate what development in reading might look like across the various elements of knowledge and skill that comprise the learning of reading. That is, for each of the

Tables 4.1 and 4.2 illustrate reading development in stages

developmental points selected, the tables provide a description of what a reader might typically know and be able to do. The tables are not meant to be used to measure the reading performance of individual readers, nor are they a set of outcomes or benchmarks upon which to plan teaching programs. (State and territory syllabus documents provide clear statements of outcomes and learning experiences and teachers should use these when planning reading programs for their students.) Rather, they are designed to show that reading skills and knowledge need to be developed concurrently, across the range of elements of knowledge and skill that make up effective reading. Focusing teaching on only one element, or on a narrow range of elements, will hinder reading development.

Reading the tables horizontally will show what a student at a particular stage of development might know and be able to do across all significant reading elements. Reading the table vertically will help to illustrate how a particular reading element might develop over time.

Learning to read

Children begin moving along the road to literacy before they come to school. They begin the journey on the day they are born, from the first time they hear a human voice. Talk leads them into making a range of meanings with spoken language and it leads them into written words and into books.

As Meek (1988) points out, 'Most children come to school with a crop of reading-like behaviours and an awareness of what they expect reading to be like'. They have come into contact

Children come to school with many early literacy experiences

with multiple literacy experiences: road signs, advertisements on television, writing on food packages, and all the mysterious letters, journals, newspapers, and books that adults read as well as those electronic images that appear on computer screens. They have already discovered writing and have made, in most cases, their early attempts at it. If they have entered the world of literacy through adults who are interested in their development, they are a further step along the way.

MULTILITERACIES

The preschool child is in one way as involved in multiliteracies and multimodal texts as older children. He responds to visual images, sound, and movement to make meaning from the texts encountered in speech, environmental print, books, and the television and computer screens. Because the preschooler cannot read words in the full sense, she relies more heavily on the other modes to produce an understanding of text: the illustrations in a book, the voice that reads the story, the images on the screen. Multiliteracy is very much part of these children's 'literate' world, although it is only later that children come to real reading through a synthesis, when words, pictures, and other modes come together.

A good example of the involvement of a preschooler or early reader with a multiliteracy experience is found in sharing a picturebook. In Anthony Browne's *Gorilla* (2003), the author sets the scene for multimodal experience in the opening paragraph: 'Hanna loved Gorillas. She read books about gorillas, she watched gorillas on the television, and drew pictures of gorillas. But she had never seen a real gorilla.' This beautifully balanced polysemic text then proceeds through the carefully wrought integration of words and pictures to explore the many themes of the story. The richness and the density of the meaning becomes more and more evident as the story is read … and re-read. The intricacies of the visual meaning can be explored through the 'visual grammar' of the text. See Unsworth et al. (2005: 9–10).

▶ LITERACY IN THE DIGITAL AGE: COMPUTER EXPERIENCE

Plan and carry out a computer session with a preschool child. Include basic things such as booting up the computer, using the mouse, becoming familiar with the keyboard and following the prompts on interactive software. Allow the child to work on the computer by herself.

Obtain some interactive software and share it with a child. Then allow her to operate the computer alone. There are many products on the market and they are, usually, reader-friendly.

Very young children are surrounded by multisensory digital stimuli at home, at the shopping centre, at preschool, and in the wider community. In fact many of their experiences before coming to school will involve digital texts. This means that children starting school now and in future years will not know what it means to live in a world without digital texts. They will not need to be introduced to concepts such as screen, button bar, mouse, interactivity, and search functions. It is important to recognise that what, for teachers, is a new way of communicating, for their students is just 'how the world works'.

To help them, young children have oral language, and when they come to school they are surprisingly sophisticated speaker-listeners: they can satisfy their own communication needs through their speech; they can use a wide variety of syntactic rules with increasing accuracy; they can understand and produce most of the important sound distinctions; and they can effectively handle the grammar of their language without explicit knowledge of how it works. This impressive array of

Oral language is essential for the acquisition of literacy

Table 4.1   Reading development: what the reader knows

	KNOWS ABOUT TEXTS IN THE WORLD (CONTEXTUAL KNOWLEDGE)	KNOWS ABOUT THE TOPIC (SEMANTIC KNOWLEDGE)	KNOWS ABOUT LANGUAGE (GRAMMATICAL KNOWLEDGE)	KNOWS ABOUT SOUNDS AND LETTERS (PHONOLOGICAL– GRAPHOLOGICAL KNOWLEDGE)
BEFORE SCHOOL	Knows that texts convey meaning. Understands the purposes of some simple texts, e.g. advertisements.	Knows about familiar topics, e.g. home, family, own community, own environment, games, food, pets, familiar animals, clothes. Knows the words for many familiar things and actions.	Talks to familiar people. Uses whole sentences. Answers questions appropriately. Uses words in right order. Retells simple events and stories. Can tell if a word is missing in speech or story read aloud. Begins to write a sentence. Understands 'story' language.	Knows words that rhyme. Recognises and interprets print, e.g. M sign. Says syllables in words, e.g. *car-pet*. May know that letters represent sounds. Can recognise own name in print. Can hear separate sounds in spoken words, e.g. *c-a-t*.
FIRST YEAR OF SCHOOL	Knows there are different kinds of texts, e.g. stories, newspapers. Can tell the difference between texts that tell stories and texts that give information.	Knows about less familiar topics, e.g. other families, other communities, animals in the world, some simple scientific topics. Knows the words for less familiar things and actions. Uses describing words, e.g. size, colour, shape.	Begins to understand about things (nouns), actions (verbs) and describing words. Talks in longer sentences. Retells more extended events or stories. Writes in sentences. Can tell if words are out of order in speech and text. Matches verb and subject.	Knows all letters and the sounds they make. Works out new words using letter–sound match. Knows some simple words by sight, e.g. *can, saw*.
THE EARLY SCHOOL YEARS	Understands that texts are written *by* people and represent real and imaginary experiences. Talks about some texts in the real world and knows how they are different.	Knows about a range of topics. e.g. other countries, other environments and cultures, endangered animals, scientific topics. Knows the words for a range of specific things, e.g. scientific words, sporting terms. Uses more specific describing words.	Can talk and write in extended sentences. Understands different types of language in texts, e.g. story, TV program, recipe, information book.	Knows most letter–sound matches. Knows a significant number of words by sight, e.g. *caught, were*. Regularly uses letter–sound matches to work out new words. Breaks long words into chunks, e.g. *in-ter-est-ing*.
MIDDLE PRIMARY YEARS	Understands the purposes of different literary and factual texts. Can talk about how text features help achieve the text's purpose, e.g. list of ingredients in a recipe helps the reader know what to get.	Knows about a wider range of topics being studied. Knows the vocabulary related to topics being studied in all learning areas.	Can understand more complex sentence and clause structures including causal connectives, e.g. because, therefore.	Knows and applies generalisations about letter–sound matches. Knows a wider range of sight words. Uses word identification strategies on texts at own reading level.
UPPER PRIMARY YEARS	Understands the effects context and purpose have on the construction of written text, e.g. a narrative for a young child differs from instructions on how to run a computer program.	Has a range of topic knowledge developed through reading and study. Understands subject-specific terminology and figurative use of language.	Understands grammatical features at clause, sentence, and text level.	Knows a range of effective word identification strategies and uses them automatically and effectively in all learning areas. Adds to sight vocabulary through own reading.

Table 4.2   Reading development: what the reader can do

The reader can:
- *decode the text (code-breaker)*
- *work out what the text means (text-participant)*
- *use the text in some way (text-user)*
- *think about who wrote the text and why (text-analyst).*

Begins to act like a reader, holds the book, turns pages, 'reads' the story from memory. Talks about the story, the characters, the events. Enjoys favourite books over and over. Knows if something is left out in the reading. May know that the print on the page is what we read rather than the pictures. Uses print in the environment, e.g. can recognise favourite breakfast cereal from the package, notices street and traffic signs or other print and knows that they are there to inform people. Knows what family members like to read, e.g. Dad reads the newspaper to find out what is happening. Wants to write, e.g. letters and greeting cards, and produces some letters or letter-like marks and tries to write own name. May be able to say the alphabet.

Uses what they know about a text to try to work out what it says (i.e. topic, language, sounds, and letters). Predicts what might happen in a story. When meeting a new word tries to work it out. Sometimes recognises when they have made a mistake and may try to correct it. Gains meaning from simple texts they can read and from more complex text read aloud to them. Thinks about the characters and events and may make speculations, e.g. I wonder what Goldilocks will do now? Empathises with characters, e.g. I wouldn't like to be Little Red Riding Hood. Learns some factual information from texts, e.g. about dinosaurs, endangered animals. With help uses simple texts in own life, e.g. uses a recipe to make chocolate crackles. Knows many products from their packaging. Knows what text to use for several purposes, e.g. a TV program to find out what's on TV. Begins to understand that texts are produced for a purpose, e.g. This book is for children, that one is for adults; the people who made that ad want us to buy that toy. May begin to understand that not all texts tell the truth.

Efficiently reads simple texts and those of growing complexity. Can work out many new words using their knowledge and skills, e.g. Asks 'What would make sense here? What would fit the sentence? What letters do I know?' Knows when they have made a mistake and works to correct it by, for example, re-reading the sentence, reading ahead, sounding out, looking for what they recognise in the word, trying different options. Understands what is happening in the text and thinks about meanings that are hinted at. Can predict what might happen in a story. Learns factual information from texts and knows how to use texts to find information, e.g. what koalas eat, where platypuses live. Often uses reading purposefully in own life, e.g. choosing a video by reading the cover, asking for something they see at the supermarket. Begins to think about the author of the text and their purpose. Knows that the purpose of advertising is to get us to buy something. Knows that not everything in an ad is always factually true. Can have a different opinion from the one in a text, e.g. does not like the breakfast cereal that 'all kids love'.

Efficiently reads more complex texts in all learning areas. Uses code-breaking strategies to work out what the text says, e.g. monitors own reading to maintain meaning, samples text, tries different options, and checks one source of information against another when meaning is temporarily lost. Constructs literal and inferential meaning from texts at own level and relates meanings in texts to own growing knowledge and experience. Begins to use graphics such as diagrams and maps in text to construct meaning. Uses a range of texts at own level in all learning areas to gain information, compares information from different sources and compares texts on the same topic from different viewpoints. Can talk about what an author might think or feel about a topic based on information in a text and discuss their own agreement or disagreement with a text's viewpoint. e.g. *Where the Forest Meets the Sea* recognises that the author doesn't want a hotel development built on the island.

Competently and confidently uses a range of code-breaking strategies depending on the text and the purpose for reading. Has developed a large bank of sight words. Constructs meaning from literary and factual texts in all learning areas including those containing maps, diagrams, tables. Confidently selects texts to use for a range of real-world and school purposes and uses texts to add to their knowledge and refine their understandings in all learning areas. Can share and justify their personal response to a text. Is developing abilities as a text-analyst and can identify opinion, bias, and point of view in a text. Can explain why people might interpret a text differently and can talk about how the language choices in a text contribute to the way the text's point of view is constructed. e.g. Understand how the selective use of positive or negative opinion adjectives presents a person in a favourable or unfavourale light.

language abilities is all the more significant if we bear in mind that it has been achieved without formal teaching. The way has been paved for acquiring literacy at school under the guidance of teachers who introduce explicit instruction in reading and writing.

Young children rely heavily on speech for communication. They share their experiences through talk with those around them. As well, parents, grandparents, and other carers introduce children to rhymes that are tiny stories in themselves, to language games, to songs, folk stories, and fables, and to books that have been written for children the world over. Indeed, young children live in a world of print and image, not only in the books that are read to them but in every social situation in which they find themselves: at home in the bedroom, living room, and kitchen; on the train; in the car; at the supermarket; watching television; looking at a computer screen; going to the beach; at the preschool or day care centre; at a party—'public print', as Meek (1982: 41) calls it, is part of the child's world of print 'and sooner or later he will notice it'. For young children these early experiences are important foundations on which the school can build. Print in the environment gives young children an awareness of how literacy is used in their community. This awareness is one of the most important things children can bring to school.

It is from books, nevertheless, that children gain the richest and most rewarding literacy experience. Books provide 'the essential link between learning to talk and learning to read,

Books provide the vital link between learning to talk and learning to read

because they are a special kind of play with language that separates it from speech. The simplest answer to the question "How does a child come to know how print works?" is by being read a story' (Meek 1982: 38–9). As has been repeatedly pointed out, a valuable preparation for school learning is a love of books.

Much-quoted studies by Durkin (1966) and Clark (1976) illustrate through research the importance of early exposure to books in the literacy development of the child. Clark, working with an experimental group of young fluent readers—children who came to school able to read—found that her subjects had certain factors in common: one was the early involvement of the parents and other interested adults in the child's progress. She did not find that the children's parents were all of a socially privileged group; on the contrary, some had left school early and had had no further training. What they had in common was time to talk with their children, listen to them, read to them, and encourage an interest in books.

The other factor was the important role played by the local library in catering for and

The library has a significant role in developing literacy

stimulating the interests of the children. Accessibility of different types of reading material was common to the group. These parents did not set out to teach their children to read. Their role was sensitising the children to the features of book language, such as conventional openings to stories ('Once upon a time'). This, Clark concludes, is probably a more valuable preparation

for school than attempting to teach the child phonics or a basic sight vocabulary.

Not all children come to school with a rich book experience behind them. It is the task of the teacher to build on the child's other early literacy experiences and to supply a rich diet of books in classroom and library.

The central role of literature is well documented in current publications (Beard 1998), the International Reading Association position statement (1998), and in ongoing curriculum

Literature is the key to literacy achievement

development in Australia. The importance of literature in the achievement of literacy is seen by the authors of this book as so important that it warrants a special part of the text (see part III).

All those who deal with small children before school must capitalise on knowledge of the language development of children. We need to be aware that the period from birth to five years is the fastest language-learning time in a child's life. Vocabulary growth alone illustrates this: as a rough rule of thumb, a 2-year-old controls about 200 words, a 3-year-old about 1000, and a 4-year-old about 2000. An average adult's vocabulary is between 4000 and 5000 words. 'With language growth goes intellectual growth because the two are intertwined: the more sophisticated the language, the more sophisticated the thinking' (Winch & Poston-Anderson 1993: 5).

Figure 4.1 Stages of speech and language development

(Winch & Poston-Anderson 1993)

The vital role of the parent must be realised as home and school develop a partnership in the child's literacy development. Parents or other carers as listener, speaker, prompter, supplier of information, asker and answerer of questions, co-reader, and co-writer are all important before and during schooling.

The important transition from preschool literacy to school itself must be transparently clear to parent and teacher alike. Children, through their early association with books and other forms of print, have become involved in what they see before them. This interaction with texts provides the untaught lessons that children have before school that help them to find out 'how the book works, how the story goes' (Meek 1988: 7).

The early literacy experience

As discussed above, the earliest literacy experiences that children bring to school are associated with their encounters with public print and quest for meaning from books. They react to street signs, advertisements on television, labels in supermarkets, and other forms of writing they see all around them.

They also carry out a quest for meaning from books that are read to them. They know that books carry stories within them; they have heard the stories read and they have investigated them in their private interactions with books and the reading-like behaviour they exhibit when they retell or 'read' the story in bed at night, in a quiet corner during the day, or out loud to an interested adult who has time to listen. Rhymes and language play are also important; they add enjoyment and help to develop children's linguistic growth. Children's own rhymes in play make the value of this form of language growth apparent.

These early literate experiences include an interpretation of the mysterious lines of print and the pictures that either reinforce the story or add another dimension to it. These lines of print are not there to be deciphered in a linguistic sense. Children, by and large, are not engaged in the business of phonic decoding to sound before they come to school. It is wrong to expect them to do so for two reasons. The first is that while they can indeed use the phonemes that carry meaning in their oral language as they speak or listen, they find it difficult to do so consciously. That is, they are not yet phonemically aware; they are unable to segment the phonemes in speech. An effective way to develop phonemic awareness in young children is to involve them in language games such as *I Spy*. In this example ('I spy with my little eye something beginning with *c*') it is better to make the onset sound rather than say the letter. Many interactive computer software packages capitalise on this principle.

Early literacy experience is about a quest for meaning through the delight of having stories read and told, not about decoding print

The second reason is that children have only primitive concepts about print. Very young children will probably not know that it is print that carries much of the meaning in the picture book they have before them, that to read print one moves from left to right with a return sweep at the end of a line, that words are entities within themselves, and that letters represent sounds in an alphabetic system of writing. To ask very young children to decode print is to ask something essentially beyond them. It is infinitely better to engage children in the delight of having stories read and told and to capitalise on the early literacy experiences that are pleasurable and rewarding to them.

It is interesting to note that Finnish children, who performed better than Australian readers on the PISA study quoted above in the Introduction, do not experience any formal teaching of literacy skills at preschool and are not expected to learn to read in that year. They are read to, exposed to texts such as fairytales, poems, and riddles and are encouraged to make up rhymes and discuss the content of stories. It is of further interest to note that preschool in Finland starts at the child's sixth birthday and at age seven children are taught to read. It should be noted also that Finnish is a much more transparent language than English (there is a very close relationship between sound and symbol).

It is interesting to note that 'real' books, which carry stories through words and pictures, build up a knowledge, implicit though it might be, of the nature and variety of written discourse and the different ways that language lets a writer tell, and the many and different ways a reader reads (Meek 1988: 21).

'Real' books are the most important resource for developing literacy

It is often sadly the case that when children come to school and they encounter stilted linguistic reading texts, they find the business of reading both difficult and uninviting. Consider the following text as an example of such dull and lifeless prose:

Sam. Pam.

Hello, I'm Sam. Hello, I'm Pam.

Hello, I'm Sam. I am six. Hello, I'm Pam. I am six, too.

In such an example 'the language reads like no language the child has heard spoken and bears little affinity to the richly rewarding stories which have come from libraries and other sources of literacy material' (Winch 1988: 6). As Halliday points out:

> Some of the failure in reading and writing of which we are all so conscious nowadays has been due at least in part to children failing to make the conceptual leap which relates writing to speech, never co-ordinating the new behaviour with an ability they already possess, the ability to speak and listen. The new experience never clicks into place alongside the old. (1979: 42)

The point is made again by Ferriero & Teberosky (1982), who argue that the text of contrived reading books may look like real sentences but they take away the learnt predictive approaches used by children because the words do not correspond to any real language they know. Children attempting to read with this material must forget all they know about home language, as if written language and the activity of reading had no relationship to real language functioning.

Real books require very young children to bring meaning and language to the pages, to draw on their past experience of stories, rhymes, characters, and, of course, words. These books allow children to build up the types of early reading experiences they need in their encounters with books and other reading material at school.

It should be noted that not every child has had a rich exposure to books written in English before coming to school. These children will have had experiences in other languages and exposure to print in different forms. It is important that positive action be taken by schools to use the different linguistic backgrounds of children and that they be cognisant of the different cultural contexts of the home. In this way a partnership in the children's literacy development can be established between home and school (Cairney 1997).

The role of the parent in early literacy

It is never too soon or too late to begin reading to your child

The parents' role in literacy development is extremely important, as pointed out above. It is wise to start sharing stories with young children at a very early age. Babies recognise and respond

The parent is vital in preschool literacy development

to the sound of a parent's voice whether or not they understand the exact meaning of the words. When we consider that the child's language learning develops most rapidly during the first five years of life, a child is never too young to begin sharing stories.

Although books themselves are the main source of the stories young children meet, the oral tradition is very important, too. Many stories are passed on by word of mouth, so storytelling

Stories should be told as well as read to young children

provides another source. Stories should be read and told to the young child. There are significant differences in the two forms. Consider the beginning of the story of Little Red Riding Hood, first as it was read and then as it was told.

You will notice that when the story is read, the reader reads the words exactly as they are written. It is formal book language with little interruption and little dramatic action to support the text. Vocal expression is very prominent, however, and the child is encouraged to follow the pictures and the print as the story is read.

When the story is told without the book, the language is much less formal and the teller actively involves the child. There are frequent interruptions to allow for questions and replies; sound effects are added, and the speaker is free to dramatise the characters and the situation, using different voices, facial expressions, and body movements.

READ

Once upon a time there was a little girl and her name was Little Red Riding Hood. She lived with her Mother on the far side of the woods. (Reader points to the picture of Little Red Riding Hood in front of her cottage.)

One morning her mother said to her, 'Little Red Riding Hood, please take this basket of good things to eat to your Grandmother.'

'Yes, Mother, I will,' Little Red Riding Hood replied. (change of voice)

Immediately she put on her red cape and started through the woods. The day was bright and she skipped happily down the path … through the woods.

TOLD

Once there was a little girl who was very much like you, except that she had a red cape. Do you know what her name was? (child responds)

Yes, that's right—Little Red Riding Hood.

One day her mother said to her, just like this,

'Yes, Mum, I will,' she said. (change of voice, nod of head)

What do you think was inside the basket? (child responds) Little Red Riding Hood started down the path The birds sang like this (twitter). The sun shone brightly and Little Red Riding Hood was so happy that she sang a little tune (hum).

(Winch & Poston-Anderson 1993: 11)

A modified approach that allows more interaction between the reader and the child can also be used. In this way the types of interruption that the straight reading of the text excludes may be introduced at different times to involve the child in the story:

> *'… please take this basket of good things to eat to your grandmother.'*
> What do you think might be in this basket?
> *'The day was bright and she skipped happily down the path …'*
> What sounds might Little Red Riding Hood have heard?

Interactive reading of this type, which can include discussion about the illustrations as well as the story, increases readers' understanding of the book and lets them take on the reader role of text-participant as they participate in constructing meaning from the text.

The child's early development in writing is closely intertwined with development in reading; the two are never really apart. Early motor skills come into play as the child puts pencil to paper in response to stories, heard and told. (See part II.)

The best books

The way to provide the best experience for a child is to find the best stories and the best books. If you are looking for books to read, select those with appealing illustrations. Young children like clear, uncluttered illustrations like those found in the books of Dick Bruna, John Burningham, and Pamela Allen, but they like other forms of illustration too. Find out which books appeal to the child.

Books should have intrinsic quality, but they must also appeal to the child.

Here are some further things to consider: Does the story read well? Is the language clear and well suited to a child of that age? Does the plot hold together and move at a lively pace? Are the characters interesting? Do they have special characteristics that make them memorable? Does the story stimulate the imagination? And, probably most important of all, do you and the child want to read the book together? If you are reading a factual book, consider answers to these questions: Is the language clear and suitable to the child's linguistic level? Do the illustrations support the text? Is the book a good example of a particular factual genre?

Award-winning books and books chosen from Reading Challenge lists give guidance, but these are not always books that children find enjoyable. Another guide is the list of books chosen for an award by the children themselves. The Koala Award is an example. A book, whatever else its attributes, must 'bring light to a child's eye. That is, it must provide enjoyment and satisfaction to a young reader' (Winch 1991: 19).

There is another useful guideline: good books stand up well to re-reading. They are often requested by children, to be read again and again.

The best stories to tell

It is important to select appealing stories containing interesting characters, plot, humour, and plenty of action

These are usually the old favourites like The Three Bears, The Billy Goats Gruff, and The Little Red Hen. These stories seem to be just right for telling. This is not surprising, considering that they were more often than not passed down by word of mouth. This accounts for the fact that there are so many versions of each tale. A teller would give his or her special twist to the story, depending on the audience, the occasion, and the storyteller's mood.

Good stories for telling can be found in classic collections such as *The Fairy Tale Treasury* by Raymond Briggs, but there are many good collections full of suitable stories in bookstores and libraries. It is important to include stories that relate to a child's social and cultural background.

Children whose first language is not English will hear stories that come from the culture and language of the country concerned. Aboriginal and Torres Strait Islander children will hear Dreaming stories told in English or, often, in their native tongue.

When choosing stories, remember that a story must hold the child's attention through its plot, its characters, its action, its humour, and, of course, the teller's presentation. It must allow the child to participate through predictable words, phrases, and longer refrains.

IN THE HOME OR CLASSROOM

1   Sharing a book with a child.

- Select a well-known and popular children's picture book such as *Rosie's Walk* by Pat Hutchins or *Each Peach Pear Plum* or *Peepo* by Janet and Allan Ahlberg. Make sure you are familiar with the book. Read the story to yourself and look carefully at the illustrations, which form a vital part of the story. Rehearse the reading and vary your voice and facial expressions.

- Now, talk to the child about the book before you start reading: discuss the cover and its illustrations, the writing on it. What does the writing mean? What might this book be about?

- Next, put into practice what you have rehearsed. Read the book to the child at a suitable pace. Slow down to enjoy the pictures. Allow time for the child to comment on what is happening, on what it all means. Make sure that the reading is a happy experience for you both. If your listener wants to become a 'reader', allow the child to do so. This reading-like behaviour is valuable as it allows the child to deal with story meaning in a different way. Children often like to engage in this activity alone and should not be pressured to perform in front of you.

- Finally, record your responses to your experience. How did you gauge your performance? What did you do well? What could you have done better? What did you observe about the child's reactions?

2 Telling a story.

- Select a story to tell to a child. Practise the story and memorise its main sequences. It does not have to be perfect; just remember how the parts fit together. Practise using your voice: pause, volume, pitch, rate; your facial expressions; your gestures. Use props if they are appropriate. They can bring life to a story. These could include parts of costumes, musical instruments, pieces of furniture.

- Now, tell your story and record your responses to the experience. Ask yourself the same questions as above: How did you gauge your performance? and so on.

3 Literacy in everyday activities.

Plan an activity with a young child, such as shopping, cooking, or making a greeting card, with scissors and paste or on the computer. Consider what literacy learning you can insert into the experience. Provide the child with opportunities to tell and show you what she has learnt about literacy.

Early literacy in the community

Modern children meet print in their early years in a wide variety of ways, and parents and carers can take advantage of print exposure, 'public print', to prepare children for reading and writing at school. These experiences are invaluable if children are to develop necessary understandings about what literacy is and how it is used in the community in which they live.

Print in the environment, 'public print': an important early literacy experience

When shopping in the local street or in a big store, such as a supermarket, children can have their attention drawn to advertisements on shop signs and labels on items of food and clothing. The child will easily predict the meaning of a word or phrase and will begin to associate the letters of the word with the meaning. Simple questions about the beginning sound of a word, or simply what it says, are examples of very valuable uses that can be made of public print.

In the kitchen at home, young children can share in the experience of preparing food and have their attention drawn to the labels on cans and bottles. Recipes can be read aloud with the child looking on, and instructions on and relating to appliances can be read aloud.

The arrival of the mail can be another literacy experience. Children will enjoy working out who wrote a letter, to whom it is addressed, and what its contents say. Junk mail has its place too. Young children become skilful at working out the gimmicks that advertisers use. Birthday and other greeting cards fill young children with delight as these examples of print and picture have a personal dimension.

The television program and the television guide are important to young children, and parents can draw their attention to the information this material contains. Television watching takes up a significant part of the day for many young children. Parents should direct them to programs that are introductions to literacy in themselves, e.g. *Sesame Street* and *Playschool*.

Information and Communication Technology is having an increasing influence on people's lives, and young children are eager to have 'a turn on the computer' whenever they have the chance. Some computer games have literacy offshoots, and instructional software for children of all ages is appearing on the market. Because of the interactional features of the software programs, activities suited to early literacy are becoming more prevalent. Examples of possible exercises featuring onset sounds and rhyming words are shown in the following figures.

Information and Communication Technology is becoming rapidly more significant at all levels of literacy

Figure 4.2   Interactional software exercises

In figure 4.2(a) the child must move the cursor to the items and click the pictures that start with the sound made by C. This exercise depends on both phonemic awareness and the graphophonic skill of knowing that 'c' stands for the sound /k/ in the two relevant examples. In figure 4.2(b) the child must click the pictures that represent words rhyming with 'hat' in the box. The young child does not need to read the word to do the exercise correctly, although the caption is presented as an additional reference.

Technological change and the availability of computers at home and in school are both increasing rapidly.

▶ LITERACY IN THE DIGITAL AGE

The digital age is reaching deeply into the literacy-learning world of the preschool child. Visual literacy is being expanded through television, the CD-ROM, and the DVD. Sound in the form of electronic talking books and television is combining to create a new semiotic system for modern preschoolers. These children are using interactive modes of multimedia presentations (IMM) as illustrated in the above example, Fig. 4.2, and are responding to animation and music. Modern preschool children ('the clickerati kids') proceed without fear and engage comfortably in fast-speed interactive experiences which many adults find daunting. This new generation can operate mouse and keyboard, use paint-and-draw programs and navigate around their favourite websites. The potential for literacy learning is enormous. (See Turbill 2004.)

▶ Summary

1 Children develop as readers and acquire knowledge and skills related to language and text that help them become proficient readers. This development shows a distinct pattern.

2 Children have made significant steps towards literacy before they come to school.

3 Children bring with them to school their early encounters with public print, information and communication technology, and a quest for gaining meaning from books.

4 Of particular importance in before-school literacy development is a close involvement with a caring adult, oral language, and stories told and read to the child.

5 Also important is an awareness of print in the environment and the way literacy is used in the child's community.

6 For preschool children, a new and changed literacy scenario in the digital age is simply part of the normal world.

Critical thinking and study exercises

1 Consider the case made for the importance of a caring, listening adult and of stories read and told for the preschool child on the road to literacy.

2 What experiences with literacy in the community are important for young children?

3 How you would provide for a child with a disability (e.g. hearing or seeing). Read about Cushla, the multiply disabled granddaughter of Dorothy Butler, in *Cushla and Her Books* (1979).

4 Consider how the information in this chapter might influence the way reading is taught during the early years of school. In particular, give attention to the children's language knowledge and book experience.

5 Consider the choice of books for children from language backgrounds other than English. How would such a choice be made?

6 Carlos is three and about to go to bed. His father tells him that when he is ready—teeth cleaned, face washed, and suitable goodnights made to Gran and Mum—he will read him a story. Carlos says he would like to hear a story in bed and he would like to select his own book. He selects *Bertie and the Bear* by Pamela Allen. 'You've had this story before,' his dad said. Carlos insisted that he have it again. And he did.

Carlos watched as his father opened the book and began to read. He managed to get in 'There's Bertie' as his father paused at the title page. Carlos loved the noisy lines and repeated them, pointing to the repetitions in the speech bubbles or the lines in the text ('Shoo, shooo you monster YOU!'). He liked the noises of the trumpet, the gong, the drum, the horn and the flute, especially, and the yip, yip, yip … of the little dog. The big word IN-CRED-IBLE was a favourite. He kept saying it after his father had turned the page.

Carlos' father slowed the reading down when the bear 'stopped quite still, turned right around, and said, "All this for me? Thank you …" and bowed very low'.

When the bear stood on his head and turned a few cartwheels and danced, Carlos burst into roars of laughter. He pointed to the pictures again and again, laughing more and more. He liked the resolution of the plot and the happy ending.

'Time for sleep now,' said Carlos' father.

'Please can I read the book myself?' asked Carlos.

'Just for a while.'

Carlos 'read' the book by himself, making up the story as he went, while, surprisingly, repeating some whole lines accurately. He did this for some time until …

'Lights off now, Carlos. Good night!'

It is a good idea to have a copy of *Bertie and the Bear* available or read the above text before carrying out these activities.

Carlos chose Pamela Allen's *Bertie and the Bear*, the Children's Book Council Picture Book of the Year 1984. Is it a good thing to have a child share a quality book with an adult, rather than a lesser text that may be a favourite of the child? Winch (1991) argues that it is not if the quality book does not bring light to the child's eye!

Here are some questions:

a   What is the advantage of reading the same book to a child, again and again, if the child wishes you to do so? What might be some disadvantages?

b   If you are reading a book to a child consider the importance of mentioning matters such as the information on the cover, the name of the author, the dedication (For Jessie Mary Allen), and the imprint page.

c   Carlos joined in with the reading of the book, particularly the 'noisy' parts. What advantages are there in having a child do this?

d   Although Carlos is obviously carried away by the sheer vitality of the text (and the pictures), would it have been of value to have included some questions to develop his concepts about print? (Where do I start to read? What words say 'Shoo, shooo you monster, YOU!'? Where is that said again?) What other concepts about print and about books generally could be included? What ways could Carlos' phonemic awareness have been developed, using this book? (Think of the onomatopoeic words throughout the text such as BLAH! BLAH, TOOT-TOOT, YIP, YIP.)

e   The word 'incredible' is popular with Carlos. What would be some ways you might capitalise on his interest in this word? (Think of word meaning, the way the word is said, other uses of the word.)

f   What are some things Carlos' spontaneous laughter tells us about reading books to children? (Consider enjoyment of reading, development of sense of humour, involvement with the story.)

g   The pictures highlight the incongruity and delightful absurdity of the text. It also shows clearly where the crisis ends and the bear changes his attitude to Bertie. What features of the pictures illustrate the change in the bear? (Think of his expression, teeth, eyes, among other things.)

h   Reading and writing are 'social things to do in any community where written language is part of our social function as human beings' (Meek 1988: 4). What social functions did Carlos experience? (Think of the whole scene from the beginning to the end and how reading was part of it.)

I   Carlos wanted to read the book by himself. What 'private lessons' would he experience? What are some things he might learn about the way a story goes?

j   What does Carlos know about reading? What parts of the reading process can he already do? How do you know?

Further reading

Ashton, J. & T. H. Cairney, 2001, 'Understanding the discourses of partnership: An examination of one school's attempts at parent involvement', *Australian Journal of Language and Literacy* 24(2): 145–56.

Cairney, T. H. 2000, 'Beyond the classroom walls: The rediscovery of the family and community as partners in education', *Educational Review* 52(2): 163–74.

Cairney, T. H. 2000, 'The construction of literacy and literacy learners', *Language Arts* 77(6): 496–505.

Cairney, T. H. 2002, 'New Directions in family literacy: Building effective partnerships between home and school'. In B. Spodek & O. Saracho (eds) *Contemporary Perspectives on Early Childhood Education*, Greenwich, Conn.: Information Age Publishing, pp. 99–126.

Cairney, T. H. 2003, 'The home-school connection in literacy and language development'. In D. Green & R. Campbell (eds) *Literacies and Learners: Current perspectives*, Sydney: Prentice Hall, pp. 17–32.

Cairney, T. H. 2003, 'Literacy in family life'. In N. Hall, J. Larson & J. Marsh (eds) *Handbook of Early Childhood Literacy*, London: SAGE Publications, pp. 85–98.

Cairney, T. H. & J. Ashton 2002, 'Three families, multiple discourses: Examining differences in the literacy practices of home and school', *Linguistics and Education* 13(3): 303–45.

Cairney, T. H. & L. Munsie, 1992, *Beyond Tokenism: Parents as partners in literacy*, Heinemann, Portsmouth, N.H.

Department of Education and Children's Services 1997, *Early Literacy Practices and Possibilities*, Adelaide.

Education Department of Western Australia 1994, *First Steps*, Longman, Melbourne.

Hill, S. 1997, 'Perspectives on early literacy and home–school connections', *Australian Journal of Language and Literacy* 20(4): 263–79.

Louden, W., M. Rohl, C. Barratt-Pugh, C. Brown, T. H. Cairney, J. Elderfield, H. House, M. Meiers, J. Rivalland & K. Rowe, 2005, 'In teachers' hands: Effective literacy teaching practices in the early years of schooling', *Australian Journal of Language & Literacy*.

Morrow, L. 1993, *Literacy Development in the Early Years: Helping children read and write*, Allyn & Bacon, Needham Heights, Mass.

Unsworth, L. A. Thomas, A. Simpson & J. Asha 2005, *Children's Literature and Computer-based Teaching*, Open University Press, Maidenhead, UK.

Web links

Early Childhood Teachers Association (ECTA Inc.): www.ecta.org.au
Department of Education Tasmania: www.tased.edu.au
Education Department of Western Australia: www.eddept.wa.edu.au

5

LEARNING TO READ: THE EARLY SCHOOL YEARS

Overview

It is during the early years of schooling that most children learn to read. Effective teaching during this time is therefore of the utmost importance. A useful example of such practice can be presented in the form of Shared, Guided, and Independent Reading in the first three years of school. The influence of multiliteracies and the changed face of literacy in the digital age must be considered when children are learning to read. The explicit and systematic teaching of reading skills is addressed.

The emergent reader: An example with Shared Reading

It is important to note that, although an example with Shared Reading is illustrated with the emergent reader, Guided and Independent Reading are also included in the reading program at this level. Likewise, the three types of reading practice apply to the developing reader also. Each of the three facets is illustrated for a different year to save repetition. The chapter should be read as a whole.

Jenny is working with her class of emergent readers. They are in their first year of school. The students come from a variety of social and cultural backgrounds and have had a wide range of different experiences with books and with print in their communities. They all display the eagerness of young children starting school, particularly an eagerness to learn to read and write.

Jenny looks at the little group sitting on the mat before her. They are on the way to becoming literate, although some will need special help before the end of the year.

How will Jenny achieve this? What does she know that will direct her teaching? What practices will she adopt?

The background of theory

As a professional teacher of some years' standing, Jenny brings both knowledge and experience to her task. She knows first of all that there is no single approach that stands out as the one way to teach a child to read. Research has pointed this out. Jenny will base her teaching on what she knows about the theory of the reading process and the teaching of reading, backed up with experience. She is well aware of the importance of speaking/listening and writing, both in sitting beside reading and as a support for reading itself. (See chapters 11 and 17.) Her approach, whatever methods she uses, will allow her to tailor her teaching to the needs of individual children.

There is no one way to teach a child to read; speaking and writing are both part of the literacy spectrum

Using the reading model

Jenny is aware that both reading and writing operate in cultural and social contexts and is sensitive to the varying backgrounds of children in her class. The bases of reading—perceptual ability, language ability, cognitive ability—will vary also. Some children who have a visual or auditory disability may require special attention; those who speak a language other than English will require extra work to build up their oral skills in what is to them a second language. Others may have difficulties of other kinds and will need extra help. And some will be able to achieve at a higher level than the rest of the class. Jenny is aware that early readers use the same cue systems as mature readers, but most children will need to experience systematic teaching before they use these systems effectively. In particular, Jenny will make sure that she teaches an understanding of sound–symbol relationships in writing along with the exposure to a variety of meaningful texts. That is, she will teach children how to use the phonological–graphological cue system along with grammatical and semantic cues. Put another way, she will include systematic code-based instruction in phonics with context-based prediction, using sentence structure and knowledge of the subject that her young readers bring to print.

Reading and writing operate in social and cultural context. Each child has different literacy learning needs. Systematic teaching is vital for all

Early readers need to learn to become increasingly phonemically aware. They need to learn how the alphabetic system codes the language and how letters represent the sounds in words. In working with a range of carefully selected texts, Jenny will give systematic attention to the sounds of letters, the way they are written, and the relationship of the two. She will give attention to the immediate recognition of words in context, to the prediction of words and repeated sentence patterns, and to the overall meaning of texts.

A balanced approach to teaching reading meets different learning needs

There is also a great deal her students will need to learn about how books work: what part of the page we read, where we start, how print travels from left to right and top to bottom, how pages follow one another in sequence, and many other concepts about print and books in general.

In her balanced approach to teaching reading, Jenny will give a suitable weighting to all aspects of the reading model, varying her approach for each child as required.

Theory into practice: Shared Reading

One practical application of theory Jenny will use frequently in her class of emergent readers is Shared Reading (also called Modelled Reading). This will usually involve the whole class and will allow Jenny to give her students structured demonstrations of what skilled readers do when they read. In the following example, Jenny has chosen a Big Book, titled *Sal and Sam at the Farm*. It is part of the Go Book series, published by Blake Education. There is ample scope in this text for teaching about graphophonic, grammatical, semantic and visual cues, about the basic strategies of reading and the various roles of the reader.

Shared Reading is one important practice in teaching the emergent reader

The Shared Reading lesson

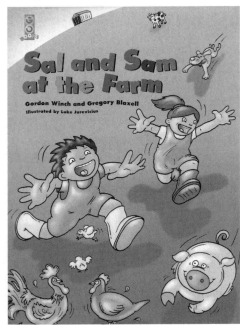

Shared reading is a whole-class experience

Before Reading

Before reading Jenny has prepared her students for a Shared Reading of the text by building up their semantic knowledge about the topic: life on a farm. She knows that children will find the text easier to read if they can form mental images to relate to words on the page and the illustrations. She has taken the class to visit a farm owned by a relative of one of the children—a very special excursion. The children, many of whom had not seen farm animals before, are now full of the experience. Some of the class have drawn pictures and 'written' about their visit. Jenny has also read them Pat Hutchins' picturebook *Rosie's Walk*, which proved a great favourite.

It is important to build up semantic knowledge about a topic before reading

The first reading of *Sal and Sam at the Farm* is mainly for overall meaning and enjoyment. Jenny begins with the whole text before looking at its parts. As she has decided to adopt the approach of 'masking' the print on this occasion—one of various introductory techniques she uses—she is ready to introduce the book. She wants to make sure that the students enjoy the first reading and respond to the book's meaning before dealing with its parts. She adopts the rule of thumb 'whole-part-whole', always coming back to the full text at the end of a reading. For instance, she has made up sight word cards of commonly used vocabulary found in the text and has noted words that are phonically regular for special treatment. Some words have been taken from the list of the most frequently used words conveniently provided by the authors on the inside back cover of the book. The words are sometimes placed in sentences written on the board to show their use in context. Words that are phonically regular are related to sound–symbol relationships that are being treated in systematic phonic instruction. Then the book is read again.

A 'whole-part-whole' method is a good rule of thumb

Introducing the book

Jenny sits her class on the big mat in front of her and holds the big book on an easel so all the children can see. She points to the front cover, with its bright, full-colour artwork, and asks the children what they think the book might be about. As the farm visit is fresh in their minds, the class is quick to point out that the book is obviously about a farm—just like the one they visited last week.

Discuss features of the book before it is read

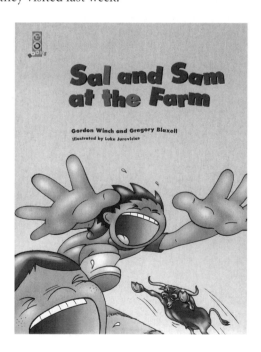

She then asks what the title of the book might be and where the title is on the page. Some children can read the title and there is talk about the children on the cover and their names. Jenny points to the names of the authors and the illustrator. There is discussion of their role in the creation of the book.

The children then turn their attention to the title page and the fierce bull chasing Sal and Sam. Will this book be about a visit like the class's visit or will there be something else? Some predictions are made about the story line. It might be an adventure story. It might contain something scary.

Reading the text

The class is led through the text with the print masked, then asked to predict the story from the illustrations. Who is that man on page 3? What are the children doing on page 4? Where are they going on page 8? What might Grandpa be telling them on page 9? What happens when the children wander off on page 11? What might be happening on page 16?

The masking paper is then removed from the text, page by page, and the story read to the children. Jenny takes special care to discuss the characters and the story line, allowing the children to predict what might be happening next and to confirm or revise the predictions they have made earlier. The last page (16) is particularly interesting because Sal and Sam have not obeyed Grandpa and their faces tell a story that goes beyond the text, allowing the children to infer what the two characters are thinking.

Reading the text should be an interesting and involving experience. It is important to link the illustrations with the words on the page

Reading strategies: some examples

Jenny demonstrates the prediction strategy of gaining significant reading cues from the illustrations in the book. She uses page 4 as an example and asks the children the question 'What did Sal and Sam do on Grandpa's farm?' while pointing to the pictures on the page, one at a time. The children are quick to respond with 'They fed the hens', 'They fed the ducks', and so on.

She is then able to move quickly to the text on the page and link the text to the picture in each case. The important idea about print, that the words themselves tell the story, is reinforced in the children's minds. The illustrations are there to assist prediction and the actual reading of the text.

The children are then directed to the words in bold type. What might these words say? Why are they in bold type? What are the sounds that the animals made? Point to the words that tell us what sounds the pigs made. Make those sounds yourselves.

They fed the hens.
Cluck! Cluck!

They fed the ducks.
Quack! Quack!

They fed the pigs.
Oink! Oink!

4

page 4

Teaching specific skills

In the classroom

Building grammatical knowledge

Focus is placed on the use of the past tense in narrative:

*They **fed** the … They **picked** the … They **collected** the …*

The class is asked to tell Jenny some other things the children did:

*They **went** for a ride … They **ran** across … They **shouted** …*

Specific subskills of reading are taught in context

Building word meaning

Words that are difficult or interesting are given special attention. *Bellowed* and *charged* are discussed and drama is used to demonstrate these words. Synonyms for the words are suggested as alternatives.

Teaching sight words

High-frequency sight words are given special attention. Words such as *said*, *the*, and *was* are held up on flash cards and then found in the text. They are then read in context. Sight word games are played with the flash cards.

Teaching letter–sound (phonic) knowledge

Initial sounds that are frequently used in the text, such as *s* as in *Sal*, *Sam*, *said*, *snake*, are emphasised. What sound does this letter make? Find me another word that starts with the *s* sound. Does anyone's name start with *s*? What letter makes the *s* sound? Go and point to the letter that makes the *s* sound on our sound chart.

Focus on punctuation

Full stops are given focus on a browse through the text. Why are they there? What purpose do speech marks serve? What is happening each time speech marks appear?

Systematic teaching

The systematic teaching of reading subskills is important in each level of the early school years. For instance, the systematic teaching of basic sight words or the teaching of essential phonic skills cannot be left to incidental reference on isolated occasions. Good teachers will develop their own approaches and use their chosen materials for specific teaching of reading subskills. The learning of such skills must be carefully monitored by the teacher. Good teachers will also ensure that the teaching of subskills is done within the context of whole text so that students can see the purpose of the skill and how it is used in text.

In the classroom

Systematic phonics in Early Stage 1 (Kindergarten/Prep)

The systematic teaching of phonics begins in Kindergarten (Prep). Approaches vary considerably. Some schools use one of the many published phonic programs; others devise their own method. Beginning teachers will be obliged to follow the approach used at a school and develop and modify it as they become more experienced. Below is an example of the approach used by one very experienced and successful teacher of children in their first year of school.

At the beginning of the year, I introduce the basic sounds, vowels and consonants, and use all kinds of examples of the sounds in words and in the stories the children meet.

There is a sound chart always at the front of the room and each morning I go over all of the sounds, almost as a drill. They love it!

When the children are writing their own stories, I hand out sound strips, 'magic wands' which they can use to build up words. I do not stress or drill the names of the letters, as children either come to school knowing them or we learn them in the 'alphabet song'.

As I introduce the sounds, I also introduce blending common consonants and short vowels, first with consonants as beginning sounds (ma, me, mi, mo, mu); then with consonants as final sounds (am, em, im, om, um). The children enjoy finding appropriate words containing the blended letters. They don't keep to CVC words; in fact the more complicated the word the better. For example, with 'me' they might say 'men', but they might also say 'member' or 'remember'. This happens with all of the sounds. The children think that this is fun and it certainly helps with decoding in reading and processing in writing.

Later in the year I introduce common blends, such as bl, cl, sl and vowel and consonant digraphs, such as ea, ee, th and ch. The children come across these less regular spellings in their sight words and recognise them readily in their phonic work.

Teachers in following years revise the sounds and add more complicated patterns, following syllabus requirements. In this way we teach phonics explicitly and systematically and apply this knowledge to the children's reading skills in wider reading.

Literal and inferential meaning

Jenny places emphasis on the literal meaning of the text (reading the lines) in the first part of the book—that is, what Sal and Sam actually do. The inferential meaning (reading between the lines) is raised in the later pages, particularly at the end when Sal and Sam are asked if they have been good. What are they thinking? What might they say? Jenny's class is very interested in the moral dimension of the story, and this is explored. Would the children tell Grandpa what they had done? Should they have wandered off? What happens when children disobey their parents or grandparents?

Literal and inferential comprehension of the text is taught within the four roles of the reader

Jenny emphasises the four roles of the reader as she proceeds with her teaching:

1   the code-breaker role (letter–sound knowledge, sight words, punctuation) in which her students are decoding the visual information of the text

2   the text-participant role (literal and inferential meaning) in which her students are involved in finding out the meaning of the text

3   the text-user role (what knowing about a farm means to me) in which students apply the text to their own situation

4   the text-analyst role (what is this author trying to tell me about responsible behaviour?) in which the students work out what the text is doing to them—finding out the underlying assumptions in the text relating to the author's intention.

Re-reading the text

Jenny re-reads the text with her class. All the children are able to participate in making the animal sounds and reading the simple sentences, which contain repetitive structures: *They picked the apples. They picked the oranges. They picked the peas.* The dramatic sections are very popular and the class joins in to read them: *The big bull bellowed and charged.* ***Roar!***

In subsequent readings of this text later in the same week, Jenny takes the opportunity to focus on a number of teaching points that her assessment shows needed further attention.

After the reading experience

The big book acts as a springboard into a wide range of literacy activities in English and other learning areas

Jenny uses the big book as a springboard into a range of varied activities for the children. These include making a language experience book with the class. It is built up by the teacher and the children and written by Jenny. The resultant 'story' is written on sheets of butcher's paper and later illustrated by the class (see chapter 11).

As the big book is supported by ten small books about Sal and Sam, also published by Blake Education, Jenny is able to introduce these publications for Guided Reading with some groups in the class. The ten books are pitched at the emergent reading level and are suitable for instructional reading during the Literacy Session (see chapter 9). During Guided Reading, Jenny reinforces the teaching points on which she has focused, including specific letters, the full stop, and common sight words.

Jenny's students are reminded of the various skills they have learnt in their lesson and are told to look out for examples of these in the Guided Reading lesson they will be having at a later time. Sight words, examples of the *s* sound, and the past tense of verbs are noted.

Assessment and Shared Reading

Assessment is made of the work of every student in his or her reading portfolio

Jenny has developed an approach to independent assessment of each student in her class. She has focused on the outcomes and indicators in her state syllabus and has drawn up an independent profile in a reading portfolio for each student in which she assesses specific skills and strategies that must be mastered. She monitors the reading development of individuals by observation in the Shared Reading lesson, makes judgments, and places checks against indicators as children achieve them. This is done each week (see chapter 17).

The Sal and Sam set

For instance, indicators relating to a desired outcome concerned with reading and viewing texts for Shared Reading may include:

- enjoys Shared Reading
- participates in Shared Reading lessons in familiar and imaginary topics
- recognises how specific letters relate to specific sounds
- recognises words in Shared Reading
- uses illustrations to assist reading
- reads text of a big book largely from memory.

Critical thinking and study exercises

1 Consider ways you might involve children who have oral language differences in a shared book experience. How would you maximise the benefits these children may gain? Consider having them say the word or words in their own language, giving them additional one-to-one assistance in Guided Reading.

2 Discuss ways the progress of children could be monitored in a Shared Reading lesson. Build on what Jenny has done. Think of running records

when the children begin to read, parental involvement, and teacher reports on progress.

3 Prepare a set of lesson notes for a Shared Reading lesson. Follow the sequence used in this chapter and add Shared Reading activities of your own. Present your lessons to a class, group, or a single child. Write a comment on your lesson. Include ways you might improve the presentation.

The developing reader: An example with Guided Reading

In their second year of school, 1G is working busily during the Literacy Session. The class has now broken up into groups. John, the class teacher, is about to take Group 2 for Guided Reading. The students in Group 2 are all approximately at the same reading level. Other groups are reading independently, reading to parent helpers, or engaged in literacy activities based on the shared text they have just read together.

After a year at school, these children are beginning to use a variety of strategies for processing text. Most can read simple texts of short duration containing two or three sentences per page; all students need to extend their reading skills with more sophisticated use of the cue systems and become more conversant with the four roles of the reader.

John has multiple copies of the book he has planned to use with Group 2. It is Danny *Dolphin's Nose*, one of a series of eight books about Danny the dolphin, and is pitched at a level that will allow the group to read between 90 and 95 per cent of the words in the text correctly. The book has been graded by the authors, but John has his own set of criteria that he applies to all books used in his classroom and he matches his students to their reading texts with care.

The Guided Reading session

Before reading

John makes sure that the rest of the class is working purposefully before he begins work with Group 2. The separate copies of *Danny Dolphin's Nose* are spread out on the desks in the group reading corner. John has a Guided Reading Record Sheet ready to record the progress of each child in the group.

Multiple copies of a book are useful for guided reading

Introducing the book

Before reading the new text John lets the students warm up by reading out aloud a text they have already mastered. Then he turns his attention to the new book. He discusses the front cover, the title, the title page, the names of the authors, the name of the illustrator, and the Go Books logo that appears first on the top left-hand corner of the front cover.

It is always important to consider the features of a book, such as the cover and the title page

John then discusses the topic, at first generally to activate the students' semantic knowledge and build on what they already know. Dolphins are very popular with the children, as many have seen them in the ocean and in marine parks. The discussion is spirited. Talk turns to the specific title. Why Danny Dolphin's nose? Is it really a nose like their noses? What is its function? Is this nose something special? This 'mini-brainstorming' session builds up the information that the students bring to print. They develop a rich schema to apply when they are actually reading the book.

Build up a schema (prior knowledge) about the topic to act as a scaffold before reading the book

Next, the talk is about the type of text this book might be. Is it a story, a narrative? Is it a factual text? If it is a factual text, what type of factual text? They think it is a factual description, a book that describes Danny, a special dolphin. We'll see.

The students have their attention drawn to the word 'dolphin'. It is a difficult word. What is hard about it? Let's look at it in two parts, the way we would say it: *dol.phin*. What says /f/ in the second part? Do we know any other words that have a /f/ that is spelt *ph*? The students supply *phone* and *photo*. The information is then related to the students' systematic phonic instruction where they have been studying the fricative consonant sounds, /f/ and /v/. What are the big words that *phone* and *photo* come from? Other words in the text that might cause difficulty are also discussed.

The students have now developed a range of knowledge that will provide a 'scaffold' or supporting context for the language and the meaning of the book they are about to read.

Reading the Book

John tells the students to turn to the title page and asks them to read it with him.

The Title Page should receive special attention What is that hard word we looked at? What were the hard letters? What did they say? Why is that apostrophe there? Let's all read the title again. What is on the title page that wasn't on the cover? I wonder why that bottle is there. We'll come back to it later.

John asks the students to turn to the next page and selects a student to read.

Danny Dolphin's mouth can open wide.

2

When the student reads 'nose' for 'mouth' John prompts her by saying, I know 'nose' makes sense here, but does it look right and sound right? Look at the first letter. The student reads on and self-corrects after picking up the meaning in context and confirming it graphophonically (It starts with the *m* sound). She is also assisted by the pictures. In this way, the student brings in multiple cues to read the word and retain meaning.

Students call on multiple cues to read with meaning

Each student is then given an opportunity to read in turn, a double-page spread at a time. As each student reads, John prompts with questions to help the student draw on what she knows in order to solve unknown words. At the end, John talks with the group about relevant aspects of the text: the meaning of the pages, what the illustrations tell the reader, and what might come next. To build up fluency and expression, he reads some of the pages himself, running his finger under the line of print. He involves the whole group also by having them read some parts of the book in unison, with emphasis on fluency and phrasing.

Each student has an opportunity to read

The students are pleased that they have predicted correctly and that the book is a factual description. One of them has predicted correctly that Danny is indeed a bottlenose dolphin and informs the group in no uncertain terms.

Danny is a bottlenose dolphin.

12

When a student has trouble with a word, John quickly identifies which cue system is causing difficulty. Is it phonological–graphological, grammatical, or semantic? As an example, does the student's problem stem from the fact that he cannot decode the printed letters with the correct sound–symbol relationships? Is the student failing to provide a word that fits the grammar of the sentence? Does he provide a word that just does not make sense?

If the student is having phonological–graphological difficulty (e.g. the word the student reads does not match the sounds that the letters on the page represent), she is told to look carefully at the word and questions like these are asked: What letters do you see? What sound does the first letter in the word make? What might the rest of the word say? Can you see any letter patterns in the word to help you? (morphemes bottle/nose; syllables *dol.phin*; onset and rime *m-outh*). Say the letters in the word. Say the sounds they make.

Various techniques are used to overcome difficulties at graphophonic, grammatical, and semantic levels

John says the sounds with the student and helps her to blend them to get the correct pronunciation of the word. The word is constantly tested in context to see that the meaning of the text is maintained. For example, a reading of 'mouth' as 'nose' is entirely inappropriate in the context of the following: *Danny Dolphin's **mouth** can open wide. It has tiny teeth in it.*

If the student is making mistakes of a grammatical nature and losing meaning as a result, John asks such questions as: Does that seem right? Is that what someone would really say? Does that word really fit into the sentence? For example, if a student reads 'cat' for 'catch' in the sentence on page 5, *He can **catch** little fish with his mouth*, John asks the questions above and finally, Would we say 'cat' then?

Semantically, if a student reads a word that fits the sentence grammatically but does not make sense in that context, such as *It can catch a **wing*** for *It can catch a **ring*** John asks: Does that make sense? Would Danny really catch a wing? Look at the picture. What is Danny really catching?

It looks like
the neck of a bottle.

11

John is careful to make sure that the students in the Guided Reading group are able to engage in the four roles of the reader in gaining understanding of the text. The first is the code-breaker role, as shown above.

Students must take on the four roles of the reader

The next is the text-participant role which is concerned with the meaning of the text. He asks literal questions such as: What things could Danny do with his mouth? He asks inferential questions such as: Why do you think Danny is called a bottlenose dolphin?

Then the text-user role. He asks questions relating to the purpose of the text, such as: Since we have decided that this book is a factual description, what did we learn about Danny and about dolphins? What information did we gain?

Finally, the text-analyst role. He asks questions relating to the author's purpose in starting out writing about Danny's mouth and then bringing in his nose. Did the author have any particular reason for saying that Danny's nose looked like the neck of a bottle and how did the illustration on page 11 help us to understand the last page 'Danny is a bottlenose dolphin'? (the text-analyst role works out what the writer wants the reader to understand or feel).

After the Guided Reading session

The students in the group then form pairs and re-read the text to each other. They are later allowed to take it home to read to their parents.

John has prepared a number of activities to reinforce the teaching points of the lesson. These include sequencing sections of the text, which he has written onto cardboard strips, and matching high-frequency words on cards and teaching the students to play matching games with them. There is also published material to support the text. As there are seven other books about Danny in the set, John flags the fact that the group will be meeting Danny again soon.

Students should re-read and take home a text they have mastered

Assessment and Guided Reading

John monitors the reading of all students in the group. He keeps a record for each student on the Guided Reading Record Sheet and makes notes to assist the student in future teaching sessions. The record sheet allows him to focus on specific indicators relating to desired outcomes in his state syllabus. This record sheet is included in each student's portfolio. For instance, *Danny Dolphin's Nose* has particular relevance to *drawing on an increasing range of skills and strategies when reading and comprehending texts.*

A Guided Reading Record Sheet is kept for each student

Specific indicators include the following:

- draws on letter–sound relationship when reading unknown words
- uses different parts of a text to access information, e.g. title page
- reads a variety of literary and factual texts
- attempts to self-correct when meaning is disrupted
- identifies sentences in written text.

Critical thinking and study exercises

1. Guided Reading is a particularly important part of reading instruction. Discuss why this is so.

2. If you are engaged in teaching a Guided Reading group, it is necessary to manage the remainder of the class effectively. Consider the best ways you might do this.

3. Prepare lesson notes for a Guided Reading lesson. Follow the sequence used in this chapter and add Guided Reading activities of your own.

4. Present your lesson to a group. Write a comment on your lesson. Include ways by which you might improve the presentation.

The developing reader: An example with Independent Reading

2D consists of children with a range of reading abilities. They are in their third year of school. Most can read independently at some level. C Group is about to engage in an Independent Reading session while Maria, their class teacher, is working with B Group on Guided Reading.

C Group goes to the class library and makes a selection from the books that are at the appropriate level. These are on the C Group shelf. Independent Reading begins.

The Independent Reading session

Before reading

Students must use their own initiative during Independent Reading

Maria has explained to the children the routine they are to follow during Independent Reading. They know that it is a special time and that they must use their own initiative for most of the period. She has introduced the children to three or so books from the C Group shelf, and has explained what each one is about and the way the books are arranged on the shelf.

Choosing a book

Maria has explained to the children in the group the best ways they might find books that would interest them during the Independent Reading session. These include choosing three

The chosen books must be interesting and at the correct level of difficulty

books that they might find interesting; looking at the cover, author's name, the title of each book, and reading the information on the back; reading the first page of the book to see if it is interesting and testing the difficulty of the book by applying a rule of thumb (more than five unknown words on a page means that the book is too hard). It is important that the children find books that interest them and they are encouraged to return books to the shelves until they find one that does.

Special attention must be given to children who are new to the technique or are having difficulty with reading alone, and Maria does this while the Guided Reading group is assembling. Simple texts must be selected that will ensure success, and encouragement and help are given when necessary.

Keeping a record

Maria requires that each student keeps a record of his or her Independent Reading. She has prepared a special sheet for the purpose and maintains an overall class progress sheet herself.

Independent Reading

Students record their own progress

The students are allowed time to read and record their progress. The Independent Reading session gives them the opportunity to practise and consolidate the skills they have learnt in Shared and Guided Reading. It is also a very pleasurable period, because they are not only demonstrating their skills but are also reading to follow their interests.

Independent Reading must be carefully monitored

Maria uses the Independent Reading session effectively by taking other groups for Guided Reading. She walks around the classroom, sometimes checking the independent readers, working with Guided Reading groups or commenting on the work of another group who are writing about their reading experience. Two parents are assisting Maria during this Literacy Session. They are listening to children as they read and filling in a checklist of skills that Maria has prepared.

The Independent Reading session is a development of DEAR (drop everything and read) and USSR (uninterrupted sustained silent reading). It is an integral part of the daily Literacy Session in Maria's class.

After Independent Reading

Maria has introduced various 'after Independent Reading' practices. These include dividing the students into groups of twos and threes and having each student tell the others something interesting from the book he or she has read; describing one of the characters from a narrative text; relating something of importance from a factual text; making a comment (with demonstration) on the illustrations in the book; offering an opinion of the author's purpose in writing the book; making a comment on the author of the book or series, where relevant, or providing a short reading from a part of the book.

Post-reading activities reinforce the experience and provide valuable information

Multiliteracies

Teachers should build on what children already know about multiliteracies when they come to school to extend and develop their knowledge and skills.

During the first three years of school, beginning and developing readers are becoming more involved with multimodal texts in an increasingly varied literacy environment. Reading material is infused with examples of visual stimuli that go well beyond the printed word. Illustration supplements story and also complements it. Some picturebooks have no meaning without the pictorial dimension, as in John Burningham's *Come Away from the Water, Shirley.* Words and pictures come together, work together rather than separately, 'bouncing off each other, juxtaposing and tipping into each other their own carriages of meaning', as Rosemary Johnston states in chapter 29 on visual literacy.

Young children are also very familiar with the combination of visual and audio modes of meaning through their experiences with TV, film, and DVDs. They understand how the images on the screen are augmented by the sounds, whether these are dialogue, sound effects, or background music. Without explicit instruction, students know when the music is 'scary' or 'funny'. They know which character is saying what, even in animations where mouth movements are sometimes quite unlike those of real people. This knowledge translates into an understanding of the part dialogue plays in paper-based texts and it is then just a small step to teach children about the print text convention of inverted commas to indicate what is being said. ("Hello," said the rabbit.)

Follow-up

Because the students spend most of their time working independently during this form of reading, Maria is careful to spend some time each week talking to each student about the books he or she has read. She uses the information to assist her in later work with the students in Guided Reading and to help her decide whether she needs to change the difficulty or type of books used in Independent Reading, both in class and at home.

The variety and scope of books available for children in the class library must be constantly monitored, and Maria adds new titles as well as removing others every week. She consults the children about the selection and makes a complete change of books at the end of term or when the class is involved in a particular theme or unit of work.

Available books must be constantly monitored

Independent Reading allows children to follow their own interests

Matching books to children

It is important that children have a range of books of various genres available to them. The books must be arranged to suit the various needs of children at a particular time. For the best results the books must be arranged in a number of predetermined levels according to the degree of difficulty. This process is known as grading or 'levelling'. (See chapter 7 for further information on how to grade or 'level' books.)

Books across a range of genres should be arranged in levels

Next, the books must be matched to individual children according to their special needs. Children then proceed from level to level of book difficulty as their reading skills develop. Naturally, books for Independent Reading at school or at home would be of a lower level of difficulty than those used for Shared or Guided Reading. Wille (1996) makes the important point that matching books to children should be only a part of a balanced literacy program and that children should also have many opportunities to choose from a wide range of ungraded texts. (See also chapter 8 for a further discussion of book matching.)

Books must be matched to students' special needs

Children should have a range of books from which to choose

▶ LITERACY IN THE DIGITAL AGE

Students in the first three years of school will become increasingly familiar with the computer and electronic texts. Depending on availability of hard and software, they will interact with talking books, videos and DVDs, CD-ROMs, text messages, email, and computer graphics. They will be able to use computer software, find information on the Internet, navigate hypertext, comprehend computer icons, and follow computer interactive directions, to name but a few. What is more, they will handle digital age equipment with a confidence that will astound many adults. The syllabuses of all Australian states and territories include the requirement that students need to be given the opportunity to access and compose a wide range of digital texts.

Two important matters must be considered, however. One is the matter of equity: not every school and certainly not every child will have the most up-to-date equipment available or be able to replace it when it becomes (rapidly) obsolete. The other is the extremely significant fact that many of the literacy benefits of the digital age are unavailable if a child in unable to read. Nevertheless, there is much evidence to show pre-literate children using and interacting with digital text through image, sound, and icon alone. In addition, many early reading programs use digital programs to begin and assist the path towards reading.

Teachers are finding many creative ways to use digital texts in the classroom. For example, one Kindergarten teacher uses the voice-recognition software program Dragon Naturally Speaking as part of her morning news session. After several children have told their news, the class decides which news item will be recorded. The teacher repeats the child's news into the microphone while the children watch the program scribe it onto the screen. As always, the program makes some errors and the children are asked to find these. The keyboard is used to correct the errors, thereby demonstrating to children how to refine and edit a text. The text is then printed, illustrated by the 'author' and inserted into a class book to become a reading resource that all children can now read.

Some further ways to include ICT reading in the digital age are as follows:

- use Avalanche Flash to create an animated cover for a book the class is reading
- use Photoshop to create a collage of a scene in a book
- use Paint to create a character, then write a literary description; produce a Cotton flow chart of the sequence of events in a story
- use Inspiration to create a mind map of the qualities of one of the characters in a book
- use Paint and Photostory to produce a summary of chapters in a book
- use Access to create a database of the books researched in developing a unit or theme
- create a Power Point presentation to expand the reading of a book
- have students record themselves and others reading a book orally.

(Part of a much wider selection provided by Linda Yeates, PLC Pymble, NSW.)

▶ Summary

1   Using the reading model with children who are beginning school requires knowledge and imagination. Aspects of the model are discussed in the context of teaching practice and a Shared Reading experience is explored with a class of emergent readers.

2   A Guided Reading lesson is explored with a class in their second year of school. Aspects of the Guided Reading lesson are explained and the teacher's approach is discussed in terms of practice before, during, and after reading.

3   Independent reading is an important part of the reading program and takes place in every Literacy Session. Independent Reading requires carefully wrought practice; it also requires planning, and considerable time spent in organisation.

4   Books from a range of genres should be matched to suit the needs of children at a particular time.

Critical thinking and study exercises

1   Independent Reading gives students the opportunity to practise and integrate the skills they have learnt in Guided Reading. It also provides pleasure. Consider ways you might encourage students to spend more time reading independently, both at school and at home.

2   A range of text-types should be made available for students during Independent Reading, depending on the reader's interest and ability. Discuss the range of text-types you would make available for a particular class.

3   Obtain a selection of books from a source such as a school or public library and place them in order of difficulty. Now divide the books into six levels. Remember that these are not Reading Recovery levels, which are much finer in gradation of difficulty.

4   Practise matching a book to a student for Independent Reading. Remember that if a student is making one or two errors in each twenty words, the book is probably at his or her instructional level and too hard for Independent Reading.

5   Begin compiling your own children's literature collection by visiting a good bookshop and selecting two or three books you particularly like. Add to your collection over time as you see new books that appeal to you. Build a poetry collection by obtaining one or two good anthologies of verse, collections from your favourite poets, and photocopies of poems you wish to use with the class. (See a good collection of recommended poetry texts such as in Winch & Poston-Anderson 1993. See also part III of this book for many examples of quality children's literature texts.)

Further reading

Students are advised to consult the current curriculum and support documents relating to the teaching of literacy and reading in their state or territory.

Cairney, T. H. 1991, *Other Worlds: The endless possibilities of literature*, Heinemann, Portsmouth, N.H.

Cairney, T. H. 1995, *Pathways to Literacy*, Cassell, London.

Cairney, T. H. & L. Munsie, 1992, *Beyond Tokenism: Parents as partners in literacy*, Heinemann, Portsmouth, N.H.

Cope, B. & M. Kalantzis (eds) 2000, *Multiliteracies: Literacy learning and the design of social futures*, Routledge, London.

Downes, T. & C. Fatouros 1995, *Learning in an Electronic World*, PETA, Sydney.

Kist, W. 2005, *New Literacies in Action: Teaching and learning in multiple media*, Teachers College Press, New York.

Unsworth, L. 2006, *E-Literature for Children: Enhancing digital literacy learning*, Routledge, London.

Unsworth, L. A. Thomas, A. Simpson & J. Asha 2005, *Children's Literature and Computer-based Learning*, Open University Press, Maidenhead, UK.

Web links

Office of the Board of Studies (NSW): www.boardofstudies.nsw.edu.au
International Reading Association: www.reading.org

6 LEARNING TO READ/ READING TO LEARN: THE MIDDLE PRIMARY YEARS

Overview

This chapter demonstrates how students in the middle years engage in more complex reading tasks and develop more sophisticated reading skills and strategies. More difficult literary and factual texts are read and comprehension skills are stressed. These skills are taught in the reading session through explicit and systemic teaching followed by ongoing assessment. A guided reading lesson is modelled and various teaching strategies are explained.

By the time children enter the middle primary years, Years 3 and 4, they have generally developed knowledge about meanings (semantic knowledge), about the structure of language (grammatical knowledge), and about sound and print relationships (phonological–graphological knowledge) to enable them to read a variety of texts. These include print and multimodal texts, both literary and factual, on topics that are largely familiar to them.

Students in Years 3 and 4 have many basic reading skills

They have also learnt to draw on and integrate their knowledge as they read. They can read texts of increasing difficulty automatically and fluently by using their growing knowledge flexibly and efficiently. When they meet an unfamiliar word, or temporarily lose meaning in the text, they can ask themselves such questions as: Does this make sense? Does this fit with what's gone before? Does this sound right? Would we say it like that? Does this look right? What words or sounds do I know that match the letters I can see?

As Clay says:

I define reading as a message-getting, problem-solving activity which increases in power and flexibility the more it is practised … Language and visual perception responses are purposefully directed by the reader in some integrated way to the problem of extracting meaning from cues in a text, in sequence, so that the reader brings a maximum of understanding to the author's message. (1991: 6)

THE TEACHER'S TASK

It is the task of the teacher in the middle primary years to assist children to increase the power and flexibility of their reading by increasing their ability to use and integrate the knowledge and skills they bring to the reading task and by broadening their experiences of unfamiliar texts.

It is most important that the teacher begins the task of developing a reading program for the class by first developing a thorough understanding of the needs and abilities of each student. This is done by using a range of assessment practices including, in particular, running records, to provide the necessary information on which to build an effective teaching program. (See chapter 8 p. xx.) Assessment also helps teachers to identify those students who will need increased support in order to reach the outcomes of their particular stage of learning.

Effective assessment is the first step in developing a reading program

A reading program has three main areas of focus.

1 **Texts**

As the core of the program, the teacher extends the range and variety of texts students encounter, and uses these texts to help students develop and strengthen their reading skills, knowledge, and strategies. Emphasis is placed on phrased and fluent reading in order to assist students to maintain the meaning and flow of the more complex texts they encounter.

2 **Reading cues or sources of information**

The teacher develops and extends each student in the four areas of *semantic knowledge, grammatical knowledge, phonological–graphological knowledge and visual knowledge* in order to increase their ability to solve unfamiliar and more complex texts. More importantly, the teacher helps children to learn to use this knowledge flexibly and efficiently as they read by using a variety of strategies, e.g. by reading on and referring back, by looking at words in context, and by cross-checking or comparing one piece of information against another (that word *looks* like 'house' but it doesn't make sense in this text).

3 **Reading practices or roles of the reader**

The teacher develops in each student the skills to be able to adopt the four reader *roles of code-breaker, text-participant, text-user, and text-analyst*. The teacher uses a text several times and in doing so supports students in thinking about the text in different ways and for different purposes.

Developing knowledge of reading cues

Semantic knowledge

Semantic knowledge plays an important part in reading for students in the middle years of primary school because it helps them access the meanings of a range of more difficult texts such as factual texts. Semantic knowledge includes real-world knowledge about topics of interest and about topics being studied at school in all learning areas. It also includes vocabulary knowledge, especially word meanings, common expressions, figurative language, and subject-specific vocabulary.

Semantic knowledge helps readers construct meaning from a text

Teachers need to be specifically conscious of the semantic knowledge students will need in order to read each new text. Teachers think about the texts they want to use as part of each unit of work, perhaps a unit on the environment, and about the understandings and vocabulary knowledge that will be needed to make meaning from the texts. During the unit of work, the students will be using their growing semantic knowledge to read the new texts and at the same time will be learning new semantic knowledge from the texts as they read them. It is important for teachers to show students how new texts can provide new knowledge and access to new vocabulary. (See Reading Factual Texts in chapter 7, p. xx.)

Perhaps one of the texts in a unit of work on the environment is a picturebook such as *Where the Forest Meets the Sea* by Jeannie Baker or *The Paddock* by Lilith Norman. What do the students already know about the topic of the text and how can they be helped to acquire the new topic knowledge they will need to read it? The teacher thinks about the vocabulary that is used in the text. Are there any words that students might not know, such as 'ecosystem' or 'habitat'? Are there any expressions that might be unfamiliar to students, such as 'life cycle'? By using these texts as part of the unit of work, the teacher is developing students' abilities both to learn to read and to read to learn.

In the classroom

Teachers use a range of strategies to help students gain new semantic knowledge. For example, students may watch a video or use a CD-ROM on the topic of the text, such as the video of *Where the Forest Meets the Sea* or one of the many excellent wildlife videos. The teacher then follows this up with much class discussion and reinforces important terminology using the chalkboard and charts. During this early part of the unit the classroom will come alive with pictures, posters, books, and charts collected from the school and local libraries, brought to school by students and the teacher, or collected from local authorities such as councils. Students may also visit a location such as a museum, zoo, or nature reserve where the concepts and understandings are explained and demonstrated on site. Materials are brought back to school to add to the classroom displays and for further reference.

Teaching strategies for building semantic knowledge

Often teachers will use the Shared Reading session to introduce students to new concepts and terminology. By introducing a new big book and reading it in a shared way with students, the teacher can pause at critical points and, often referring to the illustrations, explain concepts and terminology that may be unfamiliar to students. By using the same book over several sessions, and by providing small versions of the book for students to read on their own or refer to when writing their own texts, the teacher maximises students' exposure to the new concepts and terminology. The new terminology becomes part of the everyday classroom talk and the new semantic knowledge becomes part of each student's own working knowledge.

As students learn these new concepts and terminology, the teacher will provide opportunities for them to write, both in shared and individual sessions, so that they can use their new knowledge. In the students' writing the teacher will expect to see the new terms used with accuracy and confidence and will work with individual students if this is not happening.

It is particularly important for students who have reading difficulties to be helped to develop a strong bank of semantic knowledge about the topics they will encounter in their reading. This will give them a meaning base to decide whether their attempts at decoding a particular text make sense and it will help them to predict what might come next.

Semantic knowledge helps students with reading difficulties to decode new text

Grammatical knowledge

In the middle primary years students encounter many texts whose grammatical structure is unlike the spoken English they are used to. These texts may be literary or factual and their grammatical structure may present a challenge to students in the ways the phrases, clauses, sentences, and paragraphs are structured. These texts pose special problems for students from non-English-speaking backgrounds and for those with reading difficulties.

Texts encountered in the primary years will have more complex grammatical structures

For example, a literary text might contain this passage:

Miss Gardenia's View

There once was a woman *called* Miss Gardenia, who lived alone in a little flat in a large block of other little flats just like it. Miss Gardenia *liked* her home, for it was little just like her, and *folded* round her like a flower. Not only that—because the building was tall, and built on a hill, and because Miss Gardenia *lived* near the beach, she was able to look out her window and gaze across rooftops and backyards and pine trees and see the ocean whenever she *wanted* to.

Cassandra Golds, 'Miss Gardenia's View'

This text presents the reader with several challenges:

- complex sentences of several clauses, such as the last sentence
- past-tense verbs (lived)
- a sentence word order unlike that of everyday speech ('There once was a woman called Miss Gardenia …').

A factual text might contain the passage:

Mars has two moons, Earth has one, and Mercury and Venus have no moons at all. These last two planets are moonless *because* they are close to the sun, and the sun's powerful gravity would drag anything smaller than a planet towards itself.

David Hill, 'Night Lights', 1999b

This text also has some challenges:

- generalised statements which use the timeless present tense (Mars has two moons)
- a causal relationship represented through a complex sentence and the text connective 'because' (2nd sentence)
- use of the adjective 'one' without the noun 'moon' in the first sentence.

Both these texts could present problems for students trying to predict what might come next in each sentence. Their reading could be slowed down to word-by-word level as they attempted

Understanding the grammatical structures of texts helps students predict what might come next

to construct the flow of each sentence. In order for all students to develop effectively as readers it is important that they develop a good knowledge of what to expect in the grammatical structure of the texts they meet. Reliance on graphophonic information and the use of 'sounding out' strategies will not be enough to support their reading if their grammatical knowledge is unsatisfactory.

 # IN THE CLASSROOM

In developing students' grammatical knowledge, the teacher shows them how whole texts are structured

Teaching strategies for building grammatical knowledge

and what to expect of certain types of texts. For example, the class might look at several different narrative texts such as *The Enchanter's Daughter* by Antonia Barber, *The Paper Bag Princess* by Munsch and Marchenko, and *Wilfred Gordon McDonald Partridge* by Mem Fox, and discuss how each of these narratives is structured.

They could also look at the use of grammatical devices such as past tense and direct speech and how adjectives and adverbs are used to enhance meaning in each of the narratives. The teacher also helps them to think about how cohesion (e.g. referring words) is handled in the texts. For example, how pronouns such as 'him', 'her', and 'it' refer back to people or things already named in the text, and how grammar works at the sentence level, including recognising the subject of a sentence or clause, subject–verb agreement in person and number, verb tense, and plurals.

The use of both literary and factual texts in the development of this grammatical knowledge is essential. Students need to see how authors structure texts and use various grammatical features to achieve their desired meaning. Using real literary texts such as traditional fairytales helps students to develop a 'feel' for the sound of literary texts and a familiarity with the way literary language operates. In addition, it helps them understand the often complex and very compacted grammar that is typical of factual texts. Teachers incorporate the teaching of grammar into most aspects of the Literacy Session. By reading aloud many different texts to students, teachers cue them into the rhythm and sound of the language and can take the opportunity to discuss how the authors have used language to make meaning. (The Literacy Session is considered in detail in chapter 9.)

In Shared Reading the teacher might point out the way pronouns are used to refer to the main character in a narrative, or might ask the students to find the subject of a particular sentence or clause. Students might track the use of past-tense verbs in the text and contrast this with the use of present tense for direct speech. The teacher might read part of the text aloud, asking students to join in with appropriate phrasing and fluency to help them develop a feel for the flow of the language. After the Shared Reading students might be asked to complete a retelling of the narrative as a cloze passage (see p. xx [ch.8]) in which the pronouns have been deleted. Or they might be asked to reconstruct paragraphs from the text that have been cut up into sentences. Students might prepare a 'reader's theatre' presentation of the text (acting out the text while reading from the book) to focus their attention on the events of the narrative and the speech of each of the characters.

In Guided Reading the teacher might prompt students when they meet an unknown word by asking them to draw on their grammatical knowledge. Prompts such as 'Read that again and listen to the way it sounds. Do you think we would say it like that?' invite students to draw on their grammatical knowledge to read an unknown word or correct a *miscue*. The teacher often takes a running record of a student's reading to assess the student's reading accuracy and to check on how effectively the student is using particular knowledge and strategies. If a student is having difficulty with using grammatical knowledge it will be evident in the running record.

Writing plays an important part in the development and use of students' grammatical knowledge. As the teacher models each writing task for students, she emphasises the particular grammatical features that are part of the text being constructed. Together, in a joint construction of the text, teacher and students discuss the language choices they make in terms of their grammatical effectiveness. The teacher focuses on the particular grammatical features she wants the students to incorporate into their own writing. Later, in talking with each student about his writing, the teacher looks for the way he has used grammatical knowledge to structure the text and will ask him to explain particular grammatical choices, e.g. 'Which noun does this pronoun refer back to?' (see chapter 12).

Phonological–graphological knowledge

Students build the number of words they can recall automatically—often called 'sight words'. They also develop their ability to isolate sounds in words and combine these to make new words, a skill they have learnt in previous years. Students learn the common English spelling patterns for a range of sounds, including vowel digraphs such as *oa* and *ea*, and consonant digraphs such as *sh* and *th*. They learn to blend the sounds of the letters they see in words to work out the word (*tr-i-ck*). They learn to read multisyllabic words by breaking them into chunks, such as syllables (*un-der-take*), onset and rime (*tr-ick*) or morphemes (*under-take*). Students learn and use a growing number of letter clusters such as *br* and *str* as well as prefixes and suffixes, such as *pre* and *tion*. This knowledge improves their skill at working out unknown words.

Readers use phonological–graphological knowledge to work out how to pronounce unknown words

In developing phonological–graphological knowledge, teachers also build students' knowledge of book and screen conventions such as headings, page and screen layout. They focus on those conventions relating to factual texts, where layouts may include tables, maps, graphs, and diagrams, icons, button bars and drop-down menus.

In the classroom

Teaching strategies for building phonological–graphological knowledge

In developing students' phonological and graphological knowledge, both reading and writing play a part. Instruction in this area takes place in the context of students' attempts to read and write real texts both paper-based and digital.

For Shared Reading, teachers choose texts that demonstrate the particular text features and phonological or graphological items they want to teach. The teacher might display a book's table of contents and help students to work out how to find some of the items it lists. Students might study past-tense verbs to see how the -ed ending functions as a past-tense signal. Later the teacher will provide a writing task to enable students to practise using one or more of these text features.

The teacher usually introduces new sight words or unfamiliar letter clusters using the same shared text. New sight words might be listed on the board as they are encountered in the text and, at a later reading, students could be asked to find the words in the text by matching them with those on the board. These new sight words and words containing the new letter clusters often form part of students' individual spelling lists for the week, the level of difficulty of the lists being adjusted to each student's ability (see chapter 12).

Figure 6.1   Example of the type of word list teachers construct from Shared Reading texts

*Words ending in **ly***

*sudden**ly***
*rapid**ly***
*quick**ly***
*pleasant**ly***
*severe**ly***
*gent**ly***

In Guided Reading, where each group of students works with a text at their instructional reading level, teachers identify specific phonological–graphological items to focus on with each group. These items are usually the same as those taught during the Shared Reading lessons of the week but they will be modified to suit the reading level of each group of students. The teacher might ask students to find particular sight words in their text, and to practise writing these words quickly on small whiteboards. Using a whiteboard or the chalkboard, the teacher might write some new words using this week's letter cluster (e.g. for *str* the teacher might write 'string', 'strange') and ask students if they can use their knowledge of the new letter cluster to work out what the words say.

In Guided Reading the teacher prompts students by asking them to call on their phonological–graphological knowledge when they miscue or meet an unknown word. For a sentence such as 'There was no one to greet them', the student reads 'There was no one to get them'. A prompt from the teacher could be: 'You said *get* them. *Get* would make sense but does it match the letters you can see?' This prompt requires students to call on their phonological–graphological knowledge to resolve a mismatch. Teachers also use running records to check how well students are attending to the phonological–graphological information in the text they are reading.

After Guided Reading, students may work with small plastic letters to make the words that occurred in their text or to use the letter cluster to make new words. Teachers also monitor students' writing to see how they are using phonological–graphological knowledge as well as other knowledge in spelling.

Multiliteracies

Students in the middle years of primary school need many opportunities to engage with a range of literacies both as a significant part of their learning and also to prepare them for the communications environments they will meet outside the classroom and in the later years of schooling. This engagement can take two main forms.

1. Interpreting texts
Students need to use literary and factual texts such as television programs and advertisements, CD-ROMS, DVDs and Internet sites to

- complete tasks such as constructing a model from instructions on an Internet site
- gather information such as viewing a DVD to gain information about endangered animals
- compare information from different sources such as an Internet site and a DVD on the same topic
- evaluate the effectiveness of multimodal texts such as deciding how useful a particular Internet site is for the task they are attempting.

2. Constructing texts

Student should have many opportunities to construct multimodal texts for a range of purposes across different learning areas. They can

- use word processor programs to construct, edit and print texts
- scan images into a computer to accompany a written text
- use digital cameras to take, edit and print photographs to accompany a written text
- combine words, images, and sound to create a text, e.g. a narrative
- create e-texts, e.g. web pages, web projects
- use audiotape to record information, e.g. answers to interview questions.

Developing effective comprehension strategies

When students read they use the four sources of information (semantic, grammatical, phonological–graphological and visual) to decode the text. But this is only part of what they need to do to understand and use the text for real purposes. Readers also need to use a range of **comprehension strategies** to understand and use texts for the curriculum and social purposes they meet in their lives.

Comprehension strategies are ways of thinking about what is in the text, and combining this with what we already know, to gain maximum understanding from the text

We all know what it is like to 'read' a text and not really understand it. Perhaps the topic was new to us, or perhaps there were too many words we didn't know. Whatever the reason, we failed to fully understand, or comprehend, the text. Comprehension of a text comes when we combine what we already know with what is presented in the text to arrive at new knowledge and understandings.

The comprehension strategies presented below help students draw on and understand the information presented in a text, and identify ways this information can be accessed, organised, used, and evaluated. By helping students learn to employ these strategies, teachers assist students to become more effective as readers. These comprehension strategies can be demonstrated by the teacher in Shared and Guided Reading lessons, and then practised by the student individually or in pairs and groups.

These strategies are an essential part of reading for all students throughout primary and secondary school.

Using and building prior knowledge

Prior knowledge is knowledge that comes from past experiences with the world and with other texts. What readers know about a text before they begin to read influences their level of comprehension of that text. Students need prior knowledge about

- the topic of the text
- the text type

- the structure, layout and features
- the vocabulary.

Prior knowledge helps students to predict what they might find in the text, including vocabulary related to the topic. It reduces the number of 'surprises' or challenges for the reader.

Teaching strategies

- brainstorming and floorstorming
- categorising
- making a concept map
- predicting
- developing a visual text outline
- introducing key vocabulary.

Predicting

Predicting at the text level involves a reader considering what they expect a text to contain, or what they expect to happen in the text. It is based on prior knowledge of the world and of other texts. Predictions are confirmed as the text is read. Predicting at the word level means considering which word is likely to come next in a sentence. It is based on semantic and grammatical knowledge and readers confirm these predictions using semantic and graphophonic knowledge.

Teaching strategies

- identifying text-type and content from the cover and title
- discussing expectations of a text based on cover and title
- using the table of contents to predict the text's content
- using illustrations (with print masked) to predict the likely content of a text
- recording predictions at various points in the text and confirming through further reading.

Generating and answering questions

Effective readers ask questions as they read, and expect to have their questions answered. This gives a purpose to reading and helps comprehension because the reader is thinking about their questions as they read. Teachers can generate questions, and help students to generate their own questions about a text. Both literal and inferential questions should be asked.

Teaching strategies

- compiling questions before reading
- finding answers to questions (posed by teacher or students) during reading
- directed silent reading
- quizzes and games
- matching questions generated by students with answers gained from the text
- asking questions that draw on more than one source of information (e.g. printed text, illustration, caption)
- 'Hot Seat'.

Monitoring comprehension

Readers need to keep checking that what they are reading continues to makes sense. As we read, new information is added to what we already know. Students need strategies for checking their continuing comprehension of a text, and for what to do when meaning is lost or disrupted.

Teacher strategies

- discussing each page as it is read
- making links to previous pages
- cloze passage
- reordering jumbled text
- matching illustrations to the text
- retelling the text
- linking information found in different parts of the text
- following instructions in a text, e.g. to make something or play a game

Inferring

Inferences are information that readers supply to expand their understanding of the text. Inferring enables readers to go beyond what is stated in the text and to tap into their stored knowledge to increase their comprehension. Inferring can occur before, during, and after reading. Teaching students to infer means showing them how to combine what the text says with what they already know to arrive at conclusions, generalisations, character motivations, and feelings.

Teacher strategies

- explicitly demonstrating how to infer using facts from the text
- discussing possible inferences as the text is read
- constructing an inferences chart
- asking for factual bases of inferences made by students
- matching fact cards to likely inferences.

IN THE CLASSROOM

In assisting student to makes inferences from factual text, teachers might ask the following types of questions:

Before reading

From the title what do you think this book will be about? What information might it contain? What do you know about this topic?

I think this book will tell me about _____ because _____.

The clues I used to make my inference are _____.

What questions would you like this book to answer?

> *I want to know how/why/what causes* _____.

During reading

What is important on this page? What did you already know? What is new or surprising?

Identify facts, e.g.

> *In a blizzard* _____.

Use the facts to make inferences, e.g.

- What would it be like to …?
- What caused …?
- What would happen if …?

> *Being in a blizzard would probably be* _____.

> *I think this because the text says* _____, *and I know that severe storms are*_____.

After reading

What might happen next? i.e after the book has been read

> *I think the main character will* _____ *because he still needs to find* _____ .

Visualising

Effective readers create mental images as they read. In a literary text this might include imagining what a setting looks like or how a character moves. In a factual text it might include visualising the appearance of an animal or the sequence of events in a process such as the water cycle. It is as though the reader 'makes a movie' as they read, transforming the print into images. The process of visualising enables readers to construct and monitor meaning as they read, and to identify and correct miscues.

Teaching strategies

- drawing characters based on written descriptions
- constructing 3D models of book settings
- creating digital animation sequences based on a written text
- completing diagrams such as timelines using information in a factual text
- creating story maps from the events in a narrative
- engaging in a dramatic presentation of whole or part of a text
- turning a text such as a poem or story into a picturebook
- turning a literary text into a multimodal text.

Identifying and summarising information

Students need to work out what is the important information in a text and be able to summarise that information. This helps comprehension by focusing attention on key ideas and concepts rather than supporting facts or minor details. This is an important strategy in reading factual texts and allows the information in different texts to be compared and verified.

Teaching strategies

- using the table of contents and index to find information
- using headings and subheadings to identify the topic of parts of the text
- ordering information by listing key events in a sequence (e.g. making a timeline)
- finding main ideas (e.g. using the topic sentence of a paragraph)
- skimming a page or paragraph to find what it's mainly about
- making notes to record information on a particular topic
- retelling, rewriting or drawing significant information from a text (e.g. drawing steps in a procedure).

Responding to text

Responding to a text enables students to draw on the information and ideas contained in the text to add to and refine their own knowledge. It also allows students to evaluate texts within the context of students' own cultural understandings. Students should also understand that all texts, even factual texts that seem neutral, are written from an author's point of view. Responding to the text is one way students can question the point of view contained in the text.

Teaching strategies

- discussing issues mentioned in the text from the viewpoint of the students (e.g. a community issue)
- grouping and classifying information from the text (e.g. concept diagram)
- researching information on a topic dealt with in the text
- collecting illustrations of items mentioned in the text
- recognising writer's viewpoint (e.g. asking 'What does this writer think about …? How do you know?')
- retelling or rewriting information in the text from a different viewpoint.

▶ LITERACY IN THE DIGITAL AGE

Comprehension strategies such as visualising can be enhanced if students have access to digital texts such as DVDs and animations. Students can read part of a print text and teachers can ask them to visualise (and perhaps draw) what they think is happening (including details of the setting and character). Students can share their work with others and then watch a DVD or animation of the same scene. By comparing their own visualisations with the interpretation of the film-maker or animator, students can become much more skilled at visualising from a print text.

Teaching reading in a Year 3 class: An example with Guided Reading

In this section we will see how one teacher incorporates a Guided Reading lesson for one group into the Literacy Session for the day. A Year 3 classroom is in operation. How is the teacher working to develop each student as a competent reader? What can we see as we enter the classroom?

Classroom environment

In the classroom we can see tables and chairs arranged for small-group work as well as areas for Independent Reading and Writing. There is an easel in front of a cleared space where children can gather for Shared Reading and Writing and for class discussions. On the walls are many displays of children's work as well as posters and charts that provide models of writing and help with spelling. The room contains a large number of interesting books invitingly displayed and arranged for easy access. The computer area is organised to allow for the cooperation of two or more students on a reading or writing task. There is a busy hum of activity in the room as students work on assigned or selected tasks individually or in small groups. In one corner the teacher is working with a group of five students using a text for Guided Reading.

The classroom needs to be well organised for effective literacy learning to take place

Grouping of students

On looking more closely we can see that the students who are working with the teacher all have a copy of the same book, *Samantha Seagull's Sandals* by Gordon Winch. The teacher tells us that these students are all reading at approximately the same level and she checks this by doing a **running record** with each student fortnightly and by changing the groups if necessary. (See chapter 8 for information on how to take and interpret a running record.) The other students in the class have also been assigned to a Guided Reading group and will work with the teacher at another time during the week. Today, students not working with the teacher are completing a variety of reading tasks independently or in pairs or groups. At other times in the Literacy Session students will work as a whole class to undertake particular tasks.

At different times in the Literacy Session students will be working individually, in pairs and small groups and as a whole class

The Literacy Session

Earlier in the day the teacher introduced the Literacy Session by reviewing some of the tasks completed yesterday and by reading with students the wall stories they had created. This was followed by Shared Reading in which all students participated with the teacher in reading *The Paper Bag Princess* by Robert N. Munsch in big book form. The teacher began the Shared Reading by asking students what they would expect to find in stories with princesses, princes, and dragons in them. These predictions were listed for future reference. The teacher then read the text with the class, stopping at each page to discuss the events and the illustrations and what these revealed about the characters.

The Literacy Session is built around the reading and writing of whole texts

At several points students were invited to make predictions about the way the narrative would unfold and to compare their previous predictions with the text. During the Shared Reading the teacher focused students' attention on the implied meanings in the text and on the author's purpose in writing the text, in particular the way it departed from many of the conventions of a fairytale narrative. The class also looked at the use of past-tense verbs in the narrative and compared this with other narratives they had read.

After the Shared Reading students were directed to a number of activities designed to build on the key aspects of the shared text. Some students worked in pairs to reassemble parts of the text that had been written on sheets of paper and cut up. Others prepared a retelling of the text in their own words by using strips of paper to recall the main events in the narrative and then arranging the strips in the correct sequence. Others re-read the story using small versions of the text, while others listened to a reading of the text on an audio tape.

Reading activities are designed to further develop understanding of the shared reading text

As students finished the activities they moved on to Independent Reading, selecting a text from one of the class displays.

A Guided Reading lesson with one group

This was the time the teacher chose to begin the Guided Reading lesson with today's group. If we move over to the Guided Reading group we can hear how the teacher introduces the text, *Samantha Seagull's Sandals*, to the group and how she supports students' reading of the text.

Below is a transcript of the lesson. On the left-hand side of the table is the text and on the right-hand side is the student–teacher interaction. Also included is information about how the teacher's comments and questions scaffold and support the students as they work to solve the text by using semantic, grammatical and graphophonic knowledge and by checking the illustrations. (It is advisable to have a copy of *Samantha Seagull's Sandals* available while working on the following table.)

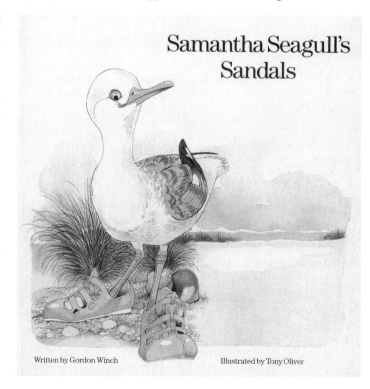

Samantha Seagull's Sandals

Written by Gordon Winch

Illustrated by Tony Oliver

Table 6.1   Guided Reading session with *Samantha Seagull's Sandals*

Text: *Samantha Seagull's Sandals*	Teacher–student interaction
	ORIENTATION TO THE TEXT
COVER	T: This is our new book for today. What can we see on the cover?
	ST: There's a bird …
Here the teacher is assisting students to prepare for reading the text by • *drawing on their knowledge of the topic* • *reading and understanding the title* • *identifying the text type*	T: What's the bird doing?
	ST: It's wearing big shoes.
	ST: It's at the beach.
	T: Let's read the title of the book together …
	T and STs: Samantha Seagull's Sandals.
	T: Does the title tell us what sort of bird this is?
	STs: A seagull.
	T: Yes, a seagull. And what is the seagull's name?
	STs: Samantha.
	T: Do you think this book will tell a story about birds or give information about birds?
	ST: Tell a story.
	T: Why do you think that?
	ST: Because the bird's wearing sandals and real birds don't wear sandals.
	T: And the bird's name is Samantha. Birds in stories have names but in information books it just says what sort of bird they are, like a seagull or a kookaburra. Now let's look through the book and see if we can find out what's happening. We'll see if we're right that the book tells a story. (Teacher and students look through the book page by page and discuss what is happening in each illustration.) Now let's turn to the front and start reading. Kim, will you read first?
Here the teacher is giving students the opportunity to build semantic knowledge that will help them to decode the text	
	READING THE TEXT

A long time ago there lived a young, silver gull who wanted to be different "Why am I the same as all the other young gulls?" She asked Hector the Hermit Crab who was old and wise. "The same grey bill,the same grey legs. The same grey feet."	ST: A long time ago the … there lived a young, silver gull who wants … wanted to be different. Her name was Samantha.	
	T: I liked the way you corrected 'wants' to 'wanted'. How did you know to do that?	*Here the teacher is making explicit the grammatical and graphophonic knowledge the student has used to self-correct an error.*
	ST: I saw it ends with 'ed'.	
	ST: "Why am I the same as all the other young seagulls?"	
	T: Have a look at this word again. (Points to 'gulls') You said 'seagulls'. It makes sense and it fits the sentence but look carefully at the letters you can see.	
	ST: gulls? she asked H … He..	

I want to be different.

I want to be different right now!"
"Ho, ho!" said Hector in a voice as deep as the ocean.
"You will be different one day. Wait and see."

Here the teacher is helping the student to use semantic information to work out the word.

But Samantha could not wait. She thought and thought until she had a bright idea.
"I know what I'll do," she said to herself.
"I'll buy some shoes. Then I will be different."

Here the teacher is helping the student to self-correct by using graphophonic information.

T: We know this is someone's name because of the capital letter. How could you work out this word? Can you see any small words you know?

ST: Hec … tor … Hector the Her … mit Crab who was old and wise.

Here the teacher is helping the student use graphophonic information to work out the word.

T: Read that sentence again so that it runs smoothly.

ST: "Why am I the same as all the other young gulls?" she asked Hector the Hermit Crab who was old and wise.

"The same grey bill, the same grey legs, the same grey feet. I want to be different. I want to be different right now!"

ST: "Ho, ho!" said Hector in a v..v..

T: What would make sense here? What would Hector use to talk to Samantha? What letters can you see?

ST: It starts with 'v'.

T: Read the sentence again and get your mouth ready for the first letter.

ST: Ho, ho!" said Hector in a … voice as deep as the …

T: Think about what would make sense here. Something very deep. What letter does it start with?

ST: o.. as deep as the o ocean. "You will be different one day. Wait and see."

T: Good reading. You looked carefully at the letters and thought about what would make sense in this story.
Let's find out what happens next. Lee, will you read from here?

ST: But S..S

T: What do you think this word could be? What can you notice?

ST: It starts with a capital. It starts with Sam..Sam an tha Samantha

T: Good reading.

ST: But Samantha could not want.

T: Do you think that makes sense? Look carefully at this word (wait). What letters can you see in the middle of the word?

ST: a..i..ai w ai t wait.

T: Read the sentence with 'wait' in it.

ST: But Samantha could not wait.

T: Good reading work. You really looked closely at that word to work it out.

ST: She thought and thought until she had a br..bright i i

T: Think about what would make sense here. If she thought and thought she might come up with a bright … what? Look at the letters you can see.

ST: idea. a bright idea. "I know what I'll do," she said to herself. "I'll buy some shoes. Then I'll be different."

Here the teacher is helping students'
comprehension by showing them how to
use their prior semantic knowledge to make
inferences about the story.

So Samantha went
to a shoe shop and
bought a pair of high-heeled
shoes.

"How smart and how
different I am," she
said as she stepped
onto the beach.

Here the teacher is helping the student
combine information from the text and
the picture to work out a word.

Here the teacher is supporting the
student to read in a phrased and fluent
way so as to maintain meaning.

Here the teacher is making explicit the
semantic and graphophonic knowledge
the student used to work out the word.

T: Look at these words here. (I will.) You said 'Then I'll be different.' That makes sense and it fits the sentence, but does it match the letters you can see?

ST: I will. Then I will be different.

T: Do you think it's a good idea for Samantha to buy a pair of shoes?

ST: No. She won't be able to wear them.

ST: They'll fall off when she flies.

ST: They'll get wet in the water.

T: Let's continue reading and find out what happens.

ST: So Samantha went to a shoe shop and b.

T: What would make sense here. What do you think Samantha did at the shoe shop?

ST: She bought shoes

Here the teacher is showing the
student how to combine two sources
of information (semantic and
graphophonic) to work out a word.

T: Yes. Do you think that word could be bought? Look carefully at the letters. What can you see at the beginning and end of the word?

ST: b t bought. bought a pair of

T: Read on to the end of the sentence. What can you see at the end?

ST: shoes

T: Yes shoes. Look at the picture and see if that can help you work out what kind of shoes.

ST: ladies' shoes … with high heels

T: Good. Now look at the word with the hyphen in

it. Can you see anything you know?

ST: high … heel high-heeled .. high-heeled shoes

T: Read that sentence again smoothly so you can hear what it says.

ST: So Samantha went to a shoe shop and bought a pair of high-heeled shoes. "How smart and how d.. diff different I am," she said as she stepped onto the beach.

T: Good reading. I liked the way you worked out different. How did you do that?

ST: Well, I looked at the letters and I saw it started with 'diff' and then I remembered that she wanted to be different.

T: Good work. Do you think she will be different now?

STs: YES

The teacher will continue to work through the text, supporting each reader with the use of prompts. She will draw out the various layers of meaning in the text by asking questions about the characters, events, and setting of the narrative and by focusing on the author's purpose in writing the text.

After Guided Reading

After reading, students in this group will work in pairs to complete a cloze passage of part of the text that focuses heavily on the use of past-tense verbs.

The teacher will take the opportunity to take a running record with Kim, who may be ready to progress to a higher reading group. After completing the cloze passage the group will begin Independent Reading while the teacher checks on the work of the rest of the class.

This will be followed by Guided Writing in which the teacher leads the class in a joint construction of a narrative, which they will later make into a big book. Students will then work independently on the narratives they are writing while the teacher works closely with four or five students in turn.

The Literacy Session will conclude with the students returning to work with the teacher as a whole class, reviewing some aspect of today's work and then listening to the teacher read aloud from their current novel.

► Summary

1   As students pass through the middle primary years at school, the reading tasks they engage in become more complex and varied.

2   They develop an interest in a wider range of print and multimodal texts and become familiar with many of the everyday and community purposes that texts serve in the modern world.

3   They develop effective comprehension strategies to help them to read and use literary and factual texts for a range of purposes.

4   They continue to participate in Shared, Guided and Independent Reading experiences that provide explicit and systematic teaching of key reading skills and strategies.

5   Examples of teaching at this level are given.

Critical thinking and study exercises

1   Imagine you are the teacher of a Year 3 class that is studying endangered animals. How will you find out what your students already know about this topic? How will you build your students' knowledge of this topic (semantic knowledge), which they will need to read and understand the texts you have chosen for the unit?

2   Select an everyday text such as a biscuit packet, chocolate bar wrapper, or drink can. Answer these questions about your text:

   a   Who wrote the text? Why?

   b   Who is the text intended for? How do you know?

   c   Which word or words are most prominent in the text? Why do you think this is?

   d   What ingredients are in the product? Are these ingredients healthy? How do you know?

   e   How would the text change if it was intended for a different audience (e.g. a younger or older group)?

   What reader roles are you adopting when you answer these questions?

3   Look carefully at the transcript of *Samantha Seagull's Shoes* in the Guided Reading lesson above. How is the teacher helping students to take on the four roles of code-breaker, text-participant, text-user, and text-analyst?

4   Select an example of quality Australian children's literature which you think is appropriate for students in the middle primary years. Read the book to a small group, showing the illustrations on each page as you read. Explain why you chose the book and how you would use it as part of the reading program for middle primary students.

5   Select a factual text that you think is appropriate as a Guided Reading text for a Year 3 or 4 class. Examine the cover carefully and list all the things you would discuss with students in your orientation to the text. Consider all the print and illustrations on the front and back cover.

6   Photocopy a page from a text and white-out every fifth word. Ask someone else to try to write in the missing words. How many were correct? How many others were appropriate for meaning and grammar? What skills and knowledge do you think the person needed to fill in the missing words correctly? What does this tell you about how effective readers operate?

Further reading

Students are advised to familiarise themselves with texts suitable for students in the middle primary years. Both literary and factual texts should be considered.

LEARNING TO READ/ READING TO LEARN: THE LATER PRIMARY YEARS

7

Overview

This chapter deals with students in the later years of primary school as they prepare to move to the secondary level. Here they are reading a wider range of texts across an extended selection of topics and building semantic knowledge. There is an emphasis on factual texts. Reading in the four roles is practised with emphasis on the text-analyst role and critical literacy. Multimodal texts are used and the Internet has a bigger place in literacy development, as do other resources of the digital age.

The later years of primary school, Years 5 and 6, are important years for students. While the early years are crucial in building the strong foundation for future learning, it is the later years that lead to secondary school with its closer focus on separate subject areas and the literacy demands that this brings. It is in the later primary years that students will refine the understandings and ways of dealing with texts that will shape their success in all subject areas in secondary school.

Reading plays an important part in learning in all subject areas and shapes success in secondary school

In Years 5 and 6 students continue to build on their earlier development of reading skills and knowledge. As they tackle more complex texts, including a wide range of print and multimodal texts, and seek to use them for a wider range of purposes, they extend and build on the knowledge and skills they have developed in earlier years. Students continue to engage in an extended Literacy Session each day, but now it is more likely that the texts they are reading and the tasks they are completing will be part of their study in curriculum areas other than English. They undertake tasks that often require them to think and work independently, to plan, research, and present information and ideas using several texts, and to study and compare texts from a range of viewpoints.

At this stage of schooling, most students have achieved a good knowledge of the basics of reading and will be able to read widely for a range of purposes. Their code-breaking skills will enable them to decode most texts written for primary-age students as well as some more complex texts such as information books and encyclopaedias. In these years it is the text-participant, text-user, and text-analyst skills that will see the greatest development.

The teacher in the later primary years will be aware of a wide range of abilities and reading competence in the class. Some students will be able to decode almost any text they meet and will be able to understand many of its literal and inferential meanings. There may be one or more students in the class who have not yet achieved the level of code-breaking skills necessary to read effectively at this level, or who may be able to decode the text but not be able to understand its meanings. For all students, accurate assessment of their reading skills and careful selection of appropriate texts for instruction will provide the basis of the reading program. For students experiencing difficulties, the type of Guided Reading lesson described in the previous chapter will help to provide the necessary 'scaffolding' for a higher level of reading proficiency.

The reading program for each student should be targeted to their assessed needs

For all students the most important component of reading development is an understanding of how to apply their knowledge and skills to a new text. They should understand what they need to do when they meet a text they find difficult or a word they can't decode. They need to acquire and refine a range of strategies for approaching a text and for unlocking its meanings. Most importantly, they should be able to articulate what they need to do in order to get to the meanings of a text.

In the later years of primary school the teacher of reading has three main tasks:

1 to continue to develop **each student's skills and knowledge** as a reader
2 to broaden **the range and types of texts**, especially factual texts and multimodal texts, that students encounter and the ways in which they use those texts
3 to develop students' abilities as **critical readers**.

Developing skills and knowledge

Semantic knowledge

Semantic knowledge includes technical vocabulary appropriate for study in all curriculum areas

Semantic knowledge is closely bound up with content learning in any new topic area. As students study topics in science, for example, their teacher helps them to develop concepts and understandings about the topic and they learn the terms that describe these concepts. A unit of work on space involves learning to be precise and accurate in the use of such words as 'planet', 'star', 'asteroid', 'orbit', 'solar system', 'galaxy', and many more.

Students increase their semantic knowledge by developing their understandings of topics in all curriculum areas and by increasing their vocabulary knowledge of word meanings, common expressions, and subject-specific terminology in these topic areas. Teachers assist students to do this by organising many real-life and lifelike experiences including excursions and field trips, and use of videos and DVDs, visiting speakers, artefacts, CD-ROMs, and the Internet, as well as a wide range of literary, factual, and everyday texts. In the extensive classroom discussions and activities around these items, teachers provide students with many opportunities to use, practise, and learn the new terminology in the context of learning about the topic. They compare the ways different texts approach a topic, and explore, compare, and contrast the information provided by different texts, to become familiar with the new body of knowledge.

In the classroom

In Years 5 and 6 the Literacy Session is used more purposefully to build students' knowledge of each topic area they are studying and to learn how to read and write texts about the topic. The teacher ensures that a great deal of discussion occurs around the Shared and Guided Reading texts that have been selected for the unit of work so that students come to understand the concepts related to the topic.

Teaching strategies for building semantic knowledge

In a unit of work on Space, teachers and students might visit the school library and local library to borrow an extensive collection of books, charts, posters, pictures, videos and DVDs, computer software, and other items about the topic. They may have already written away for brochures and other useful information from an observatory and they will participate in an excursion to an observatory or planetarium where, as part of the learning experience, the staff will introduce students to many of the terms and concepts they will meet in the unit. They will also use the Internet to access student-specific sites to gather information and to acquire new vocabulary.

The teacher will ensure that learning in this topic starts with what students already know, because it is likely that many of the students will have an interest in this area or have studied it in previous years. In particular, they will be expected to bring their growing maturity and critical judgment to their study; to think about what they read and consider it from different points of view. For example, the teacher might decide to introduce material on UFOs and reports of extraterrestrial visits to Earth, and ask students to take on the text-analyst role as they consider whether these reports can be believed.

The teacher will probably provide opportunities for students to read and discuss science fiction and fantasy novels, such as *A Wrinkle in Time* by Madeleine L'Engle, and *The Transall Saga* by Gary Paulsen, and will select some of these to read daily as class novels. Not only will this reading be interesting and exciting for its own sake, but it will also enable students to follow their own interests and to engage with texts at a level of difficulty that supports them as readers. It will also allow the teacher to demonstrate clearly the differences between narrative and factual texts on the same topic. Readers' circles will be formed for students to discuss these novels and recommend books to their friends. As part of the unit students will be encouraged to write their own texts, both narrative and factual, based on the knowledge they have gained through reading and study.

Grammatical knowledge

By the later years of primary school most students have developed a good basic understanding of English grammar and will be able to use correctly and to name a wide range of grammatical features, such as nouns (including abstract nouns), verbs, adverbs, adjectives, prepositions, sentences, clauses, and phrases. They will be familiar with more complex sentence types and will understand verb tense, subject–verb agreement, and singular and plural nouns.

Complex grammatical structures in both literary and factual texts should be clearly explained to students

Students will increasingly encounter texts in which the grammatical structures are unlike those of everyday speech. These texts will include senior novels such as *The Dark is Rising* by Susan Cooper which contains the following passage:

> Down the road with the handcart they went, Will, James, Mr Stanton, and tall Max, bigger than his father, bigger than anyone, with his long dark hair jutting in a comical fringe out of his disreputable old cap. What would Maggie Barnes think if that, Will wondered cheerfully, when she peeped roguishly as usual round the kitchen curtain to catch Max's eye; and then in the same instant he remembered about Maggie Barnes, and he thought in a rush of alarm: *Farmer Dawson is one of the Old Ones, he must be warned about her*—and he was distraught that he had not thought of it before.

Word order, complex sentences, and the use of colons, semicolons, dashes, and italics all serve to make this passage unlike everyday speech and therefore difficult for students to read easily. It is important that teachers take the time to show students how to unpack such grammatical features in order to construct meaning from texts.

In the classroom

The teacher helps students to increase their grammatical knowledge by developing wider understandings at the level of text, sentence, clause, phrase, and word. They become familiar with a wider range of text-types and their grammatical structures and features and use this knowledge to read and use a wide range of texts. They discuss the way authors use grammatical features to achieve the purpose of their text, e.g. the use of paragraphs and topic sentences to group information in an information report. They discuss the appropriateness of the way information is presented, e.g. a time-line to present events in a journey or a table to present information about features of the planets of the solar system.

Teaching strategies for building grammatical knowledge

Students consider the way a writer's choice of grammar influences a reader's interpretation of or response to a text. For example, they look at the way the use of the passive voice tends to focus a reader's attention on the information in a factual text. They consider information that is presented in running text and compare it with that presented with tables or diagrams. They look at an author's use of adjectives and adverbs in a narrative text and consider how these add to the meanings being described (see chapter 11). In Shared Reading lessons teachers can focus on particular grammatical features such as those mentioned above, and show students how they work to construct meaning in a text.

Phonological–graphological knowledge

Graphophonic knowledge continues to be important in helping students work out the many technical words they meet in all learning areas

In the later primary years students use graphophonic knowledge to help them decode a wide range of more complex texts. They learn how to segment multisyllabic words into chunks to assist pronunciation and meaning. They also continue to add to the store of words they can recognise on sight and become more skilled at seeing the relationships between words with the same base, such as 'inform' and 'information'. They also increase their phonological–graphological knowledge by learning more about the layout conventions of a range of text-types, especially factual texts and the use of graphs, maps, tables, and diagrams.

IN THE CLASSROOM

Development of phonological–graphological knowledge usually occurs during the study of a unit of work. In selecting texts for a particular unit of study the teacher will design opportunities for students to become familiar with a range of layout and illustration conventions and will also look at print and multimodal texts that present information in innovative ways. The unit will also include use of the Internet and CD-ROM texts, and so understanding of the conventions of these texts, how they are structured and accessed, will form part of the teacher's focused Shared Reading lessons.

Teaching strategies for building phonological–graphological knowledge

As part of the unit of work, students will have many opportunities to build their sight vocabulary, as new words are encountered. New words may be listed on the board or charts, made into cards for use in games and activities, and written onto labels to add to posters being constructed by students. These lists provide models of conventional spelling and become a reference point for writing during the unit. Many of these new words will be studied for their phonological or graphological features and will be incorporated into students' individual spelling lists. Students will be shown how to break the words into syllables, how to construct word families (e.g. planet, planets, planetarium, planetary) and how to break up compound words such as 'space-craft' (see chapter 14).

Teachers plan lessons to teach students about the structure and features of multimodal texts as part of the literacy session

Reading factual texts

In the later years of primary school the reading of factual texts becomes even more important. Students are expected to be able to use a wide range of print and multimodal factual texts to learn in all curriculum areas. But factual texts present a unique set of challenges for the reader. They don't work in the same way as the literary texts with which students might be familiar. They have their own structure and grammatical features, which can present traps for the unwary reader. And they use specialist vocabulary associated with the topic, which might be new to the reader. Like all texts, factual texts are constructed by someone with a particular point of view to impart. They might appear neutral, but in fact they are written from a particular point of view and employ features that serve to reinforce that point of view.

Factual texts present challenges for readers who are unfamiliar with their typical structure and language

Research has shown that students expect to read factual texts in the same way they read fiction (Lunzer & Gardner 1979). But it is quite clear that they are not the same. Teachers need to understand how factual texts employ language features in the construction of meaning, and they need to plan lessons that explicitly show students what these features are and how they work.

Factual texts are different from literary texts in several ways.

Purpose of factual texts

A factual text might

* tell real facts about the world
* describe how to do real tasks
* argue a point of view
* compare points of view
* recount events that have happened.

Structure and features of factual texts

As well, factual texts have a range of features which influence how we read them.

- Information is presented in many ways: in print text, pictures, maps, tables, etc.
- There is usually no sequence of events or 'story' structure.
- The text may have a table of contents, index, glossary.
- There will be paragraphs that 'bundle' information.
- The paragraphs may begin with topic sentences.
- There will be pictures with captions and labels.
- There may be text boxes with extra information.
- Different sections of a page are designed to complement each other (e.g. a diagram or table might add to the information in the print text).

Grammar of factual texts

The grammar of factual texts often includes:

- present tense verbs (e.g. is, have, eats)
- technical and precise vocabulary (e.g. predator, mammal, extinct)
- general nouns (e.g. whales, mountains, animals)
- moderating adjectives (e.g. most, some, few)
- phrases telling where, when, how (e.g. in their nests, at night, with sharp claws, on most occasions)
- compound and complex sentences representing complex relationships, (e.g. cause and effect;)
- logical connectives (e.g. because, so)
- comparisons (e.g. A glacier is like a frozen river of ice).

Factual texts also provide challenges in the level of technical language used. If we look at a topic such as 'Food' we can see three types of language a text might contain.

- Everyday Language (familiar to students): e.g. eat, chop, buy, cook, sandwich.
  Most students can understand these terms because they use them every day, so when they meet them in a factual text they are able to use this everyday semantic knowledge to understand the text.
- Low-level Technical Language (new to many students): e.g. harvest, crop, market, yield. Some students will know these terms but they will be new to many others. When students meet these words in a factual text they may be able to 'sound them out' but if they don't know what the words mean, sounding them out will not be enough to construct meaning from the text. Perhaps the illustrations would provide some support, but most students would find their comprehension slipping as they continue to try to make meaning of a text with several words whose meaning they don't know.
- High-level Technical Language (new to most students): e.g. production, combustion, evaporation. It is at this level of technical language that meaning can be severely disrupted. Not only are the words totally new to almost all students, but they describe processes or technical aspects of the topic that are complex and difficult to understand. Even detailed illustrations usually provide only minimal support, so the student is left struggling with a

text. They may be able to 'sound out' these words but that skill provides very little help in understanding the text. When the relationship between the words and what they mean is missing, the reader is not able to construct meaning from the text.

Looking closely at factual texts

It is important for teachers to look closely at the factual texts they intend to use to identify the features that might prove difficult for their students. New features of factual texts can be seen both as learning challenges for the student and as teaching opportunities for the teacher. By planning explicit lessons with the new features as the focus of teaching, the teacher capitalises on the resources that the factual text presents. This is why it's important not to use overly oversimplified or infantile versions of factual texts, but instead to support students to access texts appropriate to the topic they are studying.

    Some textual features that could be the focus of Shared and Guided Reading lessons are highlighted in the following example, from *The Land Around Us*, by Marian Woolley, which is part of the Alphaworld series.

Planning explicit lessons around the features of factual texts will assist students to read and understand them

Teachers should use factual texts as a regular part of their reading program.

Multiliteracies

In helping students to engage more deeply with a range of multimedia texts, teachers can provide experiences that help students understand how different media work to construct meaning. Every text is constructed with a particular message or point of view the writer wants to impart. Teachers can help students learn how writers employ the various elements of print, image, sound, and movement to construct meaning, and in particular, how writers use these elements to construct the evaluative stance they want to impart to the subject of the text.

    Students need opportunities to

- use and construct a range of media products (e.g. Internet sites, television programs)
- discuss how different media products are used for different purposes (e.g. to tell a story, to advertise a product)
- learn how different parts of a media text help to construct its overall meaning (e.g. adding illustrations to a print text)
- discuss the different ways that visual information can be presented (e.g. maps, diagrams, animation)
- discuss the ways the media combine elements to construct meaning (e.g. an Internet site with music, voice, and animation)
- experiment with the construction of media texts by manipulating print, image, sound, and movement and discuss the effects the changes have on the meaning of the text
- discuss how effective different media products are for their chosen purpose (e.g. CD versions of favourite novels)
- discuss their personal responses to different media products (e.g. responding to an anti-littering campaign which includes a TV advertisement, a poster, a brochure and a T-shirt)

Figure 7.1   Images from 'The Land Around Us'

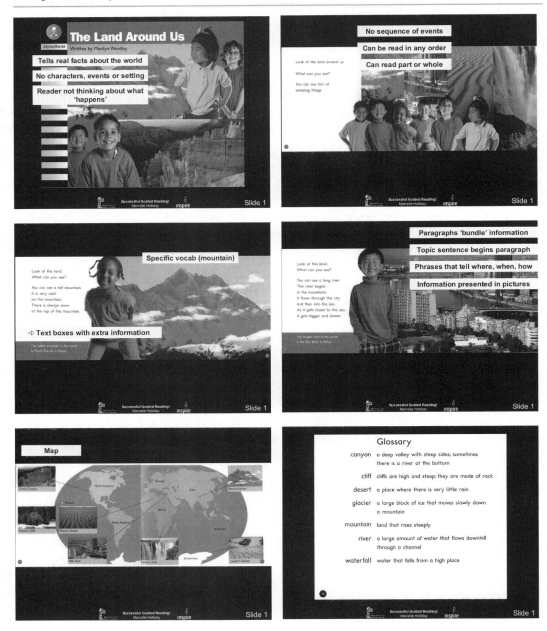

Developing the four reader roles

Developing skills in using different reading practices, or roles, enables readers to more fully interact with a text

By using the framework of the four reading practices or reader roles, developed by Alan Luke and Peter Freebody, teachers can provide a balanced development of reading skills for their students (see chapter 3). This framework prompts students to focus on their purpose for reading and on the different ways they can interact with a text to fulfil that purpose. It provides ways of moving beyond simply decoding the print to a deeper understanding and evaluation of the text on several levels. It provides flexibility and assists students to move towards independence as readers as they use their semantic, grammatical, and phonological–graphological and visual knowledge to take on these reader roles.

Code-breaker

The teacher helps students to learn code-breaking skills to read a wide range of text-types. Students become skilled at drawing on and integrating information from all sources as they read, at monitoring their own reading for a mismatch between meaning and text, and at self-correcting when they make an error. They learn how to vary their use of reading strategies to suit the demands of the particular text, such as multimodal text that contains moving images. They learn how to 'crack the code' of a range of visual features such as maps, graphs, tables, and diagrams. Their purpose for reading drives their use of strategies and how they use their knowledge and skills on a particular text. They learn how to use parts of a text such as the table of contents and index to locate information quickly, how to source information from a range of text structures, and especially how to bring what they already know about a topic to the task of decoding the text.

Readers are codebreakers when they work to decode the text

Students having difficulties in code-breaking need explicit and structured Guided Reading sessions. They need frequent opportunities to revisit and practise their understandings and skills using texts carefully matched to their reading level.

Text-participant

The teacher helps students to learn text-participant skills to build meaning from a range of literary and factual texts. Students always bring their prior knowledge to the task of understanding a new text. They learn how to relate the text to their own growing knowledge and experience, to understand the literal and inferential meanings of the text, and to be sensitive to the various layers of meaning in the text. They learn how the structure of a text, whether literary, poetic, or factual, contributes to the way the text makes meaning. And they learn how a wide range of visual elements in a text, such as illustrations and diagrams, work to add to the meaning of the print. Students learn how to construct meanings from digital texts by applying their growing understandings of print and other semiotic systems such as image and sound.

Readers are text-participants when they work to understand the meanings of the text

Text-user

The teacher also assists students to learn text-user skills to use texts for a wide range of purposes in all curriculum areas. Students learn to use a range of texts for specific purposes such as following the steps in a procedural text when they want to make or do something. They learn to use, evaluate, and compare product information when buying something and they use texts as an integral component of interaction in a range of situations. In particular, they use a wide range of print and media texts to refine their understandings and add to their knowledge in all areas of the curriculum.

Readers are text-users when they use the text for a specific social purpose

Students develop skills in effective reading for study. Skills such as skimming to get the gist of a text or section of a text, and scanning for a particular piece of information or fact, are practised and refined.

The teacher will support students in the use of a systematic information-gathering process such as this one:

- *Defining*: What do I want to find out?
- *Locating*: Where can I find the information I need?
- *Selecting*: What information do I want to use?
- *Organising*: How can I best use this information?
- *Presenting*: How can I present this information?
- *Assessing*: What did I learn from this?

Information-gathering in the digital age

Students now have access to digital resources such as the Internet to find the information they need to complete tasks at school and at home. Many of these sites, especially those designed for teachers and students, are excellent resources which provide not only up-to-date information but also interesting and creative activities in which students can engage to further their learning. It is important, however, that teachers show students how to be selective in using the Internet because there are many sites whose information is not necessarily accurate or unbiased. Showing students how to compare information from several sites as well as other sources can assist them to be discriminating in their choice of content. Teachers should also explain to students that lifting large amounts of material from an Internet site and using it as if it was written by the student himself is plagiarism and should be avoided.

Text-analyst

Teachers help students to learn text-analyst skills to think about texts within the contexts in which they were written. They consider an author's purpose in writing a text, learn how to identify opinion and bias in a text and how to compare texts on the same topic from different points of view. They look at the techniques writers use to put forward an evaluative stance on an issue, such as using words that carry positive or negative connotations. They learn to think about why people might interpret a text differently and explore how the author's choice of words and text structure contribute to the way a text portrays different social or environmental issues. In particular, they compare factual texts written by different authors that present the 'facts' of a situation or event differently. How do we decide which account is 'true'? How do we know who to believe?

Readers are text-analysts when they analyse the underlying and unstated assumptions of a text

Teaching strategies

Shared Reading

Shared Reading continues to be an important teaching strategy for students in later primary years

In Shared Reading the teacher presents many different texts, often more than one in each lesson, and 'walks' students through the processes of accessing the texts. Their purpose in reading will be uppermost as teacher and students make use of the text and its features to meet their needs. For example, using a table of contents and index of one text, they may locate the information they need, read it, and summarise it on a chart, before moving to another text to find information on the same topic for comparison. At all times the teacher is modelling or demonstrating ways of interacting with texts that will provide students with independent learning skills.

By careful questioning around a text, the teacher prompts students to draw on their knowledge and to articulate how they are using it to work out what a text is saying. For example, using a factual text on the planets of the solar system for Shared Reading, the teacher may refer to a table and ask questions such as 'Which is the largest planet? How do you know?' to prompt students to read and compare the diameters of all the planets listed in the table, or 'Which planet do you think would be the hottest? Why do you think so?' to prompt students to infer that distance from the sun determines temperature and to compare the distance of each planet from the sun.

Guided Reading

In Guided Reading the teacher provides students with opportunities to practise for themselves the skills that were demonstrated in Shared Reading, supported and guided by the teacher. On a text at their instructional reading level, their task becomes one of applying what they have seen demonstrated. Later, in Independent Reading, or as part of work in another curriculum area, students will practise the skill on their own.

In Guided Reading a student combines knowledge and skills to read an unfamiliar text

In Guided Reading, the teacher continues to help students use what they know to work on the unfamiliar text. When students meet a word they do not recognise, the teacher may prompt by asking 'What would make sense here? Is there any part of the word you know?' to help them call on the knowledge they already have.

The teacher wants the students to learn how to work out unfamiliar words by using a range of monitoring and self-correction strategies, by integrating all the information they have about the word, and by trying different options. Because the text is at the students' instructional level there will usually be several words on each page that the students do not automatically recognise. The Guided Reading lesson is designed to give them ample opportunities to refine and practise their decoding strategies, supported by the teacher. If a student can read a Guided Reading text without error it is probably too easy to provide the necessary learning and a more difficult text should be chosen.

IN THE CLASSROOM

In this section we will visit a Year 5 classroom to see how the teacher uses the study of space to extend the literacy learning of all students. At the beginning of the unit teacher and students gathered a large collection of texts, including both factual and narrative books, posters, newspaper and magazine articles, video and audiotapes, and a CD-ROM. During the unit many of the pictures, posters, and charts are displayed on the classroom walls. A large sheet of chart paper fixed to one wall contains a growing list of words associated with the topic, such as 'planet', 'star', 'solar system', 'galaxy', 'asteroid', 'meteor', 'meteorite', 'constellation'.

Teaching reading in a Year 5 class: an example

Earlier in the unit the class visited an observatory and students were able to talk with the staff about their work. They brought back to school posters and pamphlets and a three-dimensional model of the solar system. They also made an audiotape of an interview that a group of students conducted with one of the staff members. They have decided to focus their study on our solar system, and in addition, for each student to undertake an individual project on a related topic of his or her own choosing.

The class has spent considerable time discussing and mapping what they already know about space. They have enjoyed looking at DVDs and other materials and exploring the separation between fact and fiction, and between fact and opinion. They have viewed the movie *War of the Worlds* and discussed the reactions of 'Earthlings' to a reported invasion from outer space.

The Literacy Session

Teachers can choose several texts to use in a Shared Reading lesson

In today's Literacy Session students will engage in a Shared Reading lesson in which they will analyse and compare three texts on the same topic, space exploration. The class will consider the texts in terms of the text-type, audience, and purpose, and they will talk about how the structures and features of the texts contribute to the way each text communicates its information.

Today's Literacy Session began with the teacher and the whole class reviewing aspects of work done yesterday. Groups of students presented to the class the work they had done on researching the ways people have, over the centuries, gathered knowledge about space. The findings of each group were entered onto a large table for further reference.

A Shared Reading lesson

In today's Shared Reading lesson the class will look at three texts that include various aspects of modern space exploration. The texts selected are

- *Postcards from the Planets* by David Drew (big book version)
- *Put a Ring Around It* by David Hill (The School Magazine, *Touchdown*, 1999)
- a news report of the launching of a space probe to Mars as an overhead transparency

The teacher produces a large sheet of paper drawn up as a table and, together with students, labels the columns with the categories text-type, purpose, audience and text features. The rows are labelled with the names of the three chosen texts.

The teacher begins by focusing on 'purpose' and displays each of the selected texts in turn. Students are invited to comment on the purpose of each text and to support their comments by

Explicit teaching shows students how to understand the purpose and audience of different texts

reference to the text's features. As students discuss the texts the teacher begins summarising their conclusions and adding this information to the table. From time to time the teacher asks the class to review the information to ensure that they agree it represents their ideas.

The teacher works with students in this way to complete the remainder of the table. This takes quite some time and involves much discussion in which students are encouraged to support their opinions by referring to the text or by producing other evidence.

The class engages in animated discussion about which text they would select to locate the information they needed for a specific purpose. Most students realise that a combination of texts would be needed for completeness and accuracy, and others have indicated that they would check the facts in other sources.

Figure 7.2   Example of a table built up with students during a Shared Reading lesson

TEXTS: THEIR PURPOSE AND FEATURES

TEXT	TEXT TYPE	PURPOSE	AUDIENCE	TEXT FEATURES
Postcards from the Planets	Information report	To present information about the planets of our solar system. Intended to inform.	School students years 3 to 6.	
Put a Ring Around It	Factual recount	Recounts the journey of the spacecraft 'Cassini' to Saturn. Intended to record a factual event.	School students Years 5 and 6.	
Mars Space Launch	News report	Reports the launch of a space probe to Mars. Intended to inform and entertain.	The general reading public (adults and older children).	

The class then begins **Reading Activities** that include working in pairs to complete a table for a new text similar to the one completed during Shared Reading. The teacher checks that all students are working profitably, then begins Guided Reading with today's group. The text for Guided Reading is a factual text with which students will pursue the same questions they answered with the Shared Reading text. They will also have an opportunity to read aloud and to practise their code-breaker and text-participant skills, assisted by the teacher.

During **Independent Reading** students engage in reading the novels they have selected, many of which are on the theme of space travel. In one corner the teacher works with a small group in a readers' circle. Each reader presents her novel to the group in a different way. One delivers a short oral book review, another reads a short passage from an exciting part of the book, another describes the book's main characters and how they relate to each other, and a fourth talks about the book's author and other books he has written. Prompted by the teacher, the group engages in discussion about the four books, their similarities and differences.

During **Guided Writing** the teacher works with the class to construct an information report that will serve as a model for students' later writing. During this lesson the teacher will help students understand how an information report is structured, perhaps by using a structured framework like the one below.

Using this as a model, students will then begin **Independent Writing** by selecting a planet on which to write a report and beginning to research the necessary information. The teacher will remind them of the information-gathering steps they should undertake and, together with the class, will construct a list of questions to guide the research, such as:

- How big is the planet?
- How far is it from the sun?
- What are its special features?
- Has it been explored by space probes?

When the reports are finished students will combine them into a big book, which they will publish using a word-processing program.

The Literacy Session concludes with the teacher reading from the class novel.

Figure 7.3   Teachers use this type of text-structure framework to support students in Guided and Independent Writing of a new text-type

---

FRAMEWORK FOR INFORMATION REPORT

TITLE: (names the topic of the Information Report)

GENERAL STATEMENT: Identifies and classifies the topic and gives the scientific name.

DESCRIPTION: Describes the topic by giving information in 'bundles' such as

Appearance

Distance from Sun

Atmosphere

Moons

Unusual features

▶ Summary

1   As children progress through the upper primary years the reading tasks they engage in become more complex and varied. They develop an interest in a wider range of print and media texts and become familiar with many everyday and community texts.

2   Each reading task requires the child to use and integrate a growing range of skills and knowledge in order to understand and use each text effectively. Examples of teaching at this level are given.

3   When children enter the later years of primary school they have already learnt a great deal about reading and have developed the ability to read and interpret a variety of texts.

4   Reading and using factual texts become increasingly important as children select and use a range of information-gathering processes with print and multimodal texts to assist their learning in all subject areas.

5   While the focus of reading in Years 5 and 6 will continue to be on reading for enjoyment, the skills of reading to learn in all curriculum areas, of finding and using information, and of becoming an effective critical reader will begin to take prominence. Examples of teaching at this level are given.

Critical thinking and study exercises

1   Consider the teacher's purpose in the Shared Reading lesson. Do you think the choice of learning experiences will help her to achieve this purpose?

2   How would you build students' semantic knowledge of a topic such as the bird life of Antarctica? How would you prepare them for the subject-specific words they would encounter in texts on this topic?

3   Select two newspaper articles on the same topic. Compare the features of each article that contribute to the way it presents the facts of the story. In particular, focus on headline, picture, and caption, choice of nouns, verbs, and adjectives. Do both articles present the story from the same point of view? Can you discern the opinion of the reporter?

4   Select an information text that you think would be suitable for students in Year 6. Does the text have a table of contents and an index? How would you teach students to use these effectively? What features other than connected text are used to convey meaning (e.g. tables, graphs, illustrations, maps, and diagrams)? What skills and knowledge would students need in order to gain meaning from these text features? How would you teach these?

5   Select two different cereal boxes. Consider each as a text and answer the following questions:

   a   Who wrote the text? Why?

   b   Who is the audience for the text? How do you know?

   c   What words or expressions are used to persuade us that the cereal is healthy? appeals to children? is slimming? is high in energy?

   d   What illustrations are on the box? What do they tell you about the intended audience?

   e   What are the four or five most common nouns and verbs used on the box? What does this tell you?

   Would you buy either of these products? Why?

6   Ask a Year 5 or 6 student to read to you from a book he enjoys. Ask him to begin by telling you about the book, what sort of text it is, and why it is enjoyable. As you listen to the reading, try to assess what particular reading skills and strategies the student is using: self-correction, sounding out unknown words, re-reading when meaning is lost, breaking words into chunks. After the reading ask the reader some questions, such as:

   a   What do you do when you meet a word you don't know? (code-breaker)

   b   Why do you think the main character did _____? (text-participant)

   c   Would you recommend this book to a friend? (text-user)

   d   What do you think the author wanted you to think when he or she wrote this book? (text-analyst)

Further reading

Students are advised to consult the current curriculum and support documents relating to the teaching of literacy and reading in their state or territory.

Web links

Education Queensland: www.qed.qld.gov.au
Department of Education (NTDE): www.education.nt.gov.au

ASSESSMENT IN READING

Overview

This chapter stresses the importance of assessment to the whole spectrum of those engaged in literacy: from the student, the parent, the school, to the nation. Types of assessment in their varied forms are explained and demonstrated and the importance of focusing on the underachiever in order to provide assistance is stressed. Practical applications of assessment, such as the calculation of readability, are addressed.

What is assessment in reading?

Assessment is the process of identifying, gathering, and interpreting information about students' learning. The assessment process includes:

- gathering evidence of student achievement through a range of assessment techniques
- analysing the evidence to arrive at judgments about the achievement of the student in relation to expected outcomes or standards
- using the information arrived at for planning, programming, and teaching to promote further learning.

Purposes of assessment

Assessment information is used as a decision-making tool at several levels. It is used to

- identify a starting point for teaching at the beginning of a school year
- plan for ongoing teaching and learning

- place students into groups according to common learning needs
- match students to texts for Guided Reading
- identify what students have learnt as a result of the teaching program
- help teachers tailor the class program to the learning needs of their students
- identify students who are in need of extra support
- identify students who need to be extended
- report to parents/caregivers about their child's progress
- evaluate the effectiveness of teaching programs
- evaluate the effectiveness of whole-school programs
- report to governments and education authorities about the effectiveness of school programs.

How is assessment used?

Assessment in the classroom

Assessment is a crucial component of the effective teaching of reading. It provides teachers with information about what their students know and can do and so is an essential starting point for any teaching program. In addition, it is an important tool for monitoring the ongoing reading development of students and it provides teachers and schools with information about how well their programs and teaching practices are meeting the learning needs of their students.

Assessment is an essential component of effective teaching

The importance of effective assessment is highlighted in the report of the *National Inquiry into the Teaching of Literacy*: (Rowe, 2006).

> The inquiry committee came to the view that the assessment of all children by their teachers at school entry and regularly during the early years of schooling is of critical importance to the teaching of reading, and in particular, to identify children who are at risk of not making adequate progress. The early identification of children experiencing reading difficulties means that interventions to provide support for these children can be put in place early.
>
> In addition, the reading growth of individual children should be closely monitored by ongoing assessment to inform parents, as well as provide feedback information that can be used to guide teaching and learning. Information gathered from these formative assessments may then be used to shape improvements and to adjust teaching strategies that meet individual students' learning needs.

This clearly demonstrates that assessment should be carried out not just to find out how well children are progressing, but that the results of assessment should have a direct and specific bearing on the teaching programs for students.

There are many forms of reading assessment available to teachers and those that are chosen for use in the classroom should be the ones that best suit the teacher's purposes. In selecting methods, teachers should consider the following. Effective assessment should

To be an effective decision-making tool assessment must be closely linked to the content of the classroom program

- link directly to the teaching program, assess what has been taught in the program, and provide specific information for use in future programming and teaching

- mirror classroom learning experiences and require students to participate in authentic tasks to show what they know and can do
- be comprehensive, balanced, and varied and provide students with multiple opportunities in a variety of contexts to demonstrate their literacy skills
- be fair and provide all students with equitable opportunities to demonstrate their achievements, regardless of cultural and language background, gender, age, socioeconomic status, or disability
- validly assess clearly defined aspects of student achievement and provide useful and meaningful information to teachers, students, parents, and others about the progress the student is making towards targeted learning outcomes.

A teaching/learning cycle

One useful way of looking at how assessment fits into teachers' ongoing planning and teaching is to consider the teaching/learning cycle diagram below. This diagram shows that assessment plays a pivotal role in guiding a teacher's decision-making about what to teach and in showing teachers what students have learnt from the learning experiences provided in the teaching program.

Assessment occurs many times during the teaching process

Figure 8.1   This teaching/learning cycle shows the place of assessment in teachers' decision-making

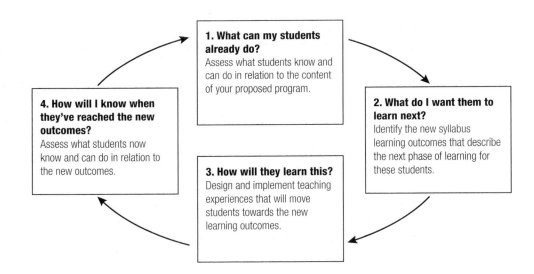

1. What can my students already do?
Assess what students know and can do in relation to the content of your proposed program.

2. What do I want them to learn next?
Identify the new syllabus learning outcomes that describe the next phase of learning for these students.

3. How will they learn this?
Design and implement teaching experiences that will move students towards the new learning outcomes.

4. How will I know when they've reached the new outcomes?
Assess what students now know and can do in relation to the new outcomes.

Assessment needs to be used throughout the teaching program, not only as a final step

By working through the steps in this cycle teachers can ensure that the learning experiences they provide will be based on what their students already know and can do, and will be effective in moving students on to the next point or stage of learning.

A process for assessing

In implementing assessment as part of their decision-making process, many teachers use the following four steps to ensure that they make the best use of the assessment information they gather.

Assessment can inform teachers' decision-making throughout the planning and teaching process

Step 1: Gathering information

Teachers decide what means they will use to gather raw information about students' reading progress. They may observe students working and take notes, or use running records. They may set questions or tasks that students complete, or they may conduct interviews with students, or set a test. This information can be recorded in many forms such as test scores, written comments, or samples of work the student has completed. Often information is gathered over time using more than one method so that a picture of a student's progress can be built up.

Step 2: Analysing information

Teachers analyse the information they have gathered by looking closely to see what it tells them about a student's reading. For example, after completing a running record a teacher needs to calculate the accuracy score, and analyse the student's errors to see what cue systems are being effectively used. If the student has completed a question-and-answer worksheet, the teacher needs to mark the sheet and identify which questions the student was able to complete and, if there are errors, what type of errors these are.

Step 3: Making informed judgments

Teachers use the analysed information to make informed judgments about a student's progress towards the achievement of syllabus outcomes. For example, the teacher might compare current assessment information with something the student completed earlier, such as the present running record with the last one that was completed for this student. Perhaps this shows that the student is self-correcting his errors more than he did previously. Or a teacher might look at how a student has answered questions which asked him to make inferences from a factual text, and decide that this student has now achieved this part of a syllabus outcome.

The effectiveness of assessment information relies on teachers' professional judgment about what the information indicates

Step 4: Using assessment information

Teachers use the knowledge they have gained through the assessment process to make decisions about the best learning experiences for their students. In many cases these will involve the development of a new class program, or modifications to the current program. Or it might include a change to class groupings. The teacher will design learning experiences with the needs of the students in mind and will modify the experiences for those students whose assessments show they have special needs. For example, one student might need extra support during Guided Reading while another needs to be extended through the use of more challenging texts.

IN THE CLASSROOM

At times, it is important for teachers to assess students individually so they can focus on each student in turn and discuss their answers with them. But this can be time-consuming. To find time to assess students individually, such as when taking running records, many teachers choose times when the rest of the class is working independently, such as completing reading activities or reading or writing independently. By assessing four or five students a day, teachers can complete this focused assessment for every student in the class over a period of a week.

Assessment at state and national levels

Assessment in reading is becoming more and more important

Assessment in reading is particularly important in schools and is becoming more so. Involvement in student assessment at state and national levels has increased steadily since the 1990s. In New South Wales the Basic Skills Tests in Aspects of Literacy for students in Years 3 and 5 have been in place for more than a decade and provide an example of assessment at a state level.

Schools and school systems throughout Australia are now required to report to the Federal Government about the achievement of their students in relation to nationally agreed benchmarks in literacy. Schools and school systems gather assessment evidence to assist in making judgments about the achievement of individual students and particular groups of students, the targeting of resources, and the effectiveness of programs.

State and national programs form an important part of literacy assessment

Assessment practices of this nature are not unique to Australia. For example, similar procedures have been developed overseas in the United Kingdom, the USA, and New Zealand. Such a widespread occurrence may be explained by a movement towards greater accountability or a general pendulum swing of teaching practice away from what was perceived as the too loosely structured assessment practices of the past. There is no doubt that greater attention is being paid in Australia and around the world to levels of literacy, as has been discussed in the introduction to this book. Effective assessment and evaluation practices by teachers are therefore increasingly important.

Assessment provides vital information for student and teacher

It should be noted that the main purpose for assessment in reading is to provide information about students' achievement and progress to inform ongoing planning and teaching. While other purposes also need to be considered, it is this central purpose that most concerns teachers in their work with students.

Information about student achievement is now being gathered at all levels from classrooms to education systems. Whether this information is being gathered by governments to map the literacy achievements of students throughout Australia or by teachers to identify the learning needs of their particular students, the procedures and processes used are showing more similarity from one setting to another. This is because of the broad general agreement that has emerged about the complexity of reading and writing and the inadequacy of narrow tests that give a single score, age, or grade norm to describe a student's achievement.

An excellent example of this is the Masters & Forster (1997b) results of the 1996 National School English Literacy Survey. Although set up as a national program to gather data about student literacy achievement throughout Australia, the project's steering committee rejected the use of norm-referenced tests as inadequate even though these would have been much quicker and cheaper to implement. The Introduction to the committee's report states:

> It was agreed that the overall purpose of the Survey was to produce a consistent factual analysis of the existing situation to be used as baseline data to monitor national performance over time and to inform strategies to improve literacy in Australian schools.
>
> The assessment methodology used for the Survey … has produced the richest picture of the literacy achievements of school students to date in this country. This Report presents achievement data on a comprehensive view of literacy, including reading and writing together with speaking, listening and viewing. It draws on detailed and valid data for students demonstrating achievement across a wide range of literacy levels. The achievement data are enriched by an analysis of those home and school variables which appear to have a significant impact on literacy achievement.
>
> The quality of the data can support a broad range of uses … Currently the Survey data are being used to inform and facilitate the development of national literacy benchmarks at Year 3 and Year 5 … System and school authorities also will be able to use the data to inform the development of literacy programs and to assist in the targeting of literacy resources.

…

> At early meetings of the Steering Committee it was agreed that
>
> * teacher judgement would be central to the methodology of the Survey
> * the methodology would model good practice in assessing English literacy and enhance the professional skills of participating teachers in the assessment of student achievement in English literacy.

…

> The underlying aim of the Steering Committee was to develop an assessment methodology which had the capacity to link the richness and validity of classroom assessment practices into the framework of a reliable national data collection process.

…

> The methodology shares some common features with a number of other assessment programs but is unique in the way it combines
>
> * the central role of the teacher in the assessment process
> * the collaborative assessment process involving teachers and external assessors
> * the integration of the assessment process with normal classroom practice over the assessment period
> * the degree and intensity of professional development for teachers and external assessors participating in the Survey
> * externally set and moderated tasks and assessment criteria, and students' best work to assess student achievement.

The report of the *National Inquiry into the Teaching of Literacy* states:

The Inquiry Committee supports the current assessment of students' literacy achievements against national benchmarks and proposes their extension so that the results for individual children are available for diagnostic and intervention purposes. The Committee noted that data from external assessments are already provided in ways that schools can evaluate, review and develop their teaching programs. Timely and reliable diagnostic information about the progress of individual children in reports to parents and other teachers are [*sic*] essential. To assist the transfer of achievement information as students move from school to school and from state to state, mechanisms are also proposed to make this process a long-overdue national reality.

System accountability

Because system accountability in literacy has assumed prominent and increasing importance in the English-speaking world since the 1990s, it is not surprising that sharp focus was placed on accountability at national and state levels in Australia.

System accountability is important at state and national levels

For example, Victorian schools are expected to structure their teaching around the Curriculum and Standards Framework (CSF). The four CSF levels are tied to particular age-grade expectations: Level 1 is the end of Prep, Level 2 is the end of Year 2, and so on. Each child's progress is reported as Beginning, Consolidating, or Established within the relevant level. Victorian schools are required to list the CSF levels and sublevels of all children in their annual reports.

In New South Wales, the Primary School Curriculum, English K–6 Syllabus (1998), is organised in stages: Early Stage 1 relates to kindergarten, the first year of school; Stage 1 relates to Years 1 and 2; Stage 2 relates to Years 3 and 4; Stage 3 relates to Years 5 and 6. A further breakdown to allow closer correspondence to grade levels refers to Mid Stage 1 and Later Stage 1, Early Stage 2 and Later Stage 2, Early Stage 3 and Later Stage 3. Another category termed Beyond Stage 3 is also included.

The NSW English K–6 Syllabus contains specific outcomes and indicators (statements of behaviour that students might display as they work towards outcomes). The outcomes state clearly what might be required of a student at a particular stage in listening, speaking, reading, and writing. Assessment in reading, for example, becomes *the process of collecting, analysing, and recording information about student progress towards achievement of syllabus outcomes.* Assessment procedures should relate to the knowledge and skills that are taught within the school program, and to the syllabus outcomes.

These examples illustrate the increased emphasis being placed on criterion-based outcomes by state departments. Similar movements are being made across Australia and the strengths of such a development in curriculum practice are obvious:

Types of assessment used at state and national levels go beyond simple scores and yield rich data about students' literacy skills and knowledge

goals are provided towards which schools may direct their teaching; there is ready accountability factored into the graded steps; classroom teaching and assessment are given a clear and uniform structure; reporting to authorities and to parents becomes much easier; and diagnostic assessment of an individual student's performance can more readily pinpoint areas of need. These and other advantages are important for the development of literacy.

In its report the National Inquiry into the Teaching of Literacy made the following recommendation:

> The committee recommends that the teaching of literacy throughout schooling be informed by comprehensive, diagnostic and developmentally appropriate assessments of every child, mapped on common scales. Further, it is recommended that:
>
> - nationally consistent assessment on-entry [*sic*] to school be undertaken for every child, including regular monitoring of decoding skills and word reading accuracy using objective testing of specific skills, and that these link to further assessments;
> - education authorities and schools be responsible for the measurement of individual progress in literacy by regularly monitoring the development of each child and reporting progress twice each year for the first three years of schooling; and
> - the Years 3, 5, 7 and 9 national literacy testing program be refocused to make available diagnostic information on individual student performance, to assist teachers to plan the most effective teaching strategies.

MULTILITERACIES

It is important that teachers use their understanding of the model of reading to decide how to assess students' knowledge and skills in all the elements of reading. There are many published tests and other assessment procedures that assess only parts of the reading process, such as graphophonic knowledge, and teachers should understand that these tests alone should not be used to give an overall picture of a student's reading ability or a so-called 'reading age'. A range of assessment items is needed to give a broad picture of a student's skills and knowledge in the various facets of the reading process.

In particular it is important to remember that reading now requires many more skills than those assessed by some of the standardised reading tests used in the past. Students should be able to read and understand a range of print and multimedia texts if they are to participate effectively in the 21st century. Assessment should focus on those attributes that the teacher believes will equip the student to achieve success in reading and using all the forms of text that they will meet in their future education, work, and community lives.

Forms of reading assessment

In gathering assessment evidence to inform decision-making processes, a number of instruments and techniques are available—from tests to a range of more inclusive data-gathering procedures. In order to select the most appropriate reading assessment techniques for their students from these many options, teachers need a thorough understanding of reading theory (see chapter 3). This understanding enables teachers to identify which reading skills and elements of knowledge a particular test or assessment technique is assessing. For example, a running record focuses chiefly on decoding an extended text and on the behaviours and knowledge the student uses to work out words and to self-correct when miscues occur. Some

Selecting the best assessment techniques relies on teachers' understanding of reading theory

other tests such as word-reading tests assess only the recognition of a list of words out of the context of a passage or text. It is important not to make assumptions about a student's overall text-reading ability, or comprehension based on the limited information that such word-reading tests provide. It is also important to remember that any instrument or technique can provide only a certain level of information and it is the teacher's role to turn that information into a professional judgment about a student's achievement.

Although there are various methods of assessment available, ranging from norm-referenced testing to school-based assessment featuring portfolios, cumulative assessment files, and profiles, a comprehensive approach where a range of assessment options is used over time is the most common practice in Australian schools. This is because most teachers recognise that collection of different sorts of information is necessary in order to understand what a student knows and can do as a reader. The disadvantages of some of the assessment techniques described in this section are often avoided if the technique is used in conjunction with other methods and not as a sole means of gaining information about a student's reading capabilities.

Norm-referenced and criterion-referenced tests

Norm-referenced tests compare an individual's score to that of a group

Norm-referenced tests allow an interpretation of an individual's test result by comparing his or her score with those of the group from which a norm was obtained. The most common outcome of norm-referenced testing is to provide a reading age for the child or a **stanine** or **decile** score. This score allows the teacher to compare the score of a student with the norming group which is considered as the 'standard'.

Criterion-referenced tests, or skills tests as they are often called, focus on a particular skill or reading criterion. Success in a test of this nature means that a student has achieved mastery over or competency in that particular reading skill. A mastery level is set, such as 80 or 90 per cent, and a

Criterion-referenced tests assess results on a particular skill

student is deemed to have achieved success in that particular reading skill after attaining such a score. In recent times many criterion-referenced assessments are reported in relation to bands of achievement, with the characteristics of each band clearly described. The NSW Basic Skills Tests in Aspects of Literacy is an example of this. It should be noted that tests may be both norm-referenced and criterion-referenced. A score can be compared with a criterion or mastery level and a set of norms.

Norm-referenced tests do supply information about students' ability on particular tests in relation to others in a sample; criterion-referenced tests do supply information about a student's ability to perform on a set of particular skills. There are serious questions raised, however, about these types of tests as sole and suitable means of assessing students' achievement in literacy, and reading in particular. In choosing to use a particular norm-referenced or criterion-referenced test, teachers should ask themselves the following:

- Does it really measure 'reading' as it claims to do?
- Does an array of questions in a norm-referenced test cover the range of reading skills that are essential to reading?
- Is a particular skill being tested for mastery of a vital reading skill?
- Does the test cover the skills being taught in the class program?

- Will the test provide the information that is required?
- Will the student's age affect the test result?
- Will the frequency of administration affect the test result?
- Will the student's language background affect the test result?

It should be noted that norm-referenced tests give no indication of a reader's specific strengths and weaknesses, nor do they indicate to the teacher the best course that might be taken to improve the student's reading.

More problematic is the fact that there is well-founded concern regarding the lack of relationship between the so-called essential skills of reading and the ability to obtain meaning from a text. Bussis (1982) described the case of a child who read effectively for meaning but performed poorly on an 'essential skills' test. Similarly, a child may master a range of so-called essential skills and still be unable to read.

Cambourne (1999), a long-time critic of what he would describe as one-off, group-administered, computer-marked, standardised tests of literacy, is particularly trenchant in his criticism. These tests, he argues, are based on quantitative measurement and view literacy as a single entity, ignoring its complexity. Added to this, the tests and their administration are not objective; the tests will not be similarly interpreted by those who take them; the tests place undue emphasis on outcomes or product and the results are not used by teachers and learners.

However, standardised tests are not in themselves bad. The problem lies in the way such tests are used or if they are used exclusively. When standardised tests are given to provide some form of indicator of a student's standard or progress, they can form a useful part of overall assessment procedure. Standardised tests in Australia are developed by reputable scholars and research bodies, such as the Australian Council for Educational Research (ACER), and refinement of their procedure is continually being carried out.

Outcomes-based assessment

As stated above, schools and teachers are increasingly structuring their programs and teaching towards the achievement of learning outcomes. These outcomes describe the knowledge, skills, attitudes, and values in each learning area that students will typically achieve at the end of a particular stage of schooling. The outcomes express the intended result of the teaching and learning programs provided for students. The set of outcomes in each stage provides a framework to help the school focus in a direct and specific way on what a student knows, understands, and can do. It provides a continuum of learning in each learning area and shows what students have achieved and where they are headed.

Outcomes-based assessment shows teachers what students know and can do in relation to stated outcomes

Teachers know that not all students will achieve the same outcomes at the same time. Some students will need more time and support to reach a particular stage, while others will achieve outcomes ahead of their age-peers.

The use of an outcomes framework to describe the expected learning provides teachers with a strategy to monitor student progress. Teachers have clearly defined outcomes on which to base their planning, teaching, and assessing; students have detailed information about what they have achieved and what they need to learn next; and parents have clear information about their children's progress and how this relates to their stage of schooling. The use of outcomes-based assessment provides a clear and understandable framework that meets the needs of all parties involved.

Outcomes-based assessment is an integral part of the teaching cycle, shown above, which includes the following:

- using assessment to identify what students already know and can do
- specifying the learning outcomes students need to work towards
- planning and implementing specific learning experiences designed to move students towards the targeted outcomes
- using ongoing assessment to identify when students have reached the targeted outcomes.

In using such an outcomes-based assessment framework, teachers are able to select and design assessment tasks for their students that meet the criteria for effective assessment described above. The National Plan assessment project in New South Wales produced a series of documents for teachers of kindergarten, Year 1, Year 3 and Year 5 that showed how this process could work. The project describes assessment tasks that children could undertake as part of their normal classroom learning to demonstrate achievement of particular learning outcomes. The tasks students complete, such as reading and writing texts, are accompanied by indicators of behaviours that students might demonstrate as they complete the tasks. Teachers make detailed observations of students working on the tasks and are able to identify those students who have achieved the particular learning outcomes associated with each task.

Authentic assessment

Using real-life or lifelike tasks as part of assessment shows teachers what students can do in actual situations

Assessment strategies, which use authentic or real-life literacy tasks and actual classroom procedures to obtain an overall picture of student achievement, are often called authentic assessment. These strategies stress an active engagement of teachers, students, and parents in the assessment process and explore new methods of collecting data. These include building portfolios of students' work, drawing up profiles of student attainment or progress, and carrying out running records of student reading. These procedures are essentially *qualitative* because they stress the quality of the particular student's reading efforts in actual literacy learning situations.

Authentic assessment values the input of the teacher, the student, and the parent. It places the emphasis on the professional in the field and can make a significant contribution to system assessment by cooperation with administrators at all levels. It places an enlarged responsibility on teachers and schools, however, and concern has been expressed at the time-consuming nature of its procedures. As Emmitt (1999) has pointed out, for authentic assessment to be successful, it must, among other things, work in the context of a clearly articulated policy. Added to this, it must be able to justify the procedures in terms of their accuracy, validity, and reliability (for a complete discussion of assessment, see chapter 17); it must be rigorous and allow time to evaluate data. It must make sound judgments, it must include parents and students, and it must take into account the possible tensions with the assessment demands of administrators.

Portfolios, running records, and informal reading inventories

Portfolios are collections of children's work that show significant aspects of development over a period of up to a year. A range of children's work and evidence of achievements can be included in the portfolio. With reference to reading, reading logs, literature responses, book reviews, reading interviews, reading profiles, running records, reading self-evaluation comments, and checklists are only some of the examples of a student's work that could be found in a portfolio. These, however, are merely collections of information or evidence. To be useful they must be analysed in the light of the outcomes to which the student is currently working in order to understand what the student has achieved.

Comparing information in a portfolio over time shows how students have progressed

Running records (Clay 1991) are a modification of Miscue Analysis and the Reading Miscue Inventory (Goodman & Burke 1972). In essence, a teacher takes a running record of the actual reading by a student of a particular piece of text. The selection of the text should be at the student's instructional level (between 90 and 95 per cent accuracy) because the reading material should be sufficiently difficult for the reader to make oral reading errors (miscues), but not so difficult that the reader loses meaning. Miscues may be of a phonological–graphological, grammatical, or semantic nature, and an experienced teacher can gain important information from the results on the reading achievement and skills of the reader concerned. Interpretation of the results is of major importance; just counting errors is to short-circuit a complex reading process (Goodman 1997). An analysis of each error is necessary. The running record shown in figure 8.2 is an example of one approach and is modified from Clay (1972).

Figure 8.2 A running record

It is wet.	√ word correct
The grass is wet.	*tree* the child's response
The fence is wet.	*fe fen fenc* various responses
The washing is wet.	*sc* self corrected
The hen is wet.	*That* child's response
The dog is wet.	*very* word inserted
Sal and Sam are dry.	*AP-TTA* appeal by child – does not get it. 10 secs.
	Teacher says: 'Try that again.' help child.

The teacher may count the errors and/or the words correct, but it is more valuable, as stated above, to analyse the types of mistakes or miscues. In the example above the reader is effectively using graphophonic skills to decipher most words, and is following the grammatical pattern and reading for meaning; reading *that* for *the* is not a serious miscue because it does not alter the meaning of the text in any significant way.

An effective way of checking the reader's understanding of the text is to ask the student to retell the story. A teacher can easily discover from such an oral response if the student has read for meaning.

Informal reading inventories are similar to running records in that a student reads a selected text and the teacher records his responses. Texts for reading inventories are divided into three levels of difficulty for a particular reader. Students progress to more and more difficult texts and the inventory serves as a rough guide to judge a reader's ability to read texts and to give clues to a reader's individual reading strategies. Criteria for judging the levels of texts are important in the informal reading inventory and texts are selected on the grounds of word recognition and comprehension. Texts are identified as Independent (requiring no teacher assistance); Instructional (requiring teacher assistance for instruction); or Frustration (requiring so much assistance that the learning would be minimal). A rule of thumb such as the following is used:

Table 8.1   Levels of texts for reading inventories

Level	Word Recognition (%)	Comprehension (%)
Independent	99–100	90–100
Instructional	90–98	75–89
Frustration	less than 90	50 or less

Informal reading inventories are not criterion-referenced tests. The information obtained from them is to be used as a guide to aid teachers in monitoring the reading progress of their students.

Reading checklists, reading profiles, and cumulative assessment files

Reading checklists provide a useful guide

Reading checklists provide a useful procedure for guiding teacher's observations and recording the results of those observations. Their contents vary but they all contain two elements: the points of behaviour to be observed and a legend (a system for coding observations). Checklists can be used widely. They can be completed by teachers, parents, and students themselves. A simple checklist for basic concepts about print is shown in figure 8.3. The points of behaviour or indicators are often related to expected learning outcomes. This is one of many ways of recording student achievement of outcomes.

Reading profiles are lists of observable reading behaviours that are considered to map the desirable reading development of a student or students. State departments develop such profiles and some schools develop their own. An example of this is found at Moonee Ponds West Primary

Figure 8.3 A simple checklist

Concepts about print	Joanna	Pedro
The front of the book	✓	✓
Print not picture tells the story	✓	✓
What is a letter?	✓	✓
What is a word?	✓	✓
What is the first letter in a word?	✓	✓
Big and little letters	✗	✗
The function of the space	✓	✗
Use of puctuation	✗	✗

School in Victoria, as reported by Davidson (1999). The school has arrived at a profile that takes into consideration a student's development from kindergarten to Year 6. The indicators on the profile are objective observable behaviours and represent collective teacher beliefs about reading and information from curriculum documents such as the Western Australian *First Steps Reading Continuum*, and the Tasmanian *Pathways* document. The profile has been refined and developed over the years and is used both as an assessment instrument and a reporting tool for parents.

Reading profiles map the reader's development

Cumulative assessment files are collections of data relating to a child's reading development. They differ from portfolios in that they contain all the available data relating to this development. At their most sophisticated, they represent an example of authentic assessment and an alternative to standardised tests. The effective operation of assessment files as a sole means of monitoring students' reading development requires serious commitment from teachers. Criticism of such assessment has focused on such points as the danger of invalidity of the data; the time-consuming nature of the approach in the development and the implementation of the criteria-based tasks; reduction of the available time for teaching; and the tensions created by external requirements at national and state levels. These problems appear to be more obvious in the secondary school (see Moni et al. Baker 1999). Again, such a collection of data is only useful if it is analysed to determine what it shows about the student's development of reading skills and knowledge.

Cumulative assessment files are an alternative to standardised tests

Diagnostic assessment

Most assessment practices will readily locate the student with difficulties. What is more important, however, is to use an assessment process that will identify (diagnose) the specific area of difficulty the student has. The term 'diagnostic assessment' is borrowed from the medical world, where it is important to accurately diagnose a patient's illness before prescribing treatment. Similarly, in the diagnosis of reading difficulty, it is important to understand exactly what is the cause of difficulty for a student before considering the provision of particular teaching procedures to overcome their reading problems.

Diagnostic assessment is often employed to identify those areas on which the program should focus when an intervention program of support is planned. An example of effective use of diagnostic assessment is to be found in the Reading Recovery program, where a series of assessment processes is used to focus attention on a range of skills and knowledge essential for beginning reading. These assessments help the teacher target instruction to the student's specific needs.

▶ ASSESSMENT IN THE DIGITAL AGE

The use of on-screen assessment techniques is growing. These programs often use sophisticated data analysis methods to provide detailed information about each student and about groups of students. As with other assessment techniques, the choice of which one to use should be based on the information the teacher wants to gather about the reading skills of their students. These techniques generally have several features in common.

- The student takes the test on a computer.
- The student is presented with questions or tasks which they answer using the keyboard or mouse.
- The questions are often multiple-choice.
- The questions can focus on one reading skill, or can require the student to complete quite complex reading tasks.
- The program recognises the student's level of skill or knowledge and terminates the test when the student is starting to struggle.
- On completion of the assessment, the student's answers are scored and analysed by the program and a report is produced highlighting strengths and weaknesses.
- If the student completes the same assessment at a later date the analysis identifies areas where the student has improved.
- When a group or whole class has completed the same assessment, the analysis provides information about common strengths and weakness.

Reading Recovery assessment methods

Reading Recovery is an early literacy intervention program developed in New Zealand by Marie Clay and designed for children who have made little progress in reading after their first year at school. The program provides individually designed and delivered lessons from a specially trained teacher. Generally, children in the lowest 20 per cent achievement range enter the program and most of these students return to the mainstream and continue with normal progression. The remaining group (about 5 per cent of the program or 1 per cent of the age group) are referred for special appraisal and long-term placement (Clay & Tuck 1991). Entry to the program is based on an early literacy survey, An Observation Survey of Early Literacy Achievement (Clay 1993). This test is composed of six tasks, administered individually. It contains a concepts about print

Reading Recovery is an early intervention program

test, a letter identification test, a word list test, a dictation test for hearing and recording sounds in words, and a writing vocabulary test over a ten-minute period during which a student writes all the words he or she knows. A summary of the results is then made to provide data for placement and guidance to help with planning a student's reading recovery program.

A cornerstone of Reading Recovery assessment during the program is the daily use of the running record described above (figure 8.2). As Sale (1995) asserts, Clay's development of this observational tool—working out how to take a record of oral reading, how to analyse the behaviour it reveals, and how to best use this information—is probably her most valuable gift to teachers. Classroom teachers who are not trained in Reading Recovery may still use running records in their everyday Literacy Sessions in Guided Reading or with remedial work.

The Reading Recovery Program uses daily running records to plot the progress of each student

Grading or levelling texts

The matter of grading texts in classrooms (or 'levelling', i.e. placing them into levels of difficulty) is of primary importance as it provides suitably graded reading material for use by students as they progress and assists teachers in monitoring reading improvement. Reading material needs to be available for all students as they engage in Shared, Guided, and Independent Reading, and teachers must be proficient in selecting a range of interesting texts and placing them in ascending order of difficulty.

Texts at students' instructional level of difficulty provide the best resource for Guided Reading.

Probably the best tool for matching students to appropriate texts is the running record, since it provides a percentage accuracy score for each child on each text. This allows the teacher to calculate whether the text is too difficult for the student or whether it is at the student's instructional or independent level. Coupled with an effective text-grading system, this information allows the teacher to select other texts which are within a child's instructional level (90–95 per cent accuracy rate) and so will provide the best resource for Guided Reading.

A running record is a very effective way of establishing a student's level of difficulty on a particular text

Of the many criteria that can be applied to the grading of texts, the following ten, developed from Wille (1996), represent the most important features that appear to be significant.

CRITERIA FOR GRADING TEXTS

Subject matter: from familiar objects to unusual fantastic happenings

Storyline: from simple to complex, with elaborated episodes or events

Syntactic patterns: from simple repetitive caption phrases and oral language structures to complex sentences and literary language

Vocabulary: particularly the number of words per page that might be difficult for the reader (long words, unfamiliar words)

Density of information: with particular reference to factual texts containing specialised vocabulary

Amount of print on the page: number of words per page and consistency throughout the book

Conventions of print: script type, size of print, layout, placement of print on the page, and punctuation

Difficulty of graphophonic patterns: numbers of phonically decodable words and sight words

Illustrations: how much they directly support the meaning of the text and complexity of the illustration itself

Organisation of text: amount of variety of organisation according to nature and purpose of the text

Specific guides for grading

The above criteria have been included in guides that give specific detail for grading texts. One guide is the *Step by Step Booklist* (1994) published by the New South Wales Department of School Education. Another is the graded list of text characteristics developed as a joint project with the New South Wales Department of Education and Training, the New South Wales Catholic Education and Commission, and the Association of Independent Schools of New South Wales and published by the Commonwealth Department of Education, Training and Youth Affairs (1998). This project devised a continuum of six text levels to assist teachers of kindergarten to Year 2. The example in figure 8.3 describes the characteristics of text suitable for readers towards the end of Year 2.

Another guide was developed by Barbara Peterson (1991). This guide applies to the twenty gradations of difficulty required by the Reading Recovery program (the gradations are collapsed into five by Peterson) and can be modified for the classroom. It is a valuable and highly specific list of criteria for grading books for early readers.

Figure 8.4 Text characteristics towards the end of Year 2

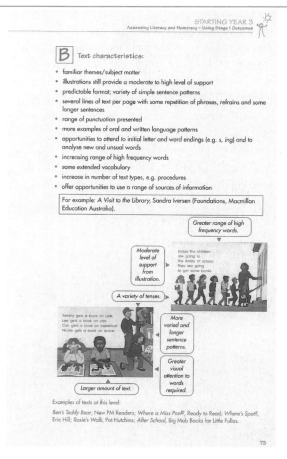

Figure 8.5 Sources of predictability in groups of levels

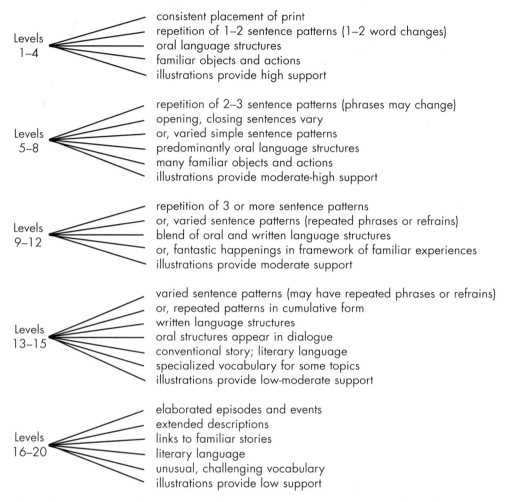

Levels 1–4
- consistent placement of print
- repetition of 1–2 sentence patterns (1–2 word changes)
- oral language structures
- familiar objects and actions
- illustrations provide high support

Levels 5–8
- repetition of 2–3 sentence patterns (phrases may change)
- opening, closing sentences vary
- or, varied simple sentence patterns
- predominantly oral language structures
- many familiar objects and actions
- illustrations provide moderate-high support

Levels 9–12
- repetition of 3 or more sentence patterns
- or, varied sentence patterns (repeated phrases or refrains)
- blend of oral and written language structures
- or, fantastic happenings in framework of familiar experiences
- illustrations provide moderate support

Levels 13–15
- varied sentence patterns (may have repeated phrases or refrains)
- or, repeated patterns in cumulative form
- written language structures
- oral structures appear in dialogue
- conventional story; literary language
- specialized vocabulary for some topics
- illustrations provide low-moderate support

Levels 16–20
- elaborated episodes and events
- extended descriptions
- links to familiar stories
- literary language
- unusual, challenging vocabulary
- illustrations provide low support

© Barbara Peterson, *Characteristics of Texts That Support Beginning Readers,* Ohio State University, 1988.

The cloze procedure

Cloze procedure involves the deletion of words from a text, leaving blank spaces in place of the words. The reader is asked to fill the spaces with words which, they think, best fit into the text. In doing this they are required to use the same cues and strategies that are used in reading. A cloze passage can indicate how effectively a student is using the cueing systems and how well they are using the strategy of prediction to work out the missing words. Psychologists call this filling in of blank spaces 'making closure'.

The cloze technique can be varied. For example, if it were applied to *Rosie's Walk* by Pat Hutchins, the book would need to be present and the words masked:

Rosie the hen went _____ *a walk*

across the _____ *around the pond*

over _____ *haycock*

past the mill _____ *the fence*

under the _____ *and got*

back in _____ *for dinner.*

Analysing answers on a cloze passage

The cloze technique can also be used to assess whether a student is using particular cue systems effectively. When used for this purpose, the student's answers on the cloze passage need to be analysed in a way similar to a running record. In other words, each incorrect substitution needs to be considered for its grammatical and semantic appropriateness. In the example below we can see how a student's incorrect answers can be analysed to provide information about the student's use of cue systems. The words in bold are incorrect answers.

On my way to school I saw a little white cat. He had a long white tail and small black eyes. **I** **ran** *over to him but he ran away* **from** *me. I thought he was* **white** *to run onto the* **road** *so I shouted for help.* **I** *girl ran out of the* **house** *house and called out to* **the** *white cat. He looked at* **her** *then turned around and* **thinks** *off down the road. The* **cat** *called and called to* **me** *but he would not* **come** *back.*

- In the fourth sentence 'white' doesn't fit grammatically with the rest of the sentence.
- In the fifth sentence 'I' and 'house' don't fit grammatically with the rest of the sentence,
- In the sixth sentence 'thinks' doesn't make sense in this text, and the verb should be in the past not the present tense.
- In the seventh sentence 'cat' and 'me' don't make sense in this text.
- So, on this text, the student is making errors in both grammatical and semantic cue systems.

► Summary

1   Effective assessment of reading is necessary in classrooms to link programming, teaching, and monitoring in the teaching–learning cycle.

2   Assessment provides information for parents, external authorities, teachers, schools, and students themselves.

3   A comprehensive assessment approach, ranging from norm-referenced tests to school-based assessment, is the most common practice in Australia.

4   There are many forms of reading assessment: standardised tests, graded lists of desirable outcomes, and authentic classroom assessment such as portfolios of students' work, informal reading inventories, running records, checklists, profiles, and cumulative assessment files.

5   'Diagnostic assessment' refers to strategies that help teachers identify the particular reading strengths and difficulties of a student.

6   Students experiencing difficulties require special assistance. Reading recovery, although not an assessment tool as such, is one specialist approach to providing that assistance.

7   Determining the level of difficulty of a text—its readability—is important. Both Wille and Peterson provide valuable practical criteria for judgment. The cloze procedure is a useful and simple 'hands-on' approach.

Critical thinking and study exercises

1   What are the benefits of assessment for the classroom teacher? How does an effective assessment program contribute to a teacher's effectiveness in meeting the learning needs of her students?

2   Who is entitled to assessment information? What uses should be made of assessment information?

3   Which assessment method or methods should be used in schools? What are the strengths and weaknesses of the various options?

4   Why are running records valuable forms of assessment for the teacher? What are their strengths and weaknesses?

5   Develop your own scenario for reading assessment procedures in a class of your choice (real or imagined). What assessment instruments would you use? How would you keep records?

6   Select a picturebook you consider to be suitable for an emergent reader of your choice (brother, sister, child next door), preferably one beginning school. Read it with the child to see if it is at his or her level in the complexity of the concepts within the text, the vocabulary, the grammar, and the book's general appeal. Write a brief report on what you found.

7   Why is the levelling of texts important? From a library, or your private collection, select five early reading books. You may include a simple book or two from a series or reading scheme. Using Peterson's grading criteria above to help you, place the books into five levels, beginning from the emergent level (the first books a child learns to read). Briefly jot down your reasons for allocating a book to a level. If there is more than one book at a level, place the books in order of difficulty. Remember that you are not looking for the fine gradations you would find in reading recovery texts.

8   Now work with a friend who has graded another set of books. Swap books and grade your friend's collection. Finally, compare the results and have a discussion about any discrepancies. This technique works well in groups who are passing a set of books around.

Further reading

Students should read the curriculum documents relating to assessment in their state or territory. They should also observe the various approaches to assessing and monitoring reading development in particular schools during practicum.

Clay, M. 1993, *Reading Recovery: A guidebook for teachers in training*, Heinemann, Auckland.

Clay, M. 2000, *Running Records for Classroom Teachers*, Heinemann, Auckland.

Derewianka, B. (ed.) 1992, *Language Assessment in Primary Classrooms*, Harcourt Brace Jovanovich, Sydney.

Web links

Curriculum Corporation: www.curriculum.edu.au
Australian Council for Educational Research: www.acer.edu.au
Primary English Teaching Association: www.peta.edu.au

THE EFFECTIVE TEACHING OF READING

9

Overview

The effective teaching of reading is a vital task. It is complex and certain procedures are paramount. They are outlined in this chapter. Shared, Guided and Independent Reading form the basis of successful literacy teaching, coupled with suitable assessment. The use of the Literacy Session is an optimal method of providing effective teaching.

There is overwhelming evidence that an effective teacher is the single most significant factor in the reading achievement of children, no matter what the children's socioeconomic status, gender, or culture. In the International Reading Association journal Reading Today of January 2006, the association's president, Richard Allington, wrote: 'study after study points to teacher expertise as the critical variable in effective literacy instruction.'

The teacher's expertise is critical in developing students' literacy

Effective teaching of reading is a complex task and requires the careful orchestration of a number of components. Effective teachers understand the needs and abilities of their students and have a repertoire of strategies to employ in meeting those needs. They design programs and employ teaching procedures in response to what they learn about their students as they watch them grow and develop as readers. There is no one foolproof teaching method or packaged program that will work for all students. As teachers learn more about the teaching of reading they, too, grow and develop in understanding and skill.

Students and teacher at work in a Literacy Session

What do effective teachers do?

Effective teachers are highly trained professionals

Effective teachers are well trained professionals. They have high expectations of their students and a belief that they will all learn to read effectively given the targeted program they have designed for them. Their classrooms are rich in print and students are encouraged to use reading and writing as part of their whole-learning program. These teachers have planned for daily, systematic reading instruction based on careful assessment of each student's needs and abilities.

Skilled teachers provide explicit and systematic instruction as part of their reading program

Literacy is taught in an integrated Literacy Session that lasts at least 90 minutes each day. These teachers have an excellent understanding of reading theory and how students learn to read, and their reading program is well balanced across the four cue systems and the four roles of the reader (see chapter 3). They provide explicit and systematic instruction across a broad range of reading skills and strategies to engage students and focus their learning on achievable, yet challenging tasks.

Their program is based on whole texts that cover a range of text-types. Texts are carefully selected and each student is matched to texts for Guided and Independent Reading. Students are flexibly grouped according to needs and abilities and instruction is differentiated for the different learning needs that students exhibit. The teacher uses the key strategies of Shared, Guided, and Independent Reading in a range of whole-class, small-group, paired, and individual groupings. Each day, the teacher reads aloud to the class, selecting from a range of high-quality children's literature. The outcomes of the particular stage of schooling are the focus of the teaching program, and teachers monitor student progress against these outcomes. There is continuous assessment of all aspects of students' literacy progress and teachers use monitoring data to adjust the program and their teaching practice. Students experiencing

Skilled teachers know how to differentiate instruction to meet the needs of each student

reading difficulties are identified promptly and effective support is provided both in the class program and in consultation with specialist support staff. A congruence is evident between the language and literacy experiences of students' home cultures and that of the school. Teachers value students' home literacy experiences and use these as starting points for the classroom program.

Effective teachers of reading accept responsibility for their own professional learning. They can articulate and reflect on their own beliefs and, as a result, classroom practice is continuously challenged and refined.

The recent report *In Teachers' Hands: Effective literacy teaching practices in the early years of schooling* clearly indicates the importance of effective teaching for the development of students' reading competence.

> The teacher research indicated the crucial importance of the individual teacher in producing effective learning outcomes. It also indicated that effective teachers have a wide repertoire of teaching practices, which they are able to skilfully employ to suit the classroom context, their purposes and the needs of their students.
>
> …
>
> The literacy research indicated that a balanced literacy curriculum that is explicitly taught and which includes word and text level knowledge and skills, particularly phonemic awareness, phonics, fluency, comprehension and oral language in addition to varied classroom practice, leads to improved literacy outcomes.

In its concluding statement the report said:

> Considered together, the findings of this study have led us to conclude that effective early literacy teaching requires teachers who
>
> ▪ can ensure high levels of student participation,
> ▪ are deeply knowledgeable about literacy learning,
> ▪ can simultaneously orchestrate a variety of classroom activities,
> ▪ can support and scaffold learners at word and text levels,
> ▪ can target and differentiate their instruction,
> ▪ and can do all this in classroom characterised by mutual respect. (Loudon et al. 2005: 5)

In this section some of the key issues in the teaching of reading, which are evident in sound practice, are addressed. They are:

• how to select and use the most effective teaching strategies to assist students to make progress as readers
• how to select texts for various components of the reading program to promote effective learning
• how to group students to enhance their learning interactions and to enable the teacher to focus instruction on students' needs and abilities
• how to manage and coordinate a daily Literacy Session to provide optimum learning experiences for all students.

IN THE CLASSROOM

Designing effective learning experiences

Effective learning experiences are those that provide explicit teaching for students. By incorporating the following ideas into their planning and teaching, teachers can provide the most effective learning experiences for their students. They can

- base new learning on what students already know and can do
- connect new learning to previous learning ('Yesterday we looked at words with two syllables, today we're going to find some words that have three syllables.')
- present new learning in small, manageable units (e.g. only one new sound–letter correspondence at a time)
- clearly explain the use and value of the new learning
- clearly explain what the new learning element is ('Today we are going to learn how to read information in a table, like this one I have here.')
- provide examples of the new learning in meaningful contexts. ('Today we're going to cook chocolate crackles for our party. We're going to read this procedure text, called a recipe, to tell us what to do.')
- explicitly model the new learning (i.e. show students exactly what to do, say or think by using a model before you ask them to try the new task for themselves)
- provide meaningful tasks to practise new learning (e.g. try to avoid the overuse of worksheets)
- cater for different students needs (i.e. differentiate instruction by providing different learning tasks to suit students' different learning needs. Have some students complete more challenging tasks)
- monitor each student's progress and provide extra support for those who need it.

Teaching strategies

Skilled teachers use a range of teaching strategies

An effective reading program uses the important teaching strategies of Shared, Guided, and Independent Reading, and Reading Aloud by the Teacher to provide students with a mix of demonstration, guidance, and opportunities to practise what they know. These key strategies are usually incorporated into a daily Literacy Session or Literacy Block—a part of the day when the teacher provides a range of whole-class, small-group, and individual learning experiences structured around selected texts.

These strategies help teachers to work with students on all parts of a balanced reading program in order to

- build an understanding of how texts relate to their contexts
- build knowledge in the cue systems: semantic, grammatical, graphological–phonological, and visual/pictorial
- build skills in reading as a code-breaker, text-participant, text-user, and text-analyst.

Shared (or Modelled) Reading

Shared/Modelled Reading shows students what effective readers do

This is called Shared Reading because it is usually done in a whole-class or shared situation. Shared Reading involves students in structured demonstrations of what effective readers know and do. During this procedure the teacher makes explicit the knowledge and skills needed to interpret a text constructed by someone else. (See also 'The emergent reader' in chapter 5.)

The students' purpose in reading will be uppermost as teacher and students make use of the text and its features to meet their needs. For example, a Year 1 class might be reading a big book of a narrative tale in which their purpose is to enjoy the story. A Year 5 class might be reading a factual text and using the table of contents and index to locate the information they need, then read and summarise it on a chart, before moving to another text to find information on the same topic for comparison. For each lesson the teacher will select a particular teaching point to become the focus of the lesson. For example, the teacher might isolate the 'sh' letter cluster and demonstrate how this is used in words in the text such as 'show', 'shape'. Or he might introduce a comprehension strategy such as inferring (see chapter 6) and demonstrate how to make inferences from the modelled reading text. At all times the teacher will have particular learning outcomes in mind for the class and for individual students as he or she models or demonstrates ways of interacting with texts that will provide students with independent learning skills.

Teachers usually work with the same text for several lessons, and on each occasion a different teaching point will be addressed. At the first reading, the teacher shares with students the thinking involved in decoding the text and in working out difficult words. He focuses on relating the text to their current knowledge, in trying to understand the literal and inferential meanings presented in the text, and in understanding how illustrations contribute to the text's meaning.

The teacher models the way effective readers read, using phrasing and expression, and pausing at difficult or unfamiliar words to demonstrate the strategies needed to work out or 'solve' the word. These might include re-reading the sentence, reading on to the end of the sentence, drawing on more than one cue system and comparing information from different cue systems against one another (e.g. 'This word looks like "house", but it doesn't make sense in this sentence'). The teacher will articulate what he is doing and will ask for student input and suggestions. On subsequent readings of the text, students will join in reading with the teacher, attempting to use the skills and strategies they have seen demonstrated. In later readings of the same text the teacher will focus on particular grammatical or phonological–graphological elements in the text as specific teaching points.

The modelled reading text is used to teach important reading skills

It is in Shared Reading that students are encouraged to think critically about the text and to question the author's purpose and point of view. Because the teacher supports them, students can access texts in Shared Reading that are beyond their Independent Reading level.

Skills in reading as a text-analyst are demonstrated during Shared Reading

Guided Reading

Guided Reading involves the teacher in working with an individual student or small group of students using a text at their instructional reading level. This is the level at which a student can read between 90 and 95 per cent of the text independently. As illustrated in chapter 5, the purpose of Guided Reading is to enable the teacher to support and guide the students as they work to read the text, to solve any words they don't know, and to focus on the text's meaning. The teacher prompts and encourages the students to recall and use the knowledge and strategies that have already been introduced in Shared Reading or previous Guided Reading sessions. Teachers also use Guided Reading to draw attention to particular features of the text such as narrative text structure or sound–letter correspondences and to provide learning experiences

Guided Reading is taken by the teacher with a small group of students with similar reading needs

Table 9.1   Shared (Modelled) Reading in action: a suggested procedure

Before the Shared Reading	■ Select an appropriate text. ■ Prepare the Shared Reading lesson. ■ Identify the teaching point you will teach with this text, e.g. the 'sh' letter cluster, the comprehension strategy of 'inferring'. ■ Prepare associated reading activities that focus on the same teaching point.
Orientation to the text	■ Introduce the text and talk about its content. ■ Discuss the cover, title, author, illustrator. ■ Activate students' topic knowledge through questioning. ■ Discuss the purpose of the text and the text-type. ■ Ask students to make predictions about the text. ■ Ask students to formulate questions they think the text might answer.
Reading the text	■ Read the text, demonstrating phrased and fluent reading. ■ Pause on each page to discuss key points, e.g. the events in a narrative, the information in a factual text. ■ Discuss how the illustrations on each page contribute to the meanings. ■ Check whether students' predictions are confirmed. ■ Check whether students' questions are answered.
Working with the text	■ Return to the text and identify an example of your teaching point. ■ Clearly explain the teaching point to students using the text. ■ Point to other examples of the teaching point or ask students to find some examples. ■ Use the board or a flipchart to further explain the teaching point and to introduce more examples.
Re-reading the text	■ Re-read the text with students participating. ■ Choose a section to model phrased and fluent reading, and ask students to practise reading in the same way. ■ Pause to identify examples of your teaching point.
After the Shared (Modelled) Reading	■ Clearly explain the activity that students are to complete, i.e. an activity which focuses on your teaching point. ■ Model how to do the activity, e.g. by doing the first example. ■ During Guided Reading ask students to find examples of the same teaching point. ■ Use this Big Book text (or a small-book version of it that is usually available) as an independent reading text for some students.

that focus on these features. (See also 'The developing reader' in chapter 5.) By supporting and guiding students as they read the new text, the teacher provides them with opportunities to practise and refine their text-processing skills and strategies. Students can later practise these skills on their own as they read independently.

In Guided Reading students work on an unfamiliar text. If the text has been carefully chosen there will be several words on each page that the student needs to work out because they will not be automatically recognised. This is where the teacher's prompts and questions help the student to draw on what she already knows in 'solving' the unknown word. The teacher will ask questions that prompt the student to think about what she knows and can see on the page that will help to work out the word. Prompts such as

In Guided Reading the student works to 'solve' the text by working out unknown words

- What would make sense here?
- Would that word sound right in this sentence?

Table 9.2   Guided Reading in action: a suggested procedure

Before the Guided Reading	■ Group students according to similar learning needs (4–5 students per group).
	■ Select an appropriate text for the group, i.e. at their instructional level.
	■ Identify the teaching point you will teach through the text, e.g. the 'sh' letter cluster, the comprehension strategy of 'inferring'.
Orientation to the text	■ Ask students to re-read a known text.
	■ Introduce the new text and talk about its content.
	■ Discuss the cover, title, author, illustrator.
	■ Activate students' topic knowledge through questioning.
	■ Discuss the purpose of the text and the text-type.
	■ Focus on any potentially difficult words and perhaps write these on the board.
Reading the text	■ Read the title page together.
	■ Have students read in turn.
	■ Prompt when a student stops at a word, e.g. What would make sense here? What letter does it start with?
	■ If a student makes an uncorrected error, return to that word and assist them to work it out.
	■ If a student loses meaning, ask them to re-read the sentence.
	■ Show students explicitly how to use strategies to work out unknown words.
	■ Pause to discuss events, characters, information, illustrations.
	■ Model phrased and fluent reading, and ask students to copy you.
Working with the text	■ Return to the text and identify an example of your teaching point.
	■ Clearly explain the teaching point to students using the text.
	■ Point to other examples of the teaching point or ask students to find some examples.
	■ Use the board or a flipchart to further explain the teaching point and to introduce more examples.
After the guided reading	■ Ask students to re-read the text in pairs.
	■ Provide activities to focus on your teaching point.
	■ Re-read today's text at the beginning of this group's next Guided Reading lesson.

- What does the word start with? Can you see any letters that you know?
- Read that part again. Get your mouth ready for the first sound.

all help to focus the reader on the cue systems and strategies that will provide her with information to solve the word.

The purpose of Guided Reading is to use each new text to teach students about the features of that text and the strategies they can employ to read it effectively. As students do this they increase their capacity to read more difficult texts and, over time, by continually moving to more difficult texts, they develop greater skill as readers.

Guided Reading provides teachers with opportunities to work with students in building their abilities to take on the four roles of the reader. As they work to solve the text, students are learning to take on the code-breaker role. Through discussion they will learn to participate in the meanings of the text (the text-participant role) such as the events in a narrative and what these reveal about the feelings and motivations of the characters or, perhaps, factors relating to environmental issues in a text such as those in *Where the Forest Meets the Sea* by Jeannie Baker. They will become text-users by using texts for specific purposes both during

In Guided Reading students learn to be code-breakers, text-participants, text-users, and text-analysts

and after Guided Reading and they will be supported through questioning to think about text-analyst issues such as who wrote this text and what its underlying messages are.

While all teaching strategies play their part in assisting students to improve as readers, Guided Reading is the strategy that focuses most closely on each reader's particular stage of development and learning needs. It is a powerful strategy for improving students' ability to process a text and is particularly effective for catering for the learning needs of students with reading difficulties. As a general rule most students should be engaged in at least one Guided Reading lesson a week. Students with reading difficulties should participate in at least three lessons a week.

Guided Reading is a powerful teaching strategy

Independent Reading

Independent Reading provides sustained, uninterrupted time when students can read to themselves to practise and consolidate the skills and knowledge they have gained in Shared and Guided Reading. Most texts for Independent Reading are easier than texts for either Shared or Guided Reading, so that the student can read at least 95 per cent of the text independently, but more challenging texts should also be available to allow for exploration.

Independent Reading enables students to spend time enjoying reading and pursuing their interests. It is significant that students who engage with Independent Reading frequently and who read a large number of varied texts make greater progress as readers than students who rarely read. The teacher's role in Independent Reading is to ensure that students have access to a wide range of quality texts from which to choose, to monitor each student's reading, and to assist in the selection of texts. An Independent Reading log is often kept by the teacher, or students themselves, to record what students have read and to provide opportunities for them to make comments. The log will often help in the selection of a new book, perhaps by the same author or on a topic of interest to the student.

In Independent Reading students can experience the best of children's literature

Table 9.3 Independent Reading in action: a suggested procedure

Preparing for Independent Reading	▪ Collect a range of interesting and appealing books, both literary and factual. ▪ Sort them into broad levels of difficulty. ▪ Display them on shelves in levels, clearly labelled. ▪ Construct a reading record sheet.
Introducing Independent Reading to the class (at the beginning of the year)	▪ Introduce students to the books, and explain the types of books available and the levels. ▪ Select one or two books, show the cover, talk about the author and read a page or two. ▪ Ask students about their favourite authors and the books they have really enjoyed. ▪ Show students how to select a book, i.e. look for topics that appeal, look for favourite authors, look at the cover, check the level of the text, read the blurb. ▪ Explain the record sheet.
During Independent Reading	▪ Allow students time to browse. ▪ Then ask them to choose two books. ▪ Provide time for students to sample the books and decide which one they want to read. ▪ Allow time for uninterrupted reading (about 15–20 minutes).
After Independent Reading	▪ Ask students to complete their record sheets. ▪ Provide opportunities for students to share information about books read. ▪ Change the selection of books frequently.

As part of Independent Reading, students can form literary circles or discussion groups that allow them to share their responses with others. Students can be asked to prepare a short presentation on their text, to give a character profile, to compare this book to one they have read previously, or to read a short extract. Other students may then have questions for the presenter that will raise interesting issues for discussion. When the teacher joins such a group he is usually a participant rather than the leader, but can nevertheless model ways of questioning and discussing that will promote student learning. (See part III for a wide range of activities that will promote students' reading and thinking about literary texts.)

Reading aloud by the teacher

Reading aloud to students from a range of quality children's literature allows teachers to

- share the best of children's literature with students, especially those who have difficulty decoding texts by themselves
- model how effective readers read
- show how to effectively phrase a sentence to enhance meaning
- show how writers construct enthralling stories using characters, plots, and settings
- provide a basis for discussion about texts and their characters, settings, themes, and events (see part III for detailed exploration of children's literature and a range of suitable class activities).

Selecting texts for the reading program

The use of whole texts is an essential component of an effective reading program, so careful selection of a range of quality texts is an extremely important part of the teacher's role. (See also 'Grading or levelling texts' in chapter 8.)

The selection of texts for each part of the reading program is an important part of a teacher's planning

Texts used in the reading program should include both print and digital text such as

- quality literary texts by recognised children's authors
- quality factual texts in a range of curriculum areas
- texts used in everyday situations such as magazines and newspapers, posters, and timetables
- texts delivered in digital formats such as DVDs and Internet sites.

SELECTING DIGITAL TEXTS FOR THE READING PROGRAM

It is important to include a range of digital texts in the reading program. These can include electronic texts such as CD-ROMs and DVDs, which can be used alongside print texts to explore their similarities and differences. Students should also have opportunities to access the Internet when they are gathering information for topics associated with curriculum areas other than English. In addition, a range of computer software programs provide experiences with literacy skills that can be of benefit to students. In particular, resources such as the Learning Federation's Learning Objects, www.thelearningfederation.edu.au, provide high-quality targeted experiences in literacy as well as other learning areas specifically designed in accordance with Australian and New Zealand curriculum requirements (see Introduction).

It is important to include a variety of texts of appropriate levels of difficulty to cater for the different learning needs of all students in the class, and care needs to be taken to match texts to the particular needs of students, especially for Guided Reading. It is also important to take account of students' cultural backgrounds and interests when selecting texts since students will be able to read texts more easily if they present ideas and situations with which children are familiar.

Texts will also provide students with access to information, ideas, and concepts beyond their current understandings. In using these texts the teacher supports students by showing them how to use the texts to find information and extend their knowledge and understanding of the world. Texts need to be selected for Shared, Guided, and Independent Reading and reading aloud by the teacher, and different criteria are needed for each purpose.

Selecting texts for Shared Reading

As stated, in Shared Reading the teacher reads an enlarged text to and with students, involving them in the process of unlocking the text's meaning. The enlarged text might be

- a Big Book, either commercially produced or made by students themselves in previous lessons
- an example of everyday text such as a poster advertising an upcoming event
- an overhead transparency or a series of overhead transparencies of suitable texts
- a text written on the chalkboard or whiteboard
- a digital text such as an Internet page.

In fact any text that can be seen by the whole class is suitable for Shared Reading provided it meets the following criteria as a text.

- The text should present a good example of an effective text, whether a factual text, a literary text, or an everyday text (which may be either factual or literary).
- Carefully chosen texts create many opportunities for interesting and extended discussions, explorations, and activities that help children learn what it means to be a reader. Part III provides a wide-ranging look at the qualities of different texts that enable students to grow as readers.
- The text should be interesting to students and give them many opportunities to enjoy and participate in its many layers of meaning. Quite often, texts produced as part of reading schemes or series do not provide the richness and variety needed to meet this criterion.
- The text should be at a level appropriate for the students in the class. Because the teacher supports students in their reading of the shared text, it is not necessary that the text be able to be read independently by all students in the class. Rather the ideas and information presented in the text and the opportunities it provides for taking on the four reader roles should be uppermost in the teacher's mind when selecting it. As the text is read and re-read over several days, students who initially found the text quite challenging will be able to access it more easily.
- The text should provide examples of the teaching points the teacher wants to present to

Shared Reading texts are enlarged examples of effective texts

students. These may include the type of text and its structure, the way it presents information or tells its story, its use of illustrations, maps, and tables or particular grammatical and phonological–graphological elements, and punctuation features. The teacher will be interested in how the text relates to the particular unit of work presently being undertaken by the class and what information or ideas will be added by this text.

- The text should provide opportunities for the teacher to demonstrate 'how to be a reader', how to use reading strategies such as predicting and self-correcting when reading, and how to take on the four reader roles.

Selecting texts for Guided Reading

In Guided Reading the reader works to 'solve' the text, bringing to bear all his knowledge and skill to work out the words he doesn't know and to construct meaning from the text. The teacher supports students as they do this, prompting and questioning to help them to draw on and integrate their semantic, grammatical, and phonological–graphological knowledge. It is important that the text for Guided Reading is at the student's instructional reading level; that is, it is easy enough for the student to read most of the words unaided so as to maintain meaning, but difficult enough to present about one word in ten that the student has to 'solve', since this is how the lesson promotes the student's learning.

Texts for Guided Reading should be at students' instructional reading level

In recent times a great deal has been said and written about the grading of texts for Guided Reading and about matching books to students. The reading recovery program has devised a system of reading text levels for the Year 1 students who are in the program. But these levels are often too finely graded to be really useful to classroom teachers and the system reaches only to about an average Year 2 level. Some schools have worked collaboratively to grade their texts and have used these grades for their Guided Reading program. Many commercial reading materials provide a statement of 'reading level' or even 'reading recovery level' on their texts.

It is important to remember that these mechanisms are only a guide to teachers. In the end it is the teacher's professional judgment about the suitability of a particular text that is the deciding factor and this is based, more than anything else, on how well the student can handle the proposed text. The level of difficulty of a text for a particular student will be influenced not only by the difficulty of the text but also by its topic (whether it is a topic familiar to the student), its use of illustrations such as maps and tables (whether the student knows how to read these), the language structures (whether the student is familiar with these), the student's interest in the topic, and how relevant the text is to the student's cultural and social background.

Selecting texts for Guided Reading, then, involves two processes:

1. Putting the class Guided Reading texts into levels or groups based on the teachers' professional judgment about what seems hard or easy and testing this over time with students.
2. Considering the needs and abilities of students and selecting texts for them that are at an appropriate level and also meet the other criteria mentioned above. This will mean the student reading the text aloud to the teacher and, if possible, the taking of a running record to ascertain the student's accuracy level on that text.

Over time, teachers will come to recognise which texts their students find particularly easy or difficult and how to gauge what will be effective texts for them. As with Shared Reading, texts for Guided Reading should be good examples of effective texts, should present students with many opportunities to enjoy and participate in their meanings, and should provide examples of the teaching points that the teacher wants to teach with that particular group of students.

Selecting texts for Independent Reading

A generous selection of high-quality independent reading texts will prompt students to read for enjoyment

In selecting texts for Independent Reading the teacher should spend some time finding out about the interests of her students and involving them in the selection of texts. It is often possible to find several texts on the same topic, and students will enjoy making comparisons between them. When particular authors become favourites with the class, or when the unit of work being studied is an author study, a selection of books by that author can be included in the Independent Reading collection. Students can be invited to include some of their own books in this collection.

The texts selected should cover the range of reading abilities in the class and should be numerous enough to provide a wide choice. Texts that have previously been used for Shared and Guided Reading are also suitable for Independent Reading since students often enjoy revisiting old favourites. The selection of Independent Reading texts should be added to frequently and changed completely every three or four months.

Grouping students

Effective teaching of reading involves the use of a range of ways of grouping students in the class. Teachers provide opportunities for students to work individually, in pairs, in small groups, and as a class. This flexibility allows teachers to

- cater for the learning needs of students with a range of abilities
- provide opportunities for students to develop self-directed learning skills

Reading with an assisting parent

- provide opportunities for students to develop collaborative learning and social interaction skills
- observe and assess students over time and in a range of situations
- use limited resources efficiently
- deliver the program in the most time-efficient manner
- work closely with individuals or groups of students on instruction targeted to their learning needs.

Grouping students in different ways enables the teacher to provide different forms of instruction to meet students' needs

Ways of grouping students are determined by the purpose of the lesson and students' ability to participate effectively. At all times teachers should ensure that all students are helped to gain the most from their learning experiences through the support, collaboration, and guidance of others, as well as being given opportunities to practise on their own and to demonstrate what they can do.

Working individually

Students work individually during such activities as Independent Reading and Independent Writing (see part II). This enables them to take responsibility for their own work and to concentrate on the details of the text they are trying to read or write. Teachers often work with individual students to assess their knowledge and skills by, for example, taking a running record of a student reading aloud or by engaging him in a writing conference. Students having difficulty with reading may need extra support from the teacher in the form of individual Guided Reading lessons.

Students take responsibility for their own work in Independent Reading

Paired reading can help students come to new understandings of texts

Working in pairs

By working in pairs, students can support each other and learn through discussion

Teachers will often ask children to work in pairs so that they can use the process of discussion to help them come to new understandings. In pair work, where one partner is helping another, both the 'learner' and the 'teacher' benefit. Children often read in pairs, helping each other with words they don't easily recognise. Pair work is also useful in reading activities where students could, for example, reassemble a cut-up story or add to a list of words that contain a particular letter cluster. Pairs can consist of students reading at approximately the same level or a more able student working with one less able.

MULTILITERACIES

It is often advisable to group students in pairs or small groups for working on mulitliteracy tasks using technologies such as computers, digital cameras, scanners and printers. This not only makes the best use of scarce digital equipment, but also enables students to share, discuss, evaluate and justify their suggestions and responses to the task they are engaged in. It is important that students take turns in using the technology, especially in the early years, since skills in operating a range of digital equipment are part of students' multiliteracy learning.

Working in small groups

Small groups can be formed in a number of ways:

- similar ability groups
- mixed ability groups
- friendship groups
- interest groups
- random groups.

Small groups can be formed with students who share particular learning needs or with students of diverse needs and abilities. Grouping together students of similar ability enables the teacher to target instruction to the needs of the group—particularly useful for Guided Reading.

Small groups are used effectively to target instruction in Guided Reading

Grouping together students with varied abilities enables students to help each other and to harness a range of viewpoints and abilities; this is especially useful in creative arts such as play-making and drama and music performance. When forming groups for Guided Reading, teachers assess the achievement of each student using an assessment device such as a running record, and place together students of similar ability. It is important, however, to monitor the progress of students in each group and to keep the membership of each group flexible. Students should be moved to another group if their performance indicates that they are progressing at a different rate from the other group members.

Small groups are used not only for Guided Reading but also for other activities during the Literacy Session where group interaction will promote student learning. The oral interaction that occurs during group work is an extremely important part of the literacy program and

Small group sharing a Big Book with the teacher

should be fostered every day. Group work enables the teacher to work closely with one group for Guided Reading while the rest of the class is profitably engaged in other literacy activities. This ensures that the teacher can work with each group, and therefore each student, over the course of a week.

Working with the whole class

There are times when working with the whole class serves an important function in the literacy program. For example, whole-class grouping allows students to participate in a shared experience such as an excursion or watching a DVD, which then becomes the basis for further discussion and learning. Whole-class grouping is useful for Shared Reading because it allows the teacher to build a common experience over several days. Teacher reading aloud is often done as a whole-class experience because participation and enjoyment does not depend on an individual student's reading ability. Whole-class groupings are also useful for the sharing of individual, pair, or group projects with the rest of the class.

Working as a whole class enables students to share experiences

The Literacy Session

Many teachers find that the most effective way to cover all the elements of a comprehensive literacy program is to organise a daily session. A daily Literacy Session enables the teacher to

The Literacy Session provides for effective teaching of reading

- provide a balanced literacy program
- focus the day's activities around whole texts
- include listening, talking, reading, and writing every day
- ensure that all students receive effective Shared, Guided, and Independent experiences in both reading and writing
- provide a range of individual, small-group, and whole-class learning experiences
- group students effectively for Guided Reading
- cater for the learning needs of the range of students in the class

- establish an effective and workable routine where students know what is expected of them and can work purposefully on tasks
- assess and monitor students' progress as part of the routine of the session
- allocate time for handwriting practice and acquisition of computer skills.

Most importantly, the Literacy Session enables the teacher to organise the flow of classroom activities so that there is enough time every day to take one or more small groups for Guided Reading while the rest of the class is purposefully engaged.

The Literacy Session or Literacy Block is being widely used in Australia. Although there are many ways of organising and carrying out such a session, certain fundamentals need to be present.

Classroom organisation

The Literacy Session enables the teacher to focus on key skills of reading and writing over an extended period

The classroom must provide a print-rich environment with, for example, wall displays, charts, word lists, labels, and samples of children's work. There must be a class library containing books of many genres in graded levels covering a range of key learning areas. There must be spaces for Shared, Guided, and Independent Reading and Writing. There must be prepared material for reading and writing activities, prepared by the teacher and/or published.

The students

Students must be familiar with the routines of the Literacy Session. They must be cooperative and share responsibility for carrying out and completing tasks. They must be familiar with assessment procedures, such as portfolios, checklists, profiles, and tests, and be ready to talk to their teacher about their work. They must be able to engage in paired reading (a stronger and a weaker reader together) and be confident to work in a group focused on a particular task.

Students working together on a literacy task

The teacher

The teacher must be able to teach flexibly and be able to move readily from task to task in the Literacy Session: from Shared to Guided Reading; from group teaching to supervision of individual students; from teaching to assessing progress. The teacher must be able to read orally with feeling and, above all, display enthusiasm about students' efforts.

Structure of a Literacy Session

An effective Literacy Session usually has the following elements.

Session introduction

This is where the teacher introduces the day's session and provides a starting point for the session to follow. During this part of the session the teacher often re-reads or revisits previous activities that link to today's activities and reviews previous skills and knowledge in order to help students make the connections that will allow them to succeed in today's activities.

Shared/Modelled Reading

This is where the teacher, for example, shares an enlarged text with the class, demonstrating what effective readers do when they read. The same text is usually used for several days. Each day the teacher engages students in reading or re-reading part or all of the text, and uses the text as a teaching focus for specific reading skills. Over a week he ensures that the reading skills dealt with will cover a balance of all four reader roles.

The Literacy Session flows from one component to the next, allowing students to build and consolidate the learning focus of the day

Reading activities

After Shared Reading students engage in a range of reading activities that allow them to practise the specific skills that have been part of the Shared Reading. They work individually or in pairs or small groups, sometimes using small versions of the enlarged text or with specially prepared task sheets or activities. Activities are designed with the particular learning needs of each student in mind (differentiated instruction), and not all students will do the tasks in the same way. It is important that the exercises or activities designed for this part of the session link to the specific focus of the day's shared text if they are to be an effective learning experience for students.

Guided Reading

During this part of the session, while the rest of the class is engaged in reading activities, the teacher works closely with a small group of four or five students who have a similar reading level. Each student has a copy of the Guided Reading text, chosen because it is at the students' instructional reading level. Therefore there will be a different text for each Guided Reading group in the class. The teacher provides specific reading instruction as students read the text one at a time, and supports each student's reading by helping him activate his knowledge and skill to 'solve' the unknown parts of the text. Today's text will be re-read as a familiar text at this group's next Guided Reading session. Over the week the teacher will expect to work in this way with all students in the class as part of a Guided Reading group.

Table 9.4 The Literacy Session at a glance

ELEMENT	PURPOSE	GROUPING	KEY FEATURES
Introduction 5–10 minutes	▪ Introduce day's activities. ▪ Provide clear focus for learning. ▪ Build on prior knowledge. ▪ Link to previous experience.	Whole class	▪ Teacher revisits previous activities and reviews skills and knowledge. ▪ Teacher makes links to today's learning. ▪ Teacher helps students access and build on their prior knowledge.
Modelled/ Shared Reading 10–15 minutes	▪ Involve students in structured demonstration of effective reading. ▪ Demonstrate specific teaching points. ▪ Allow students to join in reading in supportive situation.	Whole class	▪ Teacher demonstrates how to read a text. ▪ Teacher leads discussion about the text's meaning and features. ▪ Teacher uses the text to focus on the teaching point. ▪ Students join teacher in reading part or whole of text.
Reading activities 20 minutes	▪ Allow students to work closely with modelled text and its features. ▪ Allow students to practise skills demonstrated in Shared Reading.	Individuals or pairs	▪ Teacher structures learning experiences around the teaching point in the modelled text. ▪ Students work at own level. ▪ Teacher assists students if necessary.
Guided Reading 20–30 minutes	▪ Provide specific reading instruction at students' instructional level. ▪ Allow students to practise skills demonstrated in Shared Reading. ▪ Allow teachers to assess students' use of reading strategies.	Small group	▪ Students are grouped according to common learning needs. ▪ Students are matched to text at their instructional level. ▪ Each student reads aloud. ▪ Teacher supports each student to work out unknown words. ▪ Teacher and students discuss the text's meaning and features. ▪ Teacher uses text to focus on teaching point .
Independent Reading 10–15 minutes	▪ Provide extended opportunities for students to read independently. ▪ Allow students to practise skills and strategies introduced in Shared and Guided Reading. ▪ Enable students to access and enjoy quality literature.	Individual	▪ Teacher provides wide selection of books at students' independent reading levels. ▪ Teacher supports student to select appropriate texts. ▪ Students read independently. ▪ Students record brief information about the text read.
Guided Writing 10–15 minutes	▪ Allow students to participate in joint construction of written text. ▪ Involve students in structured demonstration of effective writing. ▪ Show students structure and features of particular text-types.	Whole class	▪ Teacher sets context and purpose for text construction. ▪ Teacher reminds students of text-type structure and features. ▪ Teacher begins writing text using '*think aloud*' strategy to involve students. ▪ Students offer suggestions and discuss possibilities. ▪ Teacher and students discuss the effectiveness of the completed text.

ELEMENT	PURPOSE	GROUPING	KEY FEATURES
Independent Writing 15–20 minutes	■ Provide opportunities for students to write independently. ■ Allow students to practise constructing a text based on the Guided Writing lesson. ■ Allow students to demonstrate creativity and an understanding of text-type structure and features.	Individual	■ Teacher sets writing task and reminds students of text structure and features. ■ Teacher provides a model or structure to assist students. ■ Students write independently. ■ Teacher assists individuals or small groups of students. ■ Students share writing. ■ NOTE: Students might take several lessons to complete one written text.
Teacher Reading Aloud 5–10 minutes	■ Allow teachers to share the best of children's literature with students. ■ Allow teachers to model effective reading. ■ Provide a shared text for discussion. ■ Allow students with reading difficulties to experience texts beyond their independent reading ability.	Whole class	■ Teacher selects text. ■ Teacher introduces book to students by e.g. linking to another book, telling about the author. ■ Teacher reads aloud, without too many pauses for discussion. ■ Teacher and students briefly discuss their responses to the text. ■ NOTE: The book may be read over several sessions as a serial.
Conclusion 5 minutes	■ Conclude the session. ■ Allow teacher to reinforce the major learning of the session. ■ Allow students to share work.	Whole class	■ Teacher recaps the day's activities. ■ Teacher invites two or three students to share their work. ■ Students' work may be displayed on classroom walls. ■ Teacher reminds students of the key points they have learnt through today's session.

Independent Reading

During this part of the session students read independently, for enjoyment and to practise the skills they have been learning. Texts for Independent Reading are usually easier for students than their Guided Reading texts, although sometimes students will want to try a 'hard' book for fun or because they are interested in the topic. The teacher ensures that there is a wide range of inviting books available for Independent Reading and that they are arranged in levels to support students' selection. Guided Reading may continue with another group while Independent Reading is in progress.

Guided Writing

In Guided Writing the teacher involves students in a joint construction of a text to demonstrate how effective writers put a text together. With the teacher or one of the students acting as scribe, teacher and students solve the problems associated with the text's construction, discussing possible alternatives and contributing ideas. The discussion centres around models of this text-type that students have previously studied.

Independent Writing

This part of the session provides opportunities for students to create their own texts, using the Guided Writing text as a model. As they write, students practise what they already know about writing and work to gain control of an increasing range of text-types. Although students write independently, they share their drafts with the teacher and each other in their efforts to create an effective text. Although Independent Writing is usually part of every day's Literacy Session, students may work on the same text for several days to bring it to publication stage.

Teacher reading

As part of each Literacy Session the teacher finds time to read aloud to students. The text chosen will be a quality example of children's literature or a factual text that relates in some way to the unit being studied. If it is a long text the teacher will read it as a serial story over several sessions. This part of the session allows students to enjoy hearing a range of texts, to listen to models of effective language use, and to experience texts that may be beyond their ability to access independently.

Session conclusion

An effective conclusion to the Literacy Session helps to focus students' attention on what they have learnt

The Literacy Session usually closes with the teacher bringing the class together to share some part of the day's activities, and perhaps to allow students to present some of their work to others. Students are encouraged to think back over the day's session and to share what they have learnt.

Although teachers often make changes to a session depending on the unit they are teaching and the particular needs of their students, it is important to remember that no matter what changes are made, the key elements of Shared, Guided, and Independent Reading and Writing should be included every day.

Planning the Literacy Session

Teachers can use the planning sheet shown in figure 9.1 to coordinate their Literacy Sessions. It is a useful guide that can be readily adapted to suit specific purposes.

Kindergarten/Prep

The Literacy Session helps to introduce students to the routines and expectations of the classroom

In the early weeks of kindergarten children are learning about the routines of the classroom and how to adapt to the new school environment. The Literacy Session plays an important role in settling a new kindergarten class into the types of classroom practices they will encounter in later months. By introducing whole-class, small-group, and individual literacy practices from the first week of kindergarten, the teacher is able to

- set up expectations for classroom behaviour within a familiar routine of enjoyable activities
- provide a link to children's literacy learning in the years before school
- gain a good understanding of what each child knows and can do, on which to build the literacy program.

Figure 9.1 The daily planner

Literacy session:
Daily planner

Week: _____   Day: _____

Session introduction

Shared Reading

Guided Reading group…	Reading activities

Guided Reading group…	Independent Reading

Guided Writing

Independent Writing

Teacher reading

Concluding the session

In the first weeks of Kindergarten the Literacy Session will run in a modified form until the class is familiar with the routines. In Week 3 or 4, after carefully observing students and their interactions with text, the teacher can begin to form Guided Reading groups. The first group will be composed of the four or five most able readers. Over the next four or five weeks the remaining Guided Reading groups will be formed one at a time. By the end of Term 1 all students will be placed in an appropriate Guided Reading group and will work with the teacher at least twice a week.

High-quality texts that appeal to students' interest form the basis of an effective Literacy Session

At the beginning of kindergarten a unit focused on 'starting school' is often a good way to begin. Children can use the shared experience of starting school as the basis of many effective listening, talking, reading, and writing experiences. There are also many books on this theme, such as *The Kinder Hat* by Morag Loh, *Timothy Goes to School* by Rosemary Wells, and *Lucy and Tom Go to School* by Shirley Hughes.

The unit extract provided here shows Day 1 of a two-week unit on starting school and is designed to be run in the early weeks of Term 1. At this stage of the year the Literacy Session will not include Guided Reading, but all other components of the Literacy Session are included.

At the beginning of the year the teacher takes the opportunity to assess the literacy achievements of each student

During the unit the teacher will carefully observe each student's interactions with text and will begin to establish an understanding of the learning outcomes each has achieved. This will allow her to develop a learning program for the class which ensures that each student engages in learning experiences to enable him to achieve the next stage of learning outcomes.

Over the two weeks of the unit, students will engage in creating and exploring text in various ways.

Year 1, Term 3

This Literacy Session takes place towards the end of the year. The classroom is an ideal place for literacy work, providing a colourful, print-rich environment with ample resources. Both the children and the teacher are well versed in the routines required for a Literacy Session to operate successfully, and parents are on hand to give assistance. Books used in this classroom have been carefully graded by the teacher, with the assistance of a specially trained reading recovery teacher.

Setting the scene

The class is sitting on the floor and the teacher has a copy of the Big Book *Bernard Was a Bikie* by Val Marshall and Bronwyn Tester (1988) on a display stand ready for Shared Reading. The class has been working on a unit called Leisure Time. The class begins by reciting the known poems 'Barbecue' by Anne Le Roy and 'Cubby-House in a Garden' by Lydia Pender. The students talk about some of the work they completed in the previous Literacy Session. They then launch into the Big Book they are going to share today.

Figure 9.2   A Kindergarten/Prep Literacy Session

Starting School: Day 1

Session introduction

Read *Timothy Goes to School* by Anthony Wells. Talk about what happens in the book and what it feels like to start school. Ask children what they liked and didn't like about the first day. Ask what they would tell a little brother or sister about starting school.

Shared Reading

Write a sentence on the board to record some of the discussion, e.g. 'We like playing at school'. Read the sentence aloud, pointing to each word. Ask children to read with you. Focus on one word, e.g. the word 'school'; ask students to read it with you. Say the word slowly and emphasise the first sound. Ask if anyone's name starts with that sound. Write the name on the board and compare the shapes of the initial letters.

Reading activities

Provide each pair of students with seven or eight captioned pictures of children doing activities at school and at home (e.g. going to bed, playing in the playground). Provide a large sheet of paper with two clearly labelled sections (at school, at home). Ask students to discuss each picture and then paste it onto the paper in the correct section. Ask them to consider what they will do with activities done both at school and home (e.g. eating lunch, putting on a raincoat). As each pair finishes they can begin Independent Reading.

Independent Reading

Ask children to choose a book from the class library and begin 'reading'. At the end of Independent Reading show students how to return their books to the shelves nearby.

Guided Writing

Tell children you are going to write about something we do at school. Discuss what you might write, e.g. 'At school we eat our lunch under the trees'. Ask children to help you write. Keep re-reading the sentence as it is built. Talk about the need for a capital letter to start and a full stop at the end. Read the sentence together when it is finished.

Independent Writing

Provide a sheet of paper for each child with the sentence beginning 'At school …' at the bottom. Ask children to draw something they like doing at school. While they work, move around the class, asking each child to tell you what their picture shows and helping them to compose a sentence and write it under the picture. Write the sentence accurately on each child's page.

Teachers' reading

Read aloud to the class *The Kinder Hat* by Morag Fraser.

Session conclusion

Ask two or three children to share their picture and writing with the class. Assist children to read their writing aloud. Collect all children's work and staple into a book. Tell children the book will go into the class library.

Big Book, *Bernard Was a Bikie*. What happened next?

Shared Reading

The teacher follows the Shared Reading sequence described above, stopping some way through the book. The question is, What happened next?—a mystery that will be solved during the next Shared Reading session.

Guided Reading

The class now breaks up into groups; some move off to reading and writing activities associated with the leisure theme; the five students of Blue Group go with the teacher to the Guided Reading section of the classroom.

While the teacher takes one group for guided reading the rest of the class is completing activities associated with the Shared Reading text

For Guided Reading with Blue Group, the teacher has chosen *Mr Gumpy's Outing* by John Burningham. This picturebook is pitched at the instructional level of the children and has been carefully graded by the teacher and his peers. Its language is sprightly and original. The book is about outdoor activities and is a very good fit for the leisure theme. The teacher follows the Guided Reading steps described above and the students are allowed to take one of the multiple copies home for further reading after the session. Every student in the group is heard by the teacher and reading progress is monitored.

A leisure-time writing display showcases the literacy efforts of all the students

Reading and writing activities

Some students complete their leisure time writing tasks and add them to the display; others place work in their portfolios; others are busy with work sheets. The main point to note is that every student is fully occupied in systematic literacy tasks.

Independent Reading and Writing

Students read material in a variety of text-types. They access the class library and move to their desks. Some engage in paired reading or work with a parent. Additional reading material, such as a Poetry Box, is available and popular with students.

Benjamin's portfolio

A portfolio entry

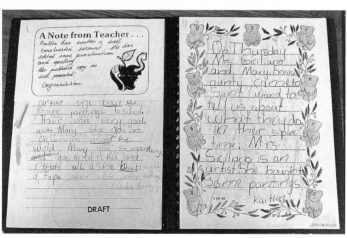

Figure 9.3 Reading record sheets

Guided Reading record

Name:.. . Group: ....

Date	Text	Book box no.	Comments	Work needed on

Independent Reading record

Name:...

Title	Author	Date finished	Comment
1.			
2.			

Browsing the classroom poetry box

Assessing student achievement

Apart from individual student portfolios that contain progressive examples of work, the teacher keeps records on each student for various aspects of literacy work. These can be readily collated and used for reporting and diagnostic assessment and teaching. The above examples are useful guides for setting up such record sheets.

Teacher reading

The teacher begins reading Bob Graham's *Greetings from Sandy Beach*. This delightful, witty book proved a big hit with the students, who could hardly wait for the next Literacy Session to hear the rest of it. The Disciples of Death bikies, who turned out to be most helpful, were particularly popular.

Conclusion

Students reported to the class about their work during the session. The teacher noted those needing further assistance. All material was returned to its proper place before children went out for recess.

▶ Summary

1 Teaching reading effectively is a complex task.
2 Effective teaching must include the three key strategies of Shared, Guided, and Independent Reading.
3 Careful selection of quality texts is a vital component of an effective reading program.
4 Students can be grouped in a variety of ways for the reading program. They can work individually, in pairs, in small groups, or with the whole class.
5 The Literacy Session is fast becoming common practice in Australia and has its equivalents around the world. It has various essential components, although it can take various forms. Two Literacy Sessions in action are provided, one in Kindergarten and another in Year 1.

Critical thinking and study exercises

1 What are the qualities of an effective teacher of reading? What would you see and hear in a classroom where the Literacy Session was operating effectively?

2 Assessment is important in the Literacy Session. How would a teacher successfully monitor each student's progress over a period of time? Consider some of the tools outlined in chapter 8.

3 Computer skills are becoming increasingly important in literacy development. Consider how the computer might be successfully incorporated into the Literacy Session.

4 The Literacy Session includes three types of strategies: Shared, Guided, and Independent. How does the role of the teacher change in employing these strategies? What role do students take when teachers employ these strategies?

5 In the Literacy Session the teacher works to help students take on the four reader roles of code-breaker, text-participant, text-user, and text-analyst. What activities could be used to help them do this? What questions can teachers ask to prompt students to take on each role?

6 Develop what you consider a suitable Literacy Session for Year 1 or 2. Make sure that you have included the basic and essential components as shown above.

7 What would be some valuable sources of reading material for students in a Literacy Session? Consider the class collection of books and of samples of print around the walls. What else?

Further reading

Students should read the various approaches to the Literacy Block or Literacy Session advocated by their state or territory documents. As noted in this chapter, such practices vary considerably but all stress a dedicated period to be set aside for literacy learning in the school curriculum. Observation should be made of schools that operate or are developing a literacy session in their programs.

Web links

Department of Education and Training (DET): www.nsw.det.gov.au
Primary English Teaching Association: www.peta.edu.au
Australian Council for Educational Research: www.acer.edu.au
International Reading Association: www.reading.org

Writing

L. LJUNGDAHL AND P. MARCH

....

Overview

Writing is an act of communication and an expression of culture. From hieroglyphics to email, people have recorded ideas, information, thoughts and feelings in a more permanent form than the speaking mode. Writing involves making visual marks on paper, other surfaces, or through the semiotics of the new electronic media. It is in fact the other side of the reading coin and is also very closely linked with speaking and listening. We can communicate with each other through the medium of writing, whether it be simply to jot down some items to remember to buy at the supermarket or to express our innermost feelings about an issue. Writing has many diverse social purposes and so can take on many different forms. Children learn most effectively when writing is used for real purposes—to inform, to entertain, to persuade, to clarify thinking. Above all, children need to regard writing as an exciting activity that is both functional and an important part of the learning process.

Chapter 10 examines the nature and role of writing in our society and presents an overview of the development of writing as a semiotic system through the ages. Chapter 11 focuses on the importance of writing as a learning tool, its place in the classroom, its power in the learning and thinking processes, its imaginative potential, and its place in the artistic process. It also discusses the way different text-types are used for different writing purposes in our society.

Chapter 12 explores the way writing develops throughout the grades and looks at writing as being a life-long process.

Chapters 13 to 16 focus on the skills of grammar, punctuation, spelling and handwriting as having important places in the writing process. They are a means to an end and must be seen in the context of the whole writing process as essential tools in the communication of meaning.

Chapter 13 emphasises the importance of grammatical knowledge in a wide range of social contexts. The use of both traditional and functional grammars is advocated to assist students to become successful writers, readers and speakers. Self-study quizzes on the Internet can help students at all grade levels.

Chapter 14 discusses the way punctuation helps to clarify meaning in writing and may be used for special or humorous effect. Punctuation marks are not just about when to make a pause for breath. Email communications and text messaging have their own kinds of 'punctuation', accepted as appropriate by users.

Chapter 15 outlines the different stages of spelling development and those multiple strategies that help students become better spellers, focussing on phonological, visual, morphemic and etymological knowledge. Students benefit from phonics instruction, particularly in the early years of learning, as well as wide reading of language and literature in many contexts.

Chapter 16 stresses that handwriting is not just a physical activity but involves the memorisation of letters and words. Students who handwrite or type with confidence (by quickly retrieving words from their memory bank), are likely to want to write more and can thus focus more easily on the quality of their ideas. Legible handwriting visually reinforces the memory for word patterns that can help in speaking, spelling and writing more effectively.

Chapter 17 explores the many ways of assessing writing, exploring assessment, evaluation and reporting practices as part of the teaching and learning cycle. Assessment to aid the learning process should be multifaceted and can be carried out by teachers, by peers or, importantly, by the students themselves. Portfolio assessment is discussed at length, with practical advice on the planning and design of language portfolios. There is a balance between theory and practice throughout the chapters, highlighting the important idea that the process of writing is part of the larger picture of literacy as a whole.

Chapter 18 discusses how information and communication technologies (ICT) have the potential for expanding the repertoire of literacy practices. Using new technologies such as the Internet can enrich teaching and writing but also change the notion of what writing is. Blogging, book raps, emoticons, and netiquette are now words in popular use from the world of computing. Multimodal texts and multimedia creations may change the linear concept of writing. While using ICT has many benefits such as accessing material and editing capabilities, the challenge for the teacher and student is to use these technologies in liberating, productive, and creative ways.

Chapter 19 has useful suggestions as to how writing can be managed and taught within the classroom. Different approaches to the teaching of writing are discussed and a functional approach is recommended. Of special importance is a detailed analysis of the nexus between talking, listening, and writing.

Of special interest in each chapter are very practical classroom suggestions and activities, together with information and ideas for teaching writing in the multiliteracy and digital age.

THE ROLE OF WRITING

Overview

Writing is a phenomenon invented by humans to help in the communication process—it has become, indeed, a social and cultural practice in most societies today. Children need writing skills in a literate society. There is a close relationship between speech and writing, each reinforcing the other in the process of language development in children.

What is writing?

Written language is organised differently from spoken language, and the world as seen in writing is different from the world as heard in speech. For Halliday & Mathiessen (2004: 7) this is a positive feature as the student's learning is reinforced by 'the functional complementarity between speech and writing'. This suggests two mutually reinforcing pictures of the world, both of which are vitally important in the learning process. Halliday & Mathiessen also see them as different ways of meaning embodied in a common system we call language.

Speech and writing are functionally complementary

Writing in fact evolved not to duplicate the functions of spoken language but to carry out new functions that arose in advancing cultures. One consequence was that writing brought language into consciousness in a new way. Learning to read and write makes it possible for children to reflect on language in the process of their learning.

Language is integral to culture and cultural process:

Some ideas/forms of language seem to exist in one culture and not in another. Language and culture are very closely interwoven; social structures and linguistic form are intimately intermeshed. This is so across larger cultures, much as it is the case in the social and cultural diversity within one society. (Kress 1988: ii)

Lankshear takes these ideas further and sees people as capable of making sense and meaning out of their experiences because they 'learn to do so through sociocultural processes of socialisation and education which initiate them into, or apprentice them to, what have variously been called "forms of life", "domains of social practice", or "discourses"' (1996: 19). Like Halliday, Mathiessen, and Kress, Lankshear sees language as central to education because it is both a necessary condition for cultural process and an outcome of that process. It has the ability to empower or disempower children at school, depending on their ability to access the many forms of texts used by our culture.

The power of language

A social-functional approach to language focuses on the power language can exert in children's lives. Because writing is a social and cultural practice, children must be given access to a wide range of discourses and practices so that they can participate fully in the society in which they live. They need an understanding of writing as a social construct, and practice in using language so that they can express themselves with confidence.

> Competence in English will enable students to learn about the role of language in their own lives, and in their own and other cultures. They will then be able to communicate their thoughts and feelings, to participate in society, to make informed decisions about personal and social issues, to analyse information and viewpoints, to use their imaginations and to think about the influence of culture on the meanings made with language. (Board of Studies NSW 1998a: 6)

It is interesting to note that although there are approximately 9000 languages in the world, only 300 of them are written. Languages such as Arabic, Chinese, English, French, German, Hindustani, Italian, Japanese, Portuguese, Russian, and Spanish all have strong written traditions. Historically, while both written and oral forms of a language pass on the knowledge and traditions of a society, the written form is a more 'permanent' record, not reliant on the presence of someone who has memorised the information. English has emerged as an important *lingua franca* among speakers of other languages partly because of its written heritage, partly because of US dominance of the computer hardware and software industries.

The evolution of language

How does a written language evolve? For the cave dwellers who produced the earliest known forms of written language in the shape of painted pictures on their cave walls, it seems that these pictures served as a mnemonic device to help in the recall of stories. The pictures apparently served this purpose very well, but problems arose when people wanted to travel. Hence the need for more portable mnemonic devices. For example, in the Inca empire, some used a *quipu* (pronounced 'key-poo') to help them remember tribal stories and to pass on information such as the number of livestock. The *quipu* was a cord with a series of coloured strings and knots that could be worn as a necklace. Different-coloured strings, different positions, and knot sizes all had meaning for the storyteller or recorder. The knots (using the decimal system) could record crop information or population counts. Recent research (*SMH*, 13–14 August 2005: 23) from Harvard University may have the key to unlocking the code of some of these knots. North American Indians used a *wampum* belt in much the same way—different-coloured shells were shaped into beads and woven into a sequence to tell a story or record an event. In many cases the colours represented different ideas: red was for war or anger; black was death or misfortune; white was peace, health, and riches; yellow was gold or tribute; purple was grief or sympathy. The number of beads used, their colour, and their order would help the teller remember the story or information.

Quipu

Wampum belt

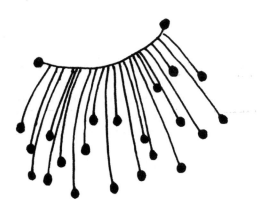

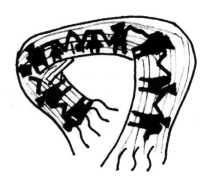

Drums were another portable mnemonic device. In fact most memorisation techniques are based on sound or vision. Hearing a sound such as a drumbeat or seeing a coloured bead can help the memory. There are some memorisation techniques that do make pictures that others can 'read'. The pictures may not tell the whole story but they give clues that even a stranger can understand. The Sioux Indians of North Dakota, for instance, made this kind of mnemonic device, called 'Lone Dog's Winter Count', a chronicle of seventy-one winters starting from the year 1800. A symbol or picture of the most important event of each winter was drawn on a buffalo hide. Even a person not familiar with the Dakota tribe can guess at many of the events represented and follow their sequence. This is a great step forward in the art of writing—for a stranger to be able to understand when you are not there to say it. *Writing does what speech cannot*: it goes beyond the barriers of time and space.

Writing has undergone many transitional stages, one of which is the pictogram stage, where pictures represent objects. Many different cultures have used pictograms. Some are easy to understand while others are unrecognisable until you know the code. Some languages, such as Chinese, use written or pictorial symbols intended to represent a whole word.

These symbols are called **logograms** or logographs (i.e. symbols representing words or phrases). Other forms are Egyptian hieroglyphs and early cuneiform writing systems such as that of the Sumerians. However, no known writing system is totally logographic; all such systems contain both logograms and symbols representing particular sounds or syllables. The ideogram is similar to the logogram and is a written or pictorial symbol intended to represent an idea or concept.

Chinese symbols

他们正在做什么

Today we often use pictures instead of words to convey messages. International symbols are used at airports and train stations to help travellers find their way around, no matter what language they speak. Pictures also feature on some maps where writing might not fit or be as appropriate.

The mythology and symbolism of Aboriginal cultures in Australia were often expressed in rock art. Thousands of 'galleries' survive across the continent with millions of individual designs. The art holds a key to understanding the origins of the regional variations that characterised Aboriginal societies. 'Aboriginal worldview was a spiritual one and many values were expressed by the scars on their bodies … and the total array of their decorative art' (Mulvaney 1987: 112). Much of the surviving rock art can throw light on what life might have been like many thousands of years ago.

MULTILITERACIES

Students in the current age not only have to master traditional literacy material in the form of books, but a burgeoning technology has provided a very rich source of other reading matter. Media such as television, the Internet, and computer games all rely on a knowledge of symbols representing language. Signs, symbols, and icons communicate messages without a printed word. The logo of a television station, a shopping trolley symbol on the World Wide Web, an icon representing a folder in word-processing software, the image of Super Mario, road traffic signs, and community symbols—these are designed to be easily recognised by the target audience. Language is conveyed through signs and symbols.

Another set of symbols

Semiotics is the study of systems of signs or symbols and how they have evolved. It comes from the same Greek word conveying 'sign' or 'meaning', as in 'semantics' and 'semaphore'. Both mathematicians and musicians write texts that employ sign systems.

Origin of the alphabet

The English alphabet developed gradually over thousands of years. Most civilisations start with pictograms, then progress to ideograms and phonograms, which become their written language. Some cultures, however, have bypassed the pictogram and ideogram stages and gone straight to a 'syllabary'.

A **syllabary** is a list of the set of written symbols, each of which represents a syllable (i.e. an element of speech) of the written language. This happens when someone who knows about the idea of writing meets a group of people who do not have a written language. For instance, a syllabary was invented for the Cree Indians of North America by James Evans. The Cree writing system that he invented to do this used fewer than fifty signs, so it was very easy to learn and their knowledge of writing spread very quickly.

The letters we use today do not look like pictures any more, but they were developed from pictures used by writers who lived in the Middle East thousands of years ago. For example, the shape of the letter 'A' comes from the Phoenicians, who lived in the Middle East about 3000 years ago. The Phoenicians had a letter shape called aleph. When letters were pictures, aleph meant ox. It was drawn like a picture of an oxhead: ◁ . The Phoenicians were great sailors and traders and when they started trading with the Greek people, the Greeks adopted the basic Phoenician letter shapes. ◁ in Phoenician became △ or ◁ and finally A in Greek. The Greek letter is called alpha (from aleph), which in Greek means the beginning—the beginning of the alphabet.

Eventually the Greeks were conquered by the Romans, who changed the alphabet to suit the sounds in their Latin language, and this actually became our alphabet, a system in which the sounds in our language are represented by written symbols.

The Romans conquered most of the Mediterranean region and some of Europe, including Britain, over many years about 2000 years ago. They consequently taught their subjects the new alphabet, carving it in stone on buildings, archways, stairways, statues, and signs. The Roman alphabet had at first only twenty-one letters, ABCDEFGHIKLMNOPQRSTVX, later adopting

The evolution of the letter 'D' illustrates the adaptation of symbols

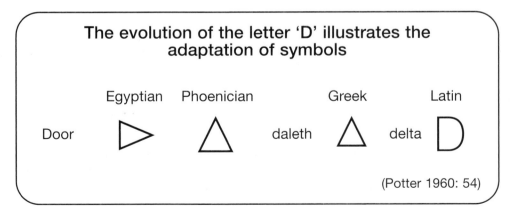

The evolution of the letter 'D' illustrates the adaptation of symbols

Door   Egyptian   Phoenician   daleth   Greek   delta   Latin

(Potter 1960: 54)

YZ for spelling foreign names. Early Roman writing was always in capital letters and only with the use of a cursive hand did the shape of our modern *u* develop from the earlier *V*. Roman *V*, when a consonant, was pronounced as modern English *w* as in *wall*, and when a vowel, could be long as in modern English *rude*, or short as in modern English *put*. Our letter *w*, originally written *uu* as the name implies, is a representation of the Roman consonant, and was first written as *w* by Norman scribes.

The twenty-six letters of English are used throughout the world today. The world's longest alphabet, Cambodian, has seventy-four letters and the shortest is 'Rotokas', from the Easter Islands, which has only eleven letters. The functions and uses of literacy vary greatly across literate cultures and historical periods, and in this sense reading and writing are not 'natural'. There are still cultures that operate without writing systems at all, and children, left to their own devices, will not 'necessarily organically or spontaneously develop or "invent" reading and writing' (Luke 1993: 26). But if children grow up in a literate culture, they will encounter, use, observe, and imitate functions and uses of literacy in everyday life.

▶ LITERACY IN THE DIGITAL AGE

One question needs to be asked: why use technology for writing?

Technology for technology's sake may not improve students' writing. However, if the positive features of the technology are capitalised upon, they may enhance writing and even make certain stages of the writing process easier, more interesting, and ultimately more satisfying. The end result may even be better!

Some of the positive features of using technology to write are being able to edit a draft easily; having access to pictorial material and being able to intertext; being able to work on a large screen, making collaborative work easier and reinforcing the social nature of learning; and retrieving and organising information, which can be done faster and more easily. The piece of writing is the end product, not the technology, but if this piece can be enhanced and improved using technology such as computers then the technology has been used judiciously.

See chapter 18 on ICT for more ideas on useful classroom practice.

In our contemporary society, literacy skills are increasingly important because they enable people to interact and satisfy their needs. English is an important language internationally because it is used by large English-speaking populations in the United Kingdom, the USA, and Canada, but also because it is used in other countries for international commerce and in communicating scientific knowledge. The spread of computer literacy may sweep English to increased popularity, although developments in voice-activated technology may change this. Even though many people do not use the written format to gain information, knowledge of writing is still a prerequisite to full participation in society. Writing is an integral part of our culture and it is generally the school's task to teach and develop it.

Literacy skills are increasingly important in contemporary society

IN THE CLASSROOM

Mrs Docherty is introducing her Grade One students to the computer and is showing the class some of the different symbols on the screen and demonstrating what some of these icons are for. The tool bar icons, in particular, can be a help when the students want to draw on the screen, cut things out and insert others, colour different parts of the text for highlighting purposes, insert bullet points and so on.

Mrs Docherty allows her students to play around with different symbols so that they can become familiar with them and able to use them appropriately when it comes to composing text and publishing their writing using word processing skills.

Mr Badgery's Year 5 students, however, are skilled at word processing and finding their way around the screen using the various icons, so much so that they are able to insert diagrams and pictures when appropriate and also present information in table or pictorial formats—this comes in very handy when doing research for HSIE and needing to present material in creative and eye-catching ways.

Writing has certainly become an integral part of the digital age in the classroom.

▶ Summary

1   Writing is a social and cultural practice. ✸

2   Children must be given access to a wide range of discourses and practices so they can participate fully in the society in which they live. They need an understanding of writing as a social construct and practice in using language so they can express themselves with confidence.

3   Students must be given access to different technologies because these can assist and enhance the writing process.

4   Written language has evolved gradually over thousands of years, the necessity for portability growing with the need to trade, communicate, and learn from others.

5   The English alphabet has its earliest origins in pictograms. It is the school's role to teach children a knowledge of writing (an alphabet system) and symbols and icons as a prerequisite to full participation in our culture.

Critical thinking and study exercises

1   Discuss the kinds of writing 'events' or experiences with print that children in our society are likely to have had before they come to school. Consider the diverse experiences that children from different social and cultural backgrounds might encounter, e.g. Aborigines or Torres Strait Islanders, immigrants, children from the city or from the country.

2   Explore ways of capitalising on the experiences of children whose first language is not English. For example, ask them to talk about their country of origin in regard to language, certain customs, different sporting activities, dress, and foods that may be different from those they are currently experiencing. Devise projects that will involve the class in learning about the writing of other cultures.

3   What are your experiences of writing in a typical day? In a small group, brainstorm and list the many times throughout the day that you are likely to encounter writing. Children may use a variety of technologies, but forms of writing can be found when accessing the telephone, television, notes between friends, textbooks, books, films, computers, even when reading the time on a clock.

Further reading

Czerniewska, P. 1992, *Learning About Writing*, Blackwell, Oxford.

Darder, A. 1991, *Culture and Power in the Classroom: A critical foundation for bicultural education*, Bergin & Garvey, New York.

Gee, P. 1996, *Social Linguistics and Literacies: Ideology in discourses*, 2nd edn, Falmer Press, London.

Heffernan, L. 2004, *Critical Literacy and Writer's Workshop: Bringing purpose and passion to student writing*, IRA, Newark, Del.

Johnson, P. 1995, *Children Making Books*, Reading and Language Information Centre, University of Reading.

Karchmer, R. A., M. H. Mallette, J. Kara-Soteriou, D. J., Leu Jr (eds) 2005, *Innovative Approaches to Literacy Education: Using the Internet to support new literacies*, IRA, Newark, Del.

Knobel, M. 1998, *Everyday Literacies: Students, discourses, and social practices*, Peter Lang, New York.

Kress, G. 1997, *Before Writing: Rethinking the paths to literacy*, Routledge, London.

Luke, A. 1993, 'The social construction of literacy in the primary school'. In L. Unsworth (ed.) *Literacy Learning and Teaching: Language as social practice in the primary school*, Macmillan, Melbourne, pp. 3–53.

Wepner, S. B., W. J. Valmont & R. Thurlow (eds) 2000, *Linking Literacy and Technology: A guide for K–8 classrooms*, IRA, Newark, Del.

Web links

International Reading Association: www.reading.org
Curriculum Council of Western Australia: www.curriculum.wa.edu.au

THE IMPORTANCE OF WRITING IN OUR SOCIETY

Overview

In spite of modern technology, writing still has a very important place in our society. In fact the technology can enhance and even make the acts of writing and editing easier. Many people find that writing is an excellent way of clarifying ideas, and thus it becomes a valuable tool in the learning process.

Writing as a collector of ideas

The philosopher Karl Popper wrote in his autobiography that learning to read and write are 'of course the major events in one's intellectual development … the three R's … are, I think, the only essentials a child has to be taught … Everything else is atmosphere, and learning through reading and thinking' (1976: 12).

By 'atmosphere' Popper means the rest of the curriculum with its many and varied subjects, all of which are dependent in some ways on learning through reading, writing, and thinking.

We learn by doing: through action, experimentation, and practice. Similar views are put forward by the Russian educator Vygotsky, who states: 'writing has occupied too narrow a place in school practice as compared to the enormous role that it plays in children's cultural development. The teaching of writing has been conceived in narrowly practical terms' (1978: 105).

Writing is at the heart of our intellectual endeavours

While the surface features of writing (spelling, handwriting, keyboarding, grammatical correctness, punctuation) are important *means* to the end product, it is that final product, that collection of clarified ideas, that is at the heart of our intellectual endeavours.

Writing, however, is not merely a tool for learning. This view undervalues what writing is and does. Writing is (or can be) learning itself: it is the protracted synthesis or coming together of our human thinking and language competence, handling a range of problems that cannot be satisfactorily managed by mental reflection or talking.

Writing is the protracted synthesis of human thinking and language competence

The excitement of this excursion for a Year 3 student is abundantly evident in her written response to an outing.

Excursion to Botany Bay

On Monday 25th 1997 3J and 3M went to Botany Bay. I left home at 7.50. I was very excited. Mr Brownlow talked to us about our manners. I couldn't keep quiet. I was so excited. We went on Baxter's coach. I sat with Bethany. We had the best parents with us. There was Mrs Johns, Mrs Masterton, Mrs Kable, Mrs Holder and Mr Thoms. It took an hour and a quarter. We went to the La Perouse Museum. It was very windy. The guides were David, Steven and Siobhan. I had David. He told us the museum used to be an old cable station. They used morse code in World War 2. Then it was used as Nurses' quarters, then used by the Salvation Army, and now it is used as the La Perouse museum. La Perouse came from the middle class. He was in love with a girl in the middle class too, but his father wanted her to be someone from the upper class. So it took ten years for his father to say yes to their marriage. La Perouse was a captain at 20 years of age. He was kind during the war with the British, he left the supply store. Many men had scurvy. They got rashes, lost hair, their teeth fell out, and black rings around their eyes. A priest died in Australia. The Aborigines kept on throwing the plaque away. La Perouse vanished in the Solomon Islands. The natives were wearing French jewellery. They found the cannon and the anchor. La Perouse's men built a raft and sailed away and vanished.

Elouisa

In retrospect and through a personal and factual recount text-type, Elouisa has been able to convey the mood of this learning experience and reinforced the knowledge she gained through the medium of writing. Elouisa's account of the history of the La Perouse Museum has given the reader a good insight into what she has gained from the excursion and also those aspects of the excursion that particularly interested her and formed part of the learning. Through writing, she has been able to clarify, order, sort, and express ideas from an occasion that was obviously worth recalling and thinking about. Elouisa is still learning to control material to present a more organised structure, but this will develop as she becomes more familiar with different text-types and their purposes.

MULTILITERACIES

Writing, then, is a great collector of ideas. In fact it has been said (Walshe et al. 1986: 164) that the chief impulse that led to the invention of writing was the need to collect and store information. This complements its value as a means of communicating from a distance. Writing, whether it be through handwriting or computerised word-processing, can collect and store ideas that arise from reflection and talk. We can then access this stored information through reading obtained from various sources such as libraries and the Internet. Since it is possible

Writing is a great collector of ideas

to store great amounts of information on a compact disk, some children may access encyclopaedias through the compact disk form rather than the hard-print version. Students need to be multiliterate in today's classroom in order to be able to utilise the many sources of information at their disposal. Louisa is able to recall her experiences at any time because she has used the written mode to record them for posterity. By writing down these experiences she will more likely remember the knowledge she gained and be able to recall it at a later date (Wray & Medwell 1998: 6–7).

Students like Elouisa can use writing about an event such as an excursion to sift out the essential from the nonessential information and develop ideas that have an impact. Obviously Elouisa was affected by quite diverse pieces of information: on the one hand the young French captain, La Perouse, and the problems he had with marrying out of his class, and on the other hand the problem with scurvy on the voyage.

Many of us tell stories of our life's experiences through writing—stories that would otherwise disappear through the oral mode. When the writer and wonderful storyteller Sally Morgan was

We write to tell our stories

asked about the beginnings of her interest in writing, Morgan replied: 'I did not have a natural interest, but as a child I loved to read. I think it actually started by what had happened to my family. I had to tell my family's story, that's what gave me the drive. Otherwise I would not have taken writing up, as it was never an ambition of mine.' Writing, then, becomes a more permanent record of the oral story.

A major advantage of writing is that it is a wonderful clarifier of thinking. A writer takes the myriad ideas in the mind, orders them, and puts the relevant ones down on paper. In this way it objectifies thought so that we can peruse it, modify it, enrich it, refine it—in general, *revise*

Good writers are good thinkers

ideas continually so that they become the best thoughts we are capable of. Thus the invention of writing introduced into human culture a huge potential for learning through its ability to collect and clarify ideas.

IN THE CLASSROOM

Mr Stevenson's Year 5 class goes on frequent excursions which are used as motivations for the students to write. The teacher builds up the students' field knowledge using the excursion strategy. When the class returns to the classroom Mr Stevenson arranges several large pieces of white butcher's paper across the chalkboard. As the class engages in active talk to review the excursion just undertaken, he records the information and impressions in note form on the paper. Later, the students use these recollections, together with their own field notes, to present a clear picture of what was learned from the excursion. Sometimes this is done in small groups, while at other times students are given freedom to present the information as individuals. Both of these strategies require students to

■   make choices
■   sort out the main ideas from the secondary ones
■   clarify their thinking through the written word
■   experiment with presenting information and impressions in different ways, including the use of digital media.

The classroom has students' work displayed on walls, on movable screens, on mobiles strung across the room, and also has 'corners of interest' which focus on displays resulting from excursions.

This Year 5 classroom considers talking and listening to be integral to the writing process. Whether it be individual or group work, students are encouraged to discuss, share and explore ideas through talk before, during, and after any writing takes place.

Mr Stevenson believes that students write best when they have something to write about, so taking the students out of the classroom gives them an invaluable stimulus for writing. These students are often allowed to respond in a text-type of their own choice. This means that final writing products are varied: information reports, explanations, poetry, recounts, and so on. Students are carefully monitored to ensure that over a period of time they have responded using a variety of text-types. Writing has become an integral part of this class's daily agenda.

When children write, they learn to be selective with their information, their choices reflecting their way of thinking and their personality. Children will also often put thoughts into writing that they will never say out loud. In this way writing becomes an important communication channel for the child.

▶ WRITING IN THE DIGITAL AGE

A lot of the writing in workplace situations is done or accessed by technology.

- Tickets for trains and buses are often accessed through machines.
- Ordering of goods is mainly done through the computer.
- Receipts are generated by computer technology.
- Record-keeping or financial statements and reporting is done through computers.
- Information for availability of products is accessed through the computer.
- Workplace presentations are done using PowerPoint technology.
- Business letters and bills are generated by computer technology.

Being able to access this technology is often a prerequisite to the workplace. Accordingly, students need keyboard skills and need to be familiar with the Internet and other sites where information is stored. Many students, in fact, are not frightened of the digital age because they are familiar with computers and can easily use them for games and surfing the Internet.

Learning through writing

When the child writes, many kinds of learning are taking place.

Physical considerations

These are the elemental aids to thinking that cluster around the physical act of writing, especially four activities that promote concentration:

- handling—the physical manipulation of pen or pencil on a page; the computer keyboard and use of the mouse
- depicting—handwriting, spelling, punctuation
- scrutinising—the constant reading back before writing on
- restating—the so-called 'shaping at the point of utterance', which is really our earliest form of editing, the editing of inner speech. (Walshe et al. 1986: 165)

Freedom and time lead to creativity

The act of writing actually frees the writer from social distractions and allows time to rethink and choose thoughts and words carefully. For the child in the classroom, however, this can happen only if time and opportunity are given to write without undue constraint and to experiment with words, phrases, sentences, and texts so that writing and reading become natural and integral to classroom activity. Peer sharing of writing develops over time and is a very rich outcome of a supportive atmosphere.

Quality process

A sensitive teacher can lift the quality of thinking to higher levels during a writing activity by emphasising quality preparation and, once a draft is achieved, the limitless potential for pondering, cutting, extending, putting aside, returning, revising again, and so on until it is 'right'. Accordingly, writing can produce a deeper kind of thinking, but this can be achieved only if children are encouraged and challenged to revisit an initial draft with a view to modifying it. Many teachers find that students will more readily engage in a revision process if they can access computers and word-processing programs.

Word-processing can often stimulate the student to write

Students like manipulating the icons of 'cut', 'paste', and 'copy' on these programs. The classroom should not become a forum for repetitive, nonchallenging, mundane writing.

When readers write

Writing can be used as a tool to enhance readers' learning about texts. Students can use writing to engage in an understanding of literacy processes, in meaningful, contextualised comprehension strategy use, and in extended and sustained opportunities to develop thoughts, knowledge, and positions (Raphael & Boyd 1997: 69; Clay 1998: 131ff.). Wide readers import language and ideas from their reading into their writing. Reading expands their range of writing practices.

Writing as a creative process

Writing is a creative process. Table 11.1 compares some major models that have contributed over the centuries to the humanities, sciences, and technologies. The four processes parallel one another closely and are part of a 'creative process'. As cognitive theory cannot easily differentiate between thinking and learning, or learning and problem-solving, or problem-solving and scientific inquiry, all four processes can be viewed as learning behaviours.

Table 11.1   Learning at its best

	Problem	*Investigate*	*Get Insights*	*Express*	*Refine*	*Announcement*	*Reaction*
Artistic process	Experience Feel challenged Decide on project	Absorption Engagement Study/research 'Imagining'	Illumination Inspiration or revelation/ 'flash'	Drafting e.g. in painting, preliminary sketching or 'roughing'	Developing Working out Crafting 'Finishing'	Communication Show to intimates Exhibit widely	Response Appreciation Criticism Evaluation
Scientific process	Problem Define as question Plan the inquiry	Observation Exploratory stratagems Data collection	Illumination e.g. methodical generalisation; or inspiration	Hypothesis Draft precisely	Experiment/test Verification or falsification Final writing	Publication Perhaps first to associates, then more widely	Response Acceptance or criticism
Problem-solving process	Problem/puzzle Define as question Plan the inquiry	Investigation Collect data Review alternatives Think laterally	Illumination 'Ah-ha' insight(s)	Formulation of best solution	Checking Error elimination Critical review	Report Demonstration Performance	Response Appreciation Criticism Evaluation
Writing process	Experience Decide to write Define writing-aim Early broad plan	Pre-writing Idea-recollection Research Brainstorming	Illumination 'See a pattern' 'Limit the subject' 'Get a lead'	Drafting Plan, or further brainstorming; then first draft	Revision Self-editing Redrafting Proofreading	Publication Show to another Read to others Circulate widely	Response Appreciation Criticism Evaluation

Writing offers *learning* power

A common sequence of thought and action runs through them. In particular, writing offers its *thinking* or *learning* power for use in any classroom learning and is a powerful tool across the subject areas.

Writing is a creative process that is truly integrated to learning

Writing, then, is more than simply a tool, markings on a page, or just a tedious service skill for writing down ideas about a subject. It is an 'offspring of the creative process', a 'learning behaviour', a 'sequence of thought and action'. Writing is truly integral to learning.

Tables like this one seldom show the full picture and this one is no exception. The table is almost exclusively concerned with verbal thinking or learning—it omits reference to feeling and emotional influences and it does not treat the nonlinguistic 'intelligences' such as the six analysed by Howard Gardner in *Frames of Mind* (1983): the logico-mathematical, spatial, musical, body-kinaesthetic, intrapersonal, and interpersonal intelligences.

Feelings and emotions are very important

Feeling and emotional influences are very important in the writing process because it is these that can be a crucial driving force behind a piece of writing. Note Elouisa's excitement about her excursion—it is this excitement that drives the piece of writing:

> … I was very excited. Mr Brownlow talked to us about our manners. I couldn't keep quiet. I was so excited. We went on Baxter's coach. I sat with Bethany. We had the best parents with us …

Elouisa is obviously eager to share her experiences with others. It is common to find emotional words or expressions in a recount of this kind of experience. While Elouisa goes through various cognitive processes to complete her recount—she needs to sort out the events of the excursion into a logical order, which she does, and she also needs to make choices about what information she will include in her work—the choice of words, phrases, and sentences is also governed by emotions. The use of emotive words such as 'very excited', 'couldn't keep quiet', 'so excited', and 'best parents' is indicative of her state of mind about the excursion. In responding to Elouisa's writing the teacher could highlight these positive aspects.

Writing provides an opportunity for *deeper thinking*

Writing means the bringing of one's inborn thinking and language *competence* to the process, and it also means the potential, the opportunity, for that *deeper thinking* that is created by the visibility of the thought-on-the-page. This is why this incredibly complex process cannot be reduced to 'x' number of 'skills'.

▶ Summary

1   Writing is a great collector of ideas, a clarifier of thinking, and a major aspect of learning itself—the protracted synthesis of our human thinking and language competence, handling a range of problems that cannot be satisfactorily managed by reflection or talking.

2   As writing is one of our tools for learning and communicating it is important for students to be genuinely interested in it and thus for teachers to be able to motivate students to write and to write often.

3 Writing can produce a deeper kind of thinking, especially when texts are being revised and edited, and can be used as a tool to enhance readers' learning about text and to engage in an understanding of literacy processes.

4 Writing is a creative process and offers a powerful thinking and learning engagement for use in any classroom learning. It is an important tool across the different subject areas.

5 Excursions are a wonderful way of building up the field for writing, for motivating students to want to write and for giving students something to write about.

Critical thinking and study exercises

1 Read the following piece of writing:

A Day To Forget

One moment it was fine and sunny and the next the rain poured down. It was the wet kind of rain, the type that sou'westers and gumboots wouldn't keep out. It seemed as if the heavens had opened. It squelched at every step and my clothes stuck to me like flies to a flypaper. After some time I came to a bus shelter. I ran for it, but inside was my old enemy Joe Harper. I stood transfixed for a second or two and then bolted out again, into the rain. As I sauntered along I came across an old friend of mine James Story. 'Nice to see you,' I said (inwardly I thought differently for James was boredom in human form). We walked along for a while, James nattering on as usual. The rain frequently drowned his voice. Presently when he realised I wasn't listening the talk began to wane rapidly and then silence at long last. A dead rat floated along the gutter frequently being pushed underwater by hailstones.

Hailstones!?! It was not until then that I had noticed it was hailing. Suddenly I broke into a run. My hair stuck up in points leaving the astonished James wondering what was the matter with me. In another shelter I sank down in a heap. A bus came along, I caught it and away we drove.

SUSAN, 11

a What is the overall tone or mood of this piece of writing? What words or phrases contribute to creating this tone? How do you think Susan is feeling? Are her feelings made clear in the writing? If so, how?

b Use the surface features, the organisation, and the content of the two samples by Elouisa and Susan to decide which is the more advanced piece of writing. Justify your choice.

c Could you give Susan any advice as to how she might make the writing clearer and/or even more interesting to the reader?

2. Examine the ways feelings manifest themselves in the following piece:

Last week daddy came home with four tickets for the circus. daddy are we going to the circus I said yes we all are said daddy we are going to night. Oh terrific I said. lets hurry and get ready now my mummy said So off we went. At the circus people were coming in and sitting down, then a lady said the acrobats It was good fun looking at them next it was red nose the clown with his pet monkey They was very funny the circus was good I said and my mummy said it was good to …

KATE, 9

a What is the child trying to do with this piece of writing? Is it largely a narrative, a recount, an information report, a combination of some or all of these? Why?

b From an initial reading of Kate's writing, list the surface features such as punctuation and spelling that may need attention. How do you balance the importance of surface features and content in a piece of writing?

c From a close reading of the piece, list the words and phrases that carry emotion and comment on the overall tone of the piece of writing.

d Make some suggestions as to what a teacher might do to help Kate write more clearly, grammatically and expressively.

e Now see if you can write a couple of paragraphs about a recent event that you felt strongly about. Pay attention to how you will structure your recount and the kinds of emotive words and phrases you will use. Take into consideration your targeted audience. Share the writing with a small group.

Further reading

Bearne, E. 2002, *Making Progress in Writing*, Routledge Falmer, London.
Cramer, R. L. 2001, *Creative Power: The nature and nurture of children's writing*, Longman, New York.

Web links

Office of the Board of Studies (NSW): www.boardofstudies.nsw.edu.au
EdNA Online, Education Network Australia: www.edna.edu.au
Department of Education and Training (NSW): www.curriculumsupport.nsw.edu.au/literacy

THE WRITING DEVELOPMENTAL CONTINUUM

12

Overview

The art of becoming a proficient writer is a developmental process and occurs over a long period of time. As with learning to talk, this process begins in the home where the child is exposed through social interaction with many different forms of writing for many different purposes. The process is continued in the school context where the formalisation of writing takes place. That is, students are introduced to text-types appropriate to different social situations and they become increasingly adept at handling these text-types as they move through the grades or stages of the primary school. At the heart of growth in the writing process is motivation and excitement with the many possibilities for learning that writing opens up.

Literacy before school

Before starting school, children are exposed to many kinds of literacy (see also chapter 4). They enter school with a vast array of literacy backgrounds. Some will already own many picturebooks and will be accustomed to the reading of books by members of the family, in the preschool environment, at the local library, or through television programs. Most households with preschoolers watch children's educational television programs and these can be valuable learning motivators.

Before entering school, children manage to learn oral language skills very proficiently. They learn that language has many uses: to get basic needs, to question, to acquire information, to control others, and so on. In fact, by the time the child enters school they have mastered the grammar of oral language very well. They haven't yet acquired a metalanguage so that they can describe what is happening with

Oral language is the precursor to written language

their language but they have internalised and can use most of the oral structures of the language. One of the main tasks of the school is to teach them to read and write. Their knowledge of oral language can be used to advantage when introducing them to the mysteries of literacy. Early writing, in fact, is often oral language structures written down.

Parents and carers play a key role in children's language acquisition since they have the opportunity to interact with children by fostering talking, reading, and writing at home. Shared language experiences promote children's confidence and self-esteem, which are important factors in promoting literacy awareness before they come to school. Through the provision of books and materials in English, and languages other than English, adults can develop children's linguistic awareness and language ability. Young children pick up their language learning in everyday situations (e.g. in verbal interaction; when parents point out and read signs, especially at places such as the supermarket; when they tell stories or read picturebooks to their listening children). Many preschools have rich language learning environments where the enjoyment of shared lullabies, stories, and rhymes fosters language ability. The encouragement of listening and speaking skills in preschoolers is very important for the later acquisition of reading and writing skills.

Many children live in a literacy-rich environment with numerous print-carrying messages where they can practise the language skills of listening, speaking, reading, and writing from a very early age. Other families rarely buy newspapers and many do not buy books but, most importantly, they still highly *value* literacy. The emergent reader will choose books, perhaps with the help of an adult, but there is no magical 'readiness' age when they should be introduced. In fact books should be introduced to children from birth, as Dorothy Butler has advocated in *Babies Need Books* (1995). The students' writing skills emerge as they progress from 'scribbling' to more purposeful and meaningful communications. Students' opportunities to develop literacy practices may be determined by their socioeconomic background—if talking, reading and writing are seen as important skills then these language abilities will be passed on to the students.

Literacy-rich environments are an advantage

Literacy at school

The role of the school should be to try to build on the knowledge and skills that children bring from the home. In this way schools can achieve success with children from all backgrounds.

What is it we look for in students' writing? What are the kinds of things we can say about a piece of writing, and how does writing change as the student develops through the different stages? As you work through this section observe how the various pieces of writing under discussion exhibit different structures and language features as the purpose varies and the audience changes for whom the pieces are written.

The school should build on the child's preschool knowledge and skills

Different syllabuses and programs contain writing samples and indicators of what to look for in children's writing. For example, the First Steps (1994) program from Western Australia has a useful continuum, which shows indicators telling us what to look for in texts and gives a good idea of how writing develops during the primary years.

The NSW English K–6 Syllabus (Board of Studies NSW 1988a) has similar outcomes and indicators but divides the continuum into four stages—Early Stage 1, Stage 1, Stage 2, and Stage 3. Each stage has its own outcomes, and support documents give examples of different text-types with discussion of indicators of achievement. These models are all helpful in giving a good idea of the writing stages students go through.

Wilkinson produced a model (after the UK 'Crediton Project') that is still useful in discussing students' writing on a developmental basis. He and his team analysed different text-types of children aged between seven and thirteen and developed some useful categories for commenting on the development in the writing. They were not only concerned with linguistic features such as sentence complexity but also with qualities of thought, feeling, and moral judgment. Wilkinson states that these assessment aspects arose from an 'interaction between our perceptions of the written materials, teachers' judgments and theoretical considerations' (Wilkinson et al. 1980: 65).

When commenting on children's writing, it is sometimes the case that readers or teachers look at the stylistic features and make comments about the surface features such as punctuation and spelling and take little notice of what the writer is actually trying to say. It is here that Wilkinson's model is particularly helpful:

Assessment needs to go beyond the *surface features*

- *Cognitive*: the writer's awareness of the world: one's ability to describe, interpret, generalise, and speculate.
- *Affective*: the writer's awareness of emotions and feelings of self and other people including the reader and one's environment and awareness of reality.
- *Moral*: the writer's awareness of a value system, attitudes, and judgments.
- *Stylistic*: the writer's awareness of syntax (the way words are organised), verbal competence, text organisation, cohesion, awareness of reader, and appropriateness of text.

In recent years, language syllabuses have tended to focus on the way texts are organised and there has been emphasis on getting students to conform to a certain text-type. This has the danger of children losing creativity or thinking that their writing must follow rigid structures. For example, when the kindergarten child is learning to manage a recount, it might be structured in this way:

Retaining creativity is vital

Orientation	*Yesterday I went to Grandma's place. She was sick.*
Record of events	*Mum cooked some food for her, then she cleaned the house.*
Reorientation	*Then I went home.*

By the time the child has reached the middle to upper primary grades, a recount would be more complex in sentence structure and idea but would contain the same overall structure. An example of a recount from a middle primary (Stage 2) student could look like the one in figure 12.1.

Figure 12.1   An example of a recount

Text structure	An Excursion to the Rock Pools	Language Structure
Orientation introduces the time, place, and characters in the event.	On Friday the 23rd of March our class went to the rock pools near Bondi Beach. We boarded the bus at nine o'clock.	Use of word families to build information e.g. rock pool, beach
Record of events.	When we arrived at the beach we went over to the rock pools. We walked around. The teacher told us to examine the shells and other sea life in the pools carefully. After a while we found a sheltered area to have morning tea.	Use of action verbs e.g. arrived, walked, found. Use of complex sentences e.g. 'When we arrived … we went'
Record of events, including evaluation.	We made lots of sketches of the shell-fish and other living things in the rock pools. We were all amazed at how many different kinds of animals and fish live in rock pools.	Use of past tense. and connections to sequence events in time e.g. when, after, then, next.
.	After lunch we were allowed to explore some sand caves. We then had a game of tip on the beach.	Use of reported speech e.g. '… teacher told us…'
Reorientation and evaluation.	We all took lots of good notes. We boarded the bus and returned to school at two o'clock. It was a really fun day.	Use of adverbial phrases of time and place e.g. 'On Friday', 'at the beach', 'in the rock pools'.

While the overall textual structure of these two pieces is similar, there are major differences in sentence complexity and sentence type. Much more information is included as the student's awareness of the world (ability to describe and interpret) has increased as well as awareness of self and others and an ability to make an evaluation ('It was a really fun day'). As the writer develops, there is an increasing ability to make meaning, which means that language choices become more complex and appropriate as the context for the writing becomes better understood.

As the writer develops, language choices become more complex

Characteristics of early writing

Children in the preschool years may be able to write certain words, such as their name or *Mum* and *Dad*, with accuracy and a knowledge of what they mean. Their teacher may have repeatedly put their name on drawings and belongings so that they learn to identify the word with their own possessions or work. Writing at the preschool stage is characterised by random marks on a page ('scribbling'), which gradually begin to form a pattern.

Early writing is very personal

Children in the early years (K–2) may find writing a difficult task. Indeed the physical act of representing all of the associated qualities of speech (tone, intonation, pause, emphasis, gesture) in a complex system of marks on paper is daunting for the beginning writer. At this stage writing activities should be short but frequent, and students should be allowed to use a variety of media for writing and/or making marks on paper. Students need something to write about, so it is important to give them lots of stimuli, including children's literature, excursions, picture study, and class talk about happenings and books.

Writing can become laborious physically—it can take a 5- to 7-year-old a long time to form the words. Young students tire easily and are inclined to do one draft only. That is, the first draft often becomes the final product. The teacher may find that the computer will provide a welcome

"The Giraffe by KP"

"The giraffe eats the leaves…"

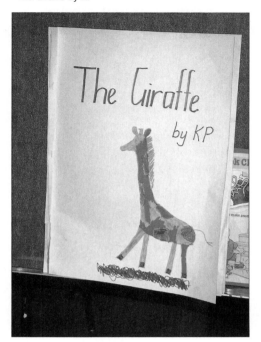

relief from the physical tedium of writing, especially for young students. Computers enable the editing process to be completed much more easily and they can make the publishing process much more satisfying for children.

The way the writing is constructed can be a challenge. Narrative or recount seems to be the easiest to do when one event follows the other in some kind of chronological order. Young writers often want to include what may appear to be irrelevant detail to the reader without getting on with the main events in the narrative or recount. The recount often tends to be disjointed. There is often mention of familiar rituals such as getting out of bed, having meals, watching TV, and going to bed. Students can use these to mark out the day, as is evident in Gary's writing:

> *I had a great day last Satiday. I got out of bed I found some prsnts on my bed it was my bithday. I opened them and found some cricket ger. I knew it was my bithday I went downsters and had brekfast I played cricket all day with my frends. For tea I had a party with frends. I watched TV and went to bed. It was a grate day.*
>
> Gary, 7

Notice how this is written from the focused view of the child. There is little awareness of others and when there is, there is little explanation about others. But the recount does have an orientation, a series of events, and a reorientation to conform to the overall structure of this particular text-type.

Students use narrative more easily than analytical writing. They find it a challenge to objectify in order to see the effects of their writing on others. Many stories at this stage have elements of the fairytale structure, which is a result of their own reading or of listening to parents or teachers sharing such tales with them. The 'once upon a time' opening and the 'lived happily ever after' conclusion can be readily found, as in Loretta and James' writing, and occasionally there is a cause–effect relationship expressed, as in Dale's writing:

> *If the stadium was burnt down I would be sad.*
>
> Dale, Year 1

> *Once upon a time there was onle one bird and it was calde a vilet and it was a pritey purpul. One day it had five eggs. When the eggs hatch there was a bird with pink with yellow with brown and with red blue perpull. and they lived happaly ever after.*
>
> Loretta, Year 1

> *Once there was an old house in the woods. It was haunted and very scary.*
>
> James, Year 1

The writing of young children often omits information that might give the reader important background in order to conceptualise the context of the writing in time, space, and place:

> *Wuns there lived a countree. It wos so hot No wun wanted to live ther. All of the tres wer folen down.*
>
> Jacinta, Year 1

It is a mark of development when awareness of the reader's needs—a sense of audience—is apparent in the writing.

The written style in these early years is often the spoken style. Obvious links such as 'and', 'then', and 'so' are used. There is wide use of common verbs such as 'be', 'have', 'go', 'say', 'take', and 'put'. Spelling is often close to pronunciation (e.g. wun = one). Nouns can be general (man, lady, policeman), often without qualification such as the use of adjectives. Concrete rather than abstract words are used. There is not much about abstract concepts such as bravery, honesty, fear, happiness, but realistic situations occur where these qualities are apparent. Sometimes direct speech is used but usually without the punctuation marks:

> *At Saterday I am going to jason house and jason bruther had a prte he was turned satnen and his perns gav sum presns to ruj. and jason sed to ruj happy bithday.*
>
> Joel, Year 1

Many of the above examples show evidence of 'temporary' or 'invented' spellings, which are a common feature in the early years. One of the best ways for students to learn to spell is to learn words by using them in real writing contexts rather than learning to spell by rote. The more students are presented with real writing models and the more they get to use words in writing, the closer their spellings will get to the correct form.

Sometimes writers in the early stages show evidence of approximating the standards of the writer in higher stages—a fact that highlights the individual nature of development. Students will progress at different rates and this will necessitate the teacher having different expectations and understandings for each student in the class. Here is a Year 1 writer producing a text that is more akin to that of a middle primary school writer:

Last holidays I went to Warragamba Dam where our water comes from. When we put our tap on hard all of the water comes rushing down the river. It is very very deep. People would drown at the bottom and die but I was too scared to look down.

Then after we went to a good view. Then I felt I could see all of Australia. It was so beautiful. We were on a cliff and I saw mountains that were so high and it was so peaceful and I had to be careful. You could see the water from the bottom on the way back. We had to go on a rocky road and it was a long way back.

When we were on a dirt road we saw a cow, like a cow but just a calf which was out of the gate. So my mum stopped the car and took me over to the calf but it was very very scared if I walked over to it. It would walk away from me eating grass. When we walked over to the car it went 'Moo, moo.' Then we went home.

Chris, Year 1

Students at all stages enjoy experimenting with new forms, phrases, and words—playing with language can be fun. Sally (Year 2) was asked to write about a topic using the letters of the word 'winter' to start her sentences (an acrostic):

Winter is cold and cloudy.
In winter we drink hot chocolate
Never go in the cold water.
The sun is often not shining in winter
Everywhere it is rainy and misty.
Read books in front of the fire.

Hale (Year 2) chose to write her piece inside the outline of a fish drawing:

If stars were trout
They would glitter through the
ocean of darkness, Swaying their
jewelled tails behind them.

Emily (also Year 2) was motivated by something she really likes and suggested some ideas about ice cream:

Ice cream
Its wriggly and smily
Smooth and creamy
and sweet
Nice

Critical thinking and study exercises

1   Read the following comments by teacher trainees about their early writing experiences and discuss in a small group your own memories of early writing:

> The foundations of my writing career are etched deeply in my mind. I was terribly distressed with my kindergarten teacher on the first day of school as she had not attempted to teach me how to write. Much to my parents' amusement, I conveyed my distress and I'm certain that this tale will be shared at my 21st party.
>
> K.

> My earliest memory of writing was in kindergarten with those orange folders that you used to put words in to make sentences. I remember that I would make the longest sentences in the whole class.
>
> T.

2   Responding with encouragement to children's work is a very important part of the writing process, to give the child early positive experiences in writing. Discuss your own experiences in response to these comments by teacher trainees, and suggest teaching methods that might overcome any problems these students encountered:

> I can recall one moment of glory in Year 2 when the teacher gave me the highest mark in the class for a very long-winded creative writing story I had written. Not only had this mark made me happy, the teacher also asked me to read the story at the parent–teacher night.
>
> K.

> I think it is very important not to criticise anybody when they write their own things, as I was sometimes criticised when I was little. I think that children should be provided with more time to write and express their own feelings and ideas. When I was little we had themes to write about that were always marked. We did not really have time provided at school when we could write anything we wanted that wasn't going to be marked.
>
> V.

> Writing for me always feels like a chore … My first and lasting memories of writing are from second grade. My teacher began each day of school by handing out a writing topic. I was always so confused over how to go about writing a story. From this time onwards I have always dreaded writing.
>
> M.

3   Compare the following two pieces of writing about koalas from Year 2 writers: Kara's poem and Simon's text.

   a   Comment on how the texts reflect the different stages of writing for each child.

   b   Decide what their different purposes are, list the positive features of the texts, and note whether they are effective in communicating information and feelings about the koala.

   ### Koalas
   Koalas eat leaves high in trees.
   They may have fleas,
   They like the breeze.
   The mother's pouch opens at base,

It is not made out of lace.
Koalas are rarely on the ground,
It's in trees the koala is found.
They don't make much sound.
Some have fluffy hair and,
Some have scruffy hair.
Beware of their claws and wide jaws.
Their feet are small and not fat at all.
When the baby is born it has no hair,
But it doesn't care.
When the koala makes a noise at night,
It might give you a fright.

Koalas

Koalas have two thumbs. They have two thumbs to make it easier to hold onto things. When the babies are born they are nearly as small as a baby bird. When the baby is born its mother licks a path for the baby to crawl up the pouch. The mother licks a path so it is easier to crawl up. I said crawl up because the Koala's pouch opens from the bottom of her. Koalas are marsupial. They eat gum leaves. They live all their life in gum trees. They are nearly all gone because of bush fires. It is very hard for Koalas to get away from bush fires. The mother or the father Koalas mixes gum leaves and waste together like cereal that we eat. Then she or he feeds the baby Koala the cereal. Some Koalas are nice to cuddle because some Koalas are very well trained. But some are NOT cuddly because they are not used to being cuddled at all.

IN THE CLASSROOM

Mrs Scott's Kindergarten class does some writing everyday. Their writing may not be very long—mostly only a sentence or two which arises from daily activities such as:

- The daily news session—an interesting item is chosen by the students themselves and the teacher writes a class sentence on the chalkboard about the item. This can also be used for reading purposes.
- The Big Book story is often used for writing—something about the story or even a sentence about how the story makes one feel.
- Excursions to the playground, local park, local shopping centre or sometimes an excursion requiring travel by bus or train are used for writing and reading purposes. Short illustrated recounts and information reports are compiled as class, group or individual pieces of writing and used to demonstrate the art of composing.
- The other KLAs are used as sources for writing, especially HSIE, Science and Environmental Studies.
- At this level whole class stories are common and students learn a lot about the conventions of writing from Big Book examples. Students, even at the Kindergarten stage can still be exposed to different text-types. Mrs Scott knows that students' personal experiences at this stage are the best sources for writing.

The developing writer

By the middle primary years students are becoming quite adventurous and can experiment with a variety of text-types (narrative, recount, information report, procedure, etc.) with a good

More adventurous— more text-types

understanding of a targeted audience. They are generally receptive to editing their work and see the sense in trying to improve their writing or in making it more appealing and meaningful for the reader as they are developing a better understanding of the concept of audience. The student will now have a store of words that can be spelt automatically, especially common words. Strategies for getting many unknown words right or nearly right, including sound–letter knowledge, use of rules and use of analogy, will be developing. Also, legible handwriting and keyboarding skills will be evident by this stage. Students will be better at talking about the grammar of texts, especially when referring to how meaning can be enhanced by the use of adjectives, adverbs, phrases, clauses, and punctuation.

The narrative form is still common at this level, but much longer stretches of text are written.

Writing is now getting less egocentric

There is less use of time markers such as getting up and meals. The student can generally begin with a significant incident without irrelevant events and without starting at the beginning of the day:

> There once was a mean drooly guard dog. He had shiny black fur with patches of brown on it. He guarded the museum which had models of cars inside. He was treated very well. He refered himself as the king of dogs and expected everyone to obbey him. Some people thought of him as a dog eater that only came out at night.
>
> One dark quiet night a female poodle passed the gate of the museum. She had luster white fur with beautiful blue eyes and she walked exactly like a show-of, dog would walk. When the museum people found out about her, they gave more love and care to her, and less to the guard dog.
>
> Two days later, the poodle was walking along the park with her owner. The poodle then saw a male poodle across the road, with fluffy brown fur. She got so carried away, that without thinking, she ran straight across the road, and got run over by a coming car. Much sorrow went around the museum. When the dog found out, he thought, 'maybe its good she died after all'.

Carol, Year 4

- More adjectives are used, together with more complex sentences and phrases ('shiny black fur with patches of brown'; 'the museum which had models of cars inside'; 'When the museum people found out about her, they gave …'; 'She had luster white fur with beautiful blue eyes …').
- Notice how Carol is able not only to advance a story with complex events but also to comment on the actions by making judgments: 'He was treated very well.'; 'Some people thought of him as a dog eater …'; 'Much sorrow went around the museum.'; 'maybe its good she died after all.'
- Carol uses dialogue to heighten interest or to further the narrative.

- Spelling: obey, show-off, it's = it is.
- There is more awareness of location and more description of setting. Some students go through a stage of writing stereotypical language:

> *… We left a note for mum and dad to say gone to get the paper and to go along the sea front. We did not wake my brother up. When we got out it was a lovely day with the sun shinning and a cool breeze. We went out of the camp site and down onto the sand. We took our sandles of and went into the sea it was cold but refreshing.*

Sandra, Year 4

The viewpoint is in many cases still egocentric and there is little comment on emotional aspects. There is more attention to other people but usually at a single dimensional level—with little attempt to enter into the mind of the other person.

Critical thinking and study exercises

1 Discuss the implications of these two statements by trainee teachers about their writing experiences in Year 4. Share ideas about what a teacher could do to overcome negative attitudes towards writing. Consider suggestions such as varying writing tasks so that boredom doesn't set in, or giving students more choice so that they can feel more in control of what they write.

> *I remember that in Year 4 we had to keep a daily journal. I loathed this chore. I often used to write lists, for example: 'Things I like, 'my favourite food', etc. Often I would simply state, 'I don't know what to write' or 'I can't think of anything'. I would also often try to be late for school as journal writing usually occurred in the morning … I still don't necessarily enjoy writing but it doesn't frighten me quite as much as it used to.*
>
> S.

> *I received the highest mark in the class so my story was read to the other 4th grade.*

> *I was so proud. Throughout that year I continued writing my very best. After 4th grade my writing skills went for a dive …*
>
> A.

2 Examine Tim's review of Roald Dahl's *George's Marvellous Medicine* as a model of a literary recount. Discuss the positive aspects of this response to a popular children's book. Consider structure, stylistic features (such as spelling, syntax, cohesion, verbal competence), and reader awareness.

> *George simply has to do something about his miserable old grandmother. She's always grouching and griping and she has the nastiest eating habits in the world. Most old ladies are nice and like to eat cream cakes; not George's grandmother. she likes caterpillars and slugs with cabbage, and earwigs with celery. She's so horrible that George decides to do something.*
>
> *He thinks of some clever ways to shake her up: bangers under her chair, snakes down her neck—but no! He decided to*

concoct a special magic brew that will either make her much nicer or make her disappear altogether. His marvellous medicine has everything in it from hair-

remover to anti-freeze. Read the book to see what happens.

TIM, YEAR 4

In the classroom

Mrs Lancaster's Year 3 class is busy with exploring the local community with a view to finding out how people in a community are dependent on each other. The opportunities for writing in this HSIE project are many and varied.

However, the teacher has chosen to introduce the exposition text-type so the focus for the unit of work is not only on the gathering of information for an information report but also the gathering of information to write an exposition or argumentative piece on where in the community the best place to live might be.

Is it near the shops or the sporting facilities or the schools or where it is quiet on the edge of the bush or …? The students have been divided into groups and each group has the responsibility of arguing their particular case for where the best place to live is.

Each group has had to go on a supervised field study of their part of the community to gather information they can use for their case.

The teacher has introduced the class to some modelled expositions so the students have a good idea as to what their final product needs to look like. As this is their first attempt at an exposition, allowances will have to be made. Mrs Lancaster is reinforcing the text-type in the oral mode by organising a debate around the same theme. Thus debating skills are gradually being introduced to this class.

As the project concerns the students' local community they have a special interest in it and are really motivated to learn.

The proficient writer

Upper primary students are beginning to manage a range of text-types with appropriate registers; they have a better awareness of appropriate language for different types of texts. They are more aware of language that is colloquial, humorous, formal, dramatic, and so on.

They make extensive use of outside models (i.e. literature, newspapers, television etc.). Students are more in control of the narrative and have more confidence in adjusting the

Upper primary students are more confident and experimental in their writing

chronological order. The capacity to write extended prose is one of the characteristics of a proficient writer. They may surprise you with their choice of a gruesome topic (in your eyes) and by their facility with words, often echoing—faintly or strongly—the novels they have read or the television stories they have watched. The following effort, titled 'Noise in the Night', is the opening paragraph in a longer story and makes good use of punctuation for effect:

I woke with a start and heard the stealthy footstep in the passage outside my door. I dived under the blankets and gave myself a pep talk 'Listen this is when you become a hero don't be a chicken!' Reappearing from under my quilt I quietly slid back my blankets and listened. Had I given myself a pep talk for nothing? Wait!!! I heard it. The step was muffled by my shut door but I heard it. I slid off my bed and tip-toed over to my closet (with teddy in my hand) and eased it open. SQUEAK!!! I stood frozen with fear. What if the person belonging to the footsteps heard my closet squeak? After what seemed like hours I moved again. Seizing my cricket bat I padded to my door. As I slowly turned the handle I found out that my body was covered in goosebumps and I was sure they weren't there because of the Arctic climate in my room. Stealing into the hallway I raised my bat.

Betsy, Year 6

Proficient writers are much more aware of the reader and can experiment with ways of developing interest and tension by keeping the reader guessing.

Better reader awareness and willingness to experiment

Karen's (Year 6) writing is the first chapter of a book titled 'Insights into the Past':

Chapter 1. It was an ordinary day

I was 12 when it happened. No one expected it. It was just one of those ordinary day things.

I was always down and nothing could cheer me up. I was comforted by my friends and family, then grew tired of all the fussing being done about me and told everyone to back off, but they just wouldn't listen.

I would sometimes just have to lock myself in my room, as it would drive me insane to keep hearing Simone are you okay? Simone, do you want something, dear, to keep you happy or Simone you've just got to stop sulking. Keeping me happy or sulking was not the issue, they simply didn't understand.

Before the tragedy I was living a normal life. I was happy and I was sad when I needed to be, instead of always being down and depressed.

My parent told me to strive high, but I couldn't think. I couldn't look at myself in the mirror. I could just see me the girl who has nothing to strive for. I wish they were still here. I miss them more than anything.

To explain how it felt is very hard. It's not just like a pet dying , because when they die you shed a few tears and that's about it, but when someone close to you dies you don't shed a few tears but a lot, and it takes time to get over them. I wish they would come home, but it will never happen.

Certainly there are still aspects of structure and ideas to be worked on here, but it can be seen how good communication is beginning to be developed. There is an awareness of self and of others as psychological beings—a movement away from egocentricity. The student shows good use of varying sentence structure to communicate ideas.

As witnessed in Neil's story about Kotic the seal, at the moral level there is an awareness of fairness and intention, and a less stereotyped method of portraying virtue and vice, good and evil, right and wrong:

> *Kotic was a seal. He had a big scar on his back. When he was two years old he was driven to the fur farm inland. One man said fire and in a few moments Kotic could not recognise any of his friends. They had all been skinned. Kotic just ran as fast as he could back to the beach but he could not. Desperately he ran round trying to get out, then a man walked up to him. Seeing the scar on Kotic's back the man flung him carelessly out of the enclosure. At that moment Kotic fainted.*
>
> *When he came to his senses Kotic was in great pain. He had broken his flipper. Very soon as he lay on the beach dieing he thought that men could have taken his skin anyway because they will probably take it when I am dead.*

Neil, 11

Empathy is developing

While Neil is having some challenges with tense and direct/indirect speech-forms, he is nevertheless able to empathise with others and convey a powerful moral message about the senseless slaughter of seals. Text-types often become mixed at this level as further experimentation takes place. The boundaries of narrative, recount, explanation, and so on can become somewhat blurred as the writer struggles with ideas and emotions.

Confidence in choice

At the level of the proficient writer there is a much more confident choice of syntax, words, and literary devices such as repetition, parallelism, irony, and disjunction (i.e. expressing an alternative, expressing choice between two words):

> *It is with some fear and apprehension that I relate to you the adventures my friend, Kerry Welsh, and I had with Spooky, the ghost, for I am rather afraid that the spirit of Spooky might come back to torment me. 'The spirit of a ghost?' I hear you ask me sardonically. 'Well,' I will answer you, 'you never know with ghosts!'*
>
> *Into the dark alley cautiously walked the affluent man. His huge, bulging bag was clutched tightly in his arm. Looking warily ahead, he then stepped uneasily in to the darkness, every now and again peering carefully behind him. Deeper and deeper he ventured, until he was a tiny dot in the distance.*

Josie, Year 6

Students have much more command of technical language, as witnessed by Carolyn's attempt at the procedural text of how to take a good photo. Terms such as 'wind the film', 'arrows', 'suitable subject', and 'telescopic lenz' are all associated with the act of taking photos:

> *You first have to select the film, either black or white or colour and put it in your camera. Wind the film from the outside of the camera until the arrows reach no. one. To take a picture you have to find a suitable subject and maybe use a telescopic lenz for best results. When taking the photo, do not move the camera. I advise you not to take fast moving photos if you are a beginner. Good luck!!!*

Carolyn, Year 6

Sometimes the writer's eagerness to write well can produce an impression of 'insincerity' where the language seems stereotyped and second-hand, and the emotions expressed appear exaggerated or overwritten. However, the experimentation with assonance and alliteration in the following piece produces some interesting effects:

We started out on a beautiful morning with a bright sky above us and a cooling south wind. Nature was in her full glory, the air smelt sweet, birds were singing loudly, squirrels scampered up trees at our approach and rabbits' tails disappeared down burrows at our presence. Lambs jumped around friskily tormenting their mothers for nourishment. Cows lay lazily chewing their cud among the buttercups. A little foal galloped alongside her mother on its spindly legs. In another field a ploughman plodded along behind his horses furrowing the field. Butterflies fluttered from flower to flower.

And so our journey went on in the presence of Nature's glory. Oh what a wonderful thing to be alive!

At Langham we refuelled ourselves and continued our journey.

John, 12

Different aspects of writing develop at different rates as the student struggles with ideas, forms, syntax, choice of word, literary devices, and so on. One of the key factors influencing writing development is the teacher, who must provide appropriate experiences to motivate and stimulate, demonstrate appropriate models, and be a sensitive facilitator who guides, nurtures, and encourages writing across a range of subject areas.

► WRITING IN THE DIGITAL AGE

Mr Black's Year 6 students can edit their writing reasonably efficiently and they can also use a variety of text-types with some skill. Many of the students enjoy word-processing, especially when they are doing the term class newspaper.

The class is divided into newspaper category groups. That is, a small group is assigned to each of the following parts of the paper:

- Lead stories: headlines are very important here as they need to be emotive and eye-catching. Stories come from events that are happening around the school, from whole-school events such as carnivals, from other classes, or from individuals who have done outstanding things.
- Sporting news: items are gathered from the whole school, not just the year 6 class. Of special interest is the 'house' competition.
- Advertisements: both buying and selling of items from the students.
- Cartoons: the dedicated artists in the class belong here.
- Letters to the editor: the 'stirrers' in the class like this group.
- Literary section: this group elicits original poetry, prose or drama pieces for publication.
- The editorial group whose responsibility it is to oversee and edit the other sections.

Each group is usually found clustered around a computer as decisions are made about what to include and from whom. Sometimes a group may access the Internet for emails from a 'sister' class in another country or for illustrative material to enhance particular articles.

Multiliteracies

Proficient writers can usually access the many forms literacy takes in our modern society. Visual literacy is just one of many forms but it is a pervasive one. Junk mail is full of visual information and students need to be discerning in being able to interpret bias and prejudice and be able to express their views in written form. Picturebooks are being written for the older student now, and once again students need to be trained to be critically literate. Having the ability to express opinion in written form on visual literature is a sign of a proficient writer. Other challenges for the student include computer literacy, and literacy involved with mobile phones, toys, emails, vending-type machines and so on.

▶ Summary

1   Literacy begins well before the child comes to school. The presence of books and print media in and around the home, and the attitude of parents and carers, are important influences on the child's literacy development. The child should be exposed to a rich variety of language in a variety of contexts, and be allowed to use and experiment with language.

2   The school needs to use and develop the language the child brings to school. As students progress through the grades they should gain greater control over their writing as they become more aware of purpose and audience.

3   Useful aspects for commenting on or assessing students' writing are: stylistic features; grammar, punctuation, handwriting, and spelling; cognitive, affective, and moral aspects; and text structure.

4   The K–6 developmental continuum generally sees the students' writing falling into three broad stages: early writing, developing writing, and proficient writing. All lines of demarcation are arbitrary as students may be at different stages for different aspects of their writing.

5   The developing writer is generally more receptive to editing writing and making it more appealing and meaningful to an audience. Also, legible handwriting and keyboarding skills are more evident at this stage.

6   The proficient writer is managing a wide range of text-types with appropriate registers and is much more aware of the reader.

Critical thinking and study exercise

Collect at least three samples of writing from different classes and see if you can assign them to stages of development. Use your syllabus to look for indicators. What does each piece tell you about the student as a writer? This activity would be best done in pairs or a small group.

Further reading

Bustamante, D. M. 2002, 'Telling our stories, finding our voices: Nurturing a community of learners', *Primary Voices K-6* 11(1): 2–6.

Christie, F. & J. Rothery 1989, *Children Writing: A reader*, Deakin University Press, Geelong, Vic.

Cushman, D. 2002, 'From scribbles to stories', *Instructor* 111(5): 32–3.

Derewianka, B. 1991, *Exploring How Texts Work*, PETA, Sydney.

Graham, L. 1995, *Writing Development: A framework*, Schools Advisory Service, London Borough of Croydon, Croydon, UK.

Graves, D. 1994, *A Fresh Look at Writing*, Heinemann, Portsmouth, N.H.

Heffernan, L. 2004, *Critical Literacy and Writer's Workshop: Bringing purpose and passion to student writing*, IRA, Newark, Del.

Kroll, B. M. & G. Wells 1983, *Explorations in the Development of Writing Theory, Research and Practice*, Wiley, Chichester, UK.

Wilde, J. 1993, *A Door Opens: Writing in fifth grade*, Heinemann, Portsmouth, N.H.

Web links

Education Department of Western Australia: www.eddept.wa.edu.au
Curriculum Council of Western Australia: www.curriculum.wa.edu.au
International Reading Association: www.reading.org

13 GRAMMAR SKILLS IN THE CLASSROOM

Overview

An understanding of grammar, the structures used in language, contributes to the achievement of high standards in written and spoken language. While linguists may simply describe language, teachers recognise the need for some prescriptive rules that their students can apply which meet general norms for language use. Teachers also recognise the wide range of social contexts where language is used, and how these different contexts determine acceptable grammatical correctness. Language changes, and what is regarded as 'correct grammar' today may be regarded as stuffy and old-fashioned by a new generation who, through force of numbers, may encourage new usage. Reasons for teaching grammar range from the improvement of literacy skills to the need for a metalanguage to talk about language use. The use of both traditional and functional grammars is advocated: traditional grammar is widely known and can contribute to the understanding of language, while functional grammar is particularly useful in studying the cohesion of whole texts. Many examples are given of how grammar can be included in classroom activities, in a wide range of contexts and subjects. Our students need to know why and how language works. An understanding of grammar is an integral part of successful writing, reading, speaking and listening.

What is grammar?

Grammar can be defined as the systematic relationships that exist between elements of the English language such as the parts of speech, the formation and arrangement of words, and sentence structure, all of which indicate meaning and determine how we use our language. 'Rules' and conventions about grammar change over time, so it is wise to recognise variations in usage. Students should be introduced to authentic materials (such as cartoons, newspapers, magazines and books) to show how grammar is used in writing and also how the 'rules' are often deliberately flouted.

Grammar concerns how language works, including a study of semantics, morphology and syntax:

a) **Semantics:** the study of the meanings of words and how they may change.
An understanding of the range and function of different grammatical features gives the student a repertoire of resources which help in expressing meaning, whether in oral or written mode.

b) **Morphology:** the patterns of word formation, which include inflections (word endings signifying grammatical meaning), prefixes and suffixes, the base or root (main body of the word carrying the meaning) derivation, and the composition of words, e.g.

- prefixes and suffixes: *un*dress, dress*es*, dress*ed*, dress*ing*, dress*y*

- derivations: *'computer' used to mean a person who made calculations; 'gay' used to mean only happy, blithe; 'sandwich' was named after the 4th Earl of Sandwich, who liked to eat meat in between slices of bread so that he didn't have to leave the gaming table to eat.*

- In the word 'inflexible', flex is the root of the word and means 'bend', so the word is built up from a negative prefix, the meaning-carrying root, and an adjectival suffix.

  Inflexible:
  in prefix;
  flex base or root word;
  -ible suffix

- The teacher can integrate the morphology of words with vocabulary expansion and spelling instruction.

c) **Syntax:** the patterns of formation of sentences and phrases from English words. For example, a common English sentence structure is:

The dog	*bit*	*the child.*
Subject	*Verb*	*Object*

This is the 'active' construction. The same sentence can also be written in the 'passive' construction, where the stress is placed on the thing done, rather than the doer of it. The indirect object becomes the subject of the passive verb. While the verb form changes, the meaning does not:

The child	*was bitten*	*by the dog.*

English syntax (or word order) is very important. See how the meaning changes with a reversed order of words.

The dog	*was bitten*	*by the child.*

These grammatical features play a major role in creating discourses beyond the sentence level. For example, we say the words *I can run* in this order because we have an implicit knowledge of the grammatical rules governing syntax, the word order in English. Changing the word order to *Run, can I!* or *Can I run?* is also possible. The English speaker can tell which meaning is intended by various clues from the context and from the word order, punctuation, and/or intonation.

Why teach grammar?

The main argument in favour of the explicit teaching of grammar is that the more we learn about the nature of language, the more efficiently we will be able to use it. A knowledge of grammatical concepts and terminology helps the development of literacy skills. The teacher's aim should be to teach grammar within the context of wide language experiences rather than as a series of isolated, decontextualised grammar lessons. Teaching and learning the difference between *saw* and *seen*, *done/have done/did*, or between *write, wrote, writing,* and *written* should be done in context. Grammatical activities at the level of word or sentence may seem irrelevant to students if they are not linked to meaningful usage.

IN THE CLASSROOM

Demonstrate how parts of speech work in a sentence. The word 'star' performs different functions, dependent on its placement in a sentence, e.g.

> *The star actor attended the first night opening. (as an adjective)*
> *The star of the film attended the first night opening. (as a noun)*
> *Heath Ledger will star in the director's next film. as a (verb)*

Make a wall chart of sentences from advertisements with labels of grammatical features such as adjective, noun and verb.

The importance of context

Grammar is best taught in context, in a rich language program

In schools, instruction about grammatical structures and strategies to teach a particular structure can be interesting and relevant if they are made part of the student's living language. Use real-life examples to explain what might be considered appropriate speech or writing in different contexts. When the excited jockey of Makybe Diva, the winner of the third successive Melbourne Cup race, said, 'She done all the work', the message was conveyed clearly, if ungrammatically. 'Thank youse all!' may be condemned outright or ignored as inconsequential. Is it being pedantic to complain about the grammatical error? The answer is that it depends on the context. Students need to recognise what is 'acceptable' and yet to be aware of how literacy skills are adjusted in different contexts. Prescriptive or value judgments about language are not made by linguists, but teachers need to prepare their students for a society that often judges people on their perceived language ability and adherence to language 'norms'. There is a linguistic consensus in English-speaking communities that says 'done' or 'youse' in the sentences above are not acceptable as 'standard English'. Some dictionaries have usage notes that explain why one form of a word is acceptable and another not. The *New Fowler's Modern English Usage* (1996) is a descriptive rather than prescriptive guide to what is currently acceptable (e.g. the prevalence of *a* instead of *to* or *of* as in *gotta/got to*, or the ungrammatical *shoulda* or *should of* instead of the standard English *should have* or *should've*).

Reasons for teaching grammar

The usefulness of grammar is clearly stated in educational syllabuses: 'grammar can be used as a tool to help students understand how sentences are structured so that they are meaningful, clear, and syntactically accurate. It also provides scope for exploring the grammatical patterns in texts to see how they build up the meaning' (NSW Board of Studies 1998a: 9). Objections to teaching grammar because it is regarded as 'boring' and 'irrelevant' can be met by referring to these reasons and by lively teaching methods that make the study of grammar relevant and meaningful. There are many reasons why gaining a knowledge of grammar is valuable.

1 *Grammar allows students to make judgments about appropriate use of English.* Students will gain some understanding of why and how people speak and write differently in various contexts. Why and when should *I done it* or *I seen it* be corrected as *I have done it* and *I saw it?*

2 *Grammar improves literacy skills.* Explicit instruction in grammar should help students choose appropriate grammatical patterns that fit the purpose and structure of their texts. Writing with grammatical accuracy is achieved over time with plenty of practice, using examples from stretches of language and from extended discourse.

3 *Grammar enriches understanding of literature.* Students are able to see patterns of language more clearly. They may identify and enjoy metaphorical language and experimental structures.

4 *Grammar assists in learning foreign languages.* Anyone who has learnt another language realises that a knowledge of English grammar can help to explain the structure of other languages. In Mandarin, the tenses are not indicated by inflections, so *Ta shi laoshi* (in pinyin) could mean 'He/she is a teacher' or 'He/she was a teacher' depending on the context in which it is used.

5 *Grammar provides a metalanguage* that allows us to talk about students' reading and writing. The terminology of grammar gives students a language to describe the language they use, hear, read, and write. While it is possible to speak and write 'grammatically' without being able to describe these features, an understanding of grammar gives students insight into how the language is constructed. Grammatical terminology provides a metalanguage to help understand how language operates in sentences, clauses, phrases, and words. It is important to show students how grammatical choices work at the level of paragraph and text. Understanding grammar is a means to an end.

Which grammar to teach?

Features of traditional grammar and functional grammar can complement one another, so the teacher is advised to draw on both. Both traditional and functional grammar can help 'crack the code' of language. The terminology of 'traditional' grammar, however, is widely known throughout the English-speaking world.

The teaching of traditional grammar dropped away in the 1960s when the new grammars (e.g. Noam Chomsky's generative grammar) emerged in universities, but it is again being taught in schools.

Chomsky believed children generated sentences and mastered grammatical rules, even if they sometimes applied them in the wrong way 'I buyed the cake'. www.chomsky.info/

- **Traditional grammar** is commonly regarded as the description of parts of speech and sentence structure.
- **Functional grammar** provides a useful focus on how language functions in particular contexts, the importance of language choices, and the analysis of extended passages of text.

Traditional grammar

These are the eight basic parts of speech in traditional English grammar:

Noun	*horse, car, day*
Pronoun	*she, he, it, they, I, we, you*
Adjective	*beautiful, small, red*
Verb	*run, laugh, eat*
Adverb	*swiftly, carefully, now*
Preposition	*over, into, under*
Conjunction	*and, but, because*
Interjection or exclamation	*oh! ugh!*

Traditional grammar has some limitations in describing how language works, particularly beyond the sentence level. It can describe written expression but it is not so capable of describing other functional varieties of language, such as formal or informal speech, which are mapped in functional grammar.

A criticism of traditional grammar is that it is based on Latin and Greek. These are inflected languages where meaning is given to nouns, verbs, and adjectives by changing the word endings (inflections). For example, in Latin, *puer* means child and *pueribus* means by, with, or from the children. In English, meaning is mostly conveyed through a combination of word order and prepositions, although inflections are still used (the -s in *stars* or -ed in *starred* are inflections). Historically, the inflectional system of the original form of English, Anglo-Saxon, withered away, but some inflections survived, particularly in verbs.

Functional grammar

Functional grammar, also known as 'systemic grammar', was developed by M. A. K. Halliday, Emeritus Professor of Linguistics at the University of Sydney (Halliday 1985a). In essence, functional grammar looks first at the general communication of a spoken or written text, giving greater attention to the importance of context (i.e. the context of culture and the context of situation). It focuses on how meaning is expressed and what forms of language express these meanings. It is clear that language is not an arbitrary set of words or structures since definite choices are made. This is different from traditional grammar, which first looks at specific items, emphasising the forms of words (morphology) and the forms of sentences (syntax). The focus of functional grammar is on the text as a whole, the extended discourse rather than the smaller unit of the sentence. Collerson expresses it well:

> A functional model of language treats language as a social phenomenon. It begins not with phonemes, words or sentences but with the social context, because this is the basis for the functions

of language and their associated meanings. A functional grammar accounts for how these are realised in texts through the choice of grammatical structures and vocabulary. It also treats variation in language usage as an essential aspect of language and gives due recognition to the grammar of both spoken and written language. (1997: 25)

We can use terminology and useful concepts from functional grammar such as field (what is happening), tenor (who is taking part), and mode (the channel of communication), which are features of the context of situation.

- **field:** the subject matter or field of a text relates to its content, who or what is involved. The field may be a shopping list, a recipe, a narrative, an explanation.
- **tenor:** the tenor of a situation determines the roles and relationships of the participants. Different language choices are made depending on factors such as age, power, and status of the individuals involved. People working in a Complaints Department are paid to be courteous to customers, and the tenor of their language reflects this.
- **mode:** the channel of communication, spoken or written, visual or contact.
- **cohesion:** the semantic relations in a text; lexicogrammatical relations. The network of connections that links references, thus contributing to the continuity of meaning in a text.
- **text-type:** the general structure of the kind of text, e.g. correspondence, legal document, newspaper editorial, narrative.

In primary schools today we can use some of the terminology of traditional grammar and build on additional terminology and concepts from functional grammar. Functional grammar can be seen as enriching traditional grammar, showing how to interpret the broad variety of discourses and registers used. It can throw light on how students use discourse in their speaking, reading, writing, and viewing.

It is not necessary to polarise the two grammars. Functional grammar extends the parameters of traditional grammar by allowing us to see how systematic language is in its structure, e.g. the hierarchical framework of sentences, clauses, phrases, words, and morphemes. As Halliday has demonstrated through many examples, 'the key to a functional interpretation of grammatical structure is the principle that, in general, linguistic items are multifunctional' (1994: 30). He illustrates this in the clause *boys throw stones*, where *boys* is both 'actor' and 'subject'.

Functional grammar is useful for understanding spoken language, which is notoriously difficult to analyse because it is so complex, spontaneous, and interactional, typically full of interruptions, hesitations, and fragments of speech. A functional approach to language sees language fulfilling the needs of people for real purposes, emphasising the role of language in communicating meaning.

The functional approach in the classroom

Beverly Derewianka in *Exploring How Texts Work* (1991) demonstrates how the functional approach can be used in writing, analysing, and assessing texts:

A functional model of language can be drawn upon during classroom activities … Such opportunities might occur, for example, during the modelling of a text, or during a conferencing session. Sometimes these opportunities can be programmed, sometimes they may be spontaneous. They can occur at the whole class, small group, or individual level. (1991: 5)

Traditional and functional perspectives can be merged, to some extent. Traditional terminology such as 'verb' is used but an additional functional aspect is added to remind students of the different ways verbs are used, e.g. an action, saying, or thinking verb. In addition, where there are different types of nouns in traditional grammar (abstract, collective, common, and proper), further examples can be added to show how these words are actually used in texts; for example, Derewianka (1998) refers to 'metaphorical nouns'.

Teaching grammar

A stimulating language environment which integrates writing, reading, speaking, and listening, will maximise literacy skills, including an awareness of grammar. Students can gain familiarity and a critical awareness of grammatical conventions through modelled teaching, guided practice, and independent writing in an environment that encourages literacy, and through opportunities for listening and speaking.

From practice in meaningful contexts, using different modes of communication, students will learn about idiomatic and more formal uses of the English language.

IN THE CLASSROOM

Idioms such as *true blue* are forms of expressions characteristic of a language. Sidney Baker, an authority on Australian language and slang, wrote that Australians' 'greatest talent is for idiomatic invention. It is a manifestation of our vital and restless investigation'.

Idiom: It was raining cats and dogs.

Literal meaning: It was raining heavily.

Collect a list of Australian idioms, and/or those from British or American English and give their definition.

Example: As flash as a rat with a gold tooth (Australian) means someone is dressed smartly, with the suggestion that the outfit is overly fashionable.

Incorporate some of these idioms in a story of your choice.

Different media can illustrate how grammar is used in a range of genres: on the Internet, in popular songs, in television programs and in current books they are reading.

New media changes old media

Using books and tapes appropriate to the student's level will help to reinforce grammatical patterns, e.g. the book and tape of *Miss Lily's Fabulous Pink Feather Boa* by Margaret Wild and Kerry Argent. Make an appeal to the students' interests such as music, sport, surfing, or their favourite DVD, but also widen their engagement with texts from different cultures, historical places, genres, and media. Exploration of these media should encourage an understanding of 'grammar in action', the recognition of acceptable grammatical patterns in both oral and written expression.

IN THE CLASSROOM

- Specific teaching/learning can be focused on the form of language (e.g. the past-tense forms of regular and irregular verbs) and punctuation conventions. Google on the Internet for lists of these.

- Story-making games and activities can help students understand the parts of speech (e.g. variations of bingo and dominoes on laminated cards with nominated parts of speech).
- In the early years, tense-sequencing cards can promote discussion and help students practise tenses. Involve students in making card sets of photographs to encourage understanding of nouns, prepositions, verbs and adjectives.
- Learning can be consolidated through writing in a journal and through class charts of shared learning experiences which have a grammar focus.

From practice in meaningful contexts, modes, and mediums, students will see grammar in action and learn how the English language works. Australian, British, and American English have their differences. Those learning English in Asia and India will also have their own forms of English that are appropriate for their particular contexts.

Grammatical terminology can be daunting for students. The teacher must decide how much detail should be given at different stages of development and whether some is too specialised such as the difference between active and passive voice. For example, 'voice' in traditional grammar indicates different relationships between the verb and its subject:

> *Mr Lee gave me a present. (active voice)*

> *A present was given to me by Mr Lee. (passive voice)*

The scope and sequence of teaching grammar can be presented in a formal program of instruction, linked to the writing of different genres. There will undoubtedly be much overlap between grammatical features in the genres. As Collerson (1997: Appendix A) advises, 'very few issues are purely grammatical' since most grammatical features have implications for broader aspects of meaning. When planning a language syllabus, grammatical features can be taught within the context of different text-types and the wider curriculum, e.g. when teaching how to write narratives, demonstrate the use of:

- nouns to refer to people, places in the story
- adjectives to describe people, events
- conjunctions to show time sequence
- past tense to indicate what has happened
- saying and thinking verbs to show what characters are feeling.

Early Stage 1

Writing a narrative is achieved by joint construction as students create a story from a Shared Reading session with the assistance of the teacher. Always write a sentence or sentences under children's drawings and encourage students to write their own sentences. At this stage they will be learning how to

- write simple sentences
- use the simple present and simple past and future tenses of verbs
- develop a story through an orientation, basic descriptions, and conclusion
- use adjectives and adverbs.

Stage 1

Here emphasis can be placed on:

- sentences and clauses using commas, capital letters, and full stops
- conjunctions to join sentences and to introduce logical relations, e.g. because, although
- pronouns used instead of nouns
- present and past tenses, e.g.

> Cartman <u>starts</u> to behave strangely. (present tense)
>
> We <u>are going</u> to the swimming pool. (present continuous tense)
>
> Cartman <u>started</u> to behave strangely. (past tense)
>
> We <u>went</u> to the swimming pool. (past tense)

Writing excerpt from Stage 1

> I am going on holidays with my nanna because she asked me to.

The teacher still plays a role in the construction of texts and may help with writing the final draft. At this stage the student has knowledge of commonly occurring words and can recognise letter–sound correspondences. Students may have keyboard skills and may type on the computer. Their writing will show more evidence of compound and complex sentences as well as pronoun references. They have more control of grammatical features and use tenses fairly accurately. There is increasing command of punctuation and the use of quoted speech. Students can edit their writing to some extent.

Stage 2

Here the following features can be emphasised:

- logical structure, e.g. using *first, second* in sentences to indicate chronological sequence
- use of modality expressing a writer or speaker's orientation towards possibility, probability, and certainty, e.g. *may, always, sometimes, usually, could, must, should*
- the difference between first- and third-person narratives, i.e. 1st person: *I, we*; 2nd person: *you*; 3rd person: *he, she, it, they*. The 1st person indicates subjecivity
- the use of dialogue and accompanying punctuation
- number, i.e. singular: *dog*, plural: *dogs*.

Writing excerpt from Stage 2

> Nanna usually goes on holidays with her two dogs. 'Come on', she said, 'you can help me look after Titch and Prince'.

Students can write a narrative that contains an orientation, a complication, a series of events, and a resolution. They have a fair degree of control over various grammatical features, especially capital letters, commas, and full stops within a sentence. At this stage they are capable of writing an individual narrative independently, perhaps based on a story they have listened to or read together. The student can write on a wide range of topics and can address different kinds of audiences. Drafting and editing work is undertaken and the student recognises more difficult aspects of writing such as the organisation of the text and the need for more expressive language that will convey the narrative.

Stage 3

Here the emphasis is on consolidating previous grammatical understanding and furthering knowledge of:

- compound sentences, e.g. Teachers want children to read, but they don't always have the books.
- adverbial phrases of manner, time, and place, e.g. The artist painted the picture *with a brush*. (how = manner)
- direct and indirect speech, e.g.

  <u>Direct</u>: '*Mirror, mirror on the wall, who is the fairest of them all?*' *she asked.*

  <u>Indirect</u> or <u>reported</u> *speech: She asked the mirror on the wall who was the fairest of them all.*

- tense structure, e.g.

  Cartman <u>will start</u> to behave strangely. (future tense)

  We <u>will be going</u> to the swimming pool. (future continuous tense)

- lexical cohesion (the cohesive effect achieved by, for example, reiteration of vocabulary in a text).

Writing excerpt from Stage 3

> *I think my nanna is an unusual person. She prefers to go on holidays with her two cocker-spaniels, Titch and Prince. Even so, last summer she invited me along. I thought she wanted me there to pamper her pooches. I found out she really wanted to pamper me!*

At this stage students write more confidently and provide more detail and coherence in texts. There is further evidence of elaboration of ideas with the appropriate grammatical structures to convey them. Students may experiment with different structures, building on the conventional narrative structure in a variety of ways. Different styles of writing and different formatting of texts may be explored. Joint constructions may still be used but students are capable of writing texts independently from the draft stages to a final edited version.

The primary school student will not need to know the terms 'anaphora', 'cataphora', or 'exophora' although the concept of how words point backwards (anaphora), forwards (cataphora), or outside a text (exophora) is extremely important. Lexical cohesion establishes continuity in a text, for example, by repeating words or synonyms of the word or by using collocations. (See also chapter 3.)

IN THE CLASSROOM

Cohesion and collocation

a) In linguistics, a collocation is a habitual arrangement of words, those generally joined together, e.g. *white as ghost*.

- Ask students to recognise collocations in their writings and in texts they read.
- Discuss when collocations become tired clichés.
- Change some collocations to more imaginative writing.

b) Within corpus linguistics, a **collocation** is defined as a sequence of two or more consecutive words that has characteristics of a syntactic and semantic unit. Collocates of *bank* are:

Corpus linguistics is the study of language as expressed in samples (corpora) or 'real-world' text

- bank account
- bank deposit
- bank manager
- merchant bank
- bank into
- bank on
- river bank

Find collocations of other words, e.g. *child*.

Cohesion

Key words throughout a text remind the reader of what is significant and lead to a cohesive and meaningful text. **Cohesion** is the 'glue' that holds writing together, to make it readable. Familiarise students with cohesive ties, getting them to spot these words in texts and to include them in their own writing. Highlight different grammatical features in coloured boxes in texts and worksheets.

Cohesive words

- Additive words: also, and, as well as, besides, in addition, likewise, moreover, too, not only … but also
- Contrast: although, but, despite, even though, however, in contrast
- Cause and effect: as, as a result, because, consequently, since, so, then, thus, therefore
- Repetition: this, these, those, that
- Sequence: afterwards, before, firstly, next, secondly, then
- Summary: finally, in conclusion

From their writing and reading, students will become familiar with many aspects of grammar but they will still need explicit instruction and considerable practice to become competent at using the dizzying potential of the English language. Make a chart of cohesive words.

Classroom ideas for teaching grammar

An eclectic and integrated approach is recommended when teaching grammar, focusing on the principles of task-based learning (Nunan 2004). These involve:

- models with teacher instruction
- student-centred activities
- authentic materials
- active learning giving students a sense of ownership
- student participation
- goals leading to task completion
- ongoing assessment for the teacher and learner.

The teaching of grammar should be linked with the reading and writing of real texts. Using games, picturebooks, poems, and writing activities, the teacher can engage the student in interesting models. In this way the features of the language, its structure, and its arrangement of words, can be taught in context, not as isolated rules of grammar. For example, verb tense can be taught with the help of tense forms that occur in children's literature read by or to students:

As he **walked** home, a priest suddenly **appeared** from nowhere.

(Junko Morimoto, *The Two Bullies*, 1997)

IN THE CLASSROOM

Sentence expander

1   Find models of vivid word choice from professional writers, everyday texts or the students' own writing. Encourage vivid and appropriate choice of words, phrases and clauses and understanding of the parts of speech by expanding sentences.

> *The girl smiled.*
> *The happy girl smiled.*
> *The happy girl smiled softly.*
> *The happy girl smiled softly to herself.*
> *The happy girl smiled softly to herself as she waited.*
> *The happy girl smiled softly to herself as she waited in the teacher's office.*
> *The happy girl smiled softly to herself as she waited in the teacher's office for the news.*

2   Expand these sentences and continue the story.

> *The house creaked.*
> *The boy dreamed and planned.*
> *Snuffy, the dog, barked.*

3   Discuss what makes a good sentence. Remind students that 'brevity is the soul of wit' and that short sentences are also effective. Effective sentences do not contain unnecessary words. A combination of short and complex sentences keeps the reader's interest.

Use Internet resources to encourage students' interest in language. Activities may be 'around the world' through ePals, blogs or webquests, or 'around the corner' through individual interactive tasks or email correspondence. (See chapter 18.)

▶ LITERACY IN THE DIGITAL AGE

Try out some of the interactive grammar sites on the Internet to see how they can help students learn grammar to improve their writing skills.

- Self-study Quizzes for ESL students < http://a4esl.org/q/h />
- Grammar Gorillas <www.funbrain.com/grammar>. The Grammar Gorillas need help identifying parts of speech. If students click on the right word in the sentence, the gorillas get a banana— Beginner (nouns and verbs only), Advanced (all parts of speech).

IN THE CLASSROOM

Grammar editing

1 Collaborate with students to make a grammar checklist. This may become a wall chart, bookmark or desk strip so that students can refer to it easily as they write and edit. Make sure the amount and type of information is appropriate for students.

2 Give students instruction and practice in using the spelling and grammar checking tools on their own word-processed texts.

3 Identify common errors in writing:

   a incomplete sentences

   b apostrophe misuse

   c non-agreement of subject and verb

   d incorrect use of verb tense.

   Identify errors (circle or underline) and write out the correct version. (N.B. Computer grammar checkers may only identify punctuation errors).

Unedited first draft

Filled with straw and gold. The room shimmer in the light. The strange little man appeared and asks the millers daughter a difficult question. Could she guess his name.

Corrections

Filled with straw and gold. (a) The room shimmer in the light. (c) The strange little man appeared and asks (d) the millers (b) daughter a difficult question. Could she guess his name?

Final version

Filled with straw and gold, the room shimmered in the light. The strange little man appeared and asked the miller's daughter a difficult question. Could she guess his name?

IN THE CLASSROOM

Teachers can help students improve their literacy skills by explaining and giving many practical examples of grammatical features. Students need to be given lots of practice in applying this knowledge so that their language works to convey meaning.

Finding out about verbs

1   Read students the short poem 'Me-Moving' by Gordon Winch:

> I dart and dash,
> I jig and jump,
> I scamper, skate
> and scramble.
> I strut and stride
> I slip and slide,
> And frequently, I amble.
> I leap and lurch,
> I crawl and creep,
> I rove and romp
> and ramble.
> I turn and trip,
> I skid and skip,
> And now and then—
> I gambol!

(Winch 1989)

2   Ask the class what the person in the poem does. Note the concept of action words, i.e. **verbs**.
3   Discuss the meanings of the words and perform some of the actions.
4   Emphasise the fact that the chosen words are about actions (what the person does). They are all 'doing' or action words, or, in grammatical terms, they are 'verbs'.
5   Encourage students to write their own verse, as a class, in pairs, or as individuals.

IN THE CLASSROOM

Verbs are very important in writing because they focus attention on what happens.

1   Find out about the various kinds of **verbs** and see how they are used in different texts.
2   Use the verbs, with acceptable grammatical usage, in writing a variety of texts.
   a   *Auxiliary* and *compound* verbs, which help to form different tenses, e.g. *be, do, have, shall/will*.
   b   *Transitive* and *intransitive* verbs, e.g. The young girl *opened* her book. (transitive verb with an object); The young girl *is singing*. (*intransitive* verb).
   c   *Regular* and *irregular* verbs

Regular verbs

Regular verbs form their tenses in a conventional way:

	Singular	Plural	Past participle
Present	I smile	We smile	smiled
	You smile	You smile	
	He, she, it smiles	They smile	
			Present participle
Past	I smiled	We smiled	smiling
	You smiled	You smiled	
	He, she, it smiled	They smiled	
Future	I will smile	We will smile	
	You will smile	You will smile	
	He, she, it will smile	They will smile	

Irregular verbs

There are several hundred irregular verbs. Here are a few examples:

Infinitive	Past tense	Past participle	Example
be	was	been	
choose	chose	(has/have, was/were) chosen	
give	gave	given	
go	went	gone	He has gone to the dogs.
lie	lay	lain	
run	ran	run	I ran into her last week.
see	saw	seen	
sink	sank	sunk	
speak	spoke	spoken	
stink	stank	stunk	
take	took	taken	
write	wrote	written	

IN THE CLASSROOM

Fun with adjectives

While individual exercises can consolidate understanding, try to use activities within an authentic context. Adjectives may be used to spark interest in making writing more interesting to a reader.

Simply, adjectives are used to describe nouns. They can go before the noun or after it:

a beautiful view
The view was beautiful.

1   Make adjectives from nouns. Try out different sentences to see which is more effective in the context of a piece of writing:

the beauty of the scenery
the beautiful scenery

2   Extend meaning with adjectives:

a surfer
a skilful surfer
a skilful, strong surfer

3   Practise using different kinds of adjectives, which modify or limit a noun, in sentences:

one, two (note that numbers are adjectives)
some, few, many

4   Check understanding of the comparative (-er) and superlative (-est) forms of adjectives:

tiny, tinier, tiniest
large, larger, largest

Remember exceptions such as *good, better, best,* or *bad, worse, worst.*

5.   Make writing more arresting by using more descriptive and/or specific words. Find synonyms for:

little, big, good

6.   Play with prefixes and suffixes to make additional adjectives. Use them in sentences as part of a longer text:

kind, unkind
dazzle, dazzling

Use a student's own writing to indicate how adding or changing adjectives can help to make a text more evocative and informative.

IN THE CLASSROOM

1   Give students practice in writing four different kinds of sentences:

declarative	*statement*	*I really like train journeys.*
interrogative	*question*	*What is your destination, miss?*
imperative	*command*	*Get off at the next stop.*
exclamative	*exclamation*	*Oh, no!*

2 Discuss with them how the concept of 'sentences' can change, depending on whether the person is speaking or writing and the different ways of interacting. Provide opportunities for students to experiment with language, extending clauses and phrases in sentences to add meaning.

> *She was holding a football. (simple sentence)*
> *She was holding a football and she wouldn't let it go. (compound sentence: two main clauses joined*
> *by a coordinating conjunction)*
> *She was holding a football, which was her birthday gift. (complex sentence)*
> *She was holding a football, which was her birthday gift, and she wouldn't let it go. (combination*
> *sentence)*

Ask students to read their texts aloud. Impress on students that a simple sentence may be the best choice. While beginning writers may write too many simple sentences, e.g. *I went to the zoo. I went on Sunday*, students who use too many complex and combination sentences may get their thinking tangled and convoluted.

As students write their texts, correct grammatical structure is further reinforced and recognised as necessary for communication. In the primary school, experience with language use should be emphasised, and complemented by formal instruction in grammar, often at the point of need. Instruction and practice can be given in:

- manipulating sentence patterns
- practising different structures
- writing different text-types
- showing the differences between spoken and written English.

TABLE 13.1   The characteristics of spoken and written language

Oracy/Spoken	Literacy/Written
speech	print
sounds	letters
impermanent	permanency
interaction with listener	no turn-taking
interruptions	continuity of text
colloquial language	more formal language
likely to be unplanned	planned text with density of content
repetition	edited text
first draft status	final draft status
vocabulary	more carefully chosen vocabulary
grammar	more polished grammar
intonation	punctuation

New developments in language study

Even though the pendulum swings in recognising the importance of teaching grammar, teachers are wise to be receptive to the new insights that linguists provide into the nature of language. Deborah Cameron (1995) in the chapter 'Dr Syntax and Mrs Grundy: the great grammar' in *Verbal Hygiene* has convincingly explained how concerns about grammar reflect societal anxieties.

Online grammar resources are increasing, many with fun interactive activities suitable for different age groups.

> ▶ LITERACY IN THE DIGITAL AGE
>
> Utilise online resources for an understanding of grammar that can help students in their writing.
>
> **www.eflnet.net**
> A Few / A Little (tutorial & quiz)
> A Lot of (count noun / noncount noun) (Beginner to Intermediate)
> A or An (tutorial & quiz)
> A or An (Beginner)
> Adjectives, Comparative and Superlative (tutorial & quiz)
> Adverbs, Comparative and Superlative (tutorial & quiz)
>
> **www.grammarbook.com**
>
> This website provides an online resource for grammar and punctuation usage with lessons, quizzes, and an optional test.

The 'grammar' of visual design

Literacy learning is increasingly multimodal, encompassing audio, visual, gestural and spatial patterns of meaning. Visual images can be read as 'text' and they possess a 'grammar' or set of features which can be analysed.

MULTILITERACIES IN THE CLASSROOM

Devise activities to illustrate the 'grammar' of visual design.

Newspapers and advertisements use photographs, changes of type face, graphics, colour, and inventive layout to convey meaning.

- Select two different advertisements that advertise products for children.
- Discuss what effect they have on a reader and how this is done.

Grammar-checking facilities on the computer are becoming increasingly sophisticated, allowing checks for run-on sentences, subject–verb disagreements, redundancies, jargon, awkward phrases, and double negatives, as well as flagging style and readability considerations.

Email communication is sometimes written like a stream of consciousness with little attention to conventional grammar or punctuation, yet written clarity is still needed if messages are to be read. The increase in text messaging has led to truncated texts with a consequent relaxation in grammatical 'correctness'. On the positive side, we can appreciate the explosion of writing that has occurred among previously reluctant writers who revel in text-messaging their friends.

Language corpus

Developments in computer technology have opened up new areas of study of linguistic features, especially with the data collection of samples of writing (corpuses) which consist of wide expanses of written and spoken text that the computer can analyse with relative ease. To construct a corpus, language data are collected from a vast range of texts so that the corpus collection is a sample of how language is actually spoken and written.

Whole sections of text may be included from newspapers, radio broadcasts, magazine articles, and conversations, and also from unpublished language such as informal letters, postcards, diaries, and printed forms. The analysis of these discourses and the compilation of dictionaries have benefited enormously from the application of such computer techniques. As well as providing raw data for linguistic research, language databases such as the International Corpus of English (ICE) or the Australian Corpus of English (ACE), which contains a million words consisting of 500 samples of written Australian English from 1986 can be used in English language teaching for syllabus and materials design.

In Roman mythology, Janus was the god of gates, beginnings and endings (*January* comes from Janus). He was depicted with two faces looking in opposite directions

Teachers need to be Janus-faced in the sense that they can look backwards and borrow useful ideas from the past and yet look to the future to see which new ideas and concepts can make their teaching and learning more effective.

► Summary

1   A study of grammar involves various elements: semantics, morphology, and syntax.

2   A knowledge of grammar allows students to make judgments about appropriate use of English; improves literacy skills; enriches understanding of literature; assists in learning foreign languages; and provides a metalanguage that allows students to talk about their reading and writing.

3   Both traditional and functional grammar can offer insights into the structure of language. The basic parts of speech in traditional English grammar are noun, pronoun, adjective, verb, adverb, preposition, conjunction, and interjection. Functional grammar assists in an understanding of cohesion, field, tenor, mode, and extended discourse.

4   Different grammatical features can be emphasised at different stages of students' understanding and development. Activities for teaching grammar should be meaningful and designed to improve students' overall communicative ability.

5   Teachers should be receptive to the new insights that linguists provide into the nature of language, including those areas opened up by developments in computer technology and multimodal texts.

Critical thinking and study exercises

1   In small groups, discuss what you would tell parents about the place of grammar in your classroom. Suggest ways that parents might be able to help the students at home with language skills. Prepare a brochure suitable for parents explaining your approach to teaching grammar.

2   Discuss appropriate strategies for teaching aspects of grammar to students from language backgrounds other than English. Use your students' own writing, the Internet, and print resources for inspiration and examples. Devise some games to assist grammar practice through oral interaction, cooperative learning, self and peer correction, and explicit teaching.

3   Explore ways of using different text-types to focus on grammatical concepts. For example, an information report identifies or highlights the following linguistic features:

   a   use of general nouns

   b   use of the timeless present tense ('platypuses have webbed feet and duckbills')

   c   use of technical terms

   d   topic sentences and paragraphs to organise material.

4   Plan a series of lessons to give students practice in writing an instructional text. Discuss in what areas of life instructional texts are mostly needed. Why is clarity and accuracy so important? What can happen if the instructions are not clear or are jumbled in some way? Clarify aspects of the text-type before you begin, such as the imperative mood with verbs; the precise language needed; the omission of articles; and so on. Provide different models of authentic texts, e.g. how to cook using a simple recipe. Encourage creativity in texts: an imaginative or imaginary recipe. Try it out if this is possible.

5   Select models of interesting language from well-known writers. Discuss what makes their writing so interesting to read. Select some grammatical features which the author uses and discuss their effectiveness with students. Award-winning children's literature, including picturebooks, will provide excellent sources. Why is it important to encourage both reading and writing? Explore strategies for using professional writing as models while encouraging students' own creative interpretation.

Further reading

Students are advised to consult the current curriculum and support documents relating to the teaching of grammar in their state or territory.

Burchfield, R. W. (ed.) 1996, *New Fowler's Modern English*, rev. 3rd edn, Clarendon Press, Oxford.

Collerson, J. 1994, *English Grammar: A functional approach*, PETA, Sydney.

Collerson, J. 1997, *Grammar in Teaching*, PETA, Sydney.

Derewianka, B. 1998, *A Grammar Companion for Primary Teachers*, PETA, Sydney.

Derewianka, B. 2002, 'Making grammar relevant to students' lives'. In G. Bull & M. Anstey, *The Literacy Lexicon*, Prentice Hall, Sydney.

Droga, L. & S. Humphrey 2003, *Grammar and Meaning: An introduction for primary teachers*, Target Texts, Berry, NSW.

Eggins, S. 1994, *An Introduction to Systemic Functional Linguistics*, Cassell, London.

Gowers, E. 1987, *The Complete Plain Words*, rev. S. Greenbaum & J. Whitout, Harmondsworth, Penguin Books.

Graham, J. & K. Alison (eds) 1998, *Writing Under Control: Teaching writing in the primary school*, Centre for Language Education and Research, David Fulton in association with Roehampton Institute, London.

Halliday, M. A. K. rev. by Christian M.I.M. Matthiessen, 2004, *An Introduction to Functional Grammar*, rev. edn, Arnold, London.

Knapp, P. & M. Watkins 1994, *Context, Text, Grammar: Teaching the genres and grammar of school writing in infants and primary classrooms*, Text Productions, Sydney.

Nunan, D. 2004, *An Introduction to Task Based Teaching*, Cambridge University Press.

Ur, P. 1988, *Grammar Practice Activities: A practical guide for teachers* (Cambridge Handbooks for Language Teachers), Cambridge University Press.

Watkins, M. & P. Knapp 2005, *Genre, Text, Grammar: Technologies for teaching and assessing writing*, UNSW Press, Sydney.

Web links

OWL, Purdue University Online Writing Lab: http://owl.english.purdue.edu/handouts/grammar

ESL Help Center: www.pacificnet.net/~sperling/wwwboard2/wwwboard.html (Twenty-four hour help for ESL/EFL students)

Dave's ESL Café: www.eslcafe.com (Resources for students and teachers)

Grammar Gorillas: www.funbrain.com/grammar

Dave Sperling's ESL Quiz Center: www.pacificnet.net/~sperling/quiz/

Zozanga ESL – grammar exercises: www.zozanga.com

PUNCTUATION SKILLS IN THE CLASSROOM

14

Overview

Punctuation marks help to clarify written language by indicating how it should be read or perceived. While it may be a matter of an author's personal style, punctuation needs to be taught in the classroom so that students can communicate effectively. The history of punctuation shows changing patterns of punctuation use, but today English punctuation is standardised. However, different contexts demand different kinds of attention to punctuation—an email communication may have little punctuation, a text message even less. On the other hand, punctuation may be used for special or humorous effect. Working with students' own texts and giving examples from a wide range of familiar contexts (such as signs and newspapers) can show how punctuation works in practice. Punctuation is essentially about meaning, not just about when to make a pause for breath.

Punctuation

Good punctuation allows the writer to show expression, to communicate rhythm, tone, and those paralinguistic features so easily conveyed in speech. It shows the reader how a text should be read aloud.

Punctuation really matters because it clarifies meaning

The importance of punctuation is often underestimated, yet a misplaced mark can significantly alter meaning, leading to obscurity and ambiguity. Poor punctuation can distract the reader and make the writer look ignorant. 'Let me be yours' is quite a different message from 'Let me be. Yours, …'. Lynne Truss (2003) advocates a zero tolerance approach to punctuation errors, pointing out that a panda that 'eats, shoots and leaves', is quite different from one that 'eats shoots and leaves'.

In the classroom

To impress on students the importance of punctuation, try to read these different versions:

theprincesslookedintothespringafterherballbutitwasverydeepsodeepthatshecouldnotseethebottomofitthens hebegantolamentherlossandsaidalasificouldonlygetmyballagainIwouldgiveallmyfineclothesandjewelsandeve rythingthatihaveintheworld

the princess looked into the spring after her ball but it was very deep so deep that she could not see the bottom of it then she began to lament her loss and said alas if i could only get my ball again I would give all my fine clothes and jewels and every thing that I have in the world

The princess looked into the spring after her ball; but it was very deep, so deep that she could not see the bottom of it. Then she began to lament her loss, and said, 'Alas! If I could only get my ball again, I would give all my fine clothes and jewels, and every thing that I have in the world.' ('The Frog Prince', Grimm's Fairy Tales)

When reading aloud:
comma (,) = pause
semicolon (;) = strong
pause
full stop (.) = hard stop

Reading aloud from an unpunctuated text highlights the need for signals to pause for breath and to give meaningful connections between the words. By this method students can quickly learn about sentence structure, and how and why to write capital letters at the beginning of sentences and a full stop at the end. They can progress fairly easily to an understanding of how commas (similar to but not identical with the pauses of speech) can divide clauses and how paragraphs can be set out so that a reader can follow the meaning of the text more easily.

Punctuation for rhetorical effect

The small symbols of punctuation carry a weight of meaning, reminding us of the Latin derivation of punctuation, *punctus,* a point.

Punctuation may not always be about breathing spaces or syntactic meaning; it is also used for *rhetorical effect*. Punctuation marks indicate the author's intentions and the different meanings to be conveyed to the reader.

In the classroom

Will Blake clean his room?
Discuss the differences between these sentences:

a   Blake promised to clean his room when he had the time.
b   Blake promised to clean his room, when he had the time.
c   Blake promised to clean his room—when he had the time.
d   Blake promised to clean his room. When he had the time.

Debate how the punctuation marks add different emphases. What is the likelihood of Blake cleaning his room in sentence 4?

Punctuation and personal style

Inventive punctuation

Students are often inventive in their use of punctuation as they try to simulate the spoken word on the printed page or to convey a particular emotion. In the following sentence a student capitalised 'died' to emphasise the magnitude of the loss:

More than fifty-five thousand Turkish soldiers DIED in the Gallipoli campaign.

IN THE CLASSROOM

Some writers punctuate for special or humorous effect. e.e. cummings, the American poet, Edward Estlin Cummings (1894–1962), directed his publishers to ignore the conventions and follow his own unorthodox typographical style. Truly case-sensitive, he found capital letters offensive. (See also chapter 26.)

Find examples of idiosyncratic punctuation from e.e. cummings and from children's literature. Highlight the need for punctuation through comparisons of texts.

Use punctuation with discrimination

To some extent, the use of punctuation is idiosyncratic. Some writers punctuate heavily, others lightly. Commas may be sprinkled like confetti among their sentences, or used sparingly

Making a point with punctuation:
Good morning.
Good morning!
Good morning?

Basic punctuation

Capitals, the full stop, and the comma are the basic punctuation marks needed in writing. Once students learn how to use features such as brackets (or parentheses), exclamation marks, and question marks, their writing can become more descriptive and meaningful because these punctuation marks mimic language features such as intonation and stress.

IN THE CLASSROOM

Punctuation in sentences
Punctuation changes the message and the meaning. Find out how a sentence changes when different punctuation marks are put at the end.

1   How does the message change in these sentences?

The bus came at 9 o'clock.	*Statement*
The bus came at 9 o'clock!	*Exclamation*
The bus came at 9 o'clock?	*Question*

2   Write an appropriate response for each sentence.

3   Encourage students to act out the different sentences, showing by intonation and body language how the meaning changes with emphasis on different words.

4   Change the intonation and stress in sentences (by italics, bold type, or underlining) to indicate how different emphasis on words changes the meaning in sentences:

> **What** is she doing?
> What **is** she doing?
> What is **she** doing?
> What is she **doing**?

Good punctuation allows a text to be read without ambiguity

In written English, punctuation can be used to show information structure, although it cannot express it fully, and most punctuation practice is a compromise between information structure (punctuation according to the intonation) and sentence structure (punctuating according to the grammar) (Halliday & Hasan 1976: 325).

The history of punctuation

An early system of punctuation was developed by the Greek scholar Aristophanes, librarian at Alexandria (not the playwright) around 200 bc. He devised a set of three points of varying heights (the later Latin technical term was *distinctiones*) to indicate longer or shorter pauses. However, these early punctuation marks fell into disuse.

The first written texts, e.g. Roman capitals on carved inscriptions, did not possess the punctuation marks we recognise today. These were added later to help in reading aloud. The standardisation of punctuation was aided by religious worship and the reading of liturgical texts. Alcuin of York in the 9th century instituted capitals to begin sentences, spaces between words, and the arrangement of text into sentences and paragraphs. These conventions are still common today.

The symbol for the question mark (?) was used first in 16th-century England, possibly derived from an abbreviation of the Latin *quaestio*, meaning *what*

The invention of the printing press in 1436–37 by Johann Gutenberg (1397–1468) was the catalyst for the development of punctuation symbols. Over the next 200 years printers experimented with punctuation and by the 1700s standardised punctuation emerged. The apostrophe, dash, exclamation point, and quotation marks were gradually added in the 17th and 18th centuries.

Punctuation may be different in other languages. For example, in French, the *acute accent* (´), *grave accent* (`), and the *accent circonflexe* (^) are marks to indicate how a word should be pronounced. The Chinese and Japanese full stop is a small circle, indicating the end of a sentence.

Everyday literacy needs and graphic symbols

It is essential that students have an understanding of the diverse ways in which information can be presented, for example, as symbols, figures, tables, graphs, pie charts, calendars, clocks, dockets, accounts, forms, maps, watches, timetables, TV guides, measurements, shapes, or labels. It cannot be assumed that students will know how to interpret this kind of symbolic language; they will need explicit instruction and plenty of practice.

Handwriting has changed from the copperplate script of the 19th and 20th centuries to a preference for writing on the computer (Sassoon 1999)

MULTILITERACIES IN THE CLASSROOM

Integrate punctuation with other projects and activities.

1   Raise students' awareness and appreciation of punctuation. Ask them to collect examples and photographs of commercial signage to illustrate the use of correct and incorrect punctuation. For models, look on the website of the Punctuation Protection Society.

2   Provide students with a current television guide. Ask them to write their own ideal program for a day, using appropriate punctuation and layout.

Modern punctuation is more complex than might be imagined. It is more than the traditional and familiar punctuation marks because it also includes various non-alphabetic marks:

$$@ \quad \# \quad \$ \quad \% \quad \& \quad *$$

Spaces and indentation can also be regarded as part of punctuation as students learn how meaning is conveyed by the way texts are organised into sentences and paragraphs.

Scope and sequence of teaching punctuation

Punctuation is best taught through students' own writings as they discover how meaning can be communicated more effectively and how punctuation signals the reading of a text.

The following sequence can be used when analysing different texts:

1   Recognition of where there is a need for punctuation
2   Explanation or discussion of which punctuation marks will assist in conveying meaning
3   Applicable 'rules' of punctuation

4 Punctuation of a student's text, with a check to see which punctuation is more effective

5 Further examples of punctuation in other contexts

6 Practice in using features of punctuation to reinforce correct usage and/or to remedy incorrect usage.

1 Recognition of where there is a need for punctuation

The capital (upper-case letter) is used for:

'Netiquette'. Why are capitals in text messaging regarded as SHOUTING?

- the first letter of the first word in a sentence
- proper nouns (e.g. Paul, Australia)
- the pronoun 'I'
- personification: 'Old Time is still a-flying'
- abbreviations and trade names, e.g. NSW or Cadbury's chocolate
- emphasis or loudness, e.g. 'Somers—S-O-M-E-R-S. Harriet spelled it out.' (D. H. Lawrence, *Kangaroo*).

2 Explanation or discussion of which punctuation marks will assist in conveying meaning

There are many 'stops' in the English language:

. The full stop indicates the end of a sentence.

, The comma indicates an interruption in the continuity of ideas expressed, or a grammatical structure signalling additional phrases or clauses.

; The semicolon separates a list of items, or is used to balance ideas in a sentence, e.g. On the one hand …; on the other hand …

: The colon marks a point in a sentence that begins a listing of some kind.

— The dash functions more strongly than the comma or parenthesis, highlighting a word or indicating an omission in a text, e.g. I—I—I was afraid.

(…) Parentheses (or brackets) contain an additional insertion in a sentence, such as a comment, explanation, or afterthought. They are also used around references such as dates.

'…' Inverted commas indicate speech marks, or quotes; the choice of single or double marks "…" is variable.

► LITERACY IN THE DIGITAL AGE

1 Look up these English punctuation marks and their rules for use on the Internet, from Kim's Korner or other sites. Discuss examples from students' own experiences and a wide range of texts.

Ampersand	*Full stop or Period*
Apostrophe	*Hyphen*
Brackets	*Italics*
Colon	*Parenthesis*
Comma	*Question Mark*
Dash	*Quotation Marks*
Ellipsis	*Semicolon*
Exclamation Point	*Underlining*

> **2** Make coloured, laminated cards with common punctuation marks such as full stops, commas, question and exclamation marks with an explanation of how they are used; give examples from authentic texts.
>
> **3** For younger students, describe punctuation marks as traffic signals telling the reader when to start and stop: a full stop is a *stop* sign; a comma a *yield* sign.
>
> **4** Make wall charts to illustrate correct use of punctuation in children's literature texts.

3   Applicable 'rules' of punctuation

Isolated rules may be forgotten by students unless they are embedded in the context of writing and 'publishing'.

Here are some examples of how different punctuation marks are used:

- the exclamation mark (!) is used after an exclamation, an outcry:

    'Oweee!' shrieked the hen and it shot straight up into the air like a rocket.

    (Roald Dahl, *George's Marvellous Medicine*)

- the question mark (?) is used after an interrogative phrase or sentence:

    'Why can't you be like the Happy Prince?' asked a sensible mother of her little boy who was crying for the moon.

    (Oscar Wilde, *The Happy Prince*)

Point out how the voice rises at the end of a question. Some speakers use the rising inflection at the end of a sentence so often that their statements sound like questions.

4   Punctuation of a student's text with a check to see which punctuation is more effective

Encourage awareness by reading texts aloud and using a punctuation checklist.

- Quotation marks (also called inverted commas) make it easier to see where dialogue is used. Both single and double quotation marks will be found in published texts. (American books usually use double quotation marks.)
- Direct and indirect (reported) speech is enclosed by single quotation marks:

    'It's disgusterous!' the BFG gurgled. 'It's sickable! It's rotsome! It's maggotwise! Try it yourself, this foulsome snozzcumber!'

    'No, thank you,' Sophie said, backing away.

    (Roald Dahl, *The BFG*)

5   Further examples of punctuation in other contexts

- Look at word-processed texts, from books or in newspapers, and check how italics, underlining and bold print are used for emphasis and other rhetorical effects.

- Check how indentation (the setting in of the text from the margin) helps the writer to organise text and give prominence to different features. Paragraphing should not be underestimated—it is part of the art of writing well:

  By establishing the order in which you wish to make the points of your exposition or your argument, to set forth the incidents of your narrative, the aspects of your description, you simultaneously and inevitably establish the division into paragraphs, and the natural, because the best—the best, because the entirely natural—order of those paragraphs. (Partridge 1953: 168)

6   *Practice in using features of punctuation to reinforce correct usage and/or to remedy incorrect usage*

The apostrophe is used to indicate:

1   possession

> *the book's cover*

2   omitted letters in contractions and or numbers in dates

The Greek word *apostrophos* means turned away, elided

> *I could've won the race if I'd 've had running shoes.*
> *I'm (I am) we're (we are)*
> *you're (you are)*
> *he's, she's (he/she is) they're (they are)*
> *The tsunami of '04.*

3   time or quantity

> *one week's holiday or two weeks' holiday*

The apostrophe (') of possession often causes problems. The 's is such a bugbear that people often put it in where it is unnecessary. It is sometimes jokingly referred to as the feral apostrophe.

It's = 'It is' or 'It has'.   Some try to avoid error by rephrasing sentences without using the apostrophe 's at all, e.g. 'The mother of the child' instead of 'The child's mother'. *It's* only ever means *It is* or *It has*; if you can't replace these words, then the correct form is 'its'. The possessive form of 'its' has no apostrophe: 'Its tentacles reached out from under the rock'.

I N   T H E   C L A S S R O O M

Learn the apostrophe rules

1   The apostrophe is used to indicate possession:
    Rule: Place the apostrophe after the last letter of the noun (owner) to indicate possession or ownership. This works for collective nouns, e.g. the children's friends. If a word is singular in number, put the apostrophe inside, unless the word ends in 's'. If plural, put an apostrophe outside the word.

Examples:

Singular

one boy's bat (singular/inside)
my only brother's sons
anybody's drink

Plural

the boys' bats (plural/outside)
her two sisters' sons
Dennis' or Dennis's guitar
Bridget Jones's Diary
Venus' bright appearance.
the Isaacs' neighbours
two babies' clothes
the fishes' scales

For collective nouns that suggest a grouping of people or objects, put the apostrophe inside:

a herd's leader
the jury's decision
sheep's wool

2   Try some of the self-tests on the Internet to check accuracy of punctuation use.
3   Place an apostrophe in the correct place in sentences made up by the class. Arrange possessive nouns in one column, contractions in another, and have one column for exceptions where the apostrophe is not used.
4   Ask students to write 'possessive case' verse, e.g.:

My dog's fleas
Your father's daughter
The pen of my aunt
La plume de ma tante
The Secret Diary of Adrian Mole
Australia's last hope

Early Stage 1

Kindergarten students can be introduced to capital letters and full stops as they write sentences. Using a full stop is easier than using inverted commas, but some Kindergarten students may be able to handle both. When students have children's literature read to them, they come across a varied range of punctuation marks. These will become increasingly familiar to them if teachers point them out in context, e.g. showing how an interrogative statement ends in a question mark.

As with most aspects of language, students may come across all the standard features of punctuation in a storybook they can read in Year 1. Nevertheless, it cannot be taken for granted that students will know how or why to use punctuation. Explicit instruction is required to teach the standard features of punctuation to signal how a text should be read: capital, full stop, comma, semicolon, colon, hyphen, dash, brackets, exclamation and question marks, inverted commas, apostrophe, italics, indentation in paragraphs.

In the classroom

Punctuation and speech marks

1   Plan a lesson to teach specific features of punctuation (e.g. inverted commas for speech) to improve students' writing of narratives.
2   Use illustrations from children's literature and everyday texts.
3   Teach some simple rules that will help the students.
4   Check grammar handbooks or Internet sites.
5   Provide interesting models.

Table 14.1   Outcomes from NSW English Syllabus

	Early Stage 1	*Stage 1*	*Stage 2*	*Stage 3*
Grammar and punctuation	WES1.10 Produces simple texts that show the emergence of the grammar and punctuation needed to achieve the purpose of the text.	WS1.10 Produces texts using the basic grammatical features and punctuation conventions of the text-type.	WS2.10 Produces texts clearly, effectively, and accurately, using the sentence structure, grammatical features, and punctuation conventions of the text-type.	WS3.10 Uses knowledge of sentence structure, grammar, and punctuation to edit own writing.

Effective literacy practices

Engage students in literacies   Teaching punctuation should be part of integrated literacy teaching so that mastery of one skill reinforces another. Students who read a lot and comprehend the meaning of different texts will also have a better command of punctuation skills. Good teachers

*   give explicit instruction about grammar and punctuation, ensuring that students of all abilities can understand
*   create classrooms that embrace various literacies with wall charts, activities, texts, and literature on display
*   provide models of written texts in the classroom
*   encourage a wide range of reading outside the classroom
*   motivate students to write with enjoyment
*   monitor student achievement
*   teach students how to edit their own texts.

In the classroom

Ten ideas for teaching punctuation

1. Search out children's books published on CD-ROM, DVD, or the Internet. Write out some book titles that interest you; try to read as many as you can; make a bookmark of one with an appropriate illustration.

2. Make a calendar, writing out the names of the months in capital letters.

3. Cut out a comic strip and ask students to write down the direct speech underneath, or their alternative versions.

4. Use macaroni shapes as speech marks. Let students stick these around direct speech. This can be fun as a Kindergarten activity, but students should quickly transfer the idea to recognisable punctuation marks on paper.

5. Make a crossword puzzle using the names of different punctuation marks (use the Internet if desired), and write out the clues for Across and Down using appropriate punctuation.

6. Use poetry to teach the importance of punctuation. Explore why line breaks are chosen by the poet. How does changing the line breaks change meaning? Illustrate the use of line breaks on simple poems such as limericks, so that students can appreciate why and how line breaks are used. Look at the effect of sounds, the visual effect of a 'shape' poem, and how sound and meaning are conveyed.

7. See how professional writers use punctuation. Read stories aloud and encourage students to listen for pauses. Make them aware of punctuation. Use Big Books to show how punctuation marks are used to convey meaning.

8. Punctuate a text, asking students to reflect on how the punctuation marks give meaning. For example, punctuate the following so that it makes sense:

   youd better be careful mrs twit said because when I see you starting to plot i watch you like a wombat

   (from Roald Dahl's *The Twits*, 1980)

9. Encourage students to edit their own texts to a publishable standard using a punctuation rubric and/or computer language checking tools. Draw an outline of the hand with these five items to be checked:
   a capitals
   b full stops
   c commas
   d end of sentences (question or exclamation marks)
   e indenting of paragraphs.

10. Encourage students to participate in email discussion groups. Use book raps (a book discussion conducted via email), and other activities that will motivate them to communicate their ideas in writing.

http://rite.ed.qut.edu.au/old_oz-teachernet/projects/book-rap/about.html

Modern punctuation

The modern trend is towards less punctuation if the meaning can still remain clear, but it is to some extent still a matter of personal preference. The apostrophe is now mostly dropped from common words such as phone (telephone, 'phone).

Current theory and practice now support a balanced view

Many advertisements and newspaper headlines use few marks.

Then	*Now*
Mr.* S.R. Durrell,	Mr* S. R. Durrell
125 Westmacott Parade,	125 Westmacott Pde
Bulli, N.S.W.	Bulli
	NSW 2516

*A full stop is put in if a contraction does not end with the original final letter: Prof. but Mr (Mister).

Unconventional punctuation may be used in emails, or none at all in text messages. Emoticons (see also chapter 18) are increasingly used in text messaging and emails.

A smiley symbol ☺ is made up of typographical colon, dash and bracket. Some word-processing programs convert the three punctuation marks instantly into the smiley

Under the influence of the Internet, different conventions arise about punctuation that encourages immediacy. While writers may sacrifice punctuation for the sake of speed in communication, 'bloggers' must still write clearly and edit their work if they want to attract and keep readers. Remember that the purpose of punctuation is to resolve uncertainty and to convey clear meaning. It is a guide to phrasing (and thus meaning) and allows the reader to hear the words in a text. Punctuation and grammar are keys to sentence structure and to complex thinking and should be woven into the overall literacy program.

▶ Summary

1   Punctuation is important because it adds significant meaning to writing.

2   Punctuation is best taught through students' own writings and reading.

3   Punctuation can accommodate personal style and be used for humorous effect.

4   The history of punctuation shows the change from the standardisation of typographical symbols used in printing to the emoticons of SMS.

5   Students need to know common graphic symbols used in everyday communication.

6   They should be familiar with: capital letters, full stop, semicolon, colon, hyphen, dash, brackets, exclamation mark, question mark, quotation marks, apostrophe, italics, and indentation in paragraphs.

7   The scope and sequence of teaching punctuation will vary depending on the age/ ability of students.

8   While the modern trend is towards less punctuation, readability is the key to its use.

Critical thinking and study exercises

1   Debate whether accurate punctuation is important. Do you get irritated by signs such as *Tomatoe's* or is this being pedantic? Is it discourteous to a reader to be lazy about punctuation? On a continuum scale of tolerance, where would you place yourself in relation to accurate punctuation? Why?

2   Do you agree with Lynne Truss?

The reason it's worth standing up for punctuation is not that it's an arbitrary system of notation known only to an over-sensitive elite who have attacks of the vapours when they see it misapplied. The reason to stand up for punctuation is that without it there is no reliable way of communicating meaning'. (2003: 20)

Look up the *New Yorker* magazine on the Internet for comments on the inconsistency of Truss' own punctuation.

3 Discuss how computer technology has affected punctuation in writing. How can you utilise students' interest in text messaging and email communication to encourage their writing ability?

4 Would you join the Apostrophe Protection Society or support a National Punctuation Day? Why? Why not? Look these up on the Web.

Further reading

Angelillo, J. & L. M. Calkins 2002, *A Fresh Approach to Teaching Punctuation: Helping young writers use conventions with precision and purpose*, Scholastic Professional Books, New York.

Derewianka, B. 1998, *A Grammar Companion for Primary Teachers*, PETA, Sydney.

Partridge, E. 1953, *You Have a Point There*, Hamish Hamilton, London.

Snooks & Co. 2002, *Style Manual For Authors, Editors and Printers*, rev. 6th edn, Snooks & Co., John Wiley & Sons, Canberra.

Truss, L. 2003, *Eats, Shoots & Leaves: The zero tolerance approach to punctuation*, Profile Books, London.

Winch, G. & G. Blaxell 1999, *The Primary Grammar Handbook: Traditional and functional grammar, punctuation and usage*, rev. edn, Horwitz Martin, Sydney.

Web links

Book raps: http://rite.ed.qut.edu.au/old_oz-teachernet/projects/book-rap/about.html

Kim's Korner: www.kimskorner4teachertalk.com

Exploring English: Punctuation: shared-visions.com/explore/english/punct.html

OWL Online Writing Labs, Purdue University

Overview of punctuation. Includes some interactive exercises with answers. http://owl.english.purdue.edu/handouts/grammar/#punctuation

University of Ottawa: Punctuation

Includes section on identifying punctuation errors with exercises and explanations for correct use. www.uottawa.ca/academic/arts/writcent/hypergrammar/node227.html

15 SPELLING SKILLS IN THE CLASSROOM

Overview

Spelling, handwriting, punctuation, and grammar are simply the visible surface beneath which lie the ideas or meaning that writers struggle to compose. Sentences carry significant meanings—experiential, interpersonal, and textual. Writers need to get the conventions right so that ideas can be conveyed with clarity, and as a courtesy to their readers. They need to master the elements of English orthography, which consists of the alphabetic and writing systems but mainly refers to spelling. Phonics instruction is essential in the early years of learning how to spell, but students benefit from many strategies, in particular the wide reading of language and literature in many contexts.

The teaching of spelling skills

Systematic instruction is needed to teach spelling, focusing on the association between sound and symbol and awareness of spelling patterns. A random approach may work with excellent readers who have already gained visual reinforcement of how to spell high-frequency words through their wide reading. A systematic approach, however, which addresses knowledge of the alphabet, phonics, segmentation of words, syllable combinations, vowels and word meanings, will be more effective. Much practice is needed in connecting the spoken and written words, i.e. the phonological and graphic similarities, to develop and improve spelling skills. Spelling behaviour needs to be evaluated so that both the teacher and student can understand why misspellings are made and how to correct them. Accurate spelling is an important tool for effective writing.

Teachers need to have a policy for teaching spelling, keeping the following general principles in mind.

1   The language skills of reading, writing, listening, and speaking are inextricably linked. The skills learnt and practised in any area and the growing knowledge of semantic, graphophonic, and syntactic information can contribute to overall language ability.

2   The main responsibility of a good teacher of writing is to motivate the students to write clearly on topics of their choice over a wide range of text-types. Students can learn to write by writing (with reinforcement from their reading).

3   Shared, Guided, and Independent Writing activities will help students to write more confidently.

4   The teacher should assist where advice is most likely to be noticed and acted upon, namely at the individual student's point of need. This will probably be when the student is actually engaged in writing and can occur at any point in the process. This is why the writing conference is so important—the student can be helped individually—and given assistance not only with the conventions of writing but also with ideas and text-types.

5   Apart from conference sessions, either individual or group, teachers can give whole-class demonstrations for common language features and/or problems.

6   The teacher should encourage a habit of self-correcting when students write. Writing partners can assist when checking needs to take place.

7   Writing intended for readers must be proofread—that is, scrutinised for conformity with standard written English. However, forms of writing such as diary entries, notes, free writing, and trial drafts, not usually intended for readers, need not be subjected to such rigorous checking/editing.

The 'skills' of writing should never be neglected, but they need to be considered in perspective. Writing needs to be approached in a way that will encourage students to write freely and to want to write—not in a way that will stifle creativity.

My family background. My pop cam for england and my great nan came from there. And my anstisers came from Island.

This is the first draft of a student writing about what it means to be an Australian. While sentence structure, spelling and punctuation may need attention, the message is communicated and he has used an appropriate word, 'ancestors'. The teacher must decide where intervention is necessary without discouraging him from wanting to write.

Spelling strategies

Key principles for strategic spelling:

1   Make spelling instruction more fun and engaging.
2   Increase student discussion, analysis, and thought.
3   Provide explicit instruction and practice with spelling strategies.
4   Increase student awareness and use of important language patterns. (Wheatley 2005: 1)

Encourage students to see accurate spelling as a worthwhile goal

Knowing how to spell accurately is acquired through increasing recognition of the patterns of words through

- phonology (how words sound)
- sight (how words look in print or writing)
- morphemes (how words are constructed from meaningful elements)
- etymology (how words are derived; word origins).

Spelling knowledge may be gained by practice in all these areas and through Guided or Shared Writing sessions. Phonemic awareness is particularly important in the early years of gaining spelling skills so that students learn about

- segmentation (e.g. words are separate units)
- isolated sounds (e.g. the first sound in a word)
- discrimination (e.g. similarity or difference between first sounds, as in thin, fat)
- substitution (e.g. making up new words by substituting letters)
- alliteration (e.g. same sound recognition).

Some people look back to a time when they think 'students knew how to spell' because of weekly spelling lists and spelling drills. Others believe that there is only one 'correct' way to spell a word and see spelling as fixed and not subject to change. The spelling of words such as colour/color or program/programme can cause controversy that appears out of proportion to its relative importance. Unlike issues of cohesion or structure, it is usually evident whether a word is spelt correctly or not and the spelling can be verified by consulting a dictionary. Inaccurate spelling is seized upon as a key indicator of a 'poor' writer, yet this is not always the case.

Spelling strategies should be taught, not 'caught', within the context of the school curriculum

At one end of the spectrum are those who say that facility in English spelling is simply acquired by wide reading and that explicit teaching is unnecessary because students will eventually 'pick up' conventional spelling. This raises the ire of those teachers, parents, and researchers who know that some students have not picked up conventional spelling skills at all. A balanced approach is to have an explicit, systematic program for teaching spelling combined with the teaching of spelling as the need arises. Wide reading is essential so that students consolidate their understanding of how words look in print (sight vocabulary).

Five spelling strategies are advocated by Bean & Bouffler (1997: 17):

1   Spelling as it sounds (this may lead to 'invented' spelling).
2   Spelling as it looks (from a student's 'sight' vocabulary).
3   Spelling as it articulates (may also depend on the student's pronunciation).
4   Spelling as it means (e.g. thankyou written as one word seen as a meaningful unit).
5   Spelling by analogy (borrowing from how other similar-sounding words are spelt).

Learners respond positively to a wide range of strategies

Students need to know which strategies can help them to spell better (e.g. by using spelling 'rules', by sounding out words, or by using the dictionary) and when and how to apply these strategies. The teacher's role is to introduce students to a range of strategies and give them practice in using them. In this way students can select those that suit their own personal learning styles and that work for them. Some learn more effectively through the phonogramic mode while others have a kinaesthetic or visual preference. Different words might require different recognition strategies.

In the classroom

1   Help students to visualise the shape and pattern of these words by highlighting particular letters (e.g. all the vowels) or by drawing a box around a selected letter or letters (e.g. segmentation of words).

   quest|ion|s   *student|s|* |*ask*|

   Lead on to similar patterns that other words make.

2   Make up crosswords or acrostics on a particular theme to aid visual recognition. Acrostics are easily done on a computer or can be invented by the students. Acrostics can be formed in lines or verses from the first, the last, or other letters to form a word or phrase.

3   Encourage the use of imagery to remember the spelling of words, e.g.

   accommodation has two c's and two m's—think of two beds;
   practice (the noun) has the word ice in it.

4   Names: make simple acrostics of students' names, e.g. Chris:

   Cheeky
   Happy
   Rowdy
   Impish
   Strong

The stages of spelling development

Spelling development varies from student to student and should not be regarded as a rigid sequence that must be followed in a lock-step manner. Even so, systematic instruction is still needed. The spelling of students must be tested regularly to find out what the problems are, why they are occurring, and what can be done about them.

Systematic spelling instruction is essential

   There are some broad stages of development in spelling that parallel the language–learning continuum as the student moves on to become an independent, effective communicator. Students will progress in their spelling ability if phonics instruction is combined with morphemic analysis. In Kindergarten, they can still be taught about morphemes as they have Big Books read aloud to them.

Spelling sequence

1   Precommunicative: letters/symbols are strung together randomly
2   Pre-phonetic: alphabet letters are recognisable and spelling is attempted by sounding out words
3   Phonetic stage: one-syllable spelling patterns and syllable combinations
4   Transitional stage: the spelling of meaningful parts of words (morphemes)
5   Correct spelling.

1. The precommunicative stage

Random letters and symbols

Although a child's writing development begins when a child first begins to use a writing tool, the first stage is usually not readable. There are usually random strings of symbols that include letters, numbers, and invented shapes. Upper and lower case letters are used indiscriminately. An example is:

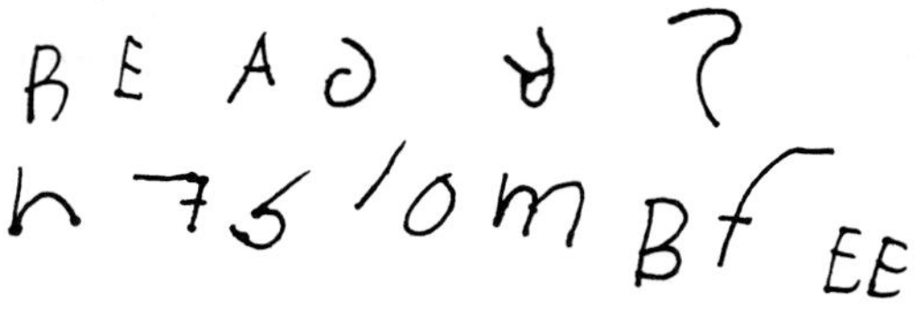

[handwritten: B E A ꝺ ꝺ ? h 7 �5 / o m B f E E]

Although this early stage is a real attempt to reproduce words, it may not conform to left-to-right progression or indicate any real knowledge of sound–letter relationship, although the *r* in mother may be accentuated. Often a striking feature in a word, such as a sound, will lead to the writing of that letter in order to spell the word:

No rigid age guidelines can be given for each developmental stage, as children learn to spell at their own rate. Those who have rich experience with books may have strong visual knowledge of words, which will help them with spelling. This early stage often corresponds to a period between two and four years old.

2. The pre-phonetic stage

At this stage children have begun to make sound–letter correspondences. Meaning is recognisable, with only two or three letters representing a word such as in TL (table), HT (hit), and BRD (bird).

Recognisable letters linked with sounds

Vowels are often introduced, sometimes incorrectly as in BET (bat) or LADE (lady). The important point is that children are making the connection between sound and symbol and are recognising the left-to-right arrangement of words and correct word segmentation, as in TD Z MDA (Today is Monday):

[handwritten: TD Z M DA / TE MSR WZ In Da Zu]

The monster was in the zoo.

The pre-phonetic stage usually covers a period between three and six years of age.

3. The phonetic stage

Matching letters and sounds

During the phonetic stage the child uses an almost perfect match between sound and symbol, even though the spelling is not standard. Like Winnie-the-Pooh, 'My spelling is Wobbly. It's good spelling but it Wobbles, and the letters get in the wrong places' (A.A. Milne: 1926). A trained reader will find a child's attempt at writing both readable and meaningful. Here are two examples:

I WUZ ONLEE FREE.

I was only three.

when I waZ sic I staid in bed.

When I was sick I stayed in bed.

Children are usually at school during the phonetic stage, which covers the period between five and seven years of age. It is at this stage that children are developing word knowledge quickly. They are experimenting with writing and should be encouraged to write freely without penalty for errors. However, the teacher analyses the misspellings and gives strategies to overcome them. Their spelling mistakes reflect a growing awareness of English spelling and they will become increasingly accurate with practice and instruction.

Weak spellers may fossilise at the phonetic stage

4. The transitional stage

In this stage, which usually covers the period between six and eight years of age, children are moving away from the purely phonetic stage and rely more on visual and morphemic modes. As writers progress through this stage, an increasing number of words are spelt accurately.

Uses phonological, sight, and morphemic knowledge

Children now include vowels in every syllable and begin to spell **digraphs** such as *wait* and *seed*. Digraphs are the single sounds made from a combination of two letters, either vowels or consonants, e.g. *ay*, *ea*, *ie*, *th*. Although the visual mode is more in evidence, children have yet to consolidate this strategy and tend to use incorrect spellings such as rec*ee*ve, bl*ea*d, or monst*o*r. Some examples are:

We nent our of the biuldng.
I waRe WITE shose on Satarday.

We went out of the building.
I wore white shoes on Saturday.

5. The correct spelling stage

Between seven and eleven-plus years of age, students become more accurate in their spelling, depending on the difficulty of the words and the general level of discourse. Now children can spell most words they meet, develop a knowledge of 'why' spelling is correct/incorrect, and attain a spelling 'conscience'. In particular, writers at this stage can deal with morphological structures, including prefixes and suffixes, contractions, compound words, derivatives, and silent letter sequences. They use the dictionary to check their spellings. A large body of words is spelt automatically. Students develop a mastery of uncommon and irregular spelling patterns and recognise when a word looks incorrect. An example is:

Thoughtful, accurate spelling

> We used to ~~thro~~ throw the ball st~~y~~ate straight at him.

It is vital to emphasise that because the stages overlap and individual differences are great in any group of students, development to the 'correct' spelling stage will vary greatly.

Misspellings for meaning and rhetorical effect

Unlike the struggling writer, the professional writer sometimes deliberately plays with spelling for rhetorical effect. To appreciate the humour one needs to know the acceptable spelling and how the author has twisted words into new shapes. Strine (Australian) speech is parodied in

It is a pity that Chawcer, who had geneyus, was so unedicated. He's the wuss speller I know of. (Artemus Ward, American humorist, 1834–67)

afferbeck lauder (alphabetical order, the pseudonym of the inventor, Alastair Morrison)

baked necks (bacon 'n' eggs)

Gloria Soame (glorious home).

James Joyce could manipulate language in an incredible way:

Rev. William Archibald Spooner (1844–1930) Warden of New College, Oxford, was noted for his slips of the tongue

All moanday, tearsday, wailsday, thumpsday, frightday, shatterday, till the fear of the Law. (Joyce, *Finnegans Wake*, 1939)

'Spoonerisms' transpose the sounds of words, as in 'weight of rages' for 'rate of wages'.

Malapropism

He is the very pineapple of politeness!

Illiterate him, I say, quite from your memory. (Sheridan, *The Rivals*, 1775).

Malaproprisms where words are misused, usually through lack of knowledge, derived from the character Mrs Malaprop in Sheridan's play *The Rivals* (1775).

Misspellings may also be used to represent accents, e.g.

I am a lone lorn creetur ... and everythink goes contrary with me. (Dickens, *David Copperfield*, 1850, Mrs Gummidge)

IN THE CLASSROOM

Read this verse aloud with students to show them how 'sounds and letters disagree'.

Sounds and letters often disagree

When the English tongue we speak
Why is 'break' not rhymed with 'freak'?
Will you tell me why it's true
We say 'sew' but likewise 'few'?
And the maker of the verse
Cannot cap his 'horse' with 'worse'?
'Beard' sounds not the same as 'heard';
'Cord' is different from 'word';
'Cow is 'cow' but 'low is 'low'
'Shoe' is never rhymed with 'foe';
Think of 'hose' and 'whose' and 'lose'
And think of 'goose' and yet of 'choose'
Think of 'comb' and 'tomb' and 'bomb'
'Doll' and 'roll' and 'home' and 'some';
And since 'pay' is rhymed with 'say',
Why not 'paid' with 'said', I pray?
We have 'blood' and 'food' and 'good',
Wherefore 'done' but 'gone' and 'lone'?
Is there any reason known?
And, in short, it seems to me
Sounds and letters disagree.

(Quoted in Williams 1977: 57)

English orthography

Orthography means the spelling system of a language (literally, 'correct writing'). There is much that is regular in the English writing system. Without conventional spelling, we would not be able to read texts. There cannot, however, be a one-to-one correspondence of sound to symbol. First, there are only twenty-six letters to represent the forty-five meaning-bearing sounds, or phonemes, that make up our speech. Second, we have taken so many words from different languages that additional variation has been included. Fortunately, there are other aspects of language that produce similarities: they are the morphemic, syntactic, and semantic elements.

Making sense of spelling requires thinking strategies, not just phonics or a good memory

English orthography is manageable if we take into account the various ways it is put together. We need to teach sound–letter relationships that are regular, as well as morphemic relationships and letter patterns and sequences. Students need to learn that words are spelt differently in different contexts.

Their home is over their.

Their home is over there.

Good spellers think about their spelling. They use phonetic strategies, meaningful relationships between words, and the visual images the words present. In this way spelling ceases to be a mystery and becomes a remarkable tool for effective and accurate writing. If students are to know how to spell accurately, they need different kinds of spelling knowledge. It is wise for a teacher to explore these different kinds of knowledge so that students can practise different strategies that suit their learning styles and consolidate their understanding of how spelling works. It is clear that instruction about spelling by sound, by pattern, and by meaning is necessary at all levels. Making sense of spelling requires thinking strategies.

Phonics and spelling

Systematic instruction in phonics will give students a better understanding of reading and spelling. In a seven-year longitudinal study of the effects of synthetic phonics teaching on reading

Teach spelling and
reading concurrently

and spelling attainment, Johnston & Watson (2005) found that a synthetic phonics program significantly improved spelling and reading ability.

IN THE CLASSROOM

Synthetic phonics

1   Teach small groups of letters quickly with magnetic letters.

> *a i n p s t*

2   Show how to make up new words which contain these letters:

> *pit, tip, sat, sit*

3   Blend the letter sounds together and pronounce the words they make.
4   Ask students to say the sounds aloud (reinforcing both spelling and reading).
5   Assess students by asking them to push letters together as they try out new blends, pronouncing them at the same time.
6   Devise games for students to play that practise arrangements of groups of letters.
7   Teach digraphs next.

> *ai oa sh th*

Embedding students' learning in meaningful contexts can be achieved by linking spelling with writing and the enjoyment of children's literature:

> whereas it is essential that children are taught the correspondences between spoken sounds at the
> level of the phoneme and their correspondences with written letters through systematic phonics
> training, in the early stages of literacy, teachers must link this with other components of literacy

including reading to children aloud for pure enjoyment of the story and providing a range of other activities such as writing and reading shopping lists or writing down and later reading telephone messages. (Australian Psychological Society 2005: 6)

Phonological knowledge

Linking a word with its sounds is essential in the early years when students are learning how language works. The sound–symbol relationships should be used in conjunction with other semantic knowledge about language. For example, the words *break*, *freak*, *beard*, and *heard* have the same symbol but different sounds.

The hard initial *c* of *crab, cancer* differs in sound from the soft initial *c* of *circle, cicada*, yet the hard *c* is the same sound but a different spelling from the *k* spelling of *kick* or *kimono*

At the pre-phonetic stage the student is beginning to recognise links between sounds and letters or words. The student may easily recognise signs and symbols and frequently seen words that are meaningful.

At the phonetic stage the student recognises sound cues but may still make errors, e.g. *bik* instead of *bike*. Also at this stage

- Words are usually spelt as they sound, e.g. dark
- Commonly seen words are spelt correctly, e.g. the.

Words may look alike but they do not always sound alike

Teaching spelling is really teaching students about words, their patterns and regularities. We can encourage students to take an interest in how words are formed and the many unusual changes words can make in different combinations. It is remarkable that the twenty-six letters of the alphabet can be moved around to create so many different words and meanings. Think of the variant pronunciations of 'ou': *tough*, *bough*, and *dough*, which are pronounced phonetically /tuf/ /bau/ /dou/. Consider also *cough* and *plough*.

Incorrect pronunciation is often the cause of incorrect spelling. This explains the spelling howler of Mt Cyanide for Mt Sinai. Work on phonemes, blends, and digraphs is therefore extremely important. Find out how students pronounce words and listen for added syllables and/or incorrect substitutions that may affect their spelling ability. For example, the following words are often mispronounced in various ways:

Spelling howlers: Moses received the Ten Commandments on Mt. Cyanide. In the 1960s women earned martial leave.

aitch = H (not haitch)	*Australia (not Austraya)*
burglar (not burgular)	*going to (not gunna)*
congratulations (not congradulations)	*library (not liberary)*

Clear articulation can be practised through songs and poems that reveal the importance of pronunciation in particular. Idiosyncratic pronunciation leads to misspellings for both children and adults.

At the kindergarten level it is helpful for students to illustrate their sentences with drawings so that they can demonstrate meaning:

- **Phonemes** are the smallest distinctive group or class of sounds ('phones') in a language. For example, *cap* consists of three different phonemes or sounds and differs from *sap*, *map*, or *cat* simply by changing one sound or phoneme.
- **Blends** are formed when different phonemes come together as in *st*reet, *bl*ue, *cr*ow, *scr*atch, and *pl*ay. Note that blends can be two or three letters in length.
- A **digraph** is a pair of letters that corresponds to a single sound, e.g. *ch* as in *chief* or *ee* as in *meet*. There are vowel and consonant digraphs.
- A **diphthong** is a sequence of two vowels produced in such a way that they are perceived to belong to one syllable, e.g. in Australian English h*o*pe, *wi*de, b*ee*r, b*ea*r.

Phonics instruction is essential in the early years

A knowledge of phonics will help students to spell accurately so that a focus is needed (especially in the early years) on the oral work of pronunciation, especially the segmentation of the spoken word. Flashcards and clapping out the sounds of syllables written on the board can help students hear the different number of syllables and help their spelling, e.g.:

one syllable: *dog*

two syllables: *teach/ er*

three syllables: *tel/ e/ phone*

four syllables: *tel/ e/ vi/ sion*

Visual knowledge

Good spellers can often see if a word looks 'right' on the page or computer screen. They can remember from previous reading and recognition of word patterns what a word looks like. Spelling is heavily dependent on our visual memories of words and their parts. Students who read a lot will have the visual reinforcement of seeing the writing of common words many times, but those students who do not read widely or for pleasure need extra opportunities. Students who write a lot from the early years will gain practice in 'cracking the code' of spelling.

There are some students who have an inability to see spelling errors. As Gentry and Gillet explain:

> The visual coding mechanism is elusive and complex. It is not simple visual memory or a learning style. Undoubtedly, it works in parallel with other processing mechanisms related to spelling. Certainly phonemic, semantic, and etymological associative linkages function in parallel with it, allowing the mind to consider input on different levels and to look for overlap and connections. (1993: 54)

Brain scan research indicates the importance of early, explicit intervention for the teaching of letters and sounds in kindergarten and first grade (Gentry: 2004). Writing skills reinforce reading skills, so that students should be taught to write as they learn to read (Gentry 2006).

A 'sight' vocabulary is very important and can be encouraged by techniques such as *Look—Cover—Write* and games with flashcards. For example, words such as *find, kind, mind,* and *wind* have *ind* in common.

> **Encourage students to be observant about spelling, making a mental picture of words they see**

Morphemic knowledge

The morphology of words refers to their form or structure, and the meaningful units of which they consist, such as word bases, prefixes, and suffixes. Students can be taught the morphemes that make up a word. For example, the word *spelling* consists of two morphemes: *spell* and *ing*. Here, the morpheme *spell* can stand alone but the morpheme (or unit) *ing* is bound to the word *spell*. Correct morphemic division is important, as well as the ability to put a word into its syllables. Students vary in their abilities to do this and it can be confusing that the pronunciation of words does not always correspond with the morphemic division, e.g.:

> **Morphemes are minimum meaningful units of language, e.g. *childish* = 2 morphemes *child* and *ish***

> *res/ig/na/tion (syllables), is pronounced resig'nation, but it is composed of three morphemes: re/sign/ation*

If students can recognise patterns in words, they can become better spellers.

At the kindergarten level, recognising the beginning letters of words, and how the main vowels are pronounced, needs to be practised, in context and with illustrations if possible, e.g. *rain, read, ride, rose, rule*. Students at the early levels will need much repetition in various guises as well as explanation to help them memorise and 'ingest' the information.

Bases of words

Knowledge of a base word will often help the student to decipher its meaning and correct spelling, and to understand that words often belong to 'families'. For example, *learn, learner, learning* have a similar base. Grammatically, the base or 'root' of a word is a morpheme that can be expanded by grammatical inflections (word endings) or by prefixes and suffixes. For example, *child* is the root of the words *children, childlike, childproof, childhood, childless, childishness*. Recognition of base words will help students become good spellers as they see the extensions and derivatives that can be built from them, such as the *-ed* past tense ending, and the *s* or *es* of plurals.

IN THE CLASSROOM

1   Students can make up card sets of some of these word roots and play a game of Snap, locating the base of a word. Many variations can be made of Snap to illustrate different elements of spelling. For example, the card pack contains words from which compounds can be made, making a 'snap' when a compound word occurs, e.g.:

> *Word bases with suffixes: friend = friendship*
>
> *Compound words, or collocations: child + proof = childproof; board + room = boardroom*

2   Make up a chart of words with Greek word elements, e.g. *geo-* is a word element from the Greek, meaning earth. From this, additions to a 'Greek' chart can be made:

GEO (Gk) = EARTH   geography, geology

Word base	Origin	Meaning	Examples
bi	Latin/Greek	two	bicycle, bimonthly
sex	Latin	six	sextet, sextuplet
bio	Greek	life	biography, biology
ology	Greek	the science of	biology, palaeontology

Prefixes

Good spellers can recognise the syllables that make up a word. They can integrate this information with other language knowledge such as the recognition of prefixes and suffixes. Students can be taught to identify prefixes, that is, those letters put before a word that add to or qualify its meaning. Thus *un-* before a word affects its meaning, implying the opposite condition. For example, *un-*, in

A prefix is put before a word to qualify its meaning

> *unkind* means *not kind*
>
> *unlike* means *not like* or *not similar*
>
> *unbolted* means *not fastened*
>
> *unprejudiced* means *not biased*.

Students will come to recognise the link between sound and meaning, e.g. in understanding various prefixes or suffixes. A recognition of parts of words, e.g. prefixes *super-*, *trans-*, *circum-*, and suffixes *-r*, *-ng*, *-sh*, *-y*, can help students to spell better if practice is given in their use and meaning.

Suffixes

Common English suffixes are: *-ble*, *-ry*, *-se*, *-ng*, *-sh*, *-sm*, *-te*, *-et*, *-ike*, *-ing*, *-ess*, *-ship*, and *-tion*. Suffixes are a little complicated because they can alter the spelling or grammatical status of a word, e.g. the addition of *-ing* changes the word *love* into *loving*. 'Rules' for adding suffixes can help students with spelling, e.g. *y* changes to *i* before *-ed* (a suffix beginning with a vowel) so that *satisfy* becomes *satisfied*.

A suffix is an addition (or affix) to a word

SUFFIXES

No change at all: appear, appeared, appearing, appearance.

Some changes: satisfy, satisfying, satisfied.

It is very rare to see double i (ii) together in words of the English language.

The silent e is dropped: dance, danced, dancing, danceable, love, loved, loving, lovable.

IN THE CLASSROOM

Word webs

Form 'word webs' to help students build up their bank of vocabulary. For example, the morphemes *-ing* or *-ed* are commonly used for participles and the teacher can indicate how some of the past tense endings change.

Present (with –ing)	Past (–ed or other)
playing	played
looking	looked
flying	flew
reading	read
sleeping	slept
running	ran

Etymological knowledge

Etymology is the study of the origin and history of individual words, the language they derived from, and how the meanings and forms have changed over time. Knowing the history of a word can sometimes stimulate interest in its meaning and encourage students to remember its spelling. For example, the word 'robot' was first used in a play, *R.U.R.* written by Karel Capek (1890–1938) and came from the Czech word *robotnik*, meaning a serf.

Etymology of *spelling*: Old English *spelian* = represent

IN THE CLASSROOM

1 Make charts to reinforce etymological knowledge, encouraging students' interest in language, e.g. the derivation of the word *electric* from the Greek *elektron* (i.e. amber, a substance that can be used to create electricity from friction). A word bank can be built up using words that are commonly used with electric:

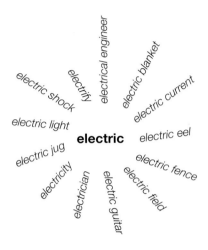

2 Many words in English are derived from other languages. Ask for suggestions, especially from multilingual students. Most English words are derived from Greek, Latin, or French words but new words or phrases are always being added from other languages or simply made up.

Construct different charts that can have words added to them as students find etymological derivations from the dictionary. Charts can be made of words or phrases of

a slang words: Which are current? Which have dropped from use? Do Australians still refer to people as 'blokes' and 'sheilas'?

b acronyms: words formed from the initial letters of other words, e.g. Anzac (Australian and New Zealand Army Corps), AIDS (acquired immune deficiency syndrome), MIRV (multiple independently targeted re-entry vehicle)

c neologisms: new words or new sense of old words (beatnik, Internet, ATM, hole-in-the-wall)

d words from other countries (blitz, junta, yum cha).

Learning styles and spelling strategies

Teachers should observe and record their students' strategies in learning how to write and spell. A record of how students actually behave when writing and spelling words will allow the teacher to build on the strategies that work for the students and introduce them to other strategies that might be helpful. Observations can be made on how students

- sound out words and then write them down
- look up words in a dictionary (or picture dictionary)
- use others (such as a peer or aide, or the teacher) to find out the spelling or meaning of a word

- have a knowledge of how words are segmented and how syllables form words
- are willing to try to spell a word
- attempt to proofread
- edit.

Asking why students have spelt a word in a certain way will often reveal the cause of a misspelling. Their spelling may be the result of visual memory of how it is spelt. If it is a new word they may borrow strategies from their previous knowledge; for example, a commonly used ending such as *-ion* may help them to spell a word such as *action*; or they may rely on how it is sounded out.

Students do not spell randomly but use reasoning processes

A student who tries to spell an unknown word may draw on all kinds of information, including phonological, morphological, and visual knowledge (sometimes for the same word). In writing the word *schools*, the student may be quite confident about the *s* and the *oo* sounds; he may realise that the word has a plural ending and register the unusual beginning of *sch-* from a sight vocabulary. The word *school* has many dictionary definitions, mostly related to educational instruction. It is pronounced /skul/. The word is mainly used as a noun and can be used colloquially, as in a two-up school. Its derivation is from Middle English, Old English, Latin, and Greek words, e.g. Greek *schole*, Latin *schola*. School originally meant 'leisure' but its meaning has changed over the years to denote how we might spend our leisure, that is, in a place for studying.

Knowledge about spelling is often drawn from a combination of factors

Here a student has misspelt words but clearly knows the message to be communicated.

Original	Student Correction
I here the bell ring.	I hear the bell ring.
I were the boots.	I wear the boots.

Spelling strategies are diverse. A common strategy often used by the poor speller is that of 'avoidance'. If unsure about a word, a student may try ignoring it altogether and try to find a different word to express meaning.

Avoidance is a spelling strategy

'Have a go' books

Students must be encouraged to attempt new spelling, to 'have a go', perhaps with a special book in which they can record their attempts so that the teacher can observe on what basis they spell a word. They need to be taught to try out their best version of spelling. 'Have a go' books encourage risk-taking, which is important for students to progress in their writing and spelling. Books are often divided into four columns: student's 1st attempt; 2nd attempt; spelling check; and personal dictionary.

Trying out variants of spelling leads to future accuracy

Accurate, independent spelling comes about with risk-taking behaviour. If students feel they are in an atmosphere where they can try out words without being criticised, they are more likely to become good spellers.

These lists provide a record for both the student and the teacher to monitor progress.

IN THE CLASSROOM

1 Encourage students to think of the most appropriate strategy to discover how to spell a word. Write down various words students have struggled with and build up a chart of strategies or key features to help in spelling. Students may find their own idiosyncratic ways of memorising, perhaps with a mnemonic:

Words	Strategy to remember
accommodation	double c and double m and three o's
separate	don't get separated from your parachute or you could be paralysed
tripod	tri means three
breakfast	two words break and fast form a compound word that means breaking your fast

2 Spell problem words and create a personal mnemonic to remember them.

Correct spelling matters

While students are engaged in the creative process of writing, it can be argued that they do not really need to know how to spell every word. This is especially true at the early level where students have the oral vocabulary to express their ideas but not the formal knowledge of transcription.

Good literacy skills are needed in schools, the community, and the workplace

However, once others want to read the text, and if it is 'published' in some form, then there is a need for accuracy. Correct spelling is needed for the meaning of the text to be communicated, as readers are easily distracted from the meaning and the message by surface features of idiosyncratic or indecipherable spelling. While 'invented' spelling is part of the developmental continuum, the aim is to progress towards conventional spelling as quickly as possible. Identifying spelling errors should be regarded as an essential editing practice after the completion of writing. Editing can be done with the teacher's help, alone, or with peers. Good spelling matters. Weak spellers may have their job applications rejected after employers read the first few lines.

Spelling lists

Vocabulary that arises from class discussion in various subject areas may be listed on the board, in the students' books, or on a general list collated by the teacher. To some extent the 'list' is an arbitrary collection that will therefore be inappropriate for all children—some will find the vocabulary beyond their reach and understanding; others may consider it a waste of time. However, relevant lists can aid vocabulary development and be used to develop spelling skills.

Here is a list of words used during the day from a Year 2–3 composite class. It includes words from an Italian lesson learnt in the school:

niece   *nephew*   *bambino*

sulk	*bulk*	*ciao*
should	*would*	*Napoli*
slave	*slaving*	*bene*
ferried	*ferry*	
carried	*carry*	
playing	*playground*	

The following list, which includes sentences, is from a Year 3–4 class after news of an earthquake disaster:

Japan, Kobe, Tokyo, tremor, earthquake, shock wave, after shock, crust, island
The capital of Japan is Tokyo.
Kobe had an earthquake.

Rote learning of spelling is not a useful technique for encouraging students to spell, because words out of context are difficult to remember. While avid readers become familiar with words and learn to spell without much explicit instruction, many students do not register this skill and remain keen readers but poor spellers. All students need to be taught how to recognise and be aware of how words are spelt, to know when a possible misspelling occurs, and to be able to consult a dictionary. While isolated words out of context might be difficult to spell, lists of commonly needed words or phrases can be made which can help the student.

A spelling list need not be random lists of words to memorise and spell

Weekly spelling lists may bore good spellers and demotivate bad spellers. To help overcome these problems:

1   Compile meaningful lists from
    • lists of words related to work done in the classroom in connection with a theme or a topic from a particular subject area
    • words centring on a topic discussed
    • words that have similar features, e.g. the -ing ending
    • word families
    • high-frequency words (e.g. from Johnson or Dolch word lists available on the Internet)
    • class or personal dictionaries made by students as they come across new words.
2   Introduce 'spelling buddies' to help one another and make a weekly test a cooperative exercise, rather than a competition.
3   Convert 'lists' into wall charts, or 'hanging wall dictionaries', so that students can check spelling as they are writing. Commercial word charts may also be useful, e.g. of the sounds of English, blends, and digraphs.
4   Encourage parent participation by asking them to help students and to sign the list of words learnt.

Edward Dolch, in 1948, made lists of commonly used words and the ninety-five most frequently used nouns

In the classroom

Personal dictionaries

- From the very beginning, students can be encouraged to keep their own personal word lists or dictionaries. They can record words, phrases, or sentences they have come across that are useful to them and that they want to reproduce accurately in their writing.
- Students may also keep an additional list of word banks, phrases or sentences from their classroom activities.
- With the help of students, teachers can compile lists that centre on a theme or a topic being discussed in class. This may help students to put words into context and remember them. Isolated words out of context do not have a 'hook' for students to peg their memory on.

Editing

There is a caveat about teaching spelling: spelling should not be taught in a manner that hampers the imagination of students so that they become fearful of making mistakes. There are clear links between children's invented spelling, the ability to segment words, and the development of phonological awareness (Silva & Alves Martins 2003). This is why 'invented' spelling is acceptable in the very early years. Our aim is to encourage students to become confident communicators who try to write in an interesting and informative way. They should not deliberately choose a simple word because they cannot spell a more difficult but more appropriate word, using the avoidance strategy.

Editing is essential for accurate spelling

Instruction about the process of writing from drafts to published product can show students how standard spelling can be arrived at. Teachers can point out that spelling errors can be edited in later drafts of the writing process, especially with computer tools that automatically check spelling. Accurate spelling is an important element of the final draft of a text.

Computer checking

Computer tools improve spelling accuracy. If the original work has been word-processed, errors picked up may be simply typographical (e.g. computers tend to correct *hte* to *the* automatically), but teachers should encourage students to take note of which spelling errors they make and why they might have made them. Berninger (2002) suggests that the spellchecker may not be useful until 5th grade, but this may vary because of teacher input and individual aptitude. Explicit instruction is needed to point out the limitations of the spellcheck facility, appreciating that this facility will not present them with an error-free text. Students will need instruction in:

- how to choose from the list of spelling options in words
- why some misspelt words may not be picked up because they are homophones, e.g. *there/their, it's/its*
- words that do not appear in the computer's thesaurus, e.g. local place names and names of people
- the common American spelling variants, e.g. *centre/center*

- spelling errors that may not be located on a computer spellcheck because they are grammatically the wrong word (though correctly spelt). For example, misspelt variants of a sentence may be picked up by a grammar checker, but not by the spellcheck: *They're* leaving! Put *their* suitcases over *there*.

▶ LITERACY IN THE DIGITAL AGE

Demonstrate to students the need to have a range of strategies for good spelling. The computer spellchecker is invaluable, but it is not enough. Give them sentences which need to be edited.

- Some students will just choose any word from a list of alternatives on the spellchecker if they are poor or lazy spellers.
- Some stewdenz (student/stewed) will just chooz (choose, chaos, chook, chokos—9 choices), eny (envy, any, deny, end) word from a list of orlternatiffs (no spelling suggestions) on the spellchecker if they are pore (not picked up on spellchecker) or lazy spellers.

Even using the spellchecker, the edited sentence may be written as:

- Some student will just choose any word from a list of orlternatiffs on the spellchecker if they are pore or lazy spellers.

Spelling 'rules' or generalisations

There are many specialised and esoteric words in the English language which are difficult to spell. There are, however, many systematic aspects of English spelling. By the end of the primary years of schooling, students should be able to

Highlight the systematic elements of English spelling

- spell frequently used words
- make an attempt at other words they have not seen before
- use the dictionary to check spelling.

Focusing on the peculiarities of the English language may be fun, but there are many more regularities that have evolved to form conventional spelling. Spelling is systematic to a great extent despite the irregular forms that make English spelling unpredictable at times.

Rhyming rule: *I* before *E* except after *C*, e.g. *ceiling, deceit, receive*

IN THE CLASSROOM

Four spelling rules

Find examples to match the rules, in context, or extended discourse, from children's literature and everyday texts:

1   Drop the e

   e.g. joke/joking, live/living

   Example: The first thing Shy could remember was living in a round, dark, leafy nest with her mother and baby brother, Spur. (Leslie Rees, *Shy the Platypus*, 1945)

2 Double the letters

e.g. *fun/funny*

3 *i* before *e* except after *c*

e.g. *believe/receive*

4 Change the *y* to *i*

e.g. *lady/ladies*

a Use linguistically accurate terminology such as *consonant*, *vowel*, etc. for advanced students.
b Double the end consonant after a short vowel.
c For one-syllable words ending with a consonant immediately after a short vowel, double the final consonant when adding a suffix that begins with a vowel, e.g. *fun/funny*.
d Discuss the exceptions to each rule, with examples, e.g. *i* before *e* except after *c*.

Exception: Drop the *e* in most cases but keep it after *c* and *g*, as in *notice/noticeable*.

Spelling plurals

The following rules, put into a meaningful context, may help in teaching plural endings:
1 Add *s* to singular nouns: dog—dogs.
2 Words that end in *fe* or *lf* are made plural by changing them to a *v* and adding *es*: knife—knives, calf—calves.
3 If a word ends in *s x z ch sh* or *zz*, an *es* is added: bus—buses, witch—witches.
4 If the last two letters of a word are a vowel followed by a *y*, add an *s*: toy—toys.
5 If the last two letters of a word are a consonant followed by *y*, change the *y* to an *i* and add *es*: fairy—fairies, ferry—ferries.
6 Those words that do not add an *s* can be taught separately: fish, sheep, deer.
7 Others are still more irregular and change their vowel: tooth—teeth, mouse—mice, or add *-en*: ox—oxen, child—children.

Teaching spelling and effective classroom practices

Teach spelling across the curricula Spelling is best taught through the work that is carried on across all the curricular areas. Specific spelling lessons may be part of a Guided and Shared Writing session, but for the most part spelling 'should be taught in the context of a talking, listening, reading or writing focus' (NSW Department of Education and Training 1998a: 7).

Much spelling instruction will occur as part of a general Literacy Session, rather than as a more formal 'lesson'. Shared, Guided, and Independent language teaching strategies will provide many opportunities for the teacher to provide informal instruction (see chapter 8).

Multiliteracies

Literacy Session on 'monsters'

1 Use different communication media such as cartoons (*The Incredible Hulk*), film (*Shrek*), audio (*Beauty and the Beast* recorded story), paintings (Uccello's *St George and the Dragon*) to show how 'monsters' are portrayed.

2 Find illustrations and information on monsters from books and the Internet, e.g. dragons, Dracula, Frankenstein, Loch Ness Monster.

3 Incorporate these ideas into students' writing tasks, using the strategies of Shared, Guided and Independent Writing.

Shared Writing

The teacher and students suggest relevant words, phrases, and sentences that might describe monsters:

> *frightening, horrible*
> *the shocking appearance; a dreadful lurch*
> *The enormous ogre turned away.*

Words from topics studied, words from the curriculum, or high-frequency words can be written on cards. These cards are then given to students who have to sort them into particular sets. For example, they may sort them into verbs and make up sentences in which the words are appropriate.

Guided Writing

The class, with assistance from the teacher, writes sentences using some of the vocabulary found on 'monsters'.

Write a dictation that uses words from the 'monsters' topic. Put the dictation on an overhead transparency with the key words highlighted. Discuss the correct version sentence by sentence so that students can easily see how the word is spelt. This activity can encourage editing and proofreading.

Independent Writing

Students look up a dictionary and a thesaurus to find synonyms for words associated with monsters, e.g. ghouls, scary, frightening, horror.

'Look, say, cover, write, say, check'

This strategy works well for a wide range of students because it appeals to different senses and visual, kinaesthetic, and cognitive aspects of learning. It may appear time-consuming but it is effective, especially in the early years. Naturally, as their ability increases and they apply the strategy almost automatically, students may choose to skip stages or say the word silently. Give students explicit instructions:

Use multisensory strategies to teach spelling

1 **Look** at a word carefully and observe its visual pattern.

2 **Say** the word aloud—this practice helps to reinforce the memory of the structure of the word, especially if the word is pronounced in its syllables.

3 **Cover**—this gives time to ruminate about what the word looked like in print.

4. **Write**—this further reinforcement mirrors the original word and reinforces the spelling pattern.

5. **Say**—by saying the word again, students may pick up whether it is accurately spelt.

6. **Check**—confirms accuracy of spelling.

In the classroom

1 With instruction from the teacher, each student makes a personal 'Look, say, cover, write, say, check' folder that includes a section for writing down frequently used words or words they find difficult, and another page for writing down spelling attempts. Encourage the use of this strategy for those students who will benefit from it.

2 Encourage all students to keep a small A–Z book which they can use as a personal dictionary, collecting words of interest to them. Environmental print and children's literature are excellent sources.

Spelling bees

Once students can spell fairly well they can take part in spelling bees, in the classroom, or held between neighbouring schools. Spelling lists can be provided including words students will encounter in different curricula, e.g. science and maths words such as *average*. A viewing of the documentary *Spellbound* (2002) may stimulate interest and motivate students about learning words, their meaning and spellings. It is important to ensure that all students achieve some improvement in their spelling ability—the spelling bee is not just for the winners or the elite spellers. Environmental print and children's literature are excellent sources.

A spelling bee is not simply a memory test

In the classroom

a Play spelling games that make learning spelling fun through games such as Sound and Word Bingo.

b Explore games that play with letters and combinations of words—such as rhymes, word play, or crossword puzzles. In the early years, alliterative rhymes and tongue-twisters can help students recognise letters, e.g. 'Peter Piper picked a peck of pickled peppers'. Remember that students from a language background other than English may not easily understand some of these. Even better are sentences or rhymes students invent themselves.

c Give students practice in awareness of homonyms and homographs, using them in context so that they can understand the meaning. Homonyms are words that are alike in some form. Technically, they are divided into homophones, words that sound the same but have different meanings (such as *fare* and *fair*) and homographs, words that look the same when written but have different meanings, such as *minute* (unit of time) and *minute* (very small), *bow* (to bend over) and *bow* (the front of a boat). Commonly confused homographs are:

  bear, bare
  by, buy

hear, here

pair, pear, pare

piece, peace

their, there, they're

to, too, two

wear, where, we're, ware

which, witch.

Using the dictionary, the thesaurus, and word banks

Students in all grades should be encouraged to own a dictionary that is appropriate to their reading level. By Years 3 and 4 they should be using dictionaries whenever they do written work. The dictionary is not just a tool to check the accuracy of conventional spelling but can open up the world of words to students. A simple dictionary entry contains a magnitude of information that may help students become aware of a word's meaning, how it is pronounced, with perhaps a phrase to illustrate what part of speech it is, whether it is used colloquially, and its etymology.

Dictionaries are indispensable aids to spelling for teachers and students

Students should be given many opportunities to familiarise themselves with the resources of dictionaries. In the early stages instruction should be given in how to locate words quickly and to practise alphabetical order. This may also be achieved through other resources such as telephone directories, indexes, street maps, or encyclopaedias.

Looking up a thesaurus can help students choose words that are the most appropriate in context and that will communicate meaning more forcefully. Students can expand their vocabulary through a range of writing activities, complemented by specific examples (from an authentic text, if possible) that focus on expansion of word knowledge. For example, different words for *big* or *little* could be substituted in sentences, encouraging students to discuss why words such as *colossal* or *petite* might be more appropriate, interesting, or more specific in conveying meaning to the reader.

Encourage the use of *Roget's Thesaurus* and the computer thesaurus

Spelling and the future

Clarity of communication is a necessity in written communication so it is likely that spelling in the future will still have established standards, accessible in dictionaries. Diversity and change will be introduced, however, through new usage and new vocabulary. Increasing numbers of people in the world speak and write English, using it as a *lingua franca*, a medium for communication, to suit their own needs. There are many Englishes.

Singlish, *no 'poblem'*, reads a T shirt from Singapore

e-spelling

Is spelling reform doomed? There have been many passionate advocates of spelling reform in the interests of clarity and economics, including George Bernard Shaw (1856–1950), who saw no reason why *bomb* should not be spelt *bom*. Relaxed (or lax) spelling standards in SMS

Figure 15.1 A page from the Oxford Dictionary

Guide to dictionary entries

Headword: the word being defined in the entry. Entries are arranged in alphabetical order of headwords.

Plural: the plural form of the headword.

Raised numbers: distinguish words with the same spelling that have separate entries for different parts of speech or unrelated meanings.

Compound: a word formed from the headword plus one or more other words.

Derivative: a word derived from the headword whose meaning can be worked out from the meaning of the headword.

Verb forms: the first form is the past tense, the second the past participle, and the third the present participle.

Phrase: a set phrase whose main word is the headword of the entry.

Verb forms: the first form is the past tense and past participle; the second is the present participle.

amnesia (*say* am-**nee**-zee-ā) *noun* loss of memory. [from Greek *a-* = without, + *-mnesis* = memory]

formal *adjective* strictly following the accepted rules or customs; ceremonious. **formally** *adverb*

kilo *noun* (*plural* **kilos**) a kilogram.

kind[1] *noun* a class of similar things or animals; a sort or type.
payment in kind payment in goods not in money.

Usage Correct use is *this kind of thing* or *these kinds of things* (not 'these kind of things').

kind[2] *adjective* friendly and helpful; considerate. **kind-hearted** *adjective*, **kindness** *noun*

kindy *noun* (*Australian informal*) kindergarten.

king *noun* **1** a man who is the ruler of a country through inheriting the position. **2** a person or thing regarded as supreme, *the lion is the king of beasts*. **3** the most important piece in chess. **4** a playing card with a picture of a king. **kingly** *adjective*, **kingship** *noun*

opt *verb* choose.
opt out decide not to join in. [from Latin *optare* = wish for]

weapon *noun* something used to do harm in a battle or fight. **weaponry** *noun*

wear[1] *verb* (**wore, worn, wearing**) **1** have something on your body as clothes, ornaments, etc. **2** damage something by rubbing or using it often; become damaged in this way, *The carpet has worn thin*. **3** last while in use, *It has worn well*. **wearable** *adjective*, **wearer** *noun*
wear off be removed by wear or use; become less intense.
wear on pass gradually, *The night wore on*.
wear out use or be used until it becomes weak or useless; exhaust.

wear[2] *noun* **1** clothes, *formal wear*. **2** damage resulting from ordinary use, *wear and tear*.

weary[1] *adjective* (**wearier, weariest**) **1** tired. **2** tiring, *It's weary work*. **wearily** *adverb*, **weariness** *noun*

weary[2] *verb* (**wearied, wearying**) tire.

worn[1] *past participle* of **wear**[1].

Pronunciation: where it is not obvious we show how to say the word. (See also p. vi.)

Etymology: the origin of the headword.

Definition: the meaning of the headword.

Usage note: a note explaining correct usage.

Usage label: indicates the word belongs to Australian English and is normally used informally. (See p. vi for more information on usage labels.)

Part of speech: describes the grammatical use of a word as a *noun*, *verb, adverb, adjective, etc.*

Numbers: used for different senses of the headword.

Example: shows how the word is used and helps to clarify the meaning.

Adjective forms: the comparative and superlative forms of the headword.

Cross-reference: refers the reader to another entry for more information.

iv

electronic messages, encouraged by truncating words to write quickly, will make some of Shaw's hopes come true. Many students are familiar with the SMS word prediction facility whereby the word is completed after typing in only the first few letters. Spelling in text messages is highly personalised and similar to informal conversation. It tends to use abbreviations without vowels, e.g. see you = cu.

TABLE 15.1   Abbreviations used in SMS, electronic communication

BCNU	be seeing you	L8R	later
BFN	bye for now	LOL	laughing out loud; lots of luck
B4	before	PCM	please call me
CU	see you	PLS	please
CUL8R	see you later	SIT	stay in touch
GR8	great	TTYL	talk to you later
FYI	for your information	TX	thanks
HTH	hope this helps	2NITE	tonight
KIT	keep in touch	2DAY	today
KWIM	know what I mean	2MORO	tomorrow
XOXOX	hugs and kisses		

The computer

The rise of computer usage has a significant impact, paradoxically to elevate the importance of spelling, or to downplay its significance. The computer provides an excellent resource for students to work independently on language skills. **Strict spelling accuracy is necessary for locating websites** Some students enjoy working with commercial products that teach spelling. If a resource is useful for a particular student, then it becomes a successful learning strategy. Innovations exist such as reading pens which, when run over written text, can spell out a word letter by letter, break it into syllables, and provide a dictionary definition. Authentic language can be found in computer-assisted learning programs and these can facilitate the spelling acquisition process. Some interactive software is excellent for practising spelling, especially that which teaches spelling through imaginative games. Talking books on the computer such as the stories from the Oxford Reading Tree allow students to highlight particular words and to hear the correct pronunciation at the same time. Subtitles on television programs and DVDs can also assist students' spelling skills.

Ideas about spelling and writing will be transformed as we enter a world of increasing technology, multiculturalism, and globalisation. As Gunther Kress points out:

> The new technologies of direct voice interaction with computing devices will make available new routes to making speech visible, not handled by the hand and the pen, or by the hand and the keyboard. This will have the most profound effects on what we think writing is and on what writing will become under the control of speech; writing will, in the very near future, be speech displayed on a screen. The whole vast machinery of spelling regulation will very likely be unmade or remade by this move. (2000: 9)

▶ Summary

1 Spelling is an aspect of literacy which should be taught in relation to other language skills of reading, writing, listening, and speaking.

2 Spelling is learnt through a combination of how words sound (phonics), by visual cues, and through knowledge of morphemes and etymology.

3 Multiple strategies should be taught for children to learn spelling.

4 There are various developmental stages in learning how to spell: the precommunicative, pre-phonetic, phonetic, transitional, and correct spelling stages.

5 Teaching activities for spelling should be varied and interesting, mostly relating to work done in the context of the curricula: word webs, 'have a go' books, spelling lists, spelling 'rules' or generalisations, 'look, say, cover, write, say, check', using the dictionary, thesaurus, and word banks.

6 With increased technology, writing is likely to become more speech-like in its features, as shown in the e-spelling of text messaging.

7 Spelling undergoes change through the influence of technology and new writing practices.

Critical thinking and study exercises

1 What do various groups in society think about the importance of spelling? Construct a survey on spelling and administer it to your peers. Include the factors that have a positive impact on spelling ability (e.g. use of a dictionary) and negative impact (e.g. lack of interest) on the ability to spell. What is your attitude to incorrect spelling by students in primary school?

2 Discuss how instruction in phonics can help students become better spellers, readers and writers. What was your own experience in learning how to spell? How do you think this will influence your teaching of spelling?

3 Read through a children's literature text or factual text and select significant words that you want students to understand and use. Analyse these words and devise appropriate strategies so that students can use them correctly in their own writing. Devise activities to use the words in appropriate contexts.

Further reading

Students are advised to consult the current curriculum and support documents relating to the teaching of spelling in their state or territory.

Bean, W. 2000, *Ways to Teach Spelling*, Pen 124, PETA, Sydney.

Bean, W. & C. Bouffler 1987, *Spell by Writing*, PETA, Sydney.

Berninger, V. W. et al. 2002, 'Teaching spelling and composition alone and together: implications for the simple view of writing', *Journal of Educational Psychology* 94(2): 291–304.

Bouffler, C. 1997, 'They don't teach spelling anymore—or do they?', *Australian Journal of Language and Literacy* 20(2): 140–7.

Department of Education and Student Services, South Australia 1997, *Spellings from Beginnings to Independence*, Darlington Materials Development Centre, Seacombe Gardens, SA.

Fresch, M. & A. Wheaton 1997, 'Sort, search and discover: spelling in the student-centred classroom', *The Reading Teacher* 51(1): 20–30.

Gentry, R. J. 2004, *The Science of Spelling: The explicit specifics that make great readers and writers (and spellers!)*, Heinemann, Portsmouth, N.H.

Gentry, R. J. & J. W. Gillett 1993, *Teaching Kids to Spell*, Heinemann, Portsmouth, N.H.

Gentry, R. J. 2006, *Breaking the Code: The new science of beginning reading and writing*, Heinemann, Portsmouth, N.H.

Heald-Taylor, B. G. 1998, 'Three paradigms of spelling instruction in Grades 3 to 6', *The Reading Teacher* 51(5): 404–13.

Johnston, R. S. & J. E. Watson 2005, *A Seven Year Study of the Effects of Synthetic Phonics Teaching on Reading and Spelling Attainment*, Scottish Executive Education Department, Edinburgh.

Roberts, J. 2001, *Spelling Recovery*, ACER, Melbourne.

Silva, A. & M. Alves Martins 2003, 'Relations between children's invented spelling and the development of phonological awareness', *Educational Psychology* 23(1): 3–16.

Snowball, D. & F. Bolton 1999, *Spelling K–8: Planning and Teaching*, Stenhouse Publishers, Maine.

Westwood, P. 1999, *Spelling: Approaches to teaching and assessment*, ACER, Melbourne.

Wheatley, J. P. 2005, *Strategic Spelling: Moving beyond word memorization in the middle grades*, IRA, Newark, Del.

Web links

First Steps program: http://www.myread.org/monitoring_first.htm
Teaching Handwriting and Spelling skills, Phonics program: www.thrass.com.au
Department of Education and Training (NSW): www.curriculumsupport.nsw.edu.au/literacy
Master Snoopy's Spelling
Monker's Spelling Submarine
Spell Dodger!
Spell It
Stickybear Spelling tutor
Super Solvers Spellbound
Zug's Spelling Adventure

16 HANDWRITING SKILLS IN THE CLASSROOM

Overview

Handwriting may be the Cinderella of the language skills but it deserves close attention because it develops skills needed for good readers and writers. Phonics instruction in the early years should be linked with practice in the writing of letters and sounds. A crucial asset for handwriting is 'the ability to code an identified language symbol (letter) in memory', not just fine motor skills (Berninger 1998: 47). Fluent writing requires the student to retrieve letters quickly. A formal program of instruction is needed to teach students the most efficient way to write and remember letters. Time invested in handwriting instruction need not be spent on old-fashioned copy drills. The acquisition of automatic handwriting skills frees the student to focus on the quality of ideas and spelling without the distraction of illegibility or worries about the appearance of written work. The aim is to write letters automatically, choosing the right ones from the choice of 26 letters. Good handwriting visually reinforces the memory for word patterns that can help in speaking, spelling and writing more effectively.

Handwriting involves memorisation of letters and words

Handwriting

Link handwriting with phonics instruction

Legible handwriting is a necessary skill so that writing can be understood by others. Handwriting should not, however, be taught in isolation from other language features. To do so can make writing a meaningless task. Recognising and memorising the shapes of letters (both upper and lower case) can be linked with lessons on:

- literature and the reading session
- pronunciation

- spelling (e.g. letter combinations to make words)
- punctuation
- graphic design: distinctive shapes communicate different meanings (e.g. the letter x can symbolise many different meanings)
- the texture of typefaces, showing that different choices result in different kinds of communications.

Examples of typography

Shown below are the different results that can be obtained by the application of selected fonts, sizes, styles, and special effects that a word-processing program can provide. Remember that there are myriad additional choices to be made from computer programs.

Fonts
Courier
Helvetica
New York
Times

Font styles
Bold
Italic
Regular

Font size
10 point

12 point

24

36

Special effects
Shadow

CAPITALISE

small caps

Outline

The quick brown fox jumped over the lazy dog.

This is written in Times font, in regular style, 12 point, with no special effects.

Encourage students to see how different typography can be used, e.g. Helvetica, bold and italic, 24 point, shadow:

The quick brown fox jumped over the lazy dog.

Multiliteracies in the classroom

Collect advertisements and a variety of print examples which use different kinds of fonts. How does the style and size of font influence meaning?

Explore the different kinds of print used in animation, comics, symbols, in digital electronic texts and visual graphics. Discuss the choices made for their effect on the reader or viewer. Are there features that students can incorporate into their own writing? The speech balloons of comics are a good source.

Teaching handwriting

Children often learn the shapes of letters through alphabet books and may be taught how to write their name before they reach formal schooling. Most students, however, need to be taught how to write legibly from kindergarten onwards. At first handwriting movements are practised, then the letter shapes are taught, and later the letters are joined for a script, popularly called 'running writing'. As Royce Holliday points out, 'The teaching emphasis is not on the shapes of letters but on the movements that produce them … Each letter is not seen as a separate phenomenon … but is taught as a member of a group of letters related by common movements and patterns' (1988: 102). Teaching the writing of letters in the A–Z alphabetic sequence may be counterproductive. A more efficient way is to link letters with sounds as part of phonics instruction and to encourage students to write common words that they need to know.

Use names and environmental print to practise handwriting

From kindergarten to grade six

There is no rigid sequence of acquisition but generally young children mimic the print they encounter and older students develop a style which is recognisably their own. Some ESL students may need particular help with directionality and the formation of letters if they are used to a different script from English. The following may help:

- copying the student's name and other familiar words
- practice in making the shapes of letters in broad movements while saying them aloud with their individual sounds
- tracing shapes and letters
- use of lined paper
- copying letters and words found in texts, linked with saying them aloud
- attention to directionality—left to right and use of slope cards
- attention to spacing of text on the page
- spacing between words
- formation of lower-case letters
- formation of upper-case letters
- appropriate size and proportion of letters
- recognition of capitalisation, punctuation and grammar
- attention to writing legibility
- development of a personal style once basic handwriting is mastered.

When introducing the letter forms, use a combination of Visual-Auditory-Kinaesthetic (VAK) associations to consolidate knowledge. Link the sight and sound of letters by focusing on the shape of the letter(s) and saying the name of the letter aloud. Practise correct formation of the letters in handwriting, following the correct pattern and direction.

A multisensory approach to the teaching of handwriting is advocated

The Foundation and Modern Cursive style

The style of handwriting preferred by education departments varies. The choice of style is usually that it is uncomplicated and easy to write. Copperplate writing is no longer taught for this reason. It is important to consult the relevant state or territory syllabus as a guide. In New South Wales, the Foundation handwriting in cursive form is taught. In this style, the downstroke is the dominant movement and letters are easily joined together to produce well-proportioned writing. Queensland also uses modern cursive handwriting. In Victoria and Western Australia, the Modern Cursive style is preferred to help students achieve fluency, legibility, and rhythm in their handwriting.

Figure 16.1   Sample of Foundation handwriting style with movement of pen strokes

This sentence is written in the Victorian Modern Cursive script:

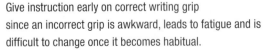

The Foundation style adopted in New South Wales is designed to involve three basic movements that reflect 'natural' drawing:

> *sloped downstroke as in l, b, d*
>
> *sloped clockwise ellipse as in b*
>
> *sloped anticlockwise ellipse as in d.*

Classroom practice

Teaching handwriting in a particular style may sound very prescriptive, but students will still develop their own individual styles in the way they form the letters, space them on a page, pay attention to layout, or even how they hold a pen. Even so, students need to be taught the rudiments of how to write and it is worth teaching aspects of handwriting such as how to hold the pen or pencil and how to sit at ease while writing.

Pen grip: illustration   Posture: illustration

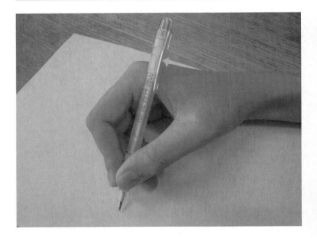

Give instruction early on correct writing grip since an incorrect grip is awkward, leads to fatigue and is difficult to change once it becomes habitual.

Advice on the physical aspects of handwriting is designed to make the task of writing easier for the student. It would be a futile exercise, however, to insist on advice that does not suit an individual student. Basically, the pen or pencil is gripped with the thumb, index finger, and middle finger. The preferred position for handwriting is to sit comfortably at a stable writing surface with the pen held at a constant angle to the page. Textbooks exist for practising handwriting through the grades, and can supplement the resources of the classroom teacher.

Practice in handwriting is more than committing writing to paper. At first, students are helped by practising the broad, gross motor movements of the shape of a letter by whole-arm movements or by tracing the shape of the letters. They can be helped to recognise letters visually by isolating individual letters or groups of letters in print. Attention needs to be paid to the correct formation of the letters, words or lines in regard to

- size and proportion to one another
- alignment
- slant
- spacing.

Handwriting is a physical exercise and there are various activities that will help students to write legibly:

- practising where to start on a page
- making sure that writing moves from left to right
- using ruled lines and slope cards for mastering spacing conventions
- practising 'patterns' that can help with fluency, e.g. 'air' writing
- tracing letter and word patterns.

Common problems that need to be assessed.

Try to alleviate these problems before they become serious barriers to legibility and/or the student's motivation to write.

1. Irregular writing that looks messy
2. Holding the pencil too tightly, producing fatigue
3. Writing too heavily, causing fatigue
4. Indecipherable letters
5. Poor fine motor skills
6. Inability to retrieve letters quickly and produce them on the page.

Writing automatism

At-risk writers need to make close connections between spoken and written texts. Writing polysyllabic words are difficult for beginning writers. Problems with writing and spelling may be masked until students meet the increased demands of written composition in the later years of school. It is very important to identify any difficulties at an early stage so students can be helped more easily.

Virginia Berninger, Professor of Educational Psychology, University of Washington, is a researcher in learning disabilities

To help struggling writers put letter retrieval and production on automatic pilot, we ask them to study a model letter with numbered arrow cues and then to follow those cues as they write the letter. We then ask children to write letters from memory to help them create retrieval routines. We gradually increase the time interval between when the child looks at the letter and when she tries to write it from memory. During each teaching trial, we name the letters at least three times: when children are asked to study the numbered arrow cues, when they are asked to cover each letter and when they are asked to write each letter from memory. In contrast to the practice of asking children to write similar letters over and over, we ask children to study and write all 26 letters of the alphabet in each instructional session. To avoid brain habituation, which is common when tasks do not vary sufficiently, children are usually asked to write each of the 26 letters only once in a practice session. Recycling through the alphabet might be done a second or third time, but never more than that. (Berninger: 1999: 21)

In the classroom

Handwriting lesson in the early years

Daily, 20 minutes.

1   Introduce a new letter(s) or sound, combined with syllable awareness training.

    a   Show the letters in context; ask students to pronounce them.

    b   Write a letter in the air ('air write)'.

    c   Alternatively, use a computer program which models the formation of letters.

    d   Trace it on the board or on worksheets, indicating direction.

    e   Copy in books

    f   Dictate a letter or word and write independently, encouraging automatic recall.

    Watch how students write and check skills.

2   Teach letters in combination to suit the way letters are written: common letters such as *e*; or those which make meaningful units, following phonics instruction e.g.

l j k l t	*oo*	*loot*
a c d g o q s	*th*	*those*
v w x y	*wh*	*why*

3   Review past letter(s) learnt.

4   Check that all students can recall and write the letters quickly. Find out why individual students have problems with particular letters/words (e.g. motivation, boredom, pencil grip etc.) and address these with appropriate strategies. Ensure that extension work is provided for those who can handwrite without problems.

Handwriting is best taught in the context of normal school work, but regular practice sessions in the early years are definitely required. In the later grades practice sessions can be used when needed. Making this practice interesting and meaningful is a challenge. For example, on a worksheet relating to the novel *Charlotte's Web*, in answer to the question 'Who is Charlotte? Tell me something she did', Daniel (8) wrote:

Charlotte is a spider. She made some words in her web like some pig, terrific, and radiant. These words saved Wilbour from being turned into Christmas ham.

Here the main task is to encourage the student to think about *Charlotte's Web*, but handwriting is practised coincidentally. Writing out short humorous poems (e.g. Spike Milligan's 'On the Ning Nang Nong'), or jokes may also motivate students.

IN THE CLASSROOM

This idea, borrowed from Chenfeld (1987: 385), will help students recognise how different styles of handwriting can achieve different effects:

> The Seven Dwarfs' Handwriting: 'Would Grumpy's handwriting look the same as Bashful's? Would Happy's handwriting look exactly the same as Sleepy's?'

Challenge the student to choose one or all the dwarfs and show samples of their writing in signatures, journal pages, letters, poems, or stories.

Left-handed writers

Being left-handed is not a barrier to good handwriting but different skills must be taught and learnt. On no account should students who naturally write with the left hand be forced to change writing hands.

There will be a different placement of the paper for left-handers so they can read their work as they are writing. Slant the paper with the upper left corner higher, the opposite to right-handers.

Keyboarding skills

Now that so much writing is done on the computer, learning to touch-type is a skill that should be acquired in the primary school classroom. Even so, students still need to be able to hand-write on those (many) occasions when a computer is not available, just as arithmetic cannot always be done on a calculator.

There are no ink blots on the computer screen

If students can do their writing on the computer, they have the instant advantage of a clean legible, attractive script with none of the irregularities of the handwritten script. Additionally, there are built-in spelling and grammar checkers. Of course, some writers love the physical act of committing words to paper. For those who appreciate the beauty of hand lettering, the many forms of calligraphy can be studied.

The New Zealand writer Janet Frame wrote of her feelings as she moved from the typewriter to word processing:

> I feel I am betraying artists by venturing into the computer world, but I love it—I am hooked …
> It produces a look-no-hands kind of letter when I could be using a turkey or goose quill dipped
> in a pot of ink. Oh how I long for all the past ways and days, like in the medieval world among the
> highwaymen and the silence and the dark nights that are gone forever. (Quoted in Michael King's
> *Wrestling With the Angel: A life of Janet Frame*, 2000: 469)

► LITERACY IN THE DIGITAL AGE

1 Introduce students to the QWERTY keyboard and encourage its use in the classroom and at home. A cardboard facsimile can be made of the keyboard for students to practise on.
2 Look up Internet programs for learning how to type (e.g. Quick Type, Ten Thumbs). Try one out in a systematic way, devoting time to developing the skill.
3 Try out voice recognition software (e.g. 'Tablet PC software'), which allows students to write with a stylus directly onto a computer screen. This handwritten text is then translated into print.
4 Try out web-based handwriting instruction programs (Leung & Komura 2006).

In the future, many teachers will still teach handwriting in a traditional way, i.e. by writing a letter or word on the board and encouraging their students to copy its formation. With the advent of computer technology there are web-based programs with 3D computer graphics and pen computing technologies (Leung & Komura 2006). While the trend is towards keyboards, not pencils, and clicking, not writing, students will still need to construct a mental image in their brain of the letter or word they want to reproduce.

► Summary

1 Handwriting should not be taught in isolation from other language features.
2 Regular practice must be given in handwriting skills, using diverse strategies to suit students' needs.
3 It is important to recognise the needs of left-handed students and ensure they receive appropriate instruction.
4 Teach touch-typing skills so that their 'published' writing is legible and attractive.

Critical thinking and study exercises

1 What is your opinion on the importance of automatic handwriting in freeing up the student's memory for higher-order thinking skills?

2 What is your own experience of handwriting? Is it easy for you to take notes or does this interfere with your comprehension of material?

Further reading

Students are advised to consult the current curriculum and support documents relating to the teaching of handwriting in their state or territory.

Berninger, V. W. et al. 1998, 'Early intervention for spelling problems: Teaching functional spelling units of varying size with a multiple-connections framework', *Journal of Educational Psychology* 90.

Berninger, V. W. 1999, 'The "Write Stuff" for preventing and treating writing disabilities: The International Dyslexia Association', *Perspectives* 25(2): 20–2.

Leung, H. & R. Komura 2006, 'Web-based handwriting education with animated virtual teacher', *International Journal of Distance Education Technologies* 4(1): 10. Article #: ITJ3032

Nightingale, G. & P. Nightingale 2005, *New Improved Foundation Handwriting 2005*, Oxford University Press, Melbourne. (Series of books from Kindergarten to Year 6)

Sassoon, R. 1999, *Handwriting of the Twentieth Century: From copperplate to the computer*, Routledge, London.

Wolf, B. J. 'Teaching handwriting'. In J. R. Birsh (ed.) *Multisensory Teaching of Basic Language Skills*, 2nd edn, Paul H. Brookes Publishing Co., Baltimore, pp. 413–38.

Web links

www.handwritingforkids.com
www.primary.thomsonlearning.com.au (NSW, Victoria and Queensland texts on handwriting)
www.oup.com.au (NSW and Victorian texts on handwriting)
www.handwritinghelpforkids.com/expert.html (Handwriting tips from Lisa Marnell on pencil grip, left-handed writing etc.)

Keyboard skills

Kid Keys
Quick Type
Ten Thumbs
Typequick

17 ASSESSMENT OF WRITING

Overview

Assessment, evaluation and reporting practices are part of the teaching and learning cycle, allowing us to gauge the relative success of both student and teacher. Good assessment tells us what the abilities of students are and their relative strengths and weaknesses. Armed with this information (gathered from data, observation or testing), the teacher and student can address individual need. Assessment to aid the learning process should be multifaceted and may be carried out by teachers or by students or their peers. A student's 'writing ability' may fluctuate, depending on the task and the variety of skills needed to construct a text. It is therefore important to have different measures of assessment over a period of time.

Assessment, evaluation and reporting

Assessment provides accountability

Assessment is a general term to describe any activities used to judge a student's performance. It involves data collection, analysis, and the recording of information about a student's progress. A student's achievement is often measured against specific outcomes and indicators. Assessment can be formative (monitoring a student's progress), summative (gauging how learning objectives have been met), or diagnostic (examining specific areas of student need). Summative assessment is usually carried out at the end of a unit of work and indicates how learning outcomes have been achieved.

Evaluation is an appraisal process undertaken by a teacher that is designed to make judgments about the effectiveness and appropriateness of teaching practices and programs, and to identify any improvements needed. The teacher then implements ongoing practices and programming in order to help students realise their potential. Formative assessment in writing could involve the judgement of texts written in class. Evaluation helps teachers judge the effectiveness of their teaching programs.

Evaluation is developmental

Reporting involves communicating information about achievement and progress to students, teachers and parents. This may be done by comparing a student's achievement against

Reporting in plain language is recommended

*   past results and achievement
*   the achievement of student's peer group (norm referenced)
*   national standards framework of syllabus outcomes (criterion referenced).

The record-keeping and reporting will depend on what is ethical, relevant or needed by stakeholders. Support of a student's learning and the improvement of teaching will be the main determinants in what is reported, and to whom. What is to be gained by ranking a students' performance against others? How confidential is the reporting?

Principles of effective assessment and reporting

*   Clear, direct links with outcomes
*   Integral to teaching and learning
*   Balanced, comprehensive and varied
*   Valid
*   Fair
*   Engages the learner
*   Values teacher judgment
*   Time-efficient and manageable
*   Recognises individual achievement and progress
*   Involves a whole school approach
*   Actively involves parents
*   Conveys meaningful and useful information

(Adapted from NSW Board of Studies 2005)

Validity and reliability are important and complementary aspects of assessment that determine how appropriate, meaningful, and useful are different assessment practices. **Validity** refers to the degree to which accumulated evidence supports the inferences (or decisions) made from looking at the results. It involves the content of what is assessed, the ways in which students are assessed, and how they actually perform. A valid assessment item might be one clearly linked to curriculum objectives; an invalid item would discriminate against students by not reflecting the content taught.

DIFFERENT KINDS OF VALIDITY

1   Concurrent validity: the extent to which performance on one writing task would be a predictor of performance on a similar task, e.g. class tasks and external examinations.

2   Construct validity: the extent to which the writing assessment measures writing skills and abilities, e.g. is cohesion of text valued more highly than neat writing?

3   Predictive validity: the extent to which performance on a writing assessment would be a predictor of performance in a related context, e.g. ability to write well in different subject fields.

Reliability (necessary for validity) concerns how much the results of assessment involve errors of measurement or extraneous factors that affect the assessment practices. If a 'test' were repeated under similar conditions, would the results be the same? Consistency is required, meaning that if an assessment item was marked by a different teacher the results would be the same.

National benchmarks in literacy

National Literacy and Numeracy Plan 1997

'every child leaving primary school should be numerate, and be able to read, write and spell at an appropriate level' (Masters & Forster 1997b: 54)

Benchmarks are agreed minimum desirable standards of achievement at particular year levels for reading, writing, spelling, and numeracy, without which students would have difficulty progressing at school. While there is a need for clear benchmarks, the creative act of writing sometimes makes it difficult to assess because it involves affective areas. Indigenous and ESL students may be disadvantaged by the cultural assumptions of questions given in Basic Skills tests which use the literacy benchmarks. It is not always easy to demonstrate particular outcomes and the teachers are likely to make subjective judgments about them. We need to think of innovative ways to assess creativity in an outcomes framework—judgement of creativity can be very subjective.

Attempts have been made at a national level in Australia to monitor and raise the literacy standards of children. The Rowe Report (Louden et al. 2005) reviews and analyses research about literacy teaching approaches. While it focuses on effective teaching practices for reading, there are clear links with general competence in writing, speaking, listening, and viewing.

Benchmarks in writing at stage 3 include the ability to write:

- logically ordered paragraphs
- a narrative with plot, characters, and setting
- simple and compound sentences
- punctuation with full stops, commas, and question marks
- spelling of most one- or two-syllable words that have regular patterns.

Level 3 Writing Benchmark Task

Write a story about having an adventure with a legendary creature such as Big Foot. See additional, corrected examples at www.online.curriculum.edu.au.

Assessment of writing in the classroom

Generally the teacher wants to assess

- how a student handles different kinds of writing tasks
- familiarity with the content and structure of different genres or text-types
- a sense of the intended audience for writing
- the ability to convey content and meaning through writing
- control over punctuation, spelling, and grammar
- the breadth of vocabulary used
- attitudes to writing
- a student's self-perception as a writer.

Three-way assessment **involves student/parent/ teacher:**

- **the parents comment on teacher-assessed work**
- **student discusses portfolio of work with teacher and parent(s)**

In the classroom

Link these strategies with a relevant learning activity. A range of writing assessment strategies can be chosen to assess literacy, dependent on the purpose of the assessment and the intended audience.

- Authentic assessment
- Collaborative assessment, e.g. three-way assessment
- Cloze tests
- Diaries or journals
- Essays and writing tasks
- Exhibitions where students present work
- Journals
- Mind maps or concept maps
- Multiple-choice tests
- Portfolios
- Projects
- Self-assessment and peer-assessment
- Standardised achievement tests
- Teacher-developed tests
- True-false tests

Benjamin S. Bloom (1913–99) His classification principles in the cognitive, affective, and psychomotor domains have been influential in learning, teaching, and assessing

A knowledge of Bloom's *Taxonomy of Educational Objectives* (1956) can help teachers understand the complexity of the learning process and can encourage assessment of different degrees of difficulty, from 'simple' knowledge to more complex judgments.

Teachers can assess different kinds of skills, such as errors in syntax, vocabulary, and spelling but also synthesis skills—the important sense and coherence of what a student has written.

Table 17.1   Bloom's taxonomy of the cognitive domain

Level	Category	Behaviour descriptors	Assessment activity
1	Knowledge	ability to remember or recall ideas, data, material	Multiple choice test Diary True–False test
2	Comprehension	ability to know, interpret, understand, and use what is communicated	Cloze tests discussion, review, explanation genre
3	Application	ability to use information in new situations	Project, Exhibition carry out procedure from directions, solve a problem, role-play
4	Analysis	ability to break down information into its constituent parts; recognition of structure	Essay compare and contrast, extrapolate (infer from what is known), value, test
5	Synthesis	ability to put parts or elements together to form a whole	Mind map Portfolios create a text, develop a plan
6	Evaluation	ability to judge the value of ideas, to make judgments or to apply criteria	Self/peer assessment review, present a case, defend or argue

The concept of 'mastering' one level before progression to another is not always applicable to the interrelatedness of skills required in the writing process. However, the levels can be useful in sorting out levels of thinking required in tasks and what is being tested. What kind of cognitive skills are to be assessed in different writing tasks: a simple recall of data in a multiple choice test or the ability to synthesise and evaluate material into a coherent whole by writing a report on a topical issue? It helps to focus attention on the different cognition skills required in basic skills of correct punctuation, spelling, and grammar as compared to the skills required in writing an imaginative story. The best writers are able to weave all the attributes into a creative whole. A multiple-choice test can assess whether the student is proficient in capitalisation but it cannot assess the ability to write extended prose.

Writing tasks are many-sided, e.g. a diary may reveal the ability to recall events, but also contain judgments, dreams, and imagination

Writing crystallises thoughts and promotes critical thinking

Data collection

Data collection for assessment purposes may be gathered through informal observation of the student or through written/oral tests of ability. A teacher's intuition is also important. Data are usually collected in a systematic way with the help of checklists, benchmarks, or some other indication that can form the basis of comparison. A student's progress can be compared with individual achievement over a period of time. Progress in writing can also be compared with other class members or with larger population groups (as with Basic Skills Tests). Analysis of the data collected will allow teachers to set up various teaching strategies to help students. The results obtained will also point towards other needs, e.g. new resources that should be acquired, specialised staff development programs, or revision of the school's language programs. Consider how data can be analysed to help the individual student and teacher.

Ask what is the purpose of an assessment. Make sure assessment focuses on appropriate rhetorical choices, not always on what is 'wrong' in spelling and punctuation. What will be done with the 'results'?

Informal and formal assessment

The key to good assessment practices is perceptive observation by the teacher, by the parents, and by the students themselves. We need to be clear about why we need a particular assessment, what aspects are to be assessed, how the assessment is to be done, and for what purposes it will be used. Often assessment is carried out for placement decisions.

The purpose and methods of assessment must be clear

Assessment that is integrated into the regular program of classroom work will feed back into the teaching and learning cycle.

The way information is recorded often reflects the purpose of the assessment. Anecdotal comments may be recorded in an A–Z book of children's names so that the teacher can remember information that would otherwise prove elusive. Other informal observation of children may be made on 'post it' notices as the teacher moves around the classroom. More formal recording is usually made through checklists that indicate what students can do, what they need to improve, and what they believe they cannot do. Assessment rubrics can often be designed with the students and used as individual assessment grids.

Writing assessment rubric
1. **Ideas and content**
2. **Organisation**
3. **Voice**
4. **Word choice**
5. **Sentence fluency**
6. **Conventions**

IN THE CLASSROOM

Using the 6 Traits model can enrich writing assessment and instruction. Make a wall chart for students to follow.

1. **Ideas:** The writer's main message and the details, evidence, or anecdotes that support or expand that message.

Is the message clear? Is the information accurate and/or persuasive?

2. Organisation: The internal structure or skeleton of a text that gives support and direction to the ideas.

   Is there a gripping opening and ending. Are there links between ideas?

3. Voice: The mix of individuality, confidence, engagement with the topic, and reader rapport that keeps readers reading.

   Does it sound like the writer?

4. Word choice: The ability to choose the right word or phrase to make meaning clear and to bring images or thoughts to life.

   Can you picture it?

5. Sentence and fluency: Rhythm and flow, the music and poetry of language.

   Is it easy to read smoothly? Is the dialogue realistic? Is there variation in the sentences?

6. Conventions: The writer's skills in using punctuation, spelling, grammar, capitalisation, and layout, to clarity and enhance meaning.

   Is it free of errors?

(adapted from Spandel 2005: 2)

Increasing recognition should be given to how the results of the assessment practices are conveyed. Are the results to be in language that the child can easily understand, or should they be addressed to an adult audience, or both? For example, the Basic Skills Test gives an individual student report that shows achievement over six bands in tabular form (for Year 5), listing the percentage of students across the state achieving in each skill band. Skills in reading, language, number, measurement, and space are itemised, indicating the skills tested in each band. These results are primarily intended for the use of teachers and parents and can be compared with the National Benchmark of the Australian Commonwealth Government.

It is sensible to include specific information about how to interpret the results of assessment, whether you are communicating with parents or students. For example, the Australian Schools English Competition (given to Year 6 students) outlines the types of questions and the individual's percentage mark gained compared with the state average for the student's year. Being placed in the 80th percentile of students from your school is quite different from being placed in the 60th percentile of students from the state, and can cause confusion and upset unless it is clearly explained.

Australian Schools English Competition		
	Your mark	*State average for your year*
Vocabulary (13 questions)		
Language (14 questions)		
Punctuation		
Standard usage		
Everyday documents, diagrams,		
data (17 questions)		
Reading comprehension (16 questions)		
detail		
judgment (low-level)		
judgment (high-level)		

Figure 17.1 Skills typical of students in each skill band

Skills typical of students in each skill band

STUDENTS IN EACH SKILL BAND GENERALLY SHOWED THE SKILLS LISTED FOR THAT BAND AND THE LOWER BANDS.

	Reading	Language	Number	Measurement	Space
6	• Locate detailed numerical information from a complex description. • Connect information provided in separate parts of a text. • Identify the speaker of dialogue when it is not directly stated.	• Recognise the incorrect use of it's. • Recognise the correct spelling of 'surrounding' not 'surrounding'. • Recognise the incorrect spelling 'enemie' for 'enemy'.	• Round off a decimal number to the nearest whole number (27.7 to 28). • Halve a four digit number selected from a table and identify values less than this. • Work out the number of five dollar notes needed to make up a given amount of money ($5 notes in $93).	• Use a scale drawing to work out the area of a shape in square kilometres. • Convert tonnes to kilograms (4.3 tonnes equals 4300kg). • Understand the concept 'second half of this century' and find dates given in a table to solve a problem.	• Understand the concept of symmetry and identify the shape that has all lines of symmetry drawn. • Understand the mathematical term "net" and identify the nets of a cube.
5	• Sort relevant information about a process. • Infer meaning using clues given by the structure of a sentence. • Understand the format of chapters and headings and identify the title of a chapter.	• Recognise the correct use of 'quite', not 'quiet'. • Recognise the conjunction 'and' as correct, not 'but'. • Identify the incorrect use of the article 'the'. • Recognise the correct spelling of 'fields' not 'feilds'.	• Use information on a map and identify the lowest decimal number to one decimal place. • Add four amounts of money (45¢ + 50¢ + $1.20 + $1.05). • Extract information from a table and subtract two four-digit numbers involving decomposition/trading (1993 - 1977).	• Estimate the area of an irregular shape using the grid supplied. • Work out the perimeter of a shape shown on a scale drawing.	• Interpret information in a graph and match with a correct statement (8 out of 24 equals one third). • Use knowledge of compass directions to describe a path taken.
4	• Interpret a table to sequence information. • Make an inference from an explanation. • Identify the meaning of figurative language in a poem.	• Recognise that a country is a proper noun and must begin with a capital letter. • Choose the correct form of a verb to be consistent in tense and number. • Select the past tense 'took' to keep the tense consistent. • Choose the personal pronoun 'their', not 'there' or 'they're'.	• Extract information from a table and add two and three-digit numbers (170 + 70). • Use subtraction or a similar strategy to work out a problem involving two-digit numbers (36 - 17 =).	• Use information given in a table and convert metres to centimetres (1.5m to 150cm). • Know that a day is 24 hours and convert 12 hours to a fraction of a day (half). • Know how many days are in April and May and add them (30 + 31).	• Identify the cross section made by cutting into a solid shape. • Identify 2D parts needed to make a 3D shape (square pyramid). • Recognise a flip as a reflection of a shape over a line.
3	• Locate and compare specific information which is organised under sub-headings. • Use a labelled diagram to identify a specific feature. • Identify a text as a recipe. • Combine and relate technical information.	• Identify the subject of a sentence. • Select the preposition "of" in a phrase that indicates possession -- of Sydney Town. • Recognise that a verb must agree with its subject.	• Interpret a place value chart and write a number containing hundreds, tens and ones (369). • Use number facts to complete a number sentence involving multiplication (6 × ? = 72). • Recognise that division is the operation needed to solve a problem.	• Understand the relative term 'lightest', use a table and compare mass of three objects to find the lightest.	• Recognise a right angle. • Recognise a set of parallel lines. • Visualise and work out the number of blocks needed to fill a partially filled box. • Use information shown on a table to complete a column graph.
2	• Locate the time of an activity shown in a timetable. • Use a table to identify specific information. • Identify the actions of characters in a story. • Find specific information from the first section in a descriptive text.	• Recognise the correct use of the apostrophe in the negative verb 'wasn't'. • Identify the incorrect use of a preposition. • Select an adverb of degree. • Recognise the need for a capital letter to begin a sentence.	• Identify three single-digit numbers to equal 18 (4 + 5 + 9).	• Understand the concept of balancing objects of the same mass. • Understand that the level of water in a container rises when an object is dropped into the container. • Compare thermometers without a scale and identify change in temperature over time.	• Use a scale to compare frequencies in a column graph. • Use coordinates to show position on a grid.
1	• Identify specific detail in a text.	• Choose the correct spelling of the word 'special', not 'speshal' or 'special'. • Select the correct conjunction to indicate time. • Recognise when to use 'for', not 'four' or 'fore'.		• Understand volume and select the container showing about half a litre.	

Basic Skills Tests

Basic Skills Tests are taken by students in Years 3 and 5 in New South Wales and South Australia. They test aspects of literacy and numeracy and provide information about where the student 'fits' on a skills band, with Band 1 being in the lowest range.

The writing test requires students to read, plan, write and edit a text. There are two writing tasks, approximately thirty minutes each:

- a factual writing task
- a literary writing task.

The reading and language questions are multiple choice or short answer questions and cover identifying correct grammar, punctuation (e.g. *its/it's*) and spelling (e.g *speshul*).

In the Year 3 test the student has to demonstrate ability in reading and language skills by

- reading a magazine and showing understanding of stories, tables, instructions, reports, and other kinds of writing
- identifying correct spelling, punctuation, and grammar.

Figure 17.1 shows the skills listed for the different skills bands.

Writing assessment in the classroom

Embedding the assessment process in daily classroom literacy tasks is a necessity, especially with the time constraints of modern classrooms.

IN THE CLASSROOM

I Wet tu
The limlies
anb i sor
horses
Tillie

Lambs jumped around friskily tormenting their mothers for nourishment. Cows lay lazily chewing their cud among the buttercups. A little foal galloped alongside her mother on its spindly legs. In another field a ploughman plodded along behind his horses furrowing the field. Butterflies fluttered from flower to flower …

John, 12

These are two very different pieces of writing. It would be meaningless to assign one a mark of 1/10 and the other 9/10. What we can say with confidence is that the writers are at different stages in the writing process. On the one hand we have a beginner writer struggling to put meanings together with letters from the alphabet, while on the other we have a writer experimenting with literary devices such as alliteration and imagery. Each finds the task challenging yet rewarding, each needs feedback and encouragement. Rather than saying X in the class is a better writer than Y, we should be saying that X is at a different stage along the writing continuum from Y.

Analyse the two texts. Write down the response you would give a) to the student, b) to the parent.

Teachers look for different **outcomes** that match different stages of ability in the student. Outcomes-based assessment poses challenges because many parents expect marks or grades to indicate proficiency and because the outcomes may be considered vague, generic, and lacking in clarity. While it is difficult to report progress accurately, stipulating 'outcomes' does serve to clarify what a student can actually do. The box below shows some sample outcomes of what a beginning writer might achieve.

OUTCOMES FOR STAGE 1 IN THE NSW ENGLISH K–6 SYLLABUS 1998 INCLUDE:

- Plans, reviews, and produces a small range of simple literary and factual texts for a variety of purposes on familiar topics for known readers.
- Produces texts using the basic grammatical features and punctuation conventions of the text-type.
- Uses knowledge of sight words and letter–sound correspondences and a variety of strategies to spell familiar words.
- Produces texts using letters of consistent size and slope in New South Wales Foundation style and using computer technology. (Board of Studies NSW 1998b: 106)

IN THE CLASSROOM

1 Construct a cloze test with a class to show them how it is done. Explain different kinds of cloze exercises, e.g. omitting every ninth or seventh word, deleting different parts of speech. Ask pairs of students to create their own exercise, eliminating every seventh word. Exchange with other pairs and see if they can select the appropriate words. As a whole class, discuss why the choices were made.

Cloze exercise: non-fiction text
Suitability: upper primary

Dinosaur is the name of a kind of reptile that lived millions of years ago. The word 'dinosaur' comes from two Greek words meaning terrible lizard. Dinosaurs were not lizards. But the size of some dinosaurs was terrifying. The biggest ones were the largest animals ever to live on land. They weighed more than 10 times as much as a full-grown elephant. Only a few kinds of whales grow to be larger than these dinosaurs (World Book Encyclopedia).

Exercise

Predict and insert words that make sense:

> *Dinosaur is the name of a ---- of reptile that lived millions of ---- ago. The word dinosaur comes from ---- Greek words meaning terrible lizard. Dinosaurs ---- not lizards. But the size of ---- dinosaurs was terrifying. The biggest ones ---- the largest animals ever to live -- land. They weighed more than 10 ---- as much as a full-grown elephant. ---- a few kinds of whales grow -- be larger than these dinosaurs.*

▶ LITERACY IN THE DIGITAL AGE

Sarah Gilpin takes full advantage of how computers can help her students with writing. She makes sure her students can understand and use the *tools* on the computer. While there are book versions of spelling/grammar, thesaurus and dictionary tools, which students may also use, they are likely to utilise the computer because of the speed and ease of use.

Provide students with a short passage to correct and/or encourage them to use their own texts.

1. Spelling and Grammar

1st draft: paul mother was happy because he was given a speshul gift of two concert ticket.
Correction: Paul's mother was happy because he was given a special gift of two concert tickets.
Ensure students understand why the corrections are made

▪ spelling	special
▪ punctuation	Paul's mother
▪ capitalisation	Paul
▪ number and agreement	two concert tickets

2. Thesaurus

Add to students' vocabulary and encourage them to make their writing interesting and clear. Ask students to look up words which can improve their sentences. Which word would you choose? Why?

- *1st draft*: *The Matrix* was a very **good** film.
- *Choices*: *The Matrix* was a first-rate/fine/superior/excellent film.
- *1st draft*: The Chinese actor, Shi Liang thinks Schezuan food is **nice**.
- *Choices*: The Chinese actor, Shi Liang, thinks Schezuan food is delicious/tasty/full of flavour/yummy/ scrumptious.
- *1st draft*: He thinks that person is **lovely**.
- *Choices*: He thinks that person is beautiful/pleasant/attractive/pretty/good-looking/gorgeous/exquisite/ charming.

3. Dictionary

Look up the word *nice* (adj.) and consider the alternative meanings in context:

- pleasant or enjoyable
- kind, or showing courtesy, friendliness, or consideration

- respectable, or of an acceptable social or moral standard
- good-looking or pleasing to look at
- skilful and accomplished
- subtle and involving delicacy of discrimination
- very concerned and careful about choosing, or being seen to do the right thing.

Models of writing and assessment

Students learn about the conventions of writing from the models they see and practise. As they learn the structures and language features of a variety of text-types, assessment is made of how well they have mastered the conventions and, increasingly, how they modify the basic outlines to suit their own purposes and audiences. For example, the model for the 'Explanation' text-type might be on the facts associated with 'What makes a kettle boil?' with accompanying demonstrations or illustrations. This might be written down quite simply with a heading (which might be a question) and a sequence of points or sentences about the phenomenon.

IN THE CLASSROOM

Choose a topic and highlight the language features, e.g. the use of general nouns, action verbs, descriptive adjectives, use of time conjunctions, e.g.

What makes a kettle boil?

Water makes lots of bubbles when it boils.
The bubbles contain gassy water.
The water turns into a gas.
Heating up the water makes it boil.
Water can boil away into gas if it keeps boiling.
Water boils when it reaches a high temperature.

Assessment of this text may focus on the accuracy of the observations and the way the student has control of the relevant language features. More scientific and technical language may be required from older students, depending on the audience.

Language portfolios

Teachers who want to enhance their students' learning and understanding find inspiration in varied assessment practices. A systematic record of observations and judgments about a student's work collected in a portfolio has many uses for the student, the teacher, and the parent. Portfolios are popular in the school context since they are a multidimensional form of assessment.

Portfolio assessment shows a student's progress over time

Definition of portfolio assessment

A systematic collection of student work that is analysed to show progress over a period of time with regard to specific instructional goals.

Language portfolios can include writing tasks, responses to reading, projects, and classroom assignments, as well as individual comments by the teacher and student. The rationale for using them lies in the educational advantages of closely linking classroom activities with assessment, involving the student more meaningfully in the learning process. 'One of the defining features of portfolio assessment is the involvement of students in selecting samples of their own work to show growth or learning over time' (O'Malley & Valdez Pierce 1996: 5). A portfolio is 'the systematic and selective collection of work that shows mastery or growth' (Walther-Thomas & Brownell 2001: 225). Collections that chart performance and achievement in the language skills of speaking, reading, writing, and listening are particularly useful for the ESL student.

The advantages of portfolios are that they provide:

- a variety in assessment procedures
- student involvement and responsibility
- suitability for the ESL student
- assessment factors
- accountability
- linking of assessment and classroom instruction or activities
- concrete evidence of students' achievement.

Variety in assessment procedures

Portfolio assessment is a useful addition to a teacher's array of assessment strategies, complementing other kinds of assessment. A survey of upper primary classroom teachers by the Schools Council, National Board of Employment, Education and Training found that:

> Respondents reported learning attainments in a variety of ways including discussions with parents, informal feedback, written report against key criteria, profiles/portfolios and interviews with the students. Taken together with the responses to other questions in the survey, it was apparent that teachers wished to use a variety of methods to report on learning attainment—choosing the method which best suited the situation and would facilitate the growth and development of the individual student. (1995: 52)

Choosing criteria for assessment can be guided by:

- developmental writing scale
- rubric for assessment of creative writing.

Student involvement and responsibility

Portfolios can engage students in monitoring their own learning and can encourage them to be reflective about the learning process. A collection of evaluated work identifies strengths and weaknesses, helping students to realise their learning potential. A portfolio collection where students have worked collaboratively with teachers on setting criteria allows students to analyse their own development more easily and improve skills. If students collaborate in the selection of content, give input into the criteria used, and reflect on the process, its potential as an assessment tool is enhanced (Stiggins 2001: 468). Brady prefers the working/process portfolio that encourages students to self-assess and to reflect on their work so that 'portfolios become a meaningful learning tool and rich assessment resource rather than just a tool for reporting' (2005: 62). Teachers and students can decide on the required and optional contents for a portfolio.

The ESL student

A particular advantage for ESL students is that the portfolio collection can gauge their ability more effectively than standardised tests, which are often measures of general knowledge and may be affected by cultural bias. The multidimensional nature of the portfolio allows a student's progress to be judged in a variety of ways and reveals improvement (or otherwise) made over a period of time.

Most assessment practices used in schools demand a high language involvement and an emphasis on written responses, so the ESL student is often at a disadvantage. By using the portfolio, students can be encouraged to respond in a variety of ways, e.g. retelling a text in their first language. If appropriate, writing in the first language can be encouraged, allowing the teacher or language aid to check whether the task could be achieved in the mother tongue.

The ESL Scales (Curriculum Corporation 1994) provide profiles for reporting linguistic development that do not put the student from a non-English-speaking background at a disadvantage. The Australian Council for Educational Research has validated the achievement levels within the language strands of reading, writing, listening, and speaking.

Assessment factors

Portfolios can provide concrete evidence of students' achievement and progress as they move from class to class or from one school to another. This is becoming increasingly important as population shifts occur for economic and social reasons. The assessment portfolio has a high degree of validity because it is a cumulative record of a student's progress. Multiple forms of assessment are commonly more reliable than isolated testing procedures.

Standardised tests such as the NSW Basic Skills Testing Program (primary school level) measure individual performance, but machine-scored tests have severe limitations. Most language tasks, especially in the areas of creative writing, critical thinking, and problem-solving, cannot be adequately assessed by multiple-choice questions. As Masters points out, 'If we allow concerns for objectivity, reliability, and ease of processing to dominate assessment practices (as we often have), then we run the risk of sending distorted messages about the kinds of learning that we wish to encourage' (1991: 11). Objectivity and reliability are still crucial concerns of portfolio assessment.

Accountability

Reporting on student progress by reference to specific learning outcomes is increasingly necessary. If planned with systematic entries and evaluations, portfolios can provide accountability to the student, parent, teacher, and members of the wider community at various stages of the school year, or, indeed, over a period of years. 'Parents are likely to be most interested in knowing how students are performing in relation to teachers' expectations and in comparison with other students of the same age or grade' (Schools Council 1995: 54). Portfolios can provide an important record of students' learning and allow teachers and parents to discuss language ability in a more focused way since samples of work can be discussed. Involving other adults in children's learning can be a positive experience, especially when parents offer encouragement and assistance. When needed, items in the portfolio can be selected to show a tangible record of the work of a class; to help in professional development activities; or to demonstrate the work of the school to the community.

Linking of assessment and classroom instruction

By linking assessment with instruction, 'student performance is evaluated in relation to instructional goals, objectives, and classroom activities' (O'Malley & Valdez Pierce 1996: 35). The portfolio gives feedback to the teacher, who can then respond flexibly to the needs of individual students. Teachers can identify a student's abilities and difficulties much more easily if systematic records are kept that incorporate the student's own view of learning development. Analysis of portfolios allows the teacher to see whether instructional objectives have been met and whether the teaching has been successful in assessing student performance relative to curricular objectives.

Planning and design of portfolios

Choose the right kind of portfolio. A working portfolio has a different purpose from a documentary or a showcase portfolio

Teachers can modify various kinds of portfolios for their own purposes:

- Working Portfolio: collection of day-to-day work.
- Documentary Portfolio: collection of work for assessment, which documents the processes used to develop items.
- Show Portfolio: where a student's 'best' work is selected. (Masters & Forster 1996: 21)

Assessment in writing may be a section within a larger Language Assessment Portfolio. This is a combination of a student's perceived 'best' work as well as a record of progress that shows the *process* by which a student has worked towards a goal (e.g. through the inclusion of notes, rough drafts, and 'final' version of a text). Each item included is evaluated on criteria collaboratively identified by the student and the teacher. For example, a story-retelling activity might nominate performance tasks such as:

- names main characters
- understands characters' motives
- recalls plot sequence
- considers genre features
- evaluates major issues.

A writing checklist based on specific criteria is an excellent way of involving students and of providing a record of learning development. It is important to assess progress as part of the regular classroom activities so that instruction and assessment are closely interwoven. The design of the portfolio can be tailored to suit the needs of particular student groups or individual students, e.g. by providing an illustration or diagram that clarifies an item, and by ensuring that the instructions are clearly written and unambiguous. Evaluation items can be changed, when appropriate, to allow students to respond in their first language.

Organisation

Planning is necessary to forestall problems and to make sense of a portfolio collection. Clear instructions and guidelines are necessary so that students, teachers, and parents are aware of their roles and responsibilities. The following practical questions (and some possible solutions to them) should be considered by teachers before embarking on portfolio assessment:

1. Why do we need a 'portfolio' collection?
2. When do we find the time to make the evaluative comments?
3. How can we ensure that work is done by the individual?
4. Who 'owns' the portfolio?
5. Where is the portfolio to be stored?
6. What happens if students lose specific items or, indeed, the whole portfolio?

Similar difficulties arise in other contexts, and often there are systematic procedures and safeguards already in place to handle them. If the idea of an assessment portfolio is new to students, parents, or colleagues, you will need to convince them with educationally valid reasons that it is a worthwhile activity. Contact parents by letter to inform them of the purpose of the portfolio; how the assessment criteria are designed to help the student; and ways in which they can contribute to the individual student's efforts.

A portfolio is a collaborative effort between teacher and student with a major role for the learner in deciding what will be included in the collection and how it will be evaluated. This kind of assessment is easier to implement and manage in learner-centred classrooms where the student is able to make some decisions about what is to be included in a portfolio and how the evidence of work will be assessed. Sufficient time must be allocated to plan, design, and respond to portfolio entries. Linking classroom-based activities and key learning areas of the curriculum to the assessment can save time. Portfolios will be burdensome and time-consuming if they are not part of regular classroom instruction.

Link portfolios with regular classroom activities

Decisions must be made on how regularly the sample items are assessed and the results conveyed to students and parents. Convenient times for a formal reporting of results might be at the end of each school term, at mid-year, and at year's end. While students may keep their pieces of writing in a folder with accompanying self-assessment checklists or comments by readers, the teacher may also want to keep additional records of observations about the student's writing behaviours and abilities.

Key features of a language portfolio are samples of a student's work, the evaluative criteria of the work done, and the opportunity for student self-assessment.

When choosing *samples of a student's work*, decisions must be made about the appropriate number of entries to be collected in a portfolio. For example, there could be:

- writing samples from classroom activities
- student choice of writing from different genres
- brief evaluation of books read
- oral interviews
- story or text retelling
- projects or exhibitions
- response to open-ended questions
- language activities from a range of curricular areas
- cloze exercises
- poetry.

IN THE CLASSROOM

Read the first poem by C. J. Dennis to the class and provide students with a copy. Brainstorm some of the criteria that make a good poem. Encourage students to write their own poem and, in a subsequent session, ask them to apply the same criteria to their own poem.

The Looking Glass

When I look in the looking-glass
I'm always sure to see—
No matter how I dodge about—
Me, looking out at me.
I often wonder as I look,
And those strange features spy,
If I, in there, think I'm as plain
As I, out there, think I.

C. J. Dennis

Example of student response:

The Looking Glass

When I look in the looking-glass,
I'm always sure to see,
A thermometer of all my thoughts,
Happy or angry.
The most infuriating thing,
Of all, I really think,
Your reflection, that stupid thing,
Will always think as you think.

O'Malley & Valdez Pierce (1996: 129) suggest the required and optional contents for a reading or writing portfolio:

Table 16.1 Contents of a reading or writing portfolio

Required	Optional
1. oral summary	1. list of books or stories read in class
2. story summary (writing or drawing independently	2. list of books or stories read
3. writing sample (teacher choice)	3. reading list inventory
4. student choice of writing	4. literacy development checklist (any type)
5. content-sample (i.e. reading)	5. student self-evaluation comprehension sample, project, report)
	6. student choice (any type)

IN THE CLASSROOM

To help understand the writing background of new students, give them a brief writing inventory:

1 Do you like to write?
2 How often do you write?
3 Are you a good writer?
4 What do others say about your writing?
5 Do you like to share your writing with others?
6 What do you like to write about?
7 What is the best writing you have done??
8 Where is your favourite place to write?
9 What is your favourite time to write?
10 What is the last creative writing you did?

Here is a sample of a diary entry from a language portfolio:

Dear Diary,

Yesterday Jacob and I went into Melbourne. Our parents dropped us off with our Aunty while they went and did Family History matters.

It was fun, we walked down the street a little and went into Time Zone and had our picture put on a sticker. We then went to a two dollar shop and had a look. We walked all the way to the end of the street and crossed the road and saw Flinders Street Station. We walked across a bridge and went past the Art Gallery and went down to the banks of the Yarra River. We walked a while down the river and got an ice cream and went back up to see some gymnasts out the front of the Art Gallery doing an act. We then caught a tram to St Kilda Beach and had KFC for lunch. I then rang my parents and we headed for Luna Park. We then met my parents at the front of Luna Park and left for my Uncle's house in the mountains and had a rest.

Daniel, Year 6

While the contents will vary according to the purposes of the portfolio (whether it is designed to showcase 'best' work or be a 'working' portfolio that reveals the process of mastering skills), it will still stand as an individual record of a student's progress towards learning goals. The cumulative entries allow comparisons that are often lost in other kinds of 'one-off' assessment. Students can clearly see how their initial attempts at the beginning of a year improve over time and thus gain some insight into their learning styles. Cover sheets and summaries of portfolio items can give a quick indication of contents.

Teaching programs that integrate the language skills of speaking, listening, reading, and writing provide authentic language tasks. Problem-solving activities can relate to meaningful, real-life situations

The charting of a student's progress is ongoing. 'There is no limit to the number of examples ('pointers') that could be assembled to enrich the description of a progress map, and there is no limit to the number of samples of student work that could be collected and used to better illustrate the nature of progress in an area of learning' (Masters & Forster 1996: 13).

There are various types of authentic assessment that teachers can incorporate into a portfolio of work, combined with observations of a student's learning development. Entries can be samples of students' writings in different genres that can be evaluated on criteria such as particular content or language features, with a rating scale that has been devised collaboratively.

MULTILITERACIES IN THE CLASSROOM

A unit of work on anti-racism may include a debate about multiculturalism as portrayed in the media, listening to different points of view, reading the speeches of politicians, looking up websites, and writing about their own perspectives. The teacher (and students) can devise relevant activities (e.g. a letter to a newspaper). Students can produce an anti-racism kit with photographs, graphics, videotapes and written materials to illustrate their message. Meaning is made in multimodal ways—through writing, visual, audio and spatial patterns. Collaborate with students on appropriate assessment criteria for the finished kit.

Formulation of useful criteria for assessment is essential

Evaluative criteria in portfolios need to be clearly stated and entries should be regularly assessed to ensure that students are realising their learning potential. Formulation of useful criteria for assessment is essential, otherwise the material simply remains a collection. Teachers (and students) can identify particular aspects that need attention and that can be addressed in mini-lessons where input is given to the class as a whole or to small groups.

Comments can be written on 'post it' notes as the teacher walks around the classroom and these can later be transferred to a student's portfolio

Writing comments is time-consuming, but the teacher still needs to make useful observations. Writing descriptive comments does take longer than assigning a numerical mark. Be aware that subjectivity, prejudices, and gender stereotypes can affect judgment about student assessment and progress. Much of the observation of students can be done by means of checklists while students are actually engaged in classroom activities.

Models of work at different levels of achievement are highly recommended so that students can see what is expected of them. Brainstorming ideas and providing contextual support for meaning will help all students to complete tasks satisfactorily. Students can become involved in constructing criteria based on their criticism of the 'benchmark' works. This can be done through group work and by the teacher eliciting appropriate criteria through a classroom discussion.

Progress maps

Portfolios can incorporate progress maps, which give a graphic display of a student's progress. The progress map (or developmental continuum) can give a broad perspective on a student's development from year to year over a long period, and show relative achievement of students of the same age or grade level.

> 'The challenge is to understand each learner's current level of progress and to provide opportunities to facilitate further growth'. (Rowe Report 2005)

Progress maps provide a framework for monitoring student growth in an area of learning. Because this growth is monitored against a described continuum, a student's estimated locations on a progress map can be interpreted and reported descriptively in terms of the skills, knowledge, and understandings typically demonstrated by students at those locations (Masters & Forster 1996: 6).

Level 1 learners can produce simple written texts with support. This is evident when they can copy simple texts or write words, phrases and simple sentences. Level 2 learners can write simple text on familiar topics. Level 3 learners can write extended texts in a variety of different genres.

A progress map describes what it means for a learner to make progress in the achievement of specific outcomes. It can indicate the knowledge, skills, values, and attitudes, which learners demonstrate at different levels. A student's educational progress, tracked over a number of years at school, provides an important record of growth and achievement.

A progress map helps teachers to know their students and how they learn.

WRITING STRATEGIES CHECKLIST

Student   Date

Writing approaches   Comments

    Works through edited drafts to finished product

    Uses mechanics of writing to aid meaning

Ability to write in different genres

- accuracy of content
- attention to logical organisation
- recognition of audience's needs
- uses correct grammar
- spells accurately
- uses resources to improve work, e.g. dictionary
- self-edits or asks peer.

IN THE CLASSROOM

Design an editing checklist suitable for senior students' (Year 6) writing. Make a wall chart suitable for the classroom. Simplify the items and make it into a bookmark for students to use.

Student self-assessment

'We teach how to read books but not how to read their own writing. Unless we show children how to read their own writing, their work will not improve'.
(Graves 1994: xvi)

If students can assess their own writing, then they can revise and edit texts to make them more accurate and meaningful. Self-assessment is an essential feature in the armoury of assessment practices.

The following aids can help students learn standards for good writing:

- checklist of strategies used for reading a particular text
- self-assessment checklist of learning goals
- knowledge of the 6 Traits model.

Portfolios encourage students to see learning as a process and to become more directly involved in their own learning. For example, a student might select a piece of work for the portfolio because it showed an improvement on an earlier piece, indicating a learning growth. Students will be more actively engaged in self- and peer-assessment if the teacher encourages these activities within the classroom. Some students may not have come from a school background that is learner-centred where they are encouraged in self-assessment.

The portfolio can help students in setting their own educational goals and developing new interests. Students can become involved in observing how standards work—whether an entry meets a standard in an exemplary fashion or whether there is much room for improvement. Once the portfolio has sufficient entries and the student teacher has assessed the work according to the agreed criteria, there is a record of what the student teacher can actually do and a judgment of relative strengths and weaknesses.

If students are given the opportunity to assess models of work in a non-threatening environment they learn to judge relative strengths and weaknesses and are more ready to apply the criteria to their own work. Benchmark models can be collected from previous years to show to new classes. Clemmons et al. (1993) suggest having a partner who can review an item and judge whether it meets criteria and how a particular text can be improved. Students need practice in setting realistic goals and in judging what their partner did well or could improve.

IN THE CLASSROOM

Here is a checklist for self- or peer-assessment that could be modified for assessing particular features of writing in relation to different genres:

Writing Assessment

Name   Date

Title of text

Genre

Writing Strategies

Purpose and organisation	Yes	No
1 I stated my purpose clearly with a main idea.		
2 I organised my thoughts in a logical way.		
3 I did some research or background reading.		
4 My work has a beginning, middle, and end.		
5 I tried to make my writing interesting to the reader.		

Use of words or sentences

6 I chose words that helped make my point.

7 I wrote complete sentences.

8 I used correct grammar with subject–verb agreement.

9 I used verb tense correctly.

Mechanics or format

10 I spelt words correctly, using a dictionary when necessary.

11 I used punctuation correctly.

12 I word-processed the text and/or wrote legibly.

Editing

13 I edited my text with a checklist and/or by reading it aloud.

14 I gained feedback from others to help edit my work.

15 I paid attention to specific features of the writing genre (different
language features could be added here).

(Adapted from O'Malley & Valdez Pierce 1996: 157)

Portfolios can complement other kinds of assessment and need not necessarily supplant existing practices. Major advantages of the portfolio assessment are the involvement of students in setting goals for their own learning and the encouragement of reflection about the process of learning. The focus on individual student growth is readily seen in a portfolio collection rather than the pass/fail information provided by some tests. The collaborative planning and design of a portfolio encourages student self-evaluation, helps to monitor progress, and links classroom instruction more closely with assessment. The work of O'Malley & Valdez Pierce (1996) provides practical examples of strategies for expanding the range of assessment practices and gives useful checklists of evaluative criteria. As many classroom teachers have discovered, the portfolio can bring about significant changes in teaching, learning, and assessment practices.

Portfolios are part of a balance of evaluation practices. To find out what students can do, use varied methods and multiple sources of information. Data drawn from a range of assessment practices will reflect more accurately an individual student's abilities.

Good writing is not always 'correct' writing, but it usually is. Poor assessment and reporting practices damage students' self-esteem and make unfair comparisons. Many problems can be deflected if students gain a sense of ownership of their writing and take pride in editing their own texts. The power of the written word cannot be underestimated: harmful comments may be remembered for a long time. Good assessment practices help students to learn and to achieve their educational potential.

▶ Summary

1   Assessment and evaluation practices gauge student performance and progress. Reporting provides accountability. Validity and reliability are fundamental considerations in assessment.

2   Assessment of writing involves familiarity with the content and structure of different genres as well as control over language features.

3   Both informal and formal assessment are needed.

4   Portfolios enhance student responsibility as independent learners by engaging them in monitoring their own learning through the selection of entries, the identification of criteria for assessment, and self- and peer-assessment.

5   Language portfolios provide variety in assessment procedures.

6   Portfolios have particular relevance for assessing the language abilities of students from diverse language backgrounds.

7   Assessment activities should be linked with classroom instruction.

Critical thinking and study exercises

1   Discuss some of the principles of classroom assessment in relation to students' writing skills. A sample of a student's writing, accompanied by a student profile, may help you to direct the discussion.

   a   What is considered 'correct' English?

   b   Why should assessment be integral to classroom activities?

   c   Why should assessment strategies be varied and cover a wide range of features?

   d   Why is it important to assess aspects such as strategies, motivation, and effort as well as other skills of writing?

   e   What relative rating should be given to a student's punctuation, grammar, and spelling as compared to a student's style, creativity, and content?

   f   What are the relative benefits of reporting by written comments, marks out of ten, alphabetical grades, achievement of outcomes?

2   Discuss the benefits of a student's self- and /or peer assessment of the writing process. Can you think of any problems and how these might be addressed by the class teacher?

   a   Suggest activities that are appropriate for self-assessment, group assessment and teacher assessment?

   b   Design a self-assessment sheet for a particular grade level and for a particular text-type. For example, list five items for a Year 2 class writing a narrative text.

3   Devise some 'authentic' writing assessment tasks for junior and/or senior grades in different areas of the curriculum, e.g. Mathematics, Music, English, Science etc. Give students a reason to write and a focus for the writing audience.

4   Integrate computer technology in tasks where it can assist understanding or efficiency e.g. websites.

5   Discuss the value of authentic assessments:

   a   activities that meet the goals of the curricula

   b   real-life performances or exhibitions (these may be multimodal)

   c   texts published on the World Wide Web

   d   newspaper competitions for writing.

6   What are some factors associated with the assessment of writing skills for ESL students? How would you apply these to specific writing tasks?

Further reading

Students are advised to consult the current curriculum and support documents relating to the assessment practices in their state or territory.

Brady, L. & K. Kennedy 2005, *Celebrating Student Achievement: Assessment and reporting*, 2nd edn, Pearson Prentice Hall, Sydney.

Breen, M. P., C. Barratt-Pugh, B. Derewianka, H. House, C. Hudson, T. Lumley & M. Rohl 1997, *Profiling ESL Children: How teachers interpret and use national and state assessment frameworks*, DEETYA, Canberra.

Brindley, G. & G. Wigglesworth 1997, *Access: Issues in language test design and delivery*, National Centre for English Language Teaching and Research, Macquarie University, Sydney.

Derewianka, B. (ed.) 1992, *Language Assessment in Primary Classrooms*, Harcourt Brace Jovanovich, Sydney.

Graves, D. 1994, *A Fresh Look at Writing*. Heinemann, Portsmouth, N.H.

Hamp-Lyons, L. 2000, 'Assessing writing', *Assessing Writing: An International Journal* 8: 5–18.

Spandel, V. 2005, *Creating Writers Through 6-Trait Writing Assessment and Instruction*, 4th edn, Pearson Education Inc., Boston.

Stiggins, R. 2001, *Student Involved Classroom Assessment*, 3rd edn, Prentice Hall, Englewood Cliffs, N.J.

Walter-Thomas, C. & M. T. Brownell 2001, 'Bonnie Jones: Using student portfolios effectively', *Intervention in School and Clinic* 36(4): 225–9.

Web links

Basic Skills Test: www.schools.nsw.edu.au

K–6 Education Resources, Board of Studies, NSW, Australia: www.bosnsw-k6.nsw.edu.au

National Centre for English Language Teaching & Research, Macquarie University: www.nceltr.mq.edu.au

Six Traits site, NWRE Laboratory (Northwest Regional Educational Laboratory): www.nwrel.org/assessment

www.cyberspaces.net

STELLA Standards for Teachers of English Language and Literacy in Australia: www.stella.org.au

18 INFORMATION AND COMMUNICATION TECHNOLOGIES

Overview

Good writing is a recursive process of moving through different stages of composition, not simply of putting words on a page. Since so much revision is needed—in thinking, changing ideas, and developing style—computer technology has become an essential tool for many writers. Used effectively, it can save valuable time and lead to writing that is accurate, well organised, and full of interesting ideas. In the classroom, teachers can use word-processing, blogs, webquests and the treasure trove of information on the Internet to motivate their students to want to write.

As educators in the 21st century, we need to accommodate the new information and communication technologies in the context of literacy education. ICT can be harnessed to exploit pedagogical potential in the classroom. There are different kinds of electronic literacies: the retrieval, recording, and storage of information (as text and pictures) and their combination in meaningful ways; and the creative process of making and publishing one's own text.

Using ICT to enhance teaching and learning

ICT is a powerful tool in the classroom because it can ignite the imagination and bridge the global divide for those fortunate enough to have access to it. The teacher needs to look at ways in which the emerging technologies can blend with traditional methods to influence and enhance students' writing and learning. Ayers, however, punctures the myth that good teachers have to make learning fun: 'Fun is distracting, amusing. Clowns are fun. Jokes can be fun. Learning can be engaging, engrossing, amazing, disorientating, and often deeply pleasurable. If it's fun, fine. But it doesn't need to be fun' (1993: 10). The application of technologies *can* enhance the curricula in imaginative ways beyond mere fun; it can add new dimensions to units of study and expand our notions of literacy. Access to a range of resources, new audiences, and a variety of media allow the teacher and student to teach and learn in new and enriching ways.

Benefits of using ICT in teaching writing

Supplementing traditional classroom programs with ICT has numerous benefits through transmitting information to students and providing discussion forums (Alexander, 1997). ICT

- develops a clearer understanding and awareness of the basic structure of written and visual texts
- provides a high quality of presentation that can motivate students who find manual writing difficult or messy
- allows students to reflect on their writing and to make changes easily by cutting and pasting text
- helps students to write more interesting texts because of access to a wide variety of information
- identifies, checks, and corrects grammatical and spelling errors
- allows students to store and retrieve texts easily
- promotes both independent and collaborative writing
- provides possibilities for multimedia creations, e.g. by employing graphic images, sound, and video with the printed text
- encourages students to write for longer periods because of the editing capacity
- allows for collaboration with other cultures, e.g. working on joint projects
- gives opportunities for publishing and communicating within the classroom and worldwide
- encourages risk-taking and creativity in writing
- enables student-centred teaching approaches
- provides 24/7 accessibility to course materials.

For each of these benefits, an antithesis can be found. For example, little understanding of language is shown if students simply plagiarise or rearrange a text from another source. A longer, neater text that is free of spelling errors is not necessarily quality writing. Preoccupation with formatting of text or poor keyboarding skills can detract from interest in the content of the writing (Armstrong & Casement 2001). Impress on students that it is the ideas that count, not decorative borders, neat presentation, or an error-free text. Good writers usually write a number of messy drafts before they produce a text that satisfies their requirements. Students may be distracted from paying attention to the quality of their writing and the need for revision by a word-processed text that gives the *appearance* of excellence.

Instruction by a teacher is needed in specific strategies and techniques for writing and information-handling, e.g. how and when to use sources and the processes of brainstorming, drafting, and revising writing. Conferencing with the teacher and with peers helps students learn how to communicate their meaning and to structure their texts in more striking and purposeful ways. The computer is not a substitute for interaction with the teacher.

Social justice issues have particular relevance to the use of emerging technologies. The teacher may work in an environment characterised by a 'digital divide' where wealthy schools possess the hardware, the software, and related resources; or the teacher has to fight for access to resources before computer-mediated technologies can be introduced into curricular programs.

Nicholas Negroponte is director of the M.I.T. Media Lab and founder of *Wired* magazine. In the One Laptop Per Child (OLPC) program he advocates a handcranked computer priced at $US100.

Equality of access should be the aim, taking care that socioeconomic disadvantage or gender bias (Spender 1995) is addressed wherever it exists. Ongoing professional development is required so that teachers can keep up to date on ways of integrating technology into their learning programs. Security and censorship issues are important, especially where young children need protection from sexist and racist sites. Copyright, intellectual property, and software privacy are areas about which teachers need to be informed for legal and ethical reasons.

A knowledgeable teacher is the key factor in how computer resources are used effectively in the classroom

The sociocultural context, the resources available, student needs and the pedagogical goals of the teacher will influence how computer and Internet resources are used. The classroom reality may show a considerable variation in each of these but the key factor is the motivated and knowledgeable teacher. Frustration with any one of the following aspects means that teachers cannot exploit the educational potential of technology:

- adequate support staff
- appropriate software
- computers and printers that 'deliver the goods'.

Conventions of writing and computers

Technology alters the way verbal and visual language is produced and understood and therefore affects the conventions of literacy practices (Snyder 1997). Does the writing become more like the spoken word? Does it tend to make students write more, or do they write more telegraphic, colloquial messages when sending by electronic mail? Students usually enjoy writing on computers and they are likely to produce longer, more 'error-free' texts than they could with pen and paper (Cochran-Smith 1991). On the other hand, the student who has writer's block with a blank sheet of paper may find the same problem sitting in front of the blank screen.

The nature of the writing process changes with the new technologies. The habits of linear thinking are subverted with the potential of hyperlinks and the ability to move rapidly between bits of information. Using technologies encourages students to read and write in a nonlinear fashion. Instead of following a single thread or text, readers have the choice of following many filaments as they click on links and move from site to site. The increase in multimodal communication means that a text may include interpolations of illustrations, photographs, sound, or moving images. Different kinds of learning opportunities are possible with an emphasis on higher-level thinking skills that require synthesis, the recognition of patterns and connection, and experiential learning. When students discuss their writing, they may change their writing practices as they work in pairs or groups on the computer. Writing on the computer may not be a private activity but may result in a lot of social interaction. This may change the nature, and content, of the writing produced.

The writing process changes with the new technologies

MULTILITERACIES IN THE CLASSROOM

1   Study models or projects that use multimodal communication and discuss what makes them successful as communicators of meaning. Look for models that have a combination of written text, illustrations, photographs, sound 'bites', and video clips. Look at 'The school I'd like' sites.
2   Organise students into small teams, or work together as a class project.
3   Select a relevant topic about which students can easily find information, e.g. 'Why I live where I live' or 'Our school today', 'The school of the future?'
4   Ensure each student has the ability and background to contribute to the final project.
5   Enlist the help of the librarian and parents to help with information and technical expertise.
6   Give students flexibility and encourage them to work on a multimodal presentation at home.
7   Deliver to the class and/or publish on the Internet.
8   Assess presentations and incorporate feedback for other projects.

Blogs (weblogs)

'Blogs', or web logs, are web pages containing diary-like entries in reverse chronological sequence. New and emerging technologies can highly motivate students to read and write. Sites for 'weblogs' can stimulate interest in keeping an online journal or diary, for private or public communication. Students can 'blog on' to a site, to write down their creative thoughts, post images, and thus become 'bloggers', sharing their musings and experiences with a worldwide audience. Blogs are not always narcissistic thoughts for others to read, but can be very important communications, stimulating discussion forums for those without a voice in the conventional media.

▶ LITERACY IN THE DIGITAL AGE

Weblog Award Winners
1   Explore suitable blog sites for students to motivate them to create their own.
2   Follow a sequence of read, reflect, organise resources, compose text, share ideas, respond to blogs, assess.

A variety of U.S. blogs can be found in the following categories:

- Best Overall Blog—Powerline
- Best New Blog (Established 2004)—Kerry Spot
- Best Group Blog—The Volokh Conspiracy
- Best Humor Blog—ScrappleFace
- Best Liberal Blog—Matthew Yglesias
- Best Conservative Blog—Captain's Quarters
- Best Election Coverage—Real Clear Politics
- Best Media/Journalist Blog—Best of the Web (Opinion Journal)
- Best Tech Blog—Engadget

- Best Culture Blog—a small victory
- Best Sports Blog—Baseball Crank
- Best Photo Blog—Chromasia
- Best LGBT Blog—Boi from Troy
- Best Military Blog—Blackfive
- Best Online Community—Fark
- Best Blog Design—Cold Fury
- Best Essayist—Victor Davis Hanson
- Best Canadian Blog—small dead animals
- Best UK Blog—Belgravia Dispatch
- Best European (Non UK) Blog—The Dissident Frogman
- Best Asian Blog—Why are you worshipping the ground I blog on?
- Best Middle East or Africa Blog—Iraq the Model
- Best Australia or New Zealand Blog—Tim Blair
- Best Latino, Caribbean, or South American Blog—Venezuela News

2004weblogawards.com

Competencies and capabilities to teach in e-literacies

Skills required by the teacher

Where is the knowledge we have lost in information?
T. S. Eliot, 'The Rock' (1934).

Using technology has great potential, but using it successfully in the classroom requires critical judgments about the educational possibilities. Skill is required to sift through the mass of information available and to find its value in terms of accuracy, authorship, and currency.

Classroom teachers mostly decide on the way computers can be used to stimulate writing practices in the classroom. However, traditional roles in the classroom may need to be renegotiated as students and teachers learn from one another. Working successfully with technology in the classroom requires from the teacher appropriate:

1 **Attitudes and values**
   - a positive attitude
   - a willingness to engage and experiment with the technologies.
2 **Knowledge and understanding**
   - knowledge and critical evaluation of the sites and software available
   - a knowledge of pedagogical issues in using technology with students (the role of the teacher; the importance of problem-solving abilities)
   - an ability to involve students, capitalising on their skills and interests
   - the skills to use the resources in teaching programs
   - the ability to integrate technologies into teaching
   - an ability to evaluate student learning from technology-based learning
   - an awareness of those developments that can enhance student learning
   - an awareness of social and ethical issues in the educational context.

3   Technical skills
- the ability to use web-based resources (epals, educational games)
- the ability to use software (databases, mind-mapping tools, spreadsheets)
- the ability to use communication software (email, simulations, online discussions).

Pedagogical matters such as classroom management, learning theories, and learning styles as well as issues of values and ethics are the background to how and why the basic competencies are taught. In order to make good use of the technologies, teachers need to be able to integrate their attitudes, understandings, and skills in response to different circumstances. In a context of rapid change, technical skills may become obsolete; teachers need to quickly become self-directed learners, willing to grasp the potential of ICT. The reflection and metacognitive awareness gained through experiential learning on computers is likely to foster ongoing learning (Phelps et al. 2001). Cognitive, problem-solving skills and successful learning strategies enable students to learn new knowledge in new contexts.

Various computer proficiency skills need to be taught, and practised frequently, so that all students are confident in using technology. To be effective, the technologies need to be incorporated into the curriculum as part of school policy. Areas of computer proficiency skills are outlined below.

I've a grand memory for forgetting, David. R. L. Stevenson, *Kidnapped* (1886)

Navigating the World Wide Web and information retrieval

The teacher's role is crucial in helping students understand the complexity of the Web and how to navigate their way through the databases, using search engines (e.g. Google, Yahoo) and hyperlinks. Students need knowledge of how to retrieve information that is relevant, accurate, up to date, and understandable at their level of knowledge.

▶ LITERACY IN THE DIGITAL AGE

Navigating the Web

A Google search on Shakespeare elicits thousands of entries. Most users only look at the first page of entries (see below). Try other search engines to see how they compare. Discuss how the best choice can be made for a particular purpose. Can you gauge that some are more authoritative than others? What are the clues to pick the best site to answer your question?

www.poets.org

William Shakespeare's biography, poems, books, essays, sonnets.

www.shakespeare.com

Shakespeare biography with guides to the plays, quotes, criticism.

www.shakespeare-online.com

Character analysis, plot synopsis, sonnets, sources used by Shakespeare.

absoluteshakespeare.com

Absolute Shakespeare, the essential resource for William Shakespeare's plays, sonnets, poems, quotes, biography and the legendary Globe Theatre.

shakespeare.palomar.edu
Mr. William Shakespeare and the Internet. An annotated guide to Shakespeare resources on the Internet.
www-tech.mit.edu/Shakespeare
The Complete Works of William Shakespeare. This site has offered Shakespeare's plays and poetry to the Internet.
www.it.usyd.edu.au/~matty/Shakespeare
The Collected Works of Shakespeare. The comments on MIT's Shakespeare site notwithstanding, this site is the web's ... Please note that I am in no way an expert on Shakespeare or his works. The complete works of Shakespeare for any word or phrase. Search results note where every instance of the query appears in his works.
www.bardweb.net
Shakespeare Resource Center. Synopses of plays, authorship debates, and a Shakespeare store.
www.shakespeare.org.uk
Shakespeare Birthplace Trust. Whether you want to find out about the man and his work or to plan your visit to Stratford-upon-Avon to explore the Shakespeare Houses— this is the site.
www.bellshakespeare.com.au
The Bell Shakespeare Company is Australia's only national touring Shakespeare theatre company.

Many sites have features such as a home page and hyperlinks, which link to other reading and discussion sources from the World Wide Web. They may have search facilities and allow interaction with the user and opportunities to communicate through a message board, via email or a discussion forum. By entering search engines such as www.google or www.yahoo and entering key words, access can be gained to books, literature, and reading sources on topics of interest. Some sites include classroom and self-teaching guides that are suitable as teaching resources.

Evaluating websites and software

Traditional criteria for evaluation are accuracy, authority, objectivity, coverage, and currency (Dodge & March 2001). However, an additional checklist relates to the challenge, attractiveness, and accessibility of Internet information resources which include:

- user friendliness
- hypertext links
- software requirements
- ability to retrieve resources
- use of search engines.

It is essential to carefully vet websites for suitability and availability, so that students are not confronted with inaccurate, slanted, or mischievous information. There is deliberate misinformation on the Internet—sometimes to persuade users to buy products or to believe in a particular point of view. Googling 'Hitler' to find accurate information may bring up propaganda sites such as the Hitler Historical Museum that makes no mention of the Holocaust or Jews. The necessary guidance could be given in the form of a list of suitable sites for students conducting research projects in the classroom so that informed choices can be made. Issues such as the developmental stage of students, racism, age, gender, and ethnicity should be considered when evaluating websites. The teacher can devise ways of teaching students how to test the credibility of sites because the amount of information that can be accessed is daunting, particularly if it is above the reading level students can handle. It is important to be able to judge the resources: will a printed book be more effective than a CD-ROM or can they complement one another? Whenever possible, check sites before students see them, especially if they are likely to contain controversial material. Try to judge whether the site is accurate, authoritative, current, has hyperlinks, objectivity, and opportunities for interactivity. How does the information on the site compare with that found in reputable print sources such as encyclopedias?

DAVE'S ESL CAFÉ `<www.eslcafe.com>`

This US site advertises itself as a meeting place for ESL/EFL students and teachers from around the world. It has accurate information from an authoritative source (a qualified TESOL teacher, Dave Sperling) and is supported by professional teacher organisations such as TESOL. The information about teaching English as a second language is presented in an objective but fun-filled manner. An open invitation is made to sponsor Dave's ESL Café through advertising and promoting products and services on the website. These sponsored links are easily recognisable but students need to be able to recognise where sites relate to advocacy, business, and marketing.

The coverage of the website is comprehensive, including many opportunities for interactivity. These links are helpfully provided in alphabetical order, e.g. Bookstore, Chat Central, Discussion Forums, FAQs, Help Center, Hint-of-the-Day. Currency is obvious from the dates of the News and Announcements. Hyperlinks allow access to other web pages. There are many practical classroom activities for teaching English on this popular site.

Word-processing and desktop publishing

Word-processing on the computer is an efficient tool for writing but it also affects how written material is structured. There are many possibilities for writing drafts and presenting an excellent copy (in transcription), cutting and pasting material, and directing readers to other hyperlinks. Although word-processing can greatly aid in revision, can it improve the quality of the writing produced? Remember that the student is doing the writing and making the choices; the computer simply facilitates planning, drafting, revising, and editing of grammatical patterns, punctuation, and spelling. The technology, however, can do much more than make writing more legible: it can help students correct, edit and revise very easily. If it is feasible, the teacher may respond to the student's writing via the computer, providing timely and effective feedback.

Cochran-Smith (1991) argues that the effectiveness of using word processing for writing instruction is embedded in the social practice of a classroom, not simply in its efficiency as a technical tool. A teacher and other students can therefore affect the quality, quantity, and processes of children's writing. A study by Haas (1998) examined the effect of word processing on the amount and kind of planning writers do and found that (1) there was less planning with word processing; (2) there was less conceptual planning and more sequential planning with word processing; (3) the effects of writing media were similar for both experienced and student writers; and (4) there were vast differences in how writers use word processing and put pen and paper together. While these writers were experienced, the results are instructive in the primary classroom context: planning is an essential part of the writing process.

Information and communication technologies have the potential to link visual and verbal information in creative ways. Students will need instruction in the preparation of graphics and artworks.

How to file and manage information

These skills include knowing how to

- use bookmarks
- make shortcuts for rapid navigation on web browsers
- use security tools
- block information deemed harmful to younger students.

The teacher has a crucial role in ensuring that the Internet is used productively. Students can easily become frustrated if they find too little, or too much, information or they do not understand what they find. For this reason, teachers are advised to 'bookmark' pages and sites that are appropriate for the developmental level of the student. However, the serendipity of searching should not be discouraged—new discoveries can be illuminating and can lead to new knowledge. The proviso is that some censorship is necessary to protect students from undesirable sites.

Ensure the Internet is used productively as students 'surf the net'

How to use presentation software

Various kinds of software can help students locate, store, and plan information so that they can maximise their understanding, e.g. databases, mind-mapping tools, and spreadsheets. Visual diagrams that organise material and show relationships between information can help students to order information. For example, the Venn diagram represents sets of elements as circles whose overlap indicates the overlap of information. A 'character' web (see Figure 18.1) can provide spaces for the discussion of attributes of a fictional character from a book, adjectives for description, and accompanying dialogue. The use of this software can greatly aid the planning process for writing.

How to use communication software

This includes how to send an email, taking part in simulations, and participating in online discussions. While many students will know how to send emails (both text and image), this knowledge cannot be assumed and needs to be taught.

Using the Internet in the classroom

'Scaffolding' the writing process on the computer

In the early years, a talking word processor (e.g. Clicker) can assist students with writing. The letter, word, or sentence is spoken once it has been typed in.

Figure 18.1 The character web

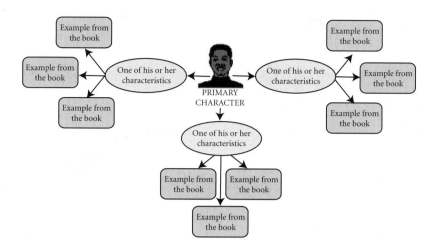

Teachers and students can use software such as Writer's Toolkit to encourage writing in a variety of genres. Three main writing 'types' are specified: imaginative (story or play); personal (story or journal); and functional (argument, letter, list, report, research, review).

Various 'scaffolds' are provided to assist the student in the writing process:

- brainstorming, aided by the facility to build up a wordbank
- gathering information; notes can be inserted into a text or edited on the screen
- planning of an outline through frameworks for different genres
- writing the text in a word-processed document
- editing the text with a spellchecker
- assessing the text through self-assessment grids/questionnaires and/or comments by teacher.

Word-processing and desktop publishing can allow students to produce texts and graphics in exciting ways (Fatouros & Walters-Moore 1997). Various programs such as Storybook Weaver or the Writing Center provide document layouts (awards, letters, newsletter, stories, reports) that can encourage students to write, read, listen, speak, and think.

IN THE CLASSROOM

Writing a classroom story

When writing a classroom story, the following ten-step program can be linked to relevant learning outcomes.

1   Decide on a topic/theme and plan an outline. Brainstorm ideas on the screen so that the outline/concept can be easily altered by addition or deletions. The plan of the story can be printed out, discussed, refined, and decided on by students.

2 Work in small student groups (or as a class) to build up the elements of the written outline. Different groups can be responsible for different sections but checks must be made for continuity and the cohesiveness of the whole story.

3 Edit the text (i.e. the ideas, structure, spelling, font, and layout) through discussion with the teacher and other students. Here the grammar checker, spellchecker, and thesaurus can be used. Focus on the purpose of the text and its intended audience to see if the text is likely to be successful.

4 If desired, graphics or sound can be chosen to complement the written text. Discuss the most appropriate placement in the text. Make decisions about size, the colour of graphics, and the relevance of sound effects.

5 Choose a format that is appropriate for the audience, e.g. whether it will be placed on a classroom wall, in a PowerPoint presentation, in digital or book format.

6 Make final editing choices by reading the text aloud and discussing its success and appeal to the intended audience. When satisfied, print out the text.

7 'Publish' the text. This could be on the Internet, on a school website, on paper that can be distributed to the class, or in book format.

8 Gauge the audience's reaction to the text.

9 Students reflect on the writing process, the final product, and the audience's response. Make a list of strategies for improvement next time.

10 The teacher evaluates the process and product.

Collaboration with other schools can be educational, encouraging students to learn about other cultures. Moore (1999: 61) describes a school in England that collected versions of the same fairy story from around the world written in the languages of the collaborating schools. All those involved ended up with a rich collection of writings that showed the diversity of language in a powerful form and led to the creation of a range of dictionaries and thesauruses, as well as a fascinating anthology that was available for subsequent use.

epals or keypals

The transition from penpals to epals has facilitated opportunities for language learning (Hennigan 1999). The speed of replies as compared with 'snail mail' is a motivating factor. Email correspondence can enhance writing skills because of the novelty of communicating with someone from another culture. It allows students to do classroom projects and transmit cultural information (geography, statistics, pictures, schools) about their countries. Since word processing eliminates illegible, clumsy handwriting, it is a boon to students whose mother tongue script is quite different from English. The writer can edit easily, move text around, and check grammar and spelling errors. Facilities for the exchange of opinions, teacher resources, technology, mentoring, projects, and research can facilitate the epal experience.

Email communication can encourage reluctant writers to expand their writing output

Written expression by email can be encouraged with class members, other classes, neighbouring and distant schools, and epals from overseas. On the other hand, it can be argued that the shortcuts of email language do not encourage students to express themselves most effectively; the formality of written prose is often undercut in emails. Technology has closed the gap between written and spoken expression.

Email communication is characterised by short paragraphs, the messages mostly being under twenty-five lines long. The brevity and truncated nature of the email has led to creative punctuation such as the smiley emoticons ☺ :) ☹ :(which use typography for visual effect. These are sometimes borrowed from the world of advertising. Communicating with an electronic penpal to practise English and to share cultures can be arranged fairly easily and contributes to multicultural education. Morriss (1997) has outlined the Internet's potential as a resource for stimulating interest in children's literature as students exchange views by electronic mail.

Choice of websites on the Internet will be determined by availability (and sometimes financial cost). Epals www.epals.com, established in 1996, is the largest online provider of student-safe email; 4.6 million students and teachers from 191 countries, and over 100 000 classroom profiles, link schools as cross-cultural learning partners and friends.

'With a word processor, writing becomes a happening; it can be scrolled up the screen so that it unfolds in time, like speech. The tape-recorder made speech more like writing; the word processor has made writing more like speech.' (Halliday, in Burns & Coffin, 2000: 188)

EPALS.COM

Projects

Take part in ePALS projects and reap the benefits of our tools and community. The projects are designed by educators to be adaptable to diverse subject areas and age levels.

ePALS Teacher Guide

Our ePALS Teacher Guide contains all the information you need to help you feel at home in the ePALS Global Network.

Online Resources

Click your way from here to many other fun and educational spots on the Web. With so many topics to be explored, think of this as your gateway to the world's biggest library!

Telecollaboration Tips

If you're new to online collaboration, you may wish to view these tips that will help you get comfortable using ePALS for projects and email exchanges.

Internet Safety Tips

This page offers some safety suggestions for online exchanges.

ePALS Case Study

A Florida teacher sees amazing results in his students with ePALS. Read the complete story.

While some have commercial links, most sites have a free educational service that allows users to start a project with another class, or to create a new friendship with someone on the other side of the globe. From most sites users can give their address, age, hobbies, and languages, and an epal from another country can be located.

Features to consider when joining an email/epals club are safety and privacy, translation facilities, ease of joining, availability of resources, and interactivity options such as discussion boards. A protected environment is needed to minimise risk so that emails can be exchanged safely and students can take part in discussion boards and chat rooms. 'Walled Gardens' can provide educationally relevant websites so that when students web-surf, they are not accessing inappropriate sites. Message monitoring is possible for students' incoming and outgoing messages if this is considered necessary. Some sites have multilingual tools for translation that can provide basic translations for a number of languages, an exciting innovation.

Finding the right match between epals is important if the communication is to continue. Search engines allow partners to key in information (hence 'keypals') such as desired location, language, subject studied (if a classroom project is desired), and age of participants. Some sites offer interesting activities and publish original student work that can motivate interest in writing. For example, in an ePALS classroom project, the results of a Space Day project are published where teams of students designed solutions to challenges confronting astronauts, in collaboration with NASA and the Johnson Space Centre. 'English-To-Go' provides lessons based on Reuters' news stories, supplemented by exercises and teachers' notes. Interactivity options through discussion boards for teachers and students encourage the exchange of opinions, the sharing of ideas, and the asking and answering of questions about new project ideas.

A real audience and a real message will help students with their writing, especially the way they must gauge what they say and how they say it so that the communication is understood. Since the messages are transferred so quickly and easily, motivation can be maintained. The teacher needs to plan in setting up the epals so that students learn from and enjoy the communications they write and receive (Teeler & Gray 2000: 75–6). These factors should be considered:

- *Finding appropriate partners for epals*
  These can be found through databases, classroom exchange programs, or EFL sites. It may be possible to arrange for collaboration with another class, and in this case the teachers will need to set up a plan and schedule to ensure success.
- *Sending messages*
  Will emails be sent by individuals or by a class? How long will they be? Will they be written in class? How much teacher input will be needed? How will they be monitored?
- *Integration in the curriculum*
  How can the correspondence help students' learning? The teacher may provide a focus for the emails, a joint project that students are involved in.
- *Response time*
  Students may become discouraged if they do not receive speedy replies.

Web quests

Web quests are guided Internet searches (usually problem-based scenarios) where students work in groups to investigate issues or problems. They give students practice in finding relevant information from the vastness of the World Wide Web, encourage cooperative learning, and develop critical thinking (Dodge 1998; March 1998a).

Web quests have appeal because of the ease and speed of seeking information from the Internet rather than from print resources. They have the potential to be creative, interesting, and challenging tasks that can focus on the students' interests. To appeal to students, a web quest should be 'real', 'rich' and 'relevant': a major advantage of the web quest is the critical investigation of an issue from many sides, as opposed to the transmission of codified knowledge or rote comprehension (March 2004).

A critical awareness of language is essential so that students have insights into why a particular discourse is chosen and how they can examine its impact (Fairclough & Wodak 1998). The information explosion on the Internet has affected both language and power relationships. Studying multiple perspectives of points of view from different websites shows students how language changes, depending on the authority and purpose of the writer, the intended audience, and the context (Fairclough 2001). Teaching students to think and argue is the cornerstone of the web quest.

In 1995, Prof. Bernie Dodge of San Diego State University created online web quests for teachers

Web quests can be linked with curricular areas that foster critical thinking. Those trialled by schools and professional teacher organisations, which contain worksheets and teaching notes, are most useful as exemplars. A web quest on Ancient Egypt may require students to complete a travel log of experiences in searching for information; or the task is to imagine you are a group of authors working for a publishing company. The assignment is to write and illustrate a book about Ancient Egypt.

When planning the web quest, take into account the level of student language skills and interests. Common features of webquests are: an outline of the task(s) to be completed with a time-line (written handout or online); the websites to consult; and a copy of an assessment rubric. Various sites are available to assist in making web quests more interesting by creating customised puzzles, word searches, mazes, matching and gap-fill, multiple-choice, short-answer, jumbled-sentence, acrostic poem exercises. Templates of online learning activities are useful for busy teachers and allow contextualisation of Internet searches, thus focusing on their students' interests and needs.

Norman Fairclough, Emeritus Professor of Linguistics at Lancaster University, is one of the founders of critical discourse analysis, which looks at the influence of power relations on the content and structure of texts

ABORIGINAL STUDIES WEB QUEST

'There has been much discussion lately on the news and in the newspapers about whether the Australian Government should make a formal apology to the Indigenous people of Australia for the Government policies of the past which have affected them.'

'The Prime Minister has requested a group be appointed to help advise himself and other central community representatives on how Australian people view saying "Sorry" to the Aboriginal People.'

'You have been appointed to that Advisors' group, which consists of an historian, a reporter, a health worker, an anthropologist and a librarian. Together with your other team members, you are required to investigate the issue and then report back your findings.'

Question: Should the Prime Minister and the Government say 'sorry' to the Aboriginal People? Why/why not? (bestwebquests.com)

Adapt web quests for an appropriate grade level and help students find useful resources such as google.earth and the *Macquarie Atlas of Aboriginal Australia* (2005).

The construction of web quests (by students or the teacher) provides a fascinating insight into the wealth of information available on the Internet that can give background knowledge

Problem-based learning activities help students to think

for areas of the curriculum. Analytical thinking and problem-solving skills are also nurtured as students are guided to apply the information they find to a particular 'quest'. Problem-based learning, where curricular content is organised into 'problem' scenarios, helps students to think. As they explore problems in groups they may find there is no predetermined answer. For example, in a web quest focusing on *The Samurai's Tale* by Erik Haugaard (1984), the novel can be explored from many perspectives—students can become journalists investigating medieval Japan.

Figure 18.2 Assessment grid for a web quest on volcanoes

	Beginning 1	Developing 2	Accomplished 3	Exemplary 4	Score
Content of Pamphlet	Facts and information presented in an unclear format and there is missing information.	There are some facts and information presented that connect to the topic of volcanoes and the formation of the Hawaiian Islands.	There is an adequate amount of information and facts presented about volcanoes and the formation of the Hawaiian Islands.	Abundance of facts and information about volcanoes and the formation of the Hawaiian Islands. I can use this pamphlet as my guide through the park!	
Research	There is not a lot of evidence of research through the websites that were provided.	Great start; has good ideas that need to be expanded through more research.	Exactly where the researcher needs to be. There are clear and detailed facts demonstrating an efficient amount of research.	More than what is expected. The facts and information presented show a significant amount of different resources.	
Pamphlet	Not enough information, the pamphlet looks rushed.	Good start, the pamphlet is easy to read, however, the reader is left with questions and it looks thrown together.	Exactly where a volcano expert needs to be; there is a lot of information and there is creativity to support the information.	More than what is expected; the audience is wowed and drawn to the pamphlet. You show an abundance of visuals that support your facts.	

An Internet web quest usually contains:

1 Introduction: An explanation of the importance or relevance of the quest, motivating the students' involvement.
2 The Quest: The problem to be solved and/or what needs to be found out.

3   The Task: What the student should be able to do after completing the web quest.
4   Roles: The roles that participants take (e.g. information-seeker, sceptic).
5   The Process: The steps needed to complete the task, including
   *   *Phase 1*—sites that give overview, general background information
   *   *Phase 2*—sites to visit for more specific information
   *   *Phase 3*—discussion of the presentation and arguments for and against
   *   *Phase 4*—how this information might be relevant in the real world.

6   Resources: A list of the main Internet sites as well as books, articles, audiovisual materials, and people to consult about the topic.
7   Evaluation: An examination of what (and how) the student has learnt to answer the quest, e.g.
   *   location of the sites
   *   an oral speech—assessment of strength of argument and support by examples
   *   written work—clarity and credibility of information
   *   reflection on the process—depth of response to show engagement with task.

Activities and games

Taking part in discussion and news groups through ICT can encourage students to engage with their learning. Students who do not participate well in the hurly-burly of the classroom situation may find online activities stimulating and conducive to learning. For example, the International Poetry Guild, a web-based language arts program, encourages students to create, edit, and publish poetry. Often eight to ten schools are involved with an editorial board, and there may be mentors from outside.

Meaningful, authentic activities are plentiful on the Internet, but much organisation is required from the teacher to plan the involvement of students so that they can learn from the experiences and enjoy them. The time students spend sitting and looking at a screen also needs to be closely monitored. It should be interspersed with talking, listening, and small-group interaction.

Many students, familiar with the rules and scenarios of video games, are practised in problem-solving skills. Popular games such as World of Warcraft (WoW) build up a fantasy universe which heightens the imagination of those who play it. Players learn how to 'read' words, graphic symbols, and non-verbal clues and can transfer this visual literacy ability into other aspects of their education (Gee 2003).

The challenge of ICT

Technological advances will affect how we teach writing and how we write. The challenge is to use ICT as a liberating, productive, and creative resource to support the curriculum. The physical well-being of students and their cognitive development needs to be considered at all times when using computer technology. Effective learning takes place if students are engaged with the task, as well as stimulated to seek and apply knowledge. The new technologies are ideally placed to assist in this quest.

The predictions of Nicholas Negroponte (1995) about ICT, intelligent agents, smart rooms, and virtual reality are being realised in a period of dynamic technological change. The integration and convergence of ICT with mobile phones and television offer exciting prospects for the teaching and learning process. The new applications of ICT offer unprecedented opportunities to the world of education. We can have an optimistic vision of ICT rather than an elegy for the Gutenberg press.

Negroponte's *Being Digital* (1995) is now available in a 'Cyberdock' version. A Cyberdock features the text as a casting-off point, from which the reader is invited to explore Internet sites linked to the Dock

Students of the future may 'write' multi-modal PowerPoint presentations that include text, visual images, sound, and video clips rather than written text on paper. When expository text moves online, it integrates multimedia. Composing effective Web texts with a non-linear structure, more relaxed syntax and grammar, an informal style, and increasing multimedia will change how we write (Kress: 2001). New media change old media.

► Summary

1 New technologies can facilitate the teaching and learning process but the pedagogical implications are of paramount concern.

2 Concepts of writing change in multimodal formats. Teachers and students need to learn how to read and write in ways that use hyperlinks and bypass habits of linearity when and where these features are inappropriate.

3 There are numerous benefits in using ICT in teaching writing, but the computer should not be a substitute for interaction with the teacher.

4 Particular skills are needed by the teacher to engage with the technologies, including an awareness of ethical issues and the need to develop some technical competence.

5 Competencies and capabilities for e-learning include navigating the Internet, evaluating websites, word-processing, and desktop publishing.

6 Various 'scaffolds' are provided by writing software, such as Writer's Toolkit, to assist the student in the writing process.

7 Ways to use the Internet in the classroom include creating a classroom story, epals and web quests.

8 Care needs to be taken that the physical and cognitive needs of students are considered when using the technologies in the classroom.

9 Teachers must be alert to new technologies that can make teaching and learning more effective.

Critical thinking and study questions

1. Discuss the value of web quests. Browse through three sites devoted to web quests. Find a web quest that interests you and that would support the curriculum and learning outcomes of the K–6 classroom. Work through one web quest as a teacher, to check that web links are available and appropriate. Modify the web quest to suit your own purposes and check for cultural relevance. Trial the web quest on a small group and evaluate as a pedagogical tool. Construct a new web quest with the help of students.

2. Explore the benefits of a class web page in the writing program. Construct a class web page, seeking technical assistance if required.

Browse through other K–6 classroom, school, and teacher sites to gather ideas. Discuss the purpose of the web page with the class and how it could/should be used.

3. Create an online newspaper. Make this a multimodal presentation with photographs, animations, texts, effects, sounds, and pictures. A variety of writing activities can be included to involve all class members: front-page news, lead stories, interviews, reporting of news events,

advertisements, book and film reviews, pet of the week, crossword puzzle, comics, opinion page on an issue, editorial, letters to the editor, cartoons, historical features, quotable quotes, classifieds, personal notices, for sale items, sports, and entertainment.

4. Conduct a research project to evaluate how students react to particular software or Internet activities, and how the use of computer technology affects their learning outcomes.

Further reading

Students are advised to consult the current curriculum and support documents relating to the teaching of ICT in their state or territory.

Burns, A. & C. Coffin (eds) 2000, *Analysing English in a Global Context: A reader*, Routledge, London.
Cochran-Smith, M. 'Word processing and writing in elementary classrooms: A critical review of related literature', *Review of Educational Research* 61(1) 1991: 107–55.
Dodge, B. 1998, WebQuests for learning, www.ozline.com
Fairclough, N. 2001, *Language and Power*, rev. 2nd edn, Longman, London.
Fatouros, C. & C. Walters-Moore 1997, *Using Software in English*, PETA, Sydney.
Gee, J. 2003, *What Video Games Have To Teach Us About Learning and Literacy*, Palgrave Macmillan, New York.
Haas, C. 1998, 'How the writing medium shapes the writing process: effects of word processing on planning', Education Resources Information Center #ED309408.
Haugaard, E. C. 1984, *The Samurai's Tale*, Houghton Mifflin, Boston.
Hennigan, H., 1999, 'Penpals to kepals', *Modern English Teacher* 8(2): 41–50.
Kress, G. & T. Van Leeuwen 2001, *Multimodal Discourse: The modes and media of contemporary communication*, Arnold, London.
March, T. 2004, 'WebQuests: The fulcrum for systemic curriculum improvement, pp. 1–15 www.ozline.com
Morriss, M. 1997, 'Children's Literature Possibilities on the Web', *Australian Journal of Language and Literacy* 20(4): 321–8.
Negroponte, N. 1995, *Being Digital*, Knopf, New York.
Schmidt, P. R. & A. W. Palliotet (eds) 2001, *Exploring Values Through Literature, Multimedia, and Literacy Events: Making connections*, IRA, Newark, Del.
Scott, A. 2002, 'Technology as a literacy tool', *Practically Primary* 7(1): 6–8.
Wepner, S. B., W. J. Valmont & R. Thurlow (eds) 2000, *Linking Literacy and Technology: A guide for K–8 classrooms*, IRA, Newark, Del.

Web links

Specific website addresses have not always been suggested as they are subject to change. Teachers should use search engines to locate current sites. If technical expertise or appropriate software is unavailable, explore other avenues for learning. Adapt suggested activities to suit the competencies of students. All software should be evaluated by the teacher before use to check its appropriateness.

Check other recommended ICT writing sources in chapters on Handwriting, Spelling and Grammar.

NSW Country Areas Program Research Modules: www.cap.nsw.edu.au
Education resources website: www.edufind.com
Charles Sturt University, Education Virtual Library: www.csu.edu.au/education
EdNA Online, Education Network Australia: www.edna.edu.au
Literacy Web Australia (Queensland Special Programs School Scheme): www.schools.ash.org.au/litweb

Software

Bailey's Book House
bestwebquests.com
Big Book Maker
epals.com
Highlighting Writing
Microsoft Creative Writer
StartWrite
Penfriend
Story Centre
Storybook Weaver
Student Writing Center
The Amazing Writing Machine
The Children's Writing and Publishing Center
Word Weaver
The Writing Centre
Writer's Toolkit

Outlines and concept mapping

Idealiner
Inspiration
Kidspiration
MaxThink

Multimedia

Clicker
Fine Artist
Kid Pix
Magpie
Media Weaver
Optima
The Multimedia Workshop

TEACHING WRITING IN THE CLASSROOM

19

Overview

The teaching of writing in the classroom should focus on the effective use of language, bearing in mind the purpose of the writing and the audience for whom it is intended. The teaching strategies of modelling the writing process and imitating written texts, guided writing, or joint construction of texts (with peers or the teacher), and practice in independent writing, will assist the child to become a confident and accurate writer. The modelling of text-types (or genres) can guide students in how writing is produced for different purposes and audiences. There must also be time for students to compose their own texts creatively, encouraging them to experiment with language.

Teaching writing should focus on the effective use of language

A sociolinguistic approach

A number of theoretical approaches can assist teachers to help students gain the understanding they need of the different aspects of literacy. The sociolinguistic approach emphasises the strong link between language and social contexts.

There is a strong link between language and social contexts

It emphasises that the communicative purpose of a text determines the appropriate structure, grammar, layout, typeface, language, and vocabulary to achieve that purpose. For example, a letter to a friend has a different structure and language from a letter of complaint about an unfair practice. A personal letter may be somewhat idiosyncratic in shape and structure but it still contains features that distinguish it from other kinds of letter writing such as a formal letter of complaint. The two kinds of letters have different functions and the writer chooses an appropriate language style to express them.

The **register** of a piece of writing or speech reflects in its vocabulary the sociocultural context in which the words are used. For example, the language children use in the playground when talking to their peers is usually more colloquial than the language used when talking to their teachers in the classroom. It is important to teach students how language appropriate for a particular context can lead to more effective communication. Familiarity with the conventions of language in different contexts and the different genres of writing will improve students' ability to make effective choices about language use when they read, write, and speak.

The genre approach

Within the context of writing, genre refers to different text-types that have recognisable characteristics, such as narratives or reports. These distinguishing characteristics, however, change over time. In literary terms, genre refers to a type of artistic creation such as the drama, novel, or poetry, and various kinds of writing such as biography or the sonnet. In the 1980s, in the field of education, genre was applied to literacy. The concept of genres or 'generic types' is based in the systemic-functional theory of language made accessible through the research of Halliday & Hasan (1976). Various researchers have classified genres: Martin & Rothery (1981), Kress (1982), and Christie (1989).

GENRE

Martin's definition of 'genre' in *Children Writing: A reader*: 'Genre refers to any staged, purposeful cultural activity, and this includes oral language genres as well as written language genres. A genre is characterized by having a schematic structure—a distinctive beginning, middle and end' (Deakin University 1984: 25).

Features of the genre-based approach

- Explicit teaching of the function, structure, organisation, and grammatical patterns of a particular genre.
- Discussion of several models of the genre and how effectively they use the text features to meet their purpose.
- Joint construction of a text to illustrate features of the genre that students are learning to write.
- Critical analysis of a text to show how communication is governed by social and cultural context, purpose, and audience.
- Class discussion about how students' own texts might be written to reflect the broad genre and to meet their imaginative and creative needs.
- Further library research to develop range and depth of writing.
- Individual writing of texts by the students.

The importance of genres

Learning to handle and manipulate the genres of the various school subjects, adapting and modifying them for different purposes, is important not only because it is a necessary part of learning the content of the subjects, but also because it is a necessary part of learning the ways of reasoning and organising the different aspects of experience that are characteristic of the different subjects. (Christie & Rothery 1990: 188).

Genres make explicit the linguistic choices that people make when they read and write, helping to explain why we choose a particular tense, or structure a text in a certain way. This should not imply that there is a fixed or 'correct' version since the conventions for a particular genre can change, either subtly or dramatically. Context and social relations are important factors that influence linguistic choices.

It is important to provide students with examples of a broad variety of text-types, mainly because models enable them to make more informed choices when they are using language. The issue of equity is central to genre theory in educational contexts. For this reason, a knowledge of different genres in a broad curriculum that is reflective of society gives children 'the possibility of the use of the resources of representation which makes possible the full participation in all aspects of the cultural and social life of a group' (Kress in Anstey & Bull 1996: 65). The types of texts selected in the curriculum should be useful and relevant to school life and society. Students can be introduced to the following text-types: narratives, personal responses, information reports, explanations, expositions, discussions, procedures, factual descriptions, factual recounts, and literary recounts.

Students should be encouraged to use a broad variety of text-types

Genres are not 'fixed' and the divisions between different types of writing are not hard and fast but change in different contexts.

A writer may choose to vary the standard format of a piece of writing and the desired format may also change over time. Even so, the reader and writer share assumptions about the linguistic features, the shape, and the structure of a genre such as a recount, expecting particular characteristics to appear. The schematic structures and linguistic features of text have multiple ways of organisation. Divisions between different genres are often arbitrary because of the mix of linguistic features.

Genres are not 'fixed'

Still, it is possible to see broad categories if not clear demarcations. Sometimes it is appropriate to organise material chronologically, e.g. when writing down the steps of a recipe or giving directions for the progress of a game. Illustrations can add to the meaning of a text but can also add to the blurring of genres.

Language features are open to change in the genres: changes eventually become acceptable, or a powerful elite of language users can exert an influence. Email may appear in several genres (recount, information report, explanation, etc.); it has affected the writing of memoranda and letters and shows how language is a social practice dependent on a particular setting. Some email messages may be brief, yet the speed and efficiency of communication can also lead to long-winded replies. It is therefore useful to see genres as on a continuum and the blending of genres as common.

Knowledge about language

Knowing how language works is, of course, useful to knowing how to use it better. Explicit teaching about the structure, organisation, and grammatical patterns of different text-types is an important contribution of the genre approach (Hammond 1996: 211). Children need a language for describing how a text communicates its meaning. Talking about what makes a particular piece of reading and writing effective will help them to become more perceptive readers and writers. Just as knowing the meanings of words such as 'climax' and 'characters' will allow children to talk with more clarity about the books they read or the television programs they watch, knowing grammatical terms and understanding how to apply this knowledge will assist their writing development. Practice in comparing patterns of language and rearranging the order of texts can reveal what works best communicatively.

The more we know about language, the better we can use it

The terminology of traditional and functional grammar helps in describing how texts are organised, providing both teachers and students with a shared **metalanguage**. Familiarity with common sentence patterns, clause and paragraph construction, and the functions of different parts of speech helps children to write with additional clarity and to analyse written texts (see chapter 13).

Critical literacy

Critical literacy can help students form better judgments

The development of a critical literacy helps children to understand and to share their likes and dislikes and also encourages them to form better judgments about what they read. For example, discussing truth and accuracy in advertising is something that kindergarten children can grasp—they know what an advertisement for new toys is trying to do to them and to their parents. Comparing their own writing with other models develops a deeper understanding of what works well in communicating ideas and meaning. (See chapter 22.)

> *Critical* is used in the special sense of aiming to show up connections which may be hidden from people—such as the connections between language, power and ideology … Critical language study analyses social interactions in a way which focuses upon their linguistic elements and which sets out to show up their generally hidden determinants in the system of social relationships, as well as hidden effects they may have upon that system. (Fairclough 1989: 5)

As students progress through the school grades they can be exposed to an increasing range of printed media (advertising brochures, literature of all kinds) and other media (TV, the Internet) in order to develop critical faculties to determine the degree of manipulation and the 'hidden effects' of such materials.

Here are some suggested questions that may help to get students thinking about critical literacy and how they might respond to media and texts:

- *Who* has produced the text? What is their point of view? Who is the intended audience?
- *Why* has it been written?
- *How* is the material presented? Are there other ways of writing about it?
- *Where* is it distributed? Who sells it?
- *What* is the piece about? What information has been left out?
- *When* was the text written and is this significant?

Luke, Comber & O'Brien point out that interconnected strategies such as the four listed below can be used in textual studies:

1. Talk about the institutional conditions of production and interpretation.
2. Talk about the textual ideologies and discourses, silences, and absences.
3. Discourse analysis of textual and linguistic techniques in relation to (1) and (2).
4. Strategic and tactical action with and/or against the text.

The reading of a diversity of genres from a broad range of texts can provide the context for the children's writing. There are many different types of writing that have evolved to suit individual authors and to meet the needs of different audiences of writing (in Bull & Anstey 1996: 38).

Some texts may deliberately subvert expectations and break conventions to communicate a message or to create a certain effect. Advertisements may set out to attract the interest of the reader by painting incongruous images or deliberately mixing and blending genres. Authors often play with conventions by subverting the expected pattern of language usage. The final paragraph in Frank McCourt's novel *Angela's Ashes* is the brief *'Tis* (this word became the title of his next book). In this context, where most readers might conventionally expect a longer paragraph, *'Tis* is entirely apposite. Playing with the conventions is not new. The English novelist Laurence Sterne (1713–68) played with all kinds of eccentricities in his novel *Tristram Shandy*: using a blank page, writing unfinished sentences, and using all manner of typographical confusions. It can be argued that children need to know the appropriate usage before they can turn it upside down. But even without this knowledge, through their own creativity they can amuse the reader by subverting expectations. The definition of generic types of writing allows the writer to see with some transparency the different textual choices that can be made.

The process approach

The 'process' approach, deriving from the work of Donald Graves (e.g. 1983; see also Calkins 1983; Cambourne 1988), emphasises writing as a systematic series of actions leading to the composition of a text:

1   Writing is a process involving pre-writing (planning), writing (drafting, editing, revising), publishing, and post-writing (response).

2   A regular time for writing is allocated to allow for planning, writing, and editing. Writing is done often, preferably every day, and at different times throughout the day.

3   Discussion (or conferencing) among teachers and students or among students is encouraged to help the writer formulate ideas, to provide a reaction to the writer, or to seek information.

4   Ownership of the topic. Usually the child chooses the topic about which to write and makes the decisions about how it should be written, taking responsibility for the final version of the text.

'Process' writing is a systematic series of actions leading to the composition of a text

The process and the genre approach can be complementary. Both advocate the need for drafting and editing in writing, both are in favour of discussing and talking about the language chosen, both help us to understand what to teach and how to teach. Both approaches can be brought together using the three teaching strategies of Shared Writing, Guided Writing, and Independent Writing. Whatever approach is used, there should be a broad and balanced selection of factual and narrative genres so that children can become familiar with different kinds of writing. Although the emphasis of both approaches is on a meaningful 'whole' text and extended pieces of writing, there is still the need for explicit and individual instruction about linguistic features such as verb tense or other grammatical features at the sentence level.

Writing can be a rapid process if the imagination is crowded with ideas or if the task is found to be easy. Even so, those children who appear to write effortlessly can usually make improvements to their writing at the drafting and editing stages. Children will vary in their writing capacity and temperament, some quickly writing down the main ideas, others labouring over the choice of words, just as some adult writers do. The French writer Gustave Flaubert (1821–80) took seven years to write his classic, *Madame Bovary*. Looking for the right word, *le mot juste*, can be an exacting business. Charles Dickens (1812–70), on the other hand, wrote quickly and prolifically.

▶ LITERACY IN THE DIGITAL AGE

Computer or technological literacy

The impact of the Internet will doubtless increase the importance of student-centred learning and help to change how we view literacies. The interactive multimedia on the Internet offer written text, graphics, and sound, pointing to how students might wish to communicate in the future. The nonlinear text is already with us and there is now the possibility of composing texts that have visual and auditory components.

At present we are mostly concerned with print literacy, but the children of the future need to have computer literacy and word-processing skills. They may increasingly rely on the computer for their language development, closing the gap between speech and writing and further blurring the boundaries between different genres of writing. Voice-activated computing may revolutionise how we view writing and possibly negate the need for typing skills.

Email

Through the Internet there is the opportunity to send messages in seconds around the world. The new media of audio, print, software, and print publications, as well as CD-ROM formats, give children an almost inexhaustible supply of information. News groups on specific topics, mailing list discussions, and chat lines all have the potential for encouraging writing and communication as respondents can send messages to many recipients at the same time.

Writing on the Internet has already introduced changes to communication. Because formatting is secondary, email emphasises *words*, although attachments also allow images to be sent. For brevity, emoticons (emotional icons) are used to convey emotion, e.g. -o = shock. Asterisks may be used for *emphasis* instead of inverted commas, underlining, or italics. Intentional misspellings may be made to amuse or to draw attention to words. Some of the Net acronyms highlight the brevity and simplicity of many messages, e.g. GDM8 = G'day mate, LOL = Laughing out loud. On the other hand the Internet may encourage writing output because it is so quick and because recipients often reply promptly. Children may therefore become more productive. (See also chapter 18.)

Ways forward

Language syllabuses, not only in Australia but also in the USA and the United Kingdom, are adopting an approach that recognises a *social view of language*, which is concerned with how people use language in a variety of social contexts. The use of computers and technology has revolutionised the way that people communicate in commerce and many other contexts.

Language choices are dependent on the social context in which a text is produced. There are many social contexts but, broadly speaking, the home, community, and school form the basis for most children's language experience. These social contexts will provide most of the text-types that students will be engaged in. Recognition of a sense of purpose and audience is a crucial consideration when composing a text. Teaching strategies will include the macro-strategies of Shared, Guided, and Independent Writing. At the same time students will be engaged in basic textual analyses as they explore typical features of the type of text they are writing. Texts are often multimodal. They will be exploiting a typical text creatively and using a critical awareness (reflecting on the socially constructed meanings they are reading and writing). Inevitably, the ways forward will include elements and best practice from previous approaches to the teaching of writing.

IN THE CLASSROOM

Following is an explanation of what a good writing classroom and best practice could look like.

Ears for my Family

'I'm coming'
Wind pushing and tugging at me
hugging my hair
scrabbling my clothes
'I want my tea'
But all is quiet
I stand straining my ears—
not moving in case I miss something
It's like a ghost house
only a creak of the stairs
and a stretching of the floor boards
I am fixed to my Sea—
my ears large
The gravel path scrunches under heavy feet
A scratched key scuffles in the lock,
stamping, coughing—it's dad:
Heavy shopping bags thump on the floor
Tins clank together. I wait for mum's deep sigh.

Christine, 11 Years (in Rosen and Rosen 1973: 105)

Christine probably had many rich, varied language experiences before she could sit down and write a poem as sensitive as this one. The poem shows that she has developed an acute sensitivity to the world around her—she understands her father's familiar 'stamping' and 'coughing' and her mother's tiredness at the end of a shopping session; 'I wait for mum's deep sigh' expresses many possibilities, and in true writerly fashion leaves things unsaid.

The honesty of expression and creativity in use of language in such phrases as 'hugging my hair', 'scrabbling my clothes', 'straining my ears', 'stretching of the floor boards', 'my ears large', 'key scuffles in the lock' indicate that Christine's senses of touch and hearing in particular have been developed to such an extent that she is able to appreciate deeply the world around her and to empathise with the feelings of others. But writing like this can take many years to develop. Parents and teachers will provide many opportunities in the home, community, and school that contribute to sensitising their children to the world around them in such a way that they will be able to communicate a part of that world to others through writing that is fresh, creative, honest, original, and exciting.

Not all writing that children do, however, is of this creative type. In fact a lot of children's writing is factual in nature and comes in the form of recounts, writing procedures, summaries, and so on. Teachers must help students to introduce creative writing into their repertoire. Students may encounter the text-types shown in Table 19.1 during their primary years.

Table 19.1   Text-types (oral and written)

Literary	*Factual*
Literary description	Discussion
Literary recount	Explanation
Narrative	Exposition
Observation	Factual description
Personal response	Factual recount
	Information report
	Procedural recount
	Procedure

It is clear that these text-types are somewhat idealised for teaching purposes and that in real life we often find 'mixed' texts. They should therefore not be seen as 'straitjackets' but as starting points. Students are in a better position to experiment with combining elements in a purposeful way when they understand that

- different types of text exist
- texts serve different purposes
- texts are typically structured in particular ways
- texts have characteristic grammatical features
- factual writing can still be creative. (Board of Studies NSW 1998a: 66–7).

The teaching of writing in these primary years, however, is not merely concerned with making sure students' writing conforms to particular forms. A major thrust should be to ensure that students are engaged in real writing for real purposes and that they are motivated to write and find it an exciting engagement with language rather than a task. It is very important, then, for the teacher to create an appropriate writing climate in the classroom.

Critical thinking and study exercises

1. Here are some comments by teacher trainees on their school experiences of writing. Consider their implications for the infants and primary school classroom and discuss what could be done to make writing an enjoyable and meaningful activity. Discuss, in particular, the kinds of topics that might stimulate good writing.

   Writing has always been a pleasure of mine. I regard it as a very important part of my sanity in life at times. From a very early age I was taught to write creatively and to use my imagination to its full capacity. My first recollection of writing was in Year 2. Our class had just come back from an excursion to Shark Island. My teacher had asked us to write a recount of what had happened and then conclude the report by drawing a picture. There were many of these experiences throughout my primary schooling years that I can recall. I still have some of my trusty 'botany books' at home somewhere.

   I have kept several journals since 1992. These have kept me sane and often let me reflect over my life problems at the time. I have maintained this diary writing to the present date. I enjoy writing in it, as it is my true feelings and life as I know it. No one reads it or ever will.

   Writing is important to me. I find it relaxing.

   N.

   When I was in Year 5 I won a competition for a story about being stranded in the middle of the ocean. I can still remember what I had written (I loved looking in the newspapers, dictionaries, thesaurus etc for new and exciting words). I remember my main character scissored her legs through the water and her salt parched lips were burning.

   S.

   My only memories of creative writing in primary school were making poems and rhymes about the teachers and handing them out to friends.

   S.

   My history as a writer is a very feeble one. I have never gone out of my way to write something off my own bat so to speak. I remember when I was participating in the Duke of Edinburgh Award Scheme and after one of the hikes I had been on I had to write a log of all the events. This was probably the best thing I have ever written. I suppose it is probably because I was there laughing and crying at the events I was writing about. Since that time I suppose it has always been a philosophy to make sure that the children experience things they are writing about.

   I would love to have the ability to pump out witty pieces of literature, but that is simply not a talent I possess.

   C.

2. What was one of your more memorable writing experiences at school? How did you deal with it? How would you handle a similar situation in your own classroom now? What can you learn from it as a teacher?

Conditions for effective writing in the classroom

The classroom climate should encourage children to want to write

One of the major challenges for the thinking teacher is to develop a 'community of writers' (Smith 1982; Graves 1994). That is, to develop a classroom climate in which children want to write and want to share their writing in order to enrich their experience of the world. Writing is a social act in so far as most writers write for audiences, whether it be the imaginative, creative type of writing or the more factual type. Remember that factual writing also requires creativity. The nature of the audience often determines the shape and formality the writing will take.

The teacher's role is to

- create an atmosphere where children will want to write and can write
- establish a climate where both teacher and pupils are sharing their writing
- provide conditions for 'real' writing for 'real' purposes
- teach different language structures
- give children equal access to writing forms and text-types that society values.

The teacher's role is crucial to developing the right atmosphere

A good Literacy Session has the advantage of linking the activities of reading, writing, and speaking, giving the child plenty of opportunities to revisit writing. It can focus on language in use as well as some explicit understanding of how language works.

Time for creativity

One of the major problems teachers have is organising their program so that students have enough time for writing. Many schools assign a block of time, usually during the morning periods, to a Literacy Session in which talking, listening, reading, and writing take place within a framework that includes Shared, Guided, and Independent Reading and Writing. During such a session writing will often occur as a natural outcome of a response to a reading activity. For example, a teacher may be presenting a Big Book such as *Possum Magic* to the class and may invite the children to respond to the story by rewriting the ending or innovating on the text (i.e. retaining the structure of the text but inserting local names and/or events) or doing character analysis and/or plot-mapping activities. (See also chapter 9.)

Sometimes a particular subject area lends itself to a writing activity. The class may be on an excursion to a rock pool or rainforest and be required to list from observation and then to categorise and/or summarise the material listed. Science experiments might need to be written up using specialised formats. For the learning area Human Society in Its Environment, students may need to write a dramatic scene to re-create events and roles from history or to respond creatively to an issue of local importance at the school or in the community. The important point is that writing is often done as an *integrated activity* and arises naturally from other subjects or other areas of the curriculum—the writing then becomes purposeful and realistic.

There is time for writing if it is integrated into the curriculum in this way. Children need time to write and to practise written language skills at various points throughout the day. Nevertheless, some children will always find that they can do their best writing alone and uninterrupted at home.

Writing is meaningful when it has direct links to what the students know in other subject areas

Choice

A good writing classroom will often give children an opportunity to choose their own topics and formats for writing. One of the ways of developing 'ownership' of a piece of writing is to give children the responsibility of choice.

Choice of topic and text-type develops ownership of writing

Even if the class is focusing on a particular text-type (e.g. writing a recount or narrative), there can be choice within the topic. If the curriculum imposes a particular format, the teacher can usually encourage a degree of freedom of choice of topic and purpose *within* the format. A degree of ownership will then develop.

Student writers will be more likely to pay more attention to a piece of writing if there is a sense of ownership—it is their writing, not the teacher's. There may be an element of 'negotiation' where the teacher helps or allows the writer to choose the topic and the purpose of the writing exercise.

Control of the process can very easily be assumed by an over-anxious teacher, who may prescribe extensive revisions or even physically write 'corrections', show disapproval through body language, try to hurry the writer, or not listen to the writer's explanations. The teacher's art is to know the appropriate time for and the degree of intervention. It is better to have fewer but better interventions; then the writer's vital sense of ownership, responsibility, and control is respected:

I never really liked writing at school. I couldn't think of what to write about when given a topic and couldn't think what to write about when I wasn't. Often my stories ended up being a recount or slightly varied version of a TV show or book I had read recently.

K.

If the child invariably chooses the topic there may be a disposition to follow a particular text-type such as the recount or narrative genre. Children need to practise and become familiar with a broad range of text-types. These should be introduced and explicit instruction given about them by teachers. The writer relies on various sources of information and inspiration and may need to use the resources of the library and the knowledge of others. For many kinds of writing, authoritative sources are needed to provide and substantiate information.

Sheer fright may set in about writing, as a student attests:

Primary school writing, as I recall, was very formulaic. You had to write about a specified topic and you were given a set period to do it in. I can still recall the terror which at times would overwhelm me, when the teacher would come in after lunch and demand that we produce a two-page story on a certain topic and constantly reiterate to us that it had to be correct, with correct grammar and spelling. Despite such constraints I was a competent writer.

K.

Another teacher trainee wrote:

If only we could all make up what we wanted [instead of set tasks], then I could be a free spirit!

T.

Students need to own their writing
Teacher-dictated topics can still engage children's sense of ownership if they are balanced with topics of their own choice. Children will often find ways of making topics interesting. For example, a simple procedure of 'how to' do some activity could be applied to 'how to make and keep friends'.

Even if children have chosen their topic, teachers will often need to 'scaffold' or provide a framework for texts so that children can be guided to make appropriate language choices and gain control of different constructions. Individual choice of topic does not necessarily negate explicit teaching about language features.

To the child who answers 'nothing' to the question 'What are you going to write about?', there is the challenge for the teacher to motivate the child to explore the range of writing that is possible. Children can find out that in the most mundane of experiences there might be something unique and worth communicating. Writing that grows out of experience is usually the best, whether that experience is an activity the child has done out of school or whether it is part of the shared environment of the classroom. Children can use their imaginations to invent stories. But there are other kinds of writing where strict accuracy of content is needed and the writer needs to impart specific information.

Integrating the language skills

There is a close relationship between the different language skills of reading, writing, listening, and speaking. Understanding and proficiency in one area can contribute to these skills in another. Knowing how to scan a text when reading has similarities to writing the headings for a first draft. Analysing how authors convey meaning through word choice, cohesion, and punctuation can provide models for children's own writing. We must give children as much practice as we can with language, allowing them to be playful and imaginative, while at the same time giving them experience of the formalities of language so that they become familiar with the possibilities of language use.

Strong links between reading, writing, listening, and speaking

Teaching children to write creatively and with clarity is a complex process. It requires planned activities that will present opportunities for children to write in a wide range of contexts for different purposes and for a variety of audiences. The use of strategies such as 'mindmapping' (Wycoff 1991) and Edward de Bono's (1970) creative thinking can help release children's imaginations. Children will obviously gain a great deal of linguistic awareness from the practice of writing itself, but they also gain from exposure, as listeners and readers, to particular kinds of writing. Through listening to a story or a variety of models they will begin to understand how a writer achieves a particular effect, and reading it independently will consolidate their understanding. Talking with their classmates, teacher, and parents will deepen a knowledge of

The processes of reading and writing should be integrated

- how a writer achieves a response in a reader
- the different responses evoked by different kinds of writing
- how individual language skills can be improved.

There are many advantages to integrating the processes of reading and writing: recognition of models and knowledge of how texts work reinforce children's ability to write their own. Reading allows them to make sense of the print, while writing can consolidate understanding. It is important to integrate reading and writing early on, in the first years of schooling. As students strive to get down their meanings on the page they listen to the sounds of the word they want to write and attempt to record those sounds using the letters they know. Through this process they are developing the sound–letter knowledge that is crucial to their reading development. Communicative ability in speaking reinforces proficiency in other modes of language such as reading and writing, and encourages children to transfer successful learning strategies from one mode to another.

Links between reading and writing

Teachers who are engaged in best practice have always recognised the strong links between reading and writing. The following principles are relevant to students engaged in literacy activities. They need to

1 Understand the purposes of literacy so they can appreciate and enjoy literacy in their lives.
    Young children need to have early experiences with print in the home context so that they can learn what print is and how it works. The preschool and Kindergarten classroom is often

saturated with print in the form of different models of writing, such as labels, captions on posters, and lists of things to do. In the early years many opportunities are given for children to *listen to* stories read aloud and to *talk about* the stories in informal discussions; more formal situations come in the later years of primary school.

2   Hear written language so they can learn its structure and take in new information and ideas.

The importance of speaking and listening in the literacy process cannot be overestimated. Although there are common vocabulary and sentence structures in oral and written versions of English, there are important differences between the oral and written modes of language, especially in grammar. The interjections, omissions, shortened forms (I'll, we've etc.), and incomplete sentences of speech are not always found in the more formal structures of book language. Pinnell & Fountas make a very strong point here: 'Children who know how to "talk like a book" are fortunate because they have had opportunities to hear the books read aloud. As they hear the same story many times, they can "absorb" the stories and make them their own' (1998: 4). (See also phonemic awareness in chapter 2.)

3   Become aware of the sounds of language in order to enjoy those sounds and to use this knowledge as a tool in becoming literate.

Young children love to experiment with familiar and unfamiliar sounds through rhymes and games. It is this playing with sound that is the beginning of phonemic awareness—the ability to hear the individual speech sounds in words. Understanding sound–letter relationships is crucial to learning to read, spell, and write, but the understanding begins in spoken language.

It is especially important for children learning English as another language to have experience in a wide range of speech activities. Repeating and expanding phrases and sentences in a natural way, so that English structures are heard again and again, are important precursors to using them with confidence. Visualisation, using pictures and concrete objects, is a useful tool in the comprehension process. Reading and rereading favourite books give children a chance to internalise the patterns of the English language.

In the early stages of language learning, children can benefit from books with understandable, repetitive, and conversational English language. A classroom and a home rich in picturebooks, rhymes, and folktales are therefore advantageous to children's language learning.

4   Have many experiences with written symbols.

It is not easy for the young child to distinguish one letter from another (Clay 1991: 266). A whole network of knowledge surrounds each letter. It has a shape, a sound, a name, it can be connected to other letters in a word, and it can appear in different ways—large, small, in colour, in different print, and so on. As well as recognising letters in isolation, children must also recognise them when the letters are embedded in print. Accordingly, lots of alphabet or letter games in both the oral and written modes should be played. Children need to see letters in a variety of print media; they need practice in writing the letters in isolation, with other letters, and in real words and phrases.

Multiliteracies

Young children not only have to cope with our alphabet system but, as mentioned earlier, there are many symbols associated with technology around the home, community, and classroom. Items like VCRs, DVDs, microwaves, computers, and numerous advertising agents such as electronic billboards are everywhere now. All of these technologies have to be 'read' and understood if the child is to function effectively in this technological age. That is, the child needs to be multiliterate and not just able to read and write in the traditional sense.

5 Explore words and learn how they work.

Some children build a network of understandings around their names. The following concepts can develop from this: their name is a word; a word consists of a sequence of letters that go together; letters in a word progress from left to right; words have meaning and are written in the same way each time; words have blank spaces on either side; sounds go with letters in a word; some words start like their own names; words have meaning when put together with other words, and so on.

The Kindergarten teacher will engage in considerable Shared Reading and Writing experiences so that children build up their visual and auditory knowledge about letters, words, phrases, sentences, and clusters of letters or patterns that are connected to sounds.

6. Read and write continuous text to expand their knowledge.

Reading and writing develop together. Not all the letters of the alphabet need to be known before beginning reading and writing. Once a start is made, lots of experimentation will occur as the child goes from the known to the unknown and learns about letter–sound relationships and print conventions. Semantic, grammatical, and graphophonic knowledge increase as engagement with text increases. The classroom teacher needs to involve the children in a wide range of language activities both at text and word level. Talking and listening activities are very important here too as experimentation with known and new sounds increases.

7 Develop flexibility and fluency to enhance comprehension and enjoyment of reading and writing.

Being a good reader and writer means more than simply being able to decipher letters or put them together to make words. It means being fluent and flexible with words, phrases, sentences, and text. The beginning writer needs to be able to let thoughts flow onto the page without being restrained by a lack of knowledge about how words are spelt and how phrases and sentences are put together. Pinnell & Fountas (1998: 11) say that fluency in writing is enhanced when children

- know a large core of words and can produce them quickly and automatically
- understand useful spelling patterns they can use to make many more words
- can associate letters and sounds quickly and easily
- can let their writing flow because they are not too distracted by the laborious processes of writing the words.

Once fluency is developed, flexibility in reading rates and in writing text-types can be gained as the child's knowledge of appropriateness to audience and purpose increases. Good readers and writers increasingly gain control over their medium.

Links between talking, listening, and writing

> Most of my life has been spent arguing for the importance of the spoken language in education … we cannot, I think, understand where writing comes into the learning process if we don't also understand where talking comes in … Writing and speech need to be seen as reinforcing each other in a total process of language development. (Halliday, in Walshe et al. 1986: 5)

Michael Halliday's research over the last three decades in particular has been concerned with a social view of language, which means that language—oral, written, and visual—can best be developed in a variety of social contexts. It recognises that there is a relationship between a text and the context in which it was generated. It also allows us to construct and interpret spoken, written, and visual texts so that we are increasingly *gaining control over meaning* in the text and seeing how the writer/reader is positioned.

There has been a major shift in thinking about how best to teach language in recent decades. Half a century ago, it was generally thought that students entering kindergarten were regarded as 'clean slates' when in fact we know that such students have an excellent grasp of their oral language and they can use it for many different purposes: they have internalised its grammatical rules and can, indeed, *make meaning* very well. In the 1960s a major shift from the 'clean slate' notion began but there were still problems with pedagogy because some thought that students beginning schooling knew all of their language and needed only to learn to write it down. While students do know a lot, there is still much to be mastered in regard to different texts, control over meaning, and genres. Another problem was that some teachers realised there had been too much concentration on errors—a paradigm of language as a set of 'table manners' or rules to be learnt and followed.

Students develop *control* over their writing over time

This resulted in a 'benevolent inertia' whereby students were allowed to talk and write almost anything without correction. The way forward is for the teacher to provide models for ways students can gain control over meaning:

> We had a big fight in the 60s getting rid of the notion that language is just about correctness—getting things right. Even today people still think of a linguist as somebody who makes rules about language; but in the University the Department of Linguistics is concerned about what the students mean, and if we can understand what they are getting at, that's fine … What you are doing when you are learning language, both spoken and written, is achieving forms of control—a social, interpersonal process, not an individual one … Writing to learn implies that there are models of how this can be done and that these can be learnt … Don't let's speak of the child *owning* the discourse, but rather of achieving *control* over it, with the help of a teacher who provides structure. (Halliday 1986: 5)

The nexus between talking and writing

It is these notions that have driven the genre or text-type approach which is an integral part of a social view of language. The nexus between talking and writing is unmistakable: although they are different ways of meaning, behind both is a common system that we call language. Writing, however, does not duplicate functions of spoken language but carries out the new functions of developing cultures. One of the advantages of writing is that it brings language into consciousness. Accordingly, it is important to see that learning to read and write makes it possible for children to *reflect* on language in the process of their learning. Sometimes this *reflection* is carried out in the oral mode through discussion or interaction with others. The written mode is a more permanent language system, although at the same time it can be modified and constantly updated to suit the needs of the communicator and the audience. This is where technology in the form of computers can play a major role with respect to word-processing.

A successful and language-rich classroom has a balanced interaction of talking and writing

Differences: Talking and writing

It is important to remember that written language tends to be organised quite differently from spoken language. It tends to have more formal language structures whereas spoken language can be characterised (depending on the formality of the occasion) by broken sentences, ellipses, non sequiturs and so on. The world as heard in speech is quite different from the world as seen in writing. This, in fact, is a positive feature because we get complementary, mutually reinforcing pictures of the world. A successful and language-rich classroom has a balanced interaction of talking and writing as some things are learned better through talking, others through writing. Halliday believes that we do not need a theory of 'literacy education' as much as a theory of learning based on language: 'The psychologists haven't given it to us. It won't come out of linguistics without the help of the classroom nor vice versa … my colleagues and I have been working for some years with teachers towards a theory of learning—of learning through language' (1986: 6).

Written language is organised differently from spoken language

IN THE CLASSROOM

The curriculum cycle

The curriculum cycle for writing model, as developed by Derewianka (1990) and further developed or modified across the nation's syllabuses, contains the kind of balance between talking/listening and writing skills that helps students to learn through and about language and also highlights an important nexus between talking and writing at whatever stage of development the student may be at.

There are three main stages in the curriculum cycle: preparation/building up the field, joint construction of text, and independent construction of text. These stages, in turn, can loosely equate to the Shared, Guided, and Independent Writing strategies. At each stage of the process, talking/listening and writing are interrelated and integral to the success of the process.

Preparation: building up the field

Very few writers can just sit down and begin to write fluently and lucidly on a topic. Most writers need something to write about. In classroom pedagogical terms this means *building up the field* and can be done in many ways with students. The teacher may take the students on an excursion, read to them, bring in an 'expert', show a video, or allow the students Internet or library time to get some 'content' or input that will spark the creative urge to put pen to paper. The kind of stimulus presented will no doubt depend on the genre or text-type in which the children are expected to write. Building up the field may involve brainstorming, predicting, using diagrams or other visuals, texts and/or videos, gathering information, selecting information, organising information and recording information—directed or *modelled* by the teacher. Using lots of talking/listening here will familiarise students with the topic or genre being explored and will introduce the students to any new vocabulary associated with the topic or field. Building up the field may give students an opportunity to respond in whole groups, small groups or even one-to-one situations and may involve students in many kinds of listening activities such as listening for information, critical listening and listening for main ideas.

The teacher's role is crucial at this stage because a new genre may need to be introduced. Modelling language and immersion in language are key elements here. Teacher talk and student listening become very important as the teacher models the genre to be explored and builds up the topic by introducing the students to new content, vocabulary and language structures.

Joint construction of text

Before engaging in *independent construction* of text, it is useful for students to participate in group writing. This activity may be jointly constructed by the whole class, by a small group, or by a teacher and a child during conferencing.

Aspects of the *field* may need to be built up in the *joint construction* of text. If the teacher has modelled this well, then the students should be able to approach this step with confidence. Talking and listening will be an integral part of this process as the students discuss, sort, and select the kind of information that might be appropriate for the genre/text-type they have chosen to use. Accordingly, researching the topic, building up data banks and the possibility of revising the genre structure provide opportunities for integrating talking and listening with composing or writing skills. Students may need language to discuss, argue, and negotiate here. During the actual joint construction of text, the students need to be allowed to contribute information and ideas while the teacher may act as a guide, questioning and making suggestions about the structure of the text. The teacher may even write down the text so that the students are free to concentrate on the *meanings* they are creating. Revision and editing should be modelled here so that students have some idea as to how the text may be modified to improve the meaning when engaged in writing their own text.

Independent construction of text

The final stage is the *independent construction* of text, which allows the students to 'have a go' at writing text. It is here that the *process* needs to be followed: motivation to write; pre-writing or preparing, drafting or translating thought to paper; revising or editing product or publication. However, the writing may not always proceed in these neat and separate stages—this terminology is needed for *discussing* the stages but, in reality, most people's composing processes are fairly 'messy'—not a smooth forward flow but rather proceeding in short bursts, pauses, retracings of steps, several starts, revisions, and so on. Graves (1994: 80–2) recognises that the writing process may not always be entirely linear.

An integrated learning process

Writing, in fact, is a *learning process* as the student attempts to make a concentrated effort to work out a problem and at the same time write in a way that appeals to a reader.

This is certainly no easy task and is more than just 'communicating'. The writer is learning: first, the problem of gathering, correcting, and clarifying ideas relevant to the given purpose of the writing (the 'content'), and second, how to express these ideas appropriately for the intended audience ('expression'). In reality, there is not a *process* of writing—there are only *processes of writing*. The process of each piece of writing varies individually and should be considered not as a series of several stages but as a number of interwoven composing behaviours between deciding to write and the end product when the writing is presented to readers. The role of *conferencing* is crucial, and can take place at any time during the *processes*. Discussing student progress and listening to what has been written are important for clarifying ideas and seeing if the language sounds 'right' and communicates the desired meanings. The teacher needs to carefully monitor student progress at all stages, which means that the links between talking/listening and writing are ever present.

Response: The writing conference

A good writing classroom invites response to children's writing so that they can be encouraged to write further, or improve what they have written, or prepare their work for publication. Response can come from the teacher, from parents, or from peers, and may be in the form of an appropriately encouraging casual comment or a more extended response, often called a 'writing conference'.

This usually occurs when a child wants to share writing with the teacher or peers in order to gain some useful feedback. The best response often comes when a child writes for a real purpose that 'works': doing a poster advertising an event to which people actually come, writing a narrative that is published in a book format and put in the school or class library, or writing a procedural text that others follow to make or do something.

Responding through conferencing is valuable

A good writing classroom will foster an environment that encourages children to share their work openly. If this is done from the Kindergarten years, by the time students reach Year 6 it will form a natural part of the writing process and will greatly contribute towards the 'community of writers'.

Writers need to share their work

Writing conferences are an ideal way of supporting a child's writing development. The teacher shows interest in the students' ideas and the way they express them by commenting or giving guidance or by answering requests for help. In a conference, each step of the writing process can be discussed and explained. The key to effective conferencing lies in the kinds of questions asked by the teacher. There is no specific structure for conferencing as there needs to be openness and spontaneity in the sharing session, but teachers should try to get the child to take the lead and avoid imposing comments or a rigid structure. Questions may be *process* questions that focus on the line of development of the writing, *development* questions that focus on the quality of ideas in the writing, or *structure* questions that deal with key ideas and the overall shape of the writing. As Ernie Tucker says:

> The conference is to be seen as an element in the process-of-writing: a potential in the teacher's hands to encourage confidence and perhaps add something to the student's thinking-discussing-drafting-revising-polishing-rewriting. Conferences are shorter when students really feel they are in control of their own writing. They work best when students have learnt to ask their own questions.
> (1986: 198)

A conference gives the learner a chance to get help from the teacher on structuring or language aspects such as word choice and syntax.

The teacher's opening remarks are very important. They should show interest in the student's work and give a chance to focus on aspects of difficulty or success. For example, remarks like

Conferences support the writer

'Well, Sam, how is your writing going?' are more likely to get a positive response than 'Well, Erin, you haven't written much yet', which may well render the student silent. The positive remark elicits comments from the student like 'I just can't think of a suitable ending' or 'I'm not sure if this paragraph is in the right place'. When the student responds then the teacher has a starting point for discussion.

Help the student to make the first statement. Sometimes a focus on the content of the writing helps rather than a focus on the spelling, grammar, or punctuation—this can come later. Even if the teacher's opening remark does not succeed in eliciting a response from the student, the teacher should resist the temptation to start talking, advising, or cajoling. The conference really begins only when the learner speaks. To stimulate that speech the teacher may need to ask the right question. Begin simply. Try not to attempt too much too soon. The teacher needs to be patient and to learn how to accept silences—the student may need time to respond and also may need to get used to the idea of talking while the teacher listens. The teacher needs to show an interest in the student's thoughts and writing and have an expectation that a final product will emerge in time.

Remember that your questions will vary according to the type of text the student is writing. Factual texts will need questions that focus on the accuracy and completeness of the information, while narrative texts will require questions that focus on the story. Different types of conference questions help children develop writing skills:

- 1. How do you like your story?
- 2. Does your title fit your story?
- 3. Do you have more than one story in your piece?
- 4. Can you add more feeling to it?
- 5. Is there more you could add?
- 6. Tell me in detail what happened.
- 7. Are there too many extra things in it that you don't really need?
- 8. Are you going to keep working on it?
- 9. Have you enjoyed writing it? (Calkins 1983: 125–6)

Here are some other questions the teacher might ask:

- What is your purpose in writing this text?
- Who is your audience?
- How did you gather information or knowledge for your text?
- Do you think your text moves in the right sequence? What have you put first? What comes next? How does it end?
- Have you told the reader the most important information?

There are several other ways of framing specific questions:

Opening questions: 'Where are you up to, Lauren?', 'How is it going, Elisha?', 'Tell me about all of this interesting work, Clare'.

Open-ended questions: These help the student to keep talking about their writing. 'That was a really interesting part—how can you bring this other information into it, do you think?' or 'Tell me more about what happened during the storm'.

Process questions: These help the student to keep a line of development. 'How will you start then?', 'Where will you go to from here?', 'Why did you change what you had?', 'Do you think your description is clear enough?', 'That's a really long passage—could you break it up more?', 'How do you think you will end the story?', 'Are you ready to end it now?'

Questions that reveal development: 'Do you think this is a better piece than last week's?', 'Is there a part you aren't happy with?', 'Why is this a better ending?'

Questions that deal with structure: These help the student to focus on the structure of the piece. 'Where is the key idea ?', 'Have you created enough tension?', 'Go through the main steps in the story', 'Does this particular part move quickly enough?'

The teacher's role is crucial in conferencing—the kind of question asked determines the kind of student response and the kind of learning that is taking place. The teacher not only assumes the role of a *questioner* but also becomes an *instructor* when some aspect of the writing needs special focus, such as spelling, grammar, or punctuation, all of which need to be handled sensitively and not overemphasised.

Asking the right questions is so important

Demonstration

IN THE CLASSROOM

A good writing classroom has a teacher who is prepared to help children by providing them with appropriate models of text-types. Children need to see good models of writing if they are going to emulate language patterns and structures found in their community, whether they be verse, fiction, or nonfiction texts, or texts from the media, including computer technology. Models of writing can be oral or written; both provide a structure that children can emulate. The models can come from many different sources: children's literature, popular newspapers, information books, journals, magazines, pamphlets, emails, or the Internet. The teacher may have many examples of such texts around the classroom. Think in terms of filling the classroom with texts—on noticeboards, mobiles, curtains, walls, display areas, interest corners, or wherever appropriate. Displays of texts need to be changed frequently so that they are always fresh and 'alive'.

Modelling texts for children is an integral part of the writing process and should enrich the children's knowledge of the kinds of texts that abound in their community and help them to select appropriate forms for their own personal writing efforts.

The classroom should be rich in language

The teacher as writer

As well as providing writing models, it is important for teachers to demonstrate their own writing. This can be done on the chalkboard, chart paper, or overhead projector and can be very effective in demonstrating writing techniques and showing drafts in progress. Artists, ceramicists, and sports people demonstrate their crafts. Writing is also a craft and needs to be demonstrated, from choosing a topic to finishing the final draft. Children need to see the teacher searching to get the right form, connections, word, or phrase. They need to realise that they are not the only ones who find the art of writing challenging, yet rewarding.

Expectation

Just as the family has an expectation that the young child will learn to talk, so too do the family and teacher have an expectation that the child will learn to write. High expectations will increase the possibility of a high standard of writing.

Physical considerations

Children must feel that they can write with ease in the classroom. Apart from a warm, supportive teacher, the classroom itself should make it easy for writing to take place:

- Writing should be an integral part of daily classroom activities.
- Procedures for sharing or conferencing should be clearly established.
- Appropriate space should be provided for the writing act, with student desks arranged suitably.

Displaying students' writing can provide a strong stimulus

- Procedures need to be in place to cope with issues such as noise or how to work with others.
- Writing folders need to be easily accessible for the children.

Assessment

Assessment generally focuses on how well the students are achieving the outcomes towards which they are working. A good writing classroom will encourage children to assess their own writing. Once again, the teacher can demonstrate here by assessing his or her own writing and by analysing samples of student writing (protecting anonymity if necessary). Using carefully selected questions, the teacher can guide the child through a self-evaluation process. This process can be aided by children being able to use the language of evaluation—that is, children can be given a metalanguage that helps them to describe what meanings are being made in their writing. The terminology of a functional grammar and/or traditional grammar may assist in this process. Children can be encouraged to question their writing at all stages of the writing process. Expertise will take time to develop, but if started in the early years of writing, children will be quite adept by the time they reach Year 6. (A longer discussion of assessment can be found in chapter 17.)

IN THE CLASSROOM

Motivation as a key factor

The classroom should be no different from the real world in that the desire to write should spring from a real purpose or need. If the need is there, this is a strong motivation. Most teachers are familiar with the child who can't get started, who doesn't know what to write about, who hasn't any ready ideas. The key to the problem is *motivation*. Some have the ability to write an imaginary story from very little or no teacher input, although many who do this may be drawing heavily on their past experiences, from their reading of imaginary stories, or from TV programs they have seen.

The onus is on the teacher to provide the child with something authentic to write about, a real purpose for writing—not simply giving the child a *topic*. This could arise from many different kinds of motivating experiences, many of which may come from the Key Learning Areas:

- a response to a book—fiction or nonfiction—shared by the teacher, e.g. a summary, a character profile, plot-mapping, writing a different ending
- a recent TV program, e.g. information report from a 'Behind The News'-type program, personal response to a cartoon or 'soapie'
- an excursion that the class has just had, e.g. organising notes from observations, thank you letter to a park ranger, further reading and writing about the place visited, emotional response through poetry-writing, summary of events, critical appraisal of what was observed
- a visitor to the class, e.g. an adult sharing aspects of their occupation with the children, visitor from overseas, a sportsperson, an artist, or a writer
- response to a cultural visit, e.g. a live performance
- a sporting event, e.g. a swimming or athletics carnival, a netball or football match

- a visit to a local community facility such as a park, library, factory, shopping centre, museum
- a classroom science experiment, art or craft activity
- a holiday to a new and exciting place
- a visit, travel in Australia or overseas.

The very best writing comes from a desire to write from a real experience that has developed the child's sensory perceptions—let the child feel the tree, smell the tree, taste the tree, see the tree, and hear the tree! Engagement with something or someone makes for active rather than passive learning. Thus many factors contribute towards a good writing classroom. Probably the most important 'condition' for effective writing is motivation—once the right atmosphere has been created, children can write with confidence and in the full knowledge that there will be a time for writing and sharing, that there will be opportunities for making choices, that writing will be for real purposes, that experimentation will be valued, that appropriate modelling will occur, and that there will be a positive expectation that their writing will be appreciated and will improve over time.

Critical thinking and study exercises

1 Creating the right conditions for writing may develop children who become lifelong writers. Discuss in a small group the following characteristics of lifelong writers and examine the teacher's role in the process. Having a reason to write is a most important characteristic.

The following is a summary of Graves' characteristics of a lifelong writer (1994: 155):

a   Initiates writing—chooses to write in order to recount, then understands experience.

b   Has a sense of the power of writing— understands its functionality.

c   Has a sense of history and of the future—the child senses where he has been and sees the past as basically healthy and foundational to the future.

d   Has a sense of audience.

e   Initiates writing at home and to affect others.

f   Senses the appropriateness of writing in a variety of genres.

What are some other important characteristics of writers? Give reasons.

2. Read the article 'Discourses on gender and literacy: changing the stories' by Pam Gilbert (in Muspratt et al. 1997) and discuss ways in which children might gain more equal access to literacy practices in the community.

3. Make a list of the positive and/or negative influences on your own writing. How do they relate to the conditions for a good writing classroom described in this chapter? Consider the role of the teacher, the role of the home, and the classroom environment as important factors.

4. Consider the classrooms you have visited and design your own reading or writing classroom incorporating the best ideas you have seen and/ or read about.

Drafting and editing

Some children find the drafting stage difficult. They are reluctant to revise, or feel they never reach a 'finished' product. Beginning writers are often unaware that professional writers may experiment with wording and edit their work constantly, searching for a more meaningful phrase or a more imaginative word or deciding that the structure of a text needs to be changed:

In writing essays at school I tended to write as I spoke with no full stops, commas, correct spelling or grammar. This meant I always seemed to be on the rough draft, everybody else on their final copy.

T.

Another teacher trainee remembers from primary school:

Each week we would be asked to write a story, a piece of creative writing. These were due on Fridays and had to be nicely presented. A lot of these stories were selected by the teacher in regards to the topic and more often than not they were, 'My life as a something'. These were a huge task, but completed anyway, first as a rough copy, and then a final copy.

J.

Here are some efforts in improving writing by using editing skills from a Year 4 student:

… Sudenly this hand groobed her leg and puled it in. Half of her body was in the bule crical. She said 'help me!' Then the bule cirlal was slowly closing up.
Sarah said 'lets get help.'
Blake said 'There is not enough time. We have to jum in!'
'But we might die,' James said.
'We have to take the risk' Blake said.
'I am jumping in.'
'So am I'. Sarah yelled.
'Wait for me' James said.

Through substitution of vocabulary and changes in spelling and punctuation, the writer adds clarity:

… Suddenly this hand grabbed her leg and pulled it in. Half of her body was in the blue circle. She said 'help me!' Then the blue circle was slowly closing up.
Sarah suggested 'Let's get help.'
Blake answered 'There is not enough time. We have to jump in!'
'But we might die,' James shouted.
'We have to take the risk,' Blake exclaimed. 'I am jumping in.'
'So am I,' Sarah yelled.
'Wait for me,' James wailed.

Students should be encouraged to edit their own writing for content, organisation, grammar, punctuation, and spelling. Individual editing checklists can be supplied as well as useful wall charts to remind students of particular features. Selected proofreading marks may be used to familiarise students with editing, e.g. symbols for:

insert	⋏	*transpose characters*	*trs*
change to capital letter	*caps*	*begin new paragraph*	*n.p.*
change to lower case	*l.c.*		

Disincentives to writing

These comments from teacher trainees provide some warning signals about what not to do when teaching writing. For many people, writing or composing is a fairly difficult task. Few of us can put pen to paper or words on the screen with total ease.

Lack of interest in the topic:

> *I remember hating having to write compositions—yes I was around then. Writing was always a very personal form of expression for me and I was very insecure about having it marked or even read by the teacher—I still have that problem today.*

> M.

The problem may be handwriting:

> *I really did try to be a pretty writer, but I received blows to my confidence ... I was one of the last children in Year 4 to get a pen licence, even after many of the naughty boys. For years I tried to conceal my real writing, but university liberated me from the confines of childhood and now I have found the real me.*

> G.

Shyness or the desire for privacy may discourage sharing of writing:

> *At school, I never particularly enjoyed writing. I remember feeling very concerned about other people reading my work. In Year 6 I tried to keep people from reading my work by writing very small.*

> S.

Lack of confidence is a common problem for the novice writer:

> *S. as writer. These two things don't really go too well together. I have a habit of writing in a style that no one really understands except for me. This lack of confidence in writing good material makes me want to write as little as possible on most occasions.*

> S.

Some don't have the urge to write until high school:

> *I guess that the pivotal moment in my life when I actually enjoyed writing was during Year 11. I had been placed into the top English class, with a brilliant teacher who I really looked up to. Ms H— not only made writing interesting and enjoyable, but she gave me the confidence to try different styles. Now, as an 'adult' (well, I think you can call me that) I enjoy writing plays and songs, short stories, letters of complaint, letters to my friends.*

> T.

Some children find inspiration for writing much later:

I was never into writing as a child. I could always think of other things to do, especially when it was homework. I am not a creative writer. I would say that I am more a researcher. I love to read and critically examine old sources.

M.

I was once in a musical and changed the words of the songs to form a poem which I would relate to all my friends. I am proud to say that it was the best piece of creative writing I have ever done.

M.

I would prefer to read than write. The exception to this would be personal letter-writing.

J.

The reluctant writer

There is no magical solution for the child who says 'I can't write anything now'. Try to give a real purpose for writing so that a child will want to write and will very likely know what to say. Start 'small'—don't be overambitious.

Get the child talking, preferably about things that have happened in very recent times—events that have been experienced at home, while shopping, at sporting fixtures, at the cinema, and so on. Either the teacher or the child can write down in the child's own words something that was enjoyable or significant about an experience; just one or two sentences will do. This is the beginning of many more encounters with the child, gradually increasing the number of sentences being recorded so that the student will eventually experience a sense of having compiled a real story or having recalled events and feelings. Work towards the student doing the writing rather than the teacher. This method relies on the one-to-one situation but is time well spent. Confidence and self-esteem will grow as well as a desire to write.

Talking is crucial for the reluctant writer

Selection of texts

The choice of texts available to children in the classroom is crucial since the selection of different text-types reflects a model of society and mirrors what the teacher considers to be important.

The texts chosen should reflect the curriculum in all its aspects and include information and storybooks relevant to the different areas of knowledge explored at school. Literacy is developed as children listen to texts, as they read and discuss them and use them as models for their own writing. A teacher's selection policy for choosing texts is based on a wide variety of factors:

Different text-types should be available in the classroom

- the kinds of writing the teacher expects students to do at different stages of their development
- textual features that will serve as models, preparing children for the kind of writing they will need in the classroom and in the wider society
- whether the texts will stimulate children to write for themselves and for others
- the clarity and accuracy of information transmitted
- the inclusion of real people and real situations
- an appeal to the imagination and creativity of the children
- texts relevant to the curriculum
- texts that contain examples of different kinds of English, e.g. standard English, Aboriginal English, formal and informal English, regional dialects
- gender-inclusiveness
- texts that reflect a culturally diverse society.

Transmitting knowledge from a single perspective or choosing texts from a powerful elite will not allow students to make balanced assessments of what they read. For example, issues of social justice such as the rights of indigenous people require texts that represent a broad range of views at a level that children can understand at their stage of literacy development. The plethora of written texts makes it necessary to be selective.

The importance of planning

To produce writing that is clear and logical, planning is essential, not only at the beginning but also throughout the process.

The amount and detail of planning varies from writer to writer and also from text to text. The amount of planning just done in the head or jotted down on paper will also vary. Early planning may involve the collection of information because the shape the writing will take may

The amount of *planning* varies from writer to writer

not be worked out until research and note-making have taken place. Children may need information and/or experiential input before a plan of the writing can take shape. Be careful, however, about prescribing planning methods since individuals prefer to work in different ways.

Some prefer to detail the steps of the writing very carefully so that when they do begin to write they know where they are going and will probably reach the end more quickly owing to the detail of the preparation. Others prefer to plan as they go so that their writing may diverge in any direction depending on the whim of the moment or a desire to follow and explore a suitable lead. Some people prefer to think as they write so that they are not constrained by a determined direction, plan, or model. It must be remembered, however, that the purpose of the writing may predetermine, to an extent, the steps of the writing.

Reluctant writers need teacher help

The reluctant writer may need a lot of teacher help to get started and it may be only through very careful questioning by a teacher and appropriate models that this kind of writer will be able to organise ideas and get started.

Investigating the topic is an important precursor to drafting

Once the topic has been decided, the writer needs to make some kind of *investigation* of it. This may include reflective thinking, observing, talking with someone, a little reading, or a great deal of research—any of which may require the taking of notes. As the writer wrestles with this initial input, insights will occur as ideas are discovered and connected. The mature writer will scribble them down for use when the real writing begins. This, of course, is a skill that develops as the child moves through the various school grades and syllabus stages of writing. When insights are not readily forthcoming or writer's block sets in, writers do many different things—they doodle, pace the floor, talk to others about it, brainstorm, or just start writing down whatever comes into their heads in the hope that good ideas will come.

Once the investigation and insights have developed sufficiently, it is time to do a *first draft*. Mature writers really appreciate an insight that gives them 'a good lead', or an opening that will focus the reader's attention and initiate a flow of well-sequenced ideas.

This draft can often command the greatest concentration of any part of the process because it is the time when initial selection from all available ideas (content) is made and when the basic shape of the form or text-type is made. This draft is often best done uninterrupted and free from the constraints of 'correctness', which can be concentrated on later. With Kindergarten writers, the first draft at this early stage of a student's writing development becomes, in fact, not only the draft but the final product. That is, the concept of *revising* the draft is a developing one and should not be imposed on beginning writers who have not yet developed the desire or the skills to 'revisit' what they have written. Very young writers are often so pleased with their initial efforts that they want to share or display them as soon as the initial effort is complete.

Drafting and **redrafting** take time to develop

A more mature writer will revisit the first draft once it is finished, or even revise during the drafting itself—a lot of re-reading and reshaping may occur. One of the hardest parts of the process is to get children to revise their writing. In the early stages of development, writers may attend to only the surface features during revision, such as spelling and punctuation. As a writer matures, a deeper revision will develop: revision of sequence and structure, of pace, and of elements of evidence and logic.

Once the final revisions have occurred, the writer has a *product* that can be *published*. In the classroom context this means making the writing available for others to see and read. If others are going to read the text, then it needs to be presented clearly and legibly, perhaps word-processed and illustrated. There are many different ways of publishing the end product:

Students like to see their writing published

- in class writing books, which are large and accessible to the children
- around the classroom walls—on charts, noticeboards, posters, writing focus boards, or corners
- on mobiles suspended from the ceiling or lines strung across the room
- in individual folders to which others can have easy access
- as part of Shared Reading time with the class, groups, pairs, and so on
- as texts sent to a real audience such as invitations to parents or letters to the local newspaper
- emails to friends; participation in chat rooms.

Response to the product or the creative work is important. When others read our writing it is encouraging to get positive, helpful comments.

In a classroom, the teacher needs to work hard at getting the children to respond positively to others' writing. Sharing writing during the process is just as important as sharing the final product. If this approach is nurtured from the

Students can benefit from *response*

very early stages then by the time the child reaches the upper primary grades, sharing and commenting will be a natural consequence of writing activities—children will get better at it and will even want to do it. In this way a positive attitude to writing will be developed.

However, young writers must not be locked into a process that contains a set number of immovable and inflexible steps. Such a process might contain: experience or problem (decision to write); pre-writing; draft; revising and editing; product and publication; reader's response;

Young writers must not be locked into a set of immovable steps

writer's attitude. The process must remain flexible: not all pieces of writing need to be polished and published; the writer may not always want to revise a piece of writing; a writer may be wise to abandon a piece halfway through, and so on.

Critical thinking and study exercises

1. Children usually have excellent innovative ideas and approaches for writing. Encourage their interests and motivate them to write more and write often. Examine the following ways literature can be used in classroom writing sessions and talk about ways of using the children's literature you are familiar with.

2. Concentrate the attention of the class on the features of, for example, fairytales and then ask them to look for other texts that have similar distinguishing characteristics. After collecting various examples, further analysis can be made to see how closely they fit the distinguishing features of a genre or subvert that genre. With further assistance from the teacher, the student can eventually construct his/her own fairytale, using the collected texts as models.

3. A variation of this might be to collect different versions of a folktale such as 'Cinderella' and analyse what makes them different and why they might appeal to different audiences. Share your findings with a small group.

4. What can you learn about the purposes of writing from the following comments by teacher

trainees? What implications do these views have for the classroom?

I don't write many stories these days. However, my writing is purposeful in expressing my views and feelings. I'm a person who often finds it difficult to verbalise my opinions/views and feelings. Writing helps me to do this … Writing for me is easier than talking.

T.

I've always wanted to be a good communicator and recognised that writing is the key. The really crucial judgments about outcomes are made in the HSC, other examinations, and written assessment.

C.

My problem is I'm very emotional and often my writing, like my speech is 'everywhere', haphazard, disjointed and quite often ending too abruptly.

M.

In the classroom

1   Generate interest in creative writing through directed discussion of popular fiction with Years 5 and 6. Examples from Paul Jennings' *Undone! More Bad Endings* illustrate the variety of openings to short stories, encouraging the reader's interest:

'A stone with a hole in it. A sort of green-coloured jewel in a leather pouch. Just lying there in the beam of my torch.' (Batty: 1)

'I, Adam Hill, agree to stand on the Wollaston Bridge at four o'clock and pull down my pants. I will then flash a moonie at Mr Bellow, the school principal.'
Who would be mad enough to sign such a thing? Suicide—flashing a bare bottom at Mr Bellow. (Moonies: 18)

Think of honey. Think of rotten, stinking fish. Put them together and what have you got? DISGUSTING COD-LIVER OIL. That's what.
'The nonsense you have just read was not written by me. My grandson Anthony wrote it. Silly boy.' (Noseweed: 31)

'I am never eating meat again,' I yelled at Dad.
He just smiled at me as if I was crazy.
You might think I'm crazy too. I mean most people who live on farms eat meat. So I'll tell you what. You be me for a while and see how you feel about it at the end.' (Thought Full: 61)

'I'm undone.
Yes, I know. I'm a fink. A rat. A creep. Nobody likes Eric Mud and it's all my own fault.
But I don't deserve this.' (Clear As Mud: 78)

2   Make mini autobiographies or autobiographical notebooks. Give each child a folder or cardboard sheet on which is placed a self-photograph or drawing. Involve the child to find out various likes and dislikes, e.g. a favourite song, favourite leisure time activity, favourite TV show, animal, book, or saying. The format will vary for different ages. This activity allows the children to find out more about each other. In retrospect, when the child becomes older, it can be revealing and often amusing to look back on earlier preferences and thoughts. The writing can be collated in book form and/or displayed in the classroom.

3   Introduce children to the *Griffin and Sabine* trilogy by Neil Bantock (1997) to encourage their interest in writing letters (some may already have penpals via email). The children can produce original postcards, cards, and letters that will help develop writing skills.

4   Involve the children in their own learning by getting them to edit and proofread their work. Provide a checklist of what to look for, such as, is the message clearly conveyed? Make sure they know how to use the spellcheck on the computer and how to use a dictionary and thesaurus. Write in front of the children (on the chalkboard or on an overhead transparency) so they can observe by your actions and running commentary how you compose your thoughts—perhaps you will hesitate, cross out a word, or rephrase a sentence. Let them know that editing and re-editing is usual and necessary even for experienced writers.

5 Encourage children to be observant writers with a curious eye. Ask them to keep a writer's diary or a notebook in which they can write about particular events or activities that impressed them or affected them in some way. These trainee students remembered writing personal diaries.

> *I have kept my diaries from previous holidays and get much enjoyment at looking back and seeing what I was doing at the time and my general outlook on life … Writing is a great way to express how you feel.*
>
> I.

> *Once I romanticised and thought I'd try to keep an accurate diary like Anne Frank—that didn't last long. I was very undisciplined, and I found myself too boring, unable to write interestingly or comically.*
>
> M.

> *The only time I can recall writing on my own initiative is when I kept a diary. I was about 9 at the time and this diary was something I completed every night. Mind you, it was one of the most boring diaries in the world, I'm sure. I simply wrote down exactly what I had done during the day, detail by detail, including about what time I got up and what TV shows I had watched—I even included the fact that I had written the diary article for the day—as if people wouldn't realise that by the fact that there were words and sentences on the page, done in my handwriting!*
>
> E.

> *I have always enjoyed writing. It allows me to express myself clearly, directly, capture thoughts, memories and ideas. I value words on a page. When I was younger I used to get homesick when my parents went away on business trips or when I stayed at a friend's house. I consulted my dear 'nanny' on this problem and she encouraged me to write my thoughts, feelings, day's events etc. in a journal. This method helped her when she was my age and experiencing similar problems. From that day, I have always recorded special events, special feelings, moments etc. in a pink diary hidden away in my cupboard. In fact, it is the same diary that my nan bought me many years ago and although it is not an everyday diary and is not written in too regularly, it contains some of the most precious moments and memories of my life.*
>
> K.

6 Expand children's vocabulary by asking them to find synonyms for different words and phrases or common expressions. Display these where they can be viewed and highlight how they can be used as appropriate choices in an extended written discourse.

> *He's nice. She's nice.*

Try these synonyms:

> *likeable, attractive, beautiful, handsome, good, helpful, kind, lovely, friendly, generous …*

Find synonyms for the following:

> *It was great. I thought it was fantastic.*

Publish children's writing. Give them time in class to start writing chapters that can develop into a book. Help the children to make a class book of their writing. They may want to collect items on similar topics or have a medley. The book may be bound and photocopied or made accessible on computer disk. Encourage individual writing at home and on the computer, and find a way for these efforts to be recognised or published.

▶ Summary

1 The sociolinguistic approach to teaching writing emphasises the importance of writing in context. This means that students must understand the social purpose of writing, the appropriate register, and how to use grammatical features to express meaning.

2 The genre approach is useful because it focuses on scaffolding and models that explain how meaning is negotiated. While the various text-types may have blurred boundaries, they are very useful models for beginning writers.

3 Having a metalinguistic knowledge can help to understand and describe what is happening in texts.

4 Students need to realise that writing is a process: brainstorming, researching, drafting, editing, and publishing are parts of this process. The first words written are rarely the finished product. Just as athletes need training, writing needs to be practised over time to improve skills.

5 Computer literacy and engaging with multiliteracies should be seen to be an integral part of writing practices. These can facilitate the process in many areas, such as access to information, possibilities for multimedia, opportunities for publishing, and revision and editing capabilities.

6 Literacy Sessions that integrate material from across the curriculum offer exciting opportunities for writing, including multimedia presentations using sound and film as well as the written text, writing collaboratively with other classrooms around the world, writing on the Internet, and engaging with social and environmental issues. Teachers can capitalise on the remarkable popularity of the Harry Potter phenomenon to encourage children to experience the joys of reading and writing.

7 A major thrust in classroom teaching should be to ensure that students are engaged in real writing for real purposes for real audiences or readers. Children should be motivated to write and should find it an exciting and interesting engagement with language. It is important that the teacher creates an appropriate writing climate in the classroom.

8 Teaching writing effectively needs time for the students to write, a degree of choice of topic and text-type, integration of language skills, adequate response to the writing, appropriate demonstration by the teacher, an expectation that writing skills will develop over time, motivation, and an appropriate classroom setting.

9 There are strong links between reading, talking, listening, and writing. Children gain a great deal of linguistic awareness from the practice of writing itself and also from reading and listening to particular kinds of writing and talking about them.

10 Activities in writing, listening, reading, and talking are best integrated to raise students' understanding of how language is used in a variety of contexts for different purposes and audiences.

11 There is no magical solution for the reluctant writer. The teacher should try to analyse the reasons for the reluctance. Quality one-to-one time may need to be spent with the student to motivate him/her and develop confidence and self esteem.

12 Students need to be competent in multiliteracies in today's schools.

Further reading

Brindley, R. & J. J. Schneider 2002, 'Writing instruction or destruction: Lessons to be learned from fourth-grade teachers' perspectives on teaching writing', *Journal of Teacher Education* 53(4): 328–41.

Christenson, T. A. 2002, *Supporting Struggling Writers in the Elementary Classroom*, IRA, Newark, Del.

Dillon, D. R. 2000, *Kids Insight: Reconsidering how to meet the literacy needs of all students*, IRA, Newark, Del.

Fu, D. & L. Lamme 2002, 'Writing lessons with Gavin Curtis', *Journal of Children's Literature* 28(1): 63 72.

Johnson, H. & L. Freedman 2005. *Developing Critical Awareness at the Middle Level: Using texts as tools for critique and pleasure*, IRA, Newark, Del.

Karchmer, R. A., M. H. Mallette, J. Kara-Sotteriou & D. Leu, Jr (eds) 2005, *Innovative Approaches to Literacy Education: Using the Internet to support new literacies*, IRA, Newark, Del.

Kinzer, C. K. & Leander, K. 2003, 'Technology and the language arts: Implications of an expanded definition of literacy'. In J. Flood, D. Lapp, J. R. Squire & J. M. Jensen (eds) *Handbook of Research on Teaching the English Language Arts*, Erlbaum, Mahwah, N.J, pp. 546–66.

Knobel, M. & A. Healy (eds) 1998, *Critical Literacies in the Primary Classroom*, PETA, Sydney.

Luke, C. 1997, *Technological Literacy*, Adult Literacy Research Network, Language Australia, Melbourne.

Moss, J. F. & M. F. Fenster 2002, *From Literature to Literacy: Bridging learning in the library and the primary grade classroom*, IRA, Newark, Del.

Neuman, S. B. & K. A. Roskos (eds) 1998, *Children Achieving: Best practices in early literacy*, IRA, Newark, Del.

Nyholm, M. 2002, 'Proofreading, editing, using authoritative sources: Getting help to get it right', *Classroom* 22(7): 38–9.

Potter, W. J. 1998, *Media Literacy*, Sage, Thousand Oaks, Calif.

Prevalet, K. 2001, 'Creativity and the importance of fourth grade', *Poets & Writers Magazine* 29(1): 51–4.

Smith, M. 2002, 'What a difference writing has made! A personal journey in the teaching of writing', *Primary Voices K–6* 11(1): 7–9.

Tyner, K. R. 1998, *Literacy in a Digital World: Teaching and learning in the age of information*, L. Erlbaum Assoc., Mahwah, N.J.

Web links

International Reading Association: www.reading.org
Office of the Board of Studies (NSW): www.boardofstudies.nsw.edu.au
OWL, Purdue University Online Writing Lab: http://owl.english.purdue.edu/handouts/grammar
K–6 Education Resources, Board of Studies, NSW, Australia: www.bosnsw-k6.nsw.edu.au

Children's Literature

PART 3

ROSEMARY ROSS JOHNSTON

Overview

This part provides a critical study of the theory and application of children's literature in pedagogy. It has a broad focus that includes both primary and secondary classrooms, and is relevant to many areas of tertiary study. It builds on parts I and II by presenting creative ways of using children's books and related multimodal digital resources to foster literate practices in reading, writing, speaking, and listening. It recognises that such practices have become more complex in an electronic age, and that the idea of literacy, always complex, has evolved and even ignited into the exciting idea, and associated challenges, of multiliteracies.

It strongly endorses children's literature as literature, and as part of an artistic continuum in which children should be encouraged to participate and share. It also argues that children need 'courteous' exposure to texts and ideas beyond their immediate capacities.

This represents part of a philosophy of Sustainable Creative Pedagogy, which in its approach to language, literacy, and children's literature is

1   *Transdisciplinary:* concerned with the perception of connections across different areas, and across different texts, genres, and textual modes; concerned with the two types of knowledge production identified by Gibbons and other learning theorists as Mode 1, which is traditional, disciplinary, homogeneous, organisationally formulated and preserved; and Mode 2, which is transdisciplinary, heterogeneous, heterarchial, and organisationally transient. Children's literature generates the production of knowledge in both modes; Mode 2 is particularly relevant to digital literacies.

2   *Subjunctive:* encourages subjunctive, hypothetical modes of thinking—'were this me, were this you, were this the situation—what if?'

3   *Speculative:* proposes opportunities for 'I wonder' experiences.

4   *Conceptual:* encourages the formulation of deep concepts and profound ideas.

5   *Cognisant of 'the truth of the other':* encourages tolerance and is generous-spirited, respectful of other 'I's. Interaction with diverse sustained narratives grows the capacity not only for words and language but for thinking, and for the imaginative leap into the recognition and understanding of otherness that is part of cultural literacy.

6   *Dialogic* rather than monologic: collaborative, interactive, listening to and interacting with many voices and many stories.

7   *Positively performative:* explicitly encodes images of success in the whole teaching cycle of 'planning, doing, reviewing and improving', strives for both do-ability and intellectual stretch in a flexible environment that encourages trial and error. This idea is informed by Bakhtin's concept of *unfinalisability*, which accepts 'unfinishedness' as part of openness to creativity (1984: 166).

8 *Discovery-oriented*: reinforces the centrality of students as explorers and of student-led experiences of learning.

Ideas of knowledge, teaching and learning are conceptualised in three inter-related ways:

i   as **story**—narratives expressed in multiple modes, texts, and media
ii   as **ecology**—webs relating humans to internal and external environments, including technology
iii as **genealogy**—ways of relating human presents to common and/or uncommon pasts.

Indigenous cultures, and in particular Australian Aboriginal culture, have traditionally passed on knowledge, wisdom, and life-learning through telling stories and describing ecologies and genealogies, not only in the language of words, but in the languages of rock art and body painting, singing and songlines and song cycles, drama and dance. These are *story arts*, multimodal communications that give shape to cultural, learning, and spiritual experience.

As this book demonstrates, technology has generated new ways of thinking about literacy and new ways of using story arts. This climate of change is a good time for leaderly initiatives. I suggest that one such initiative is to find ways of promoting mainstream inclusion of indigenous ideas about education. In the nexus of language, literacy and literature, there is an opportunity to explore teaching and learning that makes explicit connections to the centrality of story arts in indigenous learning and Western cultural experience.

The languages of children's literature are multimodal (visual, verbal, aural, oral). The story arts of children's books, creatively mined and explored, can generate innovative ideas about user-friendly, inclusive pathways into user-friendly, inclusive classrooms.

In this part, specific books have been used but only as exemplars; children's literature is rich and diverse, and augmented by increasing numbers of digital resources. Teachers can adapt these tasks and books to suit their particular teaching situations.

Chapter 20 outlines the contemporary cultural landscape of language—literacy and literature in the digital age—and readers are advised to read this chapter at least before reading any other material in part III.

Chapters 21 and 22 introduce children's literature within a context of critical literacy and link the 'pure' study of children's literature with its application in the classroom. Chapter 23 discusses the impact of the new technologies and sets current approaches in context.

Chapters 24, 25, and 26 relate children's literature theory to pedagogical practice, using theory as conceptual base, creative idea, and teaching structure. The significance of intertextuality is discussed and related to the idea of 'prior knowledge' as an important factor in children's literacy learning. Children's literature is explored as a locus of literate practices and as an inherent part of the life cycle of literacy.

Chapter 27 provides a brief sociohistorical overview of folktales and fairytales and outlines their cultural influence.

Chapter 28 discusses the special relationship between the words and pictures of picturebooks and notes the particular contribution these books can make even for older children. It also discusses the poetic language of picturebooks, and children's poetry.

This is followed by a new chapter (chapter 29) on visual literacy, which addresses the needs of both primary and secondary curricula in this area, and provides many examples from well-known and accessible children's books.

Chapters 30 and 31 consider the resources that children's literature provides in the multicultural classroom, as a forum for the discussion of social issues, and for exploring history and fantasy. Chapter 32 considers some responses to children's literature, linking literature with, among other things, popular song. It summarises children's literature in terms of theatre in the classroom.

Part III contains numerous activities designed as models for use in the primary classroom. Some activities related to theoretical ideas such as focalisation, agency, and subjectivity are suitable for secondary students. All activities can be readily adapted to meet specific teaching needs. While the 'Critical Thinking' exercises are specifically designed for tertiary students and teachers, and 'In the Classroom' for classroom practice, all activities are intended to be flexible and adaptable. There is a strong focus in all suggested activities on discovery-oriented learning, and on the principles of sustainable creative pedagogy.

The emphasis in part III is that theory informs the practice of reflective teaching, and that reflective teaching informs, refines, and inspires theoretical ideas. There is more information in this part, as in the preceding ones, than a practising teacher may need. Much of this 'bonus' material is shaded for easy reference. However, teachers, perhaps more than any other professionals, must model principles of lifelong learning. As educators, we need continually to challenge and to be challenged into developing our own ideas about what we do, how we do it, and why.

An important premise is that literature is a mosaic of multiple literacies—to reading, writing, speaking, listening we need to add visual literacy, critical literacy, cultural literacy, multimodal literacies, narrative literacy, imaginative literacy. These overlap and intersect in all sorts of ways. Most of all, we need to be aware of the capacity of literature to contribute to all aspects of children's lives, to their knowledge of the world, to their play, to their hopes and dreams, and to their creative and sustainable futures.

The Papunya School Book of Country and History, produced by the children and staff of Papunya School, in Central Australia, describes 'two-way learning': 'At Papunya School, *ngurra*—country—is at the centre of our learning. It is part of everything we need to know … But as well as learning in this traditional way, we can also find out about our country and our history by putting some of the pieces of the story into a book.' This is an example of sustainable creative pedagogy, with *Tjulkura* and *Anangu* teachers working together, using totemic honey ant imagery to connect the two knowledge systems: 'We want to see the children learning both ways and coming out bright orange and yellow together, like honey ants.'

This is a vision for Australian children—and for our future—that is creative and sustainable, and that we as educators need to dream about, work towards, and bring into being.

LANGUAGE, LITERATURE AND LITERACY IN THE DIGITAL AGE

20

Overview

Literature produced for children is a dynamic and fertile resource for the expanding practices and experiences of language and literacy in a digital age. While the term 'literacy' still expresses the significant basic idea of making meaning through and from text (whatever form that text takes, and whatever ways it is engaged with), the popularity of the term 'multiliteracies' demonstrates recognition of the burgeoning text modes that are available and accessible in classrooms and homes, and the varying skills they require. Literacy is a profound concept—as I wrote in the previous editions of this book, it is 'multi-active, multi-purpose and multi-dimensional' (Johnston 2001: 434, 2003: 483). It is in literature, and in the multimodal production of literature for children, that the diversity and range of language (both verbal and visual, both permanent and ephemeral) is arguably most interactive yet intimate, most purposeful yet playful, and most dimensional.

Children's literature is a creative art. It is of course conceived creatively but it is just as importantly reconceived by an audience which is itself in a constant state of flux and re-creation.

(R. R. Johnston)

Language and being

Language articulates what it is *to be*. The ancient Hebrews represent one of many racial groups who believed that words produced reality. J. L. Austin, in his theory of the performative (*How to Do Things With Words* 1962), argues the integral

Language articulates and produces identity

relationship of *speech* to *act*: in a performative utterance the word brings about the act which constitutes the reality, as, for example, in 'I now pronounce you man and wife'. Judith Butler extends this idea into a theory of performativity that she applies to the production of gender. Butler argues that gender and gender expectations are culturally encoded, and that they are meanings ascribed through words to a baby at the moment of birth. Thus 'It's a girl!' is an utterance that begins a process of 'girling' (*Gender Trouble* 1990). The French philosopher Jacques Derrida notes that the essence of the performative is repetition and iteration—the words used about us, repeated over and over again, come to be what we are. Derrida calls this citational doubling ('Signature event context' 1991b). These theories have, as we shall see, particular implications for the words uttered by teachers in classrooms both to and about children (consider in this context the effect of 'You're always the last to finish!' or 'Can't you do anything right!' or 'Your Maths is getting better and better!').

Language articulates thought

Language gives shape and organisation to *thought*. The genesis and production of traditional books, and the increasing amount of literary experiences available through information and communication technologies, contribute to the reservoir of words and images—visual and verbal languages—that are used to formulate and communicate thought—*thinking*.

Thinking is surely the most profound aspect of literacy. We need some sort of a language to think with, even when it involves what appears as 'wordless' appreciation or response (in reality, nothing is wordless, or at least is not wordless for long; humans strive to give words to every experience). Western society has traditionally been much influenced by the proclamation of Descartes, 'I think therefore I am'; in African traditional society the prevailing ethos is that of *ubunto*, 'I am with others, therefore I am' (Harries 2002: 140). Both philosophies imply the absolute significance of language to think with, of language to communicate. The cognitive scientist Andy Clark writes:

> Language is in many ways the ultimate artifact: so ubiquitous it is almost invisible, so intimate it is not clear whether it is a kind of tool or a dimension of the user. Whatever the boundaries, we confront at the very least a tightly linked economy in which the biological brain is fantastically empowered by some of its strangest and most recent creations: words in the air, symbols on the printed page. (1997: 218)

Literature, thinking, and the literacy of the imagination

Thoughts, T. S. Eliot writes in *Selected Essays* (1921), 'impact and subtly change the self who thinks them'. Narrative fictions—diverse and heterogeneous in story and mode of delivery, and open to all the means of response made available in an electronic age—promote 'the literacy of the imagination' (Johnston 2000a), which grows not only the capacity to think, but the capacity to make the imaginative leap into 'otherness'. It is this leap into the awareness of others as 'I's just as authentic in their needs and desires as one's own 'I', that develops moral understandings. Part of imaginative literacy is to breed a sense of human equity informed by subjunctive modes of thinking: 'Were this me, were this you, were this the situation—what if?'

The relationship between language and being is complex, and is addressed as much by philosophers as by linguists. This is reflected in folktales and fairytales in which the power of the name—that is, the naming of our being—is of great significance; it is also reflected in the cultural customs of many countries.

Ideas about language

Note the power of the name in, for example, some Aboriginal cultures: after a person dies, their name must not be mentioned because doing so may interfere with the journey to the next world.

Language creates. It is powerful and transforming, an infinity of arrangements, relationships, and networks of meaning. An observer at the launching of Apollo 17 in 1975 remarked how the wonder of that moment changed people's behaviour, made them act differently, made them more aware of each other. The wonder of language is similarly transformational, opening up what one writer has called 'windows on other worlds' (Wallace 1988: 163), but more importantly, opening up *self* to a world of *others*, and others to a world of self.

Reading books, as Brodkey notes, 'is an intimate act … because of the prolonged (or intense) exposure of one mind to another' (Booth 1988: 168). This is perhaps not so true in relation to books for young children, but it is true that the mysterious internal processing that happens between the eye taking in the marks on the page, and the making of meaning thereafter, is extremely personal, figured with private time and place and played out in individual theatres of consciousness.

However, in an age where technologies facilitate and actively encourage digital literacy learning, the opening up of self to others becomes increasingly interactive, increasingly public, through a myriad of electronic devices such as the World Wide Web (both a communication and research resource), synchronous and asynchronous chat rooms, and online communities that reach beyond the classroom and across the world, web journals or blogs (providing opportunities to publish opinions in the public domain), virtual domains—'story palaces'—in which a web persona (*avatar*) can be taken on and roles played out with international casts in sophisticated settings, digital cameras and their immediacy of image, films, mobile telephones, videos and CD ROMS, and the narratives of video games (again often played with a partner in another place).

Language in the age of e-communication

Literature as applied language

Literature is applied language. It is language in action, working parts working, a model of what Gee (1997: 5) calls many 'language-ings'. It has enormous variety. It is a multisensory experience: we see, we hear, we touch the book and

Literature as virtual reality

turn the pages, we say the words; we imagine, we enter in; our 'life-world' and the imaginative world of the text merge seamlessly if only for a moment. This does not imply that we allow ourselves to be mindlessly manipulated, or that we have to 'identify' with particular characters; we need to learn to resist such positioning and teach our students to do so. But a creative negotiation between ourselves and the words of the text takes place and, as we read, some form of a merged world is uniquely ours. Literature is a kind of virtual reality.

▶ LITERACY IN THE DIGITAL AGE

The idea of story worlds as a kind of virtual reality connects strongly to some of the e-literature experiences now available, particularly electronic literary theme parks ('real' virtual reality!). There are two main types of these:

1 *MUDs* (acronym for multi-user dungeons or domains, related to the idea of Dungeons and Dragons): synchronous chat rooms where participants log in and take on roles, using text.
2 *Story Palaces*: similar themed sites, constructed visually rather than through text. Action can be created against a backdrop of rooms that are often like cartoons, or may be elaborately decorated. Palaces may be story worlds or communal meeting places, and are built in cyberspace by a community of fans and enthusiasts, who can also construct and take on characters (*avatars*, realistic-looking or cartoon figures, available in all sorts of poses, often designed with costumes and props) and play out (in collaborative role-play) stories and action in all sorts of genres from conversation to soap opera.

Virtual literary theme parks

Participating in these sites offers a new take on the narrative and language-rich activity of role-play triggered by a storybook, and offers students the opportunity to use electronic resources in ways they find attractive, and that also develop their skills in communication, design, digital literacy, and imaginative play.

Access to palaces is through a web browser such as Internet Explorer or Netscape, or through downloading free Palace User software (http://www.paceplanet.net). The latter is worthwhile, and the free software is accompanied by clear directions.

One example of a popular palace site, suitable for children, is Middle Earth Palace, inspired by *The Lord of the Rings*, at http://www.middleearthpalace.com/palace.html. This is a sophisticated site, and children visiting the palace can wander in and out of the beautifully decorated rooms at will, assisted by drop-down help menus and a map, and sometimes accompanied by sound bytes from the movies. Part of the fun is discovering the avatars of elves, hobbits, and other characters hiding in unexpected corners.

The Middle Earth palace is owned by Tolkien fan Laurie Sorenson (nom-de-web is 'Nimue'). The palace home page opens with *Mae Govannen!*, which is Elvish for 'Welcome to Middle Earth!' and reads:

> Middle Earth is an interactive graphical chat environment, built by and for Tolkien fans! For those of you who think 'chat' on the internet is only 'text on a screen,' you are in for a pleasant surprise ... oh yes precious ... pleasant surprisssess ... Middle Earth is made up of interconnecting chart rooms that are animated and scripted. You can navigate with maps or take one of our tours of the books or the movies. Our guests can interact with the rooms and other guests by moving around on the screen, chatting, activating scripts, and by wearing avatars.

Another popular site is the Galaxy Station palace (palace://thegalaxystation.com.9998) where visitors can participate in the writing and acting out of their own *Star Wars* fiction.

MULTILITERACIES

Contexts for text

What the proliferation of MUDs and story palaces and other online story experiences demonstrate is that in these early years of the 21st century, there are many of what I am referring to as **contexts for text**. One context may be the www, one may be email, one may be a creative composition, one may be a factual research exercise, one may be a mobile text message.

'Contexts for text' and multimodes

Contexts for text and register

Each context for text unlooses its own modes of literate behaviours, its own languages, its own 'registers'. Indeed, these 'contexts for text' are closely related to traditional grammatical ideas about **register**: the variety of language used in different social situations (contexts); the need to choose language appropriate to audience, purpose, time, and place.

So contexts for texts relate to multimodes, and thus the multiliteracies that these different modes require. But there is another complication: just as contexts have changed, so what we understand as text has changed as well. Once upon a time, not so long ago, in places quite near here, 'text' referred to a body of language. In literary terms, it meant a *book*—a narrative of some description, bound and presented in printed form.

Changing ideas of 'text' and 'language'

But in our digital day, there have been two minor revolutions: first, the word 'text' has been expanded to include any communication involving language, and second, the word 'language' has burst through its conventional 20th-century usages to expand and include anything that is communicative: graphics and illustrations, images and moving images, in all sorts of combinations and often including audio. Indeed, there is now a school of thought that stresses the centrality of the image, rather than the centrality of writing, in the communication process.

In this changing world, children's literature, with its emphasis on image, on word, and on positioning them sometimes together and sometimes apart; in its postmodern development of picturebooks, that stir up meanings in the gaps where there are actually no words and no pictures; and in its switching of reading and viewing positions and jolting of conventions, provides a particularly apt field of literacy—and literary—study.

The place of literature in the classroom

Children's literature is the practice of all aspects of literacy: reading and writing, speaking in appropriate registers in different contexts, listening and communicating, accessing text in multimodes, choosing and using appropriate media, reading images as well as words (see chapter 29 on Visual Literacy). Literature is *literacy given form and artistic shape*: 'Literacy involves the integration of speaking, listening and critical thinking with reading and writing. Effective literacy is intrinsically purposeful, flexible and dynamic and continues to develop throughout the individual's lifetime' (Australian Language and Literacy Policy 1991: 9).

Children's literature encourages a wide range of literate behaviours

Literary texts and images in the mind

As ideas of literacy have become more complicated, so too have ideas of children's literature. The place of literature—expanded and multimodal—in our classrooms (primary, secondary, tertiary) needs to be confirmed, affirmed, and redefined, not only for what it reveals about language and how it develops literacy but also for what it reveals *as literature*. In all the shifting around that is going on, the idea of literature—and the literary text—as something that is intrinsically valuable, and as something significantly different from a mobile text message or an email discourse, is being re-established. There is a skill in using words well, fluently, evocatively. Perhaps, in an image-dominated world, we are renewing our respect for those who can produce the magic of mind images through words, subtly, using black marks on a white page.

There is a humanity in telling stories that are meaningful about self and others. Noam Chomsky claims that it is likely that literature will always give a far deeper insight into 'the full human person' than any model of scientific enquiry could ever hope to do.

Literature does not, however, belong only in the English class. Nor is literature in the classroom designed purely for endless analysis of its parts, or repetitive questions on each chapter or act or verse. And simply shifting such activities to the computer does not miraculously make them better.

When we admire and respect something, finding out how it works can be an edifying and exciting exercise. But before pulling something apart, an appreciation is required of what it actually looks like whole, otherwise the coherence of its essential form may be lost, or the original wholeness may not be recognised or enjoyed.

Children's literature—including its unique offspring, the picturebook—is a fundamental and integral part of this process. Pictures do help very young readers become familiar with words (verbal language). But in contemporary picturebooks, pictures are not just a prop to language but a language (visual language) in their own right. Further, and as implied above, the propinquity of words and pictures creates something more than simply the sum of those words and pictures. In fact it constitutes a 'third space' (to borrow from cognitive science), which generates properties that can be found in neither of the 'input spaces' (Turner 1996: 57–8; Johnston 1998a: 34). I very much like Noel Sanders' *verbal* image, which he uses to describe *visual* images (an interesting dichotomy to think about), in the following passage:

> Images are texts … in the very primary sense of a 'weave' … Anything woven is a fabric not only of presences (the fibres) but of the spaces between. With lace, for example, the fabric is far more absence than presence, and any cloth is likewise going to be a combination of openness and closedness. Carrying the metaphor further, it is possible to take a written text as a combination of black, written elements and the white empty spaces of the page. The closedness of newspaper text is to, say, nylon, as the openness of poetry (with its wide expanses of white paper) is to the open weave of lace … (Kress 1988: 141)

Sanders is also talking about cultural and ideological coding of images, and this is a point that will be picked up later. For now, this image helps to describe the affordances of picturebooks. Text may be dense, or—as Genette said of poetry—it may announce itself by its spaces. Pictures do not simply illustrate language, they inflate it into the making of new meaning; they add something different, stimulating an inner imaginative process that is in itself another type of 'language-ing'.

In a digital age, children's literature and its presentation in book form maintains its significance as an integral and crucial resource for the development of children's literacy—in all its multiple emphases: critical, cultural, visual, imaginative, digital—and for developing understandings and knowledge about the different sorts of language appropriate in different contexts—mobile phone text, email, and so on—which has already been noted as relating to **register**.

Indeed, children's literature becomes even more significant in an electronic age, in no small part because of the many expanded ways in which children can themselves interact with text, and interact with story worlds, through the augmentation of books by a rapidly increasing array of creative and exciting resources. These, among other things, provide access to online contexts where children, both in teaching/learning situations and in their own leisure and play time, are encouraged to explore behind the scenes of texts, to hear and watch the author speaking about the inspiration and genesis of their books and about decisions they made about characters and plot; where children can read sample chapters (e.g. http://www.morrisgleitzman.com/) and sometimes download free books (as above, and often at http://pauljennings.com.au), where they themselves can contribute to the discussion as fans, even write their own digital narratives, add chapters, create new characters and new twists in the plot.

There is another significant benefit that the online world has brought to classrooms. Books have always opened new worlds, and offered opportunities for students to enlarge perspectives of thinking and contexts of thought, in authentic and interactive ways beyond the here and now of their home and classroom. Digital technologies, in bringing the rest of the developed world into touch with the individual, must surely bring moments—in play or otherwise—when students contemplate deeper issues—such as a sense of time that is relative rather than absolute (because when you are part of an online community with a partner school in another hemisphere, you soon learn that their night may be your day), and a sense of commitment to that larger world.

Children's books have a tradition of generating meaning through the interaction of text and image (in picturebooks), they have a tradition of using experimental non-linear formats that are akin to hypertext, and they have a tradition of classroom recontextualisation—of being dramatised and acted out in school contexts and rewritten in paraphrases. **Literate behaviours and *engaged play*** They also have a long tradition of encouraging *engaged play*—I drew plans of all the houses in my favourite books (scouring the pages for any detail that would help), compiled time-lines and genealogies, even wrote my own sequels (or occasionally alternative endings). Children, through their imaginative engagement with the fictional worlds of books, play out their stories in all sorts of ways: taking on character roles, attributing roles to others—'You be Red Riding Hood'—enriching the story with their own inventions and preoccupations, with the insertion of new plots, and new characters and settings. A recent study asked a number of people to name the book that was their childhood favorite. Enid Blyton's *The Magic Faraway Tree* emerged as the most popular, but the interesting point was that when asked to name their favourite magic land from the book (such as the Roundabout Land, the Rocking Land), a significant proportion named a land that Blyton hadn't actually written. That is, at some point, as part of their imaginative engagement and play, they had added that land to the story, so cleanly and nimbly that it became for them part of the text.

In a personal true anecdote, I was talking to my son about Tigger, in A. A. Milne's *Winnie the Pooh*. He said, in the course of the discussion, 'But weren't they [the toy animals] real?' and then, 'I've never thought about them not being real. Don't they speak and stuff?'

In a comprehensive study of literacies across media, Margaret Mackie (of the University of Alberta, Canada) concludes: '[T]here is, after all, a common word that will make room for a variety of activities, with multifaceted and multimedia connotations. That word is play.' (2002: 182). She goes on to discuss the idea of 'playing the text' in the following ways:

- playing as pretending and imagining (the step into make-believe, or, as I would put it, the step into the virtual)
- playing as performing (the performance of pretending, the connection between body and text, and, the fascinating and engrossing way that the mind works, even when having what Papert calls 'hard fun' (see C. Johnston 1999:12)
- playing as engaging with the rules of the game (accepting the rules and conventions of the text, and, I would add, of the means available to engage with the text)
- playing as strategising (how to make progress through a set of alternatives)
- playing as orchestrating (learning to manage attention and automatic behaviours: 'so much of what we do when we read or watch a movie or play a computer game is unrecognised most of the time.')
- playing as interpreting (and Mackie notes that 'the individual's own private agenda may set up the warp of an interpretation …')
- playing as fooling around (exploring options without commitment: 'The capacity to experiment with texts, to fail sometimes, to try again without recrimination or penalty, and/or to abandon them, is an important part of mastering new media. This is as true for small children learning to decode print as it is for computer experts tackling a new piece of software.')
- playing as not working: 'In play, we can try things out, work through our feelings about an idea in an arena where the results are often unimportant. Naturally, this opens a zone where we can contemplate very important ideas indeed, because the risk is lowered.' (Mackie 2002: 182–8)

This last point relates of course to the power of books to stimulate profound thinking about identity and life in general; it is very much part of the ethos of our approach to children's literature. Some of these points also have a general relevance to teaching and **ICTs encourage** learning in any context: a classroom where risks can be taken without penalty **engaged play** is likely to be an environment conducive to excellence.

My concept of 'engaged play' highlights the fact that books don't just 'capture' the imagination—they arm it, they strengthen it, they exercise it and make it more supple, they engage it in possibilities and transport it to new contexts, they open it up to the virtual worlds we noted earlier.

▶ LITERACY IN THE DIGITAL AGE

ICTs can now make some aspects of these virtual worlds 'real', in that they can be seen on screen, entered into and played with. They can also be constructed. Thus there are new modes of play, new ways of imaginatively engaging with fictional narratives and of constructing individual and communal e-narratives, new ways of presenting such narratives, new forms of role-play, new ways of searching for and gathering information, new ways of interacting with such information. Increasing numbers of websites support books with interesting and up-to-date resource material. Many are developed by publishing houses to provide support material for their own authors. Many authors also have their own sites in which they offer interesting background material to their books: Harry Potter fans can visit J. K. Rowling's site at http:www//jkrowling.com/. Both primary and secondary students will find much to attract them at David Almond's site (http://www,davidalmond.com/). There are also numerous fan sites—these need to be checked, but sites such as Mugglenet, again for Potter fans (http://www.mugglenet.com/), provide playful and engaging opportunities to contribute and interact with others in a dynamic online community.

One example of a wonderful website that is well worth encouraging children to visit is that of the National Theatre in London. This site won two BAFTAs in 2005 and in November of that year was awarded the distinction of 'Best Website in the World' (it was the UK's nomination to a UN/UNESCO competition in which 168 countries took part and the award was presented by Kofi Anan).

http://www.davidalmond.com/
http:www//jkrowling.com/

Visiting websites of excellence is inspiring in itself—this one includes filmed productions of children's books that have been dramatised, including an excellent presentation of Philip Pullman's trilogy *His Dark Materials*. The *Stagework* website (www.stagework.org.uk) is an online resource that allows users behind-the-scenes access to some of England's leading theatre productions, following the creative process from initial ideas to final performance. Using interactive video, the new content—called an 'interactive scene-builder'—engages users by enabling them to choose different scenes to 'build' their own mini-production of the play. It features lead actors discussing and rehearsing different ways of presenting a key scene from the production. Users can then choose which performance they prefer and create their own 'personalised' production.

http://www.stagework.org.uk

Literature and the development of 'knowing readers'

Children need to grow into readers 'in the know' about reading

Young people in secondary school, and even students in tertiary institutions, who are required to do close textual analysis of complex literary texts need a picture—and a love—for what these texts look like whole. They don't need to see themselves in the text, but they do need to have a glimpse of what it will be like when they approach a text with fresh eyes, revisit it with a more knowledgeable appreciation, stand beside it alone, and share it in company. By the time they complete their primary school education children should be **knowing readers**—readers who not only have all the skills they need to read, but who also read with knowledge and expectation of how texts work, of how great the reading experience is, of its infinite capacity for variousness, of its personal rewards and continuing challenges, and of the deep sense of satisfaction that comes from persevering with texts that at first seem too difficult. They also need to have developed the motivation and skills to access all possible ways of exploring the text and its contexts.

So as well as the appropriate ability to use information and communication technologies, and a mindset towards keeping up to date with an ever-evolving field, children need a memory bank of reading that includes large numbers of children's books to which they have been introduced in primary school, preschool, and the home. It is this 'repertoire' (Nodelman 1996: 141) that will give them a clear understanding of what a book is and what it does, of its codes and conventions, narrative patterns and thematic structures, its word-pictures of narrative time and place. The mood, confusions, jealousy, and passion of Emily Bronte's *Wuthering Heights*, and an understanding of the representation of these in narrative, are more readily perceived in the context of a panorama of reading that has included diverse articulations of similar ideas in picturebooks such as *The Wolf* (Barbalet & Tanner 1994) and perhaps *The Werewolf Knight* (Wagner & Roennfeldt 1995), and that has seen jealousy, possessiveness, and fear at work in *John Brown, Rose and the Midnight Cat* (Wagner & Brooks 1977), and *Fox* (Wild & Brooks 2000). An apparently simple wordless picturebook such as Istvan Banyai's *Zoom* (1995), in a continual challenge to reader complacency, prepares young children for thematic ideas about

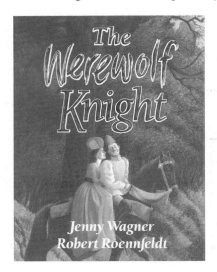

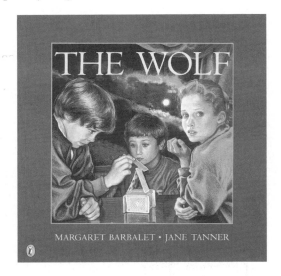

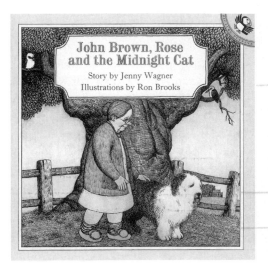

expectations and judgments that may in fact be proved incorrect, and about perspectives and ideas that may later help them to understand better the position of the various voices in Brontë's masterpiece. The complexities of Shakespeare's plays need to be read not as isolated fragments for intensive study that suddenly appear in the latter years of secondary school, but rather as part of a continuum of artistic, literary texts that includes hundreds and hundreds of children's books—humorous, sad, realistic, fantastic. In this way, books as diverse as *Leaves for Mr Walter* (Brian & Cox 1998), *The Selfish Giant* (Wilde 1888), *Playing Beatie Bow* (Park 1980), and Gleeson's *Skating on Sand* (1994) series will have foregrounded later encounters with themes of foolishness and blindness (as in *King Lear*) and of the complexities of family relationships (as in *Hamlet* and *Macbeth*).

Children's books are a vital part of a lifelong participation and engagement in literature. They may look simple but <u>they help to prepare an intellectual, aesthetic receptivity for abstract ideas and complex concepts</u>. For example, let's follow through the notion of themes noted above and consider the idea of 'outsiderness'—marginality, inclusiveness versus exclusiveness, otherness. Books can help children develop innate awarenesses of what it means to be an outsider, of how it feels to be on the margins, and of how such positioning is constructed within narrative. Consider the illustration below by Greg Rogers of the street boy looking through the window at the fat cat in Hathorn's text *Way Home* (1994), and then read Thomas Hardy's depiction of *Tess of the D'Urbervilles* as an outsider: 'She was not an existence, an experience, a structure of sensations, to anyone but herself. To all humankind, Tess was only a passing thought' (*Tess of the D'Urbervilles* chapter 14).

From the same two texts, there is something of the verbal picture of Tess and Sorrow, the young outcast mother holding the outcast baby, in the darkly shadowed visual picture of the homeless boy holding the kitten in the folds of his jacket (see Johnston 1997a). Taro Yashima's *Crow Boy* (1983) tells another story of marginality, classroom outsiderness, and difference, as does *Luke's Way of Looking* (Wheatley & Ottley 1999). Nathaniel Lachenmeyer's *Broken Beaks* (2003), beautifully illustrated by Robert Ingpen, is a moving moral representation of responses to difference:

The other sparrows did not help their friend. Some of them were frightened by the young sparrow's broken beak. Some believed—since his beak had broken and theirs had not—that he was somehow to blame. The rest assumed that someone else would help him.

Children's literature is part of an artistic continuum and it functions as a creative, enjoyable, and stimulating introduction to the great world of art and ideas, opening up that world at multiple, user-friendly points of entry. Readers are exposed, sometimes without realising it, to a mass of complex themes that, like icebergs, may show only as tiny tips. But these tips are indicators of great depths and they act as subtle and implicit guides in the development of knowing readers. Exposure to pictures of outsiderness (or *outside-ness*) in books such as *Way Home* and *Broken Beaks* prepares the way for deeper understandings of ideas relating to the social environment, or to prejudice, injustice, and exploitation—

Broken Beaks

by NATHANIEL LACHENMEYER
ILLUSTRATED by ROBERT INGPEN

ideas that may later be encountered in such diverse texts as Alexander Solzhenitsyn's *One Day in the Life of Ivan Denisovich*, Mark Twain's *Huckleberry Finn*, the music of Bob Dylan or Midnight Oil, or the contemporary novels of Toni Morrison. And, even more important (and as we shall see in chapter 22), part of critical literacy is the ability to perceive where and how we as readers are being positioned and set up, how the text is 'manipulating' us to see, to think and to feel, and what the text is implicitly and explicitly constructing as 'inside' and 'outside'.

LITERATURE AS THE PRACTICE OF ALL ASPECTS OF LITERACY

Critical focus: Bakhtin

Mikhail Mikhailovich Bakhtin (1895–1975) was a Russian literary theorist. Some of his work is complex, but he is worth browsing for his insights into how texts work. Think about this, for example:

Each large and creative verbal whole is a very complex and multifaceted system of relations. With a creative attitude towards language, there are no voiceless words that belong to no one. Each word contains voices that are sometimes infinitely distant, unnamed, almost impersonal ... almost undetectable, and voices sounding nearby and simultaneously. (1981: XX)

Bakhtin calls these voices *heteroglossia* (different voices). Consider this in the light of the classic opening lines of the fairytale, which will be discussed more fully in chapter 27. The words 'Once upon a time ...' contain, if we think about it, the 'voices' of many different fairytale texts that we have read both as children and as adults, the voices of parents and teachers from our past who may have read them to us or to others in our presence, our own voice as we have read or said those words to others, voices from other media—film, radio, television—that we have heard, perhaps the voices of small children who are saying or reading the words to others. Some of these voices are so far away in time or place that we are hardly aware of them; some may be recent and close by.

Words such as 'Once upon a time …' trigger layers of voices—read, written, spoken, heard. They access layers of different relationships, of different times and places, and of accumulated 'meaning' that go far beyond themselves.

Bakhtin is not saying that we actually 'hear' the voices—it is an inner, deeply innate experience—but he is alerting us to the richness and diversity of words and the richness and diversity of literature. There are layers and layers of speakers and listeners, readers and writers. Bakhtin's words highlight the fact that *literature is a mosaic of all aspects of literacy—reading, writing, speaking, listening.*

Children's books as mini-worlds

We have discussed the idea of virtual worlds, but it is important not to lose the idea of the mini-worlds that constitute literary text. Literature is more than a collection of texts making up a past; it is more than *cultural memory* and more than *pantheon*. Literature, and particularly children's literature, is of the moment; its focus is inherently present. Even historical books, locating action in an obvious past, are reproduced within a sense of the ideas and ideologies of the present out of which they are written (see chapter 30).

An obvious example of this is *My Place*, by Nadia Wheatley and Donna Rawlins (1987). This book clearly reconstructs a series of historical moments from the perspectives of its present—Australia on the edge of the 1988 Bicentennial; it shapes the 200 years of history it tells around 1988 ideologies and the growing moral awareness of indigenous relationships to land.

Each book is a mini-world, a microcosm of the culture that is its context. Culture is not just what things are—clothes and houses and food, for example; it is also *attitudes*: attitudes to children, to people from other races, to the roles of parents, to the shapes of families, to what little girls are and what little boys are, to grandparents, to the environment. Children's literature,

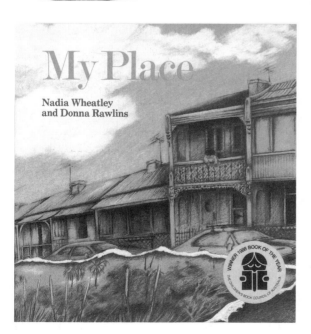

with its late-20th-century proliferation of picturebooks, represents an up-to-date, of-the-moment, highly contemporary sociocultural document. In words and pictures it shows by implication and by explication not only what life looks like, but also local and cultural ideas and attitudes about what it *should* look like and, particularly, what it should look like to children.

ICTs make another type of contribution (especially through Story Palaces) but online material at this point tends to be ephemeral. It is interesting to consider how and if MUDs and story palaces will be archived, and whether or not they will reveal as much about the culture of any given period as children's books in traditional formats do.

Children's literature and cultural literacy

Books consciously and unconsciously reflect cultures and cultural attitudes and ideas

Children's literature is a powerful resource in opening up ideas and discussions about culture and cultural perspectives, that is, about the two prongs of **cultural literacy**: knowledge of the world, and the knowledge, understanding, and appreciation of diverse ways of being. Knowledge of the world is sometimes referred to as *cultural schemata* and relates to all the bits of knowledge that we piece together in order to make sense of language and the social structures within which we live. Deep understandings of our own world should lead to respect for the world of others, which of course is a world we all share. Cultural literacy is an appreciation of this otherness, but 'otherness' is an inherently subjective and loaded concept, while the idea of 'diverse ways of being' puts us all on more equal ground. This knowledge, understanding, and appreciation of diverse ways of being doesn't mean simply including pictures of people from different races as part of a background group, or talking about different foods, clothes, and houses. It means becoming aware with integrity of the enclosures of our own thinking. *It means being open to and experimenting with different ways of doing things, different sorts of formats, different ideas about beginnings and endings, different ideas even about what language should be, and different ideas about literacy.* Cultural literacy has particular relevance to second-language learners (see chapter 29).

Real cultural literacy gives space for these diverse ways of being, and appreciates without question the fact that 'many worlds are possible' (Bruner 1993: 149). Ian Abdullah's two books, *As I Grew Older* (1992) and *Tucker* (1994), tell of one such world, and they do so in the writer's own authentic voice, allowing readers to view his expressive style of pictures and engage in what may be a different experience of the telling of story, and a cyclical rather than linear narrative frame.

Critical thinking and study exercises

Critical focus: language and diversity

Preparing for the classroom
This exercise, designed for tertiary students training to be teachers, could be adapted for secondary students and upper primary children as a preliminary to the discussion of other indigenous writing. They could also be helpful in Middle School environments, where curriculum subjects can often be more integrated.

Read *As I Grew Older* and *Tucker* by Ian Abdullah. Note the double text—Abdullah's original and the standardised English version of it.

1   Why do you think the publisher decided to add a standardised version?

2   Do you think this is helpful? Why or why not?

3   How would you introduce this text into your classroom?

4   How would you introduce it if there were Aboriginal children in your class? Would this make a difference? Should it?

5   Discuss the power of the words 'Now it is hard to find good spots along the River Murray' (*Tucker*, fifth opening). Thinking back to Bakhtin's ideas about words earlier in this chapter, what voices can you hear behind these words? What cultural ideas can you hear?

IN THE CLASSROOM

Theory into practice

The following activity not only expands children's awareness of the traditions and experiences of diverse cultures, but also enhances awareness of their own culture and of the significance of each family being able and free to create different traditions within their own mini-cultures. Making the published book (i.e. the book produced by the class), and researching the best way of publishing and distributing through online resources, will help to extend these ideas into the wider school community.

Implicit to this task are outcomes relating to cultural literacy and to the acceptance and understanding of difference. In a postmodern world of few absolutes, educators at both the primary and secondary level must seek to evolve and develop pedagogical practices that are culturally inclusive. The complex relationships between literature and language and between literature and literacy present a wide range of opportunities to develop such understandings, understandings that are of increasing significance in a multicultural, technological, and increasingly global society.

Many of these activities will be modelled on the 'Tell Me' approach of Aidan Chambers. Teachers initiate discussion through a 'tell me' invitation rather than the common 'why?' question. This approach stresses speaking and listening, anticipating, in Chambers' words, 'conversational dialogue rather than an interrogation' (1993: 49), while the open-endedness of the approach tends to be non-threatening and allows for diverse levels of response.

TEXT: *Tucker* by Ian Abdullah (1994).
Years 3–4

Before reading this with the children, begin a discussion of favourite foods. Talk about TV chefs, such as Jamie Oliver. Have they ever watched his show? Do they like to cook? Who cooks the most at home? You could tell them about his efforts to improve the diet of some English schoolchildren by cooking them school lunches with fresh vegetables. This could fit very nicely with a discussion of the importance of not eating junk food, and of the need to develop good eating habits.

1   Divide the class into small groups. (It is suggested that groups in classroom activities are flexible, and fluid, rather than fixed.)
2   Ask the children to 'tell you' about food traditions in their family. You may want to talk about celebrations such as Christmas or New Year or Easter, or birthday traditions, or picnics, or shopping expeditions, or going out for dinner. Talk about the word 'tucker'.
3   Ask children to talk to each person in the group and try to discover some tradition that is a little different from the others. Ask them to tell how this began in their family (if they know) or why they think it may have begun.
4   Each child writes a few sentences to describe that tradition.
5   Children choose to i) illustrate their sentences or ii) open Google (or another search engine) and do a search for the publisher's website to find out more about Ian Abdullah, or about TV chefs and their programs, or about recipes for their favourite food, or about the word 'tucker'. They could find other places where the word is used, e.g. 'The dog sat on the tuckerbox, Five miles from Gundagai'. Keep a list of all websites visited (this could be a special task for one of the children). Ask children to create a short description ('discovery description') of what they found out.
6   Ask children working online to note down in a designated place what they have needed to know and do, as they go. Encourage an environment of sharing information, and of children helping each other.

7 Compile all stories, illustrations, and discovery descriptions.

8 Compile these into a class book that can be called 'Tucker', or whatever other name the class likes.

9 Set this book up on a table in the classroom and invite members of other classes to come and read it at suitable times.

Years 5–6

This task can be adapted for Years 5–6 by expanding the 'discovery description', and by setting the children a research assignment to explore other texts depicting the food traditions of different cultures.

Years K–2

This task can also be adapted for Years K–2. Begin discussions by asking the class to tell about favourite foods—write them on the board. Note how everyone has different favourites. Discuss how people are different, even in the same family. Discuss some of the foods their parents like that they don't like. Emphasise the difference.

Read *Tucker* to the class. Ask them to tell about food traditions—special cakes and special foods for festivals such as Christmas and birthdays. What special birthday cake do they ask for? Tell them your favourite cake. Children may mention festivals such as Christmas and Easter, Hanukkah, and Ramadan.

Also read *Let's Eat!* by Ana Zamorano and Julie Vivas (1996).

So we have to eat without my brother.
"Ay, qué pena!" sighs Mamá.

Writing, speaking, and listening

As the 'Tucker' activity demonstrates, it is clear that as well as developing knowing readers, literature also helps to create

Literature builds knowing readers, writers, speakers, and listeners

- knowing writers, by giving children access to a variety of purposeful models, in traditional and online formats
- knowing speakers, both because of the exposure to the speaking of others beyond their immediate world (i.e. in literary texts) and because of the classroom speaking that takes place in response to literature. Class could even watch snippets of some TV cooking shows, and discuss the different ways language is used. What effect does this have?
- knowing listeners, listening with both 'inner' and 'outer' ears, not in a physical sense but in a personal one. Listening is more than hearing; it is possible to hear but not listen—consider background music in shopping centres, or a television on when one is doing something else. Listening is integral to the development of oral skills but it does not produce sound, as speaking does, nor a physical product, as writing does. Listening, like literacy in all its forms, is complex, perhaps more private than public. It is attending to, and a directing of attention. Literature gives many opportunities for motivated listening.

IN THE CLASSROOM

Years K–2

Let the children sit comfortably. Tell them you are going to read them a story and that you want them to listen carefully. Ask them to draw a picture of each animal they hear you mention. If appropriate, they could write the name of the animal. You are also going to play some soft music, and will pause between 'scenes'.

Read *Time for Bed*, by Mem Fox and Jane Dyer (1993). Play some music, then turn the tape down a little and read the first lines:

> It's time for bed, little mouse, little mouse,
> Darkness is falling all over the house.

Pause, with music gently turned up. This is an individual activity. Then continue. When finished, ask the children to tell you about the animals and write their names on the board. You may like children to choose their favourite picture and write their own story about it.

Pass the book around the class so children can link what they have heard and the mind-pictures they formed with the actual text.

Years 3–4

As above, but read *My Many Coloured Days* by Dr Seuss (1998). Play a suitable tape, and ask the children to sketch the colour and main thought of each scene:

> On Bright Red Days
> how good it feels
> to be a horse
> and kick my heels!

The first two openings are more abstract; inform the class that you will reread those at the end so that they can represent what they hear in a more informed way (when they have knowledge about the rest of the text). Circulate the book at the end.

Years 5–6

Introduce children to the idea of the literary factual text—books that convey 'real' information about a particular topic but that do so in a literary way, perhaps in story or in creative pictures or both. The increasing number of literary factual texts being published provides a rich classroom resource.

Read *Chameleons are Cool* by Martin Jenkins and Sue Shields (1997). Choose suitable music and proceed as above. Ask children to note down as many facts as they can while you read. Pause at each page turn:

> Some lizards eat bananas—chameleons don't
> Some lizards walk upside down on the ceiling—chameleons can't.
> There's even a lizard that glides from tree to tree—
> A chameleon certainly won't do that!

You could also use books such as *To the Moon and Back: The amazing Australians at the forefront of space travel plus fantastic moon facts*, by Bryan Sullivan with Jackie French (2004), *Gogo Fish!* by John Long (2004), *Animal Architects*, by John Nicholson (2003), *The Gallipoli Story*, by Patrick Carlyon (2003), *Art, History, Place,* by Christine Nicholls (2003), *Bush Babies*, by Kim Dale (2003), *I Know How We Fight Germs*, by Kate Rowan and Katherine McEwen (1988) and *A Street Through Time: A 12,000 year journey along the same street*, illustrated by Steve Noon and written by Dr Anne Millard (1998).

Websites of Children's Literature organisations provide excellent resources

Note that the Children's Book Council of Australia has a category for literary factual texts: the Eve Pownall Award for Information Books. Check out all CBC Awards at http://www.cbc.org.au/

Extension and secondary students

Play-reading provides opportunities for speaking and listening in a dramatic context. David Almond's *Wild Girl, Wild Boy* (2002) is an example of a play that lends itself to reading, even choral reading, as well as to listening. Sit the class in a circle, or in several circles to represent the different characters. Have each circle talk about the characters they represent before reading one of the scenes. Have the other circle listen to what is said, and discuss what they hear. Alternatively, have the rest of the class close their eyes (perhaps heads on desks) and listen for what is actually being said as some read the chorus of voices in Scene 2 and Scene 11.

Think about how sound is represented in texts other than aural ones—how is volume represented in print? What purpose does the soundtrack play in films and videos and DVDs?

WHAT EFFECT DO CAPITAL LETTERS, FOR EXAMPLE IN AN EMAIL, HAVE?

The interconnectedness of reading and writing

Literature, like language, is dynamic; it is significant and can be life-changing. And for the purposes of teaching children literacy, it is crucial to see in literature the intrinsic connectedness of the processes and practices of author (writing) and reader (reading). Literature in the classroom is an experience and may include everything and anything that is a part of this reading and this writing and this moment. It also includes the listening and the speaking of this moment.

It is also important to remember that while reading (the physical and cognitive process) may end when the book is closed, *reading* (dialoguing with one's own experience and worldview, past, present, and yet to come), and the role of the reader in what Bakhtin calls 'renewing the work of art' and taking it along into one's personal and private world—all this may continue for a lifetime. Reading, as well as writing, is a creative act: 'The work and the world represented in it enter the real world and enrich it, and the real world enters the work and its world as part of the process of its creation, as well as part of its subsequent life, in a continual renewing of the work through the creative perception of listeners and readers' (Bakhtin 1981: 254).

This is a realistic and helpful notion of literature for us as teachers because

- it draws attention to literature as part of the literate practices of reading and writing, speaking and listening
- it opens up windows of opportunity for discussion and exploration into a range of diverse areas, using multiple modes of discovery
- it gives children the flexibility to relate literature more authentically to their world

► Summary

1 Literature produced for children is a dynamic and fertile resource for the expanding practices and experiences of language and literacy in a digital age.

2 Increasing access to digital texts has resulted in a shifting landscape of new ideas about image as text, new ideas about contexts for text, new ideas about what language looks like, and new ideas about what constitutes literature.

3 Each context for text requires its own modes of literate behaviours, its own particular use of language. This relates to the idea of *register*: the variety of language used in different social situations (contexts); the need to choose language appropriate to audience, purpose, time, and place.

4 The contemporary emphasis on the words and images of communication is reinforcing the status of the crafted literary text. Arguably the most subtle and most magic of images are those created in minds, by words.

5 Language is powerful and articulates who and what we are.

6 Literature is applied language.

7 Children's literature is a mosaic of all aspects of literacy: reading, writing, speaking, and listening.

8 Children need to be encouraged to become knowing readers. Having access to as many books as possible, from as young an age as possible, will help children become knowing readers. Having access to as many contexts for text—that is, multimodes of text—helps children to learn and develop the specific literate skills and behaviours that are most appropriate (multiliteracies).

9 Cultural literacy has two significant aspects: knowledge of the world and the knowledge, understanding, and appreciation of diverse ways of being.

10 Knowledge of the world is sometimes called cultural schemata and relates to all the many pieces of knowledge that are used in order to make sense of language and the social structures within which we live.

11 The knowledge, understanding, and appreciation of diverse ways of being refers to more than the recognition of otherness; it means being aware of the integrity of many possible worlds, many different ways of doing things, and many different ways of thinking.

12 Engagement with literature, and with a literary text, can continue after the actual reading event.

13 Children's literature is a vital part of a lifelong participation and engagement in literature.

Further reading

Austin, J. L. 1962, *How to Do Things with Words*, Harvard University Press, Cambridge, Mass.

Bakhtin, M. M. 1986, *Speech Genres and Other Late Essays*, trans. V. W.McGee, ed. C. Emerson & M. Holquist, University of Texas Press.

Booth, W. C. 1988, *The Company We Keep: An ethics of fiction*. University of California Press, Berkeley, Calif.

Butler, J. 1990, *Gender Trouble: Feminism and the subversion of identity*, Routledge, London.

Clark, A. 1997, *Being There: Putting brain, body and mind together again*, MIT Press: Cambridge, Mass.

Derrida, J. 1991, 'Signature event context'. In P. Kamuf (ed.) *Between the Blinds: A Derrida reader*, Harvester Wheatsheaf, Hemel Hempstead, UK, pp. 82–111.

Gibbons, M., C. Limoges, H. Nowotny, S. Schwartzman, P. Scott & M. Trow 1994, *The New Production of Knowledge: The dynamics of science and research in contemporary societies*, Sage, London.

Johnston, R. R. 2000, 'The literacy of the imagination', *Bookbird* 38(1): 25–30.

Klein, J. T. 1996. *Crossing Boundaries: Knowledge, disciplinarities and interdisciplinarities.* Charlottesville, Va, University Press of Virginia.

Kress, G. (ed.) 1988, *Communication and Culture*, UNSW Press, Sydney.

Kress, G. & T. van Leeuwen 1996, *Reading Images: The grammar of visual design*, Routledge, London and New York.

Landow, G. P. 1992, *Hypertext: The convergence of contemporary critical theory and technology*, Johns Hopkins University Press, Baltimore and London.

Mackie, M. 2002, *Literacies Across Media: Playing the text*, Routledge, London and New York.

Maher, J. & J. Groves 1996, *Chomsky for Beginners*, Icon Books, Cambridge.

Morson, G. S. & C. Emerson 1990, *Mikhail Bakhtin: Creation of a Prosaics*, Stanford University Press.

Papert, S. in C. Johnston 1999, 'Children need to have hard fun,' *Times Educational Supplement* 3 September.

Children's literature websites

Teachers and students are encouraged to explore these and the rich information they contain. Some sites also have information about conferences and in-service opportunities. Go visiting!

http://www.acs.ucalgary.ca/~dkbrown/ (University of Calgary, Canada)

http://www.scils.rutgers.edu/~kvander/ChildrenLit/index.html (Kay Vandergrift at Rutgers State University, New Jersey)

http://www.ibby.org (International Board on Books for Young People)

http://www.cbc.org.au/ (Children's Book Council of Australia)

http://www.irscl.ac.uk (International Research Society for Children's Literature: check news of new publications and upcoming conferences)

http://www.scholastic.com.au

WHAT IS CHILDREN'S LITERATURE?

21

Overview

This chapter sets children's literature in postmodern contexts and explores how ideas of literature have changed, and how ideas of literacy continue to evolve. It describes children's literature as part of a literary and artistic continuum, as a fertile field of literary and cultural study, and as a rich resource for teachers, children, and parents.

Children's literature is now firmly established as a field of rigorous academic investigation and study at both undergraduate and postgraduate level in many countries. That courses in children's literature appear in different faculties in different universities—education, arts and humanities, cultural studies, social sciences, sociology, nursing—is an indicator of the many-faceted significance of this subject. Teachers, publishers, editors, writers and illustrators, librarians, journalists, psychologists, and sociologists comprise many of its students.

Professional organisations such as the International Research Society for Children's Literature and the Children's Literature Association provide forums for scholars from all over the world to share their expertise and research interests. Journals address, from a variety of perspectives, practical and theoretical approaches to historical and contemporary issues and ideas in the world of children's books.

Children's literature is usually defined as *literature for children* or, less commonly, as *literature of children*. Leaving aside the question of what constitutes 'literature', the preposition showing the relationship between *literature* and *children* is revealing. If this literature is *for* children it tends to open up obvious questions about positions of power, and about cultural and narrative ideologies and judgments: who makes the decision about the type of literature that is designed for children, and so on. The literature *of* children implies more agency on the part of the child, not as producer necessarily but as *owner*. The dilemma of children's literature is not only that so many people who are not children are involved in its processes, but that everyone has once had the experience of being a child, and therefore is a stakeholder—and an expert!

Ideas of 'literature'

The debate over what constitutes 'literature' There has always been debate about what constitutes 'literature'—in the past this has focused on an idea of quality that is 'high' (for the select) and 'low' (for the general population). There has even been a belief in some quarters that if a text is 'popular' (almost a dirty word!) it isn't 'literature.' In a lovely introduction to an edition of L. M. Montgomery's *Anne of Green Gables* (1991), novelist Margaret Atwood writes, of *Anne*, 'If it's that popular, you feel, it can't possibly be good, or good for you.' Yet Atwood goes on to place *Anne* in the orphan-heroine tradition of *Jane Eyre, Oliver Twist, Great Expectations,* and *The Secret Garden,* the fairytale tradition of *The Ugly Duckling*, and the fable tradition of the magic child who 'appears, as it seems from nowhere—like King Arthur—and proves to have qualities far superior to anyone around her'.

These connections indicate the fluidity, hybridisation, and cross-fertilisation of ideas that occur in any culture, and indeed across cultures, in story narratives.

Postmodernism, with its collapse of hierarchies, has shed such notions of 'high' and 'low culture', 'literary' and 'non-literary' texts, challenging the idea of 'grand narratives'—theories that purport to express universal 'truths'. Postmodernism asks questions about perspectives ('whose truth?') and has sought new, inclusive ways of thinking, and new **The effects of** equities. Ironically, its pervasiveness has created its own grand narrative, and **postmodernism** postmodernism has influenced and continues to influence not only literature but all the creative arts, engineering, architecture, religion, business.

We know that literature has emerged from strong oral traditions, but since Gutenberg's invention of the printing press in 1440 (and notwithstanding earlier efforts in using movable type in Korea, China and Japan) the West has held to the concept of literature not only as something made permanent—in its presentation as an artefact, in book form—but as something accorded power and respect. The late Palestinian professor of comparative literature at Columbia University in New York, Edward Said, attributed part of the ascendancy of the British Empire to the rise of the great English novel that occurred in the middle to late nineteenth century. Said (pronounced 'Say-id') believed that the novel by the 1840s had 'achieved eminence' as both aesthetic form and 'major intellectual voice' (1993–94: 85). He points to novels—literature—as a major contributing factor not only in constructing the power of the Empire but in constructing what were to become stereotypical ideas about the 'Orient', about 'natives', and about power. It was, he said, in the 'great cultural archive' that intellectual ideas and 'aesthetics in overseas dominion are made' (1993–94: xxiv).

In a completely different context, Kress & Van Leewen (1996: 20) argue that common belief in the superiority of the written word has not only tended to denigrate 'oral culture' but has similarly denigrated those cultures that, because they had no written language and communicated through visual signs, have been branded 'illiterate'. This will be discussed further in chapter 29.

Both these ideas are interesting in terms of children's literature. The idea of a 'great cultural archive' has particular relevance when we consider the protective way in which some people remember their childhoods and the books associated with it. There is a shared heritage of literature for children—for example, most English speakers, but many children from other countries as well, know about *Alice in Wonderland*, or *The Wind in the Willows*, and have come across them in some form of retelling, even if they haven't actually read the originals. So such books become arguably not only part of a nation's socioliterary capital, but part of a shared remembered environment for adults, a sort of retrospective community of cultural camaraderie. The attribution of quality to these books endows the ideologies they espouse with a type of cultural endorsement.

▶ LITERACY IN THE DIGITAL AGE

Digital multimedia in all sorts of ways has extended the reach of books, and the ways in which children can interact with story narratives.

Unsworth (2005: 2–4) describes the contemporary articulation of book and computer-based literary narratives in three main categories:

1   as *augmented* literary texts: literature published in book format only, but augmented with online resources that offer additional information about the writing of the book, the author, the characters, and so on.

2   as *recontextualised* literary texts: literature re-published as a CD ROM, or online in a variety of forms that may include free digital libraries (in which books out of copyright are transcribed or scanned), contemporary stories provided by publishers that can be downloaded at a cost, and audiofiles of current titles, which can also be downloaded at a small cost.

3   as digitally originated literary texts: literature published in digital format only, occasionally on CD ROM but more often on the Web in various forms.

Critical thinking and study exercises

Critical focus: e-literature

It is crucially important that teachers not only become familiar with what is currently available through digital media, but that they develop a readiness to engage with change. Anything currently available is likely to be upgraded, even refigured in a new technology, perhaps before this edition gets to print. Checking resources, I have discovered that some no longer exist, and that some have completely altered both what they offer and how. This highlights the need for conscious and conscientious research vigilance. It is another type of professional development, not only upgrading knowledge but the ways that knowledge is approached, to maximise the benefit in classrooms of all available and relevant ICTs.

1   Read or re-read either (or both) Philip Pullman's trilogy *His Dark Materials,* or any of the *Harry Potter* series.

2   Read chapters 3 and 4 of *E-Literature for Children: Enhancing digital literacy learning* (Unsworth 2006).

3   Go to the Pullman website sponsored by Random House: http://www.randomhouse.com/features/pullman/index.html

4   Go to the J.K. Rowling official website: http://jkrowling.com/

5 Explore the sites thoroughly, noting what skills you need to do so.

6 Using some of the material in the Unsworth book, reflect on ways in which you could use this material in the classroom. Consider how you will interface this material with the reading of the book, how you will manage the classroom (Will you have all children doing the same thing at the same time, or will you stagger the activities? Will you have some group times and some full-class sharing times? What sorts of choices will you offer children? How are you going to ensure that all children have the computer skills they need?)

7 How are you going to bring the learning experiences together—or do you need to?

8 How does using this material develop different skills and open up different possibilities for the children? Or is this just transplanting traditional approaches to new media? If so, are there imaginative ways that you can enlarge classroom experience?

9 Do a search of similar websites and compile a resource list.

Scholastic Book Club Online
http://www.scholastic.com.au/schools/curriculum/

Through Big Books and Book Clubs, Scholastic Australia has made a significant contribution to developing children's reading in both Australia and New Zealand.

Scholastic introduced the Book Club into Australian schools in 1971, at a time when there were relatively few children's books available (they had been introduced in New Zealand a few years earlier by the H. J. Ashton company). The program was supported by state departments of education. Over 90 million books have been distributed through Book Clubs.

Scholastic has a number of online resources that support teachers and children. For teachers, these include:

■ The Lexile Framework which is an online way of matching readers and books at www.mylexile.com.au

■ Free teaching notes that are made available for many of Scholastic's publications in the Curriculum Resources section of the website at http://www.scholastic.com.au/schools/curriculum/ and also through Book Club at http://www.scholastic.com.au/schools/bookclub/club_downloads_tbs.asp

■ Downloadable lesson plans and blackline masters that are made available exclusively to Book Club Bonus teachers.

For children, there is a constantly changing range of activities and information about authors and illustrators to be found at http://www.scholastic.com.au/kids/.

Ideas of 'childhood' and 'the child'

Childhood is also a very debated and subjective concept. It may be a state of remembered innocence or selfishness, holiness or unholiness. Childhood, where children live, is a space that each of us has inhabited, and that each of us now remembers in a particular way. Different cultures have different ideas about children and their relationships to society. Childhood is therefore a common but highly contested space, often loaded with nostalgia.

Views of 'the child'

The concept of *the child* is similarly a contested construct. Children in stories have been diversely represented over time as small adults, as angels, and as little devils. Norman Lindsay, both as a topical cartoonist for the *Bulletin* and as an artist, drew his small boys as 'greedy, lawless, graceless, profane'; Lindsay's biographer describes these depictions as 'little monsters, perhaps, but fearsomely authentic'. Hetherington says that these 'pleased Lindsay and pleased the *Bulletin*, but they did not please everybody'; there were 'letters of protest from sentimental adults who objected that little children were not like that' (1973: 67). Michael Benton, writing on the representations of the child in painting and literature in the period 1700–1900, describes six images in three oppositional pairs: the polite/impolite child, the innocent/sinful child, the authentic/sanitised child. His seventh representation is that of the holy child, usually with the Virgin Mary, which he describes as 'that superordinate icon which influences all writers and painters in western culture'. Benton notes that each age reinvents the child in its own image, and concludes: 'The image of childhood, in all its manifestations, was generally a construction by adults of the child they wanted to see' (1996: 57, 58–9).

Critical thinking and study exercises

Critical focus: Ideological constructions of 'the child'

It is important that teachers and all those working with children have an understanding of these ideas about the sociocultural construction of 'the child'.

1 Read Benton's paper in the international journal *Children's Literature in Education* 27(1) 1996 and critically annotate it as part of a bibliography.
2 Choose a particular period of approximately fifty years. Referring to at least five literary works containing child characters (poems, plays, books, and children's books), describe the image of the child that seems to emerge.

Discuss possible reasons for this.

This activity, designed for trainee teachers, can be modified into a useful task for secondary school students (perhaps with a focus on the representation of the adolescent and adolescence), and can also be adapted for upper primary school children. Compiling an annotated bibliography is a *literate practice* (see Morley-Warner 2000). Helping children to understand constructions and representations of childhood assists critical literacy (see chapter 19).

 I**N THE CLASSROOM**

Years 5–6

1 Choose five advertisements that feature children from as many different media as possible: televison, magazines, newspapers, computer advertising.
2 In small groups, ask the children to tell each other about the features of the child—Clean? Dirty? Attractive? Good clothes? Shabby clothes? Naughty? Good? Lots of friends? Lonely? Siblings? Parents? House? Bedroom? Tidy? Untidy? Toys?
3 Make a group list. Discuss the reasons that the advertiser has chosen to depict the child in this way.
4 Each group reports back to the class.
5 The class compiles a list of representations of different images (in words or pictures) of the child and posts examples.

Towards a definition

So, as we have seen, the term *literature* has become controversial in a postmodern, digital world. For our purposes, literature is a body of writing—fictional and factual—that includes novels, poetry, drama, biographies and autobiographies, and essays; it may also include other writings in fields such as philosophy, history, and science (think of the books of Stephen Hawking and Paul Davies). Literature is usually read in a written form, but can be performed, and in an age of new technologies may be printed or broadcast electronically as e-literature. The narratives of electronic games are not in my view literature, but they do share some literary elements—story, characters, setting, script, role-play. As such, and because of children's eagerness to play them, they can be used beneficially to develop literary awareness of these elements.

Literature is the expression of the human need to communicate, as readers and/or writers, as speakers and/or listeners, using or transgressing particular conventions and narrative modes. It is story shared, in a sustained form. The best of literature probably tells humankind's deepest stories, and addresses its deepest concerns, in a way that is not only artistically and aesthetically satisfying, but engages both senses and intellect.

Children's literature is literature that is usually written by adults, *for* children and *to* children. Thus it can become a complex revelation of what societies are concerned about and how they see themselves. The history of children's literature clearly reveals pedagogical concerns that in themselves reflect *confidence in the receptivity of the young* and *confidence in the power of story.*

Books for children were traditionally designed to 'teach' and 'socialise' and 'acculturate', in earlier times about religious and moral matters, and in later times about general education. **Literature is a body of cultural writings that reveals social and cultural concerns** Children's books of our time continue the tradition: many seek to teach (and implicitly or explicitly advocate particular stances) about the social issues that dominate contemporary political and social agendas, notably the environment, indigenous cultures, multiculturalism, the changing shape of families, and gender and gender roles.

However, children's literature is more than pedagogy and advocacy. It invites children into corporate story, and into participation in the ongoing search, which continues to confront and perplex adults, about what it is to be human. It offers the opportunity to dip into those 'deepest stories' of living: stories about change, frailty, failure, success, loss, growth, mortality and ideas of immortality, and the gamut of human emotions associated with these.

Children's literature is an artistically mediated form of communication—a conversation—that a society has with its young. It is shaped by the concerns of the many stakeholders that are part of the 'world that creates the text' (Bakhtin 1981: 253): authors and illustrators, editors and publishers, educators and critics, as well as parents and children.

Children's literature texts are characteristically forms of prose narrative, although they may also include poetry, drama, and factual writings. They have adapted the basic structure of the novel to meet the needs of their readers, and use plot, characterisation, and **Picturebooks are a unique adaptation of the novel** motivation. The protagonist is generally a child, or a stand-in child, which may be an animal or toy. Picturebooks are a unique adaptation of the novel form: very short, and using visual as well as verbal text for the carriage of story (see chapter 28).

Children's literature as *literature*

Children's literature is not something 'less than' literature—it is *part of a literature continuum*. Peter Hollindale has commented that literature read by children is children's literature (1997: 27–8); the point is that it is *literature*, no matter who is reading it. This needs to be reiterated and become an assumption underpinning the way we treat books in the classroom. Young children reading Maurice Sendak, or the Brothers Grimm, or one of the Ahlberg texts, or a Margaret Wild or Allan Baillie picturebook, are reading literature, according to their physical and intellectual capacities.

This idea of a continuum, however, means that children need a diet that is not wholly made up of 'children's books'. Continual opportunities must be made for all children to be exposed to a wide range of texts from a continuum that is continuously being supplemented and enriched with digital and other literary resources.

Exposure beyond immediate needs

Isabella and Evelyn, both aged 2, enjoy Margaret Mahy and Tim Winton. Samuel, aged 1, enters into the world of books, and Luke, aged 6 months, hears and sees that books contain story.

Sometimes, as educators, we tend to overestimate level of difficulty and underestimate the abilities of the child. Doonan notes Jerome Bruner's remarks that 'any subject could be taught to any child in an intellectually honest form at any stage of her development: it was simply a matter of finding a "courteous translation"' (1993: 49). We need to develop a similar philosophy and set about finding ways of introducing our students, courteously, to all sorts of material from across the literature continuum. This also fits in with the idea, first articulated in the context of literacy by Don Holdaway, of continually exposing children to books beyond their immediate needs—and, I would add, capacities (1979: 40).

Read aloud with children from babyhood

This is where Shared Reading (see chapter 9) is so important. Even after children can read for themselves, teachers need to continue to read with them, but to read books that are challenging, and that children may never pick up to read for themselves. *Children need to be read to and read with, even when they are competent, independent readers.*

When reading aloud to children, be bold and adventurous in the choice of texts and in your expectations of children's interactions with them. Interrogate by practice conventional ideas about the difficulty of certain texts. For example, the rhythms and rhymes of *Each Peach Pear Plum* by the Ahlbergs (1978) are not so very different from 'Ariel's Song' in Shakespeare's *The Tempest*:

> Each peach pear plum
> I spy Tom Thumb.
> Tom Thumb in the cupboard
> I spy Mother Hubbard.
> Mother Hubbard down the cellar
> I spy Cinderella.

(*Each Peach Pear Plum*)

> Where the bee sucks, there suck I:
> In a cowslip's bell I lie:
> There I couch when owls do cry.
> On the bat's back I do fly
> After summer merrily.
> Merrily, merrily shall I live now
> Under the blossoms that hang on the bough.

> (*The Tempest*)

Nor are they very different from Robert Frost's evocative lines:

> The woods are lovely, dark and deep,
> And I have promises to keep.
> And miles to go before I sleep,
> And miles to go before I sleep.

> ('Stopping By Woods on a Snowy Evening')

Allusions to the characters of nursery song and story are often no 'easier' or more readily 'known' than allusions to characters and things in poems and stories that are commonly categorised as 'literature'. These nursery characters, many of them arguably increasingly less appropriate to 21st-century children who are being encouraged to consider themselves as members of an international community, become a part of childhood knowledge achronologically (out of order, so to speak), just as the language of the Shakespeare and the Frost poems does. In fact, in *Each Peach Pear Plum* the words 'cellar', 'ditch', and 'den' are problematical in the sense that they are unlikely to be part of the average Australian small child's language. They may well be as far removed from that child's experience as the 'cowslip' of Ariel's song, and Frost's 'woods' (Australians know about the bush and the forest but 'woods' is not a term in common use).

Read such poetry to children, without worrying too much about explaining what it 'means'. In pedagogical practice, we have placed a lot of store on 'meaning' (a highly contested word in a postmodern world). But literature—like music, art, dance—is more than meaning (see Johnston 1997a). The formalists saw the essence of poetry as not what it means but what it sounds like, its euphony: its language and rhythm and cadence (Eichenbaum 1998). The symbolists stressed the importance of symbol and image. The point is that literature is a deep experience that we respond to in many different ways and at many different levels.

Literature is sound, rhythm, and 'feeling' as well as 'meaning'

Symbolism

Symbolism refers to a late-19th-century movement in French poetry that privileged symbolic over actual meanings. There was a similar movement in French art. It is interesting to read children's books, especially picturebooks, with a view to considering visual and verbal symbols and symbology (symbols of 'home', for example, and symbols of 'childhood').

Exposure to different ways of seeing the world

It is clear that books 'mean' different things to different people. This is precisely the reason children need to be exposed to a wide and diverse range of books from the whole continuum, including as a matter of course non-Western literature. It is also part of the development of cultural literacy.

In the classroom

A wonderful book for opening up discussions about different ways of seeing the world and different ways of using language is *A Caribbean Dozen*, a collection of Caribbean poetry edited by John Agard and Grace Nicholls (1994). Another is the Australian text *Do Not Go Around the Edges*, by Daisy Utemorrah and Pat Torres (1990).

Years K–2

1   Bring a mirror to class. Ask the children to look at themselves in the mirror. Then ask them to think about how they know that it is a reflection of themselves. Discuss at an appropriate level the idea of identity—of how clothes, hair colour, and language are part of their reflection. Does that tell the whole story about who they are? Ask them to tell you what other things make them who they are.

2   Read 'Who's Dat Girl?' from *A Caribbean Dozen*. Discuss how the language sounds different. What does that say about who we are? Explain any difficult words; perhaps have some props.

3   Ask children to draw a picture of themselves, showing all the things that make up who they are (family, where they live, where they used to live, how they feel about things).

Put pictures up in the classroom.

Follow-up: Do an online search on the Caribbean. Write the word on the board. Ensure that all children are familiar with a search engine, and with the idea of 'keyword'. Talk about the idea of 'keyword' in the poem ('girl'). Allow children to go exploring, and bring back any information they can relate to the poem.

Years 3–4

As above, but instead of the picture, ask the children to write a poem about seeing themselves in the mirror. Explain how poetry gives freedom from grammatical structure, allows the expression of personality in all sorts of different ways, and encourages variety of language (see chapter 28). Give an example of a structure if your class needs it:

> *I looked in the mirror*
> *And saw …*
> *   … hair,*
> *… eyes*
> *   …*
> *   But there was more …*
> *   …*
> *   …*
> *   Yes, that is me!*

(Note that this is an excellent model for encouraging creative writing in ESL and EFL classrooms. Children who are learning another language relish the freedom that writing poetry can give, and also enjoy telling their own story in different ways. Offer them opportunities to illustrate their work, or to bring in some of their own music, or books in their own language. Note too that this activity can be enlarged to explore e-poetry online. See also chapter 28.)

Years 5–6

1 Begin with as much of the above as you would like.

2 Then read *Do Not Go Around the Edges* with the class. Read in a comfortable situation if you can, and have the children as close as possible to the book.

3 Point out that this is a triple text. It contains:

   a an autobiography (life story)

   b a poetic response to Daisy's life story

   b a picture, showing another sort of response.

4 Discuss with the class the simplicity of the autobiographical sentences. Tell them that autobiography is interesting to write because we are all experts about our own lives. (If you have not covered this earlier, discuss the differences between autobiography and biography.) Refer to biographies online—author pages are a useful resource. Encourage children to share interesting sites, and to compare different ways of telling a life story: starting at birth and working forwards, or starting from the present and working backwards.

5 Ask the class to listen carefully to what they think the poems are saying about how Daisy feels now. Discuss the idea of listening with an inner ear (hearing beyond the words). Ask them to tell you what feelings and thoughts and emotions the words of the poems express that the sentences of autobiography don't.

6 In roundtable groups, or as a class, ask the children to discuss what the pictures express and what they add to the text.

7 Begin an Autobiography Project, modelled on this book, but encourage creativity. The class will produce a written autobiographical text and a poetic response to it, but may choose to do so in either written or computer text. Discuss structure: how many pages do you want, how do you want them to present their work? Encourage visuals as well—some children may like to use computer graphics, make a montage, or paint, or include a photograph as a basis for further artistic expression. If you have a scanner available, they can produce mixed media visuals.

8 Play some background music as the children work. Ask the children to bring in any tapes or CDs suitable for use in this way.

9 Use this unit either to extend or develop a continuing theme focusing on indigenous literature. Discuss the idea of 'indigenous' and explore the word 'aboriginal'—it is not a specifically Australian term but is used in other countries such as Canada as well.

Extension Activities, Year 6

Read the first chapters of *Deadly Unna*, by Phillip Gwynne (1999). (This is classified as a 'Young Adult' book; check that you are comfortable with the subject matter and language.) Read in an informal context (take the class out to the playground, or have them sit on mats on the floor, or in a circle, or read in the library). Focus on the enjoyment and challenge of a shared story. This book will open up many opportunities for discussion and enquiry, for example: 'It's like they're playing another game, with completely different rules' (p. 5).

Do you think these words describe more than a football game?

Talk about the use of the first person. What effect does it have? (The reader hears an authentic adolescent voice, understands the narrator's point of view, may feel closer to the action, may be limited to the narrator's perspectives.)

Secondary students

This activity is particularly suited to secondary students as they begin to study ideas of life story, identity, and subjectivity. It could be used as an introduction to such diverse texts as *David Copperfield* (Charles Dickens),

The Catcher in the Rye (J. D. Salinger), *Away* (Michael Gow), *A Fortunate Life* (A. B. Facey), *Wild Swans* (Jung Chang), *The True History of the Kelly Gang* (Peter Carey), *Bush Tucker Man* (Les Hiddins), or *My Place* (Sally Morgan). How are biography and autobiography shaped in narrative as personal/inner/imaginative journey? Utemorrah & Torres present three different artistic viewpoints on the past. What viewpoints do these texts create? How is time constructed? How many places (such as place then and place now) are constructed?

Read *The Book Thief* by Markus Zusak (2005), and consider the ways in which words can construct subjectivity, and construct life worlds. Refer to the discussion of the relationship of speech to identity in chapter 20.

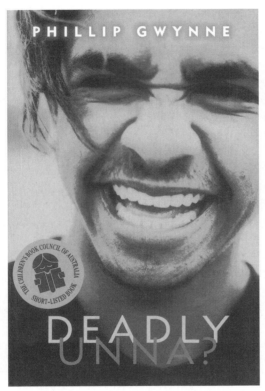

Explore online resources in all areas touched on in this bracket of lessons, and encourage each child to design a discovery activity on a related topic (biography and autobiography, life story, oral history, the Caribbean, indigenous literature). A possible question to be explored could be: 'What do poems such as 'Who's dat girl?' and Australian indigenous literature have in common? (This fits in with areas related to Empire, colonisation, postcolonialism, English as a world language or lingua franca, and the right of speakers of other languages to develop a form of English that suits them. Such discussion can focus on the question of 'what is language?', and becomes part of a discussion of visual literacy).

Teachers' reading

When appropriate, books on related themes will be suggested for teachers' enjoyment. *Angela's Ashes* by Frank McCourt (1996) tells the story of the author's early life in Ireland. *French Lessons* by Alice Kaplan (1993) is a postmodern intellectual autobiography about the power of learning a language other than one's own. A different type of autobiography again is found in Frances Mayes' *A Year in Tuscany* (1996) and *Bella Tuscany* (1999); while these are often categorised as travel books, they are more about inner journeying and the relationship between self and culture. Another different sort of autobiography is *The Bone Woman: Among the Dead in Rwanda, Bosnia, Croatia and Kosovo*, by Clea Koff (2004). Political autobiographies are also interesting, both for what they reveal about the inside workings of governments, and for a consideration of the ideologies espoused, and the way those ideologies formulate perspectives. Two recent interesting examples are *My Life*, by Bill Clinton (2004), and *Living History* (2003), by Hillary Clinton. The *Mark Latham Diaries* (2005) are not exactly autobiography, but they tell an intensely subjective but compelling story of the public years of a private life.

Multiliteracies

The above activity is one of many that lend themselves to debate. Both formal and informal debates are very worthwhile classroom activities, developing thinking, speaking, listening, and cooperative and collaborative skills.

Debates can also be reformulated into an online text activity. In this, the question is posted in whatever format most suits the classroom resources. The debate question should relate to some aspect of recent discussion, in any subject area.

Introducing the idea of the *e-debate*

I suggest that children are allowed to argue whichever side of the debate they choose, and that they argue anonymously (under an e-name), or as part of a role-play, in which they take on personas likely to have a vested influence in the debate question, arguing accordingly, e.g. an English teacher of the early 20th century, a contemporary English teacher, an indigenous writer, Shakespeare, the Prime Minister, a movie star, and so on.

After the *e-debate,* the class can choose speakers and develop the arguments into a more traditional debate. This opens all sorts of questions for discovery and class discussion:

1   What are the differences, if any, between speaking an argument and writing an argument? (discuss what the word 'argument' means in this context).
2   What factors are brought into play when arguments are spoken?
3   What factors are brought into play when arguments are written?
4   Why is listening, and reading critically, important?

Critical thinking and study exercises

Children's books and the literature of protest
This could also be developed into a suitable study for secondary and upper primary students. It is an alternative take on the old saying, 'Sticks and stones may break my bones but names will never hurt me.'

Words can constitute a language of power and agency; there is a very impressive world history of literature as protest—of texts that have changed the world, such as

■   Harriet Beecher Stowe, *Uncle Tom's Cabin*
■   Alexander Solzhenitsyn, *The Gulag Archipelago* 1918-1956, trans.Thomas P. Whitney, Collins, Melbourne.
■   Speeches by Martin Luther King, Winston Churchill.

■   Charles Dickens, *Hard Times*, *David Copperfield*, *Nicholas Nickleby*, *Oliver Twist*.

There are many texts that argue the case of the individual against oppression, or against changes in society that are believed to be detrimental, or against war. A segment of this study could focus on women's writing.

Critical focus: Language as power and agency

Texts can be as diverse as Eliot's 'The Wasteland', Paula Fox's *Slave Dancer*, Franz Kafka's *Metamorphosis*, Ken Kesey's *One Flew Over the Cuckoo's Nest*, George Orwell's *1984*, Wilfrid Owen's poems, Salinger's *The Catcher in the Rye*, Wordsworth's poems, Waris Dirie's *Desert Flower*, Toni Morrison's *Beloved*.

Consider the power of words. There is a Samoan saying that 'The young of birds are fed with flowers and fishbones but the young of humans are fed with words'. What does this mean?

Susan Price's *The Ghost Drum*, a book now unfortunately out of print, is a brilliant explication of the magic of words: ' … the sound of them, the use of them, the shock, the smart and soothing cool of them' (1987: 37). Chingis, the protagonist, is taught that 'Words can alter sight and hearing, taste, touch and smell. Used with a higher skill they can make our senses clear and protect us from the simpler magics'.

In Shakespeare's play, it is Mark Antony's word magic that changes how the mob feels about Caesar's death; Cassius warns Brutus:

> Know you how much the people may
> be moved
> By that which he will utter?

Words form, manipulate, change. To quote again from *The Ghost Drum*, consider this passage where Chingis is taught how words can be used by those in power:

> Suppose that a Czar or Czaritsa ordered their people to fight a war, a stupid war, a war that should never have been fought. Thousands of people are killed for no good reason and their families left to mourn them. Much, much money is spent on cannons and swords, so there is no money to spend on other, better, things … The Czar is afraid that if the people find out how foolish and wasteful the war was, they will be furious and do him harm. So the Czar uses word magic. He says to the people: 'The war was

> not foolish—no! It proved that our people are the bravest and best in the world because they died for us, and killed so many of the enemy. I know you are starving, my children, but that shows how noble you are and how willing to make sacrifices for the Motherland. I, your Czar, am proud of you!' He says this and repeats it over and over again, and he makes his servants repeat it over and over to everyone they meet—and the magic works. The people forget to be angry. They grow *glad* that their sons and brothers were killed, and proud that they themselves are cold and hungry. (1987: 36–7)

Consider this in relation to current events, and in conjunction with reading such books as *Onion Tears* (Diana Kidd), *Memorial* (Gary Crew and Shaun Tan 1999), *My Dog* (John Heffernan and Andrew McLean 2001), *In Flanders Fields* (Norman Jorgensen and Brian Harrison-Lever 2002).

Children's books of protest and advocacy

There are a remarkable number of children's books of protest and advocacy. These include the works of Jeannie Baker, *Where the Forest Meets the Sea, The Story of Rosy Dock, The Hidden Forest*; Anthony Browne's *Zoo*; Anthony Hill's *The Burnt Stick*; Brian Caswell and David Phu an Chiem's *Only the Heart*; Katherine Paterson's *Lyddie*; Arthur Slade's *Dust*; Anna Sewell's *Black Beauty*; Morris Gleitzman's *Girl Underground* and *Boy Overboard*.

Some protest can be unconsciously activated by the power of a personal story. Consider *The Diary of Anne Frank*, and discuss how the subjective voice exerts power. This could become an introduction to other Holocaust literature.

Literature and *jouissance*

As will be discussed in chapter 28, the language of children's books, and especially picturebooks, has much in common with poetry. Poetry is interior and exterior pictures—both the pictures that we see in front of us and the pictures-in-words and pictures-in-sounds that are a part of imagery. Poetry and literature are creative response as much as they are intellectual apprehension.

We need to remind ourselves of this. Just as we need to keep in mind the philosophical premise that as teachers we must continue to expose children to texts beyond their immediate capacities, so we must also continue to challenge ourselves. The theoretician Roland Barthes (1976) talks about the *jouissance*, the joy of the text, the pleasure of the text. In his discussions of this, Barthes makes the point that it is in persevering with texts that are difficult to understand that mere *plaisir* becomes *jouissance*, a term that is connected to orgasmic ecstasy!

Books give pleasure in many different ways

THE SCIENCE OF SIGNS AND SYMBOLS

Roland Barthes (1915–80) was a French literary critic who was particularly interested in semiotics, the science of signs and symbols. In *Mythologies* (1957) he looks at signs in everyday life, including in toys, advertisements, and wrestling. In *The Pleasure of the Text* (1970) he analyses literary text from a structuralist perspective that was to become increasingly unorthodox.

The structuralists were inspired by the work of the Swiss linguist Ferdinand de Saussure (1857–1913). They believed that texts should be analysed in terms of their structures and systems of relations.

Choose books from across the literary continuum

As adults, we are 'guests at the table of children's literature' (Hollindale 1997: 29). But the table is a long one, and it is groaning with the richness of its fare. Nor are the plates always arranged in carefully separated categories—suitable for children, suitable for adults. Just as children's books can 'replenish the completeness of a strenuous adult mind' (Hollindale 1997: 36), so texts from the wider corpus of literature can help to develop a taste for all sorts of different flavours and textures, and nourish the fledgling growth that will become that adult mind.

Literature and ideology

A cautionary note, however. The literature-based curriculum has been a boon to classroom teachers but this does not imply that books are simply a tool or resource for teaching practice. Children's books—highly visual, highly energetic, highly contemporary—are wonderful resources, and while these chapters will demonstrate many ways of using books for teaching purposes, books are much, much more than just teaching aids. It is important for teachers to keep reminding themselves of this and to reflect on the ways they use books in the classroom.

In this technological age, books are still 'wonder books'. It has become unfashionable and even suspect (as if one is ignorant of literary theory) to talk about books purely in terms of life enhancement, but we need to restore into the academy the simple acknowledgment of the fact that books give pleasure and they enhance lives. They would not exist if they didn't.

Use books in the classroom; but most of all, remember that books are to be enjoyed

However, it is also important to note and to help students understand the undoubted fact that literature reflects cultural ideologies. It not only contains *themes* that are ideologically constructed—that is, that emerge out of the writer's assumptions and beliefs about the world he or she inhabits, or out of that specific society's implicit beliefs about itself that spill over into the background world of the text, sometimes without the writer even knowing—but it also constructs its *narrative* in ways that are influenced by ideology. John Stephens argues a theory of narrative that among other things sees narrative structure as an 'ideologically powerful component of texts' (1992: 6). The decisions made by the author as to what is included and how it is represented can encourage and coerce readers into responding in particular ways. The preceding classroom activity has also highlighted the ways that language itself reflects ideologies: first, ideologies of traditional correctness, which thus implicitly attribute power to those who are able to use the language in that way, and implicitly marginalise those who cannot; and second, ideologies such as those underlying indigenous stories from many previous English colonies—that language can be used in whatever way a group of people decide is most appropriate to their country, their need, and their moment.

Every text is culturally and ideologically encoded in both what it says and how it says it. In Barthes' words, 'No text is innocent'. Even so, and indeed because of this, texts are living artefacts, anthropological and archaeological remains of the *past*—of what it was *to be* in that past and of what its culture *thought* it was to be—and sociological documents of the *present*.

If we look at any one of a number of Shirley Hughes' books, for example, we see a background picture that may be quite separate from the actual story of the book.

The picture above, seen through Hughes' eyes, is of life in a particular slice of 20th-century England: what the houses look like, what people wear, what they do, what activities are happening, what food is on the table, what the children are doing, how the children relate to their parents and the parents to their children and so on. We see what Hughes wants us to see; that is part of what I mean about narrative structure (and illustrations) being an ideological choice. She does not choose to depict a mugging or a bag-snatching incident, for example—but then, such things may not commonly occur in the suburbs that she draws anyway. And even that choice becomes significant when we consider the text as an artefact made for the edification of the construct that our society has made of *the child*.

But it goes further than the intentions of the writer and/or illustrator. In composing the shapes and pictures of their texts, every writer and illustrator unconsciously reflects ideas and attitudes that are a part of the society and culture in which they live and out of which they are writing. When Mary Grant Bruce wrote the Billabong books in the first half of the 20th century, she did not mean to be racist or classist but she unconsciously reflected the prevailing implicit cultural and national ideas of her time. Thus the book becomes ideologically marked, a representation of much more than the author ever intended. It is interesting that it is in fact the ideology that has dated such books as Billabong, Biggles, and Enid Blyton's works—and that this is what has had to be expunged in the 'sanitised', republished versions.

▶ LITERACY IN THE DIGITAL AGE

Survival of the book

Books are objects, but their essence is not in their physical form. The value of books is in the mysterious alchemy of words and narratives that somehow rises up to meet readers, privately and personally, as they engage with those black marks of print on the page. Whatever shape or form 'books' may take in the future, I am sure that *the book*—what it is within itself—will survive. In fact part of why it may survive is the very permanence of its current hard copy form, as opposed to the ephemerality of web-based material, and the propensity of children (and adults for that matter) to want to read and re-read favourites. The Web is an infinitely growing resource, but unless there are developments in the future that we cannot even imagine, it won't wipe out the book, although it may alter its look and format. Even if an electronic pocket book is developed that contains every book ever written available at the touch of a button, this would just be a different way of accessing 'books'. The exciting world of e-literature and of digital literacy resources is in fact opening up opportunities for children both at home and at school to explore book worlds and interact in fan clubs, MUDs and story palaces, and to chat and share creative ideas with others in worldwide clubs of readers and readership.

Literature as map

The latter part of the 20th century saw a growing contemporary interest in autobiography—'what writing is not [autobiographical]?' asked Sneja Gunew (1985: 107). As mentioned earlier, children's literature describes and reflects spaces that in some way are a part of a common story—the inhabiting of childhood by children. Its numerous texts constitute a type of map, an inner geography that some recognise at one point and some at another. A map gives us clues to who and where we are and helps us to claim our unique place and significance. The Canadian writer Aritha Van Herk, discovering a book written about Edmonton, remembers: 'Someone had dared to write about a place I knew, about me. I finally had a map … I now live somewhere, in a place created by Alice Monroe and Audrey Thomas, by Marian Engel and Matt Cohen, by Margaret Atwood and George Bowering … I have a map' (Olinder 1984: 71).

Such maps are of course highly subjective, and points of interest to some will be meaningless to others. Joy Hooton, in a critical study of autobiographies of childhood by Australian women, and discussing the significance of national identity as part of personal identity, writes:

Maps are subjective and culturally coded

The most striking aspect of the autobiographies studied here is that there are many different Australias. Not only is 'national' inappropriate as a descriptive term, but even 'regional' is too prescriptive, for, as George Seddon has commented, 'there is no such thing as an Australian environment,' but rather 'a great variety of different places' … Place depends on 'the logic of the perceiver's state of mind' and certainly one of the most liberating features of women's autobiography is the diversity of their subjective Australias. (1990: 341–2)

Children's literature is a map of childhood, and childhood is a diverse and subjective space. Children's literature reflects this diversity and offers children the opportunity to create their own maps and to traverse it in their own way. John Williamson's picturebook *Christmas in Australia* (and the accompanying CD; 1998) is a subjective representation of Christmas in just such a subjective Australia as Hooton describes, but there are bits that some of us may be able to relate to, if we want. *Shutting the Chooks In* by Libby Gleeson and Ann James (2003) is another version of a subjective, rural Australia; its charcoal and oil pastel illustrations poetically evoke the coming of dark that is part of the time tension of the verbal text:

Children's books offer different versions of maps through childhood

> Night has come.
> Time to run
> and run
> and run.

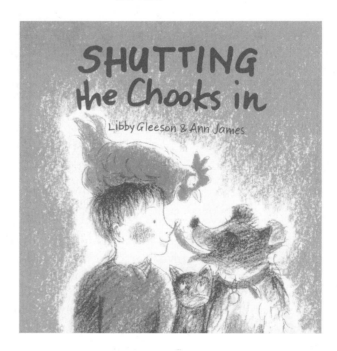

Tim Winton's *Lockie Leonard Legend* and *Blueback* (both 1997), Eleanor Spence's *Lillypilly Hill* (1960), *The Boundary Riders* (Joan Phipson 1962), Ivan Southall's *Hills End* (1962) and *Bread and Honey* (1970), *Storm Boy* (Colin Thiele 1963), *I am Susannah* (Libby Gleeson 1987), *Dancing in the Anzac Deli* (Nadia Wheatley 1984), *Beyond Duck River* (Angela Martin 2001),

Gordon Winch's *Rodney Thinks of Food* (2002), and Roland Harvey's *In the Bush* (2005) are other examples of different subjective Australias over several decades. Ursula Dubosarsky's novels for young readers give images of contemporary life in highly original stories and very elegant prose. Examples are *The Last Week in December* (1993), *The White Guinea Pig* (1994), and *The Game of the Goose* (2000).

Secondary and tertiary students may like to engage with the idea of a subjective Australia in relation to Winton's *Cloudstreet* (1991), *Dirt Music* (2001), and *The Turning* (2005). (For further discussion, see Johnston 1999, 2002c and 2004 'Australia').

Critical thinking and study questions

Critical focus: Subjectivity and subjective experience

1   Look through as many Australian picturebooks as you can.
2   List and briefly describe the different 'subjective Australias' that you find represented:

The bush	The suburbs
The city	The country
Schools	Play places
The beach	Holiday places
The house	Family and people

3   Note that what is part of the depiction of the everyday (background rather than foreground) is likely to be most revealing.
4   Think about and discuss the notion of your own 'subjective Australia'.

This task could be adapted to apply to the picturebooks of any country.

IN THE CLASSROOM

Years K–2

1   Make an overhead of one of the maps from Wheatley & Rawlins' *My Place* (choose a suitable opening).
2   Talk about the idea of maps. Ask children to discuss features of their home and neighbourhood.
3   Introduce ideas of the school as a place, a 'my place'. Ask the class to draw a map of the school, labelling as they are able.
4   Ask the children to tell you about their maps. Note that everyone sees the same place in a slightly different way, and that certain features are more important to some than to the others (the gate you come in by or leave by, for example).
5   If the class level is appropriate, you may like to draw a large composite map of the school. Divide into sections and give each group a section, then join the sections. Put up the map in class.

Years 3–4

1   Talk about the idea of books giving a map.
2   Look at *My Place*. Note the importance of the map. (It gives obvious coherence to the text and is part of the narrative structure.)
3   Ask the children to draw a map of their own place, with labels and notes, after the one in *My Place*. They can choose to do this using electronic resources.
4   Publish the maps around the classroom.

Years 5–6/secondary activities

As above, but add:

1 Encourage children to draw a map of all the spaces they inhabit: school, home, sport, family, friends, neighbourhood. Discuss.

2 Discuss ideas of ownership and of the land. You may want to relate this to other areas of the curriculum.

3 Discuss ideas of belonging to two lands: perhaps a country of birth and a new country (Australia). Share stories of different cultural backgrounds. Make a world map showing the represented countries.

4 Ask children to read John Marsden's *Tomorrow, When the War Began* (1994) (read the first few chapters in class). What ideas about land and ownership are debated within this book?

Extension activity, Year 6

Read *All in the Blue Unclouded Weather* by Robin Klein (1991). This is in part autobiographical. What picture of an Australian country town is seen in this book? When do you think this story is set? Teachers may like to read the class Tennyson's poem 'The Lady of Shalott' (the title of the book comes from a line in this poem). Why do you think the author chose this title?

> 'I love that poem,' Vivienne said. 'Specially that line that goes "All in the blue unclouded weather". It's like summer here in Wilgawa.' (Klein 1991: 57)

Ask the class to write a creative piece—poem or story—with this title.

Choose an episode in the book (each chapter tends to be an episode in a series of memories) and turn it into a playscript for either a stage or radio play (see 'The Literacy Session' in chapter 9). Choose appropriate accompanying music. Perform the play.

Teachers' reading

Dresses of Red and Gold is the sequel to *All in the Blue Unclouded Weather*. These books are not straight autobiographies but rather rememberings of memories given narrative shape: 'rememories'. *A Space for Delight* by Colleen Klein (1988) is a well-written and engrossing story about a woman looking back over her map of a subjective Australia.

An excellent book, set in France, which has recently been republished by Young Picador, and which is also semi-autobiographical, is *The Greengage Summer,* by Rumer Godden (first published 1958). This is a moving coming-of-age novel that is suitable for secondary students.

For those who want to explore ideas of memory more theoretically, read *Memory, History and Forgetting* (2004) by the eminent French philosopher Paul Ricoeur.

It is important to note that recognising maps and ideas about a subjective Australia—or a subjective France, for that matter—does not imply that we have to see ourselves in the text. Awareness of this freedom and of this choice is part of critical literacy (see chapter 22). Children don't have to identify (although some will) with the main character, or any other character for that matter. It is enough that they are for a moment viewing (observing) another equally valid way to be, which is being shaped in language.

Authors and texts

Children need the skills that will allow them to resist being manipulated into a particular reader position. Sometimes understandings of the author's background helps to achieve this. Although such ideas have been unpopular in recent literary criticism, there is no doubt that children are interested in authors: books seem to become more meaningful for them when they talk with their creators and discover, for example, that the Henry of *Henry's Bed* is a real-life boy, the son of the writer and illustrator (Perversi & Brooks 1997). We need to remind ourselves that literature is of both *reading* and *writing*. The author does not have to be 'dead' nor does the critically astute reader have to be without agency.

THE DEATH OF THE AUTHOR

Critical focus: Literary theories

Michel Foucault and Roland Barthes, in announcing the 'death of the author', were signalling the idea of the poststructuralists that the author was not the centre and principal organiser of the meaning of the text.

Poststructuralism is a theory of literature that seeks to interrogate any idea of absolute 'meanings' or 'truth' within a text, claiming that all underlying assumptions, ideas, and concepts in a literary text are open to valid questioning. In a nutshell, the poststructuralists believe that no text can mean what it seems to say, and that there are gaps and inconsistencies in all texts.

Reader response theory has grown out of poststructuralist thought. It proposes the idea that these gaps allow readers of the text to negotiate and create their own meanings.

Relationship to other genres: The *Bildungsroman*

Children's literature is a literature of growing. It commonly describes important aspects of development—the first day at school, the birth of a sibling, a significant adventure, the death of a grandparent, an epiphanal moment. It can be meaningfully related to the *Bildungsroman*, that is, the novel of development, of growing up. Everything in the *Bildungsroman*, according to Paul Ricoeur, 'seems to turn on the self-awakening of the central character' (1985: 9–10).

THE 'EDUCATION NOVEL'

The *Bildungsroman* (plural *Bildungsromane*) is a German term for the 'education novel', the novel of adolescence, of growing up, of development. It usually deals with emotional and psychological development. The original *Bildungsroman* is generally recognised as *Wilhelm Meister's Apprenticeship* (1795–96), by Johann Wolfgang von Goethe (1749–1832).

A Portrait of the Artist as a Young Man (1916) by the Irish writer James Joyce (1882–1941) is a well-known example of a 20th-century *Bildungsroman*. Children's books are commonly perceived as focusing on action rather than on character development, and so may superficially seem unrelated to the genre of the *Bildungsroman* as described by Ricoeur. However, let's consider *Each Peach Pear Plum* again.

This book is written in the first person, through the perspective and focalisation of the small child's seeing eye. (Note that **focalisation** is a technical term that alerts us to the fact that the writer has chosen to describe or depict an event from a particular viewing point, looking through particular eyes or listening with particular ears. Whose eyes we see through and whose ears we hear with in a text will tend to influence how we react as readers. (See 'Focalisation and agency' in chapter 24.)

Each Peach Pear Plum as an example of a growth journey

The child in the story looks around its world—the world of its books, itself an interesting depiction of the significance of books in a child's life—and makes connections, first to what it knows (the fictional characters in their own 'rhyme'), then by creating new connections between them and itself; that is, the child begins to write its own story. The conclusion is a triumph—everyone is now in the picture, in their place in the child's world. A moment of growing, of becoming more conscious of self in a world of others, has taken place. And doesn't the same thing happen to John Brown in *John Brown, Rose and the Midnight Cat*?

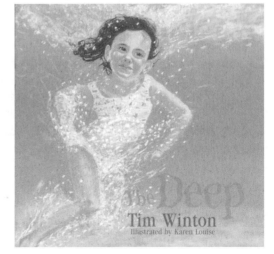

Tim Winton's *The Deep* (1998) tells about another type of growing (overcoming fear), and *Once There Were Giants* (Waddell & Dale 1989) is an interesting story about changing perspectives in which the protagonist, rather unusually for a picturebook, grows to adulthood.

A children's literature canon

Questions about definitions of children's literature open up debates about *canons*, that is, what some would define as an exclusive list that the 'Establishment' has set in place as a hierarchy of 'literary worth'. Power structures are based within some sort of ideological framework that influences decisions about acceptability and nonacceptability, in-ness and out-ness, inclusion and marginality. Ideas of a canon have become very unpopular, first because of the subjective nature of those assumptions, and second because of the groups such a hierarchy has actually excluded (groups pertaining to gender, race, and class). It is interesting to consider so-called 'classics' such as *Robinson Crusoe* (a book originally written for adults) and *The Wind in the Willows* in the light of questions about the position they assign to women, to ideas of 'lower classes' (e.g. the stoats and the weasels in *The Wind in the Willows*), and to ideas of Empire.

Books are coded to time and place, so ideas about worth and relevance differ

AN ELEMENTAL VIEW OF LITERATURE

'Literature', at its most elemental, refers to arrangements of words, formalised into particular shapes and patterns of idea and story, artistically mediated, and, in the modern period, made permanent in print. From the times of Ancient Greece, thinkers from all over the world have tried to analyse literature, to theorise it, and to evaluate it critically.

The Russian-born linguist *Roman Jacobson* wrote: 'The object of literary study is not literature but "literariness", that is, what makes a given work a literary work' (Rivkin and Ryan 1998: 8).

Jacobson (1896–1982) was born and educated in Moscow. In 1920 he left Moscow for Prague, where he produced a structural theory of language sounds. After being forced to leave Czechoslovakia in 1939, he went to Scandinavia and later emigrated to the USA. He was influenced by Russian formalism, a school in literary theory that defines literature in terms of the formal structures of the text only.

However, part of the richness of children's literature is that, while certainly there are some books with 'classic' canonical status (although whether these are actually read much by children is another matter), there are just so many diverse texts, with so many different visual and written images of the world in which we live, that they present not an exclusive picture but an increasingly inclusive one. A book such as *My Place*, by Nadia Wheatley and Donna Rawlins, not only makes a powerful implicit plea for indigenous land rights, but gives, decade by decade, every child character—girl or boy, Aboriginal or Greek or Irish or German or English or American—their own space, their own time and, most importantly, their own voice: 'My name's Johanna and this is my place.' 'My name's Bridie and this is my place.'

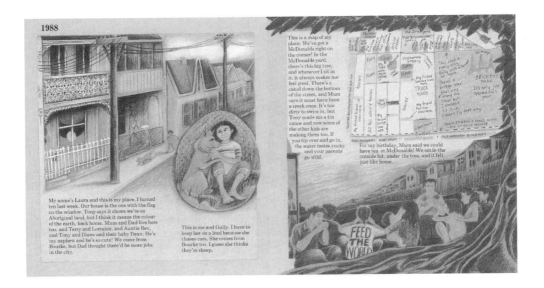

Multiliteracies

'Literature' has grown to include any reading material, as boundaries between 'high' and 'low' culture texts across society have become increasingly slippery. It is also important to note that the World Wide Web itself is a print-based medium—words are *written* and words are *read*. The Web in fact helps us to shake off any ideas of a fixed set of rules; it helps us to think in an egalitarian hypertext and challenges us to continually relocate our centre. In a diverse, technological postmodern world of many cultures, ideas of literature are expansive and exciting. Poetry, playground rhymes, drama, skipping songs, how-to-do books, books about surfing and sport, alphabet and concept books, wordless picturebooks, e-books and even comic books and magazines are all part of the collective literature of a print-based, print-rich society.

This is not to say that all literature is equal. The real test of worth is probably *longevity* and *impact*: how long and how deeply does this piece of writing stay with us? How many times can we return to it, finding something a little more, a little different, each time? How complex is the map of being that it gives us? How strong was the jolt of recognition—perhaps of self, perhaps of others, perhaps of circumstance, perhaps of predicament? How much of it do we carry to readings of other books? How much of it, if any, do we write into our own lives?

In the classroom

The real test of worth is longevity and impact

What books that were important to you in your childhood would you include in a canon? Why? Share ideas with others. Do you all agree? Why or why not? What does this show about any notion of a canon?

Read *Edward's First Day at School* by Rosemary Wells (1996).

■ What does this story reveal about ideologies of family structure?

- ■ What picture of the preschool and teacher does it convey?
- ■ What attitudes to child development does it represent?
- ■ What attitudes to the rights of the individual does it represent?
- ■ Relate this book to 20th-century constructs of the child.
- ■ Relate this story to the *Bildungsroman*.
- ■ Select other picturebooks that reveal aspects of growth and development as the frame of their narrative.

Years 5–6

1   Ask the children, as a class, to discuss ways of growing—physical, mental, emotional, being able to do something they couldn't before, learning new things about people, understanding things in a different way, learning new things about themselves. Find as many stories as you can that describe an aspect of growing. In small groups, sort them into categories: learning to do something you couldn't do before, adjusting to a new situation, moving to a new place, overcoming some difficulty, changing attitudes about something.

2   Read *Cherry Pie* by Gretel Killeen, Francesca Partridge, and Franck Dubuc (1998). In what way does the person telling the story grow? Discuss in small groups and report to class.

3   Read *Leaves for Mr Walter* by Janeen Brian and David Cox (1998). Who does the growing in this story? Does more than one person grow? In what way?

4   Who are the champions in *Champions* by Jonathan Harlen and Emma Quay (1998)? What message does this book give to us?

5. Set up a class table of growing books. Perhaps you could place other growing things on it as well—seeds, sprouts, an artwork someone is working on over a longer period than usual.

6   In groups of about six, choose a favourite piece of music and compose a dance or growing tableau. Write out your growing themes on a poster or an overhead. Set aside practice and performance times.

Years 3–4

1   Read *John Brown, Rose and the Midnight Cat.* What sort of growing takes place in this book? Who do you think grows? Why?

2   Write a poem about a time of growing.

Years K–2

1   Read any of the *Edward* books by Rosemary Wells. Discuss ideas of being ready and growing. Draw a picture and write a sentence about a time when you grew.

2   Tell the class a story about something you have seen grow.

Teachers' reading

Read *Deadly Unna* (see pages 403–4 above), even if you do not think it suitable for your class. Think about the sorts of growing and self-awakenings that are a part of this story. Middle school and secondary teachers may find ways of using these ideas to relate to other stories such as Twain's *Huckleberry Finn*, Morgan's *My Place*, Harper Lee's *To Kill A Mockingbird*, and Shakespeare's *King Lear*.

Harry Potter and the Philosopher's/Sorcerer's Stone (Rowling 1997)

To conclude, the most significant identifying characteristic of children's literature is that it is overtly (if not covertly) addressed to and designed for children, in story, language, typography, and physical format.

One of the main reasons for the phenomenal success of the *Harry Potter* books is the way the author addresses, positions, and treats her child readers, trusting them with existential (life and death) issues, as well as with some sophisticated language and ironic social commentary. From the very first paragraph, J. K. Rowling enfolds readers into a privileged position of knowing:

Trusting the child reader

> Mr and Mrs Dursley, of number four, Privet Drive, were proud to say that they were perfectly normal, thank you very much. They were the last people you'd expect to be involved in anything strange and mysterious, because they just didn't hold with such nonsense.

The use of the second person—'they were the last people you'd expect …'—immediately constructs a reader who is being taken under the wing (or cloak) of a knowledgeable narrator: 'When Mr and Mrs Dursley woke up on the dull, grey Tuesday our story starts …' (p. 7). This establishes a secure spot for a reader in the know, who already resists the Dursley point of view and, indeed, expects it to be wrong. This reader is an imaginative 'you' who becomes an 'us'—'A fine thing it would be if … the Muggles found out about us all,' says Professor McGonagall (p. 13). Rowling's book implies an addressee who is clever, perceptive, imaginative, and 'unmuggley'. She does not rely on a wiser adult to interpret the story (as C. S. Lewis sometimes does) and does not address that adult; her child reader is what Bakhtin referred to in his concept of the 'higher' superaddressee who is part of the organising structure of any text. This higher superaddressee is 'a constitutive aspect of the whole utterance', whose 'absolutely just responsive understanding is presumed' (Bakhtin 1986: 126; see also Johnston 2002b). The superaddressee of *Harry Potter* is the child/reader who will understand Harry, intimately share his adventures, and resist Muggledom.

There are also of course other reasons why these books attract readers: they are a clever generic hybrid—school story, Blyton adventure, a C. S. Lewis-type magic entrance (wardrobe/Platform Nine and Three Quarters), Tolkienesque struggle between light and dark forces, fantasy, detective novel, social commentary (especially about parenting and a consumerist society), Indiana Jones-type quest, odyssey/search for personal identity, and, most of all, fairy story (Harry is Cinderella, Dudley is the ugly sister/ugly cousin, the Dursley parents are the archetypal wicked stepmother/father/carer figures, Hagrid is the fairy godmother/helper—as well as the older, flawed hero, the Hogwarts Express is another version of the golden coach, which is the means of transporting Harry from the Muggle world where he is of little import—cinders/spidery cupboard under the stairs—to the world of school where he is very important indeed).

The *Harry Potter* books are apposite examples of the power of children's literature and the power of the reading process. When the phenomenally popular first book was made into a film, much was made about the author's and director's insistence on artistic veracity and fidelity: the film would be true to the book. The film features rich, opulent landscapes, an aristocratic cast, and brilliant special effects (some by Jim Henson's Creative Shop), while the amazing Quidditch game, with Henry winning by catching the Golden Snitch in his mouth, cost a fortune to reproduce cinematically.

The amazing magic of reading: black marks on a white page

It is indeed interesting that so many resources were needed in order to create as a *film* a highly successful book that *consisted of no more than black marks on a white page.*

▶ Summary

1 Postmodernism has dislodged hierarchical conceptions of literature as 'high' or 'select' and has brought a critical focus onto the power of words, and the impact they can have in and on culture.

2 It questions former Western attitudes that branded as 'illiterate' those cultures that communicated through visual signs and did not develop a conventional written language.

3 This has led to questions of what language is, what literature is, and what literacy looks like.

4 ICTs have compounded this through the provision of huge ranges of story and writing and playacting experiences that are 'not books' (although they may be related to them)—but that have clear connections to reading and writing, and to children's worlds.

5 So two things have come together: first, the recognition of children's literature as a field of rigorous academic study that is of interest to people from a wide range of disciplines, including educators, and second, an expanding world of digital modes and resources that can either baffle or inspire.

6 Children's literature is literature for children, but 'children' and the related concept 'childhood' are cultural constructs and depend on prevailing attitudes in society.

7 Children's literature is *literature* and is part of a literature continuum. It is an artistically mediated communication that a society has with its young.

8 Children, and adults, should be continually exposed to literature beyond their immediate needs and capacities.

9 As educators, we should always try to give children a 'courteous translation'. This means that we must develop ways of teaching that encourage children into literacy by making difficult tasks and difficult texts accessible.

10 Literature is more than 'meaning'. We need to allow the flexibility for children to enjoy texts in a range of ways, and understand that they do not always have to articulate the experience of a text.

11 Although children's literature is a powerful teaching resource, it is much more than this.

12 Children's literature gives pleasure to its readers; it is a carrier of ideologies in its themes and in its narrative structures; it provides a diverse assortment of maps of being; and it frequently addresses in different ways themes of growth and growing and can be related in this way to the *Bildungsroman*.

13 The real test of lasting worth is probably longevity and impact: how long and how deeply does this piece of writing stay with us? How many times can we return to it, finding something a little more each time? How much of it do we carry to readings of other books? How much of it, if any, do we write into our own lives?

14 Any idea of a canon has become a contested notion, but the diversity of children's books, and the sheer number of books published in the latter part of the 20th century and early part of the 21st, continues to work towards inclusivity.

Further reading

Bragg, M. 2006, *12 Books That Changed the World*, Hodder & Stoughton, London.

Bruner, J. 1993, *Actual Minds, Possible Worlds*, Harvard University Press, Boston.

Easthope, A. & K. McGowan 1992, *A Critical and Cultural Theory Reader*, Allen & Unwin, Sydney.

Chang, J. 1991, *Wild Swans*, Flamingo Books, London.

Clinton, W. 2004, *My Life*, Hutchinson, London.

Clinton, H. R.. 2003, *Living History*, Simon & Schuster, New York.

Conway, J. K. 1989, *The Road from Coorain*, Minerva, London.

Gilbert, S. M. & Gubar, S. 1979, *The Madwoman in the Attic*: *The woman writer and the nineteenth century literary imagination*, Yale University Press, New Haven, Conn.

Gow, M. 1986, *Away*, Currency Press, Sydney.

Hiddins, L. 1998, *Bush Tucker Man*, ABC Books, Sydney.

Johnston, R. R. 2002, 'Teacher-as-artist, Researcher-as-artist: Creating structures for success'. In G. Bull & M. Anstey (eds) *Crossing the Boundaries*, Pearson Australia, Sydney, pp. 311–27.

Johnston, R. R. 2003, 'Relevant or not? Literary research and literary researchers in troubled times', *Diogenes* 198, 50(2): 25–32.

Kaplan, A. 1993, *French Lessons*, University of Chicago Press.

Keneally T. 2005, *The Commonwealth of Thieves*, Random House Australia, Milsons Point, NSW.

Kertzer, A. 2002, *My Mother's Voice: Children, literature and the Holocaust*, Broadview Press, Peterborough, Ontario.

Klein, C. 1988, *A Space for Delight*, Erewhon, Sydney.

Koff, C. 2004, *The Bone Woman: Among the dead in Rwanda, Bosnia, Croatia and Kosovo*, Hodder, Sydney.

Kyi, A.S.S. 1991, *Freedom from Fear*, Penguin, London.

Latham, M. 2005, *The Latham Diaries*, Melbourne University Press.

Lechte, J. 1994, *Fifty Key Contemporary Thinkers: From poststructuralism to postmodernity*, Routledge, London and New York.

Mayes, F. 1996, *A Year in Tuscany*, Broadway Books, New York.

Mayes, F. 1999, *Bella Tuscany*, Anchor Books, Sydney.

McCourt, F. 1998, *Angela's Ashes*, HarperCollins, London [1996].

Ricoeur, P. 2004. *Memory, History, Forgetting*, University of Chicago Press.

Said, E. 1993–94, *Culture and Imperialism*, Chatto & Windus/Vintage, London and New York.

Unsworth, L. 2006, *E-literature for Children: Enhancing digital literacy learning*, Routledge/Taylor and Francis Group, London and New York.

CHILDREN'S LITERATURE AND CRITICAL LITERACY

22

Overview

Children need critical literacy not simply to analyse texts but as a life-skill. They need to be able to understand the power of the text and to determine where the language is positioning them as readers or as listeners; how it is making them feel; what it is making them feel, what it is trying to make them do and why. This is part of being a knowing reader. Children's books are in a unique position to develop knowing readers.

Critical literacy as a life-skill

Critical literacy can be described as:

- reading with a knowledge of language and how it works
- reading with a growing appreciation of the many possible contexts for text
- reading with an awareness of where the text positions a reader
- reading with a perception of the ideas and values and attitudes (and motivations) that constitute the implicit framework of the text and out of which texts are generated.

Critical literacy is a type of forensic science applied to literary text. We know that the word 'text' has come to mean any communicative graphical form from which meaning is derived. Critical literacy can also apply to visual texts, such as the illustrations of picturebooks and to moving image, such as film.

Critical literacy includes visual and cultural literacy

All texts breathe out, perceptibly or imperceptibly, a point of view, a worldview. A critically literate person examines texts for signs and clues about author intentions and about attitudes that the author may not even be aware of holding. These clues can include:

- choice of words
- choice of personal pronouns, especially those such as 'we', 'them', us', 'our'
- description of place: what the apparent 'here' of the text denotes: where the author is, where the protagonists are. Is this place inclusive or exclusive?
- if the text makes us want to do something: have a particular belief, like or dislike a certain group of people, even drive a particular car or wear a particular brand of t-shirt.

We can also examine any text through a lens that helps us to understand how we are reading it, what attitudes we are bringing to our reading, and how this may influence our reaction to characters and story.

One aspect of critical literacy is that identified by Nodelman as narrative literacy: knowledge that allows a reader/viewer to place the story in a literary and, as Nodelman (2002: 5) also argues, art world that provides contexts of understanding and recognition.

This conceptualisation of critical literacy includes **visual literacy**—reading and understanding the signs of an increasingly visual society (see also chapters 28 and 29)—and **cultural literacy**—knowledge of the world, and knowledge of diverse ways of being (see chapter 20). Books, and in particular picturebooks, provide arenas for the development of both these aspects of critical literacy, or both these critical literacies.

For example, the language of *The Fisherman and the Theefyspray* (Jennings & Tanner 1994) serves to encourage the reader into sympathy for the little fish, who is 'deep' in 'cold shadow', in a 'lonely lair'. The unusual syntax and slightly heroic feel of 'There was not one other like her now' is compounded by the alliterative description of the other fish:

Starfish swarmed. Garfish gathered.
There were twos. And threes.
And thousands.

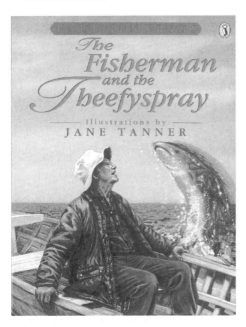

The illustrations in the text operate as a system of signs. An obvious example is the several pictures with the shadow of the boat above the mother and her hungry baby: these signify (are signs of) an imminent danger, which the reader can readily perceive. More subtle is the beautiful illustration on the last double opening: this is a picture of two worlds portrayed as a section—on the top the surface world, and the fisherman going home with his empty basket, but beneath him a vibrant world of colour and life. We read this picture as the artist intended us to—as a testimony of the marine environment and of the generous spirit of the fisherman.

Visual and critical literacy skills help us as readers to interpret the basket (without the fish, which has been returned to the ocean), a key symbol in this text, not as a sign of failure or defeat but as a sign of triumph. It is the emptiness of the basket that has contributed to the continuing vitality of the world beneath the surface. 'Truth' and 'meaning' depend on perspectives: the basket, symbol of the fishing trip, 'means' success, or lack of success, depending on your point of view. Which description is 'true' is equally problematical.

IN THE CLASSROOM

Read *The Fisherman and the Theefyspray* by Paul Jennings and Jane Tanner.

Years K–2

- Find all the signs of the fisherman in the story (the boat, the line, the basket).
- What is the underwater world like? Ask children to think of as many words as they can to describe it (bright, colourful, full of life, active etc.).
- Tell me: would you have put the theefyspray back?
- Draw a picture and write a sentence telling a story about saving something.

Years 3–4

Organise the class into small groups. Ask them to discuss the following, sharing the recording of their responses:

- Tell the story in one sentence.
- Why didn't Jennings tell the story as simply as that?
- What words make you feel sorry for the theefyspray?
- What sort of words are most of these? (adjectives) What work do these words do? (describe)
- What do these words mean?

    … a pain grew and flowered,
    deep inside her.

- Why do you think Jennings chose the word 'flowered'? What other words could he have used? Have you ever heard that word used in relation to pain before? What does it make the reader feel?

Years 5–6

Add the following:

- *Alliteration* is the name for when several words near each other start with the same letter, thus giving a similar sound, e.g. 'shrill shriek'. Find as many examples as you can.
- *Assonance* is the name for when several words near to each other have the same vowel sound but don't actually rhyme, e.g. 'deep', 'theefyspray', 'green'. Can you find any other examples of assonance?
- The class reports its findings. Discuss the poetic nature of the language and the idea that the language of poetry tries to make you see ordinary things in a new way (see also 'Picturebooks and poetry' in chapter 28).
- Individual task: write a short poem about something you have seen today or know you will see today. Try to describe it in such a way as to make your readers see the thing in a new way. The class may like to use the computer to help them set out text in innovative ways. (Show some examples of poems that do this.)

- If you were told that the fisherman was very poor and had a hungry family at home waiting for him to provide food for them, would you see the story in a different light? Discuss.

Two other deceptively 'simple' texts that can be approached in this way are *Rosie's Hat* (Julia Donaldson and Anna Currey 2005), and *Diary of a Wombat* (Jackie French and Bruce Whatley 2002). *Rosie's Hat* tells the story of a hat blowing away, and being found years later by the grown Rosie. Rosie is portrayed as a chubby figure, even on her wedding day, and she grows up to be a fireman (person!). So the author who writes in Rosie's occupation as fireman, and the illustrator who depicts in a diet-conscious age a slightly round grown woman, have collaborated in expressing or transgressing particular codes of appearance and gender expectations.

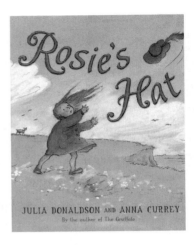

In a different way, the text of *Diary of a Wombat* is layered to encode questioning ideas about territory, perspectives, learning about difference, tolerating difference, and sharing and getting on with others—with a 'them' that is not 'me' or 'us.' (See further discussion in chapter on Visual Literacy).

Critical thinking and study exercises

Critical focus: Critical and cultural literacy

Consider:

1 Critical literacy alerts us to the assumptions and attitudes often hiding in places where we don't expect them. Read *Robinson Crusoe* (Daniel Defoe), *The Wind in the Willows* (Kenneth Grahame), and *Charlie and the Chocolate Factory* (Roald Dahl).

2 Comment on these texts and any others you consider appropriate in terms of the following ideas about an Imperialist worldview:

- cultural assumptions that indigenous people need to be 'civilised'
- cultural assumptions that the wilderness needs to be tamed and frontiers of civilisation extended
- the historical context of patriotic conquest
- the importance of power and empire
- class structure.

3 Then read some or all of the following: *Window* (Baker 1992), *Island in My Garden* (Howes &

Harvey 1998), *The Paddock* (Norman 1992), *The Story of Rosy Dock* (Baker 1995), *The Hidden Forest* (Baker 2000), *As I Grew Older* (Abdullah 1992), *Enora and the Black Crane* (Meeks 1991), *The Burnt Stick* (Hill 1994).

4 Discuss these texts in relation to a 21st-century environmental worldview:

- cultural assumptions that the wilderness must be protected against the creep of civilisation
- the significance of the natural environment in sustainable futures
- equal rights of indigenous peoples to maintain their culture.

Teachers' reading

The Testament by John Grisham (1999) is an example of an international bestseller that has a strong environmental theme underlying its story. A book you may like to share with older classes is *The Whale's Child* by Gillian Rubinstein (2002), which expresses environmental issues and moral dilemmas.

How texts work

We have already noted that in some ways a literary text is an artefact—something created by the author, turned into book form by editors and publishers, and re-created by the reader. If we consider it in a scientific way, and cut a section (i.e. the representation of a solid object as it looks when cut by an intersecting plane, so that you can see what's inside it), we would see that the text consists of a number of different levels:

- the level of story
- the level of the telling of the story
- the level of themes and significance (understory).

The level of story

There is obviously a level of story or narrative. The *story* is what is narrated. It is what you see at a glance. It emerges out of the events that take place, the actions its characters engage in, and the time and the place of the setting.

Story is events, actions, time and place

The irony of story, however, is that although it is what is seen at a glance, it is not actually what appears in the black marks on the surface of the page. For example, the story of theefyspray could be told in one sentence:

> *The last theefyspray had a baby who was hungry and was caught by a fisherman who put it back in the water because he had seen the mother's beautiful colours.*

Or the story of *Where the Wild Things Are* (Sendak 1963) could be something like this:

> *A little boy was naughty and was sent to his room but he had a fantastic (probably imaginary) adventure with some wild animals and when he came back his hot supper was waiting for him.*

The telling of the story (the telling of the text)

Neither Jennings nor Sendak have chosen to tell their stories with these words. So 'story' is a curiously insufficient term and only a superficial way of describing what happens in a text. It does not adequately describe the process of the telling of the story, a process that we need to understand if we are to be critically literate.

This *telling of the story* refers to all those choices that the author has made about the words used:

- the arrangement of the words (syntax)
- the meanings of the words (semantics)
- the sound and look of the words (graphophonics).

Syntax, semantics, graphophonics

It refers to what is actually on the page, the order in which events and characters appear, the mode or register of the narrative, and the point of view and focalisation of events, characters, and setting. For example, Jennings describes the birth of the baby fish with the words 'a pain grew and flowered, deep inside her'. The unusual use of 'flowered' in relation to 'pain' jolts readers into a new awareness of the nature of pain and into a new emphasis on pain's outcome (it is an example of what Shklovsky calls the 'roughened' language of poetry).

So, in our scientific sectioning of the text there is a paradox—what we see at a glance, the story, is not what actually appears on the surface, although readers usually think it is.

Discourse

This distinction between the story and the telling of the story, the *process of the telling* if you like, is given different names by different theorists (see e.g. Martin 1986: 107–8), but one of the most common terms, and that used by, among others, Gerard Genette (1980), Seymour Chatman (1978), Perry Nodelman (1992: 61–3), and John Stephens (1992: 17–18) is discourse.

Discourse is a term with various applications, but it commonly refers to the process of narrating, how story is told on the surface of the text. **Narrative** includes both the *story* (what is narrated) and the discourse (how it is narrated).

Readers make, create, negotiate, construct, interpret story from how they read the discourse.

Readers help to make story Discourse is the language of the text, the actual words on the page. Story appears to fly free from the page, but in reality of course it is very much dependent on it.

Understory

Underneath the discourse is a rich pool of personal and collective resources that is the reservoir out of which the author has made his or her selections in the telling of the story. Each word on the surface—the discourse—still smells and tastes of where it has come from and where it has been, and it is this smell and this taste that helps to give narrative its significance and to express its themes.

The simple term **understory** relates to this under-layer of themes and significance. It helps to explain narrative and thematic cohesion, as well as the points of connection to other texts. Narrative cohesion refers to how the elements of story (characters, actions and events, time and place) are stuck together and ordered in such a way as to make some sort of whole. Thematic cohesion is like an undercurrent, pulling together words, concepts, and pictures into a coherent and significant idea or theme that goes beyond story.

If we look at Patricia Mullins' *V for Vanishing* (1993), particularly at the powerful opening 'Xx eXtinct', the discourse—what actually appears on the page—is a very simple statement (not technically accurate anyway: 'extinct' begins with *e* not *x*) and some short scientific labels. This is a book without a

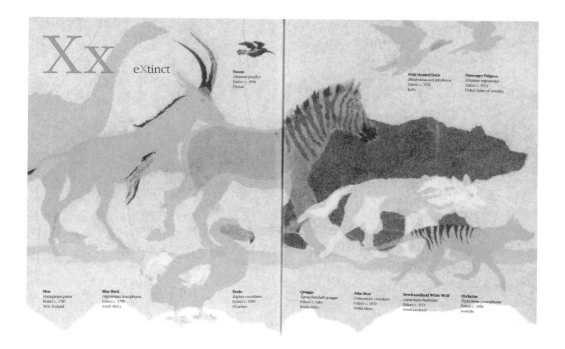

conventional 'narrative'—no traditional verbal linkages—but ordered in a recognisable generic structure, the alphabet book. However, story and theme emerge loud and clear and reach beyond the brevity of its discourse (scientific labels). The *story*, told through the poignancy of its illustrations, is about animals and how the animals it names are becoming extinct; the *theme* is about a world environment under threat. The powerful advocacies of this book (its themes and significance) come from the taste, smell, and feel of the layers and layers of visual and verbal understory that still cling to what appears on the surface, that flavour that surface, and that provide textual and intertextual connections (see also chapter 24), contrast, and cohesion. Contemporary cultural ideas about the sanctity of the environment (cultural ideologies and societal agendas) are a significant part of that understory.

In the classroom

Year 3–4

1   Read as a class *Way Home* by Libby Hathorn and Greg Rogers (1994). If you can, darken the classroom.

2   Make an overhead of the thirteenth opening. After you have finished the story, turn this overhead on and let the class reflect on it for a few minutes.

3   Discuss the idea of visual perspective or point of view:

   ■   From what other perspectives could the artist have drawn this picture?
   ■   Why has he chosen this perspective?
   ■   Where are we looking from?

4 Now look at the words on this page. You might like to introduce children to the idea of the telling of the story.

- Whose eyes are we seeing through?
- What is the advantage of direct speech as part of the telling of a text?
- What is the effect of the three lines in third person? (You may need to explain these terms to your class. If so, reinforce them as often as possible in subsequent discussions.)
- What ideas and attitudes in our society does a story like this show (concern about homeless children, the division between rich and poor, waste of resources, etc.)?

Years 5–6

Add the following:

1 Look at the pictures again. What signs in the pictures are about society?

2 Some of the above tasks can be open class discussion, or you may prefer it to be done in small groups. Divide the class into small groups now, if you have not already done so. Ask each group to think about how the story of this page could be told by a different person with a different point of view. Encourage them to give the person a name and explain their reasons for thinking the way they do. Each group writes a short script of what their person says. Then each group presents their script to the class, with one person in the group briefly explaining who the person is, another setting the scene, another presenting the script, and another describing how a point of view changes how you see things.

3 Give the class time to reflect and to take some notes.

This type of exercise can be adapted using many books. It may also be a helpful way to introduce secondary students to the literary analysis of such texts as Bronte's *Wuthering Heights*, Shakespeare's *The Tempest* (compare the different perspectives of Prospero, Caliban, Ariel), and Winton's *Cloudstreet*.

Teachers' reading

Highways to a War by Christopher Koch is an Australian story, rich in description and perspectives, about a news photographer in Vietnam. Margaret Atwood's *Alias Grace* is a psychological case study observed from differing perspectives. *The Republic of Love* by Carol Shields tells through shifting viewpoints a seductive story about love.

Multiliteracies

For Upper Primary, Middle School and Junior Secondary students

1 Plan a series of lessons around the novel *Feeling Sorry for Celia* by Jaclyn Moriarty (2001). This is set in the tradition of the *epistolary novel:* a novel in which the story is told in an exchange of letters between characters.

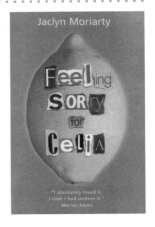

    a Introduce the novel by a discussion of the many ways—multimodes— of communication. Discuss the idea of register and contexts for text (see chapter 20) and explore the ways in which language varies according to purpose and context.

    b Read the novel, and list the different modes of communication (not all are conventional letters—there are journal entries and notes pinned on the refrigerator) and their characteristics. How does story emerge?

2   Exercise: Using the computer, write a short story employing as many different epistolary type modes as you can (for example, mobile phone text, email, letter to editor, MSN Messenger, reports, notes and post-its, formal letter to principal, greeting cards etc).

3   List the skills you need for each one. How are they the same? How are they different?

▶ Summary

1   Critical literacy is like a forensic skill. It seeks *clues* about the author's intentions, and *cues* about how the author (and illustrator if relevant) is positioning readers and viewers to react.

2   Critical literacy is: reading with a knowledge of language and how it works; reading with an awareness of where the text positions a reader; and reading with a perception of the ideas, values, and attitudes that constitute the implicit framework of the text and out of which texts are generated.

3   Critical literacy is a necessary life-skill. It includes visual literacy and cultural literacy. (Visual literacy is reading and understanding the signs of an increasingly visual society; see chapter 29.)

4   Different contexts for text and different modes of communicative text require different literacy skills and literate behaviours.

5   Exploring and discussing how texts work helps us to enhance all literacy skills, particularly critical literacy.

6   Texts consist of story (what happens) and discourse (the telling of the story). Texts also contain understory, which is a helpful term for the deep layers of theme and significance in texts. Understory includes the resources out of which textual and intertextual connections are made and which help to give cohesion.

7   Cultural ideas, assumptions, and attitudes are a part of understory; awareness, knowledge, and recognition and identification of these represent the development of critical literacy.

Further reading

Atwood, M. 1997, *Alias Grace*, Virago, London.

Grisham, J. 1999, *The Testament*, Century, London.

Koch, C. 1988, *Highways to a War*, Minerva, Melbourne.

Newton, K. M. (ed.) 1997, *Twentieth Century Literary Theory: A reader*, 2nd edn, Macmillan, London.

Nodelman, P. 2002, 'Child Readers and Narrative Literacy'. In M. Anstey and G. Bull (eds) *Crossing the Boundaries*, Prentice Hall, Sydney.

Nussbaum, M. C. 2006, *Frontiers of Justice: Disability, Nationality, Species Membership*, The Belknap Press of Harvard University Press, Cambridge, Mass., London.

Shields, C. 1992, *The Republic of Love*, Vintage Canada, Toronto.

CHILDREN'S LITERATURE AND DIGITAL LITERACIES

Overview

The book has evolved from clay tablets, through papyrus scrolls, codex, and printing and paper and ink technologies. It continues to evolve, as do ideas about language. However, in whatever complex way we understand it to be, language remains the primary technology of communication. And as digital technologies and moving images bring images to instant life, we need to assert the role that books play in fostering the literacy that most helps us to value and understand the position of others—the 'other'—that is, the literacy of the imagination.

Development of new literacies

Books first appeared as clay tablets in about 2500 bc (Kilgour 1998). Although there were some huge tablets (6 square metres) for important reference 'books' such as the Middle Assyrian Code of Laws, most early Mesopotamian tablets were usually approximately 7.6 centimetres square (sometimes oblong) pads of clay that fitted comfortably in the hand. 'A book consisted of several such tablets, kept perhaps in a leather pouch or box, so that a reader could pick up tablet after tablet in a predetermined order' (Manguel 1997: 125).

About five hundred years later came the new technology of the papyrus scroll. The look changed and the book was to remain in this form for over two thousand years. In ad 150 another new technology changed the look of the book. The codex—a sheaf of bound papers—was unsuitable for the old materials of clay and papyrus and so the new materials of parchment and vellum took over. Because it was convenient, this parchment codex became the common form of the book. It also changed the organisation of texts.

The scroll had possessed a limited surface—and, as Manguel notes, we are aware of this today, *'having returned to this ancient book-form on our computer screens, which reveal only a portion of text at a time as we "scroll" upwards or downwards'*. On the other hand, the codex allowed the reader to flip to other pages, and 'thereby retain the *sense of the whole*—a sense compounded by the fact that the entire text was usually held in the reader's hands throughout the reading' (Manguel 1997: 126–7, emphasis added). The appearance of paper in Europe (during the Crusades), and the invention of the printing press in the mid-15th century, revolutionised the crafting of books and made them increasingly accessible in the form that we know them today.

▶ LITERACY IN THE DIGITAL AGE

Many believe that the book is destined to disappear. In a paper entitled 'Electronic text: literacy medium of the future', Anderson-Inman notes the following seven advantages of digitised text. It is:

1   modifiable (easily edited, updated, and altered by both author and user)
2   programmable (adaptable to needs of the individual user)
3   linkable (user can set up nonlinear links)
4   searchable (by word or phrase)
5   collapsible (can be hidden from view)
6   collaborative (multiple users can work at different workstations from the same text at the same time) (1998: 678–82).

Those who believe that the book will survive, perhaps in new forms, could well argue that the present format of books presents similar options: books come out in new editions, they can be turned into film, they can be marked and adapted, they give references, they have indexes and glossaries, text can easily be hidden from view, and multiple copies of books mean that multiple users can work at different workstations from the same text at the same time.

The book continues to evolve

What this discussion highlights, and what is most significant to note, is that *language is the primary technology of communication*. These ideas present a basis for discussion and for the following exercise for students.

Critical thinking and study questions

This is an exercise in reading an example of the literature (that is, the academic research and discussion) about children's literature. Reading such literature is a way of consciously keeping aware of current ideas and practices. Teachers in training will want to develop their own literacy skills in reading journal articles, as many of these contain research discussions that can inform teaching practice. Reading academic literature also enhances our practice as educators by exposing us to ideas that may be beyond our immediate reach, but that, with effort, become accessible and often exciting.

The following journal article, 'The Literacy of the Imagination' (Johnston 2000a), was translated and reprinted in several European journals It sums up many of the ideas about children's literature discussed in this book. It also discusses the influences of technology and contemporary ideas about multiple literacies.

Critical focus: Critiquing academic papers

Critically read this paper.

1   Always check the date of publication. This will help to inform you about the currency of ideas. Sometimes papers published decades earlier are out of date, but sometimes they include a pivotal thought that has been responsible for opening whole new realms of thinking.

2   List and describe the new literacies mentioned here. Add any others you consider appropriate. How has the concept of muliliteracies expanded since 2000 (when this paper was published)?

3   Briefly note the main thought of each paragraph.
   - What are the three main arguments?
   - Write an abstract (no more than 250 words) describing this paper.

4   This paper was published in 2000, and there have may have been significant changes in ICT since that time. Consider any such changes, and describe them

5   Write a considered response (1000 words), describing your own position. Engage with the arguments of this paper.

This activity can be adapted for use in classrooms by using other articles such as editorials, sports commentaries, and film reviews. Web material could also be critiqued in this way. Explore sites that allow you to download relevant text.

The literacy of the imagination

'Literacy', writes Margaret Meek, 'has two beginnings: one, in the world, the other, in each person who learns to read and write' (1991: 13).

Literacy—reading and writing—is important because we are social beings in a world of others. That this is also a world of ever-increasing technologies complicates conceptions of literacy and demands of us a rethinking of the links between literacy and literature. Is the world of children's books soon to become obsolete?

The 'world' at the beginning of the new millennium is an interesting place. The 20th century began in an explosion of modernism—jarring, confrontational, exciting. It ends in a melt of postmodernism—in the collapse of canons, traditions, orders, universals, 'truths', and 'meanings'. Postmodernism has cleaned out the cupboards of the centuries, but it has left us strangely empty and vulnerable. Its essentially self-reflexive nature has helped to create the 20th-century construct of an individual-centred universe. However, in opposition to this and irrespective of the individual, technology continues inexorably to reshape the topography of the universe, both reskilling and deskilling its inhabitants.

Literacy is a plurality of complex skills. As Meek's comments imply, prescriptive language symbols are processed not only communally by sociohistorical consensus but also privately by the individual. Words on the page both hark back to the old and push towards the new. Bakhtin refers to the concept of *napravlennost*, the impulse that 'reaches out beyond' what he calls the 'naked corpse of the word' (1981: 292). When Max leaves the wild things and comes back 'into the night of his very own room where he found his supper waiting for him' (Sendak 1992), 'supper' and 'very own room' connote much more than a meal or a place of habitation, but just what precisely they connote will depend to some degree on the individual reader. Similarly, when Alice and her father 'had another cookie' at the end of Nodelman's picturebook *Alice Falls Apart*

(1996), they were doing more than assuaging hunger; the impulses that reach out beyond these words are also likely to be recognised differently by different readers. Literacy is of the world, and it is also of us, of the individual worlds that each of us inhabits.

MULTILITERACIES

Traditional concepts of literacy are expanded in this age of *new* and *multiple* literacies. Such literacies include obvious technological literacies—for example, being *computer-literate*, reading and writing with CD-ROM and desktop publishers, using faxes and email and the Internet as part of literate, communicative, goal-seeking activity. There are new 'languages'—words that have moved out of 'jargon' into popular arenas (often because of *media literacy*), and new understandings of culture and of how culture defines social practice (*cultural literacy*). In a more complex way, and directly related to postmodernism, educators are challenged by provocative and eclectic understandings of what literacy is and of what it should be—to an Aboriginal or migrant child, for example; and how much, or how little, such children should be pressured to conform to traditional notions of literacy standards.

Technology has changed our literacy habits. The Internet and the ready communication of emails and faxes have resurrected communicative writing practices as part of everyday life—creating their own discourses and giving contemporary shape to the quick note, the postcard, and the Victorian letter. I write to more people as part of my everyday activity than I have done for years. Education packages structure synchronous and asynchronous 'chat-times' within their programs; these are currently *written* chat that is interactive and contextualised. They provide great opportunities for teachers to encourage reading and writing in new ways and in meaningful contexts.

The new literacies, however, not only involve new skills, defined by social experience, but also involve new, metaphorical ways of reading the world. Thus *visual literacy* becomes more than the critical ability to read signs and images and pictures; it also becomes part of the ability to map subjects and objects, and centres and margins, as part of the process of recognising the ideologies of perspectives, focalisation, shape, and form (see also chapter 28). It lends itself to allegories of cognitive mapping and to different modalities, such as positionality and movement. Part of the vocabulary of the new literacies has been conceived at least initially out of metaphor, out of a way of thinking that imaginatively links aspects of dissimilars because of one process or one quality which they share and at which point they connect (*rapport*). I am writing this chapter using a *mouse*—although I hope that the computer I am using is free of *bugs*.

It is important to note that although understandings of what literacy is may have altered the way its *practices*, especially its educational practices, are being constructed, its *processes*, challenged as they may be, remain at the heart of these other literacies. The new literacies of course have their genesis in the old literacy and they depend on it for making meaning. Understandings of what a second language is, or responses to an indigenous appropriation of a colonial language, must connect at some point with notions of the process of literacy as learning to read and write. The simplicity (and the complexity) of this 'essence' of literacy must not be overlooked (or downgraded) amid fashionable ideological perceptions of literacy as a socially constructed tool that sets in place societal agendas. The discussion of such perceptions, however, encourages enhanced educational practices, and is the foundation of *critical literacy*—of being what I have

The new literacies have their genesis in the old

elsewhere called 'knowing readers': readers who perceive the implicit and explicit ideas, values, and attitudes that constitute the architecture of words and out of which texts are constructed.

Metaphor (and metonymy) are inherently imaginative processes. As Ricoeur and Proust have noted, metaphor both specifies and liberates (Ricoeur 1985: 198); it hones in on and pins down a specific innovative meaningfulness even as it sets previous meanings free. Reading itself is an imaginative process—linking signifiers to signifieds, decoding, analysing, making meaning, enjoying vicarious experiences through black marks on a page.

signified

signifier

Applegate & Huxley 2000, *Rain Dance*

Ferdinand de Saussure (1857–1913) introduced the terms 'signifier' and 'signified' into linguistics.
  Signifier: the word (speech sounds or written marks) used to describe the thing, e.g. 'dog', 'chien'.
  Signified: the concept of the actual thing being described, e.g. the four-legged animal that barks.
  Saussure believed that language is a system of signs, and that each sign is composed of these two parts. The relationship between the two parts is arbitrary, as the fact that different languages have different signifiers for the same signifieds indicates. Saussure's ideas emphasise the autonomy of language.

Reading is an imaginative process

It is the *literacy of the imagination* that lies at the heart of the process and practice of literacy in all its forms—reading, writing, speaking, listening. The essence of imagination is the ability to visualise, to make pictures in the mind.

The word 'imagine' derives from the Old French '*imaginer*', to make images, which in turn comes from the Latin '*imaginari*' meaning 'to picture to oneself'. Picturing to oneself not only stretches the muscles of the mind, it is also the imaginative process through which we understand otherness, the coherence of the other; as Peter Dickinson points out, it is imagination that is the core of our humanity: 'All morality, all that is in us that we regard as good and worthwhile, from the highest religious impulse to the smile at a child skipping across a bit of wasteland, derives from the imagination' (1986: 45).

Dickinson defines imagination as 'the leap of the mind that places one perception alongside another and sees that somehow they fit ... the sudden flash of thought ... the imaginative leap'

(1986: 43, 51). He notes that this leap of the mind not only enables us to recognise the validity of otherness, but also can take us, for a moment at least, into that other's place. Of course, as Bakhtin states, 'aesthetic activity proper actually begins at the point when we return into ourselves and to our place outside the other person' (1986: xiii).

This pattern—away from the safety of home, into the wild place (the place of the 'other') then back home with fresh and enlarged world-understandings and maturity—represents what has been a fundamental narrative pattern in children's literature, although, as Nikolajeva (1996b) and others have pointed out, the pattern no longer necessarily includes the resolution associated with a closed ending. It is important to note, however, that both happy endings and closed endings have been imposed by Western ideas; the fact that children's literature texts are no longer bound by such expectations reflects what Sell (1996) refers to as 'cultural mediation'. Nonetheless, they do offer endless opportunities for the imaginative leap that promotes enhanced understandings of human behaviour and of the human condition. Heidegger expresses a similar idea in his concept of 'the leap of thought' that encapsulates the search for knowledge and truth. (This relates to the 'leap of faith' of religious philosophers such as Kierkegaard.)

Children's literature opens up infinite possibilities for the leap of the question 'why?' and for that further imaginative leap that is in part its answer. Literature does not just expose, in context, the graphophonic, semantic, syntactical, and orthographic relationships in which language operates, the theoretical and practical knowledge of which gives a child what we call literacy. It does not just demonstrate to young people how language works, how it can be used to set up reader positions, how it can denote and connote otherness, how it reflects and transmits ideologies, and how it attributes power. Literature, in giving us 'images to think with' (Chambers 1985: 3) and in allowing us to 'converse with more voices than we hear from the speakers around us' (Wallace 1988: 143), nurtures and is nurtured by imagination. Concepts of rightness and wrongness are always going to be socially constructed, but literature offers possibilities and options to enter into imaginative dialogues that test these notions and experiment with them. It offers endless opportunities to take that imaginative leap into a knowledge, however fleeting, of the validity of otherness; this knowledge activates moral positioning—concepts of rightness and wrongness that represent an immanent response to shared humanity.

Television, video games, and the Internet can complement and supplement imaginative processes, but they don't of themselves provide sufficient opportunities for personal input, for interior programming, for the development of that ability of 'picturing to oneself'. And we need to explore other possibilities for the type of narratives they tell and the characters they create. We can play with the Internet and become completely engrossed in it, but whether or not we are being imaginatively creative or passively receptive is problematical. We can't play with television or film—although we may be able to retell their stories and play with the commercial products that emerge out of their ideological narratives (Luke 1996: 179). There is a physical permanence and convenience about books that should not be discounted. Media texts are fleeting, even with instant rewind and replay; despite all their technology, they are more limiting about where they can be accessed.

Television and video games present children with a world of images that are ready-made. I have written previously (Johnston 1996: 8) that programs such as *Sesame Street* fire images like bullets with the overt aim of teaching children to know their alphabet and to 'read', that is, to become literate. It all happens so quickly that children have little opportunity to visualise or to put into place their own internal pictures or images of narrative, of character, of place. The barrage of visual images to which children are subjected don't so much preclude them from that experience of picturing to oneself as make such an effort unnecessary. Why should they bother? The pictures are already there for them, with sophisticated special effects and amazing stunts that ironically, in being 'beyond imagination', cramp and inhibit the imaginative potential and capacity for the imaginative *doingness* of the child.

This is not to criticise *Sesame Street*, but it makes a convenient and valid example. Children who watch television a lot and read only a little (if at all) don't have much practice in picturing to themselves. They don't have much practice in transcribing text into their own interior images. Media texts construct a reality that the child imaginatively engages with, but not at the deepest level of making mind-pictures; moreover, these texts also construct a version of reality that children may not question. Children's images of Cinderella and Snow White and Pocahontas are now not drawn by their own imagination, or even by the illustrators of a number of books; a common picture for all has been drawn and imposed by Disney.

The immediacy of moving text has certainly expanded worldview and given children a visual topography that makes the world appear more accessible. But while television and video games teach and entertain, they do not sufficiently challenge active imaginative input. It can be argued that their extravaganza of images stimulates the imagination. It can also be argued that there is a strong imaginary component in video games. In answer to the first argument, I agree that images are *stimulated*, but they are not *created*. I drove home from the latest James Bond movie acutely conscious of a mental traffic jam of images of fast-moving cars that were not my own. In answer to the second argument, video games present their own images; imagination is required only to pretend they are real. It is my observation that video games are not so much played to imagine as for the fun of the game itself.

Books do things that the other texts can't—at the moment anyway—and it is the responsibility of educators to continue as their advocates while at the same time taking our own leap of faith into the new technological literacies. Peter Hollindale has noted that in an age of multiple literacies, literature has become 'something that you do things with … You reply to it, you rewrite it, you convert it for yourself into a message for another medium' (1995: 251). In other words, the new technologies take books into new areas.

In human terms, it is the imagination that makes connections between memory and experience, between present and future, and between past and future. Imagination is not just a learned response, like the salivation of Pavlov's dogs, although such learned responses may be a part of it. Imagination can rewrite memory, can construct patterns. Imagination is a sort of super hypertext. Memory may access particular moments, but it is imagination that sets up linkages, that overlays an individual experience or event with metaphor and significance. As in the act of reading, the experience of one moment thus accesses a hundred moments that have gone before, and anticipates a hundred others that are yet to come. The child goes to bed on Christmas Eve stirred by the experiences of other Christmas Eves and by the anticipation of the morning. The experience of the moment is given added lustre, perspective, and texture: 'This ideal morning filled my mind full of a permanent reality, identical with all similar mornings, and infected me with … cheerfulness', writes Genette (1980).

The notion of imaginative passivity versus imaginative activity is significant. Consider these opening lines of *The Violin-Maker's Gift* by Donn Kushner, a book that won the CLA Book of the Year for Children (1980).

Babette, the toll-keeper's wife, paced the corners of her look-out tower, scanning the forest below with a long brass telescope.

'Matthias!' she cried. 'The warriors are coming!'

No answer came.

Babette gasped and thrust the glass to her eye again. Past a steep ravine, on the hillside where a road just showed itself now and again between low, twisted pines, a curious object appeared …

The eye reads the signs, the brain decodes into words, the words release a tumble of the mysterious imaginative processes that create an interior picture of *mindscape*, not just *landscape*. If this were a film, the image would be there for the taking, in Technicolor; Babette would have a face, the tower a particular architecture, the forest a particular shape and form, and while the imagination may have been stimulated, it would not have been involved in its core business of 'making pictures for oneself'.

Paradoxically, picturebooks are particularly significant in this discussion. Although they present images, the images are discontinuous, moments of *thisness* (see Johnston 1998a). The narrative agendas of picturebooks are not set wholly within the verbal text nor wholly within the visual text: narrative thrust occurs in the unique spaces across, between, and beyond both. Film presents a synchronised 'reality' where image matches sound; in picturebooks the matches (and mismatches) of visual and verbal text have to be made by the reader. Picturebook images may have all the impact of a stage set, but they also allow literature's privileged access to the interior worlds of the characters. Further, picturebooks anticipate and extend worldview, promote intellectual activity rather than passive viewing, and stimulate the creative pulling together of links as an act of making meaning. They leave gaps for readers to fill in their own images, to read and write their own story. These gaps breed literate behaviour and grow the imagination.

A picturebook is a mini-world. Picturebooks uniquely accommodate the child's viewing eye and demonstrate to it a range of autonomous worldviews. This helps to grow cultural schemata and knowledge of the 'real world'. Literacy is a social activity, and reading worlds are socially constructed. As Freire (1987) writes: 'Reading the world precedes reading the word, and the subsequent reading of the word cannot dispense with continually reading the world.' Conceptualising Bakhtin's 'impulse that reaches out beyond' (which encompasses ideas of what he calls social dialects, worldviews, and individual artistic works) helps to define the delicate relationships and balances of these three interrelated notions: the significance of reader response, the significance of the literary decisions of the author (including how the text is crafted), and the significance of social world, both of author and reader. Janet and Allan Ahlberg's books for small children are successful not only because of the way they are crafted (text and illustrations) but also because of the way they cleverly represent anticipation and extension of *knowledge of the world* and, most significantly, *overtly focus on the child's worldview*. It is the child's viewing eye reading an expanding world that is at the centre of both *Each Peach Pear Plum* (1978) and *Peepo* (1981). In the former it is an 'I Spy' game:

Each Peach Pear Plum
I spy Tom Thumb

In *Peepo* a small cutout, a porthole both limiting and focusing attention, opening up and indicating a route (resembling a portal of the new media), deliberately represents what the child views and 'reads' as world knowledge, and how worldview and knowledge expand into context on turning the page. This is a literary representation of a highly reflexive process; the act of

The child's viewing eye   reading expands worldview, which expands the act of reading, which expands worldview. Response depends on context, worldview, and knowledge: the adult reader, seeing beyond the text, may glimpse beneath the gentle illustrations of this book a rich understory of war, of impending departure and the possibility of loss and grief, similar to that expressed by the young war poet, Wilfred Owen:

> What candles may be held to speed them all?
> Not in the hands of boys, but in their eyes
> Shall shine the holy glimmers of goodbyes.

All texts, including those of the media, reflect social practice and cultural assumptions; the Internet is arguably Western and non-negotiable in its implicit and explicit cultural orientation. On the other hand, children's literature theorists describe texts as 'sites of multiple meaning', places where, in the words of Bull, 'contesting literacies and literatures exist' (1995: 267). Such culturally 'contesting' conventions—of story, narrative structure, narrative time, and narrative place—promote imaginative and intellectual activity. Exposure to a rich landscape of sites of multiple meaning encourages a literate imagination to raise the threshold of tolerance and receptivity to difference. Books 'multiply possible worlds and in so doing enlarge private worlds' (Kushner 1996: 1). In the terms of the new literacies, they combine the best of RAM and the best of ROM into an interior and intensely private program that randomly accesses memory and transforms 'read only' memory into imaginative understandings that can be recalled, that can be saved, but that can endlessly be rewritten into layers and layers of new significances and meanings.

So, while we should not overstate the case, we must not downplay it. Children's literature has a unique role in encouraging imaginative literacy, not least because it is likely to be the first sustained art form that children will encounter (television is not a sustained art form, although film is). Waugh has written that the aesthetic is the 'only space of individual freedom' (1997: 22). Space, verbal and visual, gives shape to picturebooks. In fact their use of spaces, real and symbolic, could lead children's literature beyond postmodernism into hyperspace, new mindscapes, mini-worlds of infinite space. Technology has helped us to contemplate the infinite and to consider such things as virtual reality and virtual space. The illustrations of Gary Crew and Shaun Tan's picturebook, *Memorial* (1999), are a wonderful example—this book about three generations of an Australian family and their experiences at war constitutes cultural and personal spaces of remembering and forgetting, of past and present, of history and geography. While interrogating contemporary society, it leaves spaces (gaps) for different readings, it speaks in many voices (*heteroglossia*), it evokes the imagination and provokes the imaginative leap, it is intertextual (related to other spaces) and dialogic.

Meek (1991: 182) writes that literature 'is its own kind of deep play'. It is this 'deep play' that both emerges from and grows the literacy of the imagination. In turn, imaginative literacy fosters the practices and processes of other literacies and nurtures understandings of the other. It also reinterprets postmodernism into creative spaces. Far from becoming obsolete, children's literature may play a vital social role in reconceptualising postmodern voids into a new and dynamic spatialism—liberating, inspiring, and vigorous.

▶ Summary

1   The history of the book demonstrates that changes in its shape and form have taken place over the centuries. It is possible that the book may again change form (even radically), but it will survive.

2   New technologies mean that literacy has become a plurality of complex skills.

3   Visual literacy is more than the critical ability to read signs and images. It is also part of the ability to map subjects and objects, centres and margins, as part of the process of recognising the ideologies of perspectives, focalisations, shape, and form.

4   In an age of multiple literacies, literature becomes something that you 'do things with'.

5   Imagination and the imaginative process lie at the heart of the practice and process of literacy in all its forms.

Further reading

Ackroyd, P. 2002, Albion: *The Origins of the English Imagination*, Chatto & Windus, London.

Bookbird Special Issue: Children's Literature and the Media, 38(1) 2000.

Hayward, P. 1990 *Culture, Technology and Creativity*, John Libbey, London.

Hollindale P. 1997, Children's literature in an age of multiple literacy. *Australasian Journal of Language and Literacy* 18(4): 248–58.

Lankshear, C. & M. Knobel 2003, New Technologies, *Journal of Early Childhood Literacy* 3(1): 59–82.

Mackey, M. 2002, *Literacies Across Media: Playing the text*, Routledge, New York.

Unsworth, L. 2006, *E-literature for Children: Enhancing digital literacy learning*, Routledge/Taylor and Francis Group, London and New York.

24 THEORY INFORMING PRACTICE

Overview

Theory informs everything that we do. It does not have to be dry and boring, but, particularly when considered in relation to practice, can be exciting and inspiring. Literary theory is a field that has increasing applications for those involved in education. Some of this theory won't be taught, but it will support and strengthen what *is* taught. It is important for practising teachers to know much more than they will ever use in the classroom.

Tensions—a vital sign

Children's literature has been and still is to a degree fraught with tensions between, on the one side, the academics, who concentrate on theory and complex textual analysis, and on the other side, the practitioners in the field—teachers, other educators, librarians, writers, and illustrators— who have a more practical focus.

The truth is that, like most tensions, this is a very healthy one. Too much pull in any one direction will result in collapse and slackness. It has been the burgeoning of children's literature criticism and the development of a *children's literature poetics* (a formal and systematic literary study of its nature, form, and aesthetics) that have led to the growing status of children's literature as a subject of rigorous study in tertiary institutions. This would not have happened were it not for the contributions of such theorists as Perry Nodelman in Canada, John Stephens in Australia, Jean Perrot in France, Jack Zipes in the USA, Maria Nikolajeva in Sweden, and Peter Hollindale, Peter Hunt, Aidan

Critical and pedagogical theory

Chambers, and Margaret Meek in the United Kingdom. It is the richness and complexity of their writing that has both staked a place for the study of children's literature within the academy, and provided the tool for that study. Other writers in the field, who tend to concentrate on the broad overview and on practical applications rather than on the specialised intensive theoretical study of particular texts, are enlarged by the presence of the theorists; the theorists are kept in line by the practitioners. Each can help, to paraphrase a now infamous political statement, to keep the other side 'honest'.

Theory as template

A template is 'a pattern, gauge, or mould of a thin piece of wood or metal, used in shaping a piece of work'. Figuratively, it can mean 'any model on which something is formed or based'. It has more technical applications: 'a horizontal piece under a girder, beam, or any other long supporting piece to distribute downward thrust', 'a piece for supporting joists or rafters, as over a doorway or window', 'a wedge supporting the keel of a ship under construction' (*World Book Dictionary*).

All of these definitions are significant when we consider theory—both critical theory (i.e. theory about the narrative, shape, and expression of literary ideas) and pedagogical theory (i.e. theory about the actual practice of teaching).

Theory is often considered as abstract, remote from the real world, but the reality is that everything that we do is based on some sort of theory. Nowhere is this more true than when we are operating in a relationship of *teacher* with others who are *learners*.

Using theory to develop 'courteous translations'

The expression 'template' is used here in its fullest sense, and certainly not in a narrow sense of uniformity or conformity. Teaching is a dynamic activity that is characterised by and stimulated by the individuality of both teachers and students. But we have much to learn from those who have gone before, and from those who have sought to discover more about *what* is taught and *how* and *why* it is taught.

Theory, both literary and pedagogical, gives a pattern on which we can shape our teaching; it can provide useful models; it can help us distribute 'downward thrust'—that is, to prepare and teach something in such a way that it becomes do-able, not too heavy for the growing learner to bear.

This is another way of thinking about Bruner's concept of the 'courteous translation': presenting complex ideas (because they push us into thinking more deeply) but translating them with thoughtfulness and consideration for others to whom these ideas may be quite unfamiliar. If we think of this definition in relation to the shipbuilding industry, the template of theory can help to support the whole growing construction of a classroom of learners.

Translating ideas courteously means doing so with consideration for the needs of those whom we teach

Of course, theory is developed and refined through research, observation, testing, experiment, and practice. It is a symbiotic process. Nonetheless, we need to understand that any practice must be grounded in a thoughtfully formulated, intellectually articulated basis that works towards the most beneficial way of achieving desired outcomes.

The concept of 'life-world'

Philosophers talk about the idea of 'life-world'—the world in which we see ourselves as living. Life-world is fluid, changing; it is what we perceive. The life-world of children, and adults as well, is in a continuous state of what Montaigne called *becoming*. It is never complete; it is always growing, shifting, transforming.

Jürgen Habermas, a European philosopher, argues that life-world is 'the horizon-forming context of processes of reaching understanding' (1981: 135). This is an important idea for teachers—what are the contextual horizons of the children in our classrooms? Come to that, what are our own horizons (background knowledges against which we come to understandings of the world; the boundaries within which we think)?

Our task as teachers is to push out horizons, to push out boundaries, to open up possibilities of new facets and new dimensions in the child's process of becoming. Books provide wonderful resources for doing this.

Consider the picturebook *Henry's Bed*, by Margaret Perversi and Ron Brooks (1997). Understandings are enhanced when we think about this text in the light of the theory of 'life-world' as a state of *becomingness*, and as an 'horizon-forming context'.

They are also enhanced if we consider this book in relation to the ideas of the Russian theorist Vygotsky, who believed that all learning is dialogic, like a conversation; there is 'social speech' (speaking with others) and 'inner speech' (speaking within self); and there is 'talk-thinking' (talking what you think to others) and 'thought-thinking' (talking what you think to self).

Vygotsky

Lev Semionovich Vygotsky (1896–1934) was a Russian psychologist who was interested in the symbolic processes of language, and how word meanings change from emotive to concrete to abstract. He believed that higher cognitive processes are socially developed. At one stage Vygotsky worked with special needs children and brain-injured adults.

Henry's Bed tells the story of a little boy called Henry who is or has been (depending on your reading) scared to go to bed alone. Those words, however, are never actually said; readers pick them up in the interaction between words and pictures and in the way that interaction implies inner and outer voices, talk-thinking and thought-thinking.

Henry is going to sleep in his own bed tonight.

Oh yes!

Whose voice is this? It could be the parent's voice, or the parents' voices. It could be the narrator's voice. It could be two voices, a speaker and a respondent ('Oh yes!')—parent and parent, or parent and Henry, or narrator and parent, or Henry and parent. Or, as one of my students said, it could be Henry's voice, claiming growth and independence. And it could be, as another student said, a deeply ironic conversation.

Whoever's voice it is, it is clear that underneath the speaking (or behind it or above it) runs a whole dialogue of other voices and preceding conversations: the conversation recorded in this text has happened before. Reading between the lines, listening to the talk-thinking and the thought-thinking, helps us to hear the 'inner speech' of both Henry and his parents.

So, even by just touching on the theoretical ideas of Vygotsky, and remembering Bakhtin's theories about voices behind words (see chapter 20), we suddenly have a new way of seeing *Henry's Bed* and a new way of talking about it. And that gives an added dimension to our teaching (and to our own reading). Not that we are going to teach children about Vygotsky, any more than we teach them about Piaget. But we can use these enhanced theoretical understandings of teaching and language to inform what we actually do in the classroom, in our daily practices. And we use them because as teachers we want to push out horizons, to extend the limits and limitations of 'life-world', to open up new ideas and new imaginings. As Professor Snape tells Harry Potter in the fifth book of the series, *Harry Potter and the Order of the Phoenix* (2003), 'The mind is a complex and many-layered thing' (p. 469). Children's literature theory helps us to *teach* as well as helping us to teach children literature, and promotes creative ways of encouraging children into literate practices. Knowing more about golf and how the various types of clubs work helps a player choose the best club to play the stroke. Fans who follow the lives of movie stars or are interested in the art of the cinema appreciate films more because of what they know goes on behind the scenes. *Tea with Mussolini* has an added texture when we know that it is based on the story of the director's life. An understanding of postmodern shifts in time and space (past and present mixed up together) help us better to understand the phantasmic Baz Luhrmann movie extravaganza of *Moulin Rouge*.

Building up knowledge of theory helps us as teachers to perceive more about children's books and therefore enriches our teaching. It pushes and provokes us to find and describe seams and layers of meaning that enlarge our own thinking.

This is important because the best children's books have many layers. In *Henry's Bed*, for example, there is a layer of

- simple narrative (telling the story)
- parent frustration (the story behind the monologue or dialogue)
- childhood fears (implicit as what Vygotsky calls 'inner speech')
- independence and growth.

When the layers are pulled back further we find a rich seam expressing the human fear of change and loneliness; peel them back again, and there, beneath everything, is a gentle context that helps to put it all into perspective—the world of nature where everyone has a special place. We could even peel it back again and find a deep layer representing the cycle of life—day following night, season following season, even arguably death following birth.

The best children's books have many layers

So, in the simple narrative of this picturebook, *Henry's Bed*, we can recognise:

Dialogic conversation:	Narrating voice
	Responding voices
	Implicit voices
	Inner voices

IN THE CLASSROOM

Integration of theory and practice

Theory is about understanding— it 'stands under' what we do. It gives us the language and understanding to explain what is happening in texts and gives us the tools and understanding to teach critical literacy.

Considering Vygotsky's ideas about texts, construct the boxes of dialogue in *Henry's Bed*, addressing the following questions. You may like to use Chambers' 'Tell Me' approach, discussed in chapter 20.

1   What voices are heard in this text?
2   How do you know? Or, why do you think so?
3   What do you hear the inner voice of Henry saying?
4   What do you hear the inner voice of the narrator saying?

Years K–2

Pretend to be Henry. Tell me: what is he saying and doing?

Years 3–4

1   Whose voices do you hear in this book? Is it one voice or many?
2   Write a short play using the voices of Henry and his parent about what happens at Henry's bedtime. Act out the play with your partner.

Years 5–6

1   In two columns, write down the monologue or dialogue of the text. Why do you think the author has not included inverted commas?
2   What are some of the ways in which we can make sense of this text? With your partner, read it in as many different ways as you can.

Teachers' reading

Teachers will enjoy listening for the different voices in *Snow Falling on Cedars* (1995) by David Guterson, and *Beloved* (1997) by Toni Morrison. John Updike's *Gertrude and Claudius* (2000) is a brilliant 'spin-off' of Shakespeare's *Hamlet*, focusing on the characters of his mother and uncle, giving them voice to tell their story. *March* (2005) by Geraldine Brooks, winner of the Pulitzer Fiction prize, gives voice to the absent father of four famous 'little women'.

A mini-world is glimpsed on the edges of the text

Children's literature texts open up and reveal mini-worlds, microcosms of larger cultures glimpsed around the edges. These worlds are a part of the fictive life-world of the fictive child, but they can also become a part of the 'life-world' of the child reader. Children's literature, then, is not only part of a life-world but can help constitute it.

Children's books covertly and overtly, implicitly and explicitly, reflect a great deal about the world in which they are written. They are responded to out of the world in which they are read. In reading, children bring with them a parcel of ideas and realities and responses that constitute their own life-world. They encounter in the text

- the fictive world of the text (the world of the book)
- the fictive world that the text 'projects beyond itself' (Ricoeur 1985: 100) and allows readers to glimpse on the horizon of the text: the world implied beyond the text

- the world of the author (customs, values and attitudes, ideologies and agendas, beliefs and disbeliefs, innocences, and knowledges)
- their own life-world as it intersects in whatever way (e.g. identification, resistance, interrogation, rejection) with the text.

MUDs and Story palaces, as discussed in Chapter 20, offer engagement with other sorts of virtual worlds.

In the classroom

Text: *Where's Mum?* by Libby Gleeson and Craig Smith (1992)

- What is the fictive world of the text?
- What is the fictive world the text projects beyond itself?
- What can you guess about the world of the author?
- What can you guess about the world of the illustrator?

(Note that your guesses may or may not be correct.)

Note that fictive life-world will always be culturally encoded, and will similarly be decoded according to sociocultural context. A telling example of this is again *Robinson Crusoe* (see also chapter 22). When Defoe wrote this text in 1719, it reflected, implicitly and explicitly, the ideas of his life-world. It was a time of Empire, of colonisation, of the desire to 'civilise' native peoples. When Crusoe names the native who has saved his life according to the day on which he found him, and teaches him 'to say Master, and then let him know that was to be my name', he is expressing the ideals and cultural assumptions of his time. When we read these words today, however, we read them within the cultural values of our own life-world, and they jar us with their autocratic imperialism.

The Wind in the Willows is another example. It has been criticised for its treatment of women, although I don't completely agree with this criticism: the women who are there have quite a deal of agency. More interesting is the uprising in the last chapters against Toad of Toad Hall. Again, when this was written in 1908 it reflected the social attitudes of its time. When we read it today, from the point of view of our own social attitudes, we are aware of feeling that Toad was a pretty awful landlord, that Badger was very class-conscious, and that the stoats and the weasels had a strong case.

Depiction of the everyday

Because children's books represent children's life-worlds, which tend to be everyday worlds, they reveal a great deal more about that world than perhaps the writer or illustrator intended. Reading a picturebook text, we *see* a host of background material without really *noticing* it. Illustrators include clothes, furnishings, food on the table, kitchens, bedclothes, gardens, transport, classrooms, shops, houses, streets, suburbs, and cities. They also include depictions of how children and adults relate to each other, how children and teachers relate, what happens at breakfast times and what happens in schoolrooms. Kate Walker and David Cox in *Our Excursion* (1994) reveal as much about everyday life in an Australian city of the 1990s as they do about what happens on a school excursion (despite the fact that both depictions are stylised, exaggerated, and represented humorously).

It is obvious that the experiences and the purposes of author and illustrator will inevitably influence their depiction of what this everyday world looks like. But literature in general and picturebooks in particular (because of the amount of visual detail used to depict these 'seen but unnoticed' aspects of everyday life) may unwittingly disclose more deeply rooted societal ideologies, attitudes, and cultural assumptions.

Edward's First Day at School by Rosemary Wells (1996) is a late-20th-century moral tale. Both text and illustrations overtly depict an everyday world where fathers and mothers play an equal role in caring for children (the father dresses Edward, the mother feeds him his porridge, 'together they put him in the car'); where parents are supportive (both parents at school having discussions with the teacher); where children are allowed to be different ('not everyone is ready …'); and where teachers are wise.

More covertly, however, it encodes an ideological shift in societal notions of power. The 20th-century construct of the individual-centred universe is at the heart of this text. There are only two double-page illustrations: the first is of Edward being driven by his parents to playschool

Edward's First day at School reveals 20th-century ideologies of the individual

and the second is of him being driven away from it. The first shows the car against an unpeopled backdrop of houses, and only the top half of Edward's face. The second shows the car decisively turned away from the group at the school gate and pointing in the opposite direction. The car here is more whole and therefore stronger—it is drawn three-quarters on rather than side on (as in the earlier picture). In the *thisness* of this moment, Edward is also more whole, his eyes are less apprehensive, and we see part of his mouth, which looks satisfied if not triumphant. The thrust of this second picture is a celebratory *going away from* the cluster at the gate that represents society. The individual, who doesn't 'want' to paint, or slide, or conform, withdraws from the 'everybody' who cheerfully support his right to do so (Johnston 1998a).

Children's books as 'comprehensive grasps' of the world

The French philosopher Merleau-Ponty, in discussing what it is to *be*, uses the phrase 'the world contracted into a comprehensive grasp' (1986: 408). Each child's book does just that—it contracts 'world' (the large macrocosm) into part of everyday 'life-world' (microcosm). Books fit world, or versions of it, to a child's grasp.

This is not to say that all books are of the everyday—they are not. Many are fantasy. Part of the charm of children's literature, however, is how fantasy accompanies the everyday. Fantastic imaginary worlds can help to shape and make sense of the 'real' and become part of the contraction into a 'comprehensive grasp', as in Sendak's *Outside Over There* (1981), and there are many books that remind us that the world of fantasy is concomitant to the everyday world anyway; *Where the Wild Things Are* (1963), *Drac and the Gremlin* (Baillie & Tanner 1988), *Come Away from the Water, Shirley* (Burningham 1977), *Sailing Home* (Thompson & Ottley 1996), and *Rosy's Visitors* (Hindley & Craig 2002) are obvious examples.

Looking for clues about the world portrayed in a literary text

Using theory as a type of forensic science, as outlined in the previous chapter on critical literacy, reveals a great deal about the world portrayed so charmingly in Alison Lester's *Are We There Yet? A Journey Around Australia* (2004).

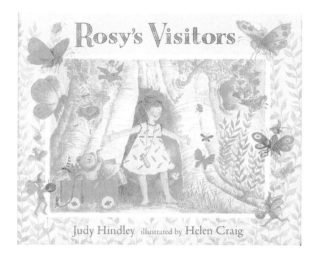

The world of *Are We There Yet?*

This book tells the story of a family travelling in an old camper trailer around Australia. The dedication (part of the peritext—the material around the text) implies that this experience is based on a real life adventure of the author.

Narrative literacy relates this story to a travel tale; it describes landscape and provides factual information as well as personal information about the places visited, and indeed is a celebration of the diversity of the Australian continent. It is organised in a type of chapter arrangement based on the familiar structure of the journey: home, away, home, with enlarged understandings of the world. It is written in the first person, but the story is told through different narrative modes that include maps and illustrations, script and labels.

Critical literacy allows us to read the following attitudes and values in the web of the text:

1   The 'us-ness' of family:

- Dad: 'I liked it better when it was just us and the whales'
- the value of family, beyond the nuclear: Nan and Poppa ('I miss our cuddles') stay to look after the animals, the adventurers stay with Uncle Pete in Sydney

- the value of doing things together as a family
- the value of home.

2   The assumption that it is good to take children to see their country, and the more implicit assumption that this is an educational experience, and that it is quite all right to miss school for 'the whole winter term'.

3   The value of the bush, of the environment, and of solitude.

4   Warm relationships of parents and children, warm relationships with the extended family of grandparents (who may live in the same house), the idea of the teenager as someone a bit separate to the two younger children.

5   Mum's lack of fear on the bungee ride at Surfers' Paradise, and Dad's fear, which deliberately interrogates gender codes.

6   Implicit in the whole book is an attitude of anti-materialism: the camper trailer 'had everything we needed'.

Cultural literacy allows us to understand the following: the depiction of how people travel in cars on long journeys (carefully belted), and what camping grounds and their shared bathrooms are like; the informal portrayal of the mother; the cat called Tigger (after A. A. Milne's *The House at Pooh Corner*); the intertextual association to the Coorong and pelicans (Thiele's *Storm Boy*); the subtle connections between whale songs and sea sirens; indigenous art traditions and ideas of the Dreamtime in the chapter titled 'The Outback.'

It also enhances understandings of phrases such as 'On the Road' as a Western idiom for getting started, the notion of cowgirl and flying doctor (could be a doctor with wings!), the play on words in 'bight' and 'bite' (and the multimodal representation of this pun), the idea of mateship and multiculturalism implicit in the episodes with the football team and the local boys and 'Luke's barramundi barbecue', and the evocation of the Australian Aboriginal flag in the watching the sunset scene.

The inculcation of social mores and morals includes the careful use of seatbelts in the visual illustrations, going to the gallery in Canberra, and wearing hats and sunscreen.

Examples of *imaginative literacy* include the use of metaphors and similes; the delightful possibility of 'creepy things in the water'.

This text will be discussed in terms of visual literacy in chapter 29.

IN THE CLASSROOM

Years K–2

1   Read *Come Away from the Water, Shirley* to the class. Perhaps you could set the scene by having a beach ball and a picture of a pirate ship. Ask the children how these two things could be connected.

2   Bring the children up close so they can see the pictures. Don't talk about the pictures until you have read the book.

3   Discuss with the class what the pictures represent. Are they a different world? Or are they pictures in Shirley's mind?

4   Ensure that children understand the unique capacity humans have for imagining.

Years 3–4

Add the following, as appropriate:

1 What are the points of connection between the two worlds? In groups, make a list of these connectors.
2 Discuss: how do the worlds affect each other? Do they change anything? If so, how? Write a story about a time when you imagined something different from what was actually happening.

Years 5–6

Choose as much as you would like to do from the above, but add:

1 In roundtable groups, write a script for what happens in the pictures.
2 Devise creative ways of acting out the two worlds of story. Children may choose to do parallel stories, or consecutive stories. They may want to run the stories together as one.
3 Groups present their play to the class.
4 Discuss the way in which imagination can be used to transform situations.

Teachers' reading

Girls in your classes may enjoy you reading L. M. Montgomery's *Anne of Green Gables* with them as an example of using imagination in everyday life. Years 1–4 (and you) will enjoy the imaginative and humorous adventure of Anne Fine's *Bill's New Frock* (1989). Other good stories include Libby Gleeson's *Eleanor, Elizabeth* (1984), Katherine Paterson's *Bridge to Terabithia* (1977), and Morris Gleitzman's *Boy Overboard* (2002). You may all enjoy reading the cartoon stories of Calvin and Hobbes.

The chronotope

In discussing books, we are used to thinking about ideas of setting – where the action of the story takes place. Literary setting doesn't just refer to environment (topography) but to an environment in time: for example, the poet Matthew Arnold's description of the English university town of Oxford as 'that sweet city with her dreaming spires' (in his poem 'Thyrsis' 1866) refers to a very different Oxford to that described by Colin Dexter in his Inspector Morse series (from 1975), and subsequently filmed as the setting for the television series of that name.

Life-world doesn't just happen in a place, it happens in a particular place at a particular time. The **chronotope**, a term introduced into literature by Bakhtin (*chronos*, time—as in 'chronicle', 'chronometer', 'chronological'; *topos*, place—see 'topography', above), refers to the relationship between people and events on the one hand, and time and space on the other. In Bakhtin's words, it is 'the organising centre for the fundamental narrative events of the novel' (1981: 250).

The chronotope shifts critical discussion beyond traditional ideas of 'setting' and 'place' and 'location' in three main ways:

1 It expands understandings of the centrality of time and place in the organisation of narrative.
2 It reformulates the notion of objective place into subjective space, that is, place and time perceived, experienced, or described from a particular point of view, or from multiple points of view.
3 It explicitly recognises that the representation of such perceptions, being subjective, are ideological and value-laden, reflecting personal and sociocultural ideas, attitudes, and experiences.

The chronotope is a more expansive way of describing and understanding genre and text-type, and gives a critical language to identify its features (e.g. see Nikolajeva's discussion of a fantasy chronotope [1996a: 122f.]). Some texts, such as *My Place* (Wheatley & Rawlins 1987), overtly use their chronotope as a structural principle.

Time and space are not separate but linked

It is important to note that the chronotope does not necessarily present time and space in 'equal' quantities; they may be combined with many differing emphases. J. K. Rowling has chosen to organise her *Harry Potter* books with the *space* element (representations of suburbs, attitudes, and language of an ironically stereotypical English social class) clearly defined from the first few lines but with the *time* element vague (see chapter 21).

Developing the concept of a *visual chronotope* expands on Bakhtin's ideas to refer to the representation of time-space in picturebook illustration. It describes the visual depiction of the relationship of people and events to time and space. This is a particularly helpful way of considering the interaction between verbal and visual text in picturebooks. Visual markers used to illustrate the relationship of people and events to time and space are easily identified and clearly reflect ideological choices and cultural attitudes. For example, a fishing basket represents the *space* of a fisherman; an empty basket may represent a specific *time* of failure, but in *The Fisherman and the Theefyspray*, as we have seen (see p. XX), is clearly intended to represent a specific time of success and a particular social attitude to the environment. *Verbal* chronotopes may match *visual* chronotopes and express a similar organisation of time and space in a text, but they may also be quite different, as in Burningham's *Come Away from the Water, Shirley*, and Baillie & Tanner's *Drac and the Gremlin*. The last illustration of Jeannie Baker's *Where the Forest Meets the Sea* projects a visual dimension of *future* into the *present* moment of verbal text, creating a chronotopical emphasis on what a different *time* may bring to the *spaces* of a threatened environment.

Clocks represent time in a close, specific sense, and the natural cycle of the day represents time in a more general, distanced sense. We could argue that representations of time-spaces in urban life tend to be hectic and hassled (think of Gleeson & Smith's *Where's Mum?*), whereas those of rural life tend to be rhythmic and gentle (think of Wagner & Brooks' *John Brown, Rose and the Midnight Cat*, which uses both a clock and the natural cycle of the day as time markers).

The chronotope is a particularly useful term for discussing children's literature because it emphasises the connectedness of time and place, and gives a way of understanding how words and pictures may be in synch or may be deliberately out of synch with each other.

At its simplest, place is, as Bal implies, 'location' (1985: 43). It is the 'somewhere' where events happen, the fictive physical situation in which the characters move. But place as location also implies a situatedness in time and a situatedness in a culture. Reflecting on the chronotopes—visual and verbal—opens up another way for understanding the complexity of picturebooks. (See also 'The visual chronotope' in chapters 28 and 29.)

In the classroom

Years 3–4

1   Discuss the idea of time-place (a bite of place and time together).

■   How many time-places can you find in *My Place*? (1987)

■   How many time-places can you find in *Peepo*? (1981)

2   How is the idea of time-place used as part of story in these books? (In *My Place* it gives the frame of the story and ties in with the history of Australia. In *Peepo* it shows the cycle of the day.)

Years 5–6

1   Depending on and as appropriate for your class, talk about the idea of time (when things happen) and place (where they happen). Note how time and place come together as space for story.

2   Build on earlier discussions about the imagination.

3   Read *Let the Celebrations Begin*, by Margaret Wild and Julie Vivas (1991). Set it in historical context, explaining that this is a story of a particular time-place.

4   Discuss the ways in which the women and children in the concentration camp used their imaginations.

5   Do you think this book makes a very terrible time in human history too trivial? (Your class may like to know that in the USA and Europe, publishers refused to give the book its Australian title, and called it *A Time for Toys*.) Or do you think it shows something strong about the human spirit?

6   Compare the representation of war in this book to that in *My Dog* by John Heffernan and Andrew McLean (2001).

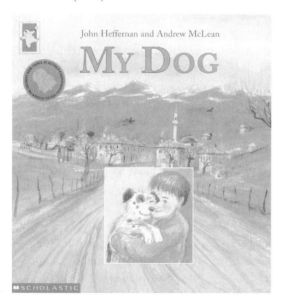

Are We There Yet? (Alison Lester) and the chronotope

An analysis of time and its intersection with *people* and events reveals that the time of the story is located in the past: time has lapsed, and 'we' are home, and perhaps have been home for quite a period. An analysis of time and its intersection with *place* reveals two senses of place: one of the country being visited as timeless and ancient compared with the transience of the family's visit, and one in terms of a human lifeline, a sense of time past, perhaps even of the transience of childhood. Note that encoded in the title of this book is a complex idea of time as at once past, present and future.

Subtle intersections of time, place and people

Teachers' reading

The Diary of Anne Frank and *Born on the Fourth of July* by Ron Kovic make interesting reading in terms of time-space issues. The movie *Forrest Gump* plays with the ideas of time-spaces, inserting pictures of Forrest in old news footage. George Clooney's film *Good Night and Good Luck*, also uses old footage, which allows historical characters to play themselves.

Philosophies of giving   An advanced class may like to extend time-place into time-space and discuss time-space in terms of being a gift. The women in *Let the Celebrations Begin* give their clothing so that the children can have toys, and the time-space for play, but they do so as a sacrifice; they have so little to give.

In a very different circumstance, but in a similar way, the mother in *Drac and the Gremlin* (Baillie & Tanner 1988) plays along with her children's game and so gives them time and space to imagine. You may like to compare this with David McKee's *Not Now Bernard* (1980).

Another type of giving is described in the fable by Jeff Brumbeau and Gail de Marcken, *The Quiltmaker's Gift* (2000).

Educators may like to introduce philosophical ideas about gifts and giving here. Jacques Derrida, a contemporary French philosopher, says that the essence of a gift is the *madness of its giving* (1991).

If you have discussed the concept of *otherness* with your class, you may also like to talk about gifts as the *affirmation of the other*. That is, gifts say how much the person we give them to is valued. You could also discuss how books, such as *Guess How Much I Love You* (McBratney 1994), give other sorts of gifts.

This could be developed into a philosophical enquiry.

Place and identity

Perceptions of place also tend to function, to adapt an idea of John Shotter, as 'extensions of ourselves'. Shotter points out the 'complex relation between people's identities and their "hook-up" to their surroundings' (1993: 21, 35).

This is particularly true of the world of children and therefore particularly significant in terms of children's literature. Think of *Anne of Green Gables*, for example. Place—often a secret place, as in *The Secret Garden* or *Bridge to Terabithia*—becomes a part of growth and psychological development. Children identify with their place: *My Place* (Wheatley & Rawlins 1987) is the most obvious of countless examples. The place may be a house, a neighbourhood, a room, a special hiding place, even a bed. *Ginger* (Voake 1997) is a story about place, and about a cat not wanting to share its place with the new kitten. *Leaves for Mr Walter* (Brian & Cox 1998) is a story about place. So also are *John Brown, Rose and the Midnight Cat* (Wagner & Brooks 1977), *The Fisherman and the Theefyspray* (Jennings & Tanner 1994), and *Window* (Baker 1992). *You and Me, Murrawee* (Hashmi & Marshall 1998) is a story of intersecting chronotopes—two little girls who live 200 years apart share a common space.

Place as subjective space

We have already noted that 'place' is a more concrete and passive term; 'space' is active and abstract, and opens up more readily to metaphor. Space is place perceived—made subjective, part of the inner as well as the outer world. Think about the common contemporary expression, 'having my own space'. *Do Not Go Around the Edges* (Utemorrah & Torres 1990) is about place, but it is much more accurately described as being about space—*perceptions* of place, perceptions of belonging and belongingness. Space is a much richer term, and a much more accurate one for discussing the 'place' of children's books. It is less geographically bounded: think of the differences between *cyberplace* and *cyberspace*.

Many of the spaces in children's books are the spaces of the mind—again, think of *Come Away from the Water, Shirley* and *Drac and the Gremlin The Great Bear* (Gleeson & Greder 1999) is about space—its chronotope is that of a folktale, a sort of nowhere/everywhere space, nowhere/everywhere time. In this book, space opens up into cosmic space. Douglas Wood's *A Quiet Place* (2002) plays with imaginative spaces and overtly celebrates inner space:

You could discover the very best quiet place of all—
  the one that's always there, no matter
  where you go or where you stay—
  the one inside you.

Yolan & Baker's *All Those Secrets of the World* (1991) thematically plays with ideas about subjective time and space, while setting the story within a clear chronotope—the USA during World War II. A film that (controversially) represents intensely subjective space within a horrific historical chronotope (a Jewish experience in Italy during World War II) is the 1999 Oscar-winner, *Life is Beautiful*. Consider this in relation to the exterior presentation of war in *Rose Blanche* (Gallaz & Innocenti 1985), by the illustrator Roberto Innocenti.

IN THE CLASSROOM

Years 3–4

1   Organise the class into small groups. Look at the first opening of *You and Me, Murrawee*.
   - 'Tell me': What can you tell about the place of the story? Each group should list its clues.
   - What can you tell about the characters in the story?
   - What do you guess about the time of the story? (Stress that right and wrong does not matter—we are still looking for clues.)

Then:

2   Let the children get comfortable but keep them in their groups. Read them the story. If they all have a copy on their roundtables, let one person turn the pages as you read.

3   Make a list of all the things that are the same for both girls—note how many times the word 'same' is used.

4   Make a list of the things that are different.

5   Choose a scribe at each roundtable. Each group will write two or three sentences explaining the last opening. Give plenty of time for discussion.

Years 5–6

Add the following:

1   Share sentences and ideas as a class. Talk about the idea of time and space coming together. If the class level is appropriate, discuss different concepts of time—time machines, Aboriginal concepts of cyclical rather than linear time, films like *Back to the Future*. Take a few weeks to read *Playing Beatie Bow* by Ruth Park (1980), which is a mixture of historical novel and time-shift fantasy.

2   Individual writing task. Write a story about time-space. It can be science fiction, or fantasy, or realistic, or about imaginary meeting places in the mind.

Extension/middle school/secondary:

1   Discuss: Literature is of:
    ■   the now-time of the writer
    ■   the now-time of the reader
    ■   the now of the time that it seeks to represent.

2   Look through a selection of picturebooks. Find examples where the above differ. What effect does this have?

Teachers' reading

An Imaginary Life by David Malouf describes the infatuation of the ageing poet Ovid with a young wolfboy. It is set in Roman times on the shores of the Black Sea, but the story it tells—of death into life—shifts it into a universal, surreal time-space that is almost folkloric. *Saturday*, by Ian McEwan (2005) is set in the specific timespace of one day post September 11, but the story it intimates is of a fallen Western world.

The implied reader

In children's literature, ideas of life-world, time, and space all relate to the fact that children's books are written for children or, in Wall's (1991: 9) words, *to* children. Children's literature is not here defined in terms of its borders, or in relation to or opposition to, the corpus of 'adult' literature (see e.g. Saxby 1997: 18–22; Stoodt et al. 1996: 4–5) because the philosophical conceptualisation in which part III is grounded is that this literature is part of an artistic continuum.

Children's literature writers compose their texts with an implicit understanding that the person reading it will be a child. This child for whom the text is written is called the **implied reader**.

The 'implied reader' is a term coined by *Wolfgang Iser* (1926–) and is used by literary theorists to describe the reader implied by the text. There will always be a tension between the real reader—real child, adult, critic, teacher, parent—and the position of reader set up within the narrative structure by the author.

Umberto Eco (1932–) uses the term 'model reader' to describe the reader inferred by the text.

Sometimes texts have a 'narratee', someone within the text to whom the story is being told. *Winnie the Pooh* is a good example of this—the story is being told to Christopher Robin, who is the narratee.

Texts make it clear who their implied reader is, in children's books usually by the interior and exterior formats and by the level of language. The implied reader relates back to ideas about the construct of the child and of childhood, because authors will either consciously or unconsciously (or both) write for the child their culture has constructed.

IN THE CLASSROOM

1   Choose three picturebooks. Consider the implied reader of each, giving your reasons.
2   Choose one picturebook.
    - Make a list of all the things that you learn about the world of the text—the fictive world.
    - What are some of the things you learn 'accidentally'?
3   Consider what you have to know before you can fully understand this book: for example, in *Where's Mum?* you would have to know what a kindergarten is. This helps us to determine the person the author has seen as implied reader of the text.

How a book looks and tells its story shows who the implied reader is

Years 5–6 (could be modified for middle primary)

Arrange the children in small groups (no more than four). Give out, or allow children to choose, a number of picturebooks.

1   Look at one book. Ask children to brainstorm a list of all the things that readers of this book must know and be able to do if they are to understand it. Model a number of examples such as *Edward's First Day at School* (Wells 1996):
    - They must understand how books work—turning the pages, beginning at the front (in Western culture), knowing what a title page is, reading the left side before the right side of an opening.
    - They must be able to read.
    - They must know what a school is.
    - They must know what a teacher does.
2   Ask children to describe the picture that the text gives of the reader of the book. You do not need to use the term 'implied reader', although you may choose to do so. What you are doing is showing children that the writer has constructed a story for a particular reader with a particular sort of cultural knowledge and knowledge about the world. You are helping children to grow into understandings of *critical literacy*, using your knowledge of theory to encourage them to have enhanced perceptions of how texts are constructed and what they do.
3   Ask children in groups to make a list of all the background things that happen in the book. What sort of world do they show?

Narrative patterns: The quest

Children's literature articulates a culture of growing. The archetypal story of all literature is the story of the quest, of the odyssey, of the voyage out and the coming back in, with equilibrium usually restored, and with growth—physical, emotional, spiritual—having taken place. Quests can be external, like Peter Rabbit venturing into Mr McGregor's garden, or they can be internal, like *You and Me, Murrawee*, which among other things is a quest for identity, for understanding of others, for reconciling shared space, and perhaps for a sense of nationality.

Subjectivity and the developing sense of self

At the heart of the quest is the search for a sense of self. Small children live in a world that is essentially solipsistic—centred on 'me'. Children's books tell stories about others but they also help to articulate a developing sense of self in relation to others, of the self as a site of consciousness and meaning. As well as this, they allow opportunities to test other selves and other ways of being.

The sense of self as a 'site of consciousness and meaning' (Webster 1990: 80) is called subjectivity in literary theory. This site of consciousness is distinct and separate from the surrounding life-world. It is formed in relationship to the others in that life-world (i.e. in intersubjective relationships). It is constructed out of what Bakhtin calls 'dialogic' encounters with those others. Bakhtin's term is specific but it is being used here in the general sense of a dialogue, a conversation, or intersubjective expression of relationship between a self and an other, or others.

Subjectivity pertains to a sense of *'I'ness* in a world of others who are also 'I's

Subjectivity is a psychoanalytical term that draws attention to the significance of this sense of self, of being an 'I' who is separate and individual from all the other 'I's in the world. As teachers, we have the opportunity to encourage children to read books offering a diversity of other, fictional subjectivities.

Literature gives privileged access to what its characters are feeling and thinking and how they define themselves as different from others. The representation of subjectivity—the sense of identity and individual being—in literature is a powerful dynamic. In children's literature the representation of subjectivity is part of deep structure. *Edward's First Day at School* is all about Edward and his life-world; *Where the Wild Things Are* is about Max and his inner and outer life-worlds.

As noted earlier, the subjectivity of the child reader, his or her sense of identity and sense of self, are in a continual state of becoming. Awareness of individual identity is formed in relationships with others, with sociocultural ideologies and with cultural ideas and attitudes. These relationships and interactions include what is read, what is talked about, what is watched on television, what happens around the family dinner table.

Critical thinking

1   Consider the multifaceted representation of Daisy's subjectivity in *Do Not Go Around the Edges*.

2   What are some of her dialogic relationships? (Think about the people of her world, and about her relationship with the land.)

3   There are many voices in this text (as noted earlier, Bakhtin referred to this as *heteroglossia*). Some are clearly heard, others are implicit (Daisy's parents, the officials who carry out government policy). What voices do you hear? List and discuss.

Teachers' reading

Read the first chapter of *David Copperfield* (1849–50) by Charles Dickens and then read the early chapters of *The Catcher in the Rye* (1951) by J. D. Salinger. Think about the different implied readers and the different representations of subjectivity.

Critical focus: Subjectivity and dialogic relationships

Focalisation and agency

Focalisation pertains to the way we see things and the way we hear things. The author chooses to write from the perspectives and ideas of a particular character, or sometimes from the more removed position of omniscient (all-knowing) narrator. The illustrator shows us how things appear from a particular angle.

One illustration from William Mayne's *Mousewing* (1987) shows how the owl saw the little mice; another shows how the mice saw the mighty wings of the owl as it swooped down on them. The illustrator's choices *instruct* viewers how to see these images. The cover positions the viewer *below* the mouse; this reflects its significance as protagonist, first by enlarging physical size, and second by letting us see more or less what it is seeing.

Focalisation asks whose eyes, whose ears?

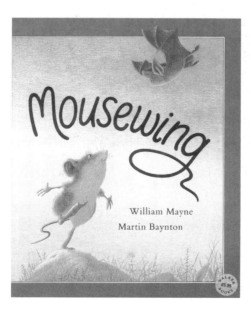

William Mayne
Martin Baynton

Understanding focalisation is a part of critical literacy because it helps us to be aware of where the verbal text is positioning its reader. Understanding how images are focalised (and read) is part of visual literacy. Such understandings give readers *agency*; that is, the knowledge and power to accept, resist, or reject such positioning. The key questions to ask about focalisation are:

- Whose eyes are we being encouraged to see with?
- Whose ears are we being encouraged to hear with?

The theoretical concept of focalisation alerts us to the significance of point of view and perspective. Perspectives relate to frameworks of seeing. Point of view has come to mean attitudes and opinions but it can also mean literally the point from which something is seen or viewed. Where we stand, of course, is likely to influence what and how we see.

Focalisation gives us a tool to interpret literary narrative in an objective way. *All Those Secrets of the World* (Yolan & Baker 1991) is overtly about literal perspective: 'When you are far away, everything is smaller' (see also the discussion of Aboriginal culture in chapter 29). But it is the implicit focalisation that is much more revealing. This text purports to be the focalisation of a child: 'I was four when my father went off to war.' The scene of her father's departure is overtly seen through her eyes: 'But everyone had a good time, except Mama, who cried all the way home …'

However, covertly, this is a retrospective, a real-life adult focalisation of a significant time and a significant learning experience of childhood. The dedications in the peritext (the writing around the actual pages of story—explanations, publishers' blurbs, etc.) make it clear that 'Janie' is Jane, the writer. We are really not seeing through little Janie's eyes; we are seeing through the eyes of the grown woman, who is nostalgic, sad, and knowing. It is precisely this focalisation, and the clever illustrations that capture the chronotope of this remembered childhood so well, that give this book its charm. The focalisation of the illustrations—what we see—is always from a grown perspective; the grown-up is looking back at the child and the child-time. The only moment when we look in any way through the child's eyes is the mirror scene. The rest of the time we view at a distance—and of course it is just this sense of distance that situates the text in its clearly delineated time-space.

In the classroom

Read *The Great Bear* by Libby Gleeson and Armin Greder (1999).

Years 3–4

1   Organise into small roundtable groups.
2   Ask children to discuss: 'Whose eyes are we seeing with?' in relation to the illustrations. Does this change? If so, when?
3   Why do you think it changes? What do you think the illustrator is trying to do?
4   Describe how the illustrator has drawn the people's faces. Why?

Years 5–6

Add the following:

1 Now look at the words of the text. We see with the eyes of a narrator, but in the last opening with verbal text we see with the eyes of the bear. What effect does this have?

2 Choose something that you feel strongly about. Write a short composition looking through the eyes of the person or thing that is being treated badly. (You may prefer to write a short play, or a poem.)

The written component of this activity could be a computer task. Ask children to experiment with using different fonts and text to represent different perspectives.

It is interesting to note the differing focalisations in *The Great Bear*, where the illustrations are strongly evocative of well-known paintings by famous artists. The faces in the crowd (focalised by the bear) remind us of the works of the Flemish painter Pieter Bruegel; the opening illustrations of distant landscapes evoke van Gogh's *Black Crows over Wheat Field*. (This particular association becomes more complex when we note that it was to these wheat fields, in Auvers near Paris, that on 27 July 1890 van Gogh took a borrowed revolver and shot himself, dying two days later.) Teachers may like to show these pictures to their class and ask students to comment on similarities and differences. What effect does knowledge of these artistic relationships have on our reading of the book?

This leads very nicely into a discussion of intertextuality.

Intertextuality

Intertextuality refers to intercourse between texts. The traditional meaning of 'intercourse' is conversation and interaction—but the common sexual implication that most of you will read there is not unhelpful.

Intertextual relationships, overt or covert, are intimate relationships that reach across, between, and beyond texts. Anthony Browne's *Voices in the Park* overtly reaches across to his earlier text, *A Walk in the Park*, setting up connections that influence our reading of the later text. Barrett & Hill's *Beware, Beware* reaches overtly into the mixed spaces between fairytales and cautionary tales, and covertly into the spaces between fairytales and adolescent 'wild side' literature. Shaun Tan's illustration of the tree in *Memorial* reaches *beyond* this book into the art world, to the famous lithograph *The Cry*, by the Norwegian artist Edward Munch. It also taps into, as part of textual understory, Munch's view of human beings as tormented, isolated, without agency.

When one text simply refers to another text, or even talks about it, it is making *allusions* or *references* to that text—which as we have seen does not have to be a literary text but can be, for example, a media text or a painting. This is not necessarily intertextuality, any more than saying someone's name necessarily means a close relationship. In a reference and allusion, the text being referred or alluded to remains more or less untouched, and all the meaning clearly stays in the text being read.

Intertextuality goes further than this. It touches. It excites and provokes. It gives new significance to reader relationships with the old text and old significances to reader relationships with the new text. These relationships make a sort of collided meaning that impacts on both. For instance, Perrault's Cinderella assumes a greater significance when we note the countless intertextual encounters it has had (particularly in feminist retellings); it gathers to a new meaning that is beyond that of its original and beyond the bare bones of the new retelling.

Intertextuality relates to the idea of prior knowledge, to cultural literacy, and to narrative literacy

Intertextuality is also significant to educators for how it interacts with learning theory. Learning theorists know that *prior knowledge*—knowing something beforehand about what is going to be taught—contributes significantly to the success of the subsequent teaching or learning experience. Intertextuality depends on and accesses prior knowledge. There is a sense of delight in recognition—a delight that encourages receptivity. Intertextuality is a narrative structure that feeds on this delight of recognition. This is not to say that it always simply corroborates prior knowledge; rather, it uses prior knowledge as a springboard to a new idea or application—extending, interrogating, or even resisting the old.

In another way, then, principles of intertextuality intersect with learning theory. Intertextuality provokes reinterpretations; it engages with ideas of altered understandings— what Saljo described as comprehending the world by reinterpreting existing knowledge (1979). Feminist retellings of fairytales have changed our understandings of the representation of gender roles and gender-specific behaviours and caused us to reinterpret and question the fairytale as cultural paradigm.

Another example of intertextuality can be seen in Pat Torres' *Jalygurr: Aussie Animal Rhymes* (1988). Consider this short poem, 'Gumbun, The Mangrove Man':

> Gumbun, Gumbun,
> Look out, look out,
> It's the Gumbun man,
> Run, run as fast as you can.

The well-known refrain of the nursery story 'The Gingerbread Man' is an obvious intertext, and Torres has told me that she deliberately sought a familiar pattern so that it would make the rhyme more accessible to non-Aboriginal children. This is a powerful intertext for another reason, however. It interacts with other aspects of the Gingerbread Man story—his cheekiness, his cockiness, and his ultimate disaster—and inflates the Gumbun with something of the same meaning. In other words, Gumbun looks scary but it's a fun scariness—don't worry too much, he won't get you. Not only that, but when children then revisit the Gingerbread Man story, they will see a little bit of Gumbun the Mangrove Man there as well.

Intertextuality can pertain to story and narrative patterns, to events and incidents, to character and character relationships. It can consist of a single deep connection at one point of a text or of a string of *motifs* and *leitmotifs* that configure the whole text.

- *Motif*: repeated image or images in a text. Imagine a gold thread running through a jumper, only showing in parts here and there but clearly visible in certain places and contributing to the overall design.
- *Leitmotif*: a strongly recurring motif (originally used in Wagner's operas).

There are many, many texts that are wholly constructed around intertextual relationships: *The Frog Prince Continued* (Scieska & Johnson 1991) (you'll never read *The Frog Prince* again in the same way!), *The Stinky Cheese Man and Other Fairly Stupid Tales* (Scieska & Smith 1992),

Yours Truly Goldilocks (Ada & Tryon 1998), *Where's Mum?* (Gleeson & Smith 1992), *Each Peach Pear Plum* (Ahlberg 1978), and so on. However, it is a more subtle text already mentioned that reveals very clearly what I now want to consider.

Beware, Beware (Hill & Barrett 1993) is an intense, intriguing picturebook. It begins with a kitchen scene that contains all the familiar elements of cosiness and security: a warm kitchen with a bright fire, spicy smells, and the sound of a kettle singing on the hearth. All of these things are comfortable symbols of home and belonging: kitchen, warmth, cooking, kettle, fire. The illustrations at first are equally comfortable. It is the human figures that are disconcerting, and that continue to disconcert; they are very separate from each other (except on the cover). However, it is the intertextuality that is of great interest here: the child venturing out by herself despite warnings (Peter Rabbit, etc.), being lost, at first without fear and then with an ever-increasing sense of terror as the text crowds with intertextual associations of fairytales and stories about all the bad things that can happen in woods:

Beware, Beware accumulates layers of meaning through intertextual associations

> Trolls Goblins
> Elves Sprites
> Mysterious lights
> Fingers beckon
> Eyes stare

The list continues. Placing these together has a cumulative effect that strengthens each of the individual intertexts and makes the 'woods' subsequently more potent. So the 'meaning' has moved from within each separate intertext to somewhere between, across, and beyond them all. Separate stories are linked and at each point of connection narrative and thematic significance is stimulated and accumulated.

IN THE CLASSROOM

Read *Where's Mum?* by Libby Gleeson and Craig Smith (1992).
Watch the DVD *Shrek* (DreamWorks LLC 2001, based upon the book by William Steig). Have the book *Shrek* in class.

Years K–2
1   Discuss all the other fairy stories that are a part of the story of this book and/or this DVD.
2   Draw pictures of all the characters.

Years 3–4
1   Organise the class into roundtable groups.
2   Ask each group to make a list of the fairytales and nursery rhymes that become a part of this story. Talk to students about how this fills the story with characters.
3   Each group chooses one intertext. Give the students a short time to prepare a creative telling of that rhyme or fairytale to the rest of the class. They can get costumes from the prop box if you like, and act it out. They may like to mime or sing or dance.
4   Performance time.

Years 5–6

1   Writing task: children make up a short story where you meet some characters from books. Perhaps these could at some point be read to the class and a big poster could be made up of all the intertexts that have been used.

2   Or, as a class, construct a story board. Organise the class into writing groups, and divide the story into parts. Each group is to write their part of the story, using a well-known intertext of their choice as a model. For example, the intertext could be *Rosie's Walk*; their story could be 'Bluey's Run', or 'Blackie's Stroll'.

3   Introduce the idea and text-type of parody (a humorous, sometimes ridiculous, imitation of something well known).

4   As a class, research the making of the film and list as many intertexts as can be found. Explore the movie site <*www.shrek.com*>. How is place represented? How is character graphically delineated? What words would you need to describe the graphic representation?

5   Discuss the idea of the book as one mode of telling the story, and the film as another. What advantages or disadvantages does each mode have? What sorts of things do you need to know to be able to read the book? What sorts of things do you need to know to access the film? What physical resources does each mode require?

Choose a story palace for children to enter (see chapter 20). Before this, discuss scriptwriting offline and online, and note the different conventions. Look at a children's play—perhaps *Skellig the Play*, by David Almond, or *Peter Pan,* by J. M Barrie. Note that the print convention of script is to have the character's name, followed by what they say, with any stage directions in brackets. Conventional script is also generally written individually. On line script is a collaborative role-play, which encourages cooperation and socialisation. In the story palace dialogue is subsumed in description of everything the character is doing as well as feeling. The Middle Earth palace site is a very good site to begin exploring and using palaces for the first time.

The Time-Warner film *Pleasantville* provides an ironic depiction of the contrast between the 1950s world of the perfect but unreal family of black-and-white sit-coms and the 1990s *fin de siècle* (end of the century) world of broken families, sexual realities, and coloured television. At one point, the 1950s female teenager gives the 1990s male teenager an apple. This immediately (but in a very confused way) sets up the story of Eve in the garden of Eden as a deliberate intertext.

▶ Summary

1   Theory helps us to understand the scope of multimodal contexts of text and provides a metalanguage (language about language) with which to discuss them.

2   Theoretical analysis discloses connections between the many different literacies and literate behaviours required by these different modes.

3   Theory and practice operate in a creative and stimulating tension.

4   A knowledge of theory helps teachers' understandings and enriches teaching practices.

Teachers, however, must find ways of teaching using 'courteous translations'—challenging children but doing so in a way that is appropriate to class and context.

5   Children's literature articulates life-worlds and helps grow them.

6   Each work of art constructs a version of the world contracted into a 'comprehensive grasp'; that is, it presents the complexity and immensity of the world in such a way as to allow the child to make sense of it.

7   The notion of the chronotope (time-space) helps us to perceive the way texts are organised. A visual chronotope is the representation of time-space in picturebook illustration.

8   The implied reader is the reader envisaged by the author when writing the text.

9   Subjectivity is a psychoanalytical term referring to the developing knowledge and awareness of a sense of self. Diverse representations of literary subjectivity offer valuable contributions to children's process of becomingness.

10 Focalisation gives us a useful tool to interpret literary narrative and encourages us to ask: Whose eyes are we being encouraged to see with? Whose ears are we being encouraged to hear with?

11 A knowledge of focalisation gives readers agency, that is, power to accept, resist, or reject what the author/illustrator is positioning them to see or think.

12 Intertextuality refers to intimate relationships between texts. Intertextuality is more than reference and allusion; it is a relationship that is part of story and structure and that pertains to thematic significance. It provokes rereadings of the old text (the intertext) as much as new readings of the new text.

Further reading

Calvin and Hobbes cartoon series.

Frank, A. 1963, *Anne Frank: The diary of a young girl*, Washington Square Press, USA.

Guterson, D. 1995, *Snow Falling on Cedars*, Bloomsbury, London.

Johnston, R. R. 2002. 'Childhood: A narrative chronotope'. In R. Sell (ed.) *Children' s Literature as Communication*, Benjamins, The Netherlands, pp. 137–57.

Kovic, R. 1996, *Born on the Fourth of July*, Pocket Books, New York [1976].

Malouf, D. 1978, *An Imaginary Life*, Chatto & Windus, London.

McEwan, I. 2005, *Saturday*. Vintage, London.

Morrison, T. 1997, *Beloved*, Vintage/Random House, London [1987].

Updike, J. 2000, *Gertrude and Claudius*, Penguin, London.

25 CHILDREN'S LITERATURE AS A LOCUS OF LITERATE PRACTICES

Overview

This chapter provides examples of the contribution children's literature can make to speaking and listening, to language study, and to philosophical enquiry. It notes the need for teachers to be careful planners of lessons that offer plenty of scope for speaking and listening, and plenty of scope for physical movement.

Life cycle of the literacy process

Literacy is for life, and the ongoing development of the multiple literacies is part of lifelong learning.

As we have seen, children's literature represents language in context. Books help us to understand how language works. As children come to appreciate the processes of language, they will grow into a more mature appreciation of the written word. We all tend to like what we understand—an interest in a particular sport encourages us to follow a particular team or a particular player, to learn more about the rules and the game; our preliminary interest thereby grows into a knowledgeable one that is intensely satisfying and promotes further and more detailed interest and investigation.

Books help us to understand language better; understanding language better helps us to further appreciate books. This is part of the life cycle of the process of literacy. We listen, we speak, we read, we write. It is not a consecutive cycle but an endlessly changing and interacting one.

Free-range reading

Children should be encouraged to be free-range readers. The important thing for educators to note is that, at whatever level children are currently reading, they need continuous and stimulating exposure beyond it, with lots of handholds and support for the next jump. (This is true for us all, no matter how old we are.) This is where the Shared Reading experience, whether it be parent and child or teacher and class, is invaluable.

As educators, we need consciously to present to children a range of texts that is as wide and diverse, as simple and as complex, as culturally similar and as culturally different, as we can possibly find.

Children need to be offered diverse reading selections

Even when children are good independent readers, they *need to be read to*, and read with, and they especially need to be read the books that they may not choose to pick up and read for themselves.

MULTIMODES OF SPEAKING AND LISTENING

Books are a dynamic and energising part of the process of literacy—not only the literacy of reading and writing but also the literacies of speaking and listening. As noted earlier (see chapter 20), literacy involves the integration of speaking, listening, and critical thinking with reading and writing. Children's literature helps us as educators to give children the opportunity to listen, to hear voices other than their own and those of their own world. It opens up a multitude of possibilities for speaking—for speaking about those other worlds and with other voices, and speaking of their own worlds and with their own voices. The common community perceptions of literacy as reading and writing need to be extended: children must also be equipped as effective speakers and effective listeners. Literature provides a locus for the activation of these speaking and listening skills, giving them purpose and direction.

In a digital age, such opportunities are extended to include speaking and listening online, in synchronous and asynchronous chat rooms, and with such programs as Messenger and Skype using audio options.

Children's literature is one of the places where children encounter in a nonthreatening way a diversity of possible perspectives on philosophical issues, worldviews, social ideas, and cultural practices. *Being literate* connects children to this diversity and connects them to *outer* worlds—to community and to society. It also, however, connects children to their *inner* worlds, to a sense of their history (the linear, vertical idea of identity: who they have been, where they have come from) and to a sense of their geography (the horizontal view of identity: where they are, the horizons and landscape of their world). We speak to the outer world and we listen in our inner world.

Literacy is a connector between outer and inner worlds

Books articulate the processes of literacy as a multitude of close encounters. In representing the ideas, thoughts, and feelings of others, and in telling *their* story, it gives shape—words and pictures—to one's *own* story, to personal ideas, thoughts, and feelings.

Literature and oracy

It is also important that we resist giving children endless written tasks about texts. You will notice that most of the tasks included in these chapters involve oral discussion—lots of group work, with children being able freely to share their spoken responses, formally and informally, around a table. Children learn from each other, and guided discussion promotes many literate oracy behaviours: it improves vocabulary, offers opportunities for more sophisticated sentence constructions and syntax, and lets children hear the sounds of words as their peers say them.

It is rarely helpful to read books and then ask for tedious written responses about story or character or whatever as a standard teaching strategy. Never underestimate the significance of getting children to talk and to listen to each other in a structured way. Aidan Chambers in his wonderful little book *Tell Me*, which provides many valuable suggestions for promoting classroom discussion, writes: 'Talking well about books is a high-value activity in itself. But talking well about books is also the best rehearsal there is for talking well about other things. So in helping children to talk about their reading, we help them to be articulate about the rest of their lives' (1993: 10).

Literature also offers children the freedom to speak out about issues and ideas that may not emerge in normal conversation. It opens up fields of discussion in the classroom in a noncontrived and nonthreatening way. As Jerome Bruner notes: 'I have tried to make the case that the function of literature as art is to open us to dilemmas, to the hypothetical, to the range of possible worlds that a text can refer to … to render the world less fixed, less banal, more susceptible to recreation' (1993: 159).

This can of course connect to other disciplines. Children's literature does not just belong in the English syllabus and in the teaching of English. It relates significantly to history, geography, the sciences, sociology, visual arts, drama, and dance.

Children's literature and philosophy

Sophie's World by Jostein Gaarder (1995) is a story that gives a very interesting introduction to the study of philosophy.

Literature of course has a strong relationship to philosophy. Current critical writing in the field of children's literature is much concerned with ideology, defined by Stephens as 'a system of beliefs by which we make sense of the world' (1992: 8). Ideology is clearly related to philosophy, which pertains to ways of understanding the world, to the study of the truth or principles of knowledge, general principles of the universe, systems for guiding life, principles of conduct, religious belief, and traditions.

Philosophy takes all knowledge for its province. The word 'philosophy' comes from the Greek *philo*, meaning 'love' and *sophos*, meaning 'of wisdom'—philosophy literally means the love of wisdom. In simple terms philosophy has a dual purpose: first to give each person a sense of a unified picture of the universe, a theoretical basis for the practice of living; and second as a practical tool to promote critical (and arguably theoretical) thinking. It involves thinking deeply about the direction of life's activity, about views of knowledge and reason and spiritual belief, and about the relationship between the individual and the community.

Sophie's World is an interesting text, although complex, which overtly introduces older children to the study of philosophy and to the idea of philosophical enquiry. But every book contains a worldview that can be discussed and debated. *Leaves for Mr Walter* (Brian & Cox 1998), for example, can be used to stimulate discussions and ideas about more than just being a good neighbour. *The Great Bear* (Gleeson & Greder 1999) can obviously stimulate discussions about issues of performing animals, but it also can be interrogated for what it says and portrays about human nature (and mobs). Anthony Browne's *Zoo* (1992) not only can open up ideas about animals in captivity but can also provoke discussions about point of view, about families, and about representations of the roles of women. *The Story of Rosy Dock* (Baker 1995) can be read as much more than a story about the introduction of a weed into the desert—it has a visual comment to make about colonisers and colonisation as well.

Books offer starting points for philosophical ideas

Critical thinking and study exercises

Gardner's idea of multiple intelligences describes the many different forms of learning: bodily/kinaesthetic as well as logical/mathematical, musical/rhythmic as well as verbal/linguistic, visual/spatial, and intrapersonal as well as interpersonal. Whereas interpersonal intelligence relates, in Gardner's words, to 'the ability to notice and make distinctions about other individuals', intrapersonal intelligence has as its core capacity *'the ability to access one's own feeling life'* (1983: 240, my italics). These are related; Gardner discusses them together, and they both clearly represent what happens in the literature/ creative arts/educational domain. But it is the latter that I think is of pivotal importance in classrooms that express moments of continuous, everyday, becoming. Children need to develop a sense of their own 'feeling life', even—particularly when—they cannot articulate it for themselves, even—particularly when—they are most divorced from any sense of it.

Read *Counting Stars*, by David Almond (2000). How does this book articulate and encourage interpersonal and intrapersonal intelligences?

Critical focus: interpersonal and intrapersonal intelligences

Using children's literature for language lessons

Reading books with children, often and in a fun way, provides a wonderful opportunity for children to see language in action. Books also provide a great resource for more formal learning about the structures of language and a locus for learning about these structures in meaningful contexts.

IN THE CLASSROOM

Text: *Rosie's Walk* by Pat Hutchins (1968)

We can use simple books in sophisticated classrooms if we use them creatively. (The converse of this is also true—we can use sophisticated texts with very young children if we translate them 'courteously' by using them creatively.) The following are some examples using *Rosie's Walk*—adjust the ideas to suit your particular class and its particular needs. *Rosie's Walk*, as well as being a wonderful little story, also shows the variety of the prepositional phrase and so is a useful instruction in grammar.

1 Children can write their own Rosie story, making up a character of their own and taking them on a similar prepositional path.

Homer Simpson went for a walk

> Over …
> Up …
> In …
> Through …
> Round …
> Under …

And …

2 Children can demonstrate the qualities of prepositions, with little labels on the two things that the prepositions relate.

The cow jumped OVER the moon
Rosie walked UNDER the bridge

Books show an abundance of varieties of sentence and paragraph constructions, and grammar in action. Again, I believe in plenty of discussions and small-group roundtables to discuss language and grammar. Endless writing and copying out of examples is nonproductive and can help take away the pleasure of the text.

3 *Living sentences*: Ask children to make labels of the parts of speech, at a level appropriate for the class. For example, as a follow-up to the exercise on *prepositions*, have children make labels (writing) for relevant prepositions and *nouns*. Children choose a label and wear it. The nouns all stand in a circle. The prepositions have to find the two nouns that they link in the story and stand together. You could add the *verbs* to this game, and *articles*, so children can construct living sentences. You could also do this as a competitive team game—if you have lots of space and can cope with the fun of this sort of grammar lesson.

4 Extend this by making a pool of different parts of speech in each corner of the room (children wearing labels) and have teams write a story by choosing words, putting them together, and making living sentences. Swap teams so that everyone has a chance to be a word and everyone has a chance to make sentences.

5 Perform *Rosie's Walk* as readers' theatre: that is, dramatic reading from the text, with lots of vocal energy but a minimum of props and movement. Have Rosie tell the story (change to first person) and then have the fox tell the story. Discuss: are there differences? Why?

6 Set up a television interview. Ask children to work in groups of four, interviewing Rosie and then interviewing the fox. How many different versions of the story does your newscast relate?

Text: *Owl Babies* by M. Waddell and P. Benson (1992)

Writing tasks about literature should be creative, rather than endless questions about story and character.

1 After reading *Owl Babies*, ask children to write their own story, real or imagined, about when they thought they were alone somewhere. You might like to read some poems about being alone (such as the relevant verses from Coleridge's 'The Rime of the Ancient Mariner'—Alone, alone, all all alone/Alone on a wide wide sea).

2 Point out some constructions you would like them to include; perhaps, in this case, it could be direct speech, with questions and exclamations. Talk over the examples in the text:

> 'Where's Mummy?' asked Sarah.
> 'Oh my goodness!' said Percy.
> 'I want my mummy!' said Bill.

As part of this story exercise, children learn what these sentence constructions are and how they are punctuated; they also learn the difference between direct and indirect speech. (Indirect speech: 'Bill said he wanted his mummy.')

3 Initiate discussions about how direct speech in books lets us hear what the characters are thinking and feeling. Find some examples in other books containing direct speech.

4 How does the direct speech in *Owl Babies* reveal character differences? How do the characters of Sarah, Percy, and Bill differ? How are they the same?

This book works well as Readers' Theatre for Years 3–4 (and possibly Years 1–2).

Text: *Tidy Titch* by Pat Hutchins (1991).

1 Appropriate to their level, children could find and discuss examples of *contractions* and the *use of the apostrophe* in *Tidy Titch*:

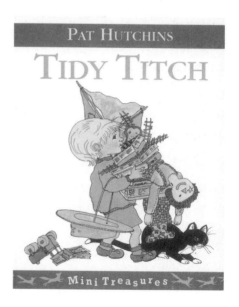

> 'I think I'll throw that old space suit out,' said Peter, 'and that cowboy outfit. They're much too small for me!'
> 'They're not too small for me!' said Titch. 'I'll have them!'
>
> …
>
> 'My room is still untidy,' said Mary. 'I think I'll get rid of this broken pram and these old games. I've played with them hundreds of times!'
> 'I haven't,' said Titch.
> 'I'll have them!'

2 Discussion ideas:

- Why does direct speech contain so many examples of contractions?
- What happens in more formal writing? Why?
- Teach *it's* as the abbreviation of *it is*.

3 Also discuss (Years 3–4) what this story shows about its culture (children have their own rooms, they have many toys, tidiness is good, useless things contribute to untidiness, things can be discarded when they are broken, children have the freedom to decide what they are going to do with their own things).

Years 5–6

Read Tohby Riddle's *The Tip at the End of the Street* (1996). Compare (note what's similar) and contrast (show what's different) these two stories (particularly the similar and different ideas about things that are discarded).

Text: *Voices in the Park* by Anthony Browne (1999)

Years 5–6

1   Read the text to the class. If possible, read Browne's earlier text, *A Walk in the Park*, as an introduction.

2   Divide the class into groups of four, to represent the four voices. Let the children read the text in groups, in their 'voices'. Then swap roles and read in at least one different voice.

3   Come back together as a class. Discuss:

- How did you feel in the character's role?
- Did your feelings change when you swapped roles? How?
- Which character do you most have sympathy with? Why do you think this is?

4   Collaborative class project: Turn the book into a movie. Discuss and allocate roles and timelines:

- Scriptwriters: write a script.
- Producers: consider how and where it will be produced. Make a schedule. Decide budget.
- Cinematographers: decide shots, background etc. Write and illustrate schedule.
- Actors: learn parts.
- Directors: rehearse with actors and cinematographers.
- Designers: make costumes and props.
- Music: write introduction and background (encourage original songs).
- If you have access to a video, make the movie. If not, act it out as if it is being shot.

(There are many other books that would lend themselves to this type of activity. Anthony Browne's *Zoo* or *Piggybook*, for example, could prove very interesting as dramatisation.)

Text: *Ginger* by Charlotte Voake (1997)

Years 3–4

1   Discuss as a class what the story is about. Can anyone relate this story to anything in his or her life?

2   This story has longer sentences than some picturebooks. After spending time enjoying the story, focus on the first opening:

Ginger was a lucky cat.
He lived with a little girl
who made him delicious meals
and gave him a beautiful basket,
where he would curl up …
and close his eyes.

3   Explore this sentence to the level appropriate to the class. You may want to label the clauses or you may choose to simply highlight the finite verbs as a clue to where the clauses are ('was', 'lived with', 'made', 'gave', 'would curl up', 'close'). You may want to discuss, for example:

- *adjectival clauses* ('who made him delicious meals')
- *coordinate clauses* ('and gave him a beautiful basket', 'and close his eyes')

- *the coordinate conjunction* ('and')
- *adverbial clauses* ('where he would curl up').

Years 5–6

Add the following:

1   Ask children to write their own sentence following as much of the pattern as you consider appropriate for their level. You could give them part of the sentence, for example:

   Kenny was a happy kookaburra.

(Or just give them the word 'happy' and let them make up the rest.)

   He ....
   who ....
   and ....
   where ....
   and ....

2   When the children have composed their sentences, let them share with each other, and peer-correct around their roundtable. Get everyone to do a finite verb check of the clauses.

3   Share sentences with the rest of the class. Encourage children to suggest any corrections.

   In all of these examples of literature as a locus of literate practices, the most important role for the teacher is that of enthuser and motivator. Demonstrate daily your own enjoyment of language, your own love of reading, and your own love of books. Tell your class about the books you are currently reading. And remember, books are wonderful teaching resources but this is not their primary purpose; they must also be made available and offered to children in classrooms as often as possible for sheer pleasure.

▶ LITERACY IN THE DIGITAL AGE

Integration of online and offline activities

In all the exciting ways that digital resources have expanded the world of children's books, making so many online activities possible, it is important for teachers to note some potential difficulties. One relates to health, and one to children's scope for developing the arts of speaking and listening.

   In relation to health, teachers need to monitor the time that children spend online as part of their school day, bearing in mind that it is likely that they may also spend hefty chunks of leisure time involved in similar activities. Physical inactivity and obesity is a problem confronting our society, in no small way because of the increased time we sit at computers, or are involved in electronic games. There is also some worrying research emerging about the deterioration of young people's eyesight, in part at least because of the time spent focused on a close screen of some type (computer, mobile phone, television etc.).

   The second potential difficulty relates to the place of speaking and listening in the classroom. There are opportunities for real electronic 'chat' (as noted above), but mostly online activities tend to focus on new ways of reading and writing.

   The affordances of ICTs are valuable, so we don't want to exaggerate these problems. They *are* problems however, and teachers must be vigilant in their daily planning to balance activities, and to surround online reading and writing with as much real talk and real movement as possible. It is worth repeating: simply moving something that could effectively be done in a more traditional way to the computer does not in itself constitute good teaching practice. Online activities can provide scope for children's socialisation, for children to explore their own pathways to a particular destination, and for collaborative and co-operative activities, but offline ones can also. All online activities need to be supported by dynamic offline action and 'chat.'

This fits in with learning theory such as Howard Gardner's idea of multiple intelligences. Gardner describes many different forms of learning: bodily/kinaesthetic, logical/mathematical, musical/rhythmic, verbal/linguistic, visual/spatial, intrapersonal and interpersonal.

▶ Summary

1 Teachers need to carefully integrate daily activities so that work online is fully supported by related speaking and listening opportunities.

2 Teachers must also be aware that children's health needs to be protected, so all online activities should be planned for maximum benefit, and again surrounded by opportunities for physical activity.

3 Children's literature provides unlimited opportunities for teaching about and practising all literacy skills, including speaking and listening. It helps children give shape to their own stories; and it presents language in a variety of authentic contexts.

4 Books help understandings of language; understanding language better means enjoying books more. This is part of the life cycle of literacy.

5 Children should be allowed to choose books freely. However, teachers must continue to share challenging books with children, and make opportunities to read such books (those that children would not choose for themselves) with them and to them. This exposure beyond immediate needs is significant in the development of knowing readers.

6 Literature gives diverse opportunities for discussion, sometimes about difficult issues.

7 Literature connects with other disciplines; it connects with philosophy and ideas about worldview.

8 Literature is a great language and grammar resource but teachers need to be creative in using it for these purposes.

9 The most important literate practice that teachers can pass on to their students is a lifelong love of language and books.

Further reading

Boxal, P. (ed.) 2006, *1001 Books You Must Read Before You Die*, ABC Books, Sydney.
Denby, D. 1996, *Great Books: My Adventures with Homer, Rousseau, Woolf and Other Indestructible Writers of the Western World*, Touchstone, New York.

THE CLASSROOM AS A COMMUNITY OF LEARNERS

26

Overview

This chapter focuses on the significance of the classroom as a physical space—as a learning space, as a space for socialisation, as a space for developing community. ICTs have not only revolutionised research and communication, they have changed the shapes of classrooms. This shape continues to evolve however, as schools adopt different ways of making technolology available.

The evolving classroom

A classroom is both a physical space and a mental space. Children will carry the memory of these spaces with them all their life. Their attitudes, not just towards literacy but also towards learning, towards discipline and self-discipline, towards challenge and difficulty, and towards self and others, will be shaped to a considerable extent by what happens in their classrooms.

Technology is having an increasing impact on the nature and directions of learning in the classroom. This is in part due to a reappraisal of some of the earlier assumptions about technology and learning, but it also reflects the skills and assumptions of an emerging generation of teachers who view technology as intrinsically involved with all aspects of their own lives. The next challenge will be how to allow the new generation of students, the digital natives, to use their 'accent' of technology seamlessly in all facets of their academic life.

The evolving classroom presents challenges about organisations of space, and teachers need to be creative. Try out different configurations, and different ways of configuring activities so that teaching and learning space is rich, vibrant, and supportive. This is our working environment as well.

Aim for creative classrooms

Classroom style will encourage certain sorts of behaviour. We want to use technology and books to encourage a sense of expectation, exploration and discovery. The two most important gifts we can give the children we teach are an *excitement about learning* that will last them all their lives, and an *excitement about who they are and what they can do*. This relates to their concept of self and their relationships to others, and as noted in chapter 20, the ability to think profoundly. It also relates to Gardner's ideas of interpersonal and intrapersonal intelligences, noted in the last chapter. Children need to be able to articulate within themselves their *'own feeling life'* (1983: 240) and to verbalise to others their own deeply held ideas. Literacy helps to articulate feeling life as a positive sense of self. It is a welcome into the world. We want to make the welcome memorable, continuous, and sustainable. We want our classrooms to be spaces that celebrate learning and that celebrate, from kindergarten until the last day of school, social and scholarly community.

The word 'celebrate' comes from the Latin *celeber*, meaning 'honoured' and also 'frequented'. 'Frequented' means, according to the *Concise Oxford Dictionary*, 'gone often or habitually to'. Educators want their students to develop *habits* of literacy, *habits* of social and scholarly community.

Literature uses language to tell the stories of communities distant in both time and place. Filling the classroom spaces with story helps to create an environment where habits of literacy and literate practices can grow, be sustained, and endure.

▶ LITERACY IN THE DIGITAL AGE

Technology has changed the shape of classrooms and the designs of schools. However, this is by no means static, and the best ways of accessing technology in classrooms continues to evolve. Gone are the blackboards, whiteboards and even the electronic whiteboards of just a few years ago. Now interactive smartboards, digital projectors, and high definition digital television have allowed a multimedia approach to learning. Wikipedia has added an interactivity to the process of knowledge discovery that encourages the student to not only read and reflect, but add to the bank of information. Wikis, blogs, and forums are opening up new possibilities as the diversity of free software strengthens a teacher's repertoire of learning tools.

The Sydney Centre for Innovation in Learning <*www.scil.nsw.edu.au*> is one institution that has established ongoing strategies for teacher professional development, looking to link technology and learning to curriculum delivery. SCIL operates on the premise that it is within a school's ability to support diversity in technological enhancement, classroom design, and digital gadgetry, and that effective and productive change will occur within the teaching sector.

Enhancing the classroom as a physical space

As much as resources allow, fill the classroom with verbal and visual story. Children's compositions and artwork make the most beautiful decorations of all—but keep them changing.

1   Set up a Book Corner (comfortable spaces to read, books to choose from, good light).
2   Make a Book Worm (or draw one). Share it around the class. Perhaps the person with the Book Worm can choose a book for Shared Reading or discussion. Perhaps the Book Worm could be a badge of some description and the person wearing it is responsible for organising

the Book Corner for that week. Stress that this is not just a tidying task but one to stimulate reading of particular books.

3   Be creative and think about how you can relate books and activities in unusual ways. (The Sustainability Unit later in this chapter is an example.)

4   Have a display of different genres: fairytales, folktales, myths, legends, adventure stories, historical fiction, family stories, fantasy, poetry, drama, cookbooks, travel books, factual texts, manuals, newspaper editorials, advertisements. Organise the class into groups looking after one category and get them to make labels and give a brief presentation.

5   You could relate this to text-types: literary text categories (narrative, poetic, dramatic); factual text categories (recounts, procedures, information reports, expositions, and general communications). Each group could present as many and as varied a sample of a particular text category as possible.

6   Introduce class to the Literary Factual Text. Find as many different examples as you can. Discuss with the class: how is this different from other factual texts?

7   Set up an Autobiography Project (see p. 403).

8   Set up an interdisciplinary display on a particular theme, e.g. 'water': books, science, poems, art, advertisements for saving water, editorials, water catchment areas for your region, and so on.

9   Many of the classroom activities in this book have talked about roundtables—children sitting around a table as a collaborative teaching and learning group. Extend the idea of the roundtable into a Reading Circle. Children could choose different groups and be part of a circle that shares books, reads to each other, and plans activities for the rest of the class based on books. For example, one circle may be interested in science fiction, another in boats, and another in stories about animals. Each Reading Circle could present a short segment to the class in any way the students choose.

10 Set up a History of Books table, and plan activities around it. Make some clay tablets. Make some scrolls (have some papyrus grass as a feature). Find examples of parchment and vellum (or something that explains what they are). Talk about ancient Chinese paper and ask children to research how paper came to Europe during the Crusades (relate to Robin Hood). Do a computer research assignment on the invention of the printing press. Relate these ideas to the new technologies. See also chapter 23.

11 Have a Fiesta of Reading and invite parents to participate. Ask parents to bring or, if they can't come, send with their child a favourite book from their own childhood. If they have a different cultural background, and if appropriate, ask them to read the book at least in part in their own language. If the child speaks the language, give the child the opportunity to read to the class in the family heritage language. Open up discussions and other stories about family heritage and customs.

12 Link this to a Family History project. Introduce children to family trees. If possible, use a software program such as Generations (Sierra) in the classroom. Use as many different research tools as possible: oral history (talking to older relatives), photograph albums, old letters, and scrapbooks, books, lists (e.g. the First Fleet), television programs, other memorabilia (books with names and dates written inside, books given as school and Sunday school prizes etc.).

13 Extend the Fiesta of Reading activity into a community program and ask local celebrities and

community officers (mayors, business proprietors, club members, etc.) to come to share their favourite books with your class.

14 Run your own Book Week. Elect judges, or institute voting procedures. Discuss categories and criteria (introduce this idea to the class if you have not previously done so). Nominate, shortlist, and select winners. Perhaps write a letter to the winning authors and illustrators— they may be happy to visit your school to receive their awards.

15 Create web pages linking to authors, children's literature organisations, and journals. Create a pool of ideas for links.

16 Create a class library of web books (i.e. write the stories on the web pages, illustrate them with graphics, set up a classification system and add as links). Discuss in a class forum this new form of the book in relation to the history of the book. What is similar? What is different? What are the problems? What are the advantages? (See also chapter 23.)

17 Set up times for synchronous and asynchronous electronic chat times, question times, times of speculation. Set e-relationships in place with other schools, other classes (use your colleagues as contacts). Work on collaborative projects on the Internet.

Assessment

Much assessment in the area of children's literature will take place either informally as observation or as part of the assessment of reading and writing (see chapters 8 and 17). The whole thrust of part III, however, is that theory informs practice. Teachers will want to confirm this for themselves and to reflect on what worked best for them in any particular situation, what didn't work so well and why, and what could be improved and how. They will also want to use their professional knowledge to adapt, modify, change or extend any activities they introduce into the classrooms, whether in children's literature or anything else.

Structured observation is important in assessment

Observation is therefore extremely important. When children are reading, the teacher needs to watch what is happening. It is tempting to use this time to catch up on marking and the thousand other things that are part of a teacher's busy day, but this wastes an opportunity to *observe the literate behaviours of children in informal contexts*. It is helpful to *structure observations*:

- Do the children procrastinate or go directly to a reading activity?
- Do they read the book or simply flip through a number of books?
- What general type of book do you notice that they choose?
- What general level of books do you notice that they choose?
- Do they commit themselves to the literature activities?
- Can you determine why or why not?
- Which of the activities do they commit to and appear to enjoy?
- Can you creatively develop more activities in this area relating to books?
- If they lack confidence as readers or writers, can you find activities that they feel more confident in and use these as a way to build up their reading and writing skills?
- If they are children from language backgrounds other than English, how can you use books and literature activities to help them find their place in the class community?

It is likely that evidence of achievement in children's literature activities will be reflected in reading and writing assessment. However, children can build up their own reading portfolio and work as roundtable groups towards extending their reading as widely as possible. Many of the activities suggested in this section could also be peer-reviewed: as teachers know, peer reviews reveal almost as much about the reviewer as they do about the person being reviewed.

There are many opportunities in children's literature activities for formal assessment, but too much emphasis on such practices is not likely to be beneficial to the long-term future of the child as a reader (this is not to say that you can't do a little formal assessment when it is obviously appropriate). Rather, use children's literature as the opportunity for observing the child:

- speak and listen
- read and write in different ways
- develop communication skills
- negotiate cultural differences
- lead discussion
- promote discussion
- initiate discussion
- engage imaginatively in a class or individual project
- work collaboratively in a team
- respond intelligently
- respond intuitively
- respond creatively
- respond emotionally
- respond spiritually.

The following three activities are designed to stimulate further creative ideas by teachers.

IN THE CLASSROOM

Text: *Each Peach Pear Plum* by Janet and Allen Ahlberg (1978)

Introduce this text to the class. Discuss these key concepts:

- sounds and rhyme
- rhythm
- game: 'I spy'
- the idea of the child's 'seeing eye'
- reader interaction: invitation to enter the text (note how the magic happens and the 'you' becomes 'I' in the text):

  In this book
  With your little eye
  Take a look
  And play 'I spy'.

- Intertextuality: what are the intertexts and how do they contribute to the book?

■ Ideology: what cultural assumptions and attitudes lie behind this text? (Think about ideas about babies and how they are treated. Think about the sort of world that is depicted. Whose world is this? Whose world isn't it?)

Table 23.1 Pointers to stimulate creative ideas

Years K–2	Years 3–4	Years 5–6
Story	Ideas of character	Structure of narrative; unity
Draw a character	Write another 'chapter'	Conclusion or finale. What does a finale represent? Visual versus verbal emphasis. Draw a diagram of the plot. How to write a story: set the scene. Genre.
Rhyme	Other rhyming games	Assonance: 'each peach'. Alliteration: peach, pear, plum.
Nursery rhyme	Other nursery rhyme characters	Who is a little different and why (Robin Hood, folktale, and oral legend)? What other folktale characters could you include (e.g. King Arthur)?
	What symbols represent what characters?	What would you draw to symbolise them and why? Discussion of symbols. Illustrations or links. What inferences (e.g. pail)?
Play 'I spy'	Play 'I spy' with letters	Make up an 'I spy' game. How do the pictures expand the text?

To think about

1 Describe the implied reader of this book.
2 What assumptions does this book make about the child's life-world?
3 What attitudes does it convey?
4 Who might find this book difficult? Why? (This could become part of a discussion on cultural literacy.)

Suggestions

1 Make a list of favourite books for children to put up in class.
2 Institute a Book of the Week.
3 Have a Fairytale Collection: ask everyone to bring in any versions they have at home. Compare the versions—illustrations and text.
4 Make up a class fairytale play. It can incorporate as many fairytale characters as you like. It can be as humorous as you like. To stimulate creative ideas, read a number of retellings such as those mentioned in chapter 25. You could also refer to the movie *Ever After*. Divide the class into groups to write different scenes, after an initial plan has been made.
5 If you haven't got a prop box in your classroom, start accumulating one. Ask for suitable old clothes from home. Old curtains make good cloaks. Make a few crowns if need be.
6 Rehearse the play and perform it at lunchtime for the other classes. You may be able to charge 20c entry and put the money towards another class book.

7 Video the performance if possible.

Activities for other curriculum areas

- Drama: Mime the story; construct a series of tableaux.
- Music: Characters march on and sing the nursery rhymes; use body percussion.
- Dance: *Play Peter and the Wolf*; choreograph different parts of the music.

IN THE CLASSROOM

Text: *Memorial* by Gary Crew and Shaun Tan (1999)

Key concepts for discussion

- place
- space
- sociocultural history
- geography
- Australian history
- the environment
- inclusivity
- subjectivity

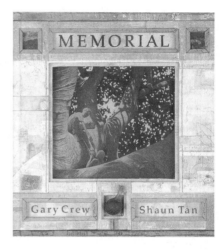

Focalisation

- Whose eyes do we see through?
- Whose voices do we hear?

Years 5–6

1 Read *Memorial* in class.

2 Discuss as many of the following concepts as are appropriate for the level of your class:

Place	Australia (but also other places experienced, e.g. France, Vietnam)
Space	Historical spaces
	The town space
	The memorial space
	Family space
	Spaces of memory
Sociocultural history	Australia from World War I until the present
Geography	An Australian country town
	Geography of the battlefield
Australian history	Involvement in wars
	Progress
	Interest in the environment
The environment	Progress
	Effect of fumes on the tree
	Attitudes towards trees
Inclusivity	The voices of four generations
	The mind-spaces of different speakers
Subjectivity	Different subjects from different generations

3   Ask children to research in groups any aspect of the above, e.g. Australia in the wars, country towns, battles of World War I, Anzac Day, changing attitudes to the environment, memorials, fashions of the interwar period.

4   If your town has a memorial you may be able to visit it as a class. What words appear on it? What pictures or sculptures? What do the words indicate is being remembered? Ask children what they think is being remembered.

5   Show the class photographs of the US Vietnam Memorial in Washington. This is a reflective memorial—it reflects the faces of those looking at it. Discuss the ideas behind building a memorial in this way.

6   Ask children to research their own family history. Have a Memorial Day and ask them to bring relevant photographs, old letters etc. to school. Stress how precious these are. Also stress that memorials do not glorify war; in fact this book is doing the opposite: showing the terrible impact that war has on everyday lives.

Exploring sustainability through children's literature

The exemplar of this activity is the idea of exploring sustainability through children's literature and the creative arts. (This activity is designed for upper primary school classes but could be adapted to suit the needs of younger children at the teacher's discretion.)

Sustainability is

- an economic and social practice which actively seeks to ensure that the demands of the marketplace do not threaten, deplete, or destroy the natural environment
- a universal imperative in a global society
- a philosophy that conceives of human wellbeing thriving in just and equitable societies where citizen rights and citizen responsibilities operate in a creative tension
- the use, conservation, and renewing of energy, including human energy.

Sustainability is using, without *using up*.

This relates sustainability to community, to inner as well as to outer environments, to the heritage and evolution of culture, and to the human spirit. A human being is more than a body that needs to be sustained and the world is more than a geographical and ecological landscape that provides physical sustenance for those who inhabit it. Sustainability is, in Ellyard's words, 'human thrival' (1997). Discussions about sustainability or thrival must take into account all aspects of human wellbeing. Sustainability is a practice for survival.

Rationale for using the creative arts

1   Using the creative arts to teach and stimulate awareness of sustainability issues is part of a long tradition. In fact the world's greatest environmentalists—those who have most celebrated the environment and who have most argued for it to be preserved, long before the terms *environmentalism* or *Green* were ever thought of—have been poets and artists. They have always known that humans and their environment are linked—by songline, by dreaming, by the need to represent an ecology of connectedness in visual forms, in aural forms, and

in kinaesthetic forms. They have always noted human interdependence as inhabitants of a shared planet.

2   The creative arts promote sustainable futures by nourishing spirit—the deepest, most intimate, and arguably the most threatened part of human beings. Individual life is a tenuous, fragile environment, briefly inhabited. Humans are connected to each other and to their environment in a worldwide web of everyday actions and mundane happenings. The creative arts allow us to explore and test and represent that connection.

3   Approaching issues of sustainability with an arts focus stimulates wide-ranging dialogues about the inner and outer habitats of a world of diverse people, all of whom are continually threatened by the processes of time and change. It promotes nonthreatening discussions about cultures and multicultures, and allows representations of a variety of cultural perspectives.

4   This activity is designed within a transdisciplinary perspective of sustainability. It will leave openings to make overt connections with history and geography, science and environmental science, as well as with arts-related fields. Mathematical activities can also be based on sustainability issues.

5   Using children's literature within a context of creative arts promotes positive outcomes:
   - the opportunity for and development of the capacity to make individual responses within a corporate experience
   - the development of complex thinking processes that can involve the whole body (and that help to physically sustain both the body and the mind)
   - the capacity to articulate being
   - interpersonal and intrapersonal communication skills
   - inner role-plays and the development of the literacy of the imagination
   - an increased capacity and confidence for creative problem solving
   - visual literacy and increased cultural literacy.

SUSTAINABILITY AND THE ENVIRONMENT

Read as many children's literature texts pertaining to sustainability and the environment as you can find:

Window by Jeannie Baker (1992)

Where the Forest Meets the Sea by Jeannie Baker (1987)

The Story of Rosy Dock by Jeannie Baker (1995)

The Hidden Forest by Jeannie Baker (2000)

The Wonder Thing by Libby Hathorn and Peter Gouldthorpe (1995)

The Paddock by Lilith Norman (1992)

Island in My Garden by Jim Howes and Roland Harvey (1998)

V for Vanishing by Patricia Mullins (1993)

The Fisherman and the Theefyspray by Paul Jennings and Jane Tanner (1994)

Memorial by Gary Crew and Shaun Tan (1999)

Pannikin & Pinta by Colin Thiele and Peter Gouldthorpe (2000)

The Rabbits by John Marsden and Shaun Tan (1998)

A Sailing Boat in the Sky by Quentin Blake (2002).

I N THE CLASSROOM

Library/Wikipedia task (for upper primary)

Theme: Find as many definitions of the verb 'to sustain' as you can:

■ keep up, keep going, keep in existence, maintain, prolong, aid, assist

■ supply with necessities or nourishment, supply with food and provisions

■ hold up, support, keep from falling or sinking, prop

■ bear, endure, support the spirits or vitality or resolution of, encourage, withstand, stand

■ suffer, experience

■ allow, admit, favour

■ agree with, confirm, corroborate, sanction, affirm the validity of.

Derivations: French from Latin *sustinere*, to hold up: *sub* (under) + *tenere* (to hold).

Writing

After sharing and noting library definitions of the verb 'to sustain', discuss the specific meanings that the noun 'sustainability' has acquired at the beginning of the 21st century. This is a great opportunity to show children that language is living and dynamic: that meanings and usages change.

Class task: Brainstorm as many ideas about sustainability as you can. Research both in the library and on the Internet. Write a class definition of 'sustainability'. Publish it in a prominent place in the classroom.

Individual writing task: Write about sustainability in the context of the classroom. What measures can be put in place to further sustainability practices? Remember to discuss sustainability in terms of human energy as well.

Publish these as part of a class newsletter to the rest of the school, to encourage discussion throughout the school. Invite responses from other classes. Include the best of these in a class newsletter to parents. For the purposes of the newsletter, elect an editor, an editorial team, illustrators, and distributors. Perhaps the class could also write a letter to the Principal, requesting that these letters are distributed at parents and friends and school council meetings.

Reading and research

Theme: Developing a concept of world heritage arts in the classroom.

Rationale: Think about the word 'ecology' in relation to the arts. 'Ecology' refers to the relationship between organisms and their environment. The arts express an ecological relationship of human beings and their environment; they have done so for thousands of years in cultures all over the world.

At the Wet Tropics World Heritage Area in Cairns, the Education building contains a plaque that reads:

This Wet Tropics World Heritage Area was created in 1988. It is one of only a handful of sites in the world that meet all four of the natural heritage criteria.

This area has several functions:

■ It represents eight major stages of the world's history.

■ It contains areas of exceptional natural beauty and aesthetic importance.

■ It represents significant ecological and biological processes in the evolution and development of plants and animals.

■ It contains significant natural habitats for conservation of biological diversity, particularly rare and threatened species.

IN THE CLASSROOM

Apply the criteria of the Wet Tropics World Heritage to a concept of a World Heritage of the Arts. (Children will need to understand that 'the arts' includes literature, drama, visual arts, drama, and dance.)

- The arts—in story, poetry and song cycle, in rock art, anecdotal sculptures, and traditional dance—represent the major stages of the experience of humankind in the world's history.
- They contain areas of exceptional beauty and aesthetic importance.
- They represent significant engagement with, and responses to, the processes of living, of being alive in a particular place at a particular time.
- They contain significant 'habitats' in which are conserved the verbal, visual, and movement stories of a world of diverse people, many of whom are already extinct, and all of whom are continually threatened by the processes of time and change.

Reading

In groups, read one of the picturebooks on the list above, or any picturebook with a related theme.

- What message about sustainable futures does this book give to its readers?
- What are the things that must be changed?
- Does the book give us any ideas about how these practices can be changed?
- Is there anything that we can do as part of our everyday life to help towards making these changes?

Literature as a continuum

1   Explore the work of the poets and writers and artists who are a part of the World Heritage of the Arts. Relate the picturebook from the Reading task and its message to other messages about sustainability and the environment within the broader continuum of literature.

'No man is an island, entire of itself. Every man is a piece of the continent, a part of the main; if a clod be washed away by the sea, Europe is the less, as well as if a promontory were … Any man's death diminishes me, because I am involved in mankind.' John Donne (1573–1631)

2   Writers and poets of all ages (e.g. the Romantic poets of Western tradition) have seen their work in many cases as a sacred trust. They have actively fought for the preservation of the environment. In 1879, Gerard Manley Hopkins (1844–89) mourned the felling of a group of trees—'not spared, not one'—and grieved that people who came after would never know the beauty that once existed.

Binsey Poplars
felled 1879

My aspens dear, whose airy cages quelled,
Quelled or quenched in leaves the leaping sun,
All felled, felled, are all felled;
Of a fresh and following folded rank
Not spared, not one
That dandled a sandalled
Shadow that swam or sank
On meadow and river and wind-wandering weed-winding bank.

O if we but knew what we do
        When we delve or hew—
Hack and rack the growing green!
        Since country is so tender
To touch, her being so slender,
That, like this sleek and seeing ball
But a prick will make no eye at all,
Where we, even where we mean
                    To mend her we end her,
        When we hew or delve:
After-comers cannot guess the beauty been.
    Ten or twelve, only ten or twelve
        Strokes of havoc unselve
            The sweet especial scene,
        Rural scene, a rural scene,
        Sweet especial rural scene.

3 John Donne's words remind us about how our world and the people in it are all connected. Think about the characteristics of living systems:

- they have diverse roles within a unity (e.g. the unity of a tree—like a poplar tree—has both soft leaves and a hard wooden trunk)
- they have permeable boundaries within the structure
- they have energy flow
- there is a synergy of the whole, that is, their energies combine to create a strength that neither leaves nor trunk possesses on its own.

An ecology of humankind sees everything as connected.

Indigenous cultures have always celebrated spirit within cultural practice: a spirit that must be encouraged and kept going if that person is to endure, to bear up, to sustain, and to be sustained. The arts work towards sustainable futures by voicing or representing experiences real or imagined in such a way as to give meaning to individual life.

Older classes: read *The Red Tree* by Shaun Tan (2001) and discuss the idea of personal sustainability.

shaun tan
THE RED TREE

IN THE CLASSROOM

Play-building exercise

1   Create a class play about sustainability. Encourage children to think of as many different aspects of sustainability as they can. Go back to the definitions at the beginning of the unit and make sure all aspects are covered. They can act, dance, mime, or sing. Encourage the use of poetry.

2   Elect a script director, director, stage manager, and choreographer.

3   Work towards a lunchtime performance for the rest of the school.

Poetry

1   Encourage children to find poems about the environment or about the human spirit.

2   Read these aloud, and tell them that it does not really matter if they don't understand every line. Concentrate on the sound and feel of the poems.

3   Some children may like to write their own poems. Some may want to paint an artistic response to issues of sustainability. Publish poems in the classroom and hang an exhibition of the paintings.

Some examples of poems from the literature continuum follow. There are countless others.

> The tide in the river
> The tide in the river
> The tide in the river runs deep
> I saw a shiver pass over the river
> As the tide turned in its sleep.
>
> (Eleanor Farjeon)

> 'Tiger! Tiger! burning bright
> In the forests of the night,
> What immortal hand or eye
> Could frame thy fearful symmetry?'
>
> (William Blake)

> Summer is y-comen in,
> Loud sing, cuckoo!
> Groweth seed and bloweth meed
> And spring'th the woode now—
>   Sing cuckoo!
> Ewe bleateth after lamb,
> Low'th after calf cow;
> Bullock starteth, buck farteth.
> Merry sing, cuckoo!
>
> (Anonymous)

Clown's Song from *Twelfth Night*

O Mistris mine where are you roaming?
O stay and heare, your true love's coming,
That can sing both high and low.
Trip no further pretty sweeting.
Journeys end in lovers meeting,
Every wise man's sonne doth know.
What is love, tis not hereafter,
Present mirth and present laughter:
What's to come is still unsure.
In delay there lies no plentie,
Then come kiss me sweet and twenty:
Youth's a stuffe will not endure.

(William Shakespeare)

maggie and milly and molly and may
went down to the beach(to play one day)
and maggie discovered a shell that sang
so sweetly she couldn't remember her troubles,and
milly befriended a stranded star
whose rays five languid fingers were;
and molly was chased by a horrible thing
which raced sideways while blowing bubbles:and
may came home with a smooth round stone
as small as a world and as large as alone.
For whatever we lose(like a you or a me)
it's always ourselves we find in the sea

(e. e. cummings)

(Note that although these tasks have been designed for upper primary, the creative teacher can adapt them for the use of younger children as well. Again, this unit has been written on the philosophical premise that children respond positively to guided exposure to concepts and tasks that challenge their existing skills.)

To consider:
The Pulitzer prize winning naturalist Annie Dillard wrote, of a creek in a Virginian field:

> Beauty and grace are performed whether or not we will sense them. The least we can do is try to be there. (Pilgrim at Tinker Creek, 1974, Harper's Magazine Press, New York.)

▶ Summary

1   The classroom is a physical and mental space that shapes attitudes that children may carry with them for life. Classroom spaces must be rich, vibrant, and supportive.

2   The most significant gifts teachers can give children are an excitement about learning and about who they are and what they can do.

Literacy constitutes a welcome into the world.

3   Teachers need to observe the literate behaviours of children in informal contexts.

4   Children's literature and the literature continuum can offer creative ways of exploring contemporary issues.

Further reading

Lovelock, J. 2006, *The Revenge of Gaia: Why the Earth is Fighting Back and How We Can Still Save Humanity*, Allenhane (Penguin), London.

27 FAIRYTALES: A PERVASIVE PARADIGM

Overview

Fairytales—in their narrative organisation, story, themes, characters and ideas—cross cultures, generations, literary genres, and media. This chapter gives a brief overview of fairytales and the powerful imageries and influences they exert.

> '*Human life is always shaped and this shaping is always ritualistic (even if only aesthetically so). The artistic image can always rely on this ritualism.*'
>
> (M. M. Bakhtin)

Fairytales as the province of children

Fairytales are a powerful understory of Western culture

Children's literature usually begins with fairytales. Note that it is not the intention of these chapters to discuss the history of children's literature; for those interested in this area there are a number of excellent texts (e.g. Hunt 1995; Saxby 1997; Saxby has written a number of books on the history of Australian children's literature).

Fairytales, however, have not historically been the province of children, and nor do they, in the history of our times, remain as the province of children. The influence of fairytales has reached deep into our culture, not only into literature but into films, advertising, and the language of everyday life. They have become pervasive cultural paradigms, artistic images that remain with us as we grow, and which, as many critics have observed, affect in diverse ways how boys and girls think about their life options.

Jack Zipes, a prominent scholar of folktales and fairytales, notes that 'the fairytale is myth' and goes on to explain: 'That is, the classical fairytale has undergone a process of mythicization' (1994: 5). 'It is the fairytale as myth that has extraordinary power in our daily lives, and its guises are manifold, its transformations astonishing' (1994: 16). Zipes is referring here to the classical tradition of ancient myths, that is, to mystical stories of sacred origin. Traditional fairytales do indeed have a 'mythic' quality in this sense, but they have also increasingly been criticised as 'myth' in that derogatory contemporary sense of being 'untrue' or separated from reality. Sacred myths were concerned with the activities of the gods, whose territory was removed from that of mortals in the ordinary world. However, the rituals of secularised myth (divorced from the sacred) are theoretically accessible to all. Zipes points out in his spirited defence of the mythic fairytales of classical tradition that modern writers of these mythic fairytales (not as appropriated and commodified by Disney) can keep alive 'alternatives for a better future' (1994: 161).

It was indeed upon such hopes that fairytales historically gained popular currency.

Children's literature and oral traditions

Fairytales emerged as one strand of the folktale (magic tale or *Zaubermärchen*) tradition (Zipes 1994: 11). Folktales were an integral part of communal story, a strong oral tradition that celebrated pasts and defined futures. In some cultures, this story was illustrated in pictures, in rock art or body paint, or in anecdotal sculpture.

Oral storytelling is a linguistic form of communication that brings a speaker and listeners together at the same time. Folktales were commonly part of social rituals and special functions and the same stories were repeated over and over again, in community. It is interesting for our purposes to note that the general features of the story told by the tale-teller did not vary greatly in content, but the actual telling of the story (words chosen and so on) did change quite radically with each retelling, depending on context and listeners.

That the form of the story changes according to audience points out the significance of the *implied reader* (see chapter 24), or in this case, implied listener. Storytellers adjust their tale to suit the moment—the listeners, the time available, the cultural time-space. Writers do the same thing, although they obviously cannot be quite so flexible and quite so variable. They write for the implied reader.

Remember the distinctions between

- story: the events, characters and setting of the narrative
- discourse: the telling of the tale, the words chosen, the shape of the chapters, the order of the telling, the way it is told (see chapter 22).

Oral storytellers may change the discourse, but they will only minimally change the story.

This helps understandings of the differences between discourse and story.

Characteristics of the oral tradition

Stories told orally tend to be repetitive, with recognisable language structures, and narrative structures clearly signalling beginnings and endings:

- *Once upon a time*: the story is starting, get ready to listen, and it's a 'no place, no time, any place, any time' story.
- *They all lived happily ever after*: the end of the story, all the threads of events have been pulled together into a perfect conclusion.

The '*playground stories*' of the Jennings type (e.g. Jennings' *Uncovered!*, 1993) are arguably a type of 20th-century folk story, telling tales about playground lore and attempting to capture in the permanence of print the ephemeral linguistic fashions of the particular school community. In these texts

- stories are told and retold
- jokes are slightly changed to suit a particular audience
- books are usually written in a very conversational, slangy way that is geared to its audience and understood by its community.

The idea of community, especially in the context of the community of children and their peers, gives us another way of understanding the success of the *Harry Potter* series. We have discussed the generic relationships of the Potter books to fairytale in chapter 22. As the popularity and media interest in the release of each book has grown, the books have almost become folktales—tales of the folk that are shared by a community and help to construct that community (see Archetypes below). Harry (the series if not the character) has become a legend in his own time, and his story is being told and retold by advertisers and commercial enterprises including filmmakers, as well as by children as they read and re-read, and tell and retell their favourite parts to each other. At the heart of the classic fairytale is magic, and the transforming power of relationship. The fifth *Harry Potter* book, *The Order of the Phoenix* (2003), tells in part about the significance of relationship (as well as the power of love); indeed Rowling dedicates the book to her husband and children who, she says, 'make my world magical'. As we shall see, there are problems with the fairytale paradigm and with the roles and behaviours they promulgate, but the Potter books, by pleasure and/or peer contagion, have generated a folk community of young readers across the world.

Archetypes

Folktales are the archetypes of our storytelling traditions. An *archetype* is an original model after which other similar things are patterned, a prototype. Carl Jung defined the archetype as an inherited idea in the individual unconscious that he argued derived from the collective experience of being human. Northrop Frye believed that all literature comes from the archetypes of folktales.

Folktales

'A real fairytale, a fairytale in its true function, is a tale within a circle of listeners.'

Karel Capek (Warner 1994: 17)

The roots of folktales, then, are in oral tales: 'tale' means 'speech', 'talk' in Anglo-Saxon. They are a part of the history of cultures all over the world but have in contemporary times become the province of retellers, collectors, interpreters, and illustrators. Their purpose was often cautionary. Common themes of folktales were greed, jealousy, love, and the need for security.

Folktales were not elitist—they belonged to the community and were stories 'of the folk'— the people. They are set in an indefinite time but usually in a specific area: the 'folk' share space and a particular region; they also share identity and history. Folktales reinforced local cultural values and operated to acculturate children into communal traditions and beliefs. They often featured magical transformations. Their structures are repetitive, using rhyme and rhythm (think of 'Chicken Licken', 'Henny Penny', 'Run run, run as fast as you can …'). Their narrative conventions, like those of fairytales, allow for unremarkable (i.e. everyone in the story accepts it as normal) communication between animals and humans, often as equals, as, for example, in 'Goldilocks and the Three Bears'.

Three Types of Folktale

1 *Myths* tell about gods and supernatural beings. Myths are often etiological, that is, they explain human origins, natural events, and geography.
2 In *legends* the main characters are often based on actual historical figures (or composites that become one figure). Legends develop their own rhetoric and their own charisma, and the stories often develop with the telling. Thus King Arthur becomes the epitome of chivalry and chivalrous behaviour, and Robin Hood becomes a hero who looks after the poor.
3 *Fables* are folktales that often use animals to explicate what a specific culture understands as a particular 'truth' about some aspect of human behaviour. They are short and snappy, and are frequently tagged at the end with a clear moral statement. The most famous examples are the fables of Aesop, which were orally transmitted from about the 6th century BC and were later translated into Latin by Phaedrus (3rd century AD) and Avianus (4th century AD). Many scholars believe that Aesop himself is a legendary character who probably never existed.

Fairytales

As we have noted, most fairytales emerged out of the oral traditions of folk literature. At their simplest, fairytales are folktales with fairies. Fairies, however, were not always the pretty little creatures in frilly skirts that we see in modern books; they were originally trickster figures. *The Faerie Queene* by the English poet Edmund Spenser (*c.* 1552–99) established a new tradition of fairies, and this was continued in the fairy world of Titania and Oberon in *A Midsummer Night's Dream* by William Shakespeare (1564–1616). However, the figure of Puck in this play relates back to earlier figures: Puck is a trickster with a range of human emotions (like Ariel in *The Tempest*). A similarly interesting representation of a fairy with 'human' emotions is Tinker Bell (in J. M. Barrie's play *Peter Pan*), who is jealous, petulant, and annoyed when she does not get her own way. Other fairy folk include sprites, goblins, elves, and brownies. Australian writers have sought with varying success to create Australian fairies—among the most interesting (and controversial) has been the attempt by Patricia Wrightson to create fairy characters based on indigenous traditions and culture.

Fairytales appear to be 'universal'—for example, more than a thousand versions of Cinderella have appeared in cultures all over the world, and the earliest extant (still in existence) version emerges from 9th-century China.

Literary fairytales

When a fairytale has no oral tradition and is created by an author, it is called a literary fairytale. The most famous writers of literary fairytales are Hans Christian Andersen and Oscar Wilde. Note that literary fairytales tend to explore particular aspects (often from a moral standpoint) of the human condition. Note also that this is not necessarily a standard definition; sometimes the classical fairytales are referred to as 'literary' (as of course they are). But the classical fairytales have clearly emerged out of a folkloric past; the literary fairytales as defined here have been created by their writers within a classical genre.

The birth of the fairytale in literature

In 1697, at the court of Louis XIV of France, one of the courtiers, Charles Perrault, put together the collection of fairy stories that would begin a tradition: *Histoires, ou contes du temps passé, avec des Moralitez* (Histories, or stories of times past, with moral lessons). These soon became known by the inscription in the frontispiece of the first edition, *Contes de ma mère L'Oye* (Mother Goose Tales). The stories included 'Cinderella' or 'The Little Glass Slipper', 'Red Riding Hood', 'Puss in Boots', 'Sleeping Beauty' (which Perrault had written and published in 1696), 'Bluebeard', and 'Tom Thumb'. The stories had a short verse-moral at the end, which of course highlights again, in the context of history, their cultural significance and explicit expectation of influence. However, these stories were written, not for children, but for the French court; Perrault's concern was with 'demonstrating how French folklore could be adapted to the tastes of French high culture and used as a new genre of art within the French civilising process' (Zipes 1994: 17).

The court of Louis XIV was a major influence on 'the look' of fairytales

Earlier, in Italy in 1550, Giovan Francesco Straparola had published a book of fairytales, and in 1634–36 Giambattista Basile published fairytale collections that included versions of 'Cinderella' and 'Beauty and the Beast'. Later, in Germany in 1812, the Brothers Grimm, German philologists, students of language and lovers of words (Wilhelm produced the first German dictionary), compiled the first edition of their fairytales. They wrote the tales in idiomatic German, the language of the folk, but this was to become the model for literary German and started a fairytale tradition.

The publication of fairytales in England began much later, with the collections of Andrew Lang. Lang drew on English literary traditions in editing *The Blue Fairy Book* in 1889. This collection included 'Beauty and the Beast' and 'Jack and the Beanstalk'.

The influence of Perrault

Perrault was to have arguably the greatest influence on perceptions of the fairytale until the advent of the 20th-century cinematic reteller, Walt Disney. He wrote in the courtly French of his day and this quickly became the language flavour of the genre. He addressed his tales to the ladies at court. Illustrators have perpetuated this French fairytale chronotope (time-space, see 'The chronotope' in chapter 24): pictorial depictions of the world of fairytale were often stylised images of the court of Louis XIV—beautiful women with pompadour hairstyles, dainty heeled slippers, and elaborate gowns; men in the court dress of the time; the carriages and architecture and social customs of the period.

We have already discussed the significance of sociocultural time-spaces in literature. Perrault wrote out of the history of his times, his historical context, and this context influenced the way the tales were told. The late 17th century (beyond the French court) was a time of mass poverty, widespread malnutrition, and the everyday presence of death. Child marriages were common, and there were large numbers of widows and orphans, and of widowers looking for mothers for their dead wife's children. So the presence of stepmothers and mothers-in-law (*belle-mères*) was a social reality. There were no state structures to care for those who could not care for themselves.

Characteristics of the fairytale

When we consider the characteristics of the fairytale within the context of the prevailing social conditions of Perrault's time, and indeed against those of later periods of history, it is not difficult to guess why this archetypal pattern of story has enjoyed such lasting popularity across the world.

Think about the ideas (and hope) inherent in the following common features of fairytales:

- the triumph of those with least agency—the youngest and the smallest (an attractive prospect to everyone younger and smaller)
- the defeat of large or threatening figures such as giants, ogres, and witches (i.e. of any frightening figures in your life)
- going out into the world to successfully make your fortune (very attractive to most people, especially those for whom this would be a nigh impossibility)
- enduring a time of trial or suffering before a happy conclusion (giving hope in tough times)
- the wicked stepmother/good true mother opposition offering contrasting responses to maternal figures (assuaging guilt about conflicting feelings)
- the resolution of conflict between an older woman and her 'daughter', with the younger one winning (again, very attractive to the younger and less-enfranchised woman)
- the transformation of the 'beast' or 'frog' bridegroom into a handsome prince (a very pleasant thought if you are married to someone much older and unattractive; it also has a clear sexual connotation)
- the attainment of wealth and power, often by supernatural means (again, an attractive prospect).

It is clear that stories incorporating these features present a very enticing escape package for people with little agency, that is, historically, for women and children.

Sanitising fairytales

Modern readers are usually shocked when they read a translation of Grimm's original 'Cinderella', where the mother urges the two sisters to cut off parts of their feet so that they will fit the slipper, and where birds pick out the sisters' eyes to punish them for what they had done (Zipes 1987). Grimm's tales met with criticism of their cruelty and harshness even in their own time and a number of 'sanitising' changes were made for the second edition. In the original 1812 version, for example, the 'stepmother' was Snow White's real mother. When the tales were republished in 1819, this was changed to the stepmother version that is common today. In 1812, Hansel and Gretel's real mother and father sent them away; in 1819 their mother became a stepmother and the father more sympathetic. It is interesting here to consider later retellings, e.g. Anthony Browne's 1981 *Hansel and Gretel* (where the witch and the stepmother are illustrated as being the same person) and Fiona French's *Snow White in New York* (1986).

A different sort of sanitising took place in the late 20th century, when the development of 'Fractured Fairytales' and other similar retellings sought to draw attention to the ways in which traditional fairytales positioned women.

Interpretations of fairytales

Fairytales are now commonly seen as children's stories, but they continue as part of the ideas and language of everyday life. The English archbishop conducting the wedding of the Prince and Princess of Wales in 1981 referred to the fairytale quality of the wedding (a sadly ironic comment in the light of future events). Films such as *Pretty Woman* (starring Richard Gere and Julia Roberts) have obvious connections to fairytales as well as, in this case, to the myth of *Pygmalion* and *Galatea*; *Erin Brockovich* (again starring Roberts) is another type of retelling.

Interest in the interpretations of fairytales began seriously with Bruno Bettelheim, a psychologist born in Vienna in 1903 who worked in the USA from 1929. Bettelheim brought a Freudian psychoanalytical perspective in his text, *The Uses of Enchantment: the meaning and importance of fairytales* (1976). One of Bettelheim's assertions was that fairytales offer a release valve; for example, they deflect children's mixed responses and ambivalences to the mother who both loves and disciplines them. Any mother then is two persons, and young children split the image so they can be angry with the 'false mother' without guilt and thus release their anger towards their own 'real' mother.

Jack Zipes, in *Breaking the Magic Spell* (1979) and a host of other publications, interprets fairytales from historical-social perspectives. Zipes pointed out that Perrault's fairytales reflected historical social reality; for example, the conflict of what today we call blended families, whereby older men with motherless children remarried younger women who then had their own children.

Marina Warner also argues the significance of historical and social perspectives in her very readable account of fairytales, *From the Beast to the Blonde* (1994). Warner takes issue with Bettelheim, and re-examines the conditions of the time. She notes that in France the word for stepmother is the same as the word for mother-in-law (*belle-mère*) and that the fairytale stereotype of wicked women may be more about mothers-in-law than stepmothers. She points out that in the custom of Perrault's time, arranged marriages between boys and girls as young as ten were common. The promised brides then lived in the homes of their husbands-to-be, and were of course ruled by their future mothers-in-law. Warner believes that Bettelheim's view is dangerous because it perpetuates and reinforces society's prejudices against women.

Deconstructing the Hero, by Margery Hourihan (1997), is a very helpful and stimulating feminist account of the construct of the hero in fairytales and literature. And Clarissa Pinkola Estès' *Women who Run with the Wolves* (1992) is a powerful Jungian analysis of fairytales and folktales concerned with discovering Wild Woman—the source of psychological/spiritual power in women that enables them to 'grow' their souls or psyches.

The complexity of fairytales

Fairytales happen in one world, 'where, within the frames of the genre, everything is possible: animals talk, wishes come true by magic, fairies give or withhold blessings, pumpkins turn into coaches, people can fly, etc. All of these supernatural elements are taken for granted, and never does the protagonist wonder at them' (Nikolajeva 1988: 13).

The irony is that these stories, which have become the classics of children's literature, are far from being simple and innocent. They can be explosive records of the worst of human behaviour and emphasise, among other things:

- sibling rivalry, e.g. the Ugly Sisters and Cinderella
- rivalry between women who all want to marry the Prince
- ambivalent attitudes towards mothers represented in images of the stepmother, the dead real mother, and the good fairy godmother
- women's dependence on finding a husband
- the idea of true worth and beauty being hidden beneath rags and surface grime (but note that the goodness still shines through—and has to be discovered, usually by a prince).

These characteristics highlight other problems inherent in the fairytale paradigm:

- The implication that goodness is useless without beauty (which is always visible when cleaned up and given fine clothes).
- The representation of goodness as meek and submissive obedience; Cinderella, for example, must not break out and go beyond the boundaries set for her: she must obey the rules and be home by midnight.

Implicit values

Fairytales are characterised by the dream that humans of the 21st century recognise as easily as those of earlier centuries did: the tempting, comforting, tantalising dream of upward social mobility.

This dream of course reinforces the significance of hierarchical structures in society: the importance of position, of becoming one of the nobility, of 'marrying money'. We have only to read the social pages of our newspapers to realise that this dream is alive and well. The implicit context of fairytales is not a pretty picture; it is a society of gross inequalities, of gross poverty, and of often equally gross treatment of the weak and helpless. In Perrault's times, wealth was recognised by its trappings (signs): coach, livery, clothes; all of these were essential for those who wanted to appear (and thus implicitly *be*) 'noble'.

Fairytales also clearly perpetuate stereotypical sex roles. Women's tasks are domestic chores; their concern is their appearance and their claims to physical beauty are of paramount concern (one wonders if much has changed when looking though women's magazines of the new millennium). Their pleasures are social rather than intellectual. Their ultimate achievement is marriage. They have little or no power of their own; their destinies are held in the hands of men—father, king, prince. The implicit ideology of fairytales is that this is the natural structure of society and that this is the proper role of women.

However, despite these all too obvious problems, fairytales have redeeming features:

- they immerse children in language, sometimes (depending on the retelling) the language of the classical tradition
- they represent and so help understandings of the human condition
- they are a fundamental part of cultural literacy
- they can be used by teachers to encourage children into critical literacy
- they lend themselves to many humorous and skewed retellings which can make children aware of the stereotypes they contain and help them to resist easy positioning
- and, yes, they do contain that element of magic that Zipes talks about, and as such, read against parodies and revisions and feminist retellings, can still captivate and, in Zipes' words, 'compel us to rethink the meaning of utopia and freedom in reality and in the realm of the fairytale as well' (1994: 161).

Characteristics of contemporary retellings

As the early chapters of part III noted, cultural ideologies influence texts both explicitly and implicitly. Retellings of fairytales in our own times reflect modern concerns. Feminist literature has helped us to rethink roles and behaviours and to resist cultural encoding that denies women freedom of choice. Thus a film such as *Ever After* (starring Drew Barrymore) features a resourceful princess who is not only quite capable of looking after herself but also saves the prince. There are many wonderful children's books that open up possibilities and potentials in retellings within the fairytale tradition. Some that come to mind are Robert Munsch and Michael Marchenko's *The Paper Bag Princess* (1980), Babette Cole's *Princess Smartypants* (1986) and *Prince Cinders* (1987), and Martin Waddell and Patrick Benson's *The Tough Princess* (1986). (See chapter 24 for some other humorous retellings of fairytales.)

A more subtle change in contemporary readings of fairytales is in our conceptions of 'the Beast'. The idea of the beast has always had sexual implications. What young girl in the time of Perrault or even in later centuries would not like to believe and hope that beneath the apparent beastliness of a beastly husband there was a prince (or anything)? A 'beast'—wild and untamed—was an apt metaphor for bad behaviour and crassness. However, we live in a different era, an era that no longer believes that everything should be 'civilised', and that has different attitudes towards beasts, and their taming. Anthony Browne's *Zoo* is an example of a new way of thinking about animals and animal rights. The world of the third millennium seeks to conserve its wilderness and its native species. So 'beasts' are no longer such an apt metaphor, and in contemporary retellings of the fairytale, beasts are not the awful things they once were; they have become more appealing—sometimes more appealing than the handsome foppish prince. The beast in Disney's film *Beauty and the Beast* was frightening perhaps, but I would argue was explicitly represented as inherently appealing, even before his transformation.

It is also interesting to note that in Grimm's original fairytale, Cinderella's ugly sisters weren't ugly, just cranky and unpleasant. They became ugly in the retellings of a society that equated ugliness of spirit with physical ugliness. However, again in the film *Ever After*, the 'ugly sisters' reverted to Grimm's original—they were unpleasant but not unattractive.

Fairytales as 'culture's sentences' and as 'socialising'

Commenting on the fairytale, Ellen Cronan Rose notes Bettelheim's comments that fairytales 'depict in imaginary and symbolic form the essential steps in growing up and achieving an independent existence' and that they 'represent in imaginative form' the 'process' of human development (1983: 209). Rose **Fairytales can be ways of reading society and social ideas** makes the point that this allows us to discuss them as *Bildungsroman*, narratives of growth and development, quoting Sandra M. Gilbert and Susan Gubar's comments that fairytales 'state and enforce culture's sentences with greater accuracy than more sophisticated literary texts because they reduce a complicated process of socialisation to its essential paradigm' (Rose 1983: 209).

Even though Bettelheim is no longer considered so authoritative (especially when gender is the issue), this reiterates the potential powers (and dangers) of the simple fairy story. The phrase 'culture's sentences' does not merely refer to an articulation or representation of cultural customs; it also indicates that these are edicts, judgments, sentences that impose a certain rule of behaviour and response. A short fairytale, say Gilbert and Gubar, can sum up everything a society thinks about what's important.

Most teachers are now alert to these issues; part of critically literate practice is to recognise this and to lead children into awareness of it. There is, however, another significance that the history of fairytales highlights, and one that we can take on board as part of our teaching philosophy. Zipes make the point that when the printing press revolutionised folklore and put it into print, it became necessarily elitist (1994). Its language changed, its audience changed, and it became the province of the educated ruling classes. In other words, it was no longer 'of the folk'.

As teachers, every time we help children into reading, every time we make something accessible that was previously inaccessible, every time we share a book in community and tell stories together, and listen to each others' stories, and every time we help children develop the skills to enable them to enter a place from which they had previously been excluded, we are helping to address such issues and to restore such equity.

IN THE CLASSROOM

(Adapt as appropriate to any level)

Fairytales are a part of our cultural *understory* — a reservoir of rich resources that have influenced not only books but also films, advertising, and other media.

1   Make a class list of as many books that you can find that are related to the fairytale.
2   Make a class list of as many films as you can think of that are related to the fairytale.
3   Set up a Fairytale Table with as many versions of one particular fairytale as you can find.

Teacher reading

Read *Eucalyptus* by Murray Bail (1998) as a fairytale. Think about the role of the daughter and the role of her would-be suitor within this paradigm. Think about analogies with the enchanted forest surrounding the home of the beautiful princess. *Eucalyptus* is a complex text with a dream-like, mythic quality that is a surreal depiction of the Australian landscape.

Critical thinking and study exercises

Critical focus: Writing the role of Woman

Woman is Sleeping Beauty, Cinderella, Snow White, she who receives and submits. In song and story the young man is seen departing adventurously in search of a woman; he slays the dragon, he battles the giants; she is locked in a tower, a palace, a garden, a cave, she is chained to a rock, a captive, sound asleep; she waits. (Simone de Beauvoir)

▪ Explore the ideas in this quote and give examples from fairytales. Find and discuss books that actively work to change this paradigm. How do they do it? Why? In what ways is this significant for us as teachers?

▪ Consider the influence of Walt Disney on the fairytale.

▪ Consider the words of Ellen Cronan Rose (above). Think through the positives and negatives of what she is saying.

▪ Start your own collection of versions and retellings that you can use in the classroom to help your students into critical literacy.

Explore the huge resources of online fairytales.

▶ Summary

1   Originally, fairytales were not particularly written for children.

2   Fairytales emerge from a rich oral, historical folkloric context.

3   Folktales are the archetypes of our storytelling traditions. The patterns of their stories were and are attractive to those with little power.

4   The most significant early collections of fairytales were those of Perrault in France, the Grimm brothers in Germany, Straparola and Basile in Italy, and Lang in England.

5   Classical fairytales need to be carefully reconsidered as they are intensely and powerfully culturally pervasive.

6   Fairytales can stimulate us to think about roles and gender issues, and about how books and films construct these in certain ways. They can also remind us about the human need to dream of more equitable futures.

7   Fairytales can provoke us as teachers to renew our efforts and inflame our philosophy to work towards helping all children into literacy and literate behaviours.

Further reading

The following books may be of interest to those who would like to explore further the writings of Jung, Frye, and other theorists, as well as critical writings on fairytales.

Gilbert, S. M. & S. Gubar 1979, *The Madwoman in the Attic: The woman writer and the nineteenth century literary imagination*, Yale University Press, New Haven, Conn.

Harland, R. 1999, *Literary Theory from Plato to Barthes: An introductory history*, Macmillan, London.

Hyde, M. & M. McGuiness 1992, *Jung for Beginners*, Icon Books, Cambridge.

Marks, E. & I. de Courtivron (eds) 1981, *New French Feminisms: An anthology*, Harvester, Brighton.

Moi, T. (1985) *Sexual Textual Politics: Feminist literary theory*, Methuen, London.

Rivkin, J. & J. Ryan (eds) 1988, *Literary Theory: An anthology*, Blackwell Publishers, Oxford.

Warner, M. 1994, *From the Beast to the Blonde*, Chatto & Windus, London.

Warner, M. 1998, *No Go the Bogeyman: Scaring, lulling and making mock*, Chatto & Windus, London.

28 PICTUREBOOKS AND POETRY

Overview

Picturebooks are a unique literary form. They tell their stories through subtle mixes of multiple modes that can include words, drawings and paintings, maps and charts, cartoon elements, photographs, montage and collage. They are a generic hybrid, adapted from the novel but often with a very strong connection to poetry. They provide a rich resource for young children learning complex and diverse literate behaviours.

Visual and verbal art

The explosion of large numbers of picturebooks in the marketplace was a 20th-century phenomenon (see Saxby 1997: 184–204). Originally such books were designed for very young children who could not yet operate as competent independent readers. Pictures, it was considered, helped children to 'read' by placing *signifier* (name) and *signified* (the thing) in close visual proximity to each other, after the style of alphabet or vocabulary books. These pictures give children clues and cues about the story and the characters, as well as helping to make the texts more attractive and aesthetically appealing.

The pictures of picturebooks, then, emerge on the one hand from a pedagogical tradition of teaching children literacy, and on the other the publishing tradition of the random use of illustrations in fiction texts. Some of these books 'with illustrations' were infuriating to the careful reader as it was quite clear that the illustrator often had not read the book, and there was frequently significant discrepancy between words and pictures. Sometimes it was only the line of text beneath the picture (caption) that gave the reader any idea of what incident in the book it was meant to represent.

In contrast, any discrepancy between the words and pictures of a modern picturebook is meant to be there. What's more, it is likely to be part of what Doonan calls the picturebook's 'narrative thrust' (1993: 39).

For example, let us look at Anthony Browne's *Zoo* (1992). This text presents readers with the focalisation of the young boy narrator, but as we progress through the story there is an increasing sense of unease and discrepancy between what he says and what the pictures 'say':

> 'We went into the elephant house which was really smelly. The elephant just stood in the corner stuffing its face.'

> 'Then we had to go and see the polar bear. It looked really stupid, just walking up and down, up and down.'

The pictures accompanying these pieces of text in both cases accurately represent the bones of the words: the elephant *is* standing in its house eating; the polar bear *is* walking, presumably up and down. However, just as the boy focaliser's language choices ('just stood', 'stuffing its face', 'really stupid', 'just walking up and down') extend meaning by conveying a particular attitude, so the pictures, while they in no way contradict what he is saying as literally true, interrogate his perspectives and work towards a moral contradiction of them.

The traditional grammatical definition of *register* refers to the way in which we make different language choices, appropriate to audience, purpose, time, and place, in different contexts

If we apply the linguistic idea of **register** to the pictures as well as to the words, it is clear that there is a deliberate mismatch of registers. The words are in one register—the colloquial language of a boy uninterested in the social situation of a family outing—and the pictures are in another, quite different register—the visual language of a deeply concerned animal-lover whose intention is to use this literary context as a protest against keeping animals in zoos.

This concept of register in relation to the pictures of picturebooks is helpful. Register pertains to the significance of the social situation in which words are uttered—who we're speaking to and where we are may not always determine what we say but it certainly influences how we say it. It draws attention to the importance of situation in how we seek to achieve our communicative purposes. Browne's visual language speaks in a noble register that is the antithesis of the slangy verbal conversation of his young narrator. This visual language is the serious and emotive language of advocacy.

The elephant stands within a space configured with sharp and heavy horizontal lines on a hard floor littered with a few pieces of either food or faeces, the only light coming from a horizontally barred ceiling, and a small door, man-size (not elephant-size, another representation of human power and animal helplessness), apparently the only way out. On this third opening, pictures and words are entering into a conversation of differing ideologies—a dialogic conflict—with each other. By the time of the polar bear (the eighth opening), the different registers used in the depiction of the bear, in its artificial and horizonless cave, are opening up textual spaces of meaning beyond either the verbal or pictorial text.

It is the way that the pictures work *against* the verbal text that tells the story of *Zoo*; the pictures would lose a major part of their argument without the words that conflate them. 'Argument' is a good word: this text argues Browne's worldview about the confining of animals in zoos for the indiscriminate and uninterested pleasure of families such as this. By the tenth opening, when the orang-utan crouches in a corner, the pictures have become such a powerful 'voice' that the narrator's perspective of 'miserable thing' rings with an awful irony.

The text opens up to further dialogic relationships when we recognise the distinct similarity between the mother and the orang-utan—it could almost be the back of her head that we see huddled in the cage.

Writers and illustrators working together

Anthony Browne is one of many children's writers who illustrate their own books, but there are also many writers who only write and illustrators who only illustrate. It is interesting to note that

**Words and pictures tell
different stories**

not so very long ago the name of the illustrator might not have appeared on the book cover; when it did it was usually much smaller and less significantly placed than that of the writer.

That this is no longer the case is an indication of increasing understandings of the literary form and structure (poetics) of this genre. Illustrators are co-producers of picturebooks and share the telling of their story. It alerts us to the fact that the pictures are not just ornaments or frills or visual embroidery but part of the narrative process.

Sometimes authors and illustrators work independently of each other. While this may or may not be desirable, it appears to be a publishing reality. This opens up provocative questions as to individual artistic conceptualisations of 'meaning'. A study of one book noted that the illustrations were carried out with very little input from the writer (Winch 1999); the anecdotes of other writers reveal that this is not an unfamiliar scenario.

Verbal and visual languages of picturebooks

We have earlier discussed Bakhtin's conceptualisation of the novel as containing many voices— *heteroglossia*. While he is not referring to picturebooks, it is interesting to consider his ideas about the verbal art of the novel in relation to what we could call the 'double languages' (verbal and visual) of the picturebook genre:

> All languages of heteroglossia, whatever the principle underlying them and making each unique, are specific points of view on the world, forms for conceptualising the world in words, specific world views, each characterised by its own objects, meanings and values. As such they may be juxtaposed to one another, mutually supplement one another, contradict one another and be interrelated dialogically. (1981: 291–2)

Zoo is clearly a heteroglossic text: its words and pictures work together to transmit many 'voices'—that of the boy focaliser, the father, the mother, Browne's philosophical position, societal ideas about zoos, and, of course, the animals.

The pictures of picturebooks in tandem with the verbal text represent a unique many-voiced language that is increasingly, deeply, intertextual, in its words and in its pictures. This intertextuality represents a conversation not only between this and other verbal texts, but also between these and other illustrations (see the earlier discussions on *Memorial* and *The Great Bear*, in chapters 23 and 24 respectively).

As Nikolajeva (1996a: 153–4) points out, intertextuality is about 'codes' and conversations between works of art or between works of art and cultural codes and practices. Anthony Browne's *Piggybook* (1986) is powerful not only because of the internal conversation between its words and pictures, and its argumentative intertextual relationship to all those books where mother does the household chores and wears an apron, but also because it contains a provocative intertextual dialogue with patriarchal and feminist discourses. This enlarges its obvious semiotic codes—the car is a 'sign' traditionally associated with masculinity, the multiplying pigs are signs not just of animals but of certain associated behaviours; the flying pigs play with the well-known idiom expressing impossibility, 'Pigs might fly'.

The internal conversation of picturebooks

At the heart of the picturebook is the dialogic conversation it has within itself, between the art of its words and the art of its pictures—the interaction it sets up in the spaces between and beyond its words and its pictures. This conversation constructs its worldview, and works in a synergistic tension extending or interrogating meaning by juxtapositions, by mutual supplementation, by contradiction, and by dialogic interrelationship. Remember that Bakhtin interprets 'dialogic' as the many voices behind and inherent in language; it is the internal and external voices we hear beyond the actual words, sentences, and pictures, which help us as readers and beholders to make meaning.

Pat Hutchins' simple little tale *Rosie's Walk* (1968) provides a great example of how words and pictures work together to create something that is across, between, and beyond each of them. This is an interdisciplinary space that is neither completely words nor completely pictures. It is a unique *third space*, which has as part of its deep structure intratextuality—a sort of within-the-text *intertextuality*. Like intertextuality, which also reaches across, between, and beyond, intratextuality sets up points of interconnectedness that are fragile and often characterised by heterogeneity.

Words and pictures also work together in dialogic conversation

For example, there is no overt connection in the words of *Rosie's Walk* with the fox who stalks her. Whether or not she is aware of its presence is a matter to debate with child readers: what is interesting in this discussion is the points of intratextual connection between the words and the pictures and the pattern that emerges from these. In terms of structure, there are obvious links to the classic narrative structure of the journey away from home and back again, a structure that children will increasingly recognise. The causal link is of course Rosie—*Rosie's Walk* is a type of **picaresque** picturebook, with either Rosie or the fox as rogue-hero. It is a story whose order and sequence of events follow the progress of its main character through a number of adventures in different places. The visual story connects, in a signifier–signified relationship, with the name of the place through which Rosie walks (across the yard, around the pond, past the mill, through the fence, etc.). This is a homogeneous, stable connection. The connection becomes more heterogeneous when what was safe for Rosie becomes a place of disaster for the fox; irony extends and amplifies the narrative way beyond the words by what is depicted as happening to the fox in Rosie's wake. Not only that, but also the pictures then infuse the words with other images about foxes getting their comeuppance—Brer Fox is an obvious example.

Counterpoint

Phillip Pullman writes: 'The complexity of interplay between picture-meaning and text-meaning … and what that interplay allows is the greatest story-telling discovery of the twentieth century: namely, counterpoint' (1989: 160). This is a helpful analogy: *counterpoint* is a musical term that refers to the musical technique of combining two or more melodic lines in such a way that they establish a harmonic relationship while retaining their linear individuality. But I am not sure that the pictures and verbal text of picturebooks, after they have been read, can maintain their 'linear individuality'. Pictures are read in nonlinear ways; children read pictures in all sorts of movements, with their eyes moving apparently randomly around the page, free from the reading of text from left to right. And although the first time we read a book we may read in a linear way, any subsequent reading is influenced by the intratextual reading that has already occurred. The second time we read *Rosie's Walk*, the pictures and meanings we made from the first reading are part of our reading repertoire. We can never recapture the innocence of a first reading.

The pleasures of predictability

Not that children want to recapture that innocence anyway. Research continually indicates the significance of *prediction*, that is, the ability of children increasingly to predict and expect, because of their past reading experience, what a word is going to be, what a story is going to do; part of predictive skill is being able to anticipate a familiar text or genre (an example of what I have already referred to as Nodelman's concept of narrative literacy). This probably explains the popularity of series books, from the Famous Five to Sweet Valley High and Goosebumps and the Animorphs. It is also significant to note that children are very highly focused close readers, as any parent or teacher who tries to skip bits of a favourite story knows. There is certainly a great pleasure in meeting the familiar; nonetheless, the particular pleasure of the picturebook and of children's literature in general is in the act of revisiting the familiar but discovering something new in the process. Margaret Meek writes that a page in a picturebook is to be 'contemplated, narrated, explicated by the viewer. It holds the story until there is a telling'. Readers have to learn 'which of the pictorial events carries the line of the story … The essential lesson of *Rosie's Walk* depends on there being no mention of the fox, but the reader knows there would be no story without him. Nowhere but in the readers' interaction with the text can this be learned' (1988).

Picturebooks have developed their own conventions: covers and title pages that reflect a significant moment; endpapers that usually reflect or symbolise thematic intent or cultural location; the convention of an illustration at every opening; sometimes decorations of words and opening initials that evoke the illustrated manuscript of past times; sometimes an afterword of explanation (usually serious and often didactic); sometimes a tiny picture on the back page representing the return to equilibrium or the new status quo.

IN THE CLASSROOM

Text: *The Fisherman and the Theefyspray* by Jennings & Tanner (1994)

Take a number of copies of the text, and an overhead print-out (on one page) of the text then

- read the verbal text from the overhead
- retell the story
- note any narrative gaps
- now look at the illustrations only
- note how the pictures help to tell the story
- now consider the whole text
- how do the pictures fill in the gaps? What do they add?

Text: *Where's Mum?* by Libby Gleeson and Craig Smith (1992)

Years K–2

1 Read the story to the class.
2 Ask children to draw pictures of all the fairytale characters.
3 Ask children to write their own fairytale.

Years 3–4

1 Read the verbal text to the class without showing them the pictures.
2 Then, in roundtable groups, read the text again, this time also reading the pictures.
3 Carefully examine the pictures in relation to the words. What do the pictures tell us that the words don't (the messiness of the house, the hassled dad)?
4 Check out the pictures for little connecting signs: e.g. dad holding an egg as they talk about Humpty Dumpty.
5 'Tell me': what is the surprise at the end of the story?

Years 5–6

As above, but add: in your group, write or script what else Mum told her family.

▶ LITERACY IN THE DIGITAL AGE

'A picture is worth a thousand words'—so the old saying goes. This statement may be challenged, but nevertheless we can see that the unique status of picturebooks is that they are *literature*—books— whose story is told in two different types of texts or 'language-ings' (i.e. words and pictures). Pictures, as noted above, are nonlinear—and the idea of 'reading the pictures' fits in very well with an increasingly electronic age in which features such as hypertext challenge previous reading hierarchies and stimulate nonlinear print cultures. Icons are visual symbols and in contemporary culture stand for everyday actions and processes as well as for representations of the abstract and/or sacred. The current debate in educational circles about *visual processing* and *visual literacy* reflects the growing awareness of the different types of texts that children engage with, and the significance of this in the reading (meaning-making) process.

MULTILITERACIES

Reading is a visual and cognitive process, and how print is arranged on a page makes a difference to how it is read. Visual processing may appear to categorise the small print on a product as less important than the large print featuring the product name—visual literacy helps us to recognise that the smallest print may contain the most important information (of course, this also represents knowledge of the ways of advertisers, which is a part of cultural and critical literacy).

Conventional ideas of illustration have obviously tacitly played with ideas of visual processing—in alphabet books for example, the child sees an apple, sees an 'Aa' and puts the two together. This is a type of *word–picture assimilation*. Picturebooks, however, have on the whole moved beyond such ideas—not to multiculturalism but to a sort of *multitextualism*, an awareness of the richness of textual difference. Words and pictures do not have to assimilate (blend together like the Aa and the picture of the apple); they can do different things and can interrogate and problematise as well as support (think of *Zoo*). This is a particularly significant attribute for children growing up in an age of multiple texts and multiple literacies.

An indication of the impact of the visual in the reading process is the current experimentation with all sorts of different representations of the verbal text in picturebooks. Words run up and around pages which may have to be tilted to be read, they hide in different parts of the page, they appear randomly and in different fonts and sizes—think of Maya Angelou's *My Painted House, My Friendly Chicken, and Me* (1994). The growing use of the term 'viewer' or 'beholder' in discussing the implied 'reader' of picturebooks reflects a challenge to (or an enlargement of) traditional notions of literacy.

Visual literacy

Teaching children about the pictures helps develop visual literacy

The particular strength of picturebooks is that their pictures as well as their words are designed to convey messages that 'mean'. We live in a world where pictures 'mean'—a world of images, symbols, and logos, a semiotic world of signs. Teaching children about how the pictures in picturebooks work, with and against the text, helps them to develop visual literacy, an increasingly important literacy in a world of diverse textual communications. Visual literacy is more than the ability to decode images (to work out what images mean). It is the ability to analyse the *power of the image* and the *how* of its meaning in its particular context. (See also 'The literacy of the imagination' in chapter 23, and chapter 29 on Visual Literacy.)

In defence of the pictures

Increased understandings of visual processing and visual literacy, and of the theory of the dialogic relationship between the words and the pictures of picturebooks, helps us to understand how important such books are in the reading history of children. But picturebooks have their critics. Protheroe writes: 'Using pictures and visual aids to subserve language learning is a very suspect activity and may not only adversely affect children's linguistic ability but permanently stunt their intellectual growth' (1992: 10).

A diet of the bland illustrations of some school reader series books may certainly be suspect, but as we have seen, the picturebooks of today are on the whole anything but bland. They are increasingly subtle and abstract. Protheroe's advocacy of the significance of the imagination for children is something with which I wholly concur, and, with a proviso, I also concur with her conclusion: 'Right from the beginning [children] need stories without pictures.'

Yes, they do. This is part of the Shared Reading process—for educators to read books without pictures, *as well as* books with pictures; to read difficult and challenging texts, while at the same time reading texts that are simple and relatively accessible. But to blame picturebooks for the promotion of illiteracy seems to me to ignore the contribution of this genre to children's literature and to fail to engage with the sophisticated processes through which picturebooks actually work.

There are a number of codes and conventions in picturebooks that we learn to accept very quickly:

- pictures are two-dimensional but they represent a three-dimensional world
- not everything can be included so some things have to be left out
- the picture is a highly limited and focused space
- sometimes there are backgrounds, sometimes there are parts of backgrounds and sometimes there is a lot of white unfilled space
- there are particular conventions for showing movement, and sometimes for indicating speech and thought (often comic book conventions are used)
- sometimes there are frames around pictures and sometimes pictures spill off the page.

Pictures can be discussed in terms of shape, proportion, colour, light and shade, space, focalisation, materials (collage, woodcuts, watercolours, oils, and pencils), use of black lines, shadows, and composition.

There are an increasing number of books and papers specialising in picturebook art. One of the first and most helpful is Perry Nodelman's *Words About Pictures* (1988). Other useful references include Jane Doonan's *Looking at Pictures in Picture Books* (1993) and *CREArTA* (2000).

The visual chronotope

In chapter 24 I noted Bakhtin's idea of the chronotope: the relationships of people and events to time and space in novels. I proposed the extension of this idea into the concept of a visual chronotope, that is, the *visual* depiction of the relationships of *people and events to time and space* in the pictures of picturebooks.

Teachers may not want to use this theoretical metalanguage in the classroom, but their own understanding of such ideas may inspire new ways of approaching picturebooks and stimulate creative classroom discussion and enquiry.

For example, *A is for Aunty* by Elaine Russell (2000) takes the traditional form of the alphabet book but is in fact deeply autobiographical; Russell uses the sequential letters of the alphabet to give narrative shape to her memories of an indigenous childhood. In the words of the text, people and events are related to time and space through the normal chronology of the narrator's lifetime: 'The mission where I lived as a child was like a small suburb outside the main town, in the bush near a river.'

Each letter of the alphabet stimulates a memory of the past:

L *is for Lagoon*

A lagoon is a great big pond way out in the bush. Wild ducks, swans, cranes and other animals gather there, mainly in the mornings or late in the evenings, to drink the water. We Aboriginal people would say this is the animals' Meeting Place, where they can rest and get together.

M *is for Mission*

The mission where I lived as a child was like a small suburb outside the main town, in the bush near a river. The government built the houses — all in rows — for the Aboriginal families to live in. There was a school, a church and a dance hall. The manager and his family lived in their own house on the mission.

I is for Inspection Day. The manager's wife visited each house on the mission to make sure our homes were clean and tidy—which they were!

So the past that is clearly expressed in words is the remembered past of an older person looking back, the past of an individual lifetime, but this does not fully explain the impact of the book. However, if we bring the concept of a visual chronotope into play, and consider how the people and events are drawn in relation to time and space in the *pictures* of the text, it is clear that the visual chronotope of this story reaches into a past that is beyond that of an individual lifetime. The past expressed in the illustrations is unbound by the restrictions of a normal lifespan; it is a dense cultural past/present that could be called a type of Dreaming chronotope. The pictures construct multiple references—to totemic figures, to the circles of sites, camps, waterholes, campfires. The roads present an imagery of paths and movement, while the river that dominates most of the illustrations reminds us of Water Dreamings, and/or of a snake or Rainbow serpent—of a type of genesis, life-giving and connecting.

In prose (without its pictures), this is a 20th-century story told in a warm but matter-of-fact way; it is a charming story of random memories, with a deep but not bitter subtext implicating sociocultural attitudes, practices, and policies in relation to indigenous people. In pictures (without its prose), this is a story that in depicting a 'modern' Australia reaches back into an Australia before white settlement. In the form of a picturebook, with both prose and pictures carrying narrative and coming together in story, the visual chronotope amplifies the verbal chronotope to something beyond an individual experience. This does not devalue that individual life experience; it enriches it. The relationship of people to the time-spaces of the illustrations is different from the relationship of people to the time-spaces of the verbal narrative, and the effect of this difference is to transpose *A is for Aunty* into a different cultural dimension.

Picturebooks and poetic language

Poetry is spare, euphonic (pleasant-sounding) language that operates very much like data compression: one word can hold and then release a tumble of information. A poet has only a short space (even in long poems) to convey his or her thoughts, and so must work towards making every word count.

Picturebook text has many similarities to poetry. It too tends to be very spare, very succinct, as Nodelman points out, and very powerful. Simple words, cohabiting with their illustrations, unleash a whole host of ideas, thoughts, feelings, meanings; they call out to other words from the understory and bring them up to play. Picturebook and poetic text depend on the semiotic (see the boxed text on Barthes in chapter 20) and semantic process of signs and symbols; the words of their discourses are much fewer than the words of their stories.

Picturebooks, like poetry, sound best read aloud—they have an acoustic function, an articulatory function, and a semantic function. Read, for example, the words of *The Fisherman and the Theefyspray*—savour the saying of them; do the same with William Mayne's beautiful little story *Mousewing* (1987). Listen to them as other people read. Think about how the words mean, and how they make you react the way that you do. In this way, picturebooks (and any books read aloud with a group) relate to the discussion of folklore in chapter 27: they offer a corporate, community experience of shared story.

This is an experience that we need to give children. Let them read aloud, not as part of oral reading—as a task—but because reading aloud is fun. Even reluctant readers feel confident when reading what looks like a short and simple text. After the reading, call attention to the words, and how the writer has put them to work. Ask children to listen to the story with pencils in their hands and jot down any words that come into their minds as they are listening (do this on a second reading of a text). Prove to them how words contain other words inside them (like those little sets of Russian dolls) and around them. Share in the activity and let the class see how much you too enjoy language.

Encourage children to read aloud, for the sheer fun of it

Formalism

Russian *formalism*, a literary theory that emerged in the early part of the 20th century, claimed that the essence of literary language was 'defamiliarisation'. That is, words are used and put together in such a way as to sound unfamiliar, different, sometimes startling. This has the effect of making readers perceive a familiar thing or consider a familiar process in a new way. Poets have to make ordinary things sound strange so that we focus on seeing them as if for the first time, rather than just knowing them from lots of other places. The formalist Shklovsky writes: 'The language of poetry is, then, a difficult, roughened, impeded language' (Rivkin & Ryan 1998: 21).

Picturebook language, like poetry, is also sometimes 'roughened' and 'impeded'—words that are quite normal and everyday and that usually glide smoothly into sentences without our even noticing them suddenly seem to stand out, surprisingly rough around the edges, not able to fit in so easily without our stopping for a microsecond (or longer), thinking about them and giving them a bit of an intellectual push. They catch and snag on each other. Then we suddenly see that this fits into place in a whole new way and we see something fresh, with 'growing eyes'.

Look at the text of *Theefyspray*:

> Deep in the still cold shadows the last
> Theefyspray looked out of her lonely lair.

'Lair' feels rough and incongruous for a fish, but when we stop and think about it as a den or a hiding place, it adds to the sense we already have of something wild and beautiful under threat.

The unusual word order, the alliteration, and the almost unconscious assonance of 'deep' and 'theefyspray' also help to roughen up the language, preventing our reading superficially. Jennings wants us to hear (and touch and feel) every word:

> There was not one other like her now.
> Not in the heavens. Or the hills.
> Or the deeps of the hushed green sea.

The *story* of these lines is that 'there was no other theefyspray'. But the discourse reaches again down to the understory and picks up strangely inappropriate words for a fish: 'Not in the heavens. Or the hills.' Nowhere in the whole wide world, or even outside it—and the alliterative 'heavens' and 'hills' release data about 'alone-ness' which some people may find almost biblical.

There are many picturebooks that are poetic in their discourse. Consider any of Sendak's texts:

> [Max] sailed off through night and day
> and in and out of weeks
> and almost a year
> to where the wild things are. (1963)
> If Ida backwards in the rain
> would only turn around again
> and catch those goblins with a tune
> she'd spoil their kidnap honeymoon! (1993)

We can savour the language of almost anything from the Ahlbergs. And what about this from *You and Me, Murrawee*?

> We walk this same brown earth—
> You and me, Murrawee.

Poetry and picturebooks share a linguistic freedom—sentences can be incomplete or ungrammatical, words can be left out; it is the sound and saying and the sense that matter:

> The boy called Shane strokes the scared fur.
> He talks and talks until growls slide into silence …
> Over the bins and garbage bags, past a row of seamed-up houses.
> 'Yeah—you're with me now, Cat. You'n me, Cat.
> And we're going way away home.
>
> (*Way Home*, Hathorn & Rogers 1994).

Most children enjoy the sounds of picturebooks. They also enjoy poetry—rhythm and rhyme and the feel and taste of words. That's why they chant rhymes in the playground, and while skipping, and on the bus, and in their games. We as teachers kill poetry when we focus on 'meaning' all the time—as edifying as that can be a little later in our development. We sometimes forget that the sounds and rhythm of words are part of their meaning and a fundamental element of the poetic experience.

Beware, Beware (Hill & Barrett 1993) is a miniature *Bildungsroman*—a story about growing, about the call of the world and the call of the wild, maybe about ambivalence and the desire to 'walk on the wild side' (Doonan 1998). Its language is intensely intertextual, as discussed earlier (see chapter 25); it is also intensely poetic:

> Setting sun
> Rose red
> Light falls
> Across the snow

This book lends itself to being spoken and acted out. Experiment with different voice combinations. Is this a monologue—a conversation with inner voices? Or is it a conversation—a cautionary one—between the little girl and her mother? And what about when she gets into the woods—are the voices she hears from inside or outside herself? Ask children to think of different ways to mime the story.

You can use picturebooks like this one as a stepping-stone to poems across the literature continuum. For example, for me, these lines evoke Tennyson's 'Blow Bugle Blow', especially the second stanza:

> O hark, O hear! How thin and clear
> And thinner, clearer, farther going!
> O sweet and far from hill and scar
> The horns of Elfland faintly blowing.
> Blow, let us hear the purple glens replying:
> Blow, bugle: answer, echoes, dying, dying, dying.

Read this, and any other poem that the story may evoke to you, to the class, but don't stress its meaning—any more than you stress the meaning of *Beware, Beware* (I am not sure exactly what the picturebook means). Sometimes we need to grow into meaning. That's part of the pleasure of literature. And sometimes meaning is beyond words anyway.

Ask the class to pick out the words that may seem related, to show them how words connect with each other, sometimes without our realising it. Doing this sets up a link between picturebooks and poetry and exposes children to the wider literature continuum, helping to build up their own capacity for understory.

You could also explore other picturebooks for connections to *Beware, Beware*. Fairytales are obvious intertexts for the adventure in the woods—perhaps the 'Rose red' plays with images from 'Snow White'. Josephine Poole's retelling of this fairytale in *Snow-White* has a much longer text than *Beware, Beware*, but the poetic type of language is still there:

> One day the queen sat by the window, stitching pearls into cloth of gold. It was winter, and very cold, and presently it began to snow.
>
> She opened the window to listen for the sound of the king's hunting horn. But as she leant out, she pricked herself with her needle, so that a drop of blood fell onto the snow. When she saw it, she wished in her heart, 'Oh, that I had a child as red as blood, as white as snow, and as black as the wood of an ebony tree!' (Poole & Barrett 1991)

Matt Ottley's *Mrs Millie's Painting* (1998) represents part of its text as a rhythmic wave that is an interesting pictorial representation of what poetry does and what it looks like:

They arrived home at dusk, as the air was filling with fireflies.

Children may like to try to write their own poetry in wavy lines, or in some other way that visually represents the sense of rhythm they are trying to create. This could be a very interesting computer task. They may also like to do a painting—perhaps to try to paint a neighbourhood, as Mrs Millie does. There are many, many wonderful poetry books for children, but the language of picturebooks is, very often, a poetic language. Understanding and becoming familiar with that language, and constructing more and more links to its understory, not only gives children confidence and enhances literacy skills but also gives them pleasure.

Children's poetry

Children—especially small children—enjoy rhythm and rhyme; they make up chants and skipping and clapping games. Children's poetry is rhythm and rhyme, sound and image; it is something that is spoken aloud and listened to. It is often a communal experience, shared with parents and carers, and with peers at play. 'Meaning' appears to be secondary—rather, it is sounds and pictures-in-words that connect and create pleasure. Nursery rhymes are examples of this; what they actually mean and their historical origins are frequently disputed (Carpenter & Prichard 1984: 384) but their attraction to children (and parents) appears to endure. Think about the somewhat dubious 'meanings' of some of the following: 'There was an Old Woman who Lived in a Shoe', 'Jack and Jill', 'Little Miss Muffet', 'Tom Tom the Piper's Son', 'Simple Simon', 'Mary Mary Quite Contrary', 'Sing a Song of Sixpence', 'Three Blind Mice', and 'Rockabye Baby on the Treetop'.

It is sad that something that children innately respond to at a very young age, and that adults actively share with children at a very young age (e.g. 'This little piggy went to market'), becomes something that many can't relate to and actively dislike by later secondary school, despite the fact that poetry is covertly an intimate part of their culture as part of popular song (see chapter 31). Many—not all!—popular songs are poetry finding its musical voice; think for example of Sting's 'Fields of Gold':

> You'll remember me, when the west wind moves
> Upon the fields of barley
> You'll forget the sun in its jealous sky
> As we walk in fields of gold.

Educators need to find ways to show that poetry is something that connects and gives expression to all sorts of emotions, some comic, some sad, some trivial, some profound. For example, play the Sting song to upper primary and secondary classes and then read with them Tennyson's 'The Lady of Shalott' with its equally passionate images of the appearance of Lancelot, seen by the lady in her mirror as he rides along the road through the fields of barley below her window:

> A bow-shot from her bower-eaves,
> He rode between the barley sheaves,
> The sun came dazzling through the leaves,

And flamed upon the brazen greaves [leg armour]
Of bold Sir Lancelot.

Poetry is an excellent resource for speaking and listening; it is something to be enjoyed, not laboured over, not endlessly explained, although teachers can give subtle clues that will help children grow into poetic understandings (e.g. showing the class one of the pre-Raphaelite depictions of 'The Lady of Shalott'). Rhyme and rhythm make poetry easy to remember and recall; talk to children about the idea of a memory bank, a resource that they start building up for life, making deposits of ideas and poems and taking them out at relevant times. Poetry is not only serious; it can be fun. A text such as *The Very Long Nose of Jonathan Jones* by Max Fatchen and Craig Smith (2001) uses rhythm and rhyme both for humour and to propel a speedy story:

When he brought it to school, students thought it was cool,
Though it got in the way of his cricket.
For bowlers would shout and the umpire said, 'OUT!'
Dismissing him, nose before wicket.

There are many wonderful collections and anthologies of children's poetry, and many wonderful books; recent publications include *The Jumblies* by Edward Lear, illustrated by Ian Beck (2001), and *Quentin Blake's ABC* (2002). The important thing to remember is that children's poetry is part of a whole artistic continuum, and *we need to bring children to poems from that wider continuum*, without always explaining 'meaning' but creating a receptive climate for children to consider and learn about poetic 'story'. Meaning is slippery, elusive, and personal; it is made not only through knowledge of words, but through connection to personal life and experience, how we are feeling, where we are as we listen to the poem, who we are with. A text such as *A Treasury of Shakespeare's Verse*, selected by Gina Pollinger and illustrated by Emma Chichester Clark (1995), provides an excellent introduction to Shakespeare; some of the songs can be used in everyday classroom situations to build up a knowledge of the world that children may not fully understand now but that is receptive to later encounters. Why not end each recess or lunchtime for a week with something like this:

Children can experience courteous exposure and classroom fun with Shakespeare

A great while ago the world began,
With hey ho, the wind and the rain,
But that's all one, our play is done,
And we'll strive to please you every day.

(*Twelfth Night*, Act 1 Scene 1)

The Australian poet Stephen Herrick uses poetry to tell story and create character, in particular the character of adolescence—*The Simple Gift* (2000), *A Place Like This* (1998), *Love, Ghosts and Nose Hair* (1996). These collections are more suitable for older children, but *My Life, My Love, My Lasagne* (1997) contains poems that describe ideas and happenings relevant to the experience of primary children:

Sarah's Dad told her
The first words she ever spoke
Were 'ball' and 'moon',
She'd point to a ball

And say 'moon, moon'.
She's point to her brother's head
and say 'ball, ball.'

Read this poem in conjunction with David McKee's *Who's a Clever Baby Then?* (1988):

'Who's a clever baby then?' said Grandma. 'And where's my oofum boofum pussy cat? Say "cat",
Baby.'

    "Dog", said Baby.

Give children the opportunity to write their own poetry—string together a series of images,
play with the sounds of words (like 'oofum boofum' above, and 'wibbly wobbly jungle jelly and
fluffy puffy whipped cream and squishy squashy chocolate fish and crunchy munchy rainbow
sprinkles', from *Desert Dessert* by Perrin Hopkins and Jenna Packer (2001)), and play with ways
of setting out ideas. Use the blackboard to brainstorm a series of classroom images, and then
set them out in such a way as to inspire children into making more pictures in words, listing
them one after another, on new lines with different starting points, using dots to fade, not
worrying about grammar or syntax. The whole point is to describe something ordinary in a new
way, to see something with a new understanding. (See also the discussion on writing poetry in
chapter 29.)

This poem by Herrick (1997:32) seems an appropriate way to conclude:

> **Poetry**
> Ms Stevrakis says,
> 'Poetry doesn't have to rhyme
> all of the time'.
> She doesn't get it
> when
> everyone laughs.
> She doesn't even get it
> when
> Sarah raises her hand and says,
> 'Miss, how much of the time
> does poetry have to rhyme?'
> But ten minutes later,
> during our quiet reading time
> she starts laughing—
> she laughs forever it seems
> and so do we.
> I didn't know poetry could be so much fun!

Australian Children's Literature Museum

Dromkeen is an historic homestead in rural Victoria, which houses a unique collection of
original artworks and manuscripts of Australian picturebooks past and present. Situated in the
small town of Riddell's Creek (about an hour's drive from the city centre of Melbourne and

thirty minutes from Melbourne International Airport) the house is listed with the National Trust and is surrounded by twenty-five acres of garden and grasslands, eucalypt and wattle trees.

Dromkeen is situated near many scenic and literary landmarks, including Mount Macedon and Hanging Rock, the latter made famous in the book (and later film) *Picnic at Hanging Rock* (the book was written by Joan Lindsay and the film directed by Peter Weir).

Dromkeen runs special programs for both teachers and students. Contact address: 1012 Riddells Creek Vic. 3431 Australia. Ph (03) 5428 6799; fax (03) 5428 6830; dromkeen@scholastic. com.au.

▶ Summary

Picturebooks develop multiliteracy skills. They offer children multiple ways of reading text, approaching text, and deriving meaning from text.

1   The words and pictures of picturebooks function together in a unique way to tell a story.

2   If we think of the pictures in picturebooks as another kind of 'language-ing', we can talk about them in terms of the linguistic idea of register: how we speak, the words we choose, and the way we say them depends on who we are with, what we are saying, and where we are. In some books the pictures are in a different register from the words.

3   Visual and verbal text are dialogic (i.e. they talk to each other) and heteroglossic (i.e. they contain many voices). Across, between, and beyond the pictures and words of picturebooks is a third space, where words and pictures meet, 'dialogue', and bounce off each other.

4   Visual literacy is more than the ability to decode images (to work out what images mean). It is the ability to recognise and analyse the *power of the image* and the *how* of its meaning in its particular context. The idea of a visual chronotope helps us to understand and describe how picturebooks work.

5   The language of picturebooks can help children to grow into understandings of poetry. Picturebook language, like poetry, has an acoustic function as well as a semantic one. Picturebooks in the classroom offer a corporate, community experience of shared story.

6   Children's poetry is rhythm, rhyme, sound, and image; it is something that is spoken aloud and listened to.

7   Children respond to poetry from a very young age. Teachers need to make connections to older children through their culture, e.g. popular songs. Children must be courteously introduced to poems from the wider literary continuum.

8   Children need to be encouraged into creating and writing their own poems.

VISUAL LITERACY: READING THE WORLD OF SIGNS

Overview

This chapter provides an overview of current thinking about visual literacy, and engages with some of its most significant issues.

Significance and heritage

Between 60 000 to 40 000 years ago, there was what Peter Watson calls a 'creative explosion' of 'cave art and carvings in abundance' (2005: endpapers). Some 35 000 odd years later, in 5500 bc, we have evidence of the first writing (in India). The world's first imaginative epic, *Gilgamesh*, appeared some time after 2900 bc.

The wheel was not invented until 2000 bc.

What does this tell us? Among other things, it informs us of the significance of visual representations and the urge to story. It implies something about the desire to depict individual experience. It implies the absolute priority of the desire to communicate. It also passes down through the centuries a sure knowledge of the interrelationships and interconnectedness between language and image. In other words, it helps us to understand that the processes and practices of what we call 'visual literacy' have a long and inspiring heritage.

Semiotics, signs and inference

Visual literacy refers to more than signs, more than signals, more than symbols, but all three are related in its theoretical heritage. Symbols are types of signs—visual objects that through common acceptance and cultural coding have come to represent or connote a particular meaning. For example, a dove has come to symbolise peace, a heart has come to symbolise love. In his study of semiotics, which he defines in terms of a theory of codes and sign production (1979: 29), and as that which pertains to 'everything that can be taken as a sign, (1979: 7), Umberto Eco refers to what he calls natural signs: physical events coming from a natural source, and human behaviour not intentionally emitted by its senders (16–17). The track of an animal is a sign that the animal was once present in that spot; a red rash as a sign of measles is written in medical books as a semiotic convention. In this early work he makes another interesting point—that smoke is only a *sign* of fire to the extent that fire is not perceived along with the smoke. A visual representation of smoke without fire is in literary terms related to metonym—where an attribute of a thing stands for the thing itself (as in 'the deep' for 'the ocean')—and synecdoche—a rhetorical term in which either the whole is taken to replace a part (for example, 'Australia won the tennis' in which the whole, 'Australia,' replaces the one or two tennis players), or the part is made to stand for the whole ('there were new faces in the team'—here a part of the body stands for the whole body). These closely related terms highlight the fact that in one sense all illustrations in books, and picturebooks, are visually synecdochal and/or metonymic: signs of wholes, signs of parts—part of a figure inferring a full figure, part of a door (e.g. the handle) inferring the whole door, and indeed the whole house—and in a very real sense, inferring and insinuating the whole world.

Problems of definition

'Visual literacy' refers to a highly contested contemporary domain of study which relates most obviously to discussions of reading and writing, but which is also relevant to such areas as visual arts, computer and software design, cartooning and illustration, and cartography, among many others.

In one sense 'visual literacy' is a tautology: 'literacy' itself (especially in respect of its common definition as 'the ability to read or write') is obviously deeply dependent on the visual (the exception is Braille). Indeed, 'reading' and 'writing' are interrelated through visual signs that may now, in the 21st century, be formalised into an alphabet, but that have in the past included and/or continue to include all sorts of other signs—symbols, pictograms, cuneiform, the rebus, hieroglyphs, and Chinese script. And of course both *reading* and *writing* are intimately connected to *speaking* and *listening*, which are nonvisual (although when we *listen* to someone *speak*, we generally—radio is one of the many exceptions—*see* them speak, and when we *read* of someone speaking, we are seeing the words). The obvious interdependence of reading, writing, speaking, and listening hinges on the notions of *transmission*, *exchange of meaning*, and *communication*; visual literacy interweaves and hinges on exactly the same things.

Let's consider the Western alphabet, the building blocks of reading and writing in many but far from all languages across the world. Readers look at them, writers organise and reproduce them in their own creative patterns (and it's amazing, is it not, to think that such diversity is possible with only twenty-six blocks!). Letters have to be sighted, sorted, interpreted through spaces, viewed in close context, and then viewed in wider context, in order for them to be 'written', in order for them to be 'read', in order for them to 'mean'. The letter 'A' is a visual sign that has a different meaning as a mark on an essay:

Well done! A

from that which it has in an alphabet book for beginning readers, where it is placed alone on a page opposite the picture of an apple:

Aa   apple

It has a different meaning again as the name of a computer drive:

$3\frac{1}{2}$ floppy (A)

and yet another meaning when it is represented as the space between the second and third of five parallel lines on a musical score:

Sketches   by   Alan   Robinson

That reading and writing even in scrupulously represented context can still be ambiguous and have different meanings for different people (as is seen, for example, in newspaper journalism as well as in literary texts, where there are endless debates about what something 'means'), and that such ambiguity is actively encouraged by postmodern thinking, are indicators of the fluidity and cultural shifting of the signs that make up our world.

   This ambiguity is particularly obvious in postmodern children's picturebooks, which as we have seen tend to reflect social issues and concerns quite rapidly. These are indeed a unique literary (and in a sense interdisciplinary) genre precisely because they have always accessed, and in fact played to, what I will call the *visuality of literacy*. **The visuality of literacy** Again as we have seen, their meaning emerges in complex encounters involving reader, (written) verbal/visual text and (illustrative/pictorial) visual text, and in a synthesising (but sometimes interrogative) coming together in the rich space (a sort of third space) that is created somewhere among and around them all. These spaces generate imaginative engagement in the ways words and pictures are presented and perceived, organised, and assimilated. Picturebooks are verbal and visual text conceived in **time** (order, duration, frequency) and **space**, and they verbally and visually arrange time and space in creative and sophisticated interplay (as in John Burningham's classic *Come Away from the Water, Shirley*). The potential of this interplay, and the complexity of reading strategies required to make meaning out of words and illustrations, is demonstrated in *Do Not Go Around the Edges* (Utemorrah & Torres) and *A is for Aunty* (Russell); each book uses words and pictures to juggle and manipulate intersecting concepts of time—as past, present, future, retrospective, retrieved, fictive.

What is visual literacy?

I have described visual literacy as 'more than the ability to decode images (to work out what images mean)—it is the ability to analyse the *power of the image* and the *how* of its meaning in its particular context' (Johnston 2000: 13). This is still a good, simple definition.

   The essence of visual literacy (and beware—many of the usages in currency at present are loose and rather muddy) is the making of meaning out of images that may be signs, objects, lines, circles, dots, tables, diagrams, charts, maps, comics, cartoons, numerals, varying mixtures of all the above, AND WORDS. The point about visual literacy is that the images listed above do not always operate as separate to words (they may do but in general practice, do not), but alongside them, around them, over them, under them. In a discussion of visual literacy, neither words nor images are necessarily privileged; they function together, both contributing to meaning-making, interdependently. However, almost always, words, either spoken or implied, are used to describe and communicate the meaning-making that has taken place.

   Visual literacy cannot and must not be divorced from traditional notions of reading and writing; it expands on them, concertinas them out. Visual literacy pertains to an idea of language, inspired by an age of visual communicative modes (film, television, DVD, video and then digital cameras, computer screens and interfaces, mobile technologies) that use other marks and signs, very often alongside the conventional marks and signs that are the letters of the alphabet, to communicate story, to describe character, to convey movement, to indicate time and place, to give shape to an abstraction, to outline a plan, to develop a thesis, to explain an idea.

Visual literacy and visual language

Thus visual literacy pertains not only to new understandings of literacy but even more importantly to new understandings of language. It pertains to a methodology of communication ('language-ing'—see chapter 20) that emerges from technologies which, just as the discovery of the printing press did in earlier times, have made digitilised and clip-art programs easily accessible, available, and usable. Visual literacy recognises a visual language that can stand alone, and often does, but is more commonly a synthesis—words and pictures coming together, working together rather than separately, bouncing off each other, juxtaposing and tipping into each other their own carriages of meaning—in much the same way they do in picturebooks.

Visual literacy and cultural codes

Visual literacy clearly relates to perception; as neuroscientists point out, perception is organised as well as experienced, and this cognitive organisation reflects our physical involvement in the world. That is, what we see is filtered through culturally encoded interpretive schemata. Indeed, visual imageries and visual language (that is, the mix of images and words in a design that may include shapes and lines and other graphics) often have a commercial or sociopolitical function—consider advertisements in glossy magazines and on television, in which the designers place objects and create visual stories that are specifically intended to trigger desire, promising something about themselves that is not of themselves (a particular sort of drink or a particular brand of clothing is associated with a good-looking partner, and a wealthy lifestyle, and an auspicious future).

These Western imageries of success (if that is what it is) stand in sharp contrast to other worldviews, but all cultural systems make the point; Caruana, discussing indigenous art, writes that 'Traditional Aboriginal society is structured by systems that organise all aspects of life and perceptions; and indeed, by which the universe is ordered' (1996: 15). He further notes that 'Unlike prose, the interpretation of Aboriginal designs and images is not a one to one equivalence. Rather, like poetry with all its ambiguities, each symbol or icon within a work may encapsulate a variety of meanings' (1996: 14).

This idea of an encapsulation of meanings is a helpful term. Just as words are coded, so too are images. If we look at the cover of the Canadian text *The Subway Mouse* (2003), by plasticine artist Barbara Reid, it is clear that this is a likeable mouse, not one to be scared of, in part because of the bright yellow background and the mouse's smiling expression. This sympathetic coding is then confirmed by the verbal language:

> Nib was a subway mouse.
> He was born into a large family that lived below the platforms of a busy subway station.
> The mice called their home Sweetfall.

The illustration of the first double page spread explains this delightful name: on the tracks, looking up at people's feet on the platform, the mice eagerly wait to catch bits of discarded rubbish. Reading both languages of the text, the visual and verbal, a charming story begins to take shape.

Visual literacy and art

Visual literacy is only in part related to art, but there are some obvious descriptors that can meaningfully be applied. Examples are terms such as colour, shape, form, proportion, texture, composition, vectors, design, density, typography, image and imageries, manipulation. These concepts, however, while they contain elements of an aesthetic, do not of themselves sufficiently demonstrate the significance of cultural marking and the attribution of meaning, the determination of which is the fundamental challenge of visual literacy.

Rather more helpful are some of the following questions; these work very well indeed when the discussion is applied to picturebooks.

- What is the time-space of the image? Seek out clues and cues about its cultural markings: is there a time code (past/present/future)? Is there a use-by date (e.g. a sign associated with summer that will become irrelevant in winter; a sign marked by age demographic)? Is the image marked in or by a visual form of jargon (a sort of slang specific to one particular group, familiar to that group and breeding a sense of exclusiveness)? Is it nationally or ethnically marked? Is it implicitly marked secret? Aboriginal art, for example, has two broad levels of interpretation, one for insiders 'of appropriate ritual standing' (Caruana 1996: 14), and one for outsiders.
- Consider the compositional pattern. What is the organising principle? Who or what is focalising and/or providing focus? Whose eyes are we seeing through? Where are we being positioned to see or hear? What are we being positioned to see or hear? How are we being set up to feel about what we are seeing or hearing? Are we lower or higher to the main image—looking down or looking up? (Film literature talks about the concept of dominant specularity—placing the viewer in a position to see everything from the highest, implicitly superior, level).
- Are the images naturalistic or surreal or traditional or ethnic or a mixture (juxtaposition)? Are they fantasy images? Is there some informing image in the fantasy? What are the links back to the real (or primary) world?
- Consider the visual schema, the centres and margins, the space and proportion, all in relation to each other.
- What materials are used? For example, in terms of picturebook images these may be collage, woodcuts, watercolours, oils, drawings, pastels, and so on, including mixtures of all of the above.
- Consider the texture: soft/hard, rough/smooth. What effect does this have? How is it expressed? How does it relate to the intentionality of the image?
- Consider shapes and their proportions, shadows, lines, and outlines.
- Are there backgrounds and borders? What effect do these have? (limiting, confining, focusing, signifying importance etc.).

- Direction of light: where is it coming from? What sort of light is it? (inside/outside, soft/harsh, daylight/nightlight). What is the source of the light? Where is the viewer positioned in relation to the light?
- Consider hue (colour), density (chroma = brightness/dullness), tonal variation (lightness/darkness): are these related or are there contrasts, and what effect does this have?

Consider the representation of relationships—interpersonal and intrapersonal—in the visual design: how are they portrayed? The Australian illustrator Julie Vivas, for example, expresses relationship through softly rounded figures overlapping, touching, and reaching out to each other across the page. Shaun Tan represents intrapersonal landscapes of the mind through images of an industrialised fast-moving world, ideologically perceived and organised as oppressive.

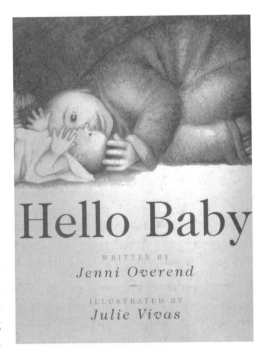

How does the image represent either implicitly or explicitly the world beyond itself? How much of that world is projected into the image? How does the projection of the world beyond affect (change, exaggerate, play down) the image? Why do we need—or do we?—some sort of a sense of wider world?

Interpreting visual language

So, visual literacy is the ability to make meaning out of visual language. We have noted already that visual language consists of combinations of words and images and shapes that operate together to convey meanings that may be sophisticated and abstract. Characteristics that may be considered include the following:

1   **Background, landscape, context, environment:** the space in which the visual language is introduced. It may be a page, a chart, a screen, a scroll, an artwork, a table, a map. Whatever it is, it will set up a generic expectation of what is to follow, and of its conventions of meaning making.

2   **Lines:** these can express containment, barrier, enclosure, exclusion, connection, relationship. Thick lines may convey boundaries; straight

lines may convey related categories; squiggly lines may convey loose or unformed relationships; jagged ones may convey disruption and dislocation, even a tearing apart or a rip of violence, such as in *Way Home*, by Libby Hathorn and Greg Rogers (1994).

3   **Space:** white space can convey freedom in some contexts and emptiness in others. It can also convey a sense of universality to whatever the actions are in the foreground—that is, the implication that actual location is unimportant. Sometimes white space emphasises the movement and actions and relationships of characters, as in the work of Julie Vivas, as seen in the illustrations above. Black space may convey darkness, loneliness, fear, or provocative mystery, as in *Imagine a Night*, by Rob Gonsalves and Sarah L. Thomson (2003). It may also convey cosiness and safety, as in the illustration of the platypus in its burrow, in Robert Roennfeldt's *The Silver Stream* (2003).

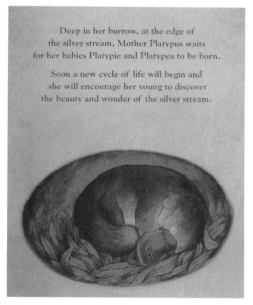

4   **Time:** We need an idea of time around which to organise narrative. Visual language tells the time—historical time, time of year (seasons), time of day—in a variety of ways. Sometimes a series of panels represents the passing of time. Sometimes there is a convention of things happening at the same time (along the lines of the medieval Simultaneous Principle); sometimes there is a time retrospective (indicated by dates in *My Place*, by Wheatley & Rawlins); sometimes there is a depiction of time moving on over a period (as in the 'wordless' picturebooks by Jeannie Baker, *Window* (1991), and its sequel, *Belonging* (2004), both of which use clues such as birthday cards on a window sill to tell the complex story of time as growth, time as years passing, time as change). Popular advertisements for Microsoft use white outlines of the future traced over the present to

represent dreams coming true; Jeannie Baker's *Where the Forest Meets The Sea* (1987) employs a similar technique to represent the nightmare of future development ruining the natural beauty of the present.

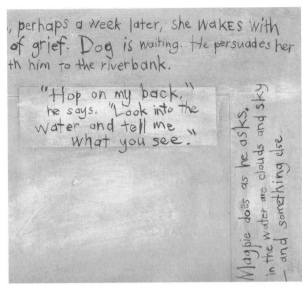

5 **Visual syntax:** This refers to the arrangement of the elements (images, lines, words, etc.). Lists are read in certain ways, usually down ways. Bullet points and numbering are part of visual syntax and help in the meaning-making process. A book such as *Fox*, by Margaret Wild and Ron Brooks (2000), plays with ideas of visual syntax, and forces the reader to turn the book in different ways, thus encouraging different perspectives.

6 **Sequencing:** How does one element lead into another element? How is visual narrative ordered? This may relate to visual syntax, but may also relate to page numbers, and narrative or visual links. Thus in *The Waterhole*, by Graeme Base (2001), the visual and verbal narrative depends on the shrinking of the secret waterhole, as well as in the progression of numbers from 1 to 10.

7 **Causality:** This refers to the representation of cause and effect, and may be explicit or implicit; sometimes cause and effect are both visually represented, and sometimes a reader's world knowledge will write in one or the other. If a ball is thrown (cause), knowledge about momentum and gravity allows us to understand that it will land somewhere (effect). A picture of children playing with a ball outside is enough for readers to discern the cause of the effect of a ball crashing through a glass window. Perry Nodelman notes that cause-and-effect relationships evoke temporal ideas about a past and future. For example, Peter Rabbit's mother walking down a path holding her basket evokes questions such as where is she going and why? Why is she carrying a basket and umbrella? (1988: 171–2). In other words, the language of the picture is implying a narrative, which we seek to express in a language of words.

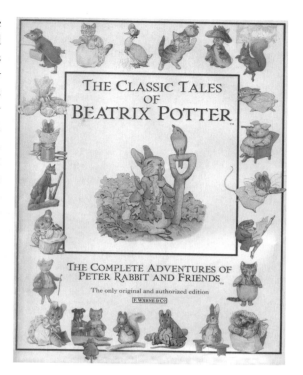

8 **Connections:** This relates to causality, but may also consist of a grouping of apparently random objects. Thus in *In Flanders Fields* (Jorgensen & Harrison-Lever 2002) the bird with the red breast, the soldier, the bayonet, the white handkerchief, and the barbed wire, set up an expectation of connections that becomes even stronger when we read the opening phrase of the story, 'Early on Christmas morning …'

9 **Direction:** A sense of movement across the page from left to right tends, at least to Western readers, to emphasise process. Kress & Van Leewen, in their formal grammar of visual design, and drawing heavily on the psychology of perception, note that in formal art theory these processes are called 'vectors',

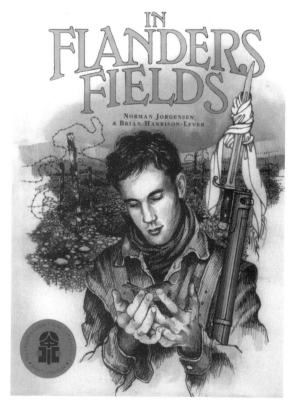

or 'tensions' or 'dynamic forces' (1996: 27). Thus as a generalisation we could say that vectors relate to verbs (doing, being, having). 'Volumes' and 'masses', each with their own 'weight' and 'gravitational pull', relate, as Kress & Van Leewen note, to participants. Thus on the cover of *Snow White* (Josephine Poole and Angela Barrett 1993), the figure of the girl running is the participant, whose 'weight' is much less heavy than the trunks of the forest trees through which she runs, and who is being pulled down in a vector which is expressed not only in her figure but in the flow of her hair and dress, in the rabbit and the wild beasts, and in the direction of the lines drawing the forest floor.

10 **Relationship:** Picturebook illustration reflects many kinds of relationships: human relationships, number relationships, letter relationships. Some relationships are expressed directly, some are expressed indirectly and indeed as mythic surrealism.

11 **Comparison:** Comparison is related to contrast: something small looks smaller still beside something big. Thus on the cover of *Wilfrid Gordon McDonald Partridge* (Mem Fox and Julie Vivas 1984), the two figures, the small boy Wilfrid and the old lady, Miss Nancy, are fairly explicitly compared as small and big, young and old, active and inactive, and more implicitly compared as hands outstretched in abandon to life and adventure, and hands gripping on to what is left.

12 Metaphor: Some images are visual metaphors, that is, their immediate 'meaning' clicks into something more abstract, perhaps through the juxtaposition of certain words or of other apparently unrelated images. The cover of Kerry Greenwood's novel for young readers, *The Long Walk* (2004), shows children walking along a dirt track, but the fact that they appear to be pushing a pram full of belongings, and the children's clothes clearly evoke the Depression Years, elaborates 'long' and 'walk' into something beyond an afternoon stroll, into something approximating a critical life journey.

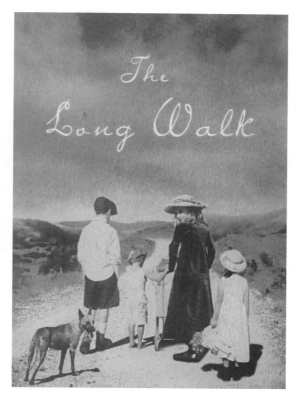

13 Satire and irony: Sometimes these are mixed with cartoons and caricatures, as in Colin Thompson's *One Big Happy Family* (2002), Roland Harvey's *In the Bush* (2005), and Lauren Child's *Beware of the Storybook Wolves* (2000).

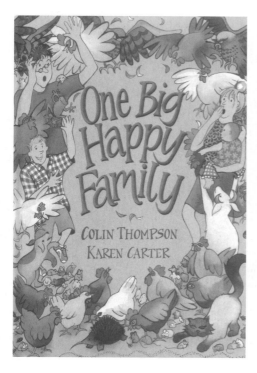

14 **Diagramming:** Diagrams usually provide information. In Lester's *Are We There Yet?* the continuing diagram of the map shows the progress of the journey, and the diagram of inside the camper trailer explains how everyone fitted in.

15 **Labelling:** Labelling provides a sense of accuracy, as in Patricia Mullins' *V is for Vanishing*.

16 **Time lines/charts:** These add perspective and context.

17 **Navigation:** This overlaps with other elements such as sequencing, labelling, direction. How readers navigate through each of the double-page openings of *My Place* depends on the flow of connections they make among diverse visual and verbal codes. (Using the dates as markers to read 'backwards' chronologically; using the big tree in the map as a point of reference in an everchanging landscape; tracing relationships between the different families; relating the events to wider world events such as world wars).

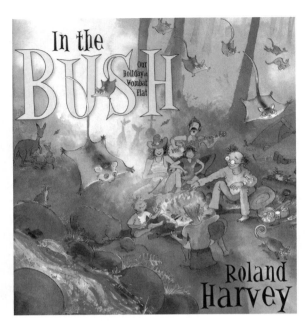

18 **Use of numbers:** Numbers are used in many different circumstances. Two interesting examples, where numbers are implicit rather than explicit, are Baker's *Window* (1991) and its sequel, *Belonging* (2004). In *Window*, *chronos*, the passing of time, is depicted not only through the scene outside but most directly through the numbers on the birthday cards on the boy's window sill. In *Belonging*, numbers are used in several print modes: cards, mugs, drawings, pencil case, diary entries.

19 **Maps:** The use of maps is common in children's books (*Winnie the Pooh*, *The Wind in the Willows*, *The Lord of the Rings*, are just a few famous examples). Indeed, J. R. R. Tolkien, the author of *The Lord of the Rings*, once said that a map is essential in an adventure story

(Grotta 1992: 89). Maps are of course powerfully loaded in meaning and are also ideologically encoded (what is important to put where, what is left out, scale, representations of distance). Maps offer a powerful sense of both continuity and change in *My Place*, by Wheatley & Rawlins. They give a visual outline of the family's journey in Alison Lester's *Are We There Yet?* (2004). The endpaper maps of Roland Harvey's *In the Bush: Our Holiday to Wombat Flat* (2005) is a good example of a subjective map.

Note the long practice of teachers encouraging children to use mind maps as 'brainstorming' and as a way of visually expressing creative ideas.

20 **Cartoon conventions:** Many examples of visual language and language-ing employ familiar cartoon conventions. *Zoo*, by Anthony Browne, and Harvey's *In the Bush* are two of many examples of picturebooks interspersing conventional text with illustrations and cartoon conventions. These may include:

- *Thoughts*: small unconnected circles leading from the character's head to the bubble of words.
- *Speech*: connected line to bubble of words.
- *Movement/motion*: speed lines usually indicate where the movement was a split second before.
- *Speed*: similar to above.
- *Impact*: the moment and place of impact may contain words such as 'BANG!' and sharp jagged lines.
- *Fear*: may be portrayed as blurred outlines representing shaking, sometimes with beads of perspiration drawn from the forehead.
- *Dimension*: size usually is portrayed as exaggerated and against a foil that gives a sense of scale.
- *Focus*: may be represented by funnel-like lines, or by central placement in the frame of the language frame.
- *Love*: a heart, often red, is a common symbol for love (as in the film *Amèlie*).
- *Sound*: this is often represented by an onomatopoeic word e.g. 'Woof-woof'; 'Rrring!' (for a telephone).
- *Emphasis*: the use of bold letters or large fonts can represent loudness; softer lines and smaller fonts may represent quietness.
- *Heat*: squiggly lines from the top of the object represent steam or excessive heat.
- *Bounce lines and hit locations*: in children's books, the throwing of a ball may employ conventions of lines indicating where the ball bounced and hit and where it now is. The visual text of *Good Night, Spot* is an excellent example.

The language of gesture

Gestural languages help us to understand the connections between reading and writing, speaking and listening. People who are hearing-impaired but can read, obviously read in the conventional way but need another type of language to 'speak' and 'listen.' Thus signing languages (such as Auslan), which are visual and made up of hand movements, are used to communicate. It is fascinating to watch someone signing in one of the languages for the deaf, and seeing the way the hands build on common conventions, such as touching the heart region in certain ways to express love.

In conventional language, too, gestures are 'read'; in linguistic theory, the term 'paralinguistic cues' refers to the ways in which gestures imply meaning. We only have to think about the ways in which we seek to communicate to someone in another language to understand how much we use hand gestures and body movements: to point, to indicate what we expect someone to do, to indicate a question; a shrug with raised shoulders and palms up is usually read as 'I don't know.'

It has become fashionable to talk about 'body language'—bodies turned away as expressing lack of interest or disharmony, as in the famous picture of the Prince and Princess of Wales in a carriage, with faces and bodies averted from each other. Yawns can express boredom, arms crossed is interpreted by some to represent aggression or defensiveness. All such stances and actions are of course read visually.

Baby signing

This is a contested but probably growing area, as there is considerable commercial interest in programs that sell parents ideas about breeding super-intelligent children. There are a number of programs that teach babies to sign words before they can speak them. There is as yet no authoritative research, and whether such practices encourage or impede the development of spoken language remains a matter for debate.

Having said that, we all know that we almost automatically use gestures and facial expressions along with voice when talking to babies and young children.

The significance of culture

It is particularly important to understand that body languages and facial expressions are culturally coded. A smile may be universal, but the ways in which we interact with others is wrapped up in all sorts of cultural conventions.

One telling example relates to early Australian history, and vestiges of it remain and can be found in the nation's literature. In Western culture, it is thought to be extremely important to look the person being addressed in the eye when speaking, or being spoken to. This is particularly so in authority situations: I can still hear a principal shouting to an errant classmate, 'Look me in the eye when I'm talking to you!'

Yet this is not so in traditional Aboriginal cultures. Richard Trudgen, in *Why Warriers Lie Down and Die*, writes the following:

Yolnu [the people of Arnhem Land] are taught to speak indirectly to a person, with almost no eye contact. Dominant culture [white] people, on the other hand, speak directly to a person with very strong eye contact.

Traditional Yolnu find strong eye contact threatening and it makes them feel very uncomfortable and vulnerable. Many Yolnu will look away or down to avoid the strong privacy-invading glare of dominant culture people. As someone said, 'Dominant culture society communicates eyeball to eyeball. In Aboriginal society, communication should be heart to heart and mind to mind.' This communication is like hearing the inner soul of a person.

Actually, the best position for communicating with a Yolnu person is side-by-side, looking at something as though there were a third party in front of the two people talking. (Trudgen 2000: 78)

Other indigenous cultures share similar ideas about the rudeness of eye contact, about offering information to an older person (thus seemingly not wanting to, or not being able to, participate in open classroom discussions). There are far too many examples in Australian literature—and children's literature—where these profound cultural differences in communication codes have resulted in unfavourable descriptions of indigenous people as, for example, 'shifty-eyed'.

Teachers must not only be aware of such differences but also be ever vigilant about the possibility of cultural differences in communicative behaviours. This tolerance and understanding must be taught as a moral imperative in all our classrooms. If we all do this, and practise it, the stretch of knowledge rather than ignorance will reach across the nation, helping to create what Yve Lomax calls 'communities of mutualities and common motives' (2000: xiv). Such communities, which reach beyond experienced cultural identity into possibility, are not grounded in expectations of *match* but rather in expectations of rich *mix*—and this makes for a happier world for us all.

The importance of teaching tolerance and understanding

The visual chronotope

In chapters 24 and 28 I introduced the idea of the visual chronotope as another theoretical lens through which to view and discuss pictures. The *visual* chronotope relates particularly to the ways in which illustrations encode designations of time and place. What elements of an illustration express place? What elements express time? How do they work together?

See also chapters 24 and 28

Sometimes the *topos* (place) element of the chronotope may be more loaded, sometimes the *chronos* (time) element, sometimes both may have more or less equal weighting. In *Run, Hare, Run! The Story of a Drawing* (2005), painter, printmaker, sculptor, ceramicist and illustrator John Winch creates an imaginative background for the famous painting *The Hare*, by Albrecht Dürer (1471–1528). The endpapers set the scene of a town that has clear markers of time and place. Through the shape of its buildings, towers, flags, and gates, the town evokes Europe as place (*topos*); the rural surrounds, lack of modern roads, lack of aerials or power lines, as well as the use of colour, evokes the medieval period as time (*chronos*). But as the story goes on, the sense of distance diminishes and the time element is played down: the trees in the forest could be of any period, as could the farmyard animals, the fruit in the basket that represents the market square, the barn, and even the artist's work bench (apart from the candle). John Winch seems

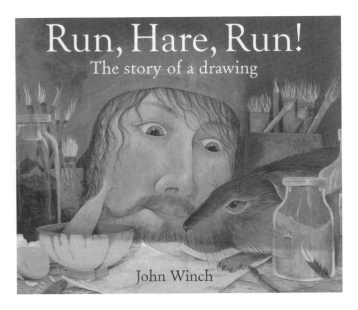

to want readers to understand that while this is the story of the painting of a 15th/16th-century painting, the love of nature expressed in the simplicity of the Dürer, and its charm, is ongoing and eternal.

Visual representations and power

Any visual representation carries meaning and power to manipulate certain viewings and certain reactions. One question always to consider relates to focalisation: where are we being positioned, what are we being positioned to see, what are we being positioned not to see, whose eyes are we seeing with? Kress & Van Leewen, in their complex study of visual design, note on the one hand the power of the visual to construct relationships in histories and products and even ideas (the idea of progress, the idea of empire), and on the other hand, the power of the visual to design the position of the viewer, through such visual characteristics as address, the gaze, size of frame and social distance, perspective and the subjective image, involvement and the horizontal angle, power and the vertical angle (1996: 119–58). They also discuss ideas of *modality*—the reliability of the image, whether what it depicts

is real or not. Of course, in many if not most picturebooks, 'realness' and 'not realness' have their own conventions. Is the graphic of the kitten on the front of *John Coltrane's Giant Steps* (remixed by Chris Raschka 2002) meant to be real, or not real? And how might 'realness' be interpreted in relation to Eric Hill's illustration of Spot (the 'real' dog?) and his teddy bear (the 'unreal' toy?) on the cover of *Goodnight, Spot*?

As noted above, *dominant specularity* is a film term that refers to a position of spectorial superiority. The covers of Jeannie Baker's *Window* and *Belonging* place the viewer/reader above the landscape, enabling us to see beyond the one house, beyond the immediately visible. Coded into this—through the authority of dominant specularity—is responsibility: you have to engage with this, do something about it, the pictures imply.

Other film terms are also helpful in providing a language to discuss pictures: examples include angle of framing, backlighting, close-up, depth of field, establishing shot, flashback, *mise-en-scène*. (See Bordwell & Simpson, *Film Art: An Introduction* [1993].)

One last point, made earlier but which bears repeating, is that the traditional language signs of the Western alphabet have in the hands of writers and poets over the centuries created imagery—pictures-in-the-mind—in the mind's eye of countless readers, out of simple black marks on a white page.

IN THE CLASSROOM

This chapter has outlined many of the ways in which we make meaning through the visual.

Teachers need to draw the attention of students to the power of images, and offer them a language to discuss the ways such images are constructed.

1   Read as many picture books in class as possible; have them accessible for children to pick up in odd moments.

2   Draw attention to the intertextuality (see chapter 24) of some illustrations, and try to show children prints of the original paintings to which they relate. Anthony Browne's *Willy's Pictures* (2000) provides a good beginning, but there are many other examples. Borrow a book of popular art reproductions from the library, again for children to browse through and discern connections.

3   Have a non-speaking hour in which all communication has to be mimed or gestured, both to demonstrate the significance of gesture and body language, and to make children aware of the frustrations of people who have to learn a second language.

4   Encourage children to become aware of the visuality of the culture that surrounds them, and of the ways in which images are designed to evoke certain responses. As a homework exercise, ask children to watch six television commercials and identify what imageries are being used to sell the product (such as looking good, attracting friends, prestige, happy family, success in something, getting married, travelling).

5   Consider the visual language of Lester's *Are We There Yet*?

MULTILITERACIES

Keep alert for all the resources available in popular culture

DreamWorks Pictures have produced the brilliantly animated and delightfully intertextual films *Shrek* and *Shrek 2*, which are full of storybook characters and which play with the conventions of the fairytale genre. Watch these films and send children on hunts, using all the digital and library resources available to them, to find other telling and retellings, including fractured fairytales. Have them write and produce their own mini-scripts, using a parade of fairytale characters and images from well-known artworks.

Spirit: Stallion of the Cimarron (DreamWorks 2002)

The same studio has produced another film which is well worthy of teachers' attention. *Spirit: Stallion of the Cimarron* (DreamWorks 2002) tells a romanticised but very strong tale about what the cover describes as 'discovering the true hero inside of yourself'. The real power of the story comes from a sustained visual metaphor that connects the story of the wild horse to the story of the 'taming' of the American West. This is a very well produced and moving film that is admirably supported by the music of Hans Zimmer and songs by Bryan Adams.

The DVD cover lists these bonus features:

1   Spirit Make-a-Movie Studio: create your own movie using real backgrounds, characters, music, and sound effects from the film. Record your own narration and import your favourite photos to personalise your movie.

2   DreamWorks Kids! Learn to draw with a DreamWorks animator. Fourteen interactive games and activities (DVD ROM and Set-Top Features including Hillside Glide, Cimarron Slam, Goal!!!, Lacota Decoder, and Teepee Tees.

3   The Animation of Spirit: A fascinating look at the integration of hand-drawn 2D and computer-generated 3D animation.

4   The songs of Spirit.

5   Storyboards.

6   Filmakers' commentaries.

These activities provide excellent resources for the practice and development of a range of multiliteracies across many curriculum areas, including English, Human Society and its Environment (and History and Geography), Art, Music, Mathematics, and Technological and Applied Sciences. Some can be shown on television; the interactive activities of course require the use of the computer.

► LITERACY IN THE DIGITAL AGE

1   The distinguished art historian E. H. Gombrich writes, in a discussion of skill and methods of production:

> But there is at least one aspect of art or of craftsmanship where nobody can deny the role of technology: this was the recipes used by the masters of the period for their pigments and their media.
>
> ...
>
> The most unassailable law of sociology I know is contained in the proverb that 'nothing succeeds like success'. The admiration for certain achievements results in an upwards spiral which manifests itself in a craze, a fashion, or even a dominant style. (1999: 101–2)

2   This observation is interesting in two ways in an age of digital literacies: first, it highlights the place that technology has always played in art and culture, and second, it notes the significance of prevailing ideas and fashions.

3   The prevailing idea and fashion of our society at present concerns the impact of Information and communication technologies, which are currently sweeping through much of the developed world. In this postmodern environment where anyone can be a star (as in television reality shows); where anyone's

ordinary life is shifted into the public domain and deemed worth watching (fitting in with postmodern emphasis on the significance of 'everydayness' rather than of the grand and the heroic; where anyone can become a publisher (through desktop publishing) and an artist (through the numerous clip art and other art programs available online); where anyone with access to MUDs and Story Palaces and electronic games can take on numerous persona and play out roles of their own choosing—in such a world, there is almost infinite scope for interaction with both verbal and visual languages. The *e-world* is full of signs and symbols and both visual and verbal languages, but it is not an archived world with privileged access (although of course, it continues to increase the gulf between the haves of the Western world and the have-nots of, say, much of Africa). For people in developed countries, this is a world with which they can interact as part of everyday activity—to chat, to research, to entertain themselves and others.

4   Some children are likely to be as skilled or even more skilled than teachers in reading the various signs, symbols and icons of digital language. The teacher's task is to observe those children who are struggling, and to ensure that they are being equipped with the skills required to read the e-world. As far as teacher's skills are concerned, education providers and teachers themselves must make sure that they access professional development opportunities, and that they continue to do so; the one most significant characteristic of information and communication technologies is their seemingly endless capacity for update and change.

▶ Summary

1   Telling stories through images has a long and inspiring heritage in cultures across the world.

2   Visual literacy is related to signs, symbols and the theory of semiotics.

3   Traditional notions of literacy have a very strong visual element and this relates to what we can call the *visuality of literacy*.

4   As all literacy does, visual literacy pertains to transmission of ideas, exchange of meaning, and communication.

5   The interest in visual literacy highlights the emergence of new ideas about *visual language*.

6   Visual language consists not only of images, but frequently of words and images working together.

7   Context plays a significant role in the reading of images, just as it does in the reading of words.

8   Picturebooks play specifically to the visuality of literacy.

9   Signs, images, and paralinguistics—unspoken but visually expressed gestures, attitudes, and expressions—are all significantly culturally coded, and care must be taken in reading what they 'mean'.

10 The concept of the *visuality of literacy*, which refers to the significance of *seeing* in literacy—seeing the letters of the alphabet and reproducing them in multiple modes for others to see in multiple contexts—reminds us that literacy, in its most elemental form, pertains to the making and releasing of meanings and imageries, through the perception of black marks (such as you are reading now) on a white page.

Further reading

Anstey, M. & G. Bull 2000, *Reading the Visual: Written and illustrated children's literature*, Harcourt Australia, Sydney.

Benterrak, K., Muecke S., Roe, P. (Rev Ed 1996), *Reading the Country: Introduction to Nomadology.* Fremantle Arts Press, South Fremantle, WA.

CREArTA 3(2) 2002–03, Issue on Music. UTS Sydney. Contributions include:

'The Graphic Score: An essential part of modern art in Czechoslovakia in the 1960s', by Lenka Stanska.

'Visual thinking in sounds and creativity: Graphic notations as means of stimulating creative thinking in music,' by Myung Sook-Auh.

'Paint that Funky Music, White Boy: Chris Raschka's *Charlie Parker Paid Be-Bop*, *The Genie in The Jar*, *Mysterious Thesalonius*, and John Coltrane's *Giant Steps*', by Megan Lambert.

Eco, U. 1979, *A Theory of Semiotics*, Indiana University Press, Bloomington, Ind.

Gombrich, E. H. 1999, *The Uses of Images: Studies in the social function of art and visual communication*, Phaidon, London.

Kress, G. & T. van Leeuwen, 1996, *Reading Images: The grammar of visual design*, Routledge, London and New York.

Lomax, Y. 2000, *Writing the Image: An adventure with art and theory*, I. B. Tauris, London and New York.

Johnston, R. R. 2000, 'The arts at the beginning of a new millennium', *CREArTA* 1(1): 4–22.

Nodelman, P. 1988, *Words About Pictures: The narrative art of children's picture books*, University of Georgia Press, Athens and London.

Trudgen, R. 2000, *Why Warriors Lie Down and Die: Towards an understanding of why the Aboriginal people of Arnhem land face the greatest crisis in health and education since European contact*. Aboriginal Resources and Development Services Inc., Darwin.

A LOCUS FOR WORLD COMMUNITY

30

Overview

Literature provides many ways of encouraging children to engage with a world wider than their own, a point of view other than their own, and commitment to issues beyond their own.

Literature and awareness of self and otherness

At a time when educators are striving to impart a sense of value and values to children (a difficult task in a world that seeks to be inclusive), literature serves a significant function in learning about what we could broadly call citizenship. This does not just mean being a citizen of a particular country but rather being a citizen of a sustainable world. The importance of some sort of conceptualisation of world citizenship is an essential component of a global society. As Radim Palous writes in *The Changing University?*:

> The drama of our times is the exodus from particularity and the advent of universal community. Mankind must relinquish individual and social games on separate playing fields. The second half of the twentieth century is an entrance onto the scene, where people take part in the common performance of the drama, 'the world'. Leaving egoistic cells and prisons and entering worldwide openness can be called education (from the Latin *educa*[*re*], 'to take out, to bring out, to lead out'). (1995: 176)

Globalisation, if it is to mean anything at all beyond consumerism and commodification, should imply not only physical connectedness but also a philosophical connectedness that transcends ideologies and politics. Classrooms and stories in the classroom can provide rich spaces for connection in this way.

This is because story is a connector, and all cultures have stories that can fill our schools and our lives with richness and diversity. These stories provide nonthreatening opportunities for encountering difference and for creatively engaging with our own differences. Each book that is read in class can become a stimulus for provoking, discussing, and challenging ideas about self and others, about ways of life that are both familiar and unfamiliar, and about customs that may at first seem strange.

Story is a connector of communities

For this reason we must not confine literature to the English class—it needs to play a part in all classes. Story gives opportunities for that imaginative leap that crosses discipline and cultural boundaries. Wise teachers can use story (and by story is meant books and plays and poems and texts about cultures and songs and picture-stories in all sorts of multimedia formats) to express community and a sense of 'home-ness'—especially when children may be suffering from a sense of *unheimlichkeit* (a German word meaning 'not-at-homeness').

Literature can also open our eyes to social problems and injustice in very powerful ways. Teachers need to remind children about the power of books to act as the social conscience of a culture. We have already noted how Anthony Browne uses *Zoo* to try to highlight his ideas about animals in cages (chapter 28). This is an important issue, but literature has engaged with, for example, the much greater issue of people in the cage of slavery. Don't just read stories, *tell* stories—that is part of a teacher's 'telling' role. Tell the story of, for example, *Uncle Tom's Cabin*, by Harriet Beecher Stowe. Stowe (1811–96) was an American woman who had worked as a teacher and who wrote this book in serial form after her brother asked her to 'write something that would make this whole nation feel what an accursed thing slavery is' (Carpenter & Prichard 1984: 500). Even read them a little of the text. It is dated and the language may be difficult, but it is part of a history of literary advocacy that we need to celebrate. Writing one's cultural story enables others to enter in and begin to understand.

There is an ever-increasing number of texts that not only tell stories of indigenous cultures but that also emerge authentically from them. *Do Not Go Around The Edges* by Daisy Utemorrah and Pat Torres (1990) is a trifurcated text—an autobiographical narrative, a poetic response, and an illustration—which presents a life story through the media of history and art. It tells of the importance of place, and describes a sense of dislocation and yearning, and the quest for ideas of 'home' and identity.

We should tell stories as well as read them

> Far far away far far away
> Is my island home
> Called Galanji
> Far far away!
> Far far away
> Is my Island home!
> Aw-aw-aw.

This text provides a wonderful beginning for talking about Aboriginal literature. Discuss the difficult issue of appropriation—taking over stories, without acknowledging ownership. (Compare it to Western concepts of breaking copyright.)

Aboriginal culture is full of stories that were told in pictures, on rock and cave walls. Read some Dreaming legends, and remind the children that there are different ways of looking at the world (and different ways of telling stories). The stories about the Dreaming are stories about

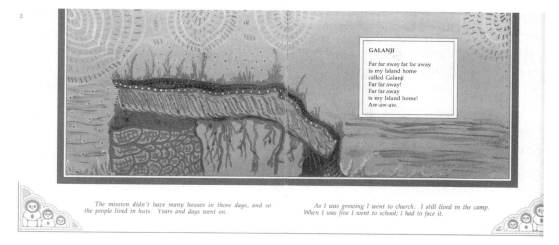

GALANJI

Far far away far far away
is my Island home
called Galanji
Far far away!
Far far away
is my Island home!
Aw-aw-aw.

The mission didn't have many houses in those days, and so the people lived in huts. Years and days went on.

As I was growing I went to church. I still lived in the camp. When I was five I went to school; I had to face it.

the beginnings of things—how the birds got their colours, how the moon got in the sky, and so on. *The Magic Fire at Warlukurlangu*, 'belonging to' Dolly Daniels Granites Nampijinpa (2003), explains how part of the country came to look as it does:

> Today the flames from this big Fire Dreaming can still be seen in that country, Warlukurlangu, in the shape of large anthills. They are there to remind the Warlpiri people of what happened in the Dreaming.

The whole concept of the Dreaming is that it is continuous, not finished; it is still going on. This is part of a different perspective of time—cyclical, rather than linear, as in Western culture. Beginnings and endings aren't so fixed. Unity happens by repetition rather than by a close relationship between what happens at the opening and closing of a story. Also discuss different ideas of *perspectives*. In Aboriginal art, the perspective is aerial—we look down on the picture from above. This clarifies some of the circular patterns and animal tracks that work in a different way from Western notions of perspective, which traditionally changes the size of what is being painted in relation to the position of the viewer. We could argue that this is a very individual-centred idea of the universe—big trees become small because of where I happen to be standing (after all, they are not really small). This opens wonderful areas of discussion and 'telling me' times.

Introduce the children to Magabala Books and Working Title Press, and encourage them to check inside for the acknowledgment of ownership of the story by tribal elders. Read with the class some of Daisy Utemorrah's poetry and discuss it in relation to issues of reconciliation. Discuss meanings of the word 'reconcile'. Dictionary definitions include:

- to re-establish friendship between
- to settle or resolve a dispute
- to bring to acceptance or acquiescence
- to make compatible or consistent
- to purify a consecrated place in a special ceremony after an act of desecration (*Readers' Digest Universal Dictionary* 1988).

What does 'reconciliation' mean in Australia today? How do books such as these help build up understanding? (Also introduce children to the *Papunya School Book of Country and History*, 2001, as a way of developing this discussion.) What sort of yearnings does Daisy express? How do the pictures emphasise these yearnings?

> Our dream and our past is buried under the ground.
> When the sun rises and begins another day
> all is empty, ground and hill shake on us,
> overwhelmed with people everywhere.
> The dream the past—where does it stand now?
> The burun burun whirrs in the night time
> And the owl calling!
> And the dingo howling!
> The moon shines on the water, all is ended—
> and the dreamtime gone.

This book can inspire children to write their own story and create both a poetic and an artistic response to it. Because the line of autobiographical narrative is so simple (sometimes only one sentence) it is a particularly encouraging creative writing model for ESL children. Remind children that they are the experts in their own story.

Note that writing a poetic response frees children from the restraints of normal sentence construction and the conventions of grammatical structure (see chapter 28). Give some examples of writing poetry, being creative in your setting out. Encourage children into writing fragments of lines, glimpses of ideas:

> **Narrative:**
> *On my first day at the new school I had lunch under the big tree in the playground.*
>
> **Poetry:**
> *Eating my lunch, under the big tree …*
> *Green marks on my legs,*
> *Grass prickles*
> *Hot sun,*
> *I eat my lunch and it tastes …*
> *like home.*

Giving ESL children the opportunity to draw an illustration for what they have written allows them to display a skill that is not hampered by lack of language, and that therefore encourages self-confidence and self-esteem in the classroom. Much research has indicated the significance of these qualities in developing literate behaviours (see Johnston 1995a).

IN THE CLASSROOM

Years 3–4

1   Write and illustrate an important moment in your life. Write a few sentences telling what happened, and a poem about how you felt about what happened. Then create a picture, which also tells something more about what you felt then, or what you feel about it now.

2   This task could also be expanded for advanced upper primary children to talk about time perspectives, historical perspectives, and cultural perspectives.

Years 5–6

Write and illustrate the story of your life, using *Do Not Go Around the Edges* as your model.

Teachers' reading

Three books that tell stories of indigenous childhoods are *My Place* by Sally Morgan and *Wandering Girl* by Glenys Ward and *Hane* by Larissa Behrendt. A story about an African childhood is *Don't Let's Go to the Dogs Tonight* by Alexandra Fuller.

Literature in the ESL multilingual classroom

Reading books draws people together in a nonthreatening way. All the second-language research indicates that 'children's literature can provide a vast language resource for teachers to draw on' (Catholic Education Office of Victoria 1990).

> Children's literature provides a vast language resource for teachers

Literature provides both the micro-context of situation and the macro-context of culture. It gives the 'knowledge of the world' (cultural schemata) that so many ESL children need in order to understand their new environment. Reading is a sociocultural activity and its difficulty is increased without a working knowledge of cultural customs and practices.

Teachers can use literature in child-friendly ways. Start with trying to find common ground.

1   Try to find as many collections of folktales and fairytales as you can from a variety of cultures. Search at fetes and second-hand bookshops. When I was teaching in an ESL/EFL class, I had a wonderful book of folktales, now out of print, from all over the world. The great thing about this book was that it had all the tales in their original languages, as well as in an English translation. This meant that children could find their own story, recognise it, and perhaps show me and the class some key words, which we could then put up around the room. This is not a language exercise—although it expands the thinking of the rest of the class about other languages, and can consolidate knowledge about parts of speech. It is first and foremost an exercise to make ESL children feel more comfortable by bringing some of their past into

the present. It is one small way of providing a 'courteous translation'. It also tends to make children more receptive to the second language.

2   When reading folktales and fairytales from different cultures, look for similarities between characters, between events, and between themes. Some of these stories tell about the beginnings of things. They tend to focus on a common world and aspects of a shared human experience.

3   Fill the classroom with as many books set in different cultures as you can find. To supplement school library books, encourage the children to go to their local library and borrow one book set in a different country—and have a special day (or week) set aside for a special class event, something like 'The World as a Global Village'.

4   Further explore similarities:
   • *story*: same basic story, different setting
   • *setting*: same country, different story
   • *character(s)*: same type of character, in different stories and places
   • *theme*: different story, characters and setting, but exploring the same underlying truths.

5   Pick up an idea that seems to emerge and expand it into creative activities. For example, the Japanese character Issunboshi (Little One-Inch) can be compared with Tom Thumb. Let children create their own miniature character and write a description and perhaps one adventure. Tell the class that they can use only one page so they must make every word count, as it does in picturebooks. Do a draft, and then peer-edit. Publish around the room.

6   The more cultures you have represented in your classroom, the more resources you have. Borrow books in other languages to show to all the class: this not only enriches the experience of the ESL children whose language it is, but also enriches the experience of everyone in the class. Note difference in writing scripts when appropriate. Consistently build up the idea, through reading and discussion, that we are all citizens in a shared world.

IN THE CLASSROOM

Text: *At the Crossroads* by Rachel Isadora (1991)

Years K–2

1   Encourage prediction of country and story from the title and cover. Look at the signs: the glimpse of the shantytown, the book, the smiling faces, the huge blue sky.

2   Read the story. Then read the story again, encouraging children to join in the refrain and use body percussion.

Years 3–4

1   Discuss what crossroads are and what they represent: more than one way to go.

2   Read the story.

3   Who is speaking? Whose eyes are we looking through? What is the grammatical name for this (first person plural)?

4   The sky is a very significant part of the illustrations and helps to tell part of the story. How? (It is the horizon of the children's world, and it shows the passing of time—morning, sunset, evening, sunrise the next morning.)

5   Look at the linguistic features of this simple text: make a word bank of the verbs (shout, sing, rush, play, beat). Note how they are all verbs of excitement and energy, and how this adds to the sense of anticipation.

6   Act out the story as a drama. Make the musical instruments: the guitar, drum, and shaker. Use body percussion. Use a chorus for the refrain: 'Our fathers are coming.'

Years 5–6

As above, but add the following as appropriate:

1   Discuss with the class how compressed but full of meaning the language is:

Warm nights blow.

The crossroads are very dark.

2   Ask them to write those two lines in another way to convey the same feeling.

3   Introduce the idea of crossroads as a metaphor.

4   Later, you could read with the children the Robert Frost poem 'The Road Less Travelled'.

5   Write a story about anticipation.

Extension reading for Year 6

Read Nancy Farmer's '21st century adventure story' and fantasy of the future, *The Ear, The Eye, and The Arm*, set in Zimbabwe. This is a very original and interesting text for older readers, with a richly drawn African setting and a strong environmental theme.

IN THE CLASSROOM

Text: *My Painted House, My Friendly Chicken, and Me* by Maya Angelou (1994)

Years K–2

1   Discuss the difference between the children's town life and home life.

2   'Tell me': which do you think they preferred?

3   Write a story sentence about your pet, real or imaginary.

Years 3–4

1   Read the story. Tell the children that Maya Angelou is also an actress, and that she appeared in the film *How to Make an American Quilt* (they won't have seen the film but it gives them another point of reference).

2   Discuss the contrasts between the children's town life and home life. Which do you think they prefer?

3   Discuss the different sizes and style of script.

4   Discuss the use of the first person singular. How does this make you feel?

Years 5–6

1   Discuss the idea of conventions of print and story. Why does this book play with these conventions? What effect does it have?

2   Ask children to write a short story about themselves, a thing, and an animal with a particular characteristic (described as an adjective): 'My Bike, My Curious Beetle, and Me'. They can use different style and size scripts if they choose, but these must be orderly, as Maya Angelou's are. Encourage them to use computer text and consider the type of illustrations they would use.

► **Summary**

1   Literature offers multiple representations of diverse ways of being. Children should understand that literature can act as social conscience and has a history of advocacy.

2   Children's books by indigenous writers and illustrators provide an authentic resource for learning about indigenous culture, perspectives, and ideas.

3   Teachers should try to find common ground with EFL/ESL children and select books such as folktales and fairytales (where stories may be similar even if the language is different); books with similar characters, themes, or events; books in different languages (to let children show you, and perhaps the class, how well they can read in their own language); books with the same stories but different settings, or about the same country but with a different story, or about similar characters in different settings.

4   The more cultures represented in a classroom, the more resources the teacher has. Work towards the idea, through reading, writing, talking, and listening, that we are all citizens of a shared world.

Further reading

Behrendt, L. 2004, *Home*, University of Queensland Press, St Lucia, Queensland.

Fuller, A. 2002, *Don't Let's Go to the Dogs Tonight: An African childhood*, Random House, New York.

Morgan, S. 1987, *My Place*, Fremantle Arts Centre Press, Fremantle, WA.

Ward, G. 1987, *Wandering Girl*, Magabala Books, Broome, WA.

A FORUM: SOCIAL ISSUES, HISTORY, AND FANTASY

31

Overview

The word 'forum' originally referred to a public square or meeting place. Books and their associated ICT resources provide many opportunities for meeting together, to consider presents, to view pasts, and to imagine fantastic futures.

Literature as meeting place

Literature is a meeting place. Its physical structures are flexible, dynamic, and often highly experimental. Books can be all shapes and sizes; they can be made of soft or hard materials (such as cloth and thick board); they can turn various ways; their words can be upside down, around the page and across the page, as in *Fox* by Margaret Wild and Ron Brooks (2000); words can be part of the illustrations; text can be different sizes; scripts can be different; there can be no words; there can be lots of words; there can be an orderly arrangement of pictures; there can be pictures scattered anywhere and everywhere.

The subject matter is equally varied. There are children's books about all aspects of life, from birth to death, from illness to divorce, from cultural difference to physical and intellectual difference and disability, from sibling rivalry to learning to live with next-door neighbours. There are picturebooks that open doors into abstract questions about the meaning of life and the consequences of the smallest action—think about Roger Vaughan Carr and Ann James' *The Butterfly* (1996), for example. There are controversial books for young adults about homosexuality, and about the social problems of incest and suicide.

Because literature contains narrative gaps, it opens up prolific and densely personal spaces across which the reader is required to construct bridges. Is Max's rumpus in *Where the Wild Things Are* a dream, a fantasy, a science fiction adventure, or is it 'real'—and what is real anyway?

Where exactly is John Burningham's *Cloudland* (1996)—and is it a fantasy, a dream or a near-death experience? What happens in *The Great Bear* (1999)—does it live, does it die? And what is 'living' and what is 'death', especially in relation to cosmic space? Such questions illustrate how problematical it is to try to categorise children's texts as either 'real' or 'fantasy'.

In the classroom, these gaps provide authentic opportunities for talk, for listening, and for sharing and testing ideas. Children's literature thus becomes a forum, a place where issues and problems can be held up to diverse points of view and discussed openly with peers. It gives connection to diverse people, diverse families, and a diverse world, as we have seen in chapter 29; it also gives connection to a thinking community. These books and discussion times don't have to be serious; a book such as Jacqueline Wilson's *The Suitcase Kid* (1992) describes the dilemma of a 10-year-old when her parents break up, but it does so with humour and compassion. Gleeson's *Skating on Sand* series gives another picture of family relationships, especially *Hannah and the Tomorrow Room* (1999), where Hannah has to give up her room to her ailing grandfather. The picturebook *Hello Baby* describes another family choosing to join in the celebration of a home birth (Overend & Vivas 1999).

Historical books use current ideas to impose meaning on the past

Social issues, history, and fantasy may seem an unlikely combination, but they interlink in many ways, and they can all be part of this forum. Historical books, that is, books written in the present about a past, usually try, from contemporary perspectives, to impose some sense and meaning on that past. Stephen Muecke writes:

> The power of history, I would suggest, is not just in its secular making-sense. Rather, its effective magic is its ability to recast our conception of the present: 'every image of the past that is not recognised by the present as one of its own concerns threatens to disappear irrevocably,' says Walter Benjamin in his thesis on the philosophy of history. (1999: 29)

For example, *My Place* (Wheatley & Rawlins 1987) is an historical unfolding of the story of Australia, but its narrative structure is unified on the principle of the social and moral issue of Aboriginal land rights. It also uses the diversity of immigration as a method of unravelling past decades and making sense of Australia's multicultural present. *Tucker* (Ian Abdullah 1994) is a retrospective of childhood, but is also a sociological document, a case study, of what it was like growing up in that particular place at that particular time.

Similarly, fantasy may be concerned with an exploration of the social problems of a 'real' world transposed to an imaginary world, within clear parameters set by the text, and set free from any restraining present-day realities. Because it tends to address the profound nature of the essential human dilemma—good versus evil, right versus wrong—fantasy is closely related to folklore, and to the construction of alternative worlds. *Outside Over There* (Maurice Sendak 1981) constructs an alternative world. So does *Cloudland*. Tolkien's *Lord of the Rings* (1954–55) and the *Narnia* books (1950–56) of C. S. Lewis are obvious examples of alternative worlds constructed out of an understory of folklore. There are many variations. *You and Me, Murrawee* (Hashmi & Marshall 1998) is a type of history–fantasy time shift, a past operating simultaneously with a present; it is a dual chronotope but its whole premise emerges from a sociological concern.

In a discussion of science fiction (a specific type of fantasy premised on future worlds moulded out of scientific achievements), Sollat notes that it consists of 'thought models in which elements of reality are separated from their actual contents and represented as estranged in a fictional future' (1997).

Fantasy itself need not of course be of the future—it can be very much of the present. Clearly, children's literature is, by convention, 'fantastic' anyway. There are talking animals, interactions between humans and animals, imaginary worlds, fairies, and all sorts of magic—magic wishes, magic drawing, magic words, and magic thresholds, such as, in Narnia, a wardrobe door.

Children's reading and social issues

The public debate about what social issues are 'suitable' for children to read about and what are not is always going to be controversial, but it is a productive argument to have. First, it shows that the community is acknowledging the significance of the books read by its children. Second, it demonstrates community desires to do the best by its young. Third, it raises the level of community awareness about difficult issues and brings them to the surface, where they may not be solved but where some of the problems that have contributed to a particular issue may be addressed.

For example, street kids may appear to be misfits in a literature that includes rural worlds such as that of Peter Rabbit and *The Wind in the Willows*, but they constitute a real and troubling issue. However, the concepts of 'reality', 'social realism', and 'realistic' pose a number of problems. Are the depictions of some of these issues 'realistic', or are they romantically contrived anyway? Hartnett's *Wilful Blue* (1994) deals with a young man's suicide, but does so in a highly fanciful way. *Sleeping Dogs* (Hartnett 1995) is powerfully written, but the language at times is so mystical that it has the surreal feel of a dream (or more accurately, nightmare). Neither of these texts are appropriate for primary school children, but teachers need to have read them, and other books like them, so that they can formulate their own position with intellectual integrity.

But what about, for example, *Way Home* (Hathorn & Rogers 1994)? How realistic is the picture of the 'real' kid in this text? It seems to me that the greatest community debates emerge when there is an unresolved or 'unhappy' ending, so in a sense this is the most realistic part of some of these texts. Life doesn't always have happy endings. But neither do 'unhappy' endings need to be without hope.

It is important that educators expose children to a diversity of texts from a diversity of points of view, and discuss openly any issues that arise out of them. Television and video have made this a generation of children from whom very little is hidden. The skewed and contorted images, purporting to be 'realistic' of life, that appear on television sets every night need to be balanced by other images, ideas, and ways of being, some of which are part of contemporary children's literature. These may not always be 'happy' but they do need to present other possibilities of thinking and doing, and of developing or challenging a worldview.

▶ LITERACY IN THE DIGITAL AGE

Digital resources have brought an easily accessible virtual world into children's homes, offering new forms of socialisation, new opportunities for communication. This is an age of intense community: young people text message, email, chat. The forum that is literature has grown exponentially with access to ICTs, which provide children and teachers with both independent and collaborative resources.

Teachers need to be sensitive to the demographics of their classrooms and choose a range of books that are authentic for this particular group of young people. Mix talking about books with talking about films. Watch Disney's *Pocahontas* and set it in its historical context. Discuss it in contemporary terms as a clash of cultures. Listen to what the children in your class are talking about and the movies they have seen, and try to find books that link up in some way. Use the Internet to find contemporary material and encourage children to conduct their own searches whenever possible. Always remember that your task as teacher is to open new horizons, not just stick to old ones.

Teachers also need to be aware that boys and girls usually have different tastes in books (Rowling's *Harry Potter* appears to be one series that appeals to both genders). There is currently great debate about literacy standards in general and boys' relatively poorer standards in particular. While this must not be overstated, it is an area of legitimate concern. John Marsden, Morris Gleitzman, Paul Jennings, and John Larkin are all writing books—some fantastic, some science fiction, some dealing with social issues—that many boys seem to enjoy. The *Tomorrow* series by John Marsden is enormously popular with boys as well as girls and has **Teachers should** been re-released for adults (1993–99). It explores ideas about fear, war, and **be aware of gender** relationships with the land. *Only the Heart* by Brian Caswell and David Phu An **preferences in** Chiem (1997) is a complex novel for older readers; it is historical (about the **reading material** Vietnam War) but also deals with the social issues of Vietnamese immigration and Cabramatta gangs. Other books for older readers are Matt Zurbo's *Idiot Pride* (1997) and Judith Clarke's *The Lost Day* (1997), which are written in a teenage idiom, very pronounced in the case of the Zurbo book. These last three books all contain sophisticated themes. However, Allan Baillie's *Secrets of Walden Rising* (1997), also a book for older readers, is one that may interest upper primary school children and could be used in the classroom. This is a well-written story about growing up, but it is set in a past–present context that is almost an allegory of the story of Australia.

Discussion of community perspectives on Aboriginal issues is fraught with political difficulties, but James Maloney, in his award-winning trilogy *Dougy*, *Gracey* and *Angela*, uses the art of narrative to throw open the differing points of view, and provoke an open discussion of all the issues. Advanced upper primary students should be encouraged to read these books; they are an honest depiction of attitudes that many Australians will recognise.

Another book to recommend for older readers is *Johnny, My Friend* (1985) by the Swedish writer Peter Pohl. This book is set in Stockholm and tells the story of a growing up, and a growing into a realisation that it is not a perfect world. Beverley Naidoo's *No Turning Back* (1995) is set in Johannesburg and tells the story of a 12-year-old boy escaping from a violent home. It is based on the real experiences of young black South Africans living on the streets.

The Sterkarm Handshake by Susan Price (1998) tells a gripping and thoughtful story about the planned exploitation of the 16th century by the developers of the 21st century, and explores a new type of time-travelling imperialism and environmental degradation.

The Running Man by Michael Gerard Bauer (2004) is a moving story about haunting fears (both of adult and child) and shifting perspectives; it has an almost dream-like conclusion. *Prep*, by Curtis Sittenfeld (2005) is a very well written story of American High School life from a female perspective; it writes of an interesting world of privilege and power, of being inside but outside the clique, and of both the näivity and precocity of adolescent relationships.

Some of these books are classified as Young Adult (YA) fiction. This category is commonly defined by the age of its readership—sometimes twelve to eighteen years, sometimes older. The most defining feature of YA novels, however, is not necessarily that they portray a person in a marginal situation (Nikolajeva 2000: 205), although they often do. Young Adult fiction does not just portray; rather, it allows the protagonist to describe events and convey perceptions, feelings, and emotions from a highly subjective point of view which is constructed by the author (and accepted by the author's culture) as an ideology of adolescence.

An ethics of hope

I want to return to the idea of hope. Many of these novels for older readers deal with difficult issues and there are others that are particularly bleak. While it is true that children must grow into an awareness of social problems, it is also true that any books we present to young people should be characterised by an **An ethics of hope implies moral and artistic integrity** *ethics of hope*. An ethics of hope does not mean that everything is always presented as perfect, or perfectly happy. Far from it. It does imply, however, moral as well as artistic integrity, and the presentation of many different possibilities of being. It recognises that children have futures and that a 'future' implies options. It represents the realities of agency in personal response (even in circumstances beyond personal control). It is also concerned to present images that are characterised by principles of positive potential and openness to freedom and creativity.

An ethics of hope engages with complex ideas of not knowing. In an age of a so-called 'knowledge society' where knowledge is all, *not knowing* appears as a deficit, even as the antithesis of what education is about. Yet education is also about equipping for the unknown, for the unknowable, for the profound mystery of life.

The books of David Almond provide some of the best examples of what I mean by this ethics of hope. As an introduction to Almond's lyrical *oeuvre*, **http://davidalmond.com/** which includes *Wild Girl Wild Boy*, *Secret Heart*, and *The Fire-Eaters*, it is worth reading *Counting Stars*, a wonderful collection of short stories that are the result of grown-up siblings, increasingly conscious of their mortality, being briefly reunited and remembering their past: 'We listen to the stories that for an impossible afternoon hold back the coming dark' (2000:157).

A shadow of mortality also hovers over the mythic realism of *Skellig* and *Skellig the Play*. Michael's baby sister is very ill and in danger of dying. In the garage at the back of their new house, he finds a roughly spoken derelict creature, who has broken and fragile angels' wings growing out of his shoulder blades. Almond uses what he calls 'Narration' in *Skellig* to guide viewing through this rite of passage into the possibility of death.

In the following passage, Michael and his friend Mina have just watched Skellig standing at the window being fed by the birds:

SKELLIG   Come to me.

They go to him. He takes their hands.

SKELLIG   Take my hand.

They make a circle.

NARRATION	He stepped sideways and they turned together,
NARRATION	And kept slowly turning
NARRATION	As if they were carefully, nervously.
NARRATION	Beginning to dance.

They turn. Michael holds back.

SKELLIG	Don't stop, Michael.
MINA	No, Michael. Don't stop!
NARRATION	He didn't stop.
NARRATION	He felt Skellig's and Mina's hearts beating alongside his own.
NARRATION	He felt their breath in rhythm with his.
NARRATION	It was as if they moved into each other,
NARRATION	As if they became one thing.
NARRATION	And for a moment he saw ghostly wings at Mina's back.
NARRATION	He felt feathers and delicate bones rising from his own
NARRATION	And he was lifted from the floor with Skellig and Mina.
NARRATION	They turned circles together through the empty air of that empty room
NARRATION	High in an old house in Crow Road …
NARRATION	And then it was over.

(Almond 2003, pp. 91–92)

The ethics of hope in this book is not so much related to the fact that the baby lives, but to growing knowledge of the possibility of beauty in the apparently unlovely, of love in unexpected places, of hope in the face of the seemingly hopeless, and of community.

Always read any book before you either recommend it or present it in class, and consider its suitability for your particular classroom context.

▶ Summary

1. Literature provides a nonthreatening, authentic forum (meeting and discussion place) where a range of issues can be contemplated.

2. Social issues relate to history and fantasy because these two genres are often concerned with the exploration of social problems, and the struggle between right and wrong. History often tries to make sense of the present by making sense of the past. Fantasy explores the profound human dilemma of good versus evil.

3. The distinctions in children's literature between fantasy and 'real' are often problematic.

4. Teachers need to be aware of the reading tastes of the girls and the boys in their classes, but not limited by them; they should also be aware of the range of literature that children can be encouraged to read as they come to leave primary school.

5. An *ethics of hope* recognises that children have futures and that a 'future' implies options.

6. Teachers should always be sensitive to the needs of their particular class and school situation.

Further reading

Marchetta, M. 2003, *Saving Francesca*, Viking, Melbourne.

Reynolds, K., G. Brennan & K. McCarron 2001, *Frightening Fiction: R. L. Stine, Robert Westall, David Almond and others*, Continuum, London and New York.

Overview

This chapter summarises children's literature in terms of responses: the responses of readers and writers to texts. It concludes with a discussion of literature as theatre in the classroom.

IN THE CLASSROOM

Texts as reader response

Mrs Prochazka	We're going to read a story about the Depression
Mai Ling (thinks)	It sounds sad—perhaps like a war—
Junko (thinks)	I wonder if there was a depression in Japan.
Naomi (thinks)	The depression wasn't as bad as the holocaust.
Ben (thinks)	My family were all still out in the country then.
Wesley (thinks)	I wish I were in the pool right now!
Mrs Prochazka	Can anyone tell me something about the Depression?
Sally	I remember my grandparents talking about it—they didn't have any money and couldn't get married for a long time—about five years I think, because my grandfather didn't have a job.
Mai Ling (thinks)	I wonder what jobs my ancestors did at that time.
Junko (thinks)	They probably did—it was all over the world I think.
Naomi (thinks)	Nothing could ever be as bad as that.
Ben (thinks)	Probably wasn't so bad in the country.

Wesley (thinks)	I wish I were in the pool right now!
Mrs Prochazka	Let's read the story.

Note how first-person dialogue such as this—even when it is inner speech rather than outer speech, as most of the above is—allows and promotes:

■ the expression of a subjective point of view, letting the reader focalise through each of the characters
■ inclusivity rather than exclusivity.

This passage reminds us that all children bring their own life-world not just to the reading of any text, but into the classroom.

Consider the different backgrounds and cultures represented in this scenario. What implications does this have for teaching?

IN THE CLASSROOM

Texts as mirrors: feeling rejection, isolation, 'out of it', different

Years 5–6

Read the following excerpts from texts. Where do they position the reader? What choices of reading do we have? (We can identify, we can empathise, we can look on.) How are these excerpts different? How are they similar? What do you think were the authors' purposes in writing these texts?

> Mr Riggs hoists a rolled-up wall-map onto the hook above the blackboard and lets it flap down over the date, 30 October 1932, chalked in blue.
> 'Who can tell me about The Granites?' he asks, tapping the red centre of Australia with his cane.
> Straight away, kids put up their hands. 'Sir, sir, me sir, please sir.'
> I don't say anything. I look away.
> Mr Riggs lost an eye in the war, and his other eye fills me with dread. I do my best to avoid it.
> Too late.
> 'Paul,' he says. 'How nice of you to be awake for a change. What can you tell me about The Granites?'
> 'Please sir,' I say, 'granite is a hard rock.'
> They laugh. They always do. I arrive some mornings and find the whole school aware of things that I've missed.
>
> (Gary Disher, *The Bamboo Flute* 1991: 12–13)

> Who's dat wide-eyed likkle girl
> Staring out at me?
> Wid her hair in beads an' braids
> An' skin like ebony?
>
>   …
>
> Who dat girl? Who dat girl?
> Pretty as poetry?
> Who dat girl in the lookin' glass?
> Yuh mean dat girl is me?
>
> (Valerie Bloom in Agard and Nicholls, *A Caribbean Dozen* 1994)

Dad was playing his music again.

Opera.

Who else's dad would be caught dead playing that kind of stuff? …

As I opened the front door, there was a quiet point in the music. His voice drifted out to me.

'Lisdalia! Non essere tardi.'

Don't be late.

'I won't be.' As usual I replied in English. My language.

I shut the door gently behind me.

(Brian Caswell, *Lisdalia* 1994)

 # IN THE CLASSROOM

Texts as mini-cultures: school and playground experience

Years 5–6

How do the following excerpts from texts represent the school experience? Do you think they were written by children? Why, or why not? Do you think they were written for children? Why, or why not? Write a story about some aspect of your school experience. Your writing may take the form of narrative; it may be poetic, it may be an *acrostic* or *limerick*, it can be a recount (retelling something that happened), information report, or media release; it may be a popular song. Set out your writing in the way you consider most appropriate. Use the computer if possible.

> *I dreamt last night of times gone by*
> *Of overflowing days and far high sky*
> *Of rainbow colours bright like tinted cellophane*
> *I dreamt last night I was a child again …*

Me (6):   The worst part is going through the gate (don't be late)
            there's a whole lot of playground (sticky when it's hot)
            and a whole lot of people and they push and they shout
            and my room's far away and my shirt's pulled out
            the worst part is going through the gate (now I'm late).

(From *Life-Times* by Rosemary Darling)

By the morning recess we all had writer's cramp and mental exhaustion, but Miss Belmont looked quite calm and relaxed as she sailed into the staffroom for coffee. I'd never cared to associate with the riff-raff in the playground at Barringa East Primary. I went into the office and asked Mrs Orlando, the school secretary, if I could lie down during recess because I had a headache. On my medical card in the office it said I was prone to nervous headaches, rhinitis, sinusitis, bee-sting allergy, rheumatism; suspected hypersensitivity to wattle pollen, horsehair, dust mite, clover and Clag glue; tested for diabetes, arthritis, gallstones and hiatus hernia; and that I didn't have to put my head under water when we went swimming because of a punctured eardrum. Mum didn't write any of that information on the sheet they'd sent home for parents to fill in; I'd supplied it to Mrs Orlando over the six years I'd been going to Barringa East Primary. (Robin Klein, *Hating Alison Ashley* 1984)

Texts as popular culture

'It seems to me you lived your life like a candle in the wind …'

Elton John

Children's literature is involved with story and feelings, with ideas and concerns, with imagery and metaphor, with the imagination. So, very often, are popular songs. We respond to these because we have an innate sense of poetic expression, rhythm, and rhyme, and because we can understand or empathise with the stories they tell.

Encourage children to bring popular songs into the classroom, and then, with them, discuss the language—simile, metaphor, abstract ideas, and concerns. Make a collection of lyrics on a noticeboard in the classroom, and vary it frequently. Children are highly motivated to look at the words of popular songs. If we can set up meaningful links to books and to poetry, poetry and books can become part of the understory of popular culture.

Story can be found in popular song

These models can be adapted in many ways. For example, in the activity 'Texts as mirrors' above I have focused on the idea of rejection and difference, but teachers could just as easily choose to discuss ideas of 'change' or 'excitement' or 'happiness'.

In the classroom

Years 5–6

Play the song to the class.

Telegraph Road (*Dire Straits*)

A long time ago came a man on a track
Walking thirty miles with a sack on his back
And he put down his load where he thought it was best
And he made a home in the wilderness.
He built a cabin and a winter store
And he ploughed up the ground by the cold lake shore
And the other travellers came riding down the track
And they never went further and they never went back
Then came the churches then came the schools
Then came the lawyers then came the rules
Then came the trains and the trucks with their loads
And the dirty old track was the telegraph road
Then came the mines—then came the ore
Then there was the hard times and then there was a war
Telegraph sang a song about the world outside
Telegraph road got so deep and wide
Like a rolling river

And my radio says tonight it's gonna freeze

People driving home from the factories

There's six lanes of traffic

Three lanes moving slow …

I used to go to work but they shut it down

I've got a right to go to work but there's no work to be found

Yes and they say we're gonna have to pay what's owed

We're gonna have to reap from some seed that's been sowed

And the birds up on the wires and the telegraph poles

They can always run away from the rain and the cold

You can hear them singing out their telegraph code

All the way down the telegraph road

You know I'd sooner forget but I remember those nights

When life was just a bet on a race between the lights

You had your head on my shoulder and your hand on my hair

Now you act a little colder like you don't seem to care

But believe in me baby and I'll take you away

From out of this darkness and into the day

From these rivers of headlights these rivers of rain

From the anger that lives on the streets with these names

'Cos I've run every red light on memory lane

I've seen desperation explode into flames

And I don't want to see it again …

From all of these signs saying sorry but we're closed

All the way down the Telegraph Road.

Responses

1   How many pictures are there in this song?

2   How many voices do you hear?

3   How many people are there in the story?

4   How many stories are there in this song?

- the story of progress

- the story of civilisation versus the untamed world

- the story of growing up

- the history of our times

- history of own growth

- history of a country's growth

- history of the world.

Compare with *Window* by Jeannie Baker.

1   Write the story of the text from the little boy's point of view.

2   Write it from the mother's point of view.

3   How have ideas about the 'wild place' changed?

4   Compare with 'The night sky' by Sally Morgan *(The Flying Emu and Other Australian Stories)*

5   Tell the story in a comic strip form. Write a text to the pictures.

6 In groups, think of some of your favourite songs. Make a draft list of the songs and what they are about. When you have a collection of songs, go to the library and see if you can find any books relating in some way to the themes of your songs. Compile a roundtable list of the song, the theme, and the book.

Children's literature as theatre

In conclusion, it is useful to consider children's literature as theatre. Perry Nodelman notes that the production process of each book represents a collaboration of different people with different skills (1988: 81). There are many ways in which we can think of both the texts of children's literature, and children's involvement with them, as theatre, as an interactive event, with a cast and a stage, with props and costumes.

Theoretically, children's books have a great deal in common with theatrical conventions. First, much of what happens between words and pictures in a text and between the words and the pictures and the reader, is *dramatic irony*: the audience (readers) knowing something that the characters on the stage (and on the page) don't (think of *Rosie's Walk*). This not only adds to the effect of the dramatic moment, but also draws young readers in, giving them a sense of superiority, offering opportunities for them to predict, to enjoy being 'in the know'. Interactive moments in children's theatre are based on this very principle: 'Where is it?' or 'Where did he go?' asks the befuddled stage character to an audience who know exactly (and will say) where it is and where he has gone.

> **Like theatre, children's books play with dramatic irony**

Second, directors seek to construct stage pictures, using lighting and sets and costumes to create images that communicate to the audience. In a play these pictures are linked by the movement of the actors; in a picturebook, the reader turns the pages (think of how this works in *The Great Bear, Hello Baby*, and *Beware, Beware*).

Third, a number of the elements of theatrical genre can be seen in picturebooks. Many stories are domestic theatre—stories about particular moments in the everyday life of a child. Pictures are moments of *thisness*—expressions of the particularity of that moment—and the theatre is a representation of *thisness*, that is, of particular moments in a continuum (perhaps a blur) of moments. Walter Benjamin refers to 'the strict, frame-like, enclosed nature of each moment' in a 'whole state of living flux' (1966: 3). The particularity of these moments can be represented in all sorts of ways, from the 'real' to the surreal. For example, the dramatist August Strindberg was an expressionist, seeking to express dramatic action as being inside the mind of a person dreaming, shifting time and space as it shifts in dreams. Many contemporary picturebooks are expressionistic—consider again Gleeson & Greder's *The Great Bear* (1999), Crew & Woolman's *The Watertower* (1994), and Crew & Rogers' *Lucy's Bay* (1992), but also consider *Come Away from the Water, Shirley* (Burningham 1977) and *Drac and the Gremlin* (Baillie & Tanner 1988) and, for that matter, *Alice in Wonderland*. On the other hand, in some children's books, particularly of the Dr Seuss type, there is a strong element of farce and slapstick. One of my students pointed out that *Rosie's Walk* is pure pantomime, complete with villain and, in her words, the 'hapless (or is she?) female', with each picture setting up for the disaster (and fun) of the next (Sinclair 1999).

Why mention this as part of a conclusion?

I want to do more than draw parallels (interesting as they are) between literature and theatrical genres. The whole underpinning philosophy of part III is that theory informs practice. As educators, we need to understand that, *in practice*, children's literature *in the classroom* is a type of theatre, the theatre of the classroom. Every time we read a book with children it is a *viewing*, as theatre is: a viewing of the text, of the imaginary experience that is the invitation of the text, and of each other's participation in that experience. Like theatre, it is a corporate experience of being involved in shared story. The word *theatre* derives from the Greek word *theatron*, meaning *a place for viewing* or *a place for seeing*. I like the idea of *the classroom as a place for seeing*. Children's literature accesses the opportunity to see beyond who we are and where we are.

A reading event is a metafictional *mise-en-scène*, a sliding between a present 'real' setting and an imagined 'un-real' setting. As classroom story (a teacher reading a book to a particular class in a particular place at a particular time) slides into the story of the book, the actual book itself takes

Reading in the classroom is a type of theatre

on a number of roles. Its physical page boundaries act like a proscenium arch, framing the scene, showing us where to look. Every turn of the picturebook page is a shift in scene; the teacher's hand turning the page is a *stagehand*. Readers are part of the *stage crew* in this reading event, getting things ready and making links between what is seen and what is unseen and filling in the gaps by running around in the backstage spaces of imagination. In the way teachers hold up picturebooks to show the pictures as they read, the book functions as much more than just a prop: sometimes it's like a puppet (something that is given voice by the person controlling its movements), sometimes it's like a narrator or chorus (making the links between the audience/viewers/readers and the action and characters of the story), sometimes it acts as an interruption to the story it tells (jolting us back to its pages). Sometimes we lose sight of it altogether and it disappears from view, like the threshold of a doorway that we have already passed through.

In practical ways, children's literature clearly lends itself very readily to drama. Every reading with a class is a dramatic performance. Children are part of the performance: they can be encouraged to play with texts and turn them into scripts, or create their own mime, Readers' Theatre, dramatic dance, tableau, radio play, television script, poem, song, artwork, or comic strip. These creative responses activate the multiple intelligences identified by Howard Gardner (1983): verbal-linguistic, logical-mathematical, natural, bodily-kinaesthetic, visual-spatial, musical-rhythmic, interpersonal, and intrapersonal. The process also stimulates real and authentic language in all its forms—speaking and listening to it, reading and writing it.

But most of all, children's literature in a generous classroom becomes a catalyst for learning about life and its unities and diversities, not only for developing and expanding traditional concepts of literacy but also for developing sophisticated skills in critical literacy, for accumulating cultural, narrative, digital and visual literacies; in other words, for building up layers of individual understory.

The well-known drama teacher Dorothy Heathcote, who sees language and communication at the core of the education system, developed and worked with a concept that she called 'the mantle of the expert'. As part of the learning process, both she and her students assume the role of experts and set about role-playing and subsequently developing expertise: focusing on what the knowledge they need to acquire might be, considering its value, and learning how.

Heathcote's teaching philosophy gives to students the space to grow and to teachers the grace to let them. They see the world with growing eyes. Teacher and students become experts together, learning collaboratively.

The way we use literature in the classroom can give similar space and grace. Reading together, writing together in a range of print and electronic media, talking together about texts with an increasing knowledge and understanding, listening and making creative responses, philosophically enquiring, and arguing sometimes, gives all of us the scope and potential to grow into experts, to communicate better, and to push beyond current capacities and skills. We can speculate; we can discover. We can perform, try on roles, engage with language not our own, and engage with new ways of using language, and indeed with new languages.

In this way, literacy becomes, appropriately in a postmodern age of new technologies, multi-active, multipurpose, and multidimensional.

Connecting communities

I began Part III by discussing language, literacy and literature in the context of sustainable creative pedagogy, and by suggesting that Australian educators should explore indigenous perspectives on teaching and learning. One last point follows. Indigenous cultures explicitly encode ideas of soul in their story arts. It is ironic that despite enhanced respect for indigenous spirituality, the mainstream hesitates to engage with such ideas. In part this is because of a desire to be inclusive of the multiple faiths of a multicultural society. In part, however, it is because 'soul' is now loaded with more taboos than any body part.

Lodge writes (2002:5):

> It is of course possible to have a concept of the self … without believing in the existence of immortal souls; but many people with no religious belief find the word 'soul' and 'spirit' useful, if not indispensable, to signify some uniquely valuable quality in human life and human awareness.

It is this sense of the uniquely human that helps individuals to commit to a moral order beyond the self and to connect to community. But there is an inherent paradox in a world that sees itself as both 'a global village'—the greatest sense of community the world has known—and 'postmodern'—celebrating individual rather than communal equities. Both globalism and postmodernism are very pervasive master narratives; in a 'globalised' world where we have all 'gotta be me', viable community, or belief beyond self, becomes problematic.

Children's literature has a significant role to play in exposing such dilemmas and ambiguities. Books are 'sites of the culture's deepest moral questionings' (Parker 1998, p.15); they express 'a sense of the density of our lives' (Murdoch 1983, pp.43–9). *Fox* (Wild and Brooks) tells a dense story: of courage ('I am blind in one eye but life is still good,' Dog tells Magpie), of community ('Fly, Dog. Fly! I will be your missing eye and you will be my wings') and of moral dilemmas (fear, jealousy, loyalty, possessiveness).

Diary of a Wombat (French and Whatley) tells the story of a wombat making friends with humans. Its last opening reads:

> Evening: Have decided that humans are easily trained and make quite good pets.
> Night: Dug new hole to be closer to them.

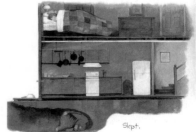

The illustration shows a cross section of three levels: the human couple soundly asleep in their bedroom on the top, the kitchen on the level below, and directly beneath, the wombat asleep in his cosy hole under the house.

This book implies that the way forward for the modern nation is to develop intimacy with difference. The wombat doesn't have to become human and the humans don't have to live in burrows. But they end up sharing the same roof.

There are great challenges and no easy answers. However, educators have the opportunity (and imperative), through story arts, to use all their expressive forms—novels and poetry and drama and visual art and music and dance—to discern connections and to create community among difference.

▶ Summary

1   Teachers can be creative in connecting books with other texts such as popular songs, and with a myriad of online resources.

2   Picturebooks have much in common with theatrical conventions.

3   The way teachers present books can be a dramatic event.

4   Children's books lend themselves to dramatic activities.

5   The idea of 'the mantle of the expert' is an inspiring teaching philosophy.

6   Teachers have the opportunity in classrooms to use texts and story arts that address profound moral concepts and that work towards creating and sustaining community.

Further reading

Gardner, H. 1983, *Frames of Mind: The theory of multiple intelligence*, Fontana, London.

Heathcote, D. & G. Bolton 1995, *Drama for Learning: Dorothy Heathcote's mantle of the expert approach to education*, Heinemann, Portsmouth, N.H.

Johnston, R. R. 'In and out of otherness: Inner-city geographies of being and children's plays as sites for the other within.' In Geraint Evans (ed.) *Text and the City*. Forthcoming.

Johnston, R. R. 'Sustainable creative pedagogy: A leaderly way forward for Australian education.' Forthcoming.

Johnston, R. R. 2003, 'Carnivals, the carnivalesque, *The Magic Puddin'*, and David Almond's *Wild Girl, Wild Boy*: Towards a theorising of children's plays', *Children's Literature in Education* 34(2): 131–46.

Johnston, R. R 2003, '"All the world's a Stage": Children's literature as performance'. In K. Reynolds (ed.) *Children's Literature and Childhood in Performance*, Pied Piper Publishing, Staffordshire, UK, pp. 57–67.

Lodge, D. 2002, *Consciousness and the Novel*, Penguin, London.

Murdoch, I. 1961, 'Against dryness: A polemical sketch', *Encounter* 16(1), pp. 16–20.

Poston-Anderson, B. 2002, '"With will there's a way". Performing a children's play: a way of learning', *CREArTA* 2(2): 20–9.

Warren, B. 1995, *Creating a Theatre in your Classroom*, Captus University Publications, Ontario, Canada.

Answers to quiz in chapter 2

i.d. hill ii. e. consonant blend iii. e. none of them iv. d. street v. d. the vi. b. thirst vii. a, fat, c. them, d. rip, g. pot, h. cuts, j. cuddle viii. a. rake, c. wine, d. been, e. coat, f. huge ix. a. see, b. bread, c. look, e. soup x. a. oil, b. out, c. ear, d. down, e. boy, g. sail xi. a. 3, b. 4, c. 3, d. 2, e. 4 xii. a.1, b. 3, c. 4, d. 2, e. 3, f. 4.

Explanation

i   The other words end in either vowels or digraphs.

ii   A consonant digraph is incorrect; it is a single consonant sound represented by two letters, e.g. the /f/ sound in 'tough' (*gh*).

iii   They begin with consonants or blends.

iv   The others are digraphs.

v   The others are 'unvoiced'. That is, they are not made using the voice box.

vi   The others use the voice box. Put your hand on your throat and notice the difference between the first sounds of *the* and *thirst*.

vii   The others are long vowels or diphthongs.

viii   The others do not say their names. (In phonics, letters that say their names are called long vowels.)

ix   In phonics, *or* in *short* is not a vowel digraph because one letter is a consonant.

x   'Catch' contains a short vowel.

xi   Try saying them out aloud until you have the separate sounds correct.

xii   Say the words and count the syllables as you do so.

Appendix: Key Australian literacy contacts

The following select list of literacy contacts contains addresses, telephone numbers, fax numbers, and websites of professional organisations, government departments, and other bodies concerned with literacy in Australia. For instance, the Australian Literacy Educators' Association supports teaching practice in literacy across all age levels and curriculum areas. It holds annual and local conferences and publishes a variety of literacy material. The Primary English Teaching Association focuses on English teaching in its many forms at the primary school level. It also holds conferences and has a large list of publications. The various states and territories of Australia produce their own curricula, while the Commonwealth Department of Education, Training and Youth Affairs deals with literacy matters at a national level.

National

Australian Association for the Teaching of English (AATE Inc.)
PO Box 3203
Norwood, SA 5067
Tel: 08 8332 2845
Fax: 08 8332 0394
Email: aatemail@nexus.edu.au

Australian Council of TESOL Association (ACTA)
25 Kimmax St
Sunnybank, Qld 4109
Tel: 07 3345 9391
Fax: 07 3345 8382
Website: www.acta.edu.au

Australia Library and Information Services Association (ALIA)
PO Box E441
Kingston, ACT 2604
Tel: 02 6285 1877
Fax: 02 6282 2249
Email: enquiry@alia.org.au

Australian Literacy Educators' Association (ALEA)
PO Box 3203
Norwood, SA 5067
Tel: 08 8332 2845
Fax: 08 8333 0394
Email: aleamail@nexus.edu.au

Australian School Library Association (Inc.) (ASLA)
PO Box 450
Belconnen, ACT 2616
Tel: 02 6231 1870
Fax: 02 6231 2092
Email: asladaw@atrax.net.au
Website: www.w3c2.com.au/asla

Australian Teachers of Media (ATOM)
Locked Bag 9
Collins St East
Melbourne, Vic. 8003
Tel: 03 9651 1310
Fax: 03 9651 1311

Children's Book Council of Australia (CBCA)
PO Box 48
Hughes, ACT 2605
Tel: 02 6287 5709
Fax: 02 6287 5709

Commonwealth Department of Education, Training and Youth Affairs (DETYA)
GPO Box 9880
Canberra, ACT 2601
Tel: 02 6240 8111
Fax: 02 6240 7111
Website: www.detya.gov.au

Curriculum Corporation
PO Box 177
Carlton, Vic. 3053
Tel: 03 9207 9600
Fax: 03 9639 1616
Email: sales@curriculum.edu.au

Early Childhood Teachers Association (ECTA Inc.)
Queensland University of Technology
PO Box 84
Spring Hill, Qld 4000
Tel: 07 3366 1288
Fax: 07 3366 1288
Website: www.ecta.org.au

Primary English Teaching Association (PETA)
PO Box 3106
Marrickville, NSW 2204
Tel: 02 9565 1277
Fax: 02 9565 1070
Email: info@peta.edu.au

ACT

Department of Education and Training
PO Box 1584
Tuggeranong, ACT 2901
Tel: 02 6207 5111
Fax: 02 6205 9333

Catholic Education Commission
Archdiocese of Canberra/Goulburn
PO Box 3317
Manuka, ACT 2603
Tel: 02 6234 5455
Fax: 02 6234 5491

Association of Independent Schools of the ACT
42 Tyrell Circuit
Kaleen, ACT 2617
Tel: 02 6241 2429
Fax: 02 6241 5923
Email: aisact@ais.act.edu.au

New South Wales

Office of the Board of Studies (NSW)
GPO Box 5300
Sydney, NSW 2001
Tel: 02 9367 8111
Fax: 02 9367 8484
Website: www.boardofstudies.nsw.edu.au

Department of Education and Training (DET)
35 Bridge St
GPO Box 33
Sydney, NSW 2001
Tel: 02 9561 8000
Fax: 02 9561 8759

Catholic Education Commission of NSW
PO Box A169
Sydney South, NSW 2000
Tel: 02 9287 1555
Fax: 02 9264 6308

Northern Territory

Department of Education (NTDE)
GPO Box 4821
Darwin, NT 0800
Tel: 08 8999 5606
Fax: 08 8999 5960
Email: infocentre.ntde@nt.gov.au

Catholic Education Council
PO Box 219
Berrimah, NT 0828
Tel: 08 8984 3833
Fax: 08 8947 1517

Association of Independent Schools of Northern Territory
GPO Box 2085
Darwin, NT 0801
Tel: 08 8950 4511
Fax: 08 8952 2131
Email: philipws@topend.com.au

Queensland

Education Queensland
PO Box 33
Brisbane, Qld 4002
Tel: 07 3237 0111
Fax: 07 3229 0265
Website: www.qed.qld.gov.au

Queensland School and Curriculum Council (QSCC)
PO Box 317
Brisbane, Qld 4002
Tel: 07 3237 0794
Fax: 07 3227 1285
Email: inquiries@qscc.qld.edu.au
Website: www.qscc.qld.edu.au

Catholic Education Commission
GPO Box 2441
Brisbane, Qld 4001
Tel: 07 3224 333
Fax: 07 3229 0907

Association of Independent Schools of Queensland
PO Box 957
Spring Hill, Qld 4004
Tel: 07 3228 1515
Fax: 07 3228 1575
Email: office@aisq.qld.edu.au

South Australia

Department of Education, Training and Employment
GPO Box 1152
Adelaide, SA 5001
Tel: 08 8226 1000
Fax: 08 8226 1234

South Australian Commission for Catholic Schools
PO Box 179
Torrensville Plaza, SA 5031
Tel: 08 8301 6600
Fax: 08 8301 6611

South Australian Independent Schools Board
301 Unley Rd
Malvern, SA 5061
Tel: 08 8373 0755
Fax: 08 8373 1116
Website: www.isb.sa.edu.au

Tasmania

Department of Education Tasmania
GPO Box 169B
Hobart, Tas. 7001
Tel: 03 6233 8011
Fax: 03 6231 1576
Website: www.tased.edu.au

Association of Independent Schools, Tasmania
Suite 15, Galleria Building
33 Salamanca Place
Hobart, Tas. 7000
Tel: 03 6224 0125
Fax: 03 6224 0174
Email: aist@tassie.net.au

Tasmanian Catholic Education Commission
PO Box 102
North Hobart, Tas. 7002
Tel: 03 6231 1033
Fax: 03 6231 1793

Victoria

Department of Education, Employment and Training (DEET)
PO Box 4367
Melbourne, Vic. 3001
Tel: 03 9637 2000
Fax: 03 9637 2020
Website: www.det.vic.gov.au

Board of Studies (Vic.)
St Nicholas Place
15 Pelham St
Carlton, Vic. 3053
Tel: 03 9651 4300
Fax: 03 9651 4324
Email: general@bos.vic.edu.edu.au

Association of Independent Schools Victoria
20 Garden St
South Yarra, Vic. 3141
PO Box 2138
Prahran, Vic. 3181
Tel: 03 9825 7200
Fax: 03 9826 6066
Website: www.ais.vic.edu.au

Catholic Education Commission of Victoria
PO Box 3
East Melbourne, Vic. 3002
Tel: 03 9267 0228
Fax: 03 9415 0325
Website: www.cecv.melb.catholic.edu.au

Western Australia

Education Department of Western Australia
151 Royal St
East Perth, WA 6004
Tel: 08 9264 4111
Fax: 08 9264 5005
Website: www.eddept.wa.edu.au

Curriculum Council of Western Australia
27 Walters Drive
Osborne Park, WA 6017
Tel: 08 9273 6300
Fax: 08 9273 6371
Website: www.curriculum.wa.edu.au

Association of Independent Schools Western Australia
3/41 Walters Drive
Osborne Park, WA 6017
Tel: 08 9244 2788
Fax: 08 9244 2786

Catholic Education Commission of Western Australia
PO Box 198
Leederville, WA 6903
Tel: 08 9388 4388
Fax: 08 9381 3201

Glossary

ACER

Australian Council for Educational Research, est. 1930. This organisation conducts general research, develops tests and materials, and provides educational services.

allophone

One of the actual sounds that make up a phoneme. The actual sound of a phoneme may differ in speech according to its position in a word or the dialect in which it is spoken, e.g. the different sounds of /l/ in *lip* and *bill* and /k/ in *cup* and *cat*. In the second example the initial consonant is modified by the following vowel.

alphabetical writing system

A writing system in which the symbols represent the sounds of speech.

analog (analogue)

Continuous and variable electrical waves that represent an infinite number of values. Information represented electronically as a continuous, varying signal. The opposite of analog is digital.

articulatory phonetics

The branch of phonetics that studies the production of speech sounds by the human vocal tract.

assessment

The process of describing and judging achievement on set tasks, against clear criteria.

authentic assessment

A selective collection of student work, teacher observations, and self-assessment that is used to show progress over time with regard to specific criteria.

avatar

See **story palaces**.

benchmark

A point of reference from which quality or achievement is measured. National literacy and numeracy benchmarks are sets of descriptors that represent nationally agreed minimum levels of literacy and numeracy at a particular year level.

blend

The combining of two or three letter sounds so that each sound can be identified, e.g. *cl* in *clown* and *str* in *string*.

Blog

Short for weblog or web log, a frequently updated personal journal on the Internet, written in reverse chronological order.

book rap

Book discussion through electronic mail.

'bottom-up' view of reading

An approach to reading and learning to read that places emphasis on word recognition and the decoding of print. It is also described as a code-based or subskill approach.

CD-ROM

(Compact Disc read-only-memory) A high-density disc that stores computer data in the form of text, graphics, and hi-fi stereo sound.

chronotope

'Time-place'. Refers to the relationship in narrative between people and events on the one hand, and time and space on the other.

cloze test

A procedure in which readers provide words that have been omitted at systematic intervals or on the basis of function.

cohesion

Particular features that link different parts of a text.

cohesive ties

Connections within a text that help to develop unity. Also termed cohesive links, these ties operate within and across sentences. There are many types of cohesive ties, e.g. reference, substitution, ellipsis, and conjunction.

collocation

Words that typically go together in a sequence (a faint hope, butt out), in associated pairs (bread and butter), or cluster around a topic (fish and chips; beach, surf, sand, sea).

comprehension strategies

Thinking techniques used by a reader to gain a deeper understanding of a text.

conferencing

In the process approach to writing or reading, the opportunity for students to meet in 'conference' to discuss draft work or material being read.

consonant

1. A sound made by the breath being partly or completely obstructed by the speech organs. For instance, /sh/ as in *show* and /t/ as in *tap*. There are twenty-four consonant sounds in Australian English.
2. The letters of the alphabet, other than the vowels.

contexts for text

This relates to multimodes of textual communication and the multiliteracies that these different types of text require. Each context for text has its own modes of literate behaviours, its own language, its own 'register'. (The traditional grammatical idea of **register** relates to the variety of language used in different social situations or contexts: the need to choose language appropriate to audience, purpose, time, and place.)

criterion-referenced test

A test used to determine whether a student has mastered a particular skill or unit of instruction.

critical literacy

An approach to literacy that aims at revealing the hidden power relationships and ideological assumptions that underlie texts.

cultural literacy

1. Knowledge of the language and social structure within which we live.
2. Awareness of the integrity of many different ways of thinking and acting.

cumulative assessment file

Collections of data that relate to a student's academic development.

curriculum cycle

This cycle has three main stages: preparation/ building up the field, joint construction of text, and independent construction of text. These stages, in turn, can loosely equate to the Shared, Guided, and Independent Writing strategies.

decile

One of the parts of a distribution of scores, each of which contains one-tenth of the cases in the complete series.

diagnostic test

A test that determines a student's strengths and weaknesses from a set number of objectives.

digital

A system that uses binary numbers (0s and 1s) rather than a continuous spectrum of values for its signals such as happens in an analog system.

digraph

A combination of two or more letters to form one speech sound, as in **bread**, **ship**.

diphthong

A blending of two vowel sounds that begins with the sound of the first vowel and glides into the other, as in the beginning of *ice, ale, old, oil, owl* and the end of *hear, chair, poor*.

directionality

In reading, the left-to-right and return sweep at the end of a line.

discourse
Communication of thought in speech or writing. In literature it refers to the process of telling the story, how the story is told on the surface of the text.

discourse analysis
The study of continuous stretches of discourse or language longer than a sentence to analyse linguistic feature of its structure.

emoticon
Keyboard character used to express emotions, e.g. 'smiley'.

ESL
English as a Second Language; sometimes ESOL is preferred, i.e. English as a Second or Other Language, to denote that many people are already bilingual or trilingual.

etymology
The derivation of words from words or word elements.

evaluation
A value judgment made by estimating the worth of something.

field
Related words in a particular context, e.g. words associated with 'vegetables'. In functional grammar the field refers to the subject matter in a discourse.

focalisation
The positioning of readers and viewers to see and hear the events of the narrative and the thoughts and ideas of the characters.

formative evaluation
Evaluation that occurs during the progress of a program in order to give feedback for improvement.

Foundation handwriting
An approach to handwriting (common in New South Wales and the Australian Capital Territory) whereby simple movements are repeated to form the shapes of letters. The letters can be joined to form cursive handwriting.

functional grammar
Grammar where the social function is central, based on the view of language as a process of social interaction and a communication of ideas. Sentences 'function' as commands, questions, and statements.

genre
In functional grammar, the description of a text in terms of the way it is structured to achieve a specific purpose (*see* **text-type**). It is a distinguishable category of text recognised by aspects such as subject matter and linguistic features.

grapheme
The written symbol of a particular phoneme.

graphological information
Visual information about letters, words, and punctuation in text.

graphophonic
Relating to the connections between sounds and letters in reading and spelling.

homonym
A word that is identical to another in pronunciation and spelling but has a different origin and meaning, e.g. *saw* (past tense of *see*) and *saw* (a cutting instrument). Can also include **homophones**, which sound the same but have different spelling and meaning, e.g. *fair* and *fare*, and **homographs**, which have the same spelling but differ in meaning and sometimes in pronunciation, e.g. *wind* (that blows) and *wind* (to wind up a clock).

hyperlink
An area of a web page or CD-ROM text or image that a user can click on in order to go to another item or source of information.

hypertext
A set of semantic associations. An area of text on a web page or CD-ROM page that acts as a link to a hyperlink.

ideogram (or ideograph)
A symbol used to represent a whole word or concept.

idiom

An idiom is a style or manner of expression peculiar to a given people. It is the usage or vocabulary that is natural to native speakers of the language.

implied reader

The person for whom a text appears to be written. Writers of children's literature compose their texts with the implicit knowledge that the person reading it will be a child.

indicator

A statement of the behaviour that students might display as they work towards the achievement of syllabus outcomes.

inferential meaning

The inferred meaning of a text. Often termed 'reading between the lines'.

inflection

A word ending that signifies grammatical meaning, e.g. -*s* (plural), -*ed* (past tense), and -*ing*.

intertextuality

Meaningful relationships and connections, overt and covert, that reach across, between, and beyond texts.

'invented' or 'temporary' spelling

Usually phonemic spelling used by a beginning writer attempting to spell a word.

knowing readers

Readers who not only have all the skills they need to read but also read with depth, knowing how texts work, how significant the rewards of the reading experience are, and the value of persevering with difficult texts.

lexical

Relating to vocabulary.

lexicogrammatical

Relating to vocabulary (*lexis*) and grammar as closely related elements of language.

lingua franca

A language used to facilitate communication between people who have different first languages.

literacy

The ability to read and write; a synthesis of language, context, and thinking that shapes meaning.

literal meaning

The plain sense meaning of a text. Often termed 'reading the lines'.

logogram (or logograph)

A symbol representing a word or phrase.

metacognitive strategies

When applied to reading, the learning strategies that provide an overall plan for gaining meaning from text, such as changing reading speed, re-reading parts of a text, asking oneself questions during reading, highlighting and summarising the text.

metalanguage

A language to describe language. Grammar is a metalanguage (adjective metalinguistic).

miscue analysis

The analysis of the oral reading errors (miscues)—graphophonic, syntactic, and semantic—that a student makes when reading a text, in order to develop improved strategies.

mode

In functional grammar, the channel of communication in a discourse, e.g. speech or writing.

morpheme

A meaning-bearing unit of language. 'Free' or 'unbound' morphemes are whole words in themselves, e.g. *boy*, or *rein* and *deer* in *reindeer*. 'Bound' morphemes are prefixes, suffixes, and inflections, e.g. *pre* in *prejudge*, *ly* in *slowly*, and *s* in *boys*.

morphology

The study of structure in language.

multiliteracies

Visual images, written and other representations. The interface of visual and linguistic meaning in multimedia.

narrative
A story. In literary theory it includes both the story (what is narrated) and the discourse (how it is narrated).

netiquette
Good manners on the Internet.

norm-referenced test
A test that allows an interpretation of an individual's test result by comparison with a group that is said to be the norm.

onset and rime
A form of segmentation of sounds in syllables. Onset is the initial consonant or consonant cluster in a syllable, e.g. *c*- in *cat*, *scr*- in *scratch*. Rime is that part of a syllable that contains a vowel and a final consonant, e.g. -*og* in *dog*.

orthography
The spelling system of a language.

outcomes
Specific statements of the results intended by a syllabus; goal statements of student achievements.

phone
A unique minimal segment of the stream of speech.

phoneme
The smallest unit of speech that distinguishes one word from another, e.g. the phonemes /s/ and /f/ in *sat* and *fat*. (*See* **allophone**.)

phonemic awareness
An understanding of the smallest sounds that make up oral language. It is characterised by a speaker's ability to hear, segment, and manipulate sounds in speech. **Phonological awareness** is a more general term that includes the ability to recognise syllables and other speech segments, such as onset and rime.

phonetics
The branch of linguistics dealing with speech sounds, their production, description, and classification. (*See* **articulatory phonetics.**)

phonics
An approach to teaching early reading, pronunciation, and spelling. Phonics refers to the relationship between written letters (graphemes) and spoken sounds (phonemes). **Phonic analysis** is a method of teaching word recognition by matching elements in writing with their corresponding sounds; **phonic synthesis** is the building up of words from the sounds within them.

phonological information
Information about the sound system of language.

phonology
The study of the sounds of language.

picaresque
In literature, especially the novel, relating to the adventures and wanderings of rogues or other colourful characters.

portfolios
Collections of students' work and observations that show significant aspects of students' development and achievement over time.

procedural texts
Texts that tell how something can be accomplished, e.g. 'How to Make a Telephone Call'.

profiles
Lists of observed behaviour that map the desired development of a student.

readability
The level of difficulty of a particular piece of reading material.

reading
A process of literate thinking during which a reader brings meaning to and takes meaning from written text in a social and cultural context.

reading recovery
An early intervention program designed to improve the literacy skills of children who have made little progress in their first year of school.

redundancy

Having more information than we need. Redundancy in reading refers to additional information that helps a reader to predict.

register

Language appropriate for its audience, context, and purpose, e.g. colloquial, scholarly, legal. In sociolinguistics, the variety of language used in different social situations.

reliability

In assessment, the consistency of measurement, procedures, or results.

rhyme

A correspondence of sounds in two or more words, especially at the ends of lines of poetry, as in *found* and *pound*.

rime

See **onset and rime**.

root

The basic meaning-carrying element of a word, e.g. *flex* in *inflexible* (i.e. un-bend-able).

running record

A record of the actual reading by a student of a particular piece of text.

saccades and fixations

Saccades or saccadic steps are the jumps a reader's eyes make when reading. Fixations are the stops or pauses that follow the saccades. A reader 'reads' during the fixations.

scaffolding

A metaphor to describe the support given to students through explicit teaching of skills and knowledge, to move students to a higher level of understanding.

scanning

The rapid viewing of reading material to locate specific information from the text.

schema

A specific type of prior knowledge that readers bring to a text when they read.

segmentation

The process of analysing speech into segments of discrete units of sound such as vowels or consonants.

semantics

The study of the meaning of words in language and how they change.

semiotics

The study of signs, focusing on the patterns of communication. Language is a sign system.

sight word

A word that is read 'on sight', as a whole, without being sounded out or analysed structurally, e.g. *said, the, was, through*.

skimming

The rapid overview of reading material to gain the overall meaning, main idea, and general tone of the text.

smiley

See **emoticons**.

sociolinguistic approach

The study of the ways in which language is used by societies in relation to class, ethnicity, gender, race, and social institutions.

standardised test

A test that has been given to various groups under uniform conditions in order to obtain norms against which the scores of other groups can be evaluated.

stanine

Contraction of 'standard of nine' in which a test population is divided into nine categories. An individual's score is given an integer from 1 to 9. The mean is 5, containing the middle 20 per cent. The bottom 4 per cent and the top 4 per cent are in the first and ninth classes.

story

A story emerges out of the events that take place, the actions the characters engage in, and the time and place, or time-space.

story palaces

Themed sites, constructed visually rather than through text and where action commonly takes place against a backdrop of rooms, which may be cartoon-like or lavishly decorated. They are built in cyberspace by a community of fans and enthusiasts, who can also construct and take on characters (*avatars*, realistic-looking or cartoon figures, available in all sorts of poses, often designed with costumes and props) and play out (in collaborative role-play) stories and action in all sorts of genres from conversation to soap opera. Access to palaces is through a web browser such as Internet Explorer or Netscape, or through downloading free Palace User software (http://www. palaceplanet.net).

structural analysis

A method of decoding in which parts of a word, such as prefixes, suffixes, compounds and syllables are separated and analysed.

subjectivity

Originally a psychoanalytical term: the developing knowledge of a sense of self.

summative assessment

Evaluation that occurs at the end of a unit or course of study, determining the extent of overall achievement according to identified learning outcomes. In contrast to formative assessment in which a student's progress is monitored or diagnostic assessment in which a student's particular strengths and weaknesses are discovered.

syllabary

A writing system in which the graphic symbols represent syllables.

syllabification

The method of dividing words into parts roughly corresponding to the syllables in speech.

syllable

A part of a written word corresponding to the spoken division uttered in a single voice impulse and containing at least one vowel or diphthong sound (but, but.ter, but.ter.fly).

syntax

The way words, phrases, and clauses are structured in sentences. In linguistics, the study of such structures.

taxonomy

Applied to education, a system of classifying educational objectives. Benjamin Bloom in the 1950s developed objectives for the cognitive domain.

tenor

In discourse, the relations among the participants in a language activity, particularly the level of formality. The style or manner in the variety of language.

text-type

Different genres in functional grammar such as recount, report, and narrative. Communication of meaning in various media that use language. Texts include written, spoken, and visual communication that can be identified. More or less synonymous with genre. (*See* **genre**.)

thesaurus

A book of words or phrases arranged by the meaning of words. Peter Mark Roget (1779–1869) produced a popular thesaurus.

'top-down' view of reading

An approach to reading and learning to read that emphasises the primary importance of meaning and what the reader brings to the text.

traditional grammar

The grammatical study (based originally on the grammar of Latin) of the structure of language, mostly within the sentence.

understory

A term relating to the layers of themes and significance in children's literature texts. It gives narrative and thematic cohesion as well as points of connection to other texts.

validity

The extent to which a measurement tool does what it is intended to do.

visual literacy

The ability to read signs, images, pictures, perspectives, focalisation, shape, and form. It is also the ability to analyse the power of images in particular contexts.

Vowel

1. A speech sound produced by the relatively unimpeded passage of air through the mouth. There are twelve vowel sounds in Australian English, nine diphthongs, and twenty-four consonants.
2. The letters *a, e, i, o, u*. In phonics, the sounds made by the names of these letters are known as 'long vowels'.

whole-language approach

Student-centred approach, emphasising motivation and interest. Reading is focused on meanings from texts such as children's literature rather than basal readers.

Bibliography

Abbreviations

ACER	Australian Council for Educational Research
ACLAR	Australasian Children's Literature Association for Research
AGPS	Australian Government Publishing Service
ALEA	Australian Literacy Educators' Association
ANU	Australian National University
CREA	Centre for Research and Education in the Arts
CREArTA	*International Journal of the Centre for Research and Education in the Arts*
DEETYA	Department of Employment, Education Training and Youth Affairs (Cth)
EFL	English as a Foreign Language
ESL	English as a Second Language
FILLM	Fédération Internationale des Langues et Litteratures Modernes
IRA	International Reading Association
IRSCL	International Research Society for Children's Literature
MIT	Massachusetts Institute of Technology
PETA	Primary English Teaching Association
SMH	*Sydney Morning Herald*
SMS	Short Message Service, i.e. text messaging on mobile phones
STELLA	Standards for Teachers of English Language and Literacy in Australia
TESOL	Teaching English to Speakers of Other Languages
UNSW	University of New South Wales
UTS	University of Technology Sydney
VAKT	Visual-Auditory-Kinaesthetic-Tactile
ZPD	Zone of Proximal Development

General references and critical texts

Adams, M. J. 1990, *Beginning to Read: Thinking and learning about print*, MIT Press, Cambridge, Mass.
—— & M. Bruck 1993, 'Word recognition: the interface of educational policies and scientific research', *Reading and Writing: An Interdisciplinary Journal* 5: 113–39.
Alexander, S., Teaching and Learning on the World Wide Web. AusWeb 97 Conference, 1997. http://ausweb. scu.edu.au/

Anderson, J. 1985, 'Microcomputers and reading'. In G. Winch and V. Hoogstad (eds), *Teaching Reading: A language experience*, Macmillan, Melbourne, pp. 203–12.

Anderson, R. C., E. H. Hiebert, J. A. Scott and I. A. G. Wilkinson 1985, *Becoming a Nation of Readers: The report of the commission on reading*, Center for the Study of Reading, Champaign, Ill.

Anderson-Inman, L. 1998, 'Electronic text: literacy medium of the future', *Journal of Adolescent and Adult Literacy* 41(8): 678–82.

Angelillo, J. & L. M. Calkins 2002, *A Fresh Approach to Teaching Punctuation: Helping young writers use conventions with precision and purpose*, Scholastic Professional Books, New York.

Anstey, M. & G. Bull 2000, *Reading the Visual: Written and illustrated children's literature*, Harcourt Australia, Sydney.

—— & —— 2003, *The Literacy Labyrinth*, 2nd edn, Pearson Prentice Hall, Sydney.

Ashton, J. & T. H. Cairney, 2001, 'Understanding the discourses of partnership: An examination of one school's attempts at parent involvement', *Australian Journal of Language and Literacy* 24(2): 145–56.

Armstrong, A. & C. Casement 2001, *The Child and the Machine: How computers put our children's education at risk*, Scribe Publications, Melbourne.

Atwood, M. 1997, *Alias Grace*, Virago, London.

Austin, J. L. 1962, *How to Do Things with Words*, Harvard University Press, Cambridge, Mass.

Australian Bureau of Statistics 1997, *Aspects of Literacy: Australia 1996*, 2 vols, AGPS, Canberra.

Australian Catholic University, unpublished action research, Centre For Communication Studies.

Australian Education Council 1989, *The Hobart Declaration on Schooling*, Australian Education Council, Melbourne.

—— 1994, *English: A Curriculum Profile for Australian Schools*, Curriculum Corporation, Melbourne.

Australian Language and Literacy Policy 1991, *Companion Volume to the Policy Paper*, AGPS, Canberra.

Ayers, W. 1993, *To Teach: The journey of a teacher*, Teachers College Press, New York.

Bakhtin, M. M. 1981, *The Dialogic Imagination*, transl. C. Emerson & M. Holquist, ed. M. Holquist, University of Texas Press.

—— 1986, *Speech Genres and Other Late Essays*, transl. V. W. McGee, ed. C. Emerson & M. Holquist, University of Texas Press.

Bal, M. 1985, *Narratology: Introduction to the theory of narrative*, University of Toronto Press.

Barrs, M. 1990, *Patterns of Learning*, Centre for Language in Primary Education, London.

Barthes, R. 1968. 'The death of the author'. In *Image-Music-Text* (1977), transl. Stephen Heath, Fontana/Collins, Glasgow.

—— 1976, *The Pleasure of the Text*, transl. Richard Miller, Jonathan Cape, London.

Bean, W. 2000, *Ways to Teach Spelling*. Pen 124, PETA, Sydney.

—— & C. Bouffler 1987, *Spell by Writing*, PETA, Sydney.

—— & —— 1997, *Spelling*, Eleanor Curtain Publishing, Melbourne.

Beard, R. 1998, *National Literacy Strategy: Review of research and other related evidence*, Department for Education and Employment, Sudbury, Suffolk, UK.

Bearne, E. 2002, *Making Progress in Writing*, Routledge Falmer, London.

Benjamin, W. 1966, *Understanding Brecht*, Verso, London.

Benton, M. 1996, 'The image of childhood: representations of the child in painting and literature, 1700–1900', *Children's Literature in Education* 27(1): 35–60.

Berninger, V. W. 1999, 'The "Write Stuff" for preventing and treating disabilities', International Dyslexia Association, *Perspectives* 25(2): 1–4.

—— et al. 2002, 'Teaching spelling and composition alone and together: implications for the simple view of writing', *Journal of Educational Psychology* 94(2): 291–304.

Bettelheim, B. 1976, *The Uses of Enchantment: The meaning and importance of fairy tales*, Vintage, New York.

Bloom B. S. (ed.) 1956, *Taxonomy of Educational Objectives: The classification of educational goals*,

Longmans, London.

Bloomfield, L. 1927, 'Literate and illiterate speech', *American Speech* 2(10): 432–9.

Board of Studies NSW 1998a, *English K–6 Syllabus*, Board of Studies NSW, Sydney.

—— 1998b, *English K–6 Student Work Samples: Talking and listening, reading, writing*, Board of Studies NSW, Sydney.

Bond, G. & R. Dykstra 1967, *Final Report*, Coordinating Center for First Grade Reading Instruction Programs, US Department of Health, Education and Welfare, University of Minnesota Press, Minneapolis. (See also the reprint, with researchers' comments, *Reading Research Quarterly* (3)1, 1999.)

Bookbird Special Issue: *Children's Literature and the Media*, 38(1) 2000.

Booth, W. C. 1988, *The Company We Keep: An ethics of fiction*, University of California Press, Berkeley, Calif.

Bordwell, D. & K. Thompson, 1993, *Film Art: An introduction*, McGraw Hill, New York.

Bouffler, C. 1987, *Spelling It out to Parents*, PETA, Sydney.

—— 1997, 'They don't teach spelling anymore—or do they?', *Australian Journal of Language and Literacy* 20(2): 140–7.

Brady, L. & Kennedy, K 2005, *Celebrating Student Achievement: Assessment and reporting*, 2nd edn, Pearson/Prentice Hall, Sydney.

Breen, M. P., C. Barratt-Pugh, B. Derewianka, H. House, C. Hudson, T. Lumley & M. Rohl 1997, *Profiling ESL Children: How teachers interpret and use national and state assessment frameworks*, DEETYA, Canberra.

Brindley, G. & G. Wigglesworth 1997, *Access: Issues in language test design and delivery*, National Centre for English Language Teaching and Research, Macquarie University, Sydney.

Brindley, R. & J. J. Schneider 2002, 'Writing instruction or destruction: lessons to be learned from fourth-grade teachers' perspectives on teaching writing', *Journal of Teacher Education* 53(4): 328–41.

Bruner, J. 1993, *Actual Minds, Possible Worlds*, Harvard University Press, Boston.

Bull, G. 1995, 'Children's literature: using text to describe reality', *Australian Journal of Language and Literacy* 18(4): 259–69.

—— & M. Anstey (eds) *Crossing the Boundaries*, Pearson Australia, Sydney.

Burchfield, R.W. (ed.) 1996, *New Fowler's Modern English*, rev. 3rd edn, Clarendon Press, Oxford.

Burns, A. & C. Coffin (eds) 2000, *Analysing English in a Global Context: A reader*, Routledge, London.

Bustamante, D. M. 2002, 'Telling our stories, finding our voices: Nurturing a community of learners', *Primary Voices K–6* 11(1): 2–6.

Butler, D. 1979, *Cushla and Her Books*, Hodder & Stoughton, London.

—— 1995, *Babies Need Books*, Bodley Head, London [1980].

Butler, J. 1990, *Gender Trouble: Feminism and the subversion of identity*, Routledge, London.

—— 1993, 'Bodies that matter: On the discursive limits of "sex"', Routledge, New York.

Cairney, T. H. 1991, *Other Worlds: The endless possibilities of literature*, Heinemann, Portsmouth, N.H.

—— 1995, *Pathways to Literacy*, Cassell, London.

—— 1997, The role of the family in children's learning: developing more effective partnerships between home and school. Unpublished manuscript.

—— 2000a, 'Beyond the classroom walls: The rediscovery of the family and community as partners in education', *Educational Review* 52(2): 163–74.

—— 2000b, 'The construction of literacy and literacy learners', *Language Arts* 77(6): 496–505.

—— 2002, 'New Directions in family literacy: Building effective partnerships between home and school'. In B. Spodek & O. Saracho (eds) *Contemporary Perspectives on Early Childhood Education*, Greenwich, Conn.: Information Age Publishing, pp. 99–126.

—— 2003a, 'The home-school connection in literacy and language development'. In D. Green & R. Campbell (eds) *Literacies and Learners: Current perspectives*, Sydney: Prentice Hall, pp. 17–32.

—— 2003b, 'Literacy in family life'. In N. Hall, J. Larson & J. Marsh (eds) *Handbook of Early Childhood Literacy*, London: SAGE Publications, pp. 85–98.

—— 2005, 'Literacy diversity: Understanding and responding to the textual tapestries of home, school and community'. In J. Anderson, M. Kendrick, T. Rogers & S. Smythe (eds) *Portraits of Literacy Across Families, Communities and Schools: Intersections and tensions*, London: Lawrence Erlbaum Associates Inc., pp. 41–61.

—— & J. Ashton 2002, 'Three families, multiple discourses: Examining differences in the literacy practices of home and school', *Linguistics and Education* 13(3): 303–45.

—— & L. Munsie, 1992, *Beyond Tokenism: Parents as partners in literacy*, Heinemann, Portsmouth, N.H.

Calfee, R. C., E. H. Hiebert & P. Afflerbach (eds) 1994, *Authentic Reading Assessment: Practices and possibilities*, IRA, Newark, Del.

Calkins, L. M. 1983, *Lessons from a Child: On the teaching and learning of writing*, Heinemann Educational, Exeter, N.H.

Cambourne, B. 1988, *The Whole Story*, Ashton Scholastic, Sydney.

—— 1999, 'What's the score on testing?', *Practically Primary* 4(1): 8–9.

Cameron, D. 1995, *Verbal Hygiene*, Routledge, London.

Carney, E. 1994, *A Survey of Spelling*, Routledge, London.

Carpenter, H. & M. Prichard 1984, *The Oxford Companion to Children's Literature*, Oxford University Press, Oxford.

Caruana, W. 1996, *Aboriginal Art*, Thames & Hudson, London.

Catholic Education Office of Victoria 1990, 'Children's literature and second language acquistion', *Diversity* 8: 1.

Chall, J. S. 1967, *Learning to Read: The great debate* (2nd edn 1983, 3rd edn 1996), McGraw-Hill, New York.

—— 1999, 'Some thoughts on reading research: Revisiting the first-grade studies', *Reading Research Quarterly* 34(1): 8–10.

Chambers, A. 1985, *Booktalk*, Bodley Head, London.

—— 1993, *Tell Me: Children, reading and talk*, Thimble Press, Stroud, Glos., UK.

Chang, J. 1991, *Wild Swans*, Flamingo Books, London.

Chapman, J. 1983, *Reading Development and Cohesion*, Heinemann, London.

Chatman, S. 1978, *Story and Discourse: Narrative structure in fiction and film*, Cornell University Press, Ithaca and London.

Chenfeld, M. D. 1987, *Teaching Language Arts Creatively*, 2nd edn, Harcourt Brace Jovanovich, New York.

Chomsky, N. 1965, *Aspects of the Theory of Syntax*, MIT Press, Cambridge, Mass.

—— & M. Halle 1968, *The Sound Pattern of English*, Harper, New York.

Christenson, T. A. 2002, *Supporting struggling writers in the elementary classroom*, IRA, Newark, Del.

Christie, F. 1989, Curriculum Genres in Early Childhood Education: A case study in writing development. Unpublished PhD thesis, University of Sydney.

—— & J. R. Martin 1997, *Genre and Institutions: Social processes in the workplace and school*, Cassell, London.

—— & J. Rothery 1989, *Children Writing: A reader*, Deakin University Press, Geelong, Vic.

—— & —— 1990, 'Literacy in the curriculum: planning and assessment'. In F. Christie (ed.), *Literacy for a Changing World*, ACER, Melbourne, pp. 187–205.

—— & R. Misson (eds) 1998, *Literacy and Schooling*, Routledge, London.

Clark, A. 1997, *Being There: Putting brain, body and mind together again*, MIT Press: Cambridge, Mass.

Clark, M. M. 1976, *Young Fluent Readers*, Heinemann, London.

Clay, M. M. 1972, *The Early Detection of Reading Difficulties: A diagnostic survey*, Heinemann, Auckland.

—— 1979, *Reading: The patterning of complex behaviour*, 2nd edn, Heinemann, Auckland.

—— 1991, *Becoming Literate: The construction of inner control*, Heinemann, Auckland.

—— 1993, *An Observation Survey of Early Literacy Achievement*, Heinemann, Auckland.

—— 1998, *By Different Paths to Common Outcomes*, Heinemann, Auckland.

—— 2000, *Running Records for Classroom Teachers*, Heinemann, Auckland.

—— & B. Tuck 1991, *A Study of Reading Recovery Subgroups: Including outcomes for children who did not satisfy discontinuing criteria*, Heinemann and University of Auckland, Auckland.

Clemmons, J., L. Laase, D. Cooper, N. Areglado & M. Dill 1993, *Portfolios in the Classroom, Grades 1–6*, Scholastic Professional Books, New York.

Clinton, H. R. 2003, *Living History*, Simon & Schuster, New York.

Clinton, W. 2004, *My Life*, Hutchinson, London.

Cochran-Smith, M. 1991, 'Word processing and writing in elementary classrooms: a critical review of related literature', *Review of Educational Research* 61(1): 107–55.

Collerson, J. 1988, *Writing for Life*, PETA, Sydney.

—— 1994, *English Grammar: A functional approach*, PETA, Sydney.

—— 1997, *Grammar in Teaching*, PETA, Sydney.

Commonwealth Department of Education, Training and Youth Affairs 1998 (draft), *Assessing Literacy: Using stage I outcomes* (Joint Project of Catholic Education Commission, Association of Independent Schools, Department of Education and Training NSW), Commonwealth of Australia, Canberra.

Conway, J. K. 1989, *The Road from Coorain*, Minerva, London.

Cope, B. & Kalantzis, M. (eds). 2000, *Multiliteracies: Literacy learning and the design of social futures*, Routledge, London.

Cope, B. & M. Kalantzis 1993, *The Power of Literacy: A genre approach to the teaching of writing*, Falmer Press, London.

Cottee, K. 1989, *First Lady: A history-making solo voyage around the world*, Pan Books, Sydney.

Cramer, R. L. 2001, *Creative Power: The nature and nurture of children's writing*, Longman, New York.

Crossman, W. 2000, 'The end of written language', *SMH* 1 January 2000. Adapted from Crossman (forthcoming), *Comspeak 2000: How talking computers will recreate an oral culture by the mid-21st century*.

Crystal, D. 1997, *English as a Global Village*, Cambridge University Press.

Curriculum Corporation 1994, *ESL Scales, A joint project of the States, Territories and the Commonwealth of Australia initiated by the Australian Education Council*, Curriculum Corporation, Melbourne.

Cushman, D. 2002, 'From scribbles to stories', *Instructor* 111(5): 32–3.

Czerniewska, P. 1992, *Learning About Writing*, Blackwell, Oxford.

Dale, E. & J. Chall 1948, 'A formula for predicting readability', *Education Research Bulletin* 27: 1120.

Darder, A. 1991, *Culture and Power in the Classroom: A critical foundation for bicultural education*, Bergin & Garvey, New York.

Davidson, J. 1999, 'All things in moderation: a whole school approach to authentic assessment', *Practically Primary* 4(1): 18–19.

Dawkins, R. 1996, *Climbing Mount Improbable*, Norton, New York.

De Bono, E. 1970, *Lateral Thinking: A textbook of creativity*, Ward Lock Educational, London.

Deakin University 1984, *Children Writing: A reader*, Deakin University Press, Geelong, Vic.

Department of Education and Children's Services 1997, *Early Literacy Practices and Possibilities*, Adelaide.

Department of Education and Student Services, South Australia 1997, *Spellings from Beginnings to Independence*, Darlington Materials Development Centre, Seacombe Gardens, SA.

Department of Education, Science and Training 2005, *Report and Recommendations, National Inquiry into the Teaching of Literacy*, www.DEST.gov.au.

Derewianka, B. 1991, *Exploring How Texts Work*, PETA, Sydney.

—— (ed.) 1992, *Language Assessment in Primary Classrooms*, Harcourt Brace Jovanovich, Sydney.

—— 1998, *A Grammar Companion for Primary Teachers*, PETA, Sydney.

—— 2002, 'Making grammar relevant to students' lives', in G. Bull & M. Anstey, *The Literacy Lexicon*, Prentice Hall, Sydney.

Derrida, J. 1991a, *Donner le Temps*, vol. 1, Galilee, Paris.

—— 1991b, 'Signature event context', in Peggy Kamuf (ed.) *Between the Blinds: A Derrida reader*, Harvester Wheatsheaf, Hemel Hempstead, UK, pp. 82–111.

Dewey, J. 1971, *English Spelling: Roadblock to reading*, Teachers College Press, Columbia University, New York.

Dickinson, P. 1986, 'Fantasy: the need for realism', *Children's Literature in Education* 17(1): 39–51.

Dillon, D. R. 2000, *Kids Insight: Reconsidering how to meet the literacy needs of all students*, IRA, Newark, Del.

Dodge, B. 1998, WebQuests for learning, www.ozline.com

—— & T. March 2001, www.kn.pacbell.com/wired/fil/#intro

Doonan, J. 1993, *Looking at Pictures in Picture Books*, Thimble Press, Stroud, Glos., UK.

—— 1998, paper presented to Beyond the Riverbank Conference, University of Exeter.

Downes, T. & C. Fatouros 1995, *Learning in an Electronic World*, PETA, Sydney.

Droga, L. & Humphrey, S. 2003, *Grammar and Meaning: An introduction for primary teachers*, Target Texts, Berry, NSW.

Durkin, D. 1966, *Children Who Read Early*, Teachers College Press, New York.

Easthope, A. & K. McGowan 1992, *A Critical and Cultural Theory Reader*, Allen & Unwin, Sydney.

Eco, U. 1979, *A Theory of Semiotics*, Indiana University Press, Bloomington, Ind.

Education Department of Western Australia 1994a, *First Steps: Writing developmental continuum*, Longman, Melbourne.

—— 1994b, *First Steps Reading Resource Book*, Longman, Melbourne.

Eggins, S. 1994, *An Introduction to Systemic Functional Linguistics*, Cassell, London.

Eichenbaum, B. 1998, 'Introduction to the Formal Method'. In Rivkin & Ryan, *Literary Theory*, pp. 8–16.

Eliot, T.S. 1951 [1921], *Selected Essays*, Faber, London.

Ellyard, P. 1997, Australian College of Education Conference, Cairns.

Emmitt, M. 1999, 'Authentic assessment—what is it?', *Practically Primary* 4(1): 5–7.

Ernst & Young 1998, Literacy, Education and Training. Their impact on the UK economy, mimeo. Quoted in R. Beard 1998, *National Literacy Strategy: Review of research and other related evidence*, Department for Education and Employment, Sudbury, Suffolk, UK.

Estès, C. P. 1992, *Women Who Run with the Wolves: Contacting the power of the wild woman*, Rider, London.

Fairclough, N. 2001, *Language and Power*, rev. 2nd edn, Longman, London.

Fatouros, C. & C. Walters-Moore 1997, *Using Software in English*, PETA, Sydney.

Ferriero, E. & A. Teberosky 1982, *Literacy Before Schooling* (English edn), Heinemann, Portsmouth, N.H.

Flesch, R. F. 1943, *Marks of Readable Style: A study of adult education*, Teachers College Press, Columbia University.

Foucault, M. 1969, 'What is an author?' In M. Foucault, *Language, Counter-Memory, Practice: Selected Essays and Interviews*, Basil Blackwell, Oxford.

Frank, A. 1963, *Anne Frank: The diary of a young girl*, Washington Square Press, USA.

Freebody, P. & A. Luke 1990, 'Literacies programs: debates and demands in cultural context', *Prospect* 5: 7–16.

Freeman, L. 1998, *Phonemic/Phonological Awareness, Literacy Discussion Paper*, Department of Education and Training, NSW.

Freire, P. 1987, 'The importance of the act of reading'. In C. Mitchell and K. Welert (eds), *Rewriting Literacy: Culture and the discourse of the other*, Bergin & Carbey, New York.

Fresch, M. & A. Wheaton 1997, 'Sort, search and discover: Spelling in the student-centred classroom', *The Reading Teacher* 51(1): 20–30.

Fry, E. 1968, 'Readability formula that saves time', *Journal of Reading* 11: 513–16, 575–8.

Fu, D. & L. Lamme 2002, 'Writing lessons with Gavin Curtis', *Journal of Children's Literature* 28(1): 63–72.

Fuller, A. 2002, *Don't Let's Go to the Dogs Tonight: An African childhood*, Random House, New York.

Gardner, H. 1983, *Frames of Mind: The theory of multiple intelligences*, Fontana, London.

Garner, A. 1976, *The Stone Book*, William Collins, London.

Gee, J. 2003, *What Video Games Have To Teach Us About Learning and Literacy*, Palgrave Macmillan, New York.

—— in Lewis, C. 2001, *Literacy Practices as Social Acts: Power, status and cultural norms in the classroom*, Mahwah, Erlbaum, N.J.

—— 1997, 'Literacy and social minds'. In Bull & Anstey (eds), *The Literacy Lexicon*, pp. 5–14.

——, G. Hull & C. Lankshear 1996, *The New Work Order: Behind the language of the new capitalism*, Allen & Unwin, Sydney.

Gee, P. 1996, *Social Linguistics and Literacies: Ideology in discourses*, 2nd edn, Falmer Press, London.

Genette, G. 1980, *Narrative Discourse: An essay in method*, Cornell University Press, Ithaca and London.

Gentry, J. R. & J. W. Gillet 1993, *Teaching Kids to Spell*, Heinemann, Portsmouth, N.H.

Gentry, R. J. 2004, *The Science of Spelling: The explicit specifics that make great readers and writers (and spellers!)*, Heinemann, Portsmouth, N.H.

—— 2006, *Breaking the Code: The new science of beginning reading and writing*, Heinemann, Portsmouth, N.H.

Gibbons, M., C. Limoges, H. Nowotny, S. Schwartzman, P. Scott, & M. Trow 1994, *The New Production of Knowledge: The dynamics of science and research in contemporary societies*, Sage, London.

Gibson, E. J. & H. Levin 1975, *The Psychology of Reading*, MIT Press, Cambridge, Mass.

Gilbert, Sandra M. & Gubar, Susan 1979, *The Madwoman in the Attic: The woman writer and the nineteenth century literary imagination*, Yale University Press, New Haven, Conn.

Golds, C. 1999, 'Miss Gardenia's View' in Jonathan Shaw (ed.), School Magazine, *Orbit* 84(4), NSW Department of Education and Training, Sydney.

Gombrich, E. H. 1999, *The Uses of Images: Studies in the social function of art and visual communication*, Phaidon, London.

Goodman, K. S. 1967, 'Reading: a psycholinguistic guessing game', *Journal of the Reading Specialist* 6: 126–35.

—— 1973, 'Psycholinguistic universals in the reading process'. In F. Smith (ed.), *Psycholinguistics and Reading*, Holt, Reinhart & Winston, New York, pp. 21–7.

—— 1986, *What's Whole in Whole Language?*, Heinemann, Portsmouth, N.H.

Goodman, Y. 1997, 'Reading diagnosis—qualitative or quantitative?', *The Reading Teacher* 50(7): 534–8.

—— & C. L. Burke 1972, *Reading Miscue Inventory Manual: Procedure for diagnosis and evaluation*, Macmillan, New York.

Gough, P. B. 1985, 'One second of reading'. In Singer & Ruddell, *Theoretical Models and Processes of Reading*. International Reading Association, Newark, Del.

Gow, M. 1986, *Away*, Currency Press, Sydney.

Graham, J. & K. Alison (eds) 1998, *Writing Under Control: Teaching writing in the primary school*, Centre for Language Education and Research, David Fulton in association with Roehampton Institute, London.

Graham, L. 1995, *Writing Development: A framework*, Schools Advisory Service, London Borough of Croydon, UK.

Graves, D. 1983, *Writing: Teachers and children at work*, Heinemann, Portsmouth, N.H.

—— 1994, *A Fresh Look At Writing*, Heinemann, Portsmouth, N.H.

Grisham, J. 1999, *The Testament*, Century, London.

Gunew, S. 1985, 'Migrant women writers: Who's on whose margins'. In C. Ferrier (ed.), *Gender, Politics and Fiction: Twentieth century Australian women's novels*, University of Queensland Press, Brisbane, pp. 163–78.

Guterson, D. 1995, *Snow Falling on Cedars*, Bloomsbury, London.

Haas, C. 1998, 'How the writing medium shapes the writing process: effects of word processing on planning', Education Resources Information Center #ED309408.

Habermas, J. 1981, *The Theory of Communicative Action*, vol. 1. Beacon Press, Boston.

Halliday, M. A. K. 1979, 'Differences between spoken and written language: Some implications for library teaching'. In G. Page, J. Elkins and B. O'Connor (eds), *Communication Through Reading*, Proceedings of the 4th ARA Conference, Australian Reading Association, Adelaide, pp. 35–52.

—— 1985, *Spoken and Written Language*, Deakin University Press, Melbourne.

—— 1986, 'Points from speakers'. In Walshe et al. (eds), *Writing and Learning in Australia*, pp. 5–6.

—— 1994, *An Introduction to Functional Grammar*, 2nd edn, Arnold, London.

—— & R. Hasan 1976, *Cohesion in English*, Longman, London.

—— rev. by C. M. I. M. Matthiessen, 2004, *An Introduction to Functional Grammar*, rev. edn, Arnold, London.

Hammond, J. 1996, 'Reading knowledge about language and genre theory'. In Bull and Anstey, *The Literacy Lexicon*, pp. 207–20.

Hamp-Lyons, L. 2000, 'Assessing writing', *Assessing Writing: An international journal* 8: 5–18.

Harland, R. 1999, *Literary Theory from Plato to Barthes: An introductory history*, Macmillan, London.

Harries, R. 2002, *God Outside the Box*, SPCK, London.

Haugaard, E.C. 1984, *The Samurai's Tale*, Houghton Mifflin, Boston.

Hayward, P. 1990, *Culture, Technology and Creativity*, John Libbey, London.

Heald-Taylor, B. G. 1998, 'Three paradigms of spelling instruction in Grades 3 to 6', *The Reading Teacher* 51(5): 404–13.

Heath, S. B. 1983, *Ways with Words: Language, life and work in communities and classroom*, Cambridge University Press.

Heathcote, D. & G. Bolton 1995, *Drama for Learning: Dorothy Heathcote's mantle of the expert approach to education*, Heinemann, Portsmouth, N.H.

Heffernan, L. 2004, *Critical Literacy and Writer's Workshop: Bringing purpose and passion to student writing*, IRA, Newark, Del.

Heidegger, M. 1968, *An Introduction to Metaphysics*, transl. Michael Heim, Yale University Press, New Haven, Conn.

Hennigan, H. 1999, 'Penpals to kepals', *Modern English Teacher* 8(2): 41–50.

Hetherington, J. 1973, *Norman Lindsay: The embattled Olympian*, Oxford University Press, Melbourne.

Hiddins, L. 1998, *Bush Tucker Man*, ABC Books, Sydney.

Hill, D. 'Night Lights' 1999, in J. Shaw (ed.), School Magazine, *Touchdown* 84(2), NSW Department Of Education and Training, Sydney.

Hill, S. 1997, 'Perspectives on early literacy and home–school connections', *Australian Journal of Language and Literacy* 20(4): 263–79.

Ho, C. 2000, 'A log-on beats a show-up for many tertiary students', *SMH* 11 January.

Holdaway, D. 1979, *The Foundations of Literacy*, Scholastic Australia, Gosford, NSW.

Holliday, R. 1988, 'Handwriting: Handwriting and the learner'. In J. Murray and F. Smith (eds), *Language Arts and the Learner*, Macmillan, Melbourne, pp. 98–124.

Hollindale, P. 1988, 'Ideology and the children's book', Thimble Press, Stroud, Glos., UK.

—— 1995, 'Children's literature in an age of multiple literacies', *Australian Journal of Language and Literacy* 18(4): 249–58.

—— 1997, *Signs of Childness in Children's Books*, Thimble Press, Stroud, Glos., UK.

Hooton, J. 1990, *Stories of Herself When Young: Autobiographies of Australian women*, Oxford University Press, Melbourne.

Hourihan, M. 1997, *Deconstructing the Hero*, Routledge, New York.

Hunt, P. 1995, *Children's Literature: An illustrated history*, Oxford University Press, Oxford and New York.

Hyde, M. & M. McGuiness 1992, *Jung for Beginners*, Icon Books, Cambridge.

International Reading Association 1998, *Phonemic Awareness and the Teaching of Reading*, IRA, Newark, Del.

Iser, W. 1980, *The Act of Reading: A theory of aesthetic response*, Johns Hopkins University Press, London.

Jacobson, R. 1998, 'Two Aspects of Language'. In Rivkin & Ryan, *Literary Theory*, pp. 91–5.

Johnson, H. & L. Freedman 2005, *Developing Critical Awareness at the Middle Level: Using texts as tools for critique and pleasure*, IRA, Newark, Del.

Johnson, P. 1995, *Children Making Books*, Reading and Language Information Centre, University of Reading.

Johnston, C. 1999, 'Children need to have hard fun,' *Times Educational Supplement*, 3 September.

Johnston, R. R. 1995a, 'Of dialogue and desire: Children's literature and the needs of the reluctant L2 reader', *Australian Journal of Language and Literacy* 18(4): 293–303.

Johnston, R. R. 1995b. 'Shaping words and shape-shifting words: The special magic of the eighties', *Children's Literature in Education* 26(4), 211–17.

Johnston, R. R. 1996, 'Connecting and community: How to encourage your child to become a reader'. In *Real Books for Real Kids*, Australian School Library Association NSW Inc., Parramatta, NSW, pp. 2–10.

Johnston, R. R. 1997a, 'Children's literature: The missing link?', *The Literature Base* 8(3): 4–11.

Johnston, R. R. 1997b, 'Reaching beyond the word: Religious themes as "deep structure" in the *Anne* books of L. M. Montgomery', *Canadian Children's Literature* 88: 25–35.

Johnston, R. R. 1998a, 'Thisness and everydayness in children's literature: The "being-in-the-world proposed by the text"', *Papers: Explorations in Children's Literature* 8(1): 25–35.

Johnston, R. R. 1998b, 'Time-space: History as palimpsest and myse-en-abyme in children's literature', *Orana* (Australian Library and Information Association Journal): 18–24.

Johnston, R. R. 1999, 'Children's literature advancing Australia', *Bookbird Special Issue: Children's Literature of Australia and New Zealand* 37(1): 13–18.

Johnston, R. R. 2000a, 'The arts at the beginning of a new millennium,' *CREArTA* 1(1): 4–22.

Johnston, R. R. 2000b, 'The literacy of the imagination', *Bookbird* 38(1): 25–30.

Johnston, R. R. 2000c, 'Connections: Literature and education research methodologies', Australian Association for Research in Education (AARE) National Conference, University of Sydney, www.Swin.edu.au/aare ISSN 1324-9339.

Johnston, R. R. 2002a, 'Teacher-as-artist, researcher-as-artist: Creating structures for success.' In G. Bull & M. Anstey (eds), *Crossing the Boundaries*, Prentice-Hall/Pearson International, Sydney.

Johnston, R. R. 2002b, 'Childhood: a narrative chronotope'. In R. Sell (ed.) *Literature as Communication*, John Benjamins, Amsterdam/Philadelphia.

Johnston, R. R. 2002c, 'The sense of "before-us": Landscape and the making of mindscapes in recent Australian children's books', *Canadian Children's Literature*, No. 104, 27(4): 26–46.

Johnston, R. R. 2002d, 'Pertinent ou non? Littérature et recherche littéraire en ces temps troubles', *Diogenes*, pp. 29–39.

Johnston, R. R. 2003a, '"All the world's a stage": Children's literature as performance', In K. Reynolds (ed.) *Children's Literature and Childhood in Performance*, Pied Piper Publishing, Staffordshire, UK, pp. 57–67.

Johnston, R. R. 2003b, 'Relevant or not? Literary research and literary researchers in troubled times',

Diogenes 198, 50(2): 25–32.

Johnston, R. R. 2003c, 'Summer holidays and landscapes of fear: Towards a comparative study of "mainstream" Canadian and Australian children's books', *Canadian Children's Literature*, 109–10.

Johnston, R. R. 2003d, 'Carnivals, the carnivalesque, *The Magic Puddin'*, and David Almond's *Wild Girl, Wild Boy*: Towards a theorising of children's plays', *Children's Literature in Education* (UK and USA) 34(2): 131–46.

Johnston, R. R. 2004a, '"Reaching beyond the Word": Religious Themes as "Deep Structure" in the Anne Books of L. M. Montgomery', *Children's Literature Review* 91, Scot Peacock (ed.), Gale, Detroit.

Johnston, R. 2004b, 'Renewing stories of childhood: Children's literature as a creative art'. In T. van der Walt (ed.) *Change and Renewal in Children's Literature, Contributions to the Study of World Literature*, No. 126. Praeger, Westport, Conn., pp. 9–15.

Johnston, R. R. 2004c, 'South seas and fabled oceans: Australian voyager literature for young people', *Litteratures d'emergence et mondialisation* (ed. Sonia Faessel et Michel Perez), Editions In Press, Paris, pp. 148–60.

Johnston, R. R. 2004d, Australia' in *International Companion Encyclopedia of Children's Literature* (Second edition) P. Hunt (ed.), Routledge, London, pp. 960–83.

Johnston, R. R. '"This world is not conclusion": Representations of soul in children's literature.' Forthcoming.

Johnston, R. R. 'In and out of otherness: Inner-city geographies of being and children's plays as sites for the other within'. In G. Evans (ed.) *Text and the City*. Forthcoming.

Johnston, R. R. 'Of connection and community: Transdisciplinarity and the arts'. In B. Nicolescu (ed.) *Transdisciplinarity: Theory and practice*, Hampton Press, USA (in press).

Johnston, R. R. 'Sustainable creative pedagogy: A leaderly way forward for Australian education.' Forthcoming.

Johnston, R. S. 1998, 'The case for orthographic knowledge: A response to Scholes 1998, the case against phonemic awareness', *Journal of Research in Reading* 21(3): 195–200.

Johnston, R. S. & J. E. Watson 2005, *A Seven Year Study of the Effects of Synthetic Phonics Teaching on Reading and Spelling Attainment*, Scottish Executive Education Department, Edinburgh.

Just, M. A. & P. A. Carpenter 1987, *The Psychology of Reading and Language Comprehension*, Allyn & Bacon, Boston.

Kalantzis, M., B. Cope & H. Fehring 2002, 'Multiliteracies: Teaching and Learning new communications environment', *PEN* 133, PETA, Sydney.

Kaplan, A. 1993, *French Lessons*, University of Chicago Press.

Karchmer, R.A., M. H. Mallette, J. Kara-Sotteriou & D. Leu, Jr (eds) 2005, *Innovative Approaches to Literacy Education: Using the Internet to support new literacies*, IRA, Newark, Del.

Kertzer, A. 2002, *My Mother's Voice: Children, literature and the Holocaust*, Broadview Press, Peterborough, Ontario.

Kervin, L. 2005, 'Students talking about home-school communication: Can technology support this process?' *Australian Journal of Language and Literacy* 28(2): 150–63.

Kilgour, G. 1998, *The Evolution of the Book*, Oxford University Press, New York.

Kinzer, C.K. & K. Leander 2003, 'Technology and the language arts: Implications of an expanded definition of literacy'. In J. Flood, D. Lapp, J. R. Squire & J. M. Jensen (eds), *Handbook of Research on Teaching the English Language Arts*, Erlbaum, Mahwah, N.J., pp. 546–66.

Kist, W. 2005, *New Literacies in Action: Teaching and learning in multiple media*, Teachers College Press, New York.

Klein, C. 1988, *A Space for Delight*, Erewhon, Sydney.

Klein, J. T. 1996, *Crossing Boundaries: Knowledge, disciplinarities and interdisciplinarities*, University Press of Virginia, Charlottesville, Va.

Knapp, P. & M. Watkins 1994, *Context, Text, Grammar: Teaching the genres and grammar of school writing in infants and primary classrooms*, Text Productions, Sydney.

Knobel, M. 1998, *Everyday Literacies: Students, discourses, and social practices*, Peter Lang, New York.

—— & A. Healy (eds) 1998, *Critical Literacies in the Primary Classroom*, PETA, Sydney.

Koch, C. 1988, *Highways to a War*, Minerva, Melbourne.

Koff, C. 2004, *The Bone Woman: Among the dead in Rwanda, Bosnia, Croatia and Kosovo*, Hodder, Sydney.

Kolers, P. A. 1973, 'Three Studies in Reading'. In F. Smith (ed.) *Psycholinguistics and Reading*, Holt Reinhart & Winston, New York, pp. 28–50.

Kovic, R. 1996, *Born on the Fourth of July*, Pocket Books, New York [1976].

Kress, G. 1982, *Learning to Write*, Routledge & Kegan Paul, London.

—— 1988, *Communication and Culture: An introduction*, UNSW Press, Sydney.

—— 1997, *Before Writing: Rethinking the paths to literacy*, Routledge, London.

—— 2000, *Early spelling: Between convention and creativity*, Routledge, London.

—— & T. van Leeuwen, 1996, *Reading Images: The grammar of visual design*, Routledge, London and New York.

—— & —— 2001, *Multimodal Discourse: The modes and media of contemporary communication*, Edward Arnold, London.

Kroll, B. M. & G. Wells 1983, *Explorations in the Development of Writing Theory, Research and Practice*, Wiley, Chichester, UK.

Kushner, D. 1980, *The Violin-Maker's Gift*, Macmillan Canada, Toronto.

Kushner, E. 1996, Liberating children's imagination. Unpublished plenary paper, International Congress, FILLM, Regensburg, Germany.

Lambert, M. 2002–03, 'Paint that funky music, white boy: Chris Raschka's *Charlie Parker Paid Be-Bop, The Genie in The Jar, Mysterious Thesalonius*, and John Coltrane's *Giant Steps*', *CREArTA* 3(2): 83–95.

Landow, G. P. (1992) *Hypertext: The convergence of contemporary critical theory and technology*, Johns Hopkins University Press, Baltimore and London,

Lanham, R. A. 1993, *The Electronic Word: Democracy, technology and the arts*, University of Chicago Press.

Lankshear, C. 1996, 'Language and cultural process'. In Bull & Anstey, *The Literacy Lexicon*, pp. 17–27.

Lankshear, C. & M. Knobel 2003, 'New Technologies', *Journal of Early Childhood Literacy*, 3(1): 59–82.

Latham, M. 2005, *The Latham Diaries*, Melbourne University Press.

Lechte, J. 1994, *Fifty Key Contemporary Thinkers: From poststructuralism to postmodernity*, Routledge, London and New York.

Lewis, A. 1992, *Writing*, Addison-Wesley, Reading, Mass.

Lievesley, D. & A. Motivans 2002, *Taking Literacy Seriously*, UNESCO Institute for Statistics, New York, www.unesco.org.

Ljungdahl, L. 1999, 'Teachers' choices and children's literature', *TESOL in Context* 9(1): 22–6.

Lokan, J., L. Greenwood & J. Cresswell 2001, *How Literate are Australia's Students*, ACER, Melbourne.

Lomax, Y. 2000, *Writing the Image: An adventure with art and theory*, I. B. Tauris, London and New York.

Louden, W., M. Rohl, C. Barratt-Pugh, C. Brown, T. H. Cairney, J. Elderfield, H. House, M. Meiers, J. Rivalland & K. Rowe, 2005, 'In teachers' hands: effective literacy teaching practices in the early years of schooling', *Australian Journal of Language & Literacy*.

Luke, A. 1993, 'The social construction of literacy in the primary school'. In L. Unsworth (ed.) *Literacy Learning and Teaching*, Macmillan, Melbourne, pp. 3–53.

—— & P. Freebody 1999, 'A map of possible practices: further notes on the Four Resources Model', *Practically Primary* 4(2): 5–8, ALEA, Adelaide.

Luke, C. 1996, 'Reading gender and culture in media discourses and texts'. In Bull & Anstey, *The Literacy Lexicon*, pp. 177–89.

—— 1997, *Technological Literacy*, Adult Literacy Research Network, Language Australia, Melbourne.

Mackie, M. 2002, *Literacies Across Media: Playing the text,* Routledge, London and New York.

Maher, J. & J. Groves 1996, *Chomsky for Beginners,* Icon Books, Cambridge.

Malouf, D. 1978, *An Imaginary Life,* Chatto & Windus, London.

Manguel, A. 1997, *A History of Reading,* HarperCollins, London.

March, T. 2004, 'WebQuests: The Fulcrum for Systemic Curriculum Improvement, pp. 1–15 www.ozline.com

Marchetta, M. 2003, *Saving Francesca,* Viking, Melbourne.

Marks, E. & I. De Courtivron (eds) 1981, *New French Feminisms: An anthology,* Harvester, Brighton.

Martin, J. R. 2001, 'Language, register and genre'. In A. Burns & C. Coffin (eds) *Analysing English in a Global Context,* Routledge, London.

—— 1992, *English Text: System and structure,* John Benjamins, Amsterdam.

—— & J. Rothery 1981, 'Writing Project 1 & 2', Department of Linguistics, University of Sydney.

—— & J.—— 1990, 'Literacy for a Lifetime', Department of Linguistics, University of Sydney.

Martin, P. 2005, 'A new chapter in the death of the book', *SMH,* 29 December.

Martin, W. 1986, *Recent Theories of Narrative,* Cornell University Press, Ithaca and London.

Masters, G. 1991, *Assessing Achievement in Australian Schools.* A discussion paper prepared for the National Industry Education Forum, National Industry Education Forum, Melbourne.

Masters, G. N. & M. Forster 1996, *Developmental Assessment: Assessment resource kit,* ACER, Melbourne.

—— & —— 1997a, *Literacy Standards in Australia,* Commonwealth of Australia, Canberra.

—— & —— 1997b, *Mapping Literacy Achievement: Results of the 1996 National School English Literacy Survey,* DEETYA, Canberra.

Mayes, F. 1996, *A Year in Tuscany,* Broadway Books, New York.

—— 1999, *Bella Tuscany,* Anchor Books, Sydney.

McCourt, F. 1998, *Angela's Ashes,* HarperCollins, London [1996].

Meek, M. 1982, *Learning to Read,* Bodley Head, London.

—— 1988, *How Texts Teach What Readers Learn,* Thimble Press, Stroud, UK. In association with PETA, Sydney.

—— 1991, *On Being Literate,* Bodley Head, London.

Merleau-Ponty, M. 1986, *Phenomenology of Perception,* Routledge & Kegan Paul, London [1962].

Milne, A.A. 1973, *Winnie-the-Pooh.* Illus. E.H. Shepard. Methuen Children's Books, London. [1926]

Moi, Toril (1985) *Sexual Textual Politics,* Feminist Literary Theory, Methuen, London.

Moni, K., C. van Krayenoord & C. Baker 1999, 'English teachers' perceptions of literacy assessment in the first year of secondary school', *Australian Journal of Language and Literacy* 22(1): 26–39.

Moore, P. 1999, 'Reading and writing the internet'. In J. Hancock (ed.), *Teaching literacy using information technology: A collection of articles from the Australian Literacy Educators' Association,* IRA and Australian Literacy Educators' Association, Melbourne.

Morley-Warner, T. 2000, *Academic Writing is …,* CREA Publications, UTS, Sydney.

Morrison, T. 1997, *Beloved,* Vintage/Random House, London [1987].

Morriss, M. 1997, 'Children's Literature Possibilities on the Web', *Australian Journal of Language and Literacy* 20(4): 321–8.

Morrow, L. 1993, *Literacy Development in the Early Years: Helping children read and write,* Allyn & Bacon, Needham Heights, Mass.

Morson, G. S. & C. Emerson 1990, *Mikhail Bakhtin: Creation of a prosaics,* Stanford University Press.

Moss, J. F. & M. F. Fenster 2002, *From Literature to Literacy: Bridging learning in the library and the primary grade classroom,* IRA, Newark, Del.

Mudd, N. 1997, *The Power of Words,* UK Reading Association, Royston.

Muecke, S. 1999, 'The sacred in history', *Humanities Research,* Humanities Research Centre, ANU, Canberra, pp. 27–37.

Muir, M. 1992, *Australian Children's Books: A bibliography,* vol. 1, Melbourne University Press.

—— & Holden, R. 1985, *The Fairy World of Ida Rentoul Outhwaite,* Craftsman House, Sydney.

Mulvaney, D. J. 1987, 'The end of the beginning: 6,000 years ago to 1788'. In D. J. Mulvaney & J. P. White (eds) *Australians to 1788*, Fairfax, Syme & Weldon, Sydney, pp. 75–114.

Muspratt, S., A. Luke & P. Freebody (eds) 1997, *Constructing Critical Literacies: Teaching and learning textual practice*, Allen & Unwin, Sydney.

Myung Sook-Auh, 'Visual thinking in sounds and creativity: Graphic notations as means of stimulating creative thinking in music', *CREArTA* 3(2): 41–57.

Naramasiaah, C. D. (ed.) 1965, *An Introduction to Australian Literature*, Jacaranda Press, Brisbane.

Negroponte, N. 1995, *Being Digital*, Knopf, New York.

Neuman, S. B. & K. A. Roskos (eds) 1998, *Children Achieving: Best practices in early literacy*, IRA, Newark, Del.

Newton, K. M. (ed.) 1997, *Twentieth Century Literary Theory: A reader*, 2nd edn, Macmillan, London.

Niall, B. 1984. *Australia Through the Looking Glass: Children's fiction 1830–1980*, Melbourne University Press.

Nightingale, G. & P. Nightingale 1985, *Foundation Handwriting*, Martin Educational, Sydney. (Series of seven books from kindergarten to Year 6.)

Nikolajeva, M. 1988, *The Magic Code: The use of magical patterns in fantasy for children*, Almqvist & Wiksell International, Stockholm.

—— 1996a, *Children's Literature Comes of Age: Towards a new aesthetic*, Garland Publishing, New York.

—— 1996b, Exit children's literature? Unpublished plenary paper, International Congress, FILLM, Regensburg, Germany.

—— 2000, *From Mythic to Linear: Time in children's literature*, Children's Literature Association and Scarecrow Press, London.

—— 2003, 'A Dear Child: By way of Introduction, *CREArTA* 3(1): 3–8.

Nodelman, P. 1988, *Words About Pictures: The narrative art of children's picture books*, University of Georgia Press, Athens and London.

—— 1996, *The Pleasures of Children's Literature*, 2nd edn, Longman, White Plains, NY [1992].

—— 2000, 'The implied viewer: Some speculations about what children's picturebooks invite children to do and to be', *CREArTA* 1(1): 23–43.

—— 2002, 'Child readers and narrative literacy'. In Bull & Anstey, *Crossing the Boundaries*, pp. 3–16.

NSW Department of Education and Training 1998a, *State Literacy Strategy: Teaching spelling K–6*, Department of Education and Training, Sydney.

—— 1998b, *English K–6: Student work samples*, Department of Education and Training, Sydney.

—— 1999a, *Literacy Strategy Evaluation 1997 and 1998*, Department of Education and Training, Sydney.

NSW Department of School Education 1994, *Step by Step Booklist*, Curriculum Directorate, Sydney.

—— 1997, *Teaching Reading: A K–6 Framework*, Department of Education and Training, Sydney.

Nunan, D. 2004, *An Introduction to Task Based Teaching*, Cambridge University Press.

Nyholm, M. 2002, 'Proofreading, editing, using authoritative sources: getting help to get it right', *Classroom* 22(7): 38–9.

O'Malley, M. & L. Valdez Pierce 1996, *Authentic Assessment for English Language Learners: Practical approaches for teachers*, Addison-Wesley, USA.

O'Neill, T. & F. O'Neill 1989, *Australian Children's Books to 1980*, Canberra: National Library of Australia.

Oakhill, J. & R. Beard (eds) 1999, *Reading Development and the Teaching of Reading: A psychological perspective*, Blackwell, Oxford.

Office for Standards in Education 1998, *The National Literacy Project 1998, an HMI Evaluation*, Office for Standards in Education, London.

Olinder, B. (ed.) 1984, *A Sense of Place*, Gothenburg University Press.

Olsen, D. R. 1977, 'From utterance to text: the bias of language in speech and writing', *Harvard Educational Review* 47: 257–81.

Organization for Economic Cooperation and Development (OECD) 2001, *Knowledge and Skills for*

Life—First Results from PISA 2000, New York, www.acer.edu.au/research/projects/pdfPISA and www.pisa.oecd.org.

Palous, R. 1995, 'The social and political vocation of the university in the global age'. In T. Schuller (ed.) *The Changing University*, Open University Press, Buckingham, UK, pp. 176–8.

Papert, S. in C. Johnston 1999, 'Children Need to Have Hard Fun,' *Times Educational Supplement* 3 September.

Parry, J. & D. Hornsby 1985, *Write On: A conference approach to writing*, Martin Educational, Sydney.

Partridge, E. 1953, *You Have a Point There*, Hamish Hamilton, London.

Perfetti, C. A. 1995, 'Cognitive research can inform reading education', *Journal of Research in Reading* 18(2): 106–15.

Peterson, B. 1988, *Characteristics of Texts That Support Beginning Readers*, Ohio State University, Columbus, Ohio.

Peterson, B. 1991, 'Selecting Books for Beginning Readers'. In D. De Ford, C. Lyons and G. Pinnell, *Bridges to Literacy: Learning from reading recovery*, Heinemann, Portsmouth, NH, pp. 119–47.

Phelps R., A. Ellis & S. Hase 2001, 'The role of metacognitive and reflective learning processes in developing capable computer users'. In G. Kennedy, M. Keppell, C. McNaught & T. Petrovic (eds) *Meeting at the Crossroads: Proceedings of the 18th Annual Conference of the Australian Society for Computers in Learning in Tertiary Education*, ASCILITE Conference, Melbourne, Biomedical Multimedia Unit, University of Melbourne, pp. 481–90.

Pinnell, G. S. & I. G. Fountas 1998, *Word Matters: Teaching phonics and spelling in the reading/writing classroom*, Heinemann, Portsmouth, N.H.

Popper, K. 1976, *Unended Quest: An intellectual autobiography*, Fontana, New York.

Poston-Anderson, B. 2002, '"With will there's a way". Performing a children's play: a way of learning', *CREArTA* 2(2): 20–9.

Potter, S. 1960, *Modern Linguistics*, Andre Deutsch, London.

Potter, W. J. 1998, *Media Literacy*, Sage Publications, Thousand Oaks. Calif.

Prevalet, K. 2001, 'Creativity and the importance of fourth grade', *Poets & Writers Magazine* 29(1): 51–4.

Protheroe, P. 1992, *Vexed Texts: How children's picture books promote illiteracy*, The Book Guild Ltd, Sussex, UK.

Pullman, P. 1989, 'Invisible pictures', *Signal* 60, September: 160–86.

Raphael, T. E. & F. B. Boyd 1997, 'When readers write'. In S. I. McMahon & T. E. Raphael (eds) with V. Goatley and L. Pardo, *The Book Club Connection: Literacy learning and classroom talk*, Teachers College Press, Columbia University, New York.

Report of the Literacy Taskforce 1999. A Report prepared for the Minister of Education, New Zealand.

Reynolds, K., G. Brennan & K. McCarron 2001, *Frightening Fiction: R. L. Stine, Robert Westall, David Almond and Others*, Continuum, London and New York.

Richards, I. A. 1969, *Practical Criticism: A study of literary judgment*, Harcourt, Brace and World, New York [1929].

Ricoeur, P. 1985, *Time and Narrative*, transl. Kathleen McLauglin & David Pellauer, University of Chicago Press.

—— 2004. *Memory, History, Forgetting*, University of Chicago Press.

Rivkin, J. & M. Ryan 1998, *Literary Theory: An anthology*, Blackwell, Oxford.

Roberts, J. 2001, *Spelling Recovery*, ACER, Melbourne.

Rose, E. C. 1983, 'Through the Looking Glass: When women tell fairy tales'. In E. Abel, M. Hirsch & E. Langland (eds), *The Voyage In: Fictions of female development*, University Press of New England, Dartmouth, New England, pp. 209–27.

Rosen, C. & H. Rosen 1973, *The Language of Primary School Children*, Penguin Books, Harmondsworth.

Rosencrans, G. 1998, *The Spelling Book: Teaching children how to spell, not what to spell*, IRA, Newark, Del.

Said, E. 1993–94, *Culture and Imperialism*, Chatto & Windus/Vintage, London and New York.

Sainsbury, M. 1998, 'Evaluation of the national literacy strategy: Summary report', National Foundation for Educational Research, Slough, UK.

Sale, C. 1995, *Demystifying Reading Recovery*, PETA, Sydney.

Saljo, R. 1979, in F. Marton, D. Hounsel & N. Entwhistle (eds) *The Experience of Learning*, Scottish University Press, Edinburgh.

Samuels, S. J. 1985, 'Word Recognition'. In Singer & Ruddell, *Theoretical Models and Processes of Reading*.

Saxby, M. 1997, *Books in the Life of a Child*, Macmillan Education Australia, Melbourne.

Schmidt, P. R. & A. W. Palliotet (eds) 2001, *Exploring Values Through Literature, Multimedia, and Literacy Events: Making connections*, IRA, Newark, Del.

Scholes, R. J. 1998, 'The case against phonemic awareness', *Journal of Research in Reading* 21(3): 177–88.

Schools Council, National Board of Employment, Education and Training 1995, *The Elements of Successful Student Outcomes: Views from upper primary classroom teachers*, Commissioned Report No. 41, Price Waterhouse, December.

Scott, A. 2002, 'Technology as a literacy tool', *Practically Primary* 7(1): 6–8.

Sell, R. 1996, 'Literary and Language Education in the mediation of Cultural Difference'. Unpublished plenary paper, International Congress, FILLM, Regensburg, Germany.

Shields, C. 1992, *The Republic of Love*, Vintage Canada, Toronto.

Shotter, J. 1993, *Cultural Politics of Everyday Life*, Open University Press, Buckingham.

Showalter, E. 1979, *A Literature of Their Own: British women novelists from Bronte to Lessing*, Virago, London.

Silva, A. and M. Alves Martins 2003, 'Relations between children's invented spelling and the development of phonological awareness', *Educational Psychology* 23(1): 3–16.

Singer, H. & R. Ruddell (eds) 1985, *Theoretical Models and Processes of Reading*, 3rd edn, IRA, Newark, Del.

Smith, F. 1971, *Understanding Reading*, Holt, Reinhart & Winston, New York.

—— (ed.) 1973, *Psycholinguistics and Reading*, Holt, Rinehart & Winston, New York.

—— 1978, *Reading*, Cambridge University Press.

—— 1982, *Writing and the Writer*, Holt, Reinhart & Winston, New York.

Smith, M. 2002, 'What a difference writing has made! A personal journey in the teaching of writing', *Primary Voices K–6* 11(1): 7–9.

Smith, N. B. 1969, 'The many faces of reading comprehension', *The Reading Teacher* 23(3): 249–59.

Snooks & Co. 2002, *Style Manual For Authors, Editors and Printers*, rev. 6th edn, Snooks & Co., John Wiley & Sons, Canberra.

Snow, C. E., M. S. Burns & P. Griffin (eds) 1998, *Preventing Reading Difficulties in Young Children*, Commission on Behavioural and Social Sciences and Education, National Research Council, National Academy Press, Washington, D.C.

Snowball, D. & F. Bolton 1999, *Spelling K–8: Planning and Teaching*, Stenhouse Publishers, Maine.

Snyder, I. (ed.) 1997, *Page to Screen: Taking literacy into the electronic era*, Allen & Unwin, Sydney.

—— 2002, *Silicon Literacies: Communication, innovation and education in the electronic age*, Routledge, London.

Sollat, K. 1997, 'The boundaries of fantasy in German children's literature', *Bookbird* 35(4): 6–11.

Spache, G. 1953, 'A new readability formula for prime grade reading materials', *Elementary School Journal* 53: 410–13.

Spandel, V. 2005, *Creating Writers Through 6-Trait Writing Assessment and Instruction*, 4th edn, Pearson Education Inc., Boston.

Spender, D. 1995, *Nattering on the Net: Women, power, and cyberspace*, Spinifex, Melbourne.

Stanovich, K. E. 1994, 'Romance and reality', *The Reading Teacher* 47(4): 280–91.

Stanovich, K. E. & J. Paula 1995, 'How research might inform the debate about early reading acquisition',

Journal of Research in Reading 18(2): 87–105.

Stanska, L., 'The graphic score: An essential part of modern art in Czechoslovakia in the 1960s', *CREArTA* 3(2): 26–40.

Stephens, J. 1992, *Language and Ideology in Children's Fiction*, Longman, London and New York.

Stephens, J. 2000. 'Modality and space in picture book art: Allen Say's Emma's Rug', *CREArTA* 1(1): 44–59.

Stewart Dore, N. 1986, *Writing and Reading to Learn*, PETA, Sydney.

Stiggins, R. 2001, *Student Involved Classroom Assessment*, 3rd edn, Prentice Hall, Englewood Cliffs, N.J.

Stoodt, B., L. Amspaugh & J. Hunt 1996, *Children's Literature*, Macmillan Education, Melbourne.

Stuart, M. 1998, 'Let the emperor retain his underclothes: A response to Scholes 1998, the case against phonemic awareness', *Journal of Research in Reading* 21(3): 189–94.

Teeler, D. & P. Gray 2000, *How to Use the Internet in ELT*, Longman, Harlow, Essex, UK.

Tierney, R. J., M. A. Carter & L. E. Desai 1991, *Portfolio Assessment in the Reading-Writing Classroom*, Christopher-Gordon, Norwood, Mass.

Treiman, R. & A. Zukowski 1996, 'Children's sensitivity to syllables, onsets, rimes and phonemes', *Journal of Experimental Child Psychology* 61: 193–215.

Trites, R. S. 2000, *Disturbing the Universe: Power and repression in adolescent literature*, University of Iowa Press.

—— 2002, 'The imaginary, Oedipus, and the capitalist order: Parental presence in adolescent literature', *CREArTA* 3(1): 9–21.

Trudgen, R. 2000, *Why Warriors Lie Down and Die: Towards an understanding of why the Aboriginal people of Arnhem Land face the greatest crisis in health and education since European contact*, Aboriginal Resources and Development Services Inc., Darwin.

Truss, L. 2003, *Eats, Shoots & Leaves: The zero tolerance approach to punctuation*, Profile Books, London.

Tucker, E. 1986. 'Conference/How To?' In Walshe et al., *Writing and Learning in Australia*, pp. 196–8.

Turbill, J. 2004, 'International Research on Literacy Research, Australia', *Reading Research Quarterly* 39(3): 356.

Turner, M. 1996, *The Literary Mind*, Oxford University Press, New York.

Tyner, K. R. 1998, *Literacy in a Digital World: Teaching and learning in the age of information*, L. Erlbaum Assoc., Mahwah, N.J.

Unsworth, L. (ed.) 1993, *Literacy Learning and Teaching: Language as social practice in the primary school*, Macmillan, Melbourne.

—— 2002, 'Changing dimensions of school literacies', *Australian Journal of Language and Literacy* 25(1): 62–77.

—— 2006, *E-literature for Children: Enhancing digital literacy learning*, Routledge/Taylor and Francis Group, London and New York.

——, A. Thomas, A. Simpson & J. Asha 2005, *Children's Literature and Computer-based Learning*, Open University Press, Maidenhead, UK.

Updike, J. 2000, *Gertrude and Claudius*, Penguin, London.

Ur, P. 1988, *Grammar Practice Activities: A practical guide for teachers* (Cambridge Handbooks for Language Teachers), Cambridge University Press.

Valencia, S. 1990, 'A portfolio approach to classroom reading assessment: The whys, whats, and hows', *The Reading Teacher* 43(4): 338–40.

—— 1991, 'Portfolios: Panacea or Pandora's Box?'. In F. L. Finch (ed.) *Educational Performance Assessment*, Riverside Publishing Co., Chicago, pp. 33–46.

Van Krayenoord, C. 1996, 'Literacy assessment'. In Bull & Anstey, *The Literacy Lexicon*, pp. 237–47.

Venezky, R. L. 1967, 'English orthography: Its graphical structure and its relation to sound', *Reading Research Quarterly* 2: 75–106.

Vygotsky, L. S. 1978, *Mind in Society*, Harvard University Press, Cambridge, Mass.

Wall, B. 1991, *The Narrator's Voice: The dilemma of children's fiction*, Macmillan, London.

Wallace, C. 1988, *Learning to Read in a Multicultural Society*, Prentice Hall, Hemel Hempstead, UK.

Walshe, R. D., P. March & D. Jensen (eds) 1986, *Writing and Learning in Australia*, Oxford/Dellasta, Melbourne.

Ward, G. 1987, *Wandering Girl*, Magabala Books, Broome, WA.

Warner, M. 1994, *From the Beast to the Blonde*, Chatto & Windus, London.

—— 1998, *No Go the Bogeyman: Scaring, lulling and making mock*, Chatto & Windus, London.

Warren, B. 1995, *Creating a Theatre in your Classroom*, Captus University Publications, Ontario, Canada.

Watkins, M. & Knapp, P. 2005, *Genre, Text, Grammar: Technologies for teaching and assessing writing*, UNSW Press, Sydney.

Waugh, P. 1997, *Revolutions of the Word*, Hodder Headline, Sydney.

Webster, R. 1990, *Studying Literary Theory*, Edward Arnold, London.

Wepner, S. B., W. J. Valmont & R. Thurlow (eds) 2000, *Linking Literacy and Technology: A guide for K–8 classrooms*, IRA, Newark, Del.

Westwood, P. 1999, *Spelling: Approaches to teaching and assessment*, ACER, Melbourne.

Wheatley, J. P. 2005, *Strategic Spelling: Moving beyond word memorization in the middle grades*, IRA, Newark, Del.

Wilde, J. 1993, *A Door Opens: Writing in fifth grade*, Heinemann, Portsmouth, N.H.

Wilkinson, A., G. P. Barnsley, P. Hanna & M. Swan 1980, *Assessing Language Development* (Oxford Studies in Education), Oxford University Press, Oxford.

Wille, C. 1996, *Matching Books to Children*, PETA, Sydney.

Williams, E. 1977, *Assignments in Punctuation and Spelling*, Edward Arnold, London.

Winch, G. 1988, 'Literature: its place in learning to read'. In A. Hanzl (ed.) *Literature: A focus for language learning*, Australian Reading Association, Melbourne, pp. 3–13.

—— 1991, 'The light in the eye: On good books for children'. In M. Saxby & G. Winch (eds) *Give Them Wings: The experience of children's literature*, 2nd edn, Macmillan Australia, Melbourne, pp. 19–25.

—— & B. Poston-Anderson 1993, *Now For a Story: Sharing stories with young children*, Phoenix Education, Melbourne.

—— & G. Blaxell 1992, *Spell Well, Teacher Resource Book 1*, Horwitz Grahame, Sydney.

—— & —— 1999, *The Primary Grammar Handbook: Traditional and functional grammar, punctuation and usage*, rev. edn, Horwitz Martin, Sydney.

—— & V. Hoogstad (eds) 1985, *Teaching Reading: A language experience*, 2nd edn, Macmillan, Melbourne.

Winch, J. 1999, The Third Space. Unpublished Masters Thesis, UTS, Sydney.

Wolf, B. J. 'Teaching handwriting'. In J. R. Birsh (ed.) *Multisensory Teaching of Basic Language Skills*, 2nd edn, Paul H. Brookes Publishing Co., Baltimore, pp. 413–38.

World Book Encyclopaedia 1986, World Book, Inc., Chicago.

Wray, D. & J. Medwell 1998, *Teaching English in Primary Schools*, Letts Educational, London.

Wycoff, J. 1991, *Mindmapping: Your personal guide to exploring creativity and problem-solving*, Berkley Books, New York.

Zipes, J. 1979, *Breaking the Magic Spell: Radical theories of folk and fairy tales*, Heinemann, London.

—— 1987, transl. *The Complete Fairy Tales of the Brothers Grimm*, Bantam, New York.

—— 1994, *Fairy Tale as Myth*, University Press of Kentucky, Lexington, Ky.

Children's books

Abdullah, I. 1992, *As I Grew Older*, Omnibus Books, Adelaide.

—— 1994, *Tucker*, Omnibus Books, Adelaide.

Ada, A. F., & L. Tryon 1998, *Yours Truly, Goldilocks*, Atheneum Books, New York.

Agard, J., & G. Nicholls (eds) 1994, *A Caribbean Dozen*, Walker Books, London.

Ahlberg, J. & A. Ahlberg 1981, *Peepo*, Kestrel Books, London.

—— & —— 1989, *Each Peach Pear Plum*, Puffin, London [1978].

—— & —— 1986, *The Jolly Postman and Other People's Letters*, William Heinemann, London.

Allen, P. 1993, *Bertie and the Bear*, Nelson, Melbourne.

Almond, D. 1998, *Skellig: The play*, Hodder, London

—— 2000, *Counting Stars,* Hodder, London.

—— 2002, *Wild Girl, Wild Boy*, Hodder Children's Books, London.

Angelou, M. 1994, *My Painted House, My Friendly Chicken, and Me*, Bodley Head, London.

Applegate, C. & D. Huxley 2000, *Rain Dance*, Margaret Hamilton Books, Sydney.

Baillie, A. 1997, *Secrets of Walden Rising*, Penguin, Melbourne.

—— & J. Tanner 1991, *Drac and the Gremlin*, Penguin Books, Melbourne [1988].

Baker, J. 1987, *Where the Forest Meets the Sea*, Julia MacRae Books, Sydney.

—— 1992, *Window*, Red Fox, London.

—— 1995, *The Story of Rosy Dock*, Random House, Sydney.

—— 2000, *The Hidden Forest*, Walker Books, London.

—— 2004, *Belonging*, Walker Books, London.

Bantock, N. 1992, *Sabine's Notebook: In which the extraordinary correspondence of Griffin continues*, Pan Macmillan Australia.

—— 1993, *The Golden Mean: In which the extraordinary correspondence of Griffin and Sabine concludes*, Pan Macmillan Australia.

—— 1997a, *Ceremony of Innocence* (computer optical disk), Real World Multimedia, UK.

—— N. 1997b, *Griffin and Sabine: An extraordinary correspondence*, Pan Macmillan Australia.

Banyai, I. 1995, *Zoom*, Viking, New York.

Barbalet, M. & J. Tanner 1994, *The Wolf*, Penguin, Melbourne.

Barber, A. 1994, *The Enchanter's Daughter*, Farr, Straus & Giroux, New York.

Base, G. 2001, *The Waterhole*, Viking, Melbourne.

Bauer, M. G. 2004, *The Running Man,* Omnibus, Adelaide.

Beck, I. illust. & E. Lear. 2001, *The Jumblies*, Picture Corgi, London.

Blake, Q. 2002, *Quentin Blake's ABC*, Red Fox, London [1989].

—— 2002, *A Sailing Boat in the Sky*, Jonathan Cape, London.

Bradbury, P. 1984, *One-Eyed Cat*, Author, New York.

Brian, J. & D. Cox 1998, *Leaves for Mr Walter*, Margaret Hamilton Books, Sydney.

Browne, A. 1981, *Hansel and Gretel*, Julia MacCrae Books, London.

Browne, A.1983, *Gorilla*, Julia MacRae Books, London.

—— 1986, *Piggybook*, Julia MacCrae Books, London.

—— 1992, *Zoo*, Red Fox, London

——1999, *Voices in the Park*, Transworld, London.

—— 2000, *Willy's Pictures*, Walker Books, London.

Brumbeau, J. & G. de Marcken 2000, *The Quiltmaker's Gift*, Scholastic New York.

Burningham, J. 1970, *Mr Gumpy's Outing*, Jonathan Cape, London.

—— 1977, *Come Away from the Water, Shirley*, Jonathan Cape, London.

—— 1996, *Cloudland*, Jonathan Cape, London.

Carr, R. V. & A. James 1996, *The Butterfly*, Random House, Sydney.

Caswell, B. 1994, *Lisdalia*, University of Queensland Press, Brisbane.

—— & D. Phu An Chiem 1997, *Only the Heart*, University of Queensland Press, Brisbane.

Child, L. 2000, *Beware of the Storybook Wolves*, Hodder, London

—— 2002, *Who's Afraid of the Big Bad Book?* Hodder, London.

Cole, B. 1986, *Princess Smartypants*, G. P. Putnam's Sons, New York.

—— 1987, *Prince Cinders*, G. P. Putnam's Sons, New York.

Crew, G. & G. Rogers 1992, *Lucy's Bay*, Jam Roll Press, Brisbane.

—— & S. Tan 1999, *Memorial*, Thomas C. Lothian, Melbourne.

—— & S. Woolman 1994, *The Watertower*, Era, Adelaide.

Dahl, R. 1984, *The BFG*, illus. Quentin Blake, Puffin Books in association with Cape, Harmondsworth.

—— 1997, *George's Marvellous Medicine*, illus. Quentin Blake, Puffin Books, Harmondsworth.

Disher, G. 1991, *The Bamboo Flute*, HarperCollins, Sydney.

Donaldson, J. & A. Currey 2005. *Rosie's Hat*, Macmillan Childrens' Books, London.

Dubosarsky, U. 2000. *The Game of the Goose*, Viking/Penguin, Melbourne.

Farmer, N. 2000, *The Ear, The Eye and The Arm: A 21st century adventure story*, Puffin, London.

Fatchen, M. & C. Smith 2001, *The Very Long Nose of Jonathan Jones*, ABC Books, Sydney.

Fine, A. 1989, *Bill's New Frock*, Mammoth Books, London.

Fox, M. 1983, *Possum Magic*, Omnibus Books, Adelaide.

—— 1984, *Wilfred Gordon McDonald Partridge*, Omnibus Books, Adelaide.

—— & J. Dyer 1993, *Time for Bed*, Omnibus Books, Adelaide.

French, F. 1986, *Snow White in New York*, Oxford University Press, London.

French, J. and B. Whatley. 2002. *Diary of a Wombat*, HarperCollins, Australia.

Gaarder, J. 1995, *Sophie's World*, Phoenix House, London.

Gallaz, C. & R. Innocenti 1985, *Rose Blanche*, Script Editions.

Gleeson, L. 1984, *Eleanor, Elizabeth*, Angus & Robertson, Sydney.

—— 1987, *I Am Susannah*, Angus & Robertson, Sydney.

—— 1994, *Skating on Sand*, Penguin, Melbourne.

—— 1999, *Hannah and the Tomorrow Room*, Penguin, Melbourne.

—— & A. Greder 1999, *The Great Bear*, Scholastic Australia, Gosford, NSW.

—— L. & A. James 2003, *Shutting the Chooks In*, Scholastic Australia, Gosford, NSW.

Gleitzman, M. 2002, *Boy Overboard*, Puffin Books, Melbourne.

Godden, R. 2004, *The Greengage Summer*, Young Picador, London [1958].

Gonsalves, R. & S. L. Thomson 2003, *Imagine a Night*, Atheneum Books, New York.

Graham, B. 1992, *Greetings from Sandy Beach*, Lothian Books, Melbourne.

Greenwood, K. 2004, *The Long Walk*, Hodder, Sydney.

Gwynne, P. 1999, *Deadly Unna*, Penguin, Melbourne.

Harlen, J. & E. Quay 1998, *Champions*, Random House, Sydney.

Hartnett, S. 1994 *Wilful Blue*, Viking, Melbourne.

—— 1995, *Sleeping Dogs*, Penguin, Melbourne.

Harvey, R. 2005, *In the Bush: Our holiday to Wombat Flat*. Allen & Unwin, Sydney.

Hashmi, K. & F. Marshall 1998, *You and Me, Murrawee*, Viking, Melbourne.

Hathorn, L. & G. Rogers 1994, *Way Home*, Random House, Sydney.

—— & P. Gouldthorpe 1995, *The Wonder Thing*, Viking/Penguin Books Australia.

Heffernan, J. & A. McLean 2001, *My Dog*, Scholastic, Gosford, NSW.

Herrick, S. 1996, *Love, Ghosts and Nose Hair*, University of Queensland Press, Brisbane.

—— 1998, *A Place Like This*, University of Queensland Press, Brisbane.

—— 1997, *My Life, My Love, My Lasagne*, University of Queensland Press, Brisbane.

—— 2000, *The Simple Gift*, University of Queensland Press, Brisbane.

Hill, A. 1994, *The Burnt Stick*, Viking, Melbourne.

Hill, E. 1999, *Good Night, Spot*, Hammersmith, Frederick Warne, London.

Hill, S. & A. Barrett 1993, *Beware, Beware*, Walker Books, London.

Hindley, J. & H. Craig 2002, *Rosy's Visitors*, Candlewick Press, Cambridge, Mass.

Hopkins, P. & J. Packer 2001, *Desert Dessert*, Scholastic, New Zealand.

Howes, J. & R. Harvey 1998, *Island in My Garden*, Roland Harvey Books, Vic.

Hughes, S. 1973, *Lucy and Tom Go to School*, Gollancz, London.

—— 1988, *Out and About*, Walker Books, London.

Hutchins, P. 1968, *Rosie's Walk*, Bodley Head, London.

—— 1991, *Tidy Titch*, Julia MacCrae Books, London.

Isadora, R. 1991, *At the Crossroads*, Red Fox, London.

Jenkins, M. & S. Shields 1997, *Chameleons Are Cool*, Walker Books, London.

Jennings, P. 1993, *Uncovered!*, Puffin Books, Melbourne.

—— & J. Tanner 1994, *The Fisherman and the Theefyspray*, Penguin, Melbourne.

Jorgensen, N. & B. Harrison-Lever 2002, *In Flanders Fields*, Sandcastle Books, Freemantle WA.

Killeen, G., F. Partridge & F. Dubuc 1998, *Cherry Pie*, Random House, Sydney.

Klein, R. 1984, *Hating Alison Ashley*, Penguin, Melbourne.

——1991, *All in the Blue Unclouded Weather*, Puffin, Melbourne.

Lachenmeyer, N. & R. Ingpen 2003, *Broken Beaks*, Michelle Anderson Publishing Company, Melbourne.

L'Engle, M. 1962, *A Wrinkle in Time*, Longman, London.

Lester, A. 2004, *Are We There Yet? A journey around Australia*, Viking, Melbourne.

Loh, M. 1985, *The Kinder Hat*, Hyland House, Melbourne.

Maloney, J. 1993, *Dougy*, University of Queensland Press, Brisbane.

Marsden, J. 1994, *Tomorrow, When the War Began*, Pan Macmillan, Sydney.

—— & S. Tan 1998, *The Rabbits*, Thomas C. Lothian, Melbourne.

Marshall, V. & B. Tester 1988, *Bernard Was a Bikie*, Ashton Scholastic, Gosford, NSW.

Martin, A. 2001 *Beyond Duck River*, Hodder, Sydney.

Mayne, W. 1987, *Mousewing*, Walker Books, London.

McBratney, S. 1994, *Guess How Much I Love You*, Walker Books, London.

McKee, D. 1980, *Not Now, Bernard*, Red Fox, London.

—— 1988, *Who's a Clever Baby Then?* Andersen Press, London.

Meeks, A. R. 1991, *Enora and the Black Crane*, Scholastic Australia, Gosford, NSW.

Montgomery, L. M. 1972 *Anne of Green Gables*, Peacock Books, London [1908].

Morgan, S. 1997 *The Flying Emu and Other Australian Stories*, Puffin Books Australia [1992].

Moriarty, J. 2000, *Feeling Sorry for Celia*, Pan Macmillan, London.

Morimoto, J. 1997, *The Two Bullies*, Random House, Sydney

Mullins, P. 1993, *V for Vanishing: An alphabet of endangered animals*, Margaret Hamilton Books, Sydney.

Munsch, R. & M. Marchenko 1980, *The Paper Bag Princess*, Annick Press, Toronto.

Naidoo, B. 1995, *No Turning Back*, Viking, London.

Nampijinpa, D.D.G. 2003, *The Magic Fire at Warlukurlangu*, Working Title Press, Adelaide.

Nodelman, P. 1996, *Alice Falls Apart*, Bain & Cox, Winnipeg.

Noon, S. & A. Millard 1998, *A Street Through Time*: *A 12,000 year journey along the same street*, Dorling-Kindersley, London.

Norman, L. 1992, *The Paddock*, Random House, Sydney.

Ottley, M. 1998, *Mrs Millie's Painting*, Hodder Headline, Sydney.

Overend, J. & J. Vivas 1999, *Hello Baby*, ABC Books, Sydney.

Papunya School 2001, *Papunya School Book of Country and History*, Allen & Unwin, Sydney.

Park, R. 1980, *Playing Beatie Bow*, Penguin, Melbourne.

Paulsen, G. 1998, *The Transall Saga*, Delacorte, New York.

Perversi, M. & R. Brooks 1997, *Henry's Bed*, Viking, Melbourne.

Phipson, J. 1962, *The Boundary Riders*, Penguin, London.

Pohl, P. 1991, *Johnny, My Friend*, transl. Laurie Thompson, Turton & Chambers, Stroud, UK [1985].

Pollinger, G. & E. C. Clark 1995, *A Treasury of Shakespeare's Verse*, Kingfisher, New York.

Poole, J. & A. Barrett 1993, *Snow-White*, Red Fox, London [1991].

Potter, B. 1902, *The Tale of Peter Rabbit*, Frederick Warne & Co., London.

Price, S. 1987, *The Ghost Drum*, Faber & Faber, London.

—— 1998, *The Sterkarm Handshake*, Scholastic Press, London.

Raschka, C. 2002, *John Coltrane's Giant Steps*, Atheneum Books, New York.

Riddle, T. 1996, *The Tip at the End of the Street*, HarperCollins, Sydney.

Reid, B. 2003, *The Subway Mouse*, North Winds Press (Scholastic Canada), Markham, Ontario.

Roennfeldt, R. 2003, *The Silver Stream*, Working Title Press, Adelaide.

Rowan, K. & K. McEwen 1988, *I Know How We Fight Germs*, Walker Books, London.

Rowling, J. K. 1997, *Harry Potter and the Philosopher's Stone*, Bloomsbury, London.

—— 2003, *Harry Potter and the Order of the Phoenix*, Bloomsbury, London.

Rubinstein, G. 1989, *Skymaze*, Omnibus/Puffin Books, Melbourne.

—— 2002, *The Whale's Child*, Hodder Headline, Sydney.

Russell, E. 2000, *A is for Aunty*, ABC Books, Sydney.

Scieska, J. & S. Johnson 1991, *The Frog Prince Continued*, Viking, New York.

—— & L. Smith 1992, *The Stinky Cheese Man and Other Fairly Stupid Tales*, Puffin, London.

Sendak, M. 1992, *Where the Wild Things Are*, HarperCollins, London [1963].

—— 1993, *Outside Over There*, HarperCollins, London [1981].

Seuss, Dr, S. Johnson & L. Fancher 1998, *My Many Coloured Days*, Hutchinson, London.

Sittenfeld, C. 2005, New York and Toronto: Random House, in press.

Southall, I. 1962, *Hills End*, Angus & Robertson, Sydney.

—— 1970, *Bread and Honey*, Angus & Robertson, Sydney.

Spence, E. 1960, *Lillypilly Hill*, Oxford University Press, London.

Tan, S. 2001, *The Red Tree*, Lothian Books, Melbourne.

Thiele, C. 1963, *Storm Boy*, Rigby, Adelaide.

—— & P. Gouldthorpe 2000, *Pannikin & Pinta*, Lothian Books, Melbourne.

Thompson, C. & K. Carter 2002, *One Big Happy Family*, Hodder, Sydney.

Thompson, C. & M. Ottley 1996, *Sailing Home*, Hodder Headline, Sydney.

Torres, P. 1994, *Jalygurr: Aussie Animal Rhymes*, Magabala Books, Broome, WA [1988].

Utemorrah, D. & P. Torres 1990, *Do Not Go Around the Edges*, Magabala Books, Broome, WA.

Voake, C. 1997, *Ginger*, Walker Books, London.

Waddell, M. & P. Benson 1986, *The Touch Princess*, Philomel Books, New York.

—— & —— 1992, *Owl Babies*, Walker Books, London.

—— & P. Dale 1989, *Once There Were Giants*, William Heinemann Australia.

Wagner, J. & R. Brooks 1977, *John Brown, Rose and the Midnight Cat*, Puffin, London.

Wagner, J. & R. Roennfeldt 1995, *The Werewolf Knight*, Random House, Sydney.

Walker, K. & D. Cox 1994, *Our Excursion*, Omnibus Books, Adelaide.

Wells, R. 1981, *Timothy Goes to School*, Dial, New York.

—— 1996, *Edward's First Day at School*, Walker Books, London.

Westwood, P. 1999, *Spelling: Approaches To Teaching and Assessment*, ACER, Melbourne.

Wheatley, N. & D. Rawlins 1987, *My Place*, Longman, Melbourne.

—— 1984, *Dancing in the Anzac Deli*, Oxford University Press, Melbourne.

——. & M. Ottley 1999, *Luke's Way of Looking*, Hodder Headline, Sydney.

White, E. B. 1952, *Charlotte's Web*, Harper & Row, New York.

Wild, M. & K. Argent 1999, *Miss Lily's Fabulous Pink Feather Boa*, Puffin, Melbourne.

—— & R. Brooks 2000, *Fox*, Allen & Unwin, Sydney.

—— & J. Vivas 1991, *Let the Celebrations Begin*, Omnibus Books, Adelaide.

Wilde, O. 1977, *The Happy Prince and Other Stories*, Puffin, Pandora's Books Ltd, London.

—— 1979, *The Selfish Giant*, Evans Bros, London [1888].

Williamson, J. & G. Singleton 1998, *Christmas in Australia*, Ashton Scholastic, Sydney.

Wilson, J. 1992, *The Suitcase Kid*, Corgi Yearling, London.

Winch, G. 1985, *Samantha Seagull's Sandals*, Childerset, Adelaide.

—— 1989, 'Me Moving'. In *Words Come Out to Play*, Rigby, Melbourne, pp. 10–11.

—— & G. Blaxell 1996, *Danny Dolphin's Nose*, Blake Education, Sydney.

—— & —— 1997, *Sal and Sam at the Farm*, Blake Education, Sydney.

—— & T. Oliver 2002, *Rodney Thinks of Food*, New Frontier Publishing, Sydney.

Winton, T. 1993, *Lockie Leonard: Human Torpedo*, Puffin Books, Melbourne.

—— 1997, *Lockie Leonard Legend*, Pan Macmillan Australia, Sydney.

—— 1997, *Blueback*, Scribner, New York.

—— 1998, *The Deep*, Sandcastle Books, Fremantle, WA.

Wood, D. 2002, *A Quiet Place*, Simon & Schuster, New York.

Yashima, T. 1983, *Crow Boy*, Puffin, New York.

Yolan, J. & L. Baker 1991, *All Those Secrets of the World*, Little, Brown & Co., Boston.

Zamorano, A. & J. Vivas 1996, *Let's Eat!*, Omnibus Books, Adelaide.

Zurbo, M. 1997, *Idiot Pride*, Penguin, Melbourne.

Zusak, M. 2005, *The Book Thief*, Picador, Sydney.

Children's literature journals

Bookbird
The Lion and the Unicorn
Canadian Children's Literature
Magpies
Children's Literature in Education
Orana
CHLA Quarterly
Papers
CREArTA (an interdisciplinary arts focus)
Signal
Literature Base
Reading Time

Name and Title Index

This index includes names of authors discussed in the book and the titles of films and children's books.

Subject and Organisation Index

This index covers subjects, organisations and glossary entries.